WileyPLUS Learning Space

An easy way to help your students learn, **collaborate,** and **grow.**

Personalized Experience

Students create their own study guide while they interact with course content and work on learning activities.

Flexible Course Design

Educators can quickly organize learning activities, manage student collaboration, and customize their course—giving them full control over content as well as the amount of interactivity among students.

Clear Path to Action

With visual reports, it's easy for both students and educators to gauge problem areas and act on what's most important.

Instructor Benefits

- Assign activities and add your own materials
- Guide students through what's important in the interactive e-textbook by easily assigning specific content
- Set up and monitor collaborative learning groups
- Assess learner engagement
- Gain immediate insights to help inform teaching

Student Benefits

- Instantly know what you need to work on
- Create a personal study plan
- Assess progress along the way
- Participate in class discussions
- Remember what you have learned because you have made deeper connections to the content

We're dedicated to supporting you from idea to outcome.

10th Edition

Information Technology for Management

Digital Strategies for Insight, Action, and Sustainable Performance

EFRAIM TURBAN

LINDA VOLONINO, Canisius College

GREGORY R. WOOD, Canisius College

Contributing authors:

JANICE C. SIPIOR, Villanova University

GUY H. GESSNER, Canisius College

WILEY

VP & EXECUTIVE PUBLISHER:	Don Fowley
EXECUTIVE EDITOR:	Beth Lang Golub
SPONSORING EDITOR:	Mary O'Sullivan
PROJECT EDITOR:	Ellen Keohane
ASSOCIATE EDITOR:	Christina Volpe
MARKETING MANAGER:	Margaret Barrett
MARKETING ASSISTANT:	Elisa Wong
SENIOR CONTENT MANAGER:	Ellinor Wagner
SENIOR PRODUCTION EDITOR:	Ken Santor
SENIOR PHOTO EDITOR:	Lisa Gee
DESIGNER:	Kristine Carney
COVER DESIGNER	Wendy Lai
COVER IMAGE	© Ajgul/Shutterstock

This book was set by Aptara, Inc. Cover and text printed and bound by RR Donnelley Kendallville.

This book is printed on acid free paper.

Founded in 1807, John Wiley & Sons, Inc. has been a valued source of knowledge and understanding for more than 200 years, helping people around the world meet their needs and fulfill their aspirations. Our company is built on a foundation of principles that include responsibility to the communities we serve and where we live and work. In 2008, we launched a Corporate Citizenship Initiative, a global effort to address the environmental, social, economic, and ethical challenges we face in our business. Among the issues we are addressing are carbon impact, paper specifications and procurement, ethical conduct within our business and among our vendors, and community and charitable support. For more information, please visit our website: www.wiley.com/go/citizenship.

ISBN   978-1-118-89778-2

BRV ISBN   978-1-118-99429-0

Printed in the United States of America

10 9 8 7 6 5 4 3 2

BRIEF CONTENTS

CONTENTS

Business strategy and operations are driven by data, digital technologies, and devices. Five years from now, we will look back upon today as the start of a new era in business and technology. Just like the way e-business started with the emergence of the Web, this new era is created by the convergence of social, mobile, big data, analytics, cloud, sensor, software-as-a-service, and data visualization technologies. These technologies enable real-time insights, business decisions, and actions. Examples of how they determine tomorrow's business outcomes are:

- **Insight.** Combining the latest capabilities in big data analytics, reporting, collaboration, search, and machine-to-machine (M2M) communication helps enterprises build an agility advantage, cut costs, and achieve their visions.
- **Action.** Fully leveraging real-time data about operations, supply chains, and customers enables managers to make decisions and take action in the moment.
- **Sustainable performance.** Deploying cloud services, managing projects and sourcing agreements, respecting privacy and the planet, and engaging customers across channels are now fundamental to sustaining business growth.
- **Business optimization.** Embedding digital capability into products, services, machines, and business processes optimizes business performance—and creates strategic weapons.

In this tenth edition, students learn, explore, and analyze the three dimensions of business performance improvement: *digital technology, business processes,* and *people*.

What Is New in the Tenth Edition—and Why It Matters

Most Relevant Content. Prior to and during the writing process, we attended practitioner conferences and consulted with managers who are hands-on users of leading technologies, vendors, and IT professionals to learn about their IT/business successes, challenges, experiences, and recommendations. For example, during an in-person interview with a Las Vegas pit boss, we learned how real-time monitoring and data analytics recommend the minimum bets in order to maximize revenue per minute at gaming tables. Experts outlined opportunities and strategies to leverage cloud services and big data to capture customer loyalty and wallet share and justify significant investments in leading IT.

More Project Management with Templates. In response to reviewers' requests, we have greatly increased coverage of project management and systems development lifecycle (SDLC). Students are given templates for writing a project business case, statement of work (SOW), and work breakdown structure (WBS). Rarely covered, but critical project management issues included in this edition are project post-mortem, responsibility matrix, go/no go decision factors, and the role of the user community.

New Technologies and Expanded Topics. New to this edition are 3D printing and bioprinting, project portfolio management, the privacy paradox, IPv6, outsource relationship management (ORM), and balanced scorecard. With more purchases and transactions starting online and attention being a scarce resource, students learn how search, semantic, and recommendation technologies function to improve revenue. The value of Internet of Things (IoT) has grown significantly as a result of the compound impact of connecting people, processes, data, and things.

Easier to Grasp Concepts. A lot of effort went into making learning easier and longer-lasting by outlining content with models and *text graphics* for each opening case (our version of infographics) as shown in Figure P-1—from the Chapter 12 opening case.

Engaging Students to Assure Learning

The tenth edition of *Information Technology for Management* engages students with up-to-date coverage of the most important IT trends today. Over the years, this IT textbook had distinguished itself with an emphasis on illustrating the use of cutting edge business technologies for achieving managerial goals and objectives. The tenth edition continues this tradition with more hands-on activities and analyses.

Each chapter contains numerous case studies and real world examples illustrating how businesses increase productivity, improve efficiency, enhance communication and collaboration, and gain a competitive edge through the use of ITs. Faculty will appreciate a variety of options for reinforcing student learning, that include three **Case Studies** per chapter, including an opening case, a business case and a video case.

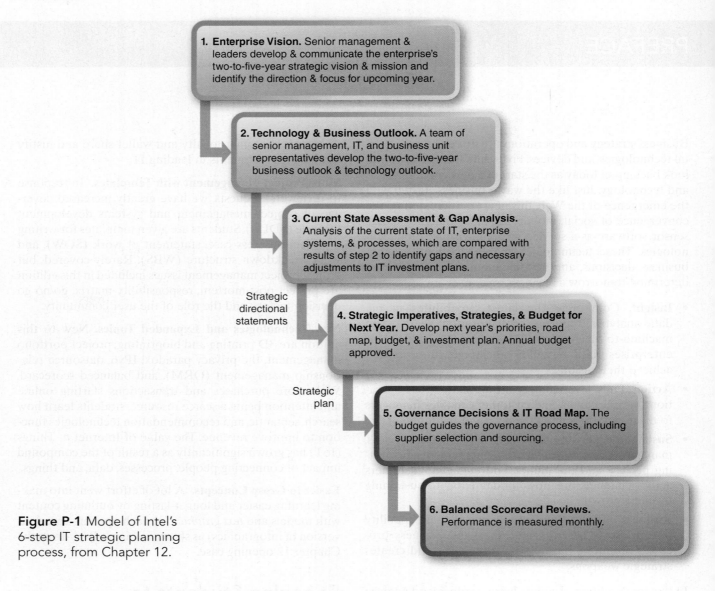

1. **Enterprise Vision.** Senior management & leaders develop & communicate the enterprise's two-to-five-year strategic vision & mission and identify the direction & focus for upcoming year.

2. **Technology & Business Outlook.** A team of senior management, IT, and business unit representatives develop the two-to-five-year business outlook & technology outlook.

3. **Current State Assessment & Gap Analysis.** Analysis of the current state of IT, enterprise systems, & processes, which are compared with results of step 2 to identify gaps and necessary adjustments to IT investment plans.

Strategic directional statements

4. **Strategic Imperatives, Strategies, & Budget for Next Year.** Develop next year's priorities, road map, budget, & investment plan. Annual budget approved.

Strategic plan

5. **Governance Decisions & IT Road Map.** The budget guides the governance process, including supplier selection and sourcing.

6. **Balanced Scorecard Reviews.** Performance is measured monthly.

Figure P-1 Model of Intel's 6-step IT strategic planning process, from Chapter 12.

Throughout each chapter are various learning aids, which include the following:

- **Learning Outcomes** are listed at the beginning of each chapter to help students focus their efforts and alert them to the important concepts that will be discussed.
- The **Chapter Snapshot** provides students with an overview of the chapter content.
- **IT at Work** boxes spotlight real-world cases and innovative uses of IT.
- Definitions of **Key Terms** appear in the margins throughout the book.
- **Tech Note** boxes explore topics such as "4G and 5G Networks in 2018" and "Data transfers to mainframes."
- **Career Insight** boxes highlight different jobs in the IT for management field.

At the end of each chapter are a variety of features designed to assure student learning:

- **Critical Thinking Questions** are designed to facilitate student discussion.
- **Online and Interactive Exercises** encourage students to explore additional topics.
- **Analyze and Decide** questions help students apply IT concepts to business decisions.

Details of New and Enhanced Features of the Tenth Edition

The textbook consists of fourteen chapters organized into four parts. All chapters have new sections as well as updated sections, as shown in Table P-1.

TABLE P-1 Overview of New and Expanded IT Topics and Innovative Enterprises Discussed in the Chapters

Chapter	New and Expanded IT and Business Topics	Enterprises in a Wide Range of Industries
1: Doing Business in Digital Times	• *Era of Mobile-Social-Cloud-Big Data* • Digital connectivity and convergence • Internet of Things (IoT), or machine-to-machine (M2M) technology • Farm-to-fork traceability • Business process management • Near-field communication (NFC)	• McCain Foods Ltd • Zipcar • Pei Wei Asian Diner • Teradata
2: Data Governance and IT Architecture Support Long-Term Performance	• Data governance and quality • Master data management (MDM) • Cloud services • Collaboration • Virtualization and business continuity • software-, platform-, infrastructure-, and data-as-a-service	• Intel Security • Liberty Wines • Unilever • Vanderbilt University Medical Center
3: Data Management, Big Data Analytics and Records Management	• Big data analytics and machine-generated data • Business intelligence (BI) • Hadoop • NoSQL systems • Active data warehouse apps • Compliance	• Coca-Cola • Hertz • First Wind • Argo Corp. • Wal-Mart • McDonalds • Infinity Insurance • Quicken Loans, Inc. • U.S. military • CarMax
4: Networks for Efficient Operations and Sustainability	• IPv6 • API • 4G and 5G networks • Net neutrality • Location-aware technologies • Climate change • Mobile infrastructure • Sustainable development	• Sony • Google Maps • Fresh Direct • Apple • Spotify • Caterpillar, Inc.
5: Cyber Security and Risk Management	• BYOD and social risks • Advanced persistent threats (APT), malware, and botnets • IT governance • Cloud security • Fraud detection and prevention	• Target • LinkedIn • Boeing
6: Attracting Buyers with Search, Semantic and Recommendation Technology	• Search technology • Search engine optimization (SEO) • Google Analytics • Paid search strategies	• Nike • Netflix • Wine.com

(continued)

TABLE P-1 Overview of New and Expanded IT Topics and Innovative Enterprises Discussed in the Chapters *(continued)*

Chapter	New and Expanded IT and Business Topics	Enterprises in a Wide Range of Industries
7: Social Networking, Engagement and Social Metrics	• Social network services (SNS) • Web 2.0 tools for business collaboration • Crowdfunding • Privacy	• Citibank • American Express • Facebook • Twitter • Cisco
8: Retail, E-commerce and Mobile Commerce Technology	• Innovation in traditional and web-based retail • Omni-channel retailing • Visual search • Mobile payment systems	• Macys • Chegg • Amazon
9: Effective and Efficient Business Functions	• Customer experience (CX) • eXtensible Business Reporting Language (XBRL) • Order fulfillment process • Transportation management systems • Computer-integrated manufacturing (CIM) • SaaS • TQM • Auditing information systems	• Ducati Motor Holding • HSBC • SAS • United Rentals • First Choice Ski
10: Strategic Technology and Enterprise Systems	• 3D printing, additive manufacturing • Enterprise social platforms • Yammer, SharePoint, and Microsoft Cloud	• Avon • Procter & Gamble • Organic Valley Family of Farms • Red Robin Gourmet Burgers, Inc. • Salesforce.com • Food and Drug Administration (FDA) • U.S. Army Materiel Command (AMC) • 1-800-Flowers
11: Data Visualization and Geographic Information Systems	• Data visualization • Mobile dashboards • Geospatial data and geocoding • Geographic Information Systems (GIS) • Supply chain visibility • Reporting tools; analytical tools • Self-service mashup capabilities	• Safeway • PepsiCo • eBay • Tableau • Hartford Hospital • General Motors (GM)
12: IT Strategy and Balanced Scorecard	• IT strategic planning process • Value drivers • Outsource relationship management (ORM) • Service level agreements (SLAs) • Outsourcing lifecycle • Applications portfolio	• Intel • AstraZeneca • IBM • Commonwealth Bank of Australia (CBA)

(continued)

TABLE P-1 Overview of New and Expanded IT Topics and Innovative Enterprises Discussed in the Chapters *(continued)*

Chapter	New and Expanded IT and Business Topics	Enterprises in a Wide Range of Industries
13: Project Management and SDLC	• Project management lifecycle • Project Portfolio Management (PPM) • Project business case • Project business case, statement of work (SOW), work breakdown structure (WBS), milestone schedule, and Gantt chart • Triple constraint • Critical path • Systems feasibility studies	• Denver International Airport • U.S. Census • Mavenlink Project Management and Planning Software
14: Ethical Risks and Responsibilities of IT Innovations	• Privacy paradox • Social recruitment and discrimination • Responsible conduct • Vehicle-to-vehicle (V2V) technology • Ethics of 3D printing and bioprinting • Tech addictions • Tech trends	• Google Glass • Apple's CarPlay • SnapChat • Target

Supplementary Materials

An extensive package of instructional materials is available to support this tenth edition. These materials are accessible from the book companion Web site at *www.wiley.com/college/turban*.

- **Instructor's Manual.** The Instructor's Manual presents objectives from the text with additional information to make them more appropriate and useful for the instructor. The manual also includes practical applications of concepts, case study elaboration, answers to end-of-chapter questions, questions for review, questions for discussion, and Internet exercises.

- **Test Bank.** The test bank contains over 1,000 questions and problems (about 75 per chapter) consisting of multiple-choice, short answer, fill-ins, and critical thinking/essay questions.

- **Respondus Test Bank.** This electronic test bank is a powerful tool for creating and managing exams that can be printed on paper or published directly to Blackboard, ANGEL, Desire2Learn, Moodle, and other learning systems. Exams can be created offline using a familiar Windows environment, or moved from one LMS to another.

- **PowerPoint Presentation.** A series of slides designed around the content of the text incorporates key points from the text and illustrations where appropriate.

E-book

Wiley E-Textbooks offer students the complete content of the printed textbook on the device of their preference—computer, iPad, tablet, or smartphone—giving students the freedom to read or study anytime, anywhere. Students can search across content, take notes, and highlight key materials. For more information, go to www.wiley.com/college/turban.

Acknowledgments

Many individuals participated in focus groups or reviewers. Our sincere thanks to the following reviewers of the tenth edition who provided valuable feedback, insights, and suggestions that improved the quality of this text:

Joni Adkins, Northwest Missouri State University
Ahmad Al-Omari, Dakota State University
Rigoberto Chinchilla, Eastern Illinois University
Michael Donahue, Towson University
Samuel Elko, Seton Hill University
Robert Goble, Dallas Baptist University
Eileen Griffin, Canisius College
Binshan Lin, Louisiana State University in Shreveport
Thomas MacMullen, Eastern Illinois University
James Moore, Canisius College
Beverly S. Motich, Messiah College

Barin Nag, Towson University
Luis A. Otero, Inter-American University of Puerto Rico, Metropolitan Campus
John Pearson, Southern Illinois University
Daniel Riding, Florida Institute of Technology
Josie Schneider, Columbia Southern University
Derek Sedlack, South University
Eric Weinstein, The University of La Verne
Patricia White, Columbia Southern University
Gene A. Wright, University of Wisconsin–Milwaukee

We are very thankful to our assistants, Samantha Palisano and Olena Azarova. Samantha devoted many hours of research, provided clerical support, and contributed to the writing of Chapter 6. Olena assisted with research and development of graphics for Chapter 7. We are fortunate and thankful for the expert and encouraging leadership of Margaret Barrett, Beth Golub, Ellen Keohane, and Mary O'Sullivan. To them we extend our sincere thanks for your guidance, patience, humor, and support during the development of this most recent version of the book. Finally, we wish to thank our families and colleagues for their encouragement, support, and understanding as we dedicated time and effort to creating this new edition of *Information Technology for Management.*

*Linda Volonino
Greg Wood*

Chapter 1

Doing Business in Digital Times

Learning Outcomes

1. Describe the use of digital technology in every facet of business and how digital channels are being leveraged.

2. Explain the types, sources, characteristics, and control of enterprise data, and what can be accomplished with near real time data.

3. Identify the five forces of competitive advantage and evaluate how they are reinforced by IT.

4. Describe enterprise technology trends and explain how they influence strategy and operations.

5. Assess how IT adds value to your career path and performance, and the positive outlook for IT management careers.

Chapter Snapshot

Make no mistake. Businesses are experiencing a *digital transformation* as digital technology enables changes unimaginable a decade ago. High-performance organizations are taking advantage of what is newly possible from innovations in mobile, social, cloud, **big data, data analytics**, and **visualization** technologies. These digital forces enable unprecedented levels of connectivity, or connectedness, as listed in Figure 1.1.

Think how much of your day you have your phone nearby—and how many times you check it. Nearly 80 percent of people carry their phone for all but two hours of their day; and 25 per cent of 18- to 44-year-olds cannot remember *not* having their phone with them (Cooper, 2013).

As a business leader, you will want to know what steps to take to get a jump on the mobile, social, cloud,

Big data are datasets whose size and speed are beyond the ability of typical database software tools to capture, store, manage, and analyze. Examples are machine-generated data and social media texts.

Data analytics refers to the use of software and statistics to find meaningful insight in the data, or better understand the data.

Data visualization (viz) tools make it easier to understand data at a glance by displaying data in summarized formats, such as dashboards and maps, and by enabling drill-down to the detailed data.

An estimated 15 billion devices are connected to the Internet—forecasted to hit 50 billion by 2020 as more devices connect via mobile networks.
Over 1 million websites engage in *Facebook e-commerce*.
Over 200 million social media users are *mobile only*, never accessing it from a desktop or laptop. Mobile use generates 30% of Facebook's ad revenue.
More data are collected in a day now than existed in the world 10 years ago. Half of all data are in the cloud and generated by mobile and social activities—known as big data.

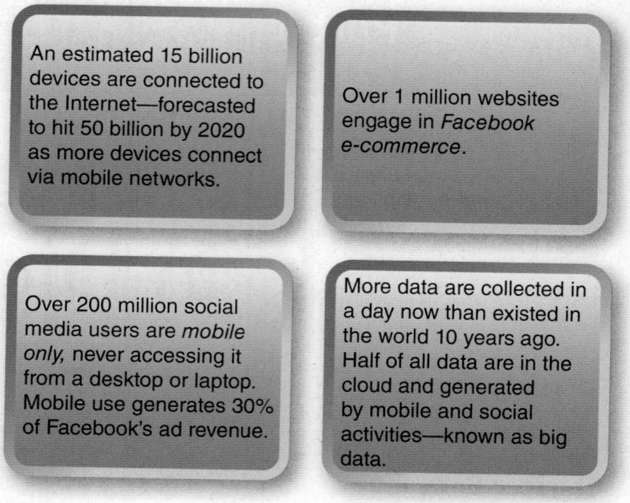

Figure 1.1 We are in the *era of mobile-social-cloud-big data* that shape business strategies and day-to-day operations.

big data, analytics, and visualization technologies that will move your businesses forward. Faced with opportunities and challenges, you need to know how to leverage them before or better than your competitors.

In this opening chapter, you read about the powerful impacts of digital technology on management, business, government, entertainment, society, and those it will have on the future. You learn of the latest digital trends taking place across industries and organizations—small and medium businesses, multinational corporations, government agencies, the health-care industry, and nonprofits.

CASE 1.1 OPENING CASE

McCain Foods' Success Factors: Dashboards, Innovation, and Ethics

COMPANY OVERVIEW

You most likely have eaten McCain Foods products (Figure 1.2, Table 1.1). McCain is a market leader in the frozen food industry—producing one-third of the world's supply of french fries. The company manufactures, distributes, and sells more than

McCain Foods, Ltd.
Brand
Frozen food manufacturer
Market leader in french fries
Global Reach
Sales offices in 110 countries
55 production plants on 6 continents
22,000 employees
Corporate Culture
Good ethics is good business.
Good food, better life.
Digital Technology
Dashboards
Data analytics
Real time reporting systems

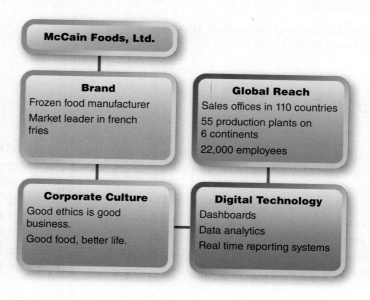

Figure 1.2 McCain Foods, Ltd. overview.

TABLE 1.1   Opening Case Overview

Company	McCain Foods, Ltd. www.mccain.com
Industry	The global company manufactures, sells, and distributes frozen food products.
Product lines	More than 100 oven-ready frozen food products
Digital technology	Dashboards are implemented throughout the organization from boardrooms to factory floors. Dashboards have drill-down capabilities.
Business challenges	The frozen food industry faced tough challenges from health and nutrition trends that are emphasizing fresh foods. Industry is highly competitive because it is expected to experience slow growth through 2018.
Taglines	"Good food. Better life." and "It's all good."

Business-to-business (B2B) commerce. The selling of products and services to other businesses.

100 oven-ready frozen foods—pizzas, appetizers, meals, and vegetables. McCain is a global **business-to-business (B2B)** manufacturer with 55 production facilities on 6 continents. The company sells frozen foods to other businesses—wholesalers, retailers, and restaurants from sales offices in 110 countries. McCain supplies frozen fries to Burger King and supermarket chains (Figure 1.3).

Voisin/Phanie/SuperStock

Figure 1.3 Frozen food is one of the most dynamic and largest sectors of the food industry.

Supply chain. All businesses involved in the production and distribution of a product or service.

Food manufacturers must be able to trace all ingredients along their **supply chain** in case of contamination. Achieving end-to-end traceability is complex given the number of players in food supply chains. Several communication and tracking technologies make up McCain's supply chain management (SCM) system to keep workers informed of actual and potential problems with food quality, inventory, and shipping as they occur. McCain's SCM system ensures delivery of the best products possible at the best value to customers. In addition, the company strives to prevent food shortages worldwide by analyzing huge volumes of data to predict crop yields.

FROZEN FOOD INDUSTRY CHALLENGES

McCain Foods had to deal with three major challenges and threats:

1. **Drop in demand for frozen foods.** McCain operated in an industry that was facing tougher competition. Health-conscious trends were shifting customer demand toward fresh food, which was slowing growth in the frozen foods market.

2. **Perishable inventory.** Of all the types of manufacturing, food manufacturers face unique inventory management challenges and regulatory requirements. Their inventory of raw materials and finished goods can spoil, losing all their value, or food can become contaminated. Regulators require food manufacturers to able to do recalls quickly and effectively. Food recalls have destroyed brands and been financially devastating.

3. **Technology-dependent.** Food manufacturers face the pressures that are common to all manufacturers. They need information reporting systems and digital devices to manage and automate operations, track inventory, keep the right people informed, support decisions, and collaborate with business partners.

© DustyPixel/iStockphoto

Figure 1.4 McCain Foods and Burger King jointly developed *Satisfries*—a french fry innovation with 30 percent less fat and 20 percent fewer calories than BK's current fries and 40 percent less fat and 30 percent fewer calories than McDonald's fries.

McCain Foods worked with Burger King (BK) to develop lower-calorie fries called *Satisfries* (Figure 1.4). These crinkle-cut fries have 30 percent less fat and 20 percent fewer calories than BK's classic fries. This food innovation has shaken up the fast-food industry and given BK an advantage with end-consumers who are demanding healthier options.

McCAIN FOODS' BUSINESS AND IT STRATEGIES

The McCain brothers, who founded the company, follow this simple philosophy: "Good ethics is good business." McCain prides itself on the quality and convenience of its products, which is reflected in the *It's All Good* brand image. The *It's All Good* branding effort was launched in 2010 after surveys found that customers were concerned about the quality and nutrition of frozen foods. Since then, many of products have been improved and manufactured in healthier versions.

Managing with Digital Technology McCain had integrated its diverse sources of data into a single environment for analysis. Insights gained from its **data analytics** helped improve manufacturing processes, innovation, and competitive advantage.

McCain Foods invested in data analytics and visualization technologies to maximize its capability to innovate and gain insights from its huge volumes of data. The company tracks, aggregates, and analyzes data from operations and business customers in order to identify opportunities for innovation in every area of the business. The results of data analytics are made available across the organization—from executive boardrooms to the factory floors—on dashboards. **Dashboards** are data visualizations (data viz) that display the current status of **key performance indicators (KPIs)** in easy-to-understand formats (Figure 1.5). KPIs are business metrics used to evaluate performance in terms of critical success factors, or strategic and operational goals.

Dashboards Create Productive Competition Among Factory Workers

McCain implemented 22,000 reports and 3,000 personal reporting systems that include dashboards. Dashboards display summarized data graphically in a clear and concise way. By clicking a graph, the user can drill down to the detailed data. The dashboards reach most of McCain's 18,000 employees worldwide.

Dashboards have created healthy competition that has led to better performance. Ten-foot dashboards hang on factory walls of plants around the world. They are strategically placed near the cafeteria so employees can see the KPIs and performance metrics of every plant. With this visibility, everyone can know in near real time exactly how well they are doing compared to other plants. The competition among factories has totally transformed the work environment—and organizational culture—in the plants and increased production performance.

Better Predictions, Better Results The CEO, other executives, and managers view their dashboards from mobile devices or computers. They are able to monitor operations in factories and farms around the globe. Dashboards keep management informed because they can discover answers to their own questions by drilling down. Data are used to forecast and predict crop yields—and ultimately combine weather and geopolitical data to predict and avoid food shortages. By integrating all of its data into one environment and making the results available in near real time to those who need it, the organization is increasing its bottom line and driving innovation.

Figure 1.5 Data visualizations of KPIs make them easy to understand at a glance.

© Delices/Shutterstock

Questions

Food Safety Modernization Act (FSMA), signed into law in early 2011, requires all companies in food supply chains to be able to trace foods back to the point of origin (*farm*) and forward to the consumer's plate (*fork*). The term for the effort is **farm-to-fork traceability**. Public health is the chief concern, followed by potential liability and brand protection issues.

1. All it takes is one compromised ingredient to contaminate food and to put human lives at risk. Delays in communicating contaminated food increase the health risk and fines for violating the **Food Safety Modernization Act**. How can the SCM system help McCain Foods reduce the risks related to low-quality or contaminated frozen foods reaching consumers?
2. What three challenges or threats facing McCain Foods and what is the reason for each challenge or threat?
3. How have dashboards on the factory floors impacted performance at McCain Foods?
4. What might be the KPIs of a frozen food manufacturer such as McCain Foods?
5. Explain how visibility about operations and performance created healthy competition among McCain's factory workers.
6. Being able to make reliable predictions can improve business performance. Explain why.

Sources: Compiled from Smith (2013), Transparency Market Research (2013), and McCain Foods Teradata video (2013).

1.1 Every Business Is a Digital Business

Digital business is a social, mobile, and Web-focused business.

Business model is how a business makes money.

Digital business model defines how a business makes money digitally.

Customer experience (CX) is about building the digital infrastructure that allows customers to do whatever they want to do, through whatever channel they choose to do it.

Today, a top concern of well-established corporations, global financial institutions, born-on-the-Web retailers, and government agencies is how to design their **digital business models** in order to:

- deliver an incredible customer experience;
- turn a profit;
- increase market share; and
- engage their employees.

In the digital (online) space, the **customer experience (CX)** must measure up to the very best the Web has to offer. Stakes are high for those who get it right—or get it wrong. Forrester research repeatedly confirms there is a strong relationship between the quality of a firm's CX and loyalty, which in turn increases revenue (Schmidt-Subramanian et al., 2013).

This section introduces the most disruptive and valuable digital technologies, which you will continue to read about throughout this book.

DIGITAL TECHNOLOGIES OF THE 2010S—IN THE CLOUD, HANDHELD, AND WEARABLE

Consumers expect to interact with businesses anytime anywhere via mobile apps or social channels using technology they carry in their pockets. Mobile apps have changed how, when, and where work is done. Employees can be more productive when they work and collaborate effortlessly from their handheld or wearable devices.

Cloud computing is a style of computing in which IT services are delivered on-demand and accessible via the Internet. Common examples are Dropbox, Gmail, and Google Drive.

Cloud Computing

Enterprises can acquire the latest apps and digital services as they are needed and without large upfront investments by switching from owning IT resources to **cloud computing** (Figure 1.6). Cloud computing ranges from storing your files in Dropbox to advanced cloud services. In short, with the cloud, resources no longer depend on buying that resource. For example, Amazon Elastic Compute Cloud, known as

Figure 1.6 Cloud computing is an important evolution in data storage, software, apps, and delivery of IT services. An example is Apple iCloud—a cloud service used for online storage and synchronization of mail, media files, contacts, calendar, and more.

EC2, eliminates the need to invest in hardware up front, so companies can develop and deploy applications faster. EC2 enables companies to quickly add storage capacity as their computing requirements change. EC2 reduces the time it takes to acquire server space from weeks to minutes.

Machine-to-Machine Technology

Internet of things (IoT) refers to a set of capabilities enabled when physical things are connected to the Internet via sensors.

Sensors can be embedded in most products. Objects that connect themselves to the Internet include cars, heart monitors, stoplights, and appliances. Sensors are designed to detect and react, such as Ford's rain-sensing front wipers that use an advanced optical sensor to detect the intensity of rain or snowfall and adjust wiper speed accordingly. **Machine-to-machine (M2M) technology** enables sensor-embedded products to share reliable real time data via radio signals. M2M and the **Internet of Things (IoT)** are widely used to automate business processes in industries ranging from transportation to health care. By adding sensors to trucks, turbines, roadways, utility meters, heart monitors, vending machines, and other equipment they sell, companies can track and manage their products remotely.

TECH NOTE 1.1 The Internet of Things

The phrase *Internet of Things* was coined by Kevin Ashton in 1999 while he was employed at Procter & Gamble. It refers to objects (e.g., cars, refrigerators, roadways) that can sense aspects of the physical world, such as movement, temperature, lighting, or the presence or absence of people or objects, and then either act on it or report it. Instead of most data (text, audio, video) on the Internet being produced and used by people, more data are generated and used by machines communicating with other machines—or M2M, as you read at the start of this chapter. Smart devices use IP addresses and Internet technologies like Wi-Fi to communicate with each other or directly with the cloud. Recent advances in storage and computing power available via cloud computing are facilitating adoption of the IoT.

The IoT opens new frontiers for improving processes in retail, health care, manufacturing, energy, and oil and gas exploration. For instance, manufacturing processes with embedded sensors can be controlled more precisely or monitored for hazards and then take corrective action, which reduces injuries, damage, and costs. IoT combined with big data analytics can help manufacturers improve the efficiency of their machinery and minimize energy consumption, which often is the manufacturing industry's second-biggest expense.

The health sector is another area where IoT can help significantly. For example, a person with a wearable device that carries all records of his health could be monitored constantly. This connectivity enables health services to take necessary measures for maintaining the wellbeing of the person.

Big Data

There is no question that the increasing volume of data can be valuable, but only if they are processed and available when and where they are needed. The problem is that the amount, variety, structure, and speed of data being generated or collected by enterprises differ significantly from traditional data. Big data are what high-volume, mostly text data are called. Big data stream in from multiple channels and sources, including:

- mobile devices and M2M sensors embedded in everything from airport runways to casino chips. Later in this chapter, you will read more about the Internet of Things.
- social content from texts, tweets, posts, blogs.
- clickstream data from the Web and Internet searches.
- video data and photos from retail and user-generated content.
- financial, medical, research, customer, and B2B transactions.

Big data are 80 to 90 per cent unstructured. **Unstructured data** do not have a predictable format like a credit card application form. Huge volumes of unstructured data flooding into an enterprise are too much for traditional technology to process and analyze quickly. Big data tend to be more time-sensitive than traditional (or small) data.

The exploding field of big data and analytics is called **data science**. Data science involves managing and analyzing massive sets of data for purposes such as target marketing, trend analysis, and the creation of individually tailored products and services. Enterprises that want to take advantage of big data use real time data from tweets, sensors, and their big data sources to gain insights into their customers' interests and preference, to create new products and services, and to respond to changes in usage patterns as they occur. Big data analytics has increased the demand for data scientists, as described in Career Insight 1.1.

CAREER INSIGHT 1.1 HOT CAREER

Data Scientist

Big data, analytics tools, powerful networks, and greater processing power have contributed to growth of the field of data science. Enterprises need people who are capable of analyzing and finding insights in data captured from sensors, M2M apps, social media, wearable technology, medical testing, and so on. Demand for data scientists is outpacing the supply of talent. It is projected that the data scientist career option will grow 19 per cent by 2020—surpassed only by video game designers. Talent scarcity has driven up salaries. According to

Glassdoor data (glassdoor.com, 2014), the median salary for data scientists in the United States is $117,500. By contrast, a business analyst earns an average of $61,000.

Profiles of Data Scientists at Facebook, LinkedIn, and Bitly

- **Facebook's Jeff Hammerbacher.** Jeff helped Facebook make sense out of huge volumes of user data when he joined the company in 2006. Facebook's data science team analyzes the self-reported data on each user's Facebook page in order to target ads based on things the user actually likes.

- **LinkedIn's DJ Patil.** DJ worked at LinkedIn as chief data scientist. Many of the cool products on LinkedIn were built using data from self-reporting and machine learning.

- **Bitly's Hilary Mason.** Hilary was chief scientist at Bitly, which offers URL shortening and redirection services with real time link tracking. Bitly sees behavior from billions of people a month by analyzing tens of millions of links shared per day, which are clicked hundreds of millions times. The clickstreams generate an enormous amount of real time data. Using data analytics, Hillary and her team detected and solved business problems that were not evident.

Data Science Is Both an Art and a Science

In their 2012 Harvard Business Review article titled "Data Scientist: The Sexiest Job of the 21st Century," authors Thomas Davenport and D. J. Patil define a data scientist as a "high-ranking professional with the training and curiosity to make discoveries in the world of big data" (Davenport & Patil, 2012). They described how data scientist Jonathan Goldman transformed LinkedIn after joining the company in 2006. At that time, LinkedIn had less than 8 million members. Goldman noticed that existing members were inviting their friends and colleagues to join, but they were not making connections with other members at the rate executives had expected. A LinkedIn manager said, "It was like arriving at a conference reception and realizing you don't know anyone. So you just stand in the corner sipping your drink—and you probably leave early." Goldman began analyzing the data from user profiles and looked for patterns that to predict whose networks a given profile would land in. While most LinkedIn managers saw no value in Goldman's work, Reid Hoffman, LinkedIn's cofounder and CEO at the time, understood the power of analytics because of his experiences at PayPal. With Hoffman's approval, Goldman applied data analytics to test what would happen if member were presented with names of other members they had not yet connected with, but seemed likely to know. He displayed the three best new matches for each member based on his or her LinkedIn profile. Within days, the click-through rate on those matches skyrocketed and things really took off. Thanks to this one feature, LinkedIn's growth increased dramatically.

The LinkedIn example shows that good data scientists do much more than simply try to solve obvious business problems. Creative and critical thinking are part of their job—that is, part analyst and part artist. They dig through incoming data with the goal of discovering previously hidden insights that could lead to a competitive advantage or detect a business crisis in enough time to prevent it. Data scientists often need to evaluate and select those opportunities and threats that would be of greatest value to the enterprise or brand.

Sources: Kelly (2013), Lockhard & Wolf (2012), Davenport & Patil (2012), U.S. Department of Labor, Bureau of Labor Statistics (2014).

SOCIAL-MOBILE-CLOUD MODEL

The relationship among **social, mobile,** and **cloud** technologies is shown in Figure 1.7. The cloud consists of huge data centers accessible via the Internet and forms the core by providing 24/7 access to storage, apps, and services. Handhelds and wearables, such as Google Glass, Pebble, and Sony Smartwatch (Figure 1.8), and their users form the edge. Social channels connect the core and edge. The SoMoClo integration creates the technical and services infrastructure needed for digital business. This infrastructure makes it possible to meet the expectations of employees, customers, and business partners given that almost everyone is connected (social), everywhere they go (mobile), and has 24/7 access to data, apps, and other services (cloud).

© scanrail/iStockphoto

Figure 1.7 Model of the integration of cloud, mobile, and social technologies. The cloud forms the core. Mobile devices are the endpoints. Social networks create the connections.

Here are three examples of their influence:

1. **Powerful social influences impact advertising and marketing:** Connections and feedback via social networks have changed the balance of influence. Consumers are more likely to trust tweets from ordinary people than recommendations made by celebrity endorsements. And, negative sentiments posted or tweeted can damage brands.

2. **Consumer devices go digital and offer new services.** The Nike+ Fuelband wristband helps customers track their exercise activities and calories burned. The device links to a mobile app that lets users post their progress on Facebook.

3. **eBay's move to cloud technology improves sellers' and buyers' experiences.** The world's largest online marketplace, eBay, moved its IT infrastructure to the cloud. With cloud computing, eBay is able to introduce new types of landing pages and customer experiences without the delay associated with having to buy additional computing resources.

The balance of power has shifted as business is increasingly driven by individuals for whom mobiles are an extension of their body and mind. They expect to use location-aware services, apps, alerts, social networks, and the latest digital capabilities at work and outside work. To a growing extent, customer loyalty and revenue growth depend on a business's ability to offer unique customer experiences that wow customers more than competitors can.

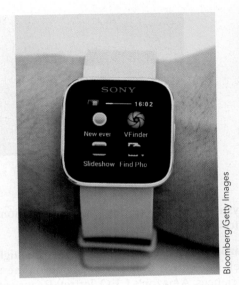

Bloomberg/Getty Images

Matthew Shaw/Getty Images

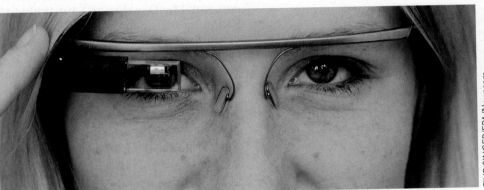

FILIP SINGER/EPA/Newscom

Figure 1.8 Strong interest in smart wearable technology reflects growing consumer desire to be more digitally connected at all times using a collection of multiple devices. A smartwatch used at work, such as in a retail store, can provide shop floor staff with a screen to check stock availability.

DIGITAL BUSINESS MODELS

Business models are the ways enterprises generate revenue or sustain themselves. Digital business models define how businesses make money via digital technology. Companies that adopt digital business models are better positioned to take advantage of business opportunities and survive, according to the Accenture *Technology Vision* 2013 report (Accenture, 2013). Figure 1.9 contains examples of new technologies that destroyed old business models and created new ones.

Figure 1.9 Digital business models refer to how companies engage their customers digitally to create value via websites, social channels, and mobile devices.

Twitter dominates the reporting of news and events as they are still happening.

Facebook became the most powerful sharing network in the world.

Location-aware technologies track items through production and delivery to reduce wasted time and inefficiency in supply chains and other business-to-business (B2B) transactions.

Smartphones, tablets, other touch devices, and their apps reshaped how organizations interact with customers—and how customers want businesses to interact with them.

Figure 1.10 MayDay video chat tech support.

The ways in which market leaders are transitioning to digital business models include the following:

- **Amazon gains a competitive edge with high-tech tech support.** Amazon is well known for radically changing online shopping and e-book reading experiences. Amazon's CEO Jeffrey Bezos set a new standard for tech support with MayDay (Figure 1.10). Within 15 seconds of touching the MayDay button on their Kindle Fire HDX tablet, customers get free, 24/7/365 tech support via video chat. MayDay works by integrating all customer data and instantly displaying the results to a tech agent when a customer presses the MayDay button. Plus, tech agents can control and write on a customer's Fire screen. By circling and underlining various buttons on the display, it is dead simple for new Fire owners to become expert with their devices. Amazon's objective is to educate the consumer rather than just fix the problem. In the highly competitive tablet wars, Amazon has successfully differentiated its tablet from those of big players like Apple, Samsung, and Asus (manufacturer of Google's Nexus 7) with the MayDay button.

- **NBA talent scouts rely on sports analytics and advanced scouting systems.** NBA talent scouts used to crunch players' stats, watch live player performances, and review hours of tapes to create player profiles (Figure 1.11). Now software that tracks player performance has changed how basketball and soccer players are evaluated. For example, STATS' SportVU technology is revolutionizing the way sports contests are viewed, understood, played, and enjoyed. SportVU uses six palm-sized digital cameras that track the movement of every player on the court, record ball movement 25 times per second, and convert movements into statistics. SportVU produces real time and highly complex statistics to complement the traditional play-by-play. Predictive sport analytics can provide a 360-degree view of a player's performance and help teams make trading decisions.

Figure 1.11 Sports analytics and advanced scouting systems evaluate talent and performance for the NBA—offering teams a slight but critical competitive advantage.

© lisegagne/iStockphoto

Figure 1.12 Casinos are improving the profitability of table games by monitoring and analyzing betting in real time.

Sports analytics bring about small competitive advantages that can shift games and even playoff series.

• **Dashboards keep casino floor staff informed of player demand.** Competition in the gaming industry is fierce, particularly during bad economic conditions. The use of manual spreadsheets and gut-feeling decisions did not lead to optimal results. Casino operators facing pressure to increase their bottom line have invested in analytic tools, such as Tangam's Yield Management solution (TYM). TYM is used to increase the yield (profitability) of blackjack, craps, and other table games played in the pit (Figure 1.12). The analysis and insights from real time apps are used to improve the gaming experience and comfort of players.

THE RECENT PAST AND NEAR FUTURE—2010S DECADE

We have seen great advances in digital technology since the start of this decade. Figure 1.13 shows releases by tech leaders that are shaping business and everyday life. Compare the role of your mobiles, apps, social media, and so on in your personal life and work in 2010 to how you use them today. You can expect greater changes going forward to the end of this decade with the expansion of no-touch interfaces, mobility, wearable technology, and the IoT.

Companies are looking for ways to take advantage of new opportunities in mobile, big data, social, and cloud services to optimize their business processes. The role of the IT function within the enterprise has changed significantly—and will evolve rapidly over the next five years. As you will read throughout this book, the IT function has taken on key strategic and operational roles that determine the enterprise's success or failure.

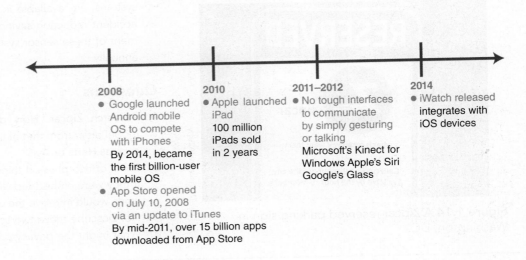

2008
• Google launched Android mobile OS to compete with iPhones By 2014, became the first billion-user mobile OS
• App Store opened on July 10, 2008 via an update to iTunes By mid-2011, over 15 billion apps downloaded from App Store

2010
• Apple launched iPad 100 million iPads sold in 2 years

2011–2012
• No tough interfaces to communicate by simply gesturing or talking Microsoft's Kinect for Windows Apple's Siri Google's Glass

2014
• iWatch released integrates with iOS devices

Figure 1.13 Digital technology released since 2010.

IT at Work 1.1

Zipcar and Other Connected Products

More objects are being embedded with sensors and gaining the ability to communicate with the Internet. This communication improves business processes while reducing costs and risks. For example, sensors and network connections can be embedded in rental cars. Zipcar has pioneered the *car rental by the hour* business model. See Figure 1.14. Cars are leased for short time spans to registered members, making retail rental centers unnecessary. Traditional car rental agencies are starting to experiment with sensors so that each car's use can be optimized to increase revenue.

When devices or products are embedded with sensors, companies can track their movements or monitor interactions with them. Business models can be adjusted to take advantage of what is learned from this behavioral data. For example, an insurance company offers to install location sensors in customers' cars. By doing so, the company develops the ability to price the drivers' policies on how a car is driven and where it travels. Pricing is customized to match the actual risks of operating a vehicle rather than based on general proxies—driver's age, gender, or location of residence.

Opportunities for Improvement

Other applications of embedded physical things are:

- In the oil and gas industry, exploration and development rely on extensive sensor networks placed in the earth's crust. The sensors produce accurate readings of the location, structure, and dimensions of potential fields.

Figure 1.14 A Zipcar-reserved parking sign in Washington, DC.

The payoff is lower development costs and improved oil flows.

- In the health-care industry, sensors and data links can monitor patients' behavior and symptoms in real time and at low cost. This allows physicians to more precisely diagnose disease and prescribe treatment regimens. For example, sensors embedded in patients with heart disease or chronic illnesses can be monitored continuously as they go about their daily activities. Sensors placed on congestive heart patients monitor many of these signs remotely and continuously, giving doctors early warning of risky conditions. Better management of congestive heart failure alone could reduce hospitalization and treatment costs by $1 billion per year in the U.S.

- In the retail industry, sensors can capture shoppers' profile data stored in their membership cards to help close purchases by providing additional information or offering discounts at the point of sale.

- Farm equipment with ground sensors can take into account crop and field conditions, and adjust the amount of fertilizer that is spread on areas that need more nutrients.

- Billboards in Japan scan people passing by, assessing how they fit consumer profiles, and instantly change the displayed messages based on those assessments.

- The automobile industry is developing systems that can detect imminent collisions and take evasive action. Certain basic applications, such as automatic braking systems, are available in high-end autos. The potential accident reduction savings resulting from wider deployment of these sensor systems could exceed $100 billion annually.

Questions

1. Research Zipcar. How does this company's business model differ from that of traditional car rental companies, such as Hertz or Avis?
2. Think of two physical things in your home or office that, if they were embedded with sensors and linked to a network, would improve the quality of your work or personal life. Describe these two scenarios.
3. What might the privacy concerns be?

Questions

1. What are the benefits of cloud computing?
2. What is machine-to-machine (M2M) technology? Give an example of a business process that could be automated with M2M.
3. Describe the relationships in the SoMoClo model.
4. Explain the cloud.
5. Why have mobile devices given consumers more power in the marketplace?
6. What is a business model?
7. What is a digital business model?
8. Explain the Internet of Things.

IT at Work 1.2

Wearable Technology

By 2016 wearable electronics in shoes, tattoos, and accessories will become a $10 billion industry, according to Gartner (2012).

Wearable technology builds computing, connectivity, and sensor capabilities into materials. The latest wearables are lightweight and may be found in athletic shoes, golf accessories, and fitness trackers. The wearables can include data analysis apps or services that send feedback or insights to the wearer. For example, Zepp Labs manufactures sensor-embedded gloves for golf, tennis, and baseball that analyze 1,000 data points per second to create 3D representations of a player's swing. The sensors track every inch of a golfer's swing, analyzes the movements, and then sends the wearers advice on how to improve their game. Sensors that weigh only half an ounce clip onto the glove. Another example is Sony's SmartBand, a wristband that synchs with your phone to track how many steps you take, the number of calories you burn each day, and how well you sleep. The Lifelog app is the key to the Smartband. The app gives a visual display of a timeline and your activity, with boxes monitoring your steps, calories, kilometers walked, and more. Lifelog goes beyond just fitness by also monitoring time spent on social networks and photos taken.

The major sources of revenue from wearable smart electronics are items worn by athletes and sports enthusiasts and devices used to monitor health conditions, such as automatic insulin delivery for diabetics.

Applications and services are creating new value for consumers, especially when they are combined with personal preferences, location, biosensing, and social data. Wearable electronics can provide more detailed data to retailers for targeting advertisements and promotions.

Questions

1. Discuss how wearable electronics and the instant feedback they send to your mobile device could be valuable to you.
2. How can data from wearable technology be used to improve worker productivity or safety?
3. What are two other potentially valuable uses of instant feedback or data from wearable technology?
4. How can wearable devices impact personal privacy?

1.2 Business Process Management and Improvement

Objectives define the desired benefits or expected performance improvements. They do not and should not describe what you plan to do, how you plan to do it, or what you plan to produce, which is the function of processes.

All functions and departments in the enterprise have tasks that they need to complete to produce outputs, or deliverables, in order to meet their **objectives. Business processes** are series of steps by which organizations coordinate and organize tasks to get work done. In the simplest terms, a **process** consists of activities that convert inputs into outputs by doing work.

The importance of efficient business processes and continuous process improvement cannot be overemphasized. Why? Because 100 per cent of an enterprise's performance is the result of its processes. Maximizing the use of inputs in order to carry out similar activities better than one's competitors is a critical success factor. IT at Work 1.3 describes the performance gains at AutoTrader.com, the automobile industry's largest online shopping marketplace, after it redesigned its *order-to-cash* process.

IT at Work 1.3

AutoTrader Redesigns Its Order-to-Cash Process

Figure 1.15 AutoTrader.com car search site.

© NetPhotos/Alamy

AutoTrader.com is the leading automotive marketplace, listing several million new and pre-owned vehicles, as shown in Figure 1.15. AutoTrader.com is one of the largest local online advertising entities, with profits of $300 million on $1.2 billion in revenues in 2013. The site attracts over 15 million unique visitors each month.

Outdated Order-to-Cash Process

AutoTrader processes thousands of orders and contracts each month. Its cross-functional order fulfillment process, or order-to-cash process, was outdated and could not handle the sales volume. The legacy process was run on *My AutoTrader* (MAT), a system based on Lotus Notes/Domino. MAT took an average of 6.3 to 8.3 days to fulfill orders and process contracts, as Figure 1.16 shows. MAT created a bottleneck that slowed the time from order to cash, or revenue generation. With over 100 coordinated steps, the process was bound to be flawed, resulting in long and error-prone cycle times. **Cycle time** is the time required to complete a given process. At AutoTrader, cycle time is the time between

the signing and delivery of a contract. Customers were aggravated by the unnecessary delay in revenue.

Redesigning the Order Fulfillment Process with BPM

Management had set three new objectives for the company: to be agile, to generate revenue faster, and to increase customer satisfaction. They invested in a BPM (business process management) solution—selecting webMethods from Software AG (softwareag.com, 2011). The BPM software was used to document how tasks were performed using the legacy system. After simplifying the process as much as possible, remaining tasks were automated or optimized. The new system cuts down the order fulfillment process to 1 day, as shown in Figure 1.17. Changes and benefits resulting from the redesigned process are:

- There are only six human tasks even though the process interacts with over 20 different data sources and systems, including the inventory, billing, and contract fulfillment.

- Tasks are assigned immediately to the right people, who are alerted when work is added to their queues.

- Fewer than five percent of orders need to go back to sales for clarification—a 400 percent improvement.

- Managers can check order fulfillment status anytime using webMethods Optimize for Process, which provides real time visibility into performance. They can measure key performance indicators (KPIs) in real time to see where to make improvements.

- Dealers can make changes directly to their contracts, which cut costs for personnel. Software and hardware costs are decreasing as the company retires old systems.

Sources: Compiled from Walsh (2012), softwareag.com (2011), Alesci & Saitto (2012).

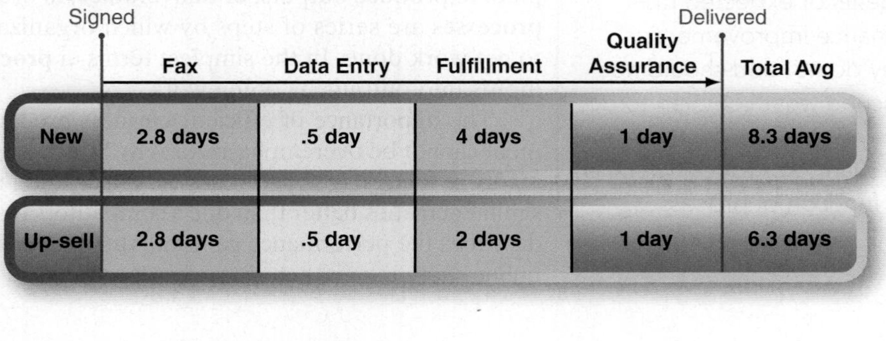

Figure 1.16 AutoTrader's legacy order fulfillment process had an average cycle time of up to 8.3 days.

		Contract Signed				Contract Delivered
		Fax	**Data Entry**	**Fulfillment**	**Quality Assurance**	**Total Avg**
New		2.8 days	.5 day	4 days	1 day	8.3 days
Up-sell		2.8 days	.5 day	2 days	1 day	6.3 days

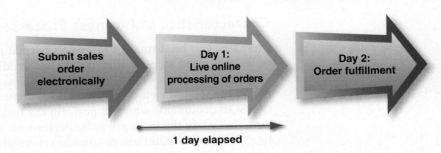

Figure 1.17 AutoTrader's objective is to process and fill orders within one day.

Questions

1. Discuss how the redesigned order process supports the company's three new business objectives.

2. How does the reduced cycle time of the order fulfillment process improve revenue generation and customer satisfaction?

3. Does reducing the cycle time of a business process also reduce errors? Why or why not?

THREE COMPONENTS OF BUSINESS PROCESSES

Business processes have three basic components, as shown in Figure 1.18. They involve people, technology, and information.

Examples of common business processes are:

- **Accounting:** Invoicing; reconciling accounts; auditing
- **Finance:** Credit card or loan approval; estimating credit risk and financing terms
- **Human resources (HR):** Recruiting and hiring; assessing compliance with regulations; evaluating job performance
- **IT or information systems:** Generating and distributing reports and data visualizations; data analytics; data archiving
- **Marketing:** Sales; product promotion; design and implementation of sales campaigns; qualifying a lead
- **Production and operations:** Shipping; receiving; quality control; inventory management
- **Cross-functional business processes:** Involving two or more functions, for example, order fulfillment and product development

Deliverables are the outputs or tangible things that are produced by a business process. Common deliverables are products, services, actions, plans, or decisions, such as to approve or deny a credit application. Deliverables are produced in order to achieve specific objectives.

Designing an effective process can be complex because you need a deep understanding of the inputs and outputs (**deliverables**), how things can go wrong, and how to prevent things from going wrong. For example, Dell had implemented a new process to reduce the time that tech support spent handling customer service calls. In an effort to minimize the length of the call, tech support's quality dropped so much that customers had to call multiple times to solve their problems. The new process had backfired—increasing the time to resolve computer problems and aggravating Dell customers.

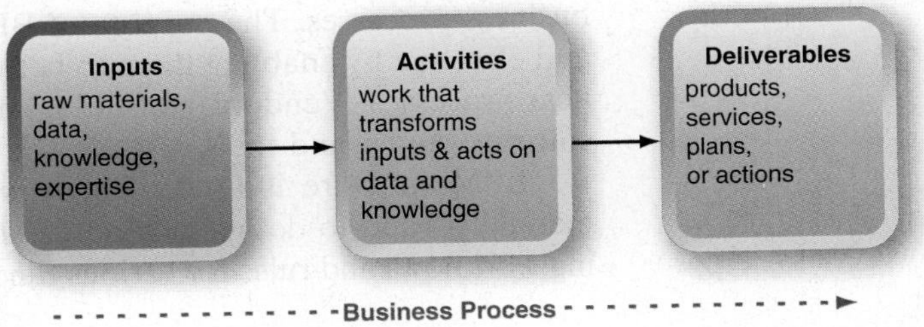

Inputs
raw materials, data, knowledge, expertise

Activities
work that transforms inputs & acts on data and knowledge

Deliverables
products, services, plans, or actions

- - - - - - - - - - - - - - Business Process - - - - - - - - - - - - - ▶

Figure 1.18 Three components of a business process.

Characteristics of Business Processes

Processes can be formal or informal. **Formal processes** are documented and have well-established steps. Order taking and credit approval processes are examples. Routine formal processes are referred to as **standard operating procedures**, or **SOPs**. A SOP is a well-defined and documented way of doing something. An effective SOP documents who will perform the tasks; what materials to use; and where, how, and when the tasks are to be performed. SOPs are needed for the handling of food, hazardous materials, or situations involving safety, security, or compliance. In contrast, **informal processes** are typically undocumented, have inputs that may not yet been identified, and are knowledge-intensive. Although enterprises would prefer to formalize their informal processes in order to better understand, share, and optimize them, in many situations process knowledge remains in people's heads.

Processes range from slow, rigid to fast-moving, adaptive. Rigid processes can be structured to be resistant to change, such as those that enforce security or compliance regulations. Adaptive processes are designed to respond to change or emerging conditions, particularly in marketing and IT.

Process Improvement

Given that a company's success depends on the efficiency of its business processes, even small improvements in key processes have significant payoff. Poorly designed, flawed, or outdated business processes waste resources, increasing costs, causing delays, and aggravating customers. For example, when customers' orders are not filled on time or correctly, customer loyalty suffers, returns increase, and reshipping increases costs. The blame may be flawed order fulfilment processes and not employee incompetence, as described in IT at Work 1.2.

Simply applying IT to a manual or outdated process will not optimize it. Processes need to be examined to determine whether they are still necessary. After unnecessary processes are identified and eliminated, the remaining ones are redesigned (or reengineered) in order to automate or streamline them. Methods and efforts to eliminate wasted steps within a process are referred to as **business process reengineering (BPR)**. The goal of BPR is to eliminate the unnecessary, non-value-added processes, then to simplify and automate the remaining processes to significantly reduce cycle time, labor, and costs. For example, reengineering the credit approval process cuts time from several days or hours to minutes or less. Simplifying processes naturally reduces the time needed to complete the process, which also cuts down on errors.

After eliminating waste, digital technology can enhance processes by (1) automating existing manual processes; (2) expanding the data flows to reach more functions in order to make it possible for sequential activities to occur in parallel; and (3) creating innovative business processes that, in turn, create new business models. For instance, consumers can scan an image of a product and land on an e-commerce site, such as Amazon.com, selling that product. This process flips the traditional selling process by making it customer-centric.

Business Process Management

BPR is part of the larger discipline of **business process management (BPM)**, which consists of methods, tools, and technology to support and continuously improve business processes. The purpose of BPM is to help enterprises become more agile and effective by enabling them to better understand, manage, and adapt their business processes. Vendors, consulting and tech firms offer BPM expertise, services, software suites, and tools.

BPM software is used to map processes performed either by computers or manually—and to design new ones. The software includes built-in templates showing workflows and rules for various functions, such as rules for credit approval. These templates and rules provide consistency and high-quality outcomes. For example, Oracle's WebLogic Server Process Edition includes server software and process integration tools for automating complex business processes, such as handling an insurance claim.

But, BPM initiatives can be extremely challenging, and in order to be successful, BPM requires buy-in from a broad cross section of the business, the right technology selection, and highly effective change management processes. You will read more about optimizing business processes and BPM's role in the alignment of IT and business strategy in Chapter 13.

Questions

1. What is a business process? Give three examples.
2. What is the difference between business deliverables and objectives?
3. List and give examples of the three components of a business process.
4. Explain the differences between formal and informal processes.
5. What is a standard operating procedure (SOP)?
6. What is the purpose of business process management (BPM)?

1.3 The Power of Competitive Advantage

In business, as in sports, companies want to win—customers, market share, and so on. Basically, that requires gaining an edge over competitors by being first to take advantage of market opportunities, providing great customer experiences, doing something well that others cannot easily imitate, or convincing customers why it is a more valuable alternative than the competition.

BUILDING BLOCKS OF COMPETITIVE ADVANTAGE

Agility means being able to respond quickly.

Responsiveness means that IT capacity can be easily scaled up or down as needed, which essentially requires cloud computing.

Flexibility means having the ability to quickly integrate new business functions or to easily reconfigure software or apps.

Having a competitive edge means possessing an advantage over your competition. Once an enterprise has developed a competitive edge, maintaining it is an ongoing challenge. It requires forecasting trends and industry changes and what the company needs to do to stay ahead of the game. It demands that you continuously track your competitors and their future plans and promptly take corrective action. In summary, competitiveness depends on IT **agility** and **responsiveness**. The benefit of IT agility is being able to take advantage of opportunities faster or better than competitors.

Closely related to IT agility is **flexibility**. For example, mobile networks are flexible—able to be set up, moved, or removed easily, without dealing with cables and other physical requirements of wired networks. Mass migration to mobile devices from PCs has expanded the scope of IT beyond traditional organizational boundaries—making location practically irrelevant.

IT agility, flexibility, and mobility are tightly interrelated and fully dependent on an organization's IT infrastructure and architecture, which are covered in greater detail in Chapter 2.

With mobile devices, apps, platforms, and social media becoming inseparable parts of work life and corporate collaboration and with more employees working from home, the result is the rapid consumerization of IT. **IT consumerization** is the migration of consumer technology into enterprise IT environments. This shift has occurred because personally owned IT is as capable and cost-effective as its enterprise equivalents.

COMPETITIVE ADVANTAGE

Two key components of corporate profitability are:

1. **Industry structure:** An industry's structure determines the range of profitability of the average competitor and can be very difficult to change.
2. **Competitive advantage:** This is an edge that enables a company to outperform its average competitor. Competitive advantage can be sustained only by continually pursuing new ways to compete.

IT plays a key role in competitive advantage, but that advantage is short-lived if competitors quickly duplicate it. Research firm Gartner defines competitive advantage as a difference between a company and its competitors *that matters to customers.*

It is important to recognize that some types of IT are commodities, which do not provide a special advantage. **Commodities** are basic things that companies need to function, such as electricity and buildings. Computers, databases, and network services are examples of commodities. In contrast, how a business applies IT to support business processes transforms those IT commodities into competitive assets. Critical business processes are those that improve employee performance and profit margins.

STRATEGIC PLANNING AND COMPETITIVE MODELS

Strategy planning is critical for all organizations, including government agencies, health care providers, educational institutions, the military, and other nonprofits. We start by discussing strategic analysis and then explain the activities or component parts of strategic planning.

What Is Strategic (SWOT) Analysis?

There are many views on strategic analysis. In general, strategic analysis is the scanning and review of the political, social, economic, and technical environments of an organization. For example, any company looking to expand its business operations into a developing country has to investigate that country's political and economic stability and critical infrastructure. That strategic analysis would include reviewing the U.S. Central Intelligence Agency's (CIA) *World Factbook*. The *World Factbook* provides information on the history, people, government, economy, geography, communications, transportation, military, and transnational issues for 266 world entities. Then the company would need to investigate competitors and their potential reactions to a new entrant into their market. Equally important, the company would need to assess its ability to compete profitably in the market and impacts of the expansion on other parts of the company. For example, having excess production capacity would require less capital than if a new factory needed to be built.

The purpose of this analysis of the environment, competition, and capacity is to learn about the strengths, weaknesses, opportunities, and threats (SWOT) of the expansion plan being considered. **SWOT analysis**, as it is called, involves the evaluation of strengths and weaknesses, which are internal factors, and opportunities and threats, which are external factors. Examples are:

- **Strengths:** Reliable processes; agility; motivated workforce
- **Weaknesses:** Lack of expertise; competitors with better IT infrastructure
- **Opportunities:** A developing market; ability to create a new market or product
- **Threats:** Price wars or other fierce reaction by competitors; obsolescence

SWOT is only a guide. The value of SWOT analysis depends on how the analysis is performed. Here are several rules to follow:

- Be realistic about the strengths and weaknesses of your organization.
- Be realistic about the size of the opportunities and threats.
- Be specific and keep the analysis simple, or as simple as possible.
- Evaluate your company's strengths and weaknesses in relation to those of competitors (better than or worse than competitors).
- Expect conflicting views because SWOT is subjective, forward-looking, and based on assumptions.

SWOT analysis is often done at the outset of the strategic planning process. Now you will read answers to the question, "What is strategic planning?"

What Is Strategic Planning?

Strategic planning is a series of processes in which an organization selects and arranges its businesses or services to keep the organization healthy or able to function even when unexpected events disrupt one or more of its businesses, markets, products, or services. Strategic planning involves environmental scanning and prediction, or SWOT analysis, for each business relative to competitors in that business's market or product line. The next step in the strategic planning process is strategy.

What Is Strategy?

Strategy defines the plan for how a business will achieve its mission, goals, and objectives. The plan specifies the necessary financial requirements, budgets, and resources. Strategy addresses fundamental issues such as the company's position in its industry, its available resources and options, and future directions. A strategy addresses questions such as:

- What is the long-term direction of our business?
- What is the overall plan for deploying our resources?
- What trade-offs are necessary? What resources will need to be shared?
- What is our position compared to that of our competitors?
- How do we achieve competitive advantage over rivals in order to achieve or maximize profitability?

Two of the most well-known methodologies were developed by Michael Porter.

Porter's Competitive Forces Model and Strategies

Michael Porter's **competitive forces model**, also called the **five-forces model**, has been used to identify competitive strategies. The model demonstrates how IT can enhance competitiveness. Professor Porter discusses this model in detail in a 13-minute YouTube video from Harvard Business School.

Video 1-1
Five Competitive Forces that Shape Strategy, by Michael Porter: youtube.com/ watch?v=mYF2_FBCvXw

The model recognizes five major forces (think of them as pressures or drivers) that influence a company's position within a given industry and the strategy that management chooses to pursue. Other forces, including new regulations, affect all companies in the industry, and have a rather uniform impact on each company in an industry.

According to Porter, an industry's profit potential is largely determined by the intensity of competitive forces within the industry, shown in Figure 1.19. A good understanding of the industry's competitive forces and their underlying causes is a crucial component of strategy formulation.

Basis of the competitive forces model Before examining the model, it is helpful to understand that it is based on the fundamental concept of profitability and **profit margin:**

PROFIT = TOTAL REVENUES minus TOTAL COSTS

Profit is increased by increasing total revenues and/or decreasing total costs. Profit is decreased when total revenues decrease and/or total costs increase:

PROFIT MARGIN = SELLING PRICE minus COST OF THE ITEM

Profit margin measures the amount of profit per unit of sales, and does not take into account all costs of doing business.

Five industry forces According to Porter's competitive forces model, the five major forces in an industry affect the degree of competition, which impact profit margins and ultimately profitability. These forces interact, so while you read about them individually, their interaction determines the industry's profit potential. For example, while profit margins for pizzerias may be small, the ease of entering that

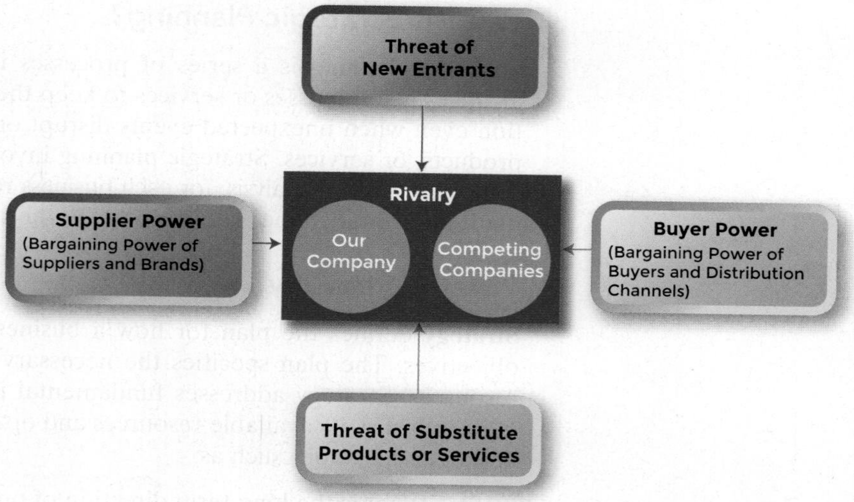

Figure 1.19 Porter's competitive forces model.

industry draws new entrants. Conversely, profit margins for delivery services may be large, but the cost of the IT needed to support the service is a huge barrier to entry into the market.

The five industry (or market) forces are:

1. **Threat of entry of new competitors.** Industries that have large profit margins attract entrants into the market to a greater degree than industries with small margins. The same principle applies to jobs—people are attracted to higher-paying jobs, provided that they can meet the criteria or acquire the skills for that job. In order to gain market share, entrants usually need to sell at lower prices as an incentive. Their tactics can force companies already in the industry to defend their market share by lowering prices—reducing profit margin. Thus, this threat puts downward pressure on profit margins by driving down prices.

   This force also refers to the strength of the **barriers to entry** into an industry, which is how easy it is to enter an industry. The threat of entry is lower (less powerful) when existing companies have ITs that are difficult to duplicate or very expensive. Those ITs create barriers to entry that reduce the threat of entry.

2. **Bargaining power of suppliers.** Bargaining power is high where the supplier or brand is powerful, such as Apple, Microsoft, and auto manufacturers. Power is determined by how much a company purchases from a supplier. The more powerful company has the leverage to demand better prices or terms, which increase its profit margin. Conversely, suppliers with very little bargaining power tend to have small profit margins.

3. **Bargaining power of customers or buyers.** This force is the reverse of the bargaining power of suppliers. Examples are Walmart and government agencies. This force is high when there are few large customers or buyers in a market.

4. **Threat of substituting products or services.** Where there is product-for-product substitution, such as Kindle for Nook, there is downward pressure on prices. As the threat of substitutes increases, the profit margin decreases because sellers need to keep prices competitively low.

5. **Competitive rivalry among existing firms in the industry.** Fierce competition involves expensive advertising and promotions, intense investments in research and development (R&D), or other efforts that cut into profit margins. This force is most likely to be high when entry barriers are low, the threat of substitute products is high, and suppliers and buyers in the market attempt to control it. That is why this force is placed in the center of the model.

The strength of each force is determined by the industry's structure. Existing companies in an industry need to protect themselves against these forces. Alternatively, they can take advantage of the forces to improve their position or to challenge industry leaders. The relationships are shown in Figure 1.19.

Companies can identify the forces that influence competitive advantage in their marketplace and then develop their strategy. Porter (1985) proposed three types of strategies—cost leadership, differentiation, and niche strategies. In Table 1.2, Porter's three classical strategies are listed first, followed by a list of nine other general strategies for dealing with competitive advantage. Each of these strategies can be enhanced by IT.

TABLE 1.2   Strategies for Competitive Advantage

Strategy	Description
Cost leadership	Produce product/service at the lowest cost in the industry.
Differentiation	Offer different products, services, or product features.
Niche	Select a narrow-scope segment (market niche) and be the best in quality, speed, or cost in that segment.
Growth	Increase market share, acquire more customers, or sell more types of products.
Alliance	Work with business partners in partnerships, alliances, joint ventures, or virtual companies.
Innovation	Introduce new products/services; put new features in existing products/services; develop new ways to produce products/services.
Operational effectiveness	Improve the manner in which internal business processes are executed so that the firm performs similar activities better than its rivals.
Customer orientation	Concentrate on customer satisfaction.
Time	Treat time as a resource, then manage it and use it to the firm's advantage.
Entry barriers	Create barriers to entry. By introducing innovative products or using IT to provide exceptional service, companies can create entry barriers to discourage new entrants.
Customer or supplier lock-in	Encourage customers or suppliers to stay with you rather than going to competitors. Reduce customers' bargaining power by locking them in.
Increase switching costs	Discourage customers or suppliers from going to competitors for economic reasons.

Primary activities are those business activities directly involved in the production of goods. Primary activities involve the purchase of materials, the processing of materials into products, and delivery of products to customers. The five primary activities are:

1. **Inbound logistics**, or acquiring and receiving of raw materials and other inputs
2. **Operations**, including manufacturing and testing
3. **Outbound logistics**, which includes packaging, storage, delivery, and distribution
4. **Marketing and sales** to customers
5. **Services,** including customer service

The primary activities usually take place in a sequence from 1 to 5. As work progresses, value is added to the product in each activity. To be more specific, the incoming materials (1) are processed (in receiving, storage, etc.) in activities called inbound logistics. Next, the materials are used in operations (2), where significant value is added by the process of turning raw materials into products. Products need to be prepared for delivery (packaging, storing, and shipping) in the outbound logistics activities (3). Then marketing and sales (4) attempt to sell the products to customers, increasing product value by creating demand for the company's products. The value of a sold item is much larger than that of an unsold one. Finally, after-sales service (5), such as warranty service or upgrade notification, is performed for the customer, further adding value.

Primary activities rely on the following **support activities**:

1. The firm's infrastructure, accounting, finance, and management
2. Human resources (HR) management (For an IT-related HR trend, see IT at Work 1.4.)
3. Technology development, and research and development (R&D)
4. Procurement, or purchasing

Each support activity can be applied to any or all of the primary activities. Support activities may also support each other, as shown in Figure 1.20.

Innovation and adaptability are **critical success factors**, or **CSFs**, related to Porter's models. CSFs are those things that must go right for a company to achieve its mission.

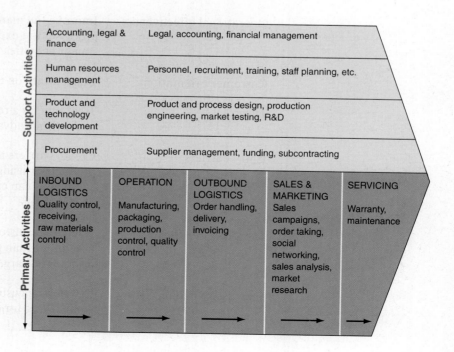

Figure 1.20 A firm's value chain. The arrows represent the flow of goods, services, and data.

IT at Work 1.4

Finding Qualified Talent

Managers at a global energy services company could not find or access their best talent to solve clients' technical problems because of geographic boundaries and business unit barriers. The company's help desks supported engineers well enough for common problems, but not for difficult issues that needed creative solutions. Using Web technologies to expand access to experts worldwide, the company set up new innovation communities across its business units, which have improved the quality of its services.

Dow Chemical set up its own social network to help managers identify the talent they need to carry out projects across its diverse business units and functions. To expand its talent pool, Dow extended the network to include former employees and retirees.

Other companies are using networks to tap external talent pools. These networks include online labor markets such as Amazon Mechanical Turk and contest services such as InnoCentive that help solve business problems.

- Amazon Mechanical Turk is a marketplace for work that requires human intelligence. Its web service enables companies to access a diverse, on-demand workforce.

- InnoCentive is an "open innovation" company that takes R&D problems in a broad range of areas such as engineering, computer science, and business and frames them as "challenge problems" for anyone to solve. It gives cash awards for the best solutions to solvers who meet the challenge criteria.

Sources: Compiled from McKinsey Global Institute (mckinsey.com/insights/mgi.aspx), Amazon Mechanical Turk (aws.amazon.com/mturk), and InnoCentive (Innocentive.com).

Questions

1. Visit and review the Amazon Mechanical Turk website. Explain HITs. How do they provide an on-demand workforce?
2. Visit and review the InnoCentive website. Describe what the company does and how.

Questions

1. What are the characteristics of an agile organization?
2. Explain IT consumerization.
3. What are two key components of corporate profitability?
4. Define competitive advantage.
5. Describe strategic planning.
6. Describe SWOT analysis.
7. Explain Porter's five-forces model, and give an example of each force.

1.4 Enterprise Technology Trends

At the end of his iPhone presentation at MacWorld 2007, Apple's visionary leader Steve Jobs displayed advice once expressed by legendary hockey player Wayne Gretzky (Figure 1.21): "I skate to where the puck is going to be, not where it has been." Steve Jobs added: "And we've always tried to do that at Apple. Since the very very beginning. And we always will." He was telling us that Apple always moves toward where it expects the future will be.

Looking at Apple's history, you see innovative products and services that shaped the future. For example, launching the iTunes store in April 2003 jumpstarted the

Jeff Vinnick/Getty Images

© ZUMA Wire Service/Alamy

Figure 1.21 Wayne Gretzky's strategy for success in hockey was to skate to where the puck was going to be. Steve Jobs followed a similar forward-looking strategy. In October, 2003, Jobs announced a Windows version of the iTunes store, saying "Hell froze over," which brought a big laugh from the audience in San Francisco.

digital music industry. iTunes was a significant breakthrough that forever changed the music industry and the first representation of Apple's future outside its traditional computing product line. You are familiar with the success of that future-driven business model.

Three IT directions for the late 2010s are outlined next. Throughout all the chapters in this book, you will learn how these and other digital technology are transforming business and society.

MORE MOBILE BUSINESS APPS, FEWER DOCS ON DESKTOPS

The direction is away from the traditional *desktop and documents era* and toward business apps in the cloud. Why? Google Apps offers apps that provide workers with information and answers with low effort—instead of having to complete tedious actions, such as logging in or doing extensive searches. This ongoing *move to mobile* raises data security issues. Data stored on mobiles are at higher risk, in part because the devices can be stolen or lost.

MORE SOCIALLY ENGAGED—BUT SUBJECT TO REGULATION

Engaging customers via mobiles and social media sites—and those customers who do not tolerate delays—is the norm. However, customers probably do not know of restrictions on financial institutions and health–care providers that make it illegal to respond to individuals publicly via social media. That is, for regulatory purposes, financial institutions cannot post or respond to comments or e-mails through social media sites because of privacy and security.

MORE NEAR-FIELD COMMUNICATION (NFC) TECHNOLOGY

Near-field communication (NFC) technology is an umbrella description covering several technologies that communicate within a limited distance. Using **radio frequency identification (RFID)** chip-based tags, as shown in Figure 1.22, devices relay identifying data, such as product ID, price, and location, to a nearby reader that captures the data. It is projected that the global market for NFC handsets will reach 1.6 billion units by 2018, according to a recent Global Industry Analysts research report. According to the report, strong demand is "driven by growing penetration of mobile phones, continued rise in demand and production of smartphones, rising penetration of NFC in consumer devices, and chip level technology developments"

Figure 1.22 NFC technology relies on sensors or RFID chips. NFC is used for tracking wine and liquor to manage the supply chain efficiently. NFC smartphones are being integrated into payment systems in supermarkets so customers can pay for purchases without cash or credit cards.

(*NFC World*, 2014). Innovative ways in which businesses are applying NFC include the following:

- Amsterdam's Schiphol Airport has installed an NFC boarding gate allowing passengers to validate their boarding pass with a touch of their NFC smartphone.
- French leather goods brand Delage has partnered with NFC object identification specialist Selinko to integrate NFC tags into its range of premium leather bags. Each bag will have a unique chip and a unique digital serial number. Consumers with an NFC smartphone equipped with Selinko's free mobile app will be able to use the tag to access information about their product and confirm its authenticity as well as access marketing offers.
- iPhone owners in the United States can make Isis payments following AT&T's introduction of a range of phone cases that add NFC functionality to the devices. To use the Isis Mobile Wallet on an iPhone, the owner selects the Isis-ready NFC case, slides the iPhone in, downloads the Isis Mobile Wallet app from the App Store, and taps the iPhone at hundreds of thousands of merchants nationwide for a quick way to pay.

These trends are forces that are changing competition, business models, how workers and operations are managed, and the skills valuable to a career in business.

Questions

1. What was the significance of Apple's introduction of the iPhones music store?
2. What are three IT trends?
3. What are three business applications of NFC?

1.5 How Your IT Expertise Adds Value to Your Performance and Career

Every tech innovation triggers opportunities and threats to business models and strategies. With rare exceptions, every business initiative depends on the mix of IT, knowledge of its potential, the requirements for success, and, equally important, its limitations. Staying current in emerging technologies affecting markets is essential to the careers of knowledge workers, entrepreneurs, managers, and business leaders—not just IT and chief information officers (CIOs).

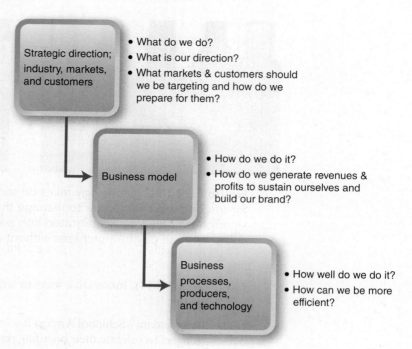

Figure 1.23 Key strategic and tactical questions.

WHAT COMPANIES CAN DO DEPENDS ON THEIR IT

What companies can do depends on what their information technology and data management systems can do. For over a decade, powerful new digital approaches to doing business—and getting through your day—have emerged. And there is sufficient proof to expect even more rapid and dramatic changes due to IT breakthroughs and advances. Understanding trends that affect the ways business is done and getting in front of those trends give you a career edge.

Key strategic and tactical questions that determine an organization's profitability and management performance are shown in Figure 1.23. Answers to each question will entail understanding the capabilities of mundane to complex ITs, which ones to implement, and how to manage them.

IT CAREERS OUTLOOK

Having a feel for the job market helps you improve your career options. According to the U.S. Department of Labor, and the University of California Los Angeles (UCLA), the best national jobs in terms of growth, advancement, and salary increases in 2013 are in the fields of IT, engineering, health care, finance, construction, and management. It is projected that these job categories will see above-average national growth over the next several years. The U.S. Department of Labor projections are generally 6–10 years in reference.

With big data, data science, and M2M, companies are increasing their IT staff. In addition, many new businesses are seeking more programmers and designers. Data security threats continue to get worse. The field of IT covers a wide range that includes processing of streaming data, data management, big data analytics, app development, system analysis, information security, and more.

Job growth is estimated at 53 percent by 2018, according to the U.S. Department of Labor; and salaries in many IT jobs will increase by 4 to 6 percent. The lack of skilled IT workers in the U.S. is a primary reason for the outsourcing of IT jobs.

Digital Technology Defines and Creates Businesses and Markets

Digital technology creates markets, businesses, products, and careers. As you continue to read this book, you will see that exciting IT developments are changing how organizations and individuals do things. New technologies and IT-supported functions, such as 4G or 5G networks, embedded sensors, on-demand workforces, and e-readers, point to ground-breaking changes. CNN.com, one of the most respected news media, has created a new market whose impacts are yet to be realized. Visit iReport.com where a pop-up reads, "iReport is the way people like you report the news. The stories in this section are not edited, fact-checked or screened before they post."

IT as a Career: The Nature of IS and IT Work

IT managers play a vital role in the implementation and administration of digital technology. They plan, coordinate, and direct research on the computer-related activities of firms. In consultation with other managers, they help determine the goals of an organization and then implement technology to meet those goals.

Chief technology officers (CTOs) evaluate the newest and most innovative technologies and determine how they can be applied for competitive advantage. CTOs develop technical standards, deploy technology, and supervise workers who deal with the daily IT issues of the firm. When innovative and useful new ITs are launched, the CTO determines implementation strategies, performs cost-benefit or SWOT analysis, and reports those strategies to top management, including the CIO.

IT project managers develop requirements, budgets, and schedules for their firm's information technology projects. They coordinate such projects from development through implementation, working with their organization's IT workers, as well as clients, vendors, and consultants. These managers are increasingly involved in projects that upgrade the information security of an organization.

IT Job Prospects

Workers with specialized technical knowledge and strong communications and business skills, as well as those with an MBA with a concentration in an IT area, will have the best prospects. Job openings will be the result of employment growth and the need to replace workers who transfer to other occupations or leave the labor force (Bureau of Labor Statistics, 2012–2013).

Questions

1. Why is IT a major enabler of business performance and success?
2. Explain why it is beneficial to study IT today.
3. Why are IT job prospects strong?

Key Terms

agility	competitive advantage	inbound logistics	productivity
barriers to entry	competitive forces model	industry structure	radio frequency
big data	(five-forces model)	informal process	identification (RFID)
business model	critical success factor (CSF)	Internet of Things (IoT)	real time system
business process	cross-functional business	IT consumerization	responsiveness
business process	process	IT project manager	services
management (BPM)	customer experience (CX)	key performance	social, mobile, and cloud
business process	cycle time	indicators (KPIs)	(SoMoClo)
reengineering (BPR)	dashboards	machine-to-machine	standard operating
business-to-business	data analytics	(M2M) technology	procedures (SOPs)
(B2B)	data science	near-field communication	supply chain
chief technology officer	dashboard	(NFC) technology	support activities
(CTO)	deliverables	objectives	SWOT analysis
cloud computing	digital business model	operations	unstructured data
commodity	formal process	process	wearable technology

Assuring Your Learning

DISCUSS: Critical Thinking Questions

1. Why are businesses experiencing a digital transformation?

2. More data are collected in a day now than existed in the world 10 years ago. What factors have contributed to this volume of data?

3. Assume you had no smartphone, other mobile device, or mobile apps to use for 24 hours. How would that mobile blackout disrupt your ability to function?

4. What were three highly disruptive digital technologies? Give an example of one disruption for each technology.

5. Why are enterprises adopting cloud computing?

6. What is the value of M2M technology? Give two examples.

7. Starbucks monitors tweets and other sources of big data. How might the company increase revenue from big data analytics?

8. Select three companies in different industries, such as banking, retail store, supermarket, airlines, or package delivery, that you do business with. What digital technologies does each company use to

engage you, keep you informed, or create a unique customer experience? How effective is each use of digital technology to keeping you a loyal customer?

9. Describe two examples of the influence of SoMoClo on the financial industry.

10. What is a potential impact of the Internet of things on the health-care industry?

11. How could wearable technology be used to create a competitive edge in the athletic and sportswear industry?

12. Why does reducing the cycle time of a business process also help to reduce errors?

13. Research firm Gartner defines competitive advantage as a difference between a company and its competitors *that matters to customers.* Describe one use of M2M technology that could provide a manufacturer with a competitive advantage.

14. What IT careers are forecasted to be in high demand? Explain why.

15. Why or how would understanding the latest IT trends influence your career?

EXPLORE: Online and Interactive Exercises

16. Research the growing importance of big data analytics. Find two forecasts of big data growth. What do they forecast?

17. Go to the U.S. Department of Commerce website and search for U.S. Economy at a Glance: Perspective from the BEA Accounts.

   a. Review the BEA homepage to learn the types of information, news, reports, and interactive data available. Search for the page that identifies who

uses BEA measures. Identify two users of industry data and two users of international trade and investment data.

   b. Click on the Glossary. Use the Glossary to explain GDP in your own words.

   c. Under the NEWS menu, select U.S. Economy at a Glance. Review the GDP current numbers for the last two reported quarters. How did GDP change in each of these two quarters?

ANALYZE & DECIDE: Apply IT Concepts to Business Decisions

18. A transportation company is considering investing in a truck tire with embedded sensors—the Internet of Things. Outline the benefits of this investment. Would this investment create a long-term competitive advantage for the transportation company?

19. Visit the website of UPS (ups.com), Federal Express (fedex.com), and one other logistics and delivery company.

   a. At each site, what information is available to customers before and after they send a package?

   b. Compare the three customer experiences.

20. Visit YouTube.com and search for two videos on Michael Porter's strategic or competitive forces models. For each video, report what you learned. Specify the complete URL, video title, who uploaded the video and the date, video length, and number of views.

21. Visit Dell.com and Apple.com to simulate buying a laptop computer. Compare and contrast the selection process, degree of customization, and other buying features. What are the barriers to entry into this market, based on what you learned from this exercise?

CASE 1.2
Business Case: Restaurant Creates Opportunities to Engage Customers

Back when phones were used only to make calls, few retailers and restaurants could have predicted that mobile technology was going to transform their industries. Smartphones and other portable devices are access points to customers. Companies can push real time, personally targeted ads to customers' phones using text messages, or interact with them using location-aware mobile apps. And potential customers can access product or brand information using 2D codes, and comparison-shop right in the store.

Brands are always looking for more effective ways to integrate social media with traditional media, such as print and TV, when implementing marketing campaigns. Managing these campaigns and interactions requires specialized software, and possibly support from the vendor or consulting firm if the company lacks in-house expertise.

Pei Wei Asian Diner's Mobile and Cloud Campaign

Pei Wei Asian Diner (www.peiwei.com), a fast-food casual restaurant chain owned by P.F. Chang's China Bistro, is an example of a company that invested in technology to manage multichannel (also called *cross-channel*) marketing campaigns. In mid-2011 Pei Wei introduced a new entrée, Caramel Chicken. The company integrated traditional in-store promotions with mobile and Web-based marketing efforts to motivate people to subscribe to its e-mail marketing campaign. It also reached out to fans via Facebook and Twitter. The success of the new campaign depended on investing in appropriate software and expertise. With thousands of tweets, Facebook posts, and Google searches per second, companies need IT support to understand what people are saying about their brands.

Campaign Management Software Vendor

Software vendor ExactTarget was selected to run and manage Pei Wei's marketing campaigns. Famous brands—like Expedia, Best Buy, Nike, and Papa John's—also used ExactTarget to power their mission-critical messages. With ExactTarget's software, Pei Wei invited guests to join (register) its e-mail list via text, the Web, Twitter, or Facebook in order to receive a buy-one, get-one free (BOGO) coupon.

Using ExactTarget's software and infrastructure, clients such as Pei Wei can send more than thousands of e-mails per second and millions of messages in 15 minutes. A massive infrastructure and architecture are needed to meet the demands of high-volume senders.

Another feature of ExactTarget is the ability to respond in a real time environment. Companies need to be able to react to the real time actions that their customers are taking across all channels. That is why it is necessary to be able to quickly and easily configure messages that are triggered by external events like purchases or website interactions. Finally, software helps companies immediately respond to customers with burst sending capabilities—sending millions of e-mails in a few minutes.

Why the Campaign Was a Success

Within two weeks, about 20,000 people had responded to the offer by registering. The BOGO coupon redemption rate at Pei Wei's 173 locations was 20 percent. It was the restaurant chain's most successful new e-mail list growth effort to date.

Effective marketing requires companies or brands to create opportunities with which to engage customers. Pei Wei was successful because it used multiple interactive channels to engage—*connect with*—current and potential customers. Brands have a tremendous opportunity to connect with consumers on their mobiles in stores and on Twitter and Facebook.

A 2010 ExactTarget study of more than 1,500 U.S. consumers entitled *The Collaborative Future* found that:

- 27 percent of consumers said they are more likely to purchase from a brand after subscribing to e-mail.
- 17 percent of consumers are more likely to purchase after liking a brand on Facebook.

A study by Forrester Consulting found that 48 percent of interactive marketing executives ranked *understanding customers' cross-channel interactions* as one of the top challenges facing marketing today.

Questions

1. What software capabilities did Pei Wei need to launch its marketing campaign?
2. What factors contributed to the success of Pei Wei's campaign?
3. Why is a high-capacity (massive) infrastructure needed to launch e-mail or text campaigns?
4. Visit ExactTarget.com. Identify and describe how the vendor makes it easy for companies to connect via e-mail and Twitter.
5. What solutions for small businesses does ExactTarget offer?

CASE 1.3

Video Case: What Is the Value of Knowing More and Doing More?

Teradata (Teradata.com) is a leading provider of big data and data analytics solutions. In a video, Teradata explains that when you know the right thing to do, you can do more of what truly matters for your business and your customers. View the video entitled "What Would You Do If You Knew?"™ at http://www.teradata.com/Resources/Videos/What-would-you-do-if-you-knew/

Questions

1. What did you learn from the video?
2. What is the value of knowing and doing more?

References

Accenture Technology Vision 2013.

Alesci, C. & S. Saitto. "AutoTrader.Com Said to Be in Talks About Possible IPO of Buyer-Seller Site." *Bloomberg,* February 4, 2012.

Bureau of Labor Statistics. *Occupational Outlook Handbook.* U.S. Department of Labor, 2012–2013.

Central Intelligence Agency (CIA). *World Factbook.*

Cooper, B. B. "10 Surprising Social Media Statistics That Will Make You Rethink Your Social Strategy." *Fast Company,* November 18, 2013.

Davenport, T.H. & D.J. Patil. "Data Scientist: The Sexiest Job of the 21st Century." *Harvard Business Review Magazine.* October 2012.

"Gartner Reveals Top Predictions for IT Organizations and Users for 2013 and Beyond." *Gartner Newsroom.* October 24, 2012.

glassdoor.com. "Data Analyst Salaries." May 8, 2014.

Gnau, S. "Putting Big Data in Context." *Wired,* September 10, 2013.

Joy, O. "What Does It Mean to Be a Digital Native?" *CNN,* December 8, 2012.

Kelly, M. "Data Scientists Needed: Why This Career Is Exploding Right Now." *VentureBeat.com,* November 11, 2013.

Lockard, C.B. & M. Wolf. "Occupational Employment Projections to 2020." *Monthly Labor Review,* January 2012.

McCain Foods. "McCain Foods: Integrating Data from the Plant to the Boardroom to Increase the Bottom Line." *Teradata.com,* 2013.

NFC World. "News in Brief." February 2014.

Pogue, D. "Embracing the Mothers of Invention." *The New York Times,* January 25, 2012.

Porter, M. E. *The Competitive Advantage: Creating and Sustaining Superior Performance.* NY: Free Press. 1985.

Porter, M. E. "Strategy and the Internet." *Harvard Business Review,* March 2001.

Schmidt-Subramanian, M., H. Manning, J. Knott, & M. Murphy. "The Business Impact of Customer Experience, 2013." *Forrester Research,* June 10, 2013.

Smith, Gavin. "Frozen Food Production in the US Industry Market Research Report from IBISWorld Has Been Updated." *PRWeb,* March 27, 2013.

softwareag.com. "Orders Are in the Fast Lane at AutoTrader.com—Thanks to BPM." 2011.

Transparency Market Research. "Frozen Food Market—Global Industry Analysis, Size, Share, Growth, Trends and Forecast, 2013–2019." September 2013.

U.S. Department of Labor, Bureau of Labor Statistics. 2014.

Walsh, M. "Autotrader.com Tops In Local Online Ad Dollars." *MediaPost.com,* April 3, 2012.

2 Data Governance and IT Architecture Support Long-Term Performance

Chapter Snapshot

Case 2.1 Opening Case: Detoxing Dirty Data with Data Governance at Intel Security

2.1 Information Management

2.2 Enterprise Architecture and Data Governance

2.3 Information Systems: The Basics

2.4 Data Centers, Cloud Computing, and Virtualization

2.5 Cloud Services Add Agility

Key Terms

Assuring Your Learning

- **Discuss:** Critical Thinking Questions
- **Explore:** Online and Interactive Exercises
- **Analyze & Decide:** Apply IT Concepts to Business Decisions

Case 2.2 Business Case: Data Chaos Creates Risk

Case 2.3 Video Case: Cloud Computing: Three Case Studies

References

Learning Outcomes

1. Explain the business benefits of information management and how data quality determines system success or failure.

2. Describe how enterprise architecture (EA) and data governance play leading roles in guiding IT growth and sustaining long-term performance.

3. Map the functions of various types of information systems to the type of support needed by business operations and decision makers.

4. Describe the functions of data centers, cloud computing, and virtualization and their strengths, weaknesses, and cost considerations.

5. Explain the range of cloud services, their benefits, and business and legal risks that they create.

Chapter Snapshot

High performance is about outperforming rivals again and again, even as the basis of competition in an industry changes. Markets do not stand still and the basis of competition is changing at a faster pace. By the time a company's financial performance starts tapering off, it might be too late to start building new market-relevant capabilities. To stay ahead, today's leaders seek out new ways to grow their businesses during rapid technology changes, more empowered consumers and employees, and more government intervention.

Effective ways to thrive over the long term are to launch new business models and strategies or devise new ways to outperform competitors. In turn, these performance capabilities depend on a company's enterprise IT architecture and data governance. The *enterprise IT architecture,* or simply the **enterprise architecture (EA)**, guides the evolution and expansion of information systems, digital technology, and business processes. This guide is needed in order to leverage IT capability for competitive advantage and growth. **Data governance**, or *information governance,* is the control of enterprise data through formal policies and procedures. A goal of data governance is to provide employees and business partners with high-quality data they trust and can access on demand.

CASE 2.1 OPENING CASE

Detoxing Dirty Data with Data Governance at Intel Security

TABLE 2.1	Opening Case Overview
Company	McAfee was renamed **Intel Security** in 2014. It is a subsidiary of Intel Corp. headquartered in Santa Clara, CA. Has more than $2 billion in revenues annually, over 7,600 employees, and over 1 million customers.
Industry	Cybersecurity software, hardware, and services.
Product lines	The company develops, markets, distributes, and supports cybersecurity products that protect computers, networks, and mobile devices. They offer managed security services to protect endpoints, servers, networks, and mobile devices. Consulting, training and support services are also provided.
Digital technology	Data governance and master data management (MDM) in order to build a best-in-class customer data management capability to facilitate the company's vision.
Business vision	To become the fastest-growing dedicated security company in the world.

COMPANY OVERVIEW

Intel Security protects data and IT resources from attack and unauthorized access. The company provides cybersecurity services to large enterprises, governments, small- and medium-sized businesses, and consumers. A significant portion of its revenues comes from postsales service, support, and subscriptions to its software and managed services. The company sells directly and also through resellers to corporations and consumers in the United States, Europe, Asia, and Latin America.

CUSTOMER-CENTRIC BUSINESS MODEL

Customer-centric business models strive to create the best solution or experience for the customer. In contrast, product-centric models are internally focused on creating the best product.

Intel Security management recognized that it needed to implement a best-practices **customer-centric** business model. In the fiercely competitive industry, the ability to connect with customers, anticipate their needs, and provide flawless customer service is essential to loyalty and long-term growth. Why? Mostly because social and mobile technology is forcing businesses to offer excellent customer experiences (CX) across every available touchpoint, including chat, video, mobile apps, and alerts (Figure 2.2). A **touchpoint** is "any influencing action initiated through communication, human contact or physical or sensory interaction" (De Clerck, 2013).

Most customers search for and exchange detailed information about the good and bad of their encounters with companies. (You will read about Yelp and the

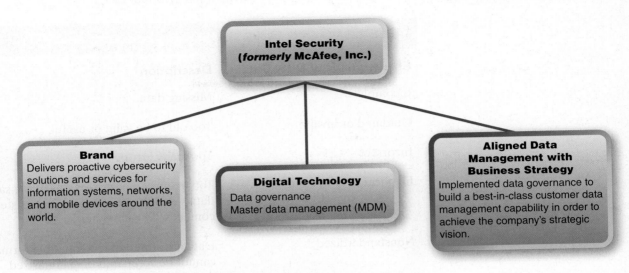

Figure 2.1 Intel Security overview.

United Breaks Guitar video in Chapter 7.) This transparency gives companies a strong incentive to work harder to make customers happy before, during, and after their purchases.

By creating a customer-centric business model, Intel Security can track what is working for its customers and what is not. Using digital technology and data analytics to understand customer touchpoints would enable the company to connect with customers in meaningful ways. Committing to a better experience for customers can increase revenue and promote loyalty—and achieve the company's growth objective.

BUSINESS CHALLENGES FROM POOR-QUALITY CUSTOMER DATA

Dirty data are data of such poor quality that they cannot be trusted or relied upon for decisions.

Intel Security is following a growth-driven business strategy. Its vision is to become the fastest-growing dedicated security company in the world. Management recognized that accurate customer data are the foundation of top-notch customer service. But, they faced a common business problem—poor-quality customer data. Characteristics of poor-quality data, also known as **dirty data**, are listed in Table 2.2.

Duplicate customer records and incomplete customer data were harming sales. The company could not effectively **cross-sell** (sell complementary products or services) or **up-sell** (sell more expensive models or features). Opportunities to get customers to renew their software licenses—and keep them loyal—were being lost. Data errors degraded sales forecasts and caused order-processing mistakes. Time was wasted trying to find, validate, and correct customer records and manually reconcile month-end sales and calculate sales commissions. Until the causes of dirty data were identified and corrected, the growth strategy could not be achieved.

Figure 2.2 Providing excellent service to customers via their preferred touchpoints, such as online chat, has never been more important as consumers use social media to rate brands, expose bad service, and vent their frustrations.

TABLE 2.2 Characteristics of Poor-Quality or Dirty Data

Characteristic of Dirty Data	Description
Incomplete	Missing data.
Outdated or invalid	Too old to be valid or useful.
Incorrect	Too many errors.
Duplicated or in conflict	Too many copies or versions of the same data—and the versions are inconsistent or in conflict with each other.
Nonstandardized	Data are stored in incompatible formats—and cannot be compared or summarized.
Unusable	Data are not in context to be understood or interpreted correctly at the time of access.

DATA QUALITY SOLUTION: DATA GOVERNANCE

Data governance is the control of enterprise data through formal policies and procedures to help ensure that data can be trusted and are accessible.

BENEFITS OF DATA GOVERNANCE AND MDM

Master data management (MDM) methods synchronize all business-critical data from disparate systems into a master file, which provides a trusted data source.

Working with consulting company First San Francisco Partners, Intel Security planned and implemented **data governance** and **master data management (MDM)**. **Master data** are the business-critical information on customers, products, accounts, and other things that is needed for operations and business transactions. Master data were stored in disparate systems spread across the enterprise. MDM would link and synchronize all critical data from those disparate systems into one file, called a **master file**, that provided a common point of reference. Data governance and MDM manage the availability, usability, integrity, and security of the data used throughout the enterprise. Intel Security's data governance strategy and MDM were designed after a thorough review of its 1.3 million customer records, sales processes, and estimated future business requirements.

Data governance and MDM have improved the quality of Intel Security's customer data, which were essential for its customer-centric business model. With high-quality data, the company is able to identify up-sell and cross-sell sales opportunities. Best practices for customer data management improved customer experiences that translated into better customer retention and acquisition. The key benefits achieved after implementing data governance and the MDM architecture to improve data quality are:

- Better customer experience
- Greater customer loyalty and retention
- Increased sales growth
- Accurate sales forecasts and order processing

Intel Security has successfully aligned its IT capabilities to meet business needs. All these efforts benefit the business by improving productivity as a result of reduced data-cleansing efforts, and by increasing sales as a result of better customer experiences.

Sources: Compiled from mcafee.com (2013), De Clerck, (2013), First San Francisco Partners (2009), and Rich (2013).

Questions

1. What is the difference between customer-centric and product-centric business models?
2. Explain the business challenges caused by Intel Security's dirty data.
3. What is the function of data governance?
4. Describe the function of master data.
5. Why is it important to keep data synchronized across disparate systems?
6. Why did Intel Security need master data management (MDM)?
7. How did MDM and data governance enable the company to achieve its vision?
8. What benefits did the company achieve as a result of implementing data governance and MDM?

2.1   Information Management

Most business initiatives succeed or fail based on the quality of their data. Effective planning and decisions depend on systems being able to make data available to decision makers in usable formats on a timely basis. Most everyone manages information. You manage your social and cloud accounts across multiple mobile devices and computers. You update or synchronize ("synch") your calendars, appointments, contact lists, media files, documents, and reports. Your productivity depends on the compatibility of devices and apps and their ability to share data. Not being able to transfer and synch whenever you add a device or app is bothersome and wastes your time. For example, when you switch to the latest mobile device, you might need to reorganize content to make dealing with data and devices easier. To simplify add-ons, upgrades, sharing, and access, you might leverage cloud services such as iTunes, Instagram, Diigo, and Box.

Information management is the use of IT tools and methods to collect, process, consolidate, store, and secure data from sources that are often fragmented and inconsistent.

This is just a glimpse of the **information management** situations that organizations face today—and why a continuous plan is needed to guide, control, and govern IT growth. As with building construction (Figure 2.3), blueprints and models help guide and govern future IT and digital technology investments.

INFORMATION MANAGEMENT HARNESSES SCATTERED DATA

Business information is generally scattered throughout an enterprise, stored in separate systems dedicated to specific purposes, such as operations, supply chain management, or customer relationship management. Major organizations have over 100 data repositories (storage areas). In many companies, the integration of these disparate systems is limited—as is users' ability to access all the information they

Figure 2.3 Blueprints and models, like those used for building construction, are needed to guide and govern an enterprise's IT assets.

© Martin Barraud/Alamy

need. Therefore, despite all the information flowing through companies, executives, managers, and workers often struggle to find the information they need to make sound decisions or do their jobs. The overall goal of information management is to eliminate that struggle through the design and implementation of data governance and a well-planned enterprise architecture.

Providing easy access to large volumes of information is just one of the challenges facing organizations. The days of simply managing structured data are over. Now, organizations must manage semistructured and unstructured content from social and mobile sources even though that data may be of questionable quality.

Information management is critical to data security and compliance with continually evolving regulatory requirements, such as the Sarbanes-Oxley Act, Basel III, the Computer Fraud and Abuse Act (CFAA), the USA PATRIOT Act, and the Health Insurance Portability and Accountability Act (HIPAA).

Issues of information access, management, and security must also deal with information degradation and disorder—where people do not understand what data mean or how they can be useful.

REASONS FOR INFORMATION DEFICIENCIES

Companies' information and decision support technologies have developed over many decades. During that time span, there have been different management teams with their own priorities and understanding of the role of IT; technology advanced in unforeseeable ways, and IT investments were cut or increased based on competing demands on the budget. These are some of the contributing factors. Other common reasons why information deficiencies are still a problem include:

Data silos are stand-alone data stores. Their data are not accessible by other ISs that need it or outside that department.

1. **Data silos.** Information can be *trapped* in departments' **data silos** (also called *information silos*), such as marketing or production databases. Data silos are illustrated in Figure 2.4. Since silos are unable to share or exchange data, they cannot consistently be updated. When data are inconsistent across multiple enterprise applications, data quality cannot (and should not) be trusted without extensive verification. Data silos exist when there is no overall IT architecture to guide IS investments, data coordination, and communication. Data silos support a single function and, as a result, do not support an organization's cross-functional needs.

   For example, most health-care organizations are drowning in data, yet they cannot get reliable, actionable insights from these data. Physician notes, registration forms, discharge summaries, documents, and more are doubling every five years. Unlike structured machine-ready data, these are messy data that take

Figure 2.4 Data (or information) silos are ISs that do not have the capability to exchange data with other ISs, making timely coordination and communication across functions or departments difficult.

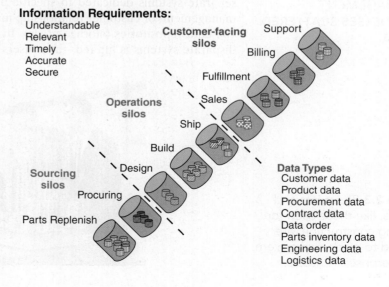

Information Requirements:
Understandable
Relevant
Timely
Accurate
Secure

Customer-facing silos
Support
Billing
Fulfillment
Sales
Ship

Operations silos
Build
Design

Sourcing silos
Procuring
Parts Replenish

Data Types
Customer data
Product data
Procurement data
Contract data
Data order
Parts inventory data
Engineering data
Logistics data

too much time and effort for health-care providers to include in their business analysis. So, valuable messy data are routinely left out. Millions of patient notes and records sit inaccessible or unavailable in separate clinical data silos because historically there has been no easy way to analyze the information.

2. **Lost or bypassed data.** Data can get lost in transit from one IS to another. Or, data might never get captured because of inadequately tuned data collection systems, such as those that rely on sensors or scanners. Or, the data may not get captured in sufficient enough detail, as described in Tech Note 2.1.

3. **Poorly designed interfaces.** Despite all the talk about user-friendly interfaces, some ISs are horrible to deal with. Poorly designed interfaces or formats that require extra time and effort to figure out increase the risk of errors from misunderstanding the data or ignoring them.

4. **Nonstandardized data formats.** When users are presented with data in inconsistent or nonstandardized formats, errors increase. Attempts to compare or analyze data are more difficult and take more time. For example, if the Northeast division reports weekly gross sales revenues per product line and the Southwest division reports monthly net sales per product, you cannot compare their performance without converting the data to a common format. Consider the extra effort needed to compare temperature-related sales, such as air conditioners, when some temperatures are expressed in degrees Fahrenheit and others in Centigrade.

5. **Cannot hit moving targets.** The information that decision makers want keeps changing—and changes faster than ISs can respond to because of the first four reasons in this list. Tracking tweets, YouTube hits, and other unstructured content requires expensive investments—which managers find risky in an economic downturn.

Without information management, these are the data challenges managers have to face. Companies undergoing fast growth or merger activity or those with decentralized systems (each division or business unit manages its own IT) will end up with a patchwork of reporting processes. As you would expect, patchwork systems are more complicated to modify, too rigid to support an agile business, and yet more expensive to maintain.

TECH NOTE 2.1 Need to Measure in Order to Manage

A residential home construction company had two divisions: standard homes and luxury homes. The company was not capturing material, labor, and other costs associated with each type of construction. Instead, these costs were pooled, making it impossible to allocate costs to each type of construction and then to calculate the profit margins of each division. They had no way of calculating profit margins on each type of home within the divisions. Without the ability to measure costs, they did not have any cost control.

After upgrading their ISs, they began to capture detailed data at the house level. They discovered a wide profit margin on standard homes, which was hiding the negative margins (losses) of the luxury home division. Without cost control data, the profitable standard homes division had been subsidizing the luxury home division for many years.

IT at Work 2.1

Data Quality Determines Systems Success and Failure

Executives at a large chemical corporation were supported by an information system specifically designed for their needs—called an **executive information system (EIS)**. The EIS was designed to provide senior managers with internal and external data and key performance indicators (KPIs) that were relevant to their specific needs. Tech Note 2.2 describes KPIs. As with any system, the value of the EIS depends on the data quality.

Too Much Irrelevant Data

The EIS was a failure. Executives found that only half of the data available through the EIS related to their level of analysis and decision making—the corporate level. A worse problem was that the data they needed were not available when and how they wanted them. For example, executives needed current detailed sales revenue and cost data for every strategic business unit (SBU), product line, and operating business. Sales and cost data were needed for analysis and to compare performance. But, data were not in standardized format as is needed for accurate comparisons and analysis. A large part of the problem was that SBUs reported sales revenues in different time frames (e.g., daily, weekly, monthly, or quarterly), and many of those reports were not available because of delays in preparing them. As a result, senior management could not get a *trusted* view of the company's current overall performance and did not know which products were profitable.

There were two reasons for the failure of the EIS:

1. **IT architecture was not designed for customized reporting.** The design of the IT architecture had been based on financial accounting rules. That is, the data were organized to make it easy to collect and consolidate the data needed to prepare financial statements and reports that had to be submitted to the SEC (Securities and Exchange Commission) and other regulatory agencies. These statements and reports have well-defined or standardized formats and only need to be prepared at specific times during the year, typically annually or quarterly. The organization of the data (for financial reporting)

did not have the flexibility needed for the customized ad hoc (unplanned) data needs of the executives. For example, it was nearly impossible to generate customized sales performance (nonfinancial) reports or do ad hoc analyses, such as comparing inventory turnover rates by product for each region for each sales quarter. Because of lags in reports from various SBUs, executives did not trust the underlying data.

2. **Complicated user interface.** Executives could not easily review the KPIs. Instead, they had to sort through screens packed with too much data—some of interest and some irrelevant. To compensate for poor interface design, several IT analysts themselves had to do the data and KPI analyses for the executives—delaying response time and driving up the cost of reporting.

Solution: New Enterprise IT Architecture with Standardized Data Formats

The CIO worked with a task force to design and implement an entirely new EA. Data governance policies and procedures were implemented to standardize data formats companywide. Data governance eliminated data inconsistencies to provide reliable KPI reports on inventory turns, cycle times, and profit margins of all SBUs.

The new architecture was business-driven instead of financial reporting-driven. It was easy to modify reports—eliminating the costly and time-consuming ad hoc analyses. Fewer IT resources are needed to maintain the system. Because the underlying data are now relatively reliable, EIS use by executives increased significantly.

Questions

1. Why was an EIS designed and implemented?
2. What problems did executives have with the EIS?
3. What were the two reasons for those EIS problems?
4. How did the CIO improve the EIS?
5. What are the benefits of the new IT architecture?
6. What are the benefits of data governance?

TECH NOTE 2.2 KPIs

KPIs are performance measurements. These measures demonstrate the effectiveness of a business process at achieving organizational goals. KPIs present data in easy-to-comprehend and comparison-ready formats. Examples of key comparisons are actual vs. budget, actual vs. forecasted, and this year vs. prior years. KPIs help reduce the complex nature of organizational performance to a small number of understandable measures, including:

- Financial KPIs: current ratio; accounts payable turnover; inventory turnover; net profit margin
- Social media KPIs: social traffic and conversions (number of visitors who are converted to customers); likes; new followers per week; social visits and leads
- Sales and marketing KPIs: cost per lead; how much revenue a marketing campaign generates
- Operational and supply chain KPIs: units per transaction; carrying cost of inventory; order status; back order rate
- Environmental and carbon-footprint KPIs: energy, water, or other resource use; spend by utility; weight of landfill waste

FACTORS DRIVING THE SHIFT FROM SILOS TO SHARING AND COLLABORATION

Senior executives and managers know about their data silos and information management problems, but they also know about the huge cost and disruption associated with converting to newer IT architectures. A Tech CEO Council Report estimated that Fortune 500 companies waste $480 billion every year on inefficient business processes (techceocouncil.org, 2010). However, business process improvements are being made. An IBM study of more than 3,000 CIOs showed that more than 80 percent plan to simplify internal processes, which includes integrated siloed global applications (IBM Institute, 2011). Companies are struggling to integrate thousands of siloed global applications, while aligning them to business operations. To remain competitive, they must be able to analyze and adapt their business processes quickly, efficiently and without disruption.

Greater investments in collaboration technologies have been reported by the research firm Forrester (Keitt, 2011). The three factors that Forrester identified as driving the trend toward collaboration and data sharing technology are shown in Figure 2.5.

BUSINESS BENEFITS OF INFORMATION MANAGEMENT

Based on the examples you have read, the obvious benefits of information management are the following:

1. **Improves decision quality.** Decision quality depends on accurate and complete data.
2. **Improves the accuracy and reliability of management predictions.** It is essential for managers to be able to predict sales, product demand, opportunities, and competitive threats. Management predictions focus on "what is going to happen" as opposed to financial reporting on "what has happened."

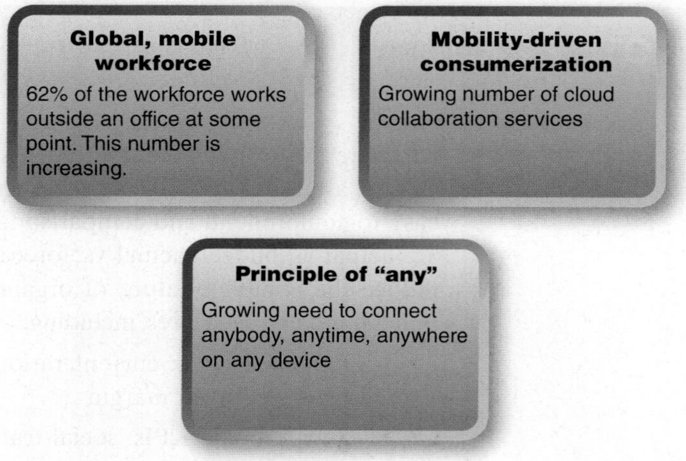

Global, mobile workforce
62% of the workforce works outside an office at some point. This number is increasing.

Mobility-driven consumerization
Growing number of cloud collaboration services

Principle of "any"
Growing need to connect anybody, anytime, anywhere on any device

Figure 2.5 Factors that are increasing demand for collaboration technology.

3. **Reduces the risk of noncompliance.** Government regulations and compliance requirements have increased significantly in the past decade. Companies that fail to comply with laws on privacy, fraud, anti-money laundering, cybersecurity, occupational safety, and so on face harsh penalties.

4. **Reduces the time and cost** of locating and integrating relevant information.

Questions

1. Explain information management.
2. Why do organizations still have information deficiency problems?
3. What is a data silo?
4. Explain KPIs and give an example.
5. What three factors are driving collaboration and information sharing?
6. What are the business benefits of information management?

2.2 Enterprise Architecture and Data Governance

Enterprise architecture (EA) is the way IT systems and processes are structured. EA is an ongoing process of creating, maintaining, and leveraging IT. It helps to solve two critical challenges: *where an organization is going* and *how it will get there.*

Every enterprise has a core set of information systems and business processes that execute the transactions that keep it in business. Transactions include processing orders, order fulfillment and delivery, purchasing inventory and supplies, hiring and paying employees, and paying bills. The **enterprise architecture (EA)** helps or impedes day-to-day operations and efforts to execute business strategy.

Success of EA and data governance is measured in financial terms of profitability and return on investment (ROI), and in the nonfinancial terms of improved customer satisfaction, faster speed to market, and lower employee turnover.

MAINTAINING IT–BUSINESS ALIGNMENT

As you read in Chapter 1, the volume, variety, and velocity of data being collected or generated have grown exponentially. As enterprise information systems become more complex, the importance of long-range IT planning increases dramatically. Companies cannot simply add storage, new apps, or data analytics on an as-needed basis and expect those additions to work with the existing systems.

The relationship between complexity and planning is easier to see in physical things such as skyscrapers and transportation systems. If you are constructing a simple cabin in a remote area, you do not need a detailed plan for expansion or to make sure that the cabin fits into its environment. If you are building a simple, single-user, nondistributed system, you would not need a well-thought-out growth plan either. Therefore, it is no longer feasible to manage big data, content from mobiles and social networks, and data in the cloud without the well-designed set of plans, or blueprint, provided by EA. The EA guides and controls software add-ons and upgrades, hardware, systems, networks, cloud services, and other digital technology investments.

ONGOING PROCESS OF LEVERAGING IT

According to consulting firm Gartner, enterprise architecture is the ongoing process of creating, maintaining, and leveraging IT. It helps to solve two critical challenges: *where an organization is going* and *how it will get there*.

Shared Vision of the Future

EA has to start with the organization's target—*where it is going*—not with where it is. Gartner recommends that an organization begin by identifying the strategic direction in which it is heading and the business drivers to which it is responding. The goal is to make sure that everyone understands and shares a single vision. As soon as managers have defined this single shared vision of the future, they then consider the implications of this vision on the business, technical, information, and solutions architectures of the enterprise. The shared vision of the future will dictate changes in all these architectures, assign priorities to those changes, and keep those changes grounded in business value.

Strategic Focus

There are two problems that the EA is designed to address:

1. **IT systems' complexity.** IT systems have become unmanageably complex and expensive to maintain.
2. **Poor business alignment.** Organizations find it difficult to keep their increasingly expensive IT systems aligned with business needs.

Business and IT Benefits of EA

Having the right architecture in place is important for the following reasons:

- EA cuts IT costs and increases productivity by giving decision makers access to information, insights, and ideas where and when they need them.
- EA determines an organization's competitiveness, flexibility, and IT economics for the next decade and beyond. That is, it provides a long-term view of a company's processes, systems, and technologies so that IT investments do not simply fulfill immediate needs.
- EA helps align IT capabilities with business strategy—to grow, innovate, and respond to market demands, supported by an IT practice that is 100 percent in accord with business objectives.
- EA can reduce the risk of buying or building systems and enterprise apps that are incompatible or unnecessarily expensive to maintain and integrate.

Basic EA components are listed and described in Table 2.3. IT at Work 2.2 describes Gartner's view of EA.

TABLE 2.3	Components of Enterprise Architecture
Business architecture	The processes the business uses to meet its goals.
Application architecture	How specific applications are designed and how they interact with each other.
Data architecture	How an enterprise's data stores are organized and accessed.
Technical architecture	The hardware and software infrastructure that supports applications and their interactions.

IT at Work 2.2

EA Is Dynamic

In order to keep IT and business in alignment, the EA must be a dynamic plan. As shown in the model in Figure 2.6, the EA evolves toward the target architecture, which represents the company's future IT needs. According to this model, EA defines the following:

1. The organization's mission, business functions, and future direction
2. Information and information flows needed to perform the mission
3. The current baseline architecture
4. The desired target architecture
5. The sequencing plan or strategy to progress from the baseline to the target architecture.

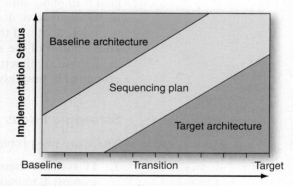

Figure 2.6 The importance of viewing EA as a dynamic and evolving plan. The purpose of the EA is to maintain IT–business alignment. Changes in priorities and business are reflected in the target architecture to help keep IT aligned with them (GAO, 2010).

CAREER INSIGHT 2.1

Essential Skills of an Enterprise Architect

Enterprise architects need much more than technology skills. The job performance and success of such an architect—or anyone responsible for large-scale IT projects—depend on a broad range of skills.

• Interpersonal or people skills. The job requires interacting with people and getting their cooperation.

• Ability to influence and motivate. A large part of the job is motivating users to comply with new processes and practices.

• Negotiating skills. The project needs resources—time, money, and personnel—that must be negotiated to get things accomplished.

- Critical-thinking and problem-solving skills. Architects face complex and unique problems. Being able to expedite solutions prevents bottlenecks.

- Business and industry expertise. Knowing the business and industry improves the outcomes and the architect's credibility.

Managing EA implementations requires someone who is able to handle multiple aspects of a project at one time. Project management is covered in Chapter 13.

DATA GOVERNANCE: MAINTAINING DATA QUALITY AND COST CONTROL

Data governance is the process of creating and agreeing to standards and requirements for the collection, identification, storage, and use of data. The success of every data-driven strategy or marketing effort depends on data governance. Data governance policies must address structured, semistructured, and unstructured data (discussed in Section 2.3) to ensure that insights can be trusted.

Enterprisewide Data Governance

With an effective data governance program, managers can determine where their data are coming from, who owns them, and who is responsible for what—in order to know they can trust the available data when needed. Data governance is an enterprise-wide project because data cross boundaries and are used by people throughout the enterprise. New regulations and pressure to reduce costs have increased the importance of effective data governance. Governance eliminates the cost of maintaining and archiving bad, unneeded, or wrong data. These costs grow as the volume of data grows. Governance also reduces the legal risks associated with unmanaged or inconsistently managed information.

Three industries that depend on data governance to comply with regulations or reporting requirements are the following:

- **Food industry.** In the food industry, data governance is required to comply with food safety regulations. Food manufacturers and retailers have sophisticated control systems in place so that if a contaminated food product, such as spinach or peanut butter, is detected, they are able to trace the problem back to a particular processing plant or even the farm at the start of the food chain.

- **Financial services industry.** In the financial services sector, strict reporting requirements of the Dodd–Frank Wall Street Reform and Consumer Protection Act of 2010 are leading to greater use of data governance. The Dodd–Frank Act regulates Wall Street practices by enforcing transparency and accountability in an effort to prevent another significant financial crisis like the one that occurred in 2008.

- **Health-care industry.** Data are health care's most valuable asset. Hospitals have mountains of electronic patient information. New health-care accountability and reporting obligations require data governance models for transparency to defend against fraud and to protect patients' information.

As you read in the Intel Security opening case, data governance and MDM are a powerful combination. As data sources and volumes continue to increase, so does the need to manage data as a strategic asset in order to extract its full value. Making business data consistent, trusted, and accessible across the enterprise is a critical first step in customer-centric business models. With data governance, companies are able to extract maximum value from their data, specifically by making better use of opportunities that are buried within behavioral data. According to Adele Pugliese, data governance director of Toronto-based Scotiabank, "If we are able to leverage and understand the data, and achieve integrity and a level of accuracy with that data, in terms of our touchpoints with the customers, we should be able to change that customer experience and take it to the next level where we know a lot more about our customers" (Hamilton, 2013).

Master Data and MDM

Master data describe key entities such as customers, products and services, vendors, locations, and employees around which business is conducted. Master data are typically quite stable—and fundamentally different from the high volume, velocity, and variety of big data and traditional data. For example, when a customer applies for automobile insurance, data provided on the application become the master data for that customer. In contrast, if the customer's vehicle has a device that sends data about his or her driving behavior to the insurer, those machine-generated data are transactional or operational, but not master data.

Data are used in two ways—both depend on high-quality trustworthy data:

1. **For running the business:** Transactional or operational use
2. **For improving the business:** Analytic use

Strong data governance is needed to manage the availability, usability, integrity, and security of the data used throughout the enterprise so that data are of sufficient quality to meet business needs. The characteristics and consequences of weak or nonexistent data governance are listed in Table 2.4.

MDM solutions can be complex and expensive. Given their complexity and cost, most MDM solutions are out of reach for small and medium companies. Vendors have addressed this challenge by offering cloud-managed MDM services. For example, in 2013 Dell Software launched its next-generation Dell Boomi MDM. Dell Boomi provides MDM, data management, and data quality services (DQS)—and they are 100 percent cloud-based with near real time synchronization.

Politics: The People Conflict

In an organization, there may be a culture of distrust between the technology and business employees. No enterprise architecture methodology or data governance can bridge this divide unless there is a genuine commitment to change. That commitment must come from the highest level of the organization—senior management. Methodologies cannot solve people problems; they can only provide a framework in which those problems can be solved.

TABLE 2.4 Characteristics and Consequences of Weak or Nonexistent Data Governance
<ul><li>Data duplication causes isolated data silos.</li><li>Inconsistency exists in the meaning and level of detail of data elements.</li><li>Users do not trust the data and waste time verifying the data rather than analyzing them for appropriate decision making.</li><li>Leads to inaccurate data analysis.</li><li>Bad decisions are made on perception rather than reality, which can negatively affect the company and its customers.</li><li>Results in increased workloads and processing time.</li></ul>

1. Explain the relationship between complexity and planning. Give an example.
2. Explain enterprise architecture.
3. What are the four components of EA?
4. What are the business benefits of EA?
5. How can EA maintain alignment between IT and business strategy?
6. What are the two ways that data are used in an organization?
7. What is the function of data governance?
8. Why has interest in data governance and MDM increased?
9. What role does personal conflict or politics play in the success of data governance?

2.3 Information Systems: The Basics

Information systems (ISs) are built to achieve specific goals, such as processing customer orders and payroll. In general, ISs process data into meaningful information and knowledge.

DATA, INFORMATION, AND KNOWLEDGE

Data, or raw data, describe products, customers, events, activities, and transactions that are recorded, classified, and stored. Data are the raw material from which information is produced; the quality, reliability, and integrity of the data must be maintained for the information to be useful. Examples are the number of hours an employee worked in a certain week or the number of new Toyota vehicles sold in the first quarter of 2015.

A **database** is a repository or data store that is organized for efficient access, search, retrieval, and update.

Information is data that have been processed, organized, or put into context so that they have meaning and value to the person receiving them. For example, the quarterly sales of new Toyota vehicles from 2010 through 2014 is information because it would give some insight into how the vehicle recalls during 2009 and 2010 impacted sales. Information is an organization's most important asset, second only to people.

Knowledge consists of data and/or information that have been processed, organized, and put into context to be meaningful, and to convey understanding, experience, accumulated learning, and expertise as they apply to a current problem or activity. Knowing how to manage a vehicle recall to minimize negative impacts on new vehicle sales is an example of knowledge. Figure 2.7 shows the differences in data, information, and knowledge.

ISs collect or input and process data, distribute reports or other outputs that support decision making and business processes. Figure 2.8 shows the input-processing-output (IPO) model.

Figure 2.9 shows how major types of ISs relate to one another and how data flow among them. In this example,

1. Data from online purchases are captured and processed by the TPS, or transaction processing system and then stored in the transactional database.
2. Data needed for reporting purposes are extracted from the database and used by the MIS (management information system) to create periodic, ad hoc, or other types of reports.

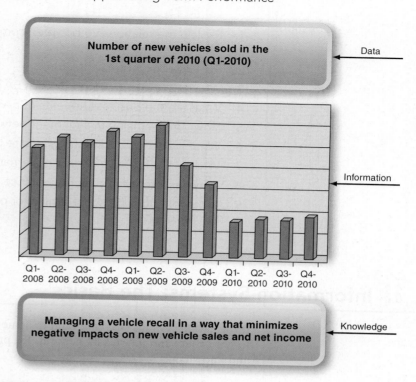

Figure 2.7 Examples of data, information, and knowledge.

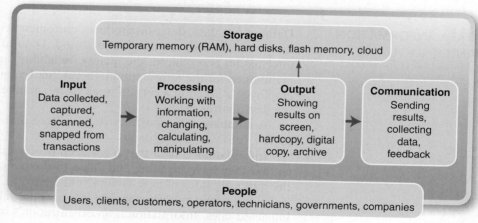

Figure 2.8 Input-processing-output model.

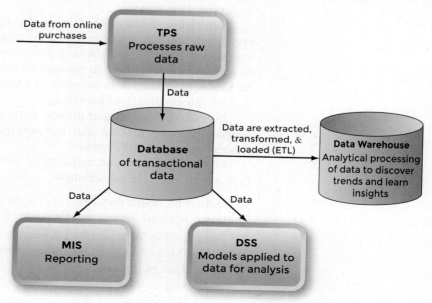

Figure 2.9 Flow of data from the point of sale (POS) through processing, storage, reporting, decision support, and analysis. Also shows the relationships among information systems.

3. Data are output to a decision-support system (DSS) where they are analyzed using formulas, financial ratios, or models.

Data collected by the TPS are converted into reports by the MIS and analyzed by the DSS to support decision making. Corporations, government agencies, the military, health care, medical research, major league sports, and nonprofits depend on their DSSs at all levels of the organization. Innovative DSSs create and help sustain competitive advantages. DSSs reduce waste in production operations, improve inventory management, support investment decisions, and predict demand. The model of a DSS consists of a set of formulas and functions, such as statistical, financial, optimization, and/or simulation models.

Customer data, sales, and other critical data are selected for additional analysis, such as trend analysis or forecasting demand. These data are extracted from the database, transformed into a standard format, and then loaded into a data warehouse.

TRANSACTION PROCESSING SYSTEMS

Transaction processing systems (TPSs) are designed to process specific types of data input from ongoing transactions. TPSs can be manual, as when data are typed into a form on a screen, or automated by using scanners or sensors to capture barcodes or other data (Figure 2.10).

Organizational data are processed by a TPS—sales orders, payroll, accounting, financial, marketing, purchasing, inventory control, and so forth. Transactions are either:

- **Internal transactions** that originate within the organization or that occur within the organization. Examples are payroll, purchases, budget transfers, and payments (in accounting terms, they are referred to as *accounts payable*).
- **External transactions** that originate from outside the organization, for example, from customers, suppliers, regulators, distributors, and financing institutions.

TPSs are essential systems. Transactions that are not captured can result in lost sales, dissatisfied customers, and many other types of data errors with financial impacts. For example, if the accounting department issued a check to pay an invoice (bill) and it was cashed by the recipient, but information about that transaction was not captured, then two things happen. First, the amount of cash listed on the company's financial statements is wrong because no deduction was made for the amount of the check. Second, the accounts payable (A/P) system

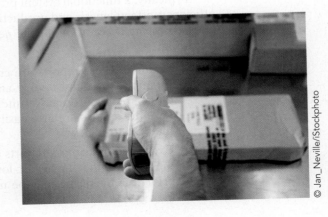

Figure 2.10 Scanners automate the input of data into a transaction processing system (TPS).

© Jan_Neville/iStockphoto

will continue to show the invoice as unpaid, so the accounting department might pay it a second time. Likewise, if services are provided, but the transactions are not recorded, the company will not bill for them and thus not collect that service revenue.

Batch vs. Online Real Time Processing

Data captured by a TPS are processed and stored in a database; they then become available for use by other systems. Processing of transactions is done in one of two modes:

1. **Batch processing:** A TPS in batch processing mode collects all transaction for a day, shift, or other time period, and then processes the data and updates the data stores. Payroll processing done weekly or bi-weekly is an example of batch mode.

2. **Online transaction processing (OLTP) or real time processing:** The TPS processes each transaction as it occurs, which is what is meant by the term *real time processing*. In order for OLTP to occur, the input device or website must be directly linked via a network to the TPS. Airlines need to process flight reservations in real time to verify that seats are available.

Batch processing costs less than real time processing. A disadvantage is that data are inaccurate because they are not updated immediately, in real time.

Processing Impacts Data Quality

As data are collected or captured, they are validated to detect and correct obvious errors and omissions. For example, when a customer sets up an account with a financial services firm or retailer, the TPS validates that the address, city, and postal code provided are consistent with one another and also that they match the credit card holder's address, city, and postal code. If the form is not complete or errors are detected, the customer is required to make the corrections before the data are processed any further.

Data errors detected later may be time-consuming to correct or cause other problems. You can better understand the difficulty of detecting and correcting errors by considering identity theft. Victims of identity theft face enormous challenges and frustration trying to correct data about them.

MANAGEMENT INFORMATION SYSTEMS

Functional areas or departments—accounting, finance, production/operations, marketing and sales, human resources, and engineering and design—are supported by ISs designed for their particular reporting needs. General-purpose reporting systems are referred to as **management information systems (MISs)**. Their objective is to provide reports to managers for tracking operations, monitoring, and control.

Typically, a functional system provides reports about such topics as operational efficiency, effectiveness, and productivity by extracting information from databases and processing it according to the needs of the user. Types of reports include the following:

- **Periodic:** These reports are created or run according to a pre-set schedule. Examples are daily, weekly, and quarterly. Reports are easily distributed via e-mail, blogs, internal websites (called *intranets*), or other electronic media. Periodic reports are also easily ignored if workers do nott find them worth the time to review.

- **Exception:** Exception reports are generated only when something is outside the norm, either higher or lower than expected. Sales in hardware stores prior to a hurricane may be much higher than the norm. Or sales of fresh

© Damir Karan/iStockphoto

Figure 2.11 Sample report produced by an MIS.

produce may drop during a food contamination crisis. Exception reports are more likely to be read because workers know that some unusual event or deviation has occurred.

- **Ad hoc, or on demand:** Ad hoc reports are unplanned reports. They are generated to a mobile device or computer on demand *as needed*. They are generated on request to learn more about a situation, problem, or opportunity.

Reports typically include interactive data visualizations, such as column and pie charts, as shown in Figure 2.11.

Functional information systems that support business analysts and other departmental employees can be fairly complex, depending on the type of employees supported. The following examples show the support that IT provides to major functional areas.

1. Bolsa de Comercio de Santiago, a large stock exchange in Chile, processes high-volume trading in microseconds using IBM software. The stock exchange increased its transaction capacity by 900 percent by 2011. The Chilean stock exchange system can do the detective work of analyzing current and past transactions and market information, learning and adapting to market trends and connecting its traders to business information in real time. Immediate throughput in combination with analytics allows traders to make more accurate decisions.

2. According to the *New England Journal of Medicine*, 1 in 5 patients suffers from preventable readmissions, which cost taxpayers over $17 billion a year. Beginning in 2012, hospitals have been penalized for high readmission rates with cuts to the payments they receive from the government (Miliard, 2011). Using a DSS and predictive analytics, the health-care industry can leverage unstructured information in ways not possible before, according to Charles J. Barnett, president/CEO of Seton Health Care. "With this solution, we can access an integrated view of relevant clinical and operational information to drive more informed decision making. For example, by predicting which patients might be readmitted, we can reduce costly and preventable readmissions, decrease mortality rates, and ultimately improve the quality of life for our patients" (Miliard, 2011).

DECISION SUPPORT SYSTEMS

Decision support systems (DSSs) are interactive applications that support decision making. Configurations of a DSS range from relatively simple applications that support a single user to complex enterprisewide systems. A DSS can support the analysis and solution of a specific problem, evaluate a strategic opportunity, or support ongoing operations. These systems support unstructured and semistructured decisions, such as make-or-buy-or-outsource decisions, or what products to develop and introduce into existing markets.

Degree of Structure of Decisions

Decisions range from structured to unstructured. Structured decisions are those that have a well-defined method for solving and the data necessary to reach a sound decision. An example of a structured decision is determining whether an applicant qualifies for an auto loan, or whether to extend credit to a new customer—and the terms of those financing options. **Structured decisions** are relatively straightforward and made on a regular basis, and an IS can ensure that they are done consistently.

At the other end of the continuum are **unstructured decisions** that depend on human intelligence, knowledge, and/or experience—as well as data and models to solve. Examples include deciding which new products to develop or which new markets to enter. Semistructured decisions fall in the middle of the continuum. DSSs are best suited to support these types of decisions, but they are also used to support unstructured ones. To provide such support, DSSs have certain characteristics to support the decision maker and the overall decision-making process.

Three Defining DSS Characteristics

These characteristics of DSSs include:

1. An easy-to-use interactive interface
2. Models or formulas that enable sensitivity analysis, what-if analysis, goal seeking, and risk analysis
3. Data from multiple sources—internal and external sources plus data added by the decision maker who may have insights relevant to the decision situation

Having models is what distinguishes DSS from MIS. Some models are developed by end users through an interactive and iterative process. Decision makers can manipulate models to conduct experiments and sensitivity analyses, for example, w*hat-if* and *goal seeking*. **What-if analysis** refers to changing assumptions or data in the model to observe the impacts of those changes on the outcome. For example, if sale forecasts are based on a 5 percent increase in customer demand, a what-if analysis would replace the 5 percent with higher and/or lower estimates to determine *what* would happen to sales *if* demand changed. With **goal seeking**, the decision maker has a specific outcome in mind and needs to figure out how that outcome could be achieved and whether it is feasible to achieve that desired outcome. A DSS can also estimate the risk of alternative strategies or actions.

California Pizza Kitchen (CPK) uses a DSS to support inventory decisions. CPK has 77 restaurants located in various states in the United States. Maintaining optimal inventory levels at all restaurants was challenging and time-consuming. A DSS was built to make it easy for the chain's managers to maintain updated records and make decisions. Many CPK restaurants increased sales by 5 percent after implementing a DSS.

Building DSS Applications

Planners Lab is an example of software for building DSSs. The software is free to academic institutions and can be downloaded from plannerslab.com. Planners Lab includes:

- An easy-to-use model-building language
- An easy-to-use option for visualizing model output, such as answers to what-if and goal-seeking questions, to analyze the impacts of different assumptions

These tools enable managers and analysts to build, review, and challenge the assumptions upon which their decision scenarios are based. With Planners Lab, decision makers can experiment and play with assumptions to assess multiple views of the future.

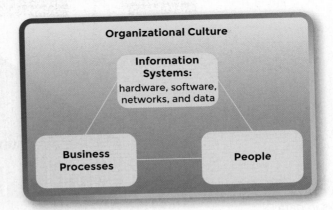

Figure 2.12 Organizational culture plays a significant role in the use and benefits of Information systems.

DATABASE VOLATILITY AND DATA WAREHOUSING

Given the huge number of transactions, the data in databases are constantly in use or being updated. This characteristic of databases—referred to as **volatility**—makes it impossible to use them for complex decision-making and problem-solving tasks. For this reason, data are extracted from the database transformed (processed to standardize the data), and then loaded into a data warehouse. As a result of the extract, transformation, and load (ETL), operations data in the data warehouse are better formatted for analyses.

ISs EXIST WITHIN A CULTURE

ISs do not exist in isolation. They have a purpose and a social (organizational) context. A common *purpose* is to provide a solution to a business problem. The *social context* of the system consists of the values and beliefs that determine what is admissible and possible within the culture of the organization and among the people involved. For example, a company may believe that superb customer service and on-time delivery are critical success factors. This belief system influences IT investments, among other factors.

The business value of IT is determined by the people who use them, the business processes they support, and the culture of the organization. That is, IS value is determined by the relationships among ISs, people, and business processes—all of which are influenced strongly by organizational culture, as shown in Figure 2.12.

Questions

1. Contrast data, information, and knowledge.
2. Define TPS and give an example.
3. When is batch processing used?
4. When are real time processing capabilities needed?
5. Explain why TPSs need to process incoming data before they are stored.
6. Define MIS and DSS and give an example of each.
7. Why are databases inappropriate for doing data analysis?

2.4 Data Centers, Cloud Computing, and Virtualization

On-premises data centers, virtualization, and cloud computing are types of **IT infrastructures** or computing systems. Long ago, there were few IT infrastructure options. Mostly, companies owned their servers, storage, and network components to support their business applications and these computing resources were on their premises. Now, there are several choices for an IT infrastructure

Figure 2.13 A row of network servers in data center.

strategy—including virtualization and cloud computing. As is common to IT investments, each infrastructure configuration has strengths, weaknesses, and cost considerations.

| DATA CENTERS

A **data center** consists of a large number of network servers (Figure 2.13) used for the storage, processing, management, distribution, and archiving of data, systems, Web traffic, services, and enterprise applications. Data center also refers to the building or facility that houses the servers and equipment. Here are some examples of data centers:

- **National Climatic Data Center.** The National Climatic Data Center is an example of a public data center that stores and manages the world's largest archive of weather data.

- **U.S. National Security Agency.** The National Security Agency's (NSA) data center in Bluffdale, UT, shown in Figure 2.14, opened in the fall of 2013. It is the largest spy data center for the NSA. People who think their correspondence and postings through sites like Google, Facebook, and Apple are safe from prying eyes should rethink that belief. You will read more about reports exposing government data collection programs in Chapter 5.

- **Apple.** Apple has a 500,000-square-foot data center in Maiden, NC, that houses servers for various iCloud and iTunes services. The center plays a vital role in the company's back-end IT infrastructure. In 2014 Apple expanded this center with a new, smaller 14,250 square-foot tactical data center that also includes office space, meeting areas, and breakrooms.

Companies may own and manage their own on-premises data centers or pay for the use of their vendors' data centers, such as in cloud computing, virtualization, and software, as service arrangements (Figure 2.15).

Figure 2.14 The NSA data center (shown under construction) opened in the fall of 2013 in Bluffdale, UT. It is the largest spy data center for the NSA. People who believe their correspondence and postings through sites like Google, Facebook, and Apple are safe from prying eyes should think again.

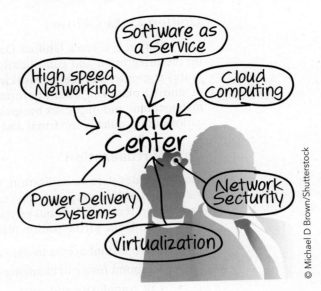

Figure 2.15 Data centers are the infrastructure underlying cloud computing, virtualization, networking, security, delivery systems, and software as a service. Many of these issues are discussed in this chapter.

Since only the company owns the infrastructure, a data center is more suitable for organizations that run many different types of applications and have complex workloads. A data center, like a factory, has limited capacity. Once it is built, the amount of storage and the workload the center can handle does not change without purchasing and installing more equipment.

When a Data Center Goes Down, so Does Business

Data center failures disrupt all operations regardless of who owns the data center. Here are two examples.

- **Uber.** The startup company Uber experienced an hour-long outage in February 2014 that brought its car-hailing service to a halt across the country. The problem was caused by an outage at its vendor's West Coast data center. Uber users flooded social media sites with complaints about problems kicking off Uber's app to summon a driver-for-hire.

- **WhatsApp.** WhatsApp also experienced a server outage in early 2014 that took the service offline for 2.5 hours. WhatsApp is a smartphone text-messaging service that had been bought by Facebook for $19 billion. "Sorry we currently experiencing server issues. We hope to be back up and recovered shortly," WhatsApp said in a message on Twitter that was retweeted more than 25,000 times in just a few hours. The company has grown rapidly to 450 million active users within five years, nearly twice as many as Twitter. More than two-thirds of these global users use the app daily. WhatsApp's' server failure drove millions of users to a competitor. Line, a messaging app developed in Japan, added 2 million new registered users within 24 hours of WhatsApp's outage—the biggest increase in Line's user base within a 24-hour period.

These outages point to the risks of maintaining the complex and sophisticated technology needed to power digital services used by millions or hundreds of millions of people.

INTEGRATING DATA TO COMBAT DATA CHAOS

An enterprise's data are stored in many different or remote locations—creating data chaos at times. And some data may be duplicated so that they are available in multiple locations that need a quick response. Therefore, the data needed for planning, decision making, operations, queries, and reporting are scattered or duplicated across numerous servers, data centers, devices, and cloud services. Disparate data must be unified or integrated in order for the organization to function.

Unified Data Center

One solution is Cisco's Unified Data Center (UDC). UDC can significantly speed up the integration and consolidation of data and cut data center costs. UDC integrates compute, storage, networking, virtualization, and management into a single or unified platform. That platform provides an infrastructure that simplifies data management and improves business agility or responsiveness. UDC can run applications more quickly in virtual and cloud computing environments.

Data Virtualization

Cisco provides data virtualization, which gives greater IT flexibility. Using virtualization methods, enterprises can respond to change more quickly and make better decisions in real time without physically moving their data, which significantly cuts costs. Cisco Data Virtualization makes it possible to:

- Have instant access to data at any time and in any format.
- Respond faster to changing data analytics needs.
- Cut complexity and costs.

Compared to traditional (nonvirtual) data integration and replication methods, Cisco Data Virtualization accelerates time to value with:

- **Greater agility:** speeds 5 to 10 times faster than traditional data integration methods
- **Streamlined approach:** 50 to 75 percent time savings over data replication and consolidation methods
- **Better insight:** instant access to data

Cisco offers videos on cloud computing, virtualization, and other IT infrastructures at its video portal at video.cisco.com.

CLOUD COMPUTING INCREASES AGILITY

In a business world where first movers gain the advantage, IT responsiveness and agility provide a competitive edge. Yet, many IT infrastructures are extremely expensive to manage and too complex to easily adapt. A common solution is cloud computing. **Cloud computing** is the general term for infrastructures that use the Internet and private networks to access, share, and deliver computing resources. The National Institute of Standards and Technology (NIST) more precisely defines cloud computing as "a model for enabling convenient, on-demand network access to a shared pool of configuration computing resources that can be rapidly provisioned and released with minimal management effort or service provider interaction" (NIST, 2012).

SELECTING A CLOUD VENDOR

Because cloud is still a relatively new and evolving business model, the decision to select a cloud service provider should be approached with even greater diligence than other IT decisions. As cloud computing becomes an increasingly important part of the IT delivery model, assessing and selecting the right cloud provider also become the most strategic decisions that business leaders undertake. Providers are not created equally, so it is important to investigate each provider's offerings prior to subscribing. When selecting and investing in cloud services, there are several service factors a vendor needs to address. These evaluation factors are listed in Table 2.5.

Vendor Management and Service-Level Agreements

The move to the cloud is also a move to vendor-managed services and cloud **service-level agreements (SLAs)**. An SLA is a negotiated agreement between a company

TABLE 2.5	Service Factors to Consider when Evaluating Cloud Vendors or Service Providers
Factors	**Examples of Questions to Be Addressed**
Delays	What are the estimated server delays and network delays?
Workloads	What is the volume of data and processing that can be handled during a specific amount of time?
Costs	What are the costs associated with workloads across multiple cloud computing platforms?
Security	How are data and networks secured against attacks? Are data encrypted and how strong is the encryption? What are network security practices?
Disaster recovery and business continuity	How is service outage defined? What level of redundancy is in place to minimize outages, including backup services in different geographical regions? If a natural disaster or outage occurs, how will cloud services be continued?
Technical expertise and understanding	Does the vendor have expertise in your industry or business processes? Does the vendor understand what you need to do and have the technical expertise to fulfill those obligations?
Insurance in case of failure	Does the vendor provide cloud insurance to mitigate user losses in case of service failure or damage? This is a new and important concept.
Third-party audit, or an unbiased assessment of the ability to rely on the service provided by the vendor	Can the vendor show objective proof with an audit that it can live up to the promises it is making?

and service provider that can be a legally binding contract or an informal contract. You can review an example of the Google Apps SLA by visiting its website at Google.com and searching for "SLA." Staff experienced in managing outsourcing projects may have the necessary expertise for managing work in the cloud and policing SLAs with vendors. The goal is not building the best SLA terms, but getting the terms that are most meaningful to the business.

The Cloud Standards Customer Council published the *Practical Guide to Cloud Service Level Agreements* (2012), which brings together numerous customer experiences into a single guide for IT and business leaders who are considering cloud adoption. According to this guide, an SLA serves:

as a means of formally documenting the service(s), performance expectations, responsibilities and limits between cloud service providers and their users. A typical SLA describes levels of service using various attributes such as: availability, serviceability, performance, operations, billing, and penalties associated with violations of such attributes. (Cloud Standards Customer Council, 2012, pp. 5–6.)

Implementing an effective management process is an important step in ensuring internal and external user satisfaction with cloud services.

CLOUD VS. DATA CENTER: WHAT IS THE DIFFERENCE?

A main difference between a cloud and data center is that a cloud is an off-premise form of computing that stores data on the Internet. In contrast, a data center refers to on-premises hardware and equipment that store data within an organization's local network. Cloud services are outsourced to a third-party cloud provider who manages the updates, security, and ongoing maintenance. Data centers are typically run by an in-house IT department.

Cloud computing is the delivery of computing and storage resources as a service to end-users over a network. Cloud systems are *scalable*. That is, they can be adjusted to meet changes in business needs. At the extreme, the cloud's capacity is unlimited depending on the vendor's offerings and service plans. A drawback of the cloud is control because a third party manages it. Companies do not have as much control as they do with a data center. And unless the company uses a **private cloud** within its network, it shares computing and storage resources with other cloud users in the vendor's **public cloud**. Public clouds allow multiple clients to access the same virtualized services and utilize the same pool of servers across a public network. In contrast, private clouds are single-tenant environments with stronger security and control for regulated industries and critical data. In effect, private clouds retain all the IT security and control provided by traditional data center infrastructures with the advantage of cloud computing.

Companies often use an arrangement of both on-premises data centers and cloud computing (Figure 2.16).

A data center is physically connected to a local network, which makes it easier to restrict access to apps and information to only authorized, company-approved people and equipment. However, the cloud is accessible by anyone with the proper credentials and Internet connection. This accessibility arrangement increases exposure to company data at many more entry and exit points.

CLOUD INFRASTRUCTURE

The cloud has greatly expanded the options for enterprise IT infrastructures because any device that accesses the Internet can access, share, and deliver data. Cloud computing is a valuable infrastructure because it:

1. Provides a dynamic infrastructure that makes apps and computing power available on demand. Apps and power are available on demand because they are provided *as a service*. For example, any software that is provided on demand is referred to as **software as a service**, or **SaaS**. Typical SaaS products are Google Apps and Salesforce.com. Section 2.5 discussed SaaS and other cloud services.

2. Helps companies become more agile and responsive while significantly reducing IT costs and complexity through improved workload optimization and service delivery.

Move to Enterprise Clouds

A majority of large organizations have hundreds or thousands of software licenses that support business processes, such as licenses for Microsoft Office, Oracle database management, IBM CRM (customer relationship management), and various network security software. Managing software and their licenses involves deploying, provisioning, and updating them—all of which are time-consuming and expensive. Cloud computing overcomes these problems.

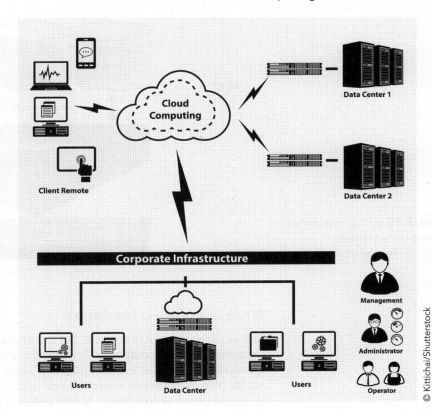

Figure 2.16 Corporate IT infrastructures can consist of an on-premises data center and off-premises cloud computing.

ISSUES IN MOVING WORKLOADS FROM THE ENTERPRISE TO THE CLOUD

Building a cloud strategy is a challenge, and moving existing apps to the cloud is stressful. Despite the business and technical benefits, the risk exists of disrupting operations or customers in the process. With the cloud, the network and WAN (wide area network) become an even more critical part of the IT infrastructure. Greater network bandwidth is needed to support the increase in network traffic. And, putting part of the IT architecture or workload into the cloud requires different management approaches, different IT skills, and knowing how to manage vendor relationships and contracts.

Infrastructure Issues

There is a big difference because cloud computing runs on a shared infrastructure, so the arrangement is less customized to a specific company's requirements. A comparison to help understand the challenges is that outsourcing is like renting an apartment, while the cloud is like getting a room at a hotel.

With cloud computing, it may be more difficult to get to the root of performance problems, like the unplanned outages that occurred with Google's Gmail and Workday's human resources apps. The trade-off is cost vs. control.

Increasing demand for faster and more powerful computers, and increases in the number and variety of applications are driving the need for more capable IT architectures.

VIRTUALIZATION AND VIRTUAL MACHINES

Computer hardware had been designed to run a single operating system (OS) and a single app, which leaves most computers vastly underutilized. Virtualization is a technique that creates a virtual (i.e., nonphysical) layer and multiple virtual machines (VMs) to run on a single physical machine. The virtual (or virtualization) layer makes it possible for each VM to share the resources of the hardware. Figure 2.17 shows the relationship among the VMs and physical hardware.

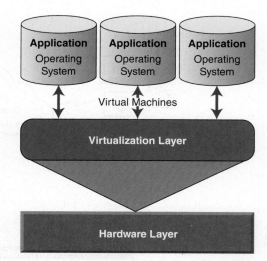

Figure 2.17 Virtual machines running on a simple computer hardware layer.

What Is a Virtual Machine?

Just as *virtual reality* is not real, but a software-created world, a virtual machine is a software-created computer. Technically, a **virtual machine (VM)** is created by a software layer, called the *virtualization layer,* as shown in Figure 2.17. That layer has its own Windows or other OS and apps, such as Microsoft Office, as if it were an actual physical computer. A VM behaves exactly like a physical computer and contains its own virtual—that is, *software-based*—CPU, RAM (random access memory), hard drive, and network interface card (NIC). An OS cannot tell the difference between a VM and a physical machine, nor can apps or other computers on a network tell the difference. Even the VM thinks it is a "real" computer. Users can set up multiple real computers to function as a single PC through virtualization to pool resources to create a more powerful VM.

Virtualization is a concept that has several meanings in IT and therefore several definitions. The major type of virtualization is hardware virtualization, which remains popular and widely used. Virtualization is often a key part of an enterprise's disaster recovery plan. In general, virtualization separates business applications and data from hardware resources. This separation allows companies to pool hardware resources—rather than dedicate servers to applications—and assign those resources to applications as needed.

The major types of virtualization are the following:

- *Storage virtualization* is the pooling of physical storage from multiple network storage devices into what appears to be a single storage device managed from a central console.

- *Network virtualization* combines the available resources in a network by splitting the network load into manageable parts, each of which can be assigned (or reassigned) to a particular server on the network.

- *Hardware virtualization* is the use of software to emulate hardware or a total computer environment other than the one the software is actually running in. It allows a piece of hardware to run multiple operating system images at once. This kind of software is sometimes known as a virtual machine.

Virtualization Characteristics and Benefits

Virtualization increases the flexibility of IT assets, allowing companies to consolidate IT infrastructure, reduce maintenance and administration costs, and prepare for strategic IT initiatives. Virtualization is not primarily about cost-cutting, which is a tactical reason. More importantly, for strategic reasons, virtualization is used because it enables flexible sourcing and cloud computing.

The characteristics and benefits of virtualization are as follows:

1. **Memory-intensive.** VMs need a huge amount of RAM (random access memory, or primary memory) because of their massive processing requirements.

2. **Energy-efficient.** Minimizes energy consumed running and cooling servers in the data center—representing up to a 95 percent reduction in energy use per server.

3. **Scalability and load balancing.** When a big event happens, such as the Super Bowl, millions of people go to a website at the same time. Virtualization provides load balancing to handle the demand for requests to the site. The VMware infrastructure automatically distributes the load across a cluster of physical servers to ensure the maximum performance of all running VMs. Load balancing is key to solving many of today's IT challenges.

Virtualization consolidates servers, which reduces the cost of servers, makes more efficient use of data center space, and reduces energy consumption. All of these factors reduce the total cost of ownership (TCO). Over a three-year life cycle, a VM costs approximately 75 percent less to operate than a physical server.

IT at Work 2.3

Business Continuity with Virtualization

Liberty Wines supplies to restaurants, supermarkets, and independent retailers from its headquarters in central London. Recipient of multiple international wine awards—including the International Wine Challenge on Trade Supplier of the Year for two years running—Liberty Wines is one of the United Kingdom's foremost wine importers and distributors.

IT Problems and Business Needs

As the business expanded, the existing servers did not have the capacity to handle increased data volumes, and maintenance of the system put a strain on the IT team of two employees. Existing systems were slow and could not provide the responsiveness that employees expected.

Liberty Wines had to speed up business processes to meet the needs of customers in the fast-paced world of fine dining. To provide the service their customers expect, employees at Liberty Wines needed quick and easy access to customer, order, and stock information. In the past, the company relied on 10 physical servers for apps and services, such as order processing, reporting, and e-mail.

Virtualized Solution

Liberty Wines deployed a virtualized server solution incorporating Windows Server 2008 R2. The 10 servers were replaced with 3 physical servers, running 10 virtual servers. An additional server was used as part of a backup system, further improving resilience and stability.

By reducing the number of physical servers from 10 to 4, power use and air conditioning costs were cut by 60 percent. Not only was the bottom line improved, but the carbon footprint was also reduced, which was good for the environment.

The new IT infrastructure cut hardware replacement costs by £45,000 (U.S. $69,500) while enhancing stability with the backup system. Apps now run faster, too, so employees can provide better customer service with improved productivity. When needed, virtual servers can be added quickly and easily to support business growth.

Questions

1. What business risks had Liberty Wines faced?
2. How does Liberty Wines' IT infrastructure impact its competitive advantage?
3. How did server virtualization benefit Liberty Wines and the environment?

Questions

1. What is a data center?
2. Describe cloud computing.
3. What is the difference between data centers and cloud computing?
4. What are the benefits of cloud computing?
5. How can cloud computing solve the problems of managing software licenses?
6. What is an SLA? Why are SLAs important?
7. What factors should be considered when selecting a cloud vendor or provider?
8. When are private clouds used instead of public clouds?
9. Explain three issues that need to be addressed when moving to cloud computing or services.
10. How does a virtual machine (VM) function?
11. Explain virtualization.
12. What are the characteristics and benefits of virtualization?
13. When is load balancing important?

2.5 Cloud Services Add Agility

Managers want streamlined, real time data-driven enterprises, yet they may face budget cuts. Sustaining performance requires the development of new business apps and analytics capabilities, which comprise the *front end*—and the data stores and digital infrastructure, or back end, to support them. The back end is where the data reside. The problem is that data may have to navigate through a congested IT infrastructure that was first designed decades ago. These network or database bottlenecks can quickly wipe out the competitive advantages from big data, mobility, and so on. Traditional approaches to increasing database performance—manually tuning databases, adding more disk space, and upgrading processors—are not enough when you are have streaming data and real time big data analytics. Cloud services help to overcome these limitations.

XAAS: "AS A SERVICE" MODELS

The cloud computing model for on-demand delivery of and access to various types of computing resources also extends to the development of business apps. Figure 2.18 shows four "as a service" (XaaS) solutions based on the concept that the resource—software, platform, infrastructure, or data–can be provided on demand regardless of geolocation.

CLOUD COMPUTING STACK

Figure 2.19 shows the **cloud computing stack**, which consists of the following three categories:

- **SaaS** apps are designed for end-users.
- **PaaS** is a set of tools and services that make coding and deploying these apps faster and more efficient.
- **IaaS** consists of hardware and software that power computing resources—servers, storage, operating systems, and networks.

Figure 2.18 Four as-a-service solutions: software, platform, infrastructure, and data as a service.

© Vallepu/Shutterstock

Software as a Service

Software as a service (SaaS) is a widely used model in which software is available to users as needed. Specifically, in SaaS, a service provider hosts the application at its data center and customers access it via a standard Web browser. Other terms for SaaS are *on-demand computing* and *hosted services.* The idea is basically the same: Instead of buying and installing expensive packaged enterprise applications, users can access software apps over a network, with an Internet browser being the only necessity.

A SaaS provider licenses an application to customers either on-demand, through a subscription, based on usage (pay-as-you-go), or increasingly at no cost when the opportunity exists to generate revenue from advertisements or through other methods.

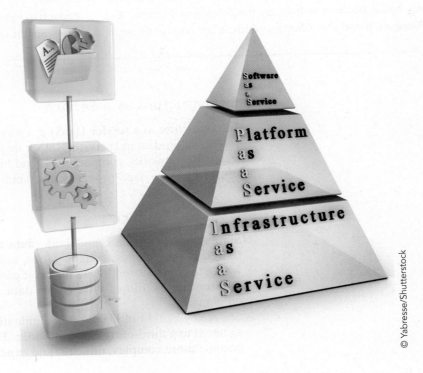

Figure 2.19 The cloud computing stack consists of SaaS, PaaS, and IaaS.

© Yabresse/Shutterstock

The SaaS model was developed to overcome the common challenge to an enterprise of being able to meet fluctuating demands on IT resources efficiently. It is used in many business functions, primarily customer relationship management (CRM), accounting, human resources (HR), service desk management, and collaboration.

There are thousands of SaaS vendors. Salesforce.com is one of the most widely known SaaS providers. Other examples are Google Docs and collaborative presentation software Prezi. For instance, instead of installing Microsoft Word on your own computer, and then loading Word to create a document, you use a browser to log into Google Docs. Only the browser uses your computer's resources.

Platform as a Service

Platform as a service (PaaS) benefits software development. PaaS provides a standard unified platform for app development, testing, and deployment. This computing platform allows the creation of Web applications quickly and easily without the complexity of buying and maintaining the underlying infrastructure. Without PaaS, the cost of developing some apps would be prohibitive. The trend is for PaaS to be combined with IaaS. For an example of the value of SaaS and PaaS, see IT at Work 2.4.

IT at Work 2.4

Unilever

Within only 12 weeks, Unilever had its new digital social platform built and implemented. The platform was designed to support Unilever Global Marketing by connecting its marketers, brand managers, and partners in 190 countries. The new social platform is built on the Salesforce Platform and leverages Salesforce Chatter, which is an enterprise social networking technology. It enables Unilever marketers to share knowledge, best practices, and creative assets across the network. According to Mark McClennon, the CIO Consumer at Unilever, "We've gone from a blank piece of paper all the way through to rolling out the first release of the platform in about three months using Salesforce technology" (Accenture, 2013).

Infrastructure as a Service

Infrastructure as a service (IaaS) is a way of delivering cloud computing infrastructure as an on-demand service. Rather than purchasing servers, software, data center space, or networks, companies instead buy all computing resources as a fully outsourced service. IaaS providers are Amazon Web Services (AWS) and Rackspace.

Data as a Service

Similar to SaaS, PaaS, and IaaS, **data as a service (DaaS)** enables data to be shared among clouds, systems, apps, and so on regardless of the data source or where they are stored. DaaS makes it easier for data architects to select data from different pools, filter out sensitive data, and make the remaining data available on demand.

A key benefit of DaaS is the elimination of the risks and burdens of data management to a third-party cloud provider. This model is growing in popularity as data become more complex, difficult, and expensive to maintain.

At-a-Service Models are Enterprisewide and Can Trigger Lawsuits

The various at-a-service models are used in various aspects of business. You will read how these specific services, such as CRM and HR management, are being used for operational and strategic purposes in later chapters. Companies are frequently adopting software, platform, infrastructure, data management and starting to embrace *mobility as a service* and *big data as a service* because they typically no longer have to worry about the costs of buying, maintaining, or updating their own data servers. Both hardware and human resources expenses can be cut significantly. Service arrangements all require that managers understand the benefits and trade-offs—and how to negotiate effective SLAs. Regulations mandate that confidential data be protected regardless of whether the data are on-premises on in the cloud. Therefore, a company's legal department needs to get involved in these IT decisions. Put simply, moving to cloud services is not simply an IT decision because the stakes around legal and compliance issues are very high.

GOING CLOUD

Cloud services can advance the core business of delivering superior services to optimize business performance. Cloud can cut costs and add flexibility to the performance of critical business apps. And, it can improve responsiveness to end-consumers, application developers, and business organizations. But to achieve these benefits, there must be IT, legal, and senior management oversight because a company still must meet its legal obligations and responsibilities to employees, customers, investors, business partners, and society.

Questions

1. What is SaaS?
2. Describe the cloud computing stack.
3. What is PaaS?
4. What is IaaS?
5. Why is DaaS growing in popularity?
6. How might companies risk violating regulation or compliance requirements with cloud services?

Key Terms

ad hoc report
batch processing
cloud computing
cloud computing stack
cross-sell
customer-centric
data
data as a service (DaaS)
data center
data governance
data silo
database
decision support system (DSS)

dirty data
enterprise architecture (EA)
exception report
executive information system (EIS)
goal seeking
information
information management
infrastructure as a service (IaaS)
IT infrastructure
knowledge
management information system (MIS)

master data
master data management (MDM)
master file
model
online transaction processing (OLTP)
platform as a service (PaaS)
private cloud
public cloud
real time processing
service-level agreements (SLAs)

software as a service (SaaS)
structured decisions
transaction processing system (TPS)
touchpoint
unstructured decisions
up-sell
virtualization
virtual machine (VM)
volatility
what-if analysis

Assuring Your Learning

DISCUSS: Critical Thinking Questions

1. Why is a strong market position or good profit performance only temporary?

2. Explain the difference between customer-centric and product-centric business models.

3. Assume you had:
   a. A tall ladder with a sticker that listed a weight allowance only 5 pounds more than you weighed. You know the manufacturer and model number.
   b. Perishable food with an expiration date 2 days into the future.
   c. A checking account balance that indicated you had sufficient funds to cover the balance due on an account.

   In all three cases, you cannot trust the data to be exactly correct. The data could be incorrect by about 20 percent. How might you find the correct data for each instance? Which data might not be possible to verify? How does dirty data impact your decision making?

4. If business data are scattered throughout the enterprise and not synched until the end of the month, how does that impact day-to-day decision making and planning?

5. Assume a bank's data are stored in silos based on financial product—checking accounts, saving accounts, mortgages, auto loans, and so on. What problems do these data silos create for the bank's managers?

6. Why do managers and workers still struggle to find information that they need to make decisions or

take action despite advances in digital technology? That is, what causes data deficiencies?

7. According to a Tech CEO Council Report, Fortune 500 companies waste $480 billion every year on inefficient business processes. What factors cause such huge waste? How can this waste be reduced?

8. Explain why organizations need to implement enterprise architecture (EA) and data governance.

9. What two problems can EA solve?

10. Name two industries that depend on data governance to comply with regulations or reporting requirements. Given an example of each.

11. Why is it important for data to be standardized? Given an example of unstandardized data.

12. Why are TPSs critical systems?

13. Explain what is meant by data volatility. How does it affect the use of databases for data analysis?

14. Discuss why the cloud acts as the *great IT delivery frontier.*

15. What are the immediate benefits of cloud computing?

16. What are the functions of data centers?

17. What factors need to be considered when selecting a cloud vendor?

18. What protection does an effective SLA provide?

19. Why is an SLA a legal document?

20. How can virtualization reduce IT costs while improving performance?

EXPLORE: Online and Interactive Exercises

21. When selecting a cloud vendor to host your enterprise data and apps, you need to evaluate the service level agreement (SLA).
    a. Research the SLAs of two cloud vendors, such as Rackspace, Amazon, or Google.
    b. For the vendors you selected, what are the SLAs' uptime percent? Expect them to be 99.9 percent or less.
    c. Does each vendor count both scheduled downtime and planned downtime toward the SLA uptime percent?
    d. Compare the SLAs in terms of two other criteria.
    e. Decide which SLA is better based on your comparisons.
    f. Report your results and explain your decision.

22. Many organizations initiate data governance programs because of pressing compliance issues that impact data usage. Organizations may need data governance to be in compliance with one or more regulations, such as the Gramm–Leach Bliley Act (GLB), HIPAA, Foreign Corrupt Practices Act (FCPA), Sarbanes–Oxley Act, and several state and federal privacy laws.
    a. Research and select two U.S. regulations or privacy laws.
    b. Describe how data governance would help an enterprise comply with these regulations or laws.

23. Visit eWeek.com Cloud Computing Solutions Center for news and reviews at eweek.com/c/s/Cloud-Computing. Select one of the articles listed

under Latest Cloud Computing News. Prepare an executive summary of the article.

24. Visit Rackspace.com and review the company's three types of cloud products. Describe each of those cloud solutions.

25. Visit Oracle.com. Describe the types of virtualization services offered by Oracle.

26. Visit YouTube.com and search for two videos on virtualization. For each video, report what you learned. Specify the complete URL, video title, who uploaded the video and the date, video length, and number of views.

ANALYZE & DECIDE: Apply IT Concepts to Business Decisions

27. Financial services firms experience large fluctuations in business volumes because of the cyclical nature of financial markets. These fluctuations are often caused by crises—such as the subprime mortgage problems, the discovery of major fraud, or a slowdown in the economy. These fluctuations require that executives and IT leaders have the ability to cut spending levels in market downturns and quickly scale up when business volumes rise again. Research SaaS solutions and vendors for the financial services sector. Would investment in SaaS help such firms align their IT capacity with their business needs and also cut IT costs? Explain your answer.

28. Despite multimillion-dollar investments, many IT organizations cannot respond quickly to evolving business needs. Also, they cannot adapt to large-scale shifts like mergers, sudden drops in sales, or new product introductions. Can cloud computing help organizations improve their responsiveness and get better control of their IT costs? Explain your answer.

29. Describe the relationship between enterprise architecture and organizational performance.

30. Identify four KPIs for a major airline (e.g., American, United, Delta) or an automobile manufacturer (e.g., GM, Ford, BMW). Which KPI would be the easiest to present to managers on an online dashboard? Explain why.

CASE 2.2

Business Case: Data Chaos Creates Risk

Data chaos often runs rampant in service organizations, such as health care and the government. For example, in many hospitals, each line of business, division, and department has implemented its own IT applications, often without a thorough analysis of its relationship with other departmental or divisional systems. This arrangement leads to the hospital having IT groups that specifically manage a particular type of application suite or data silo for a particular department or division.

Data Management

When apps are not well managed, they can generate terabytes of irrelevant data, causing hospitals to drown in such data. This data chaos could lead to medical errors. In the effort to manage excessive and massive amounts of data, there is increased risk of relevant information being lost (missing) or inaccurate—that is, faulty or dirty data. Another risk is data breaches.

- **Faulty data:** By 2016 an estimated 80 percent of health-care organizations will adopt electronic health records, or EHRs (IDC MarketScape, 2012). It is well known that an unintended consequence of EHR is faulty data. According to research done at Columbia University, data in EHR systems may not be as accurate and complete as expected (Hripscak & Albers, 2012). Incorrect lab values, imaging results, or physician documentation lead to medical

errors, harm patients, and damage the organization's accreditation and reputation.

- **Data breaches:** More than 25 million people have been affected by health-care system data breaches since the Office for Civil Rights, a division of the U.S. Department of Health and Human Services, began reporting breaches in 2009. Most breaches involved lost or stolen data on laptops, removable drives, or other portable media. Breaches are extremely expensive and destroy trust.

Accountability in health care demands compliance with strong data governance efforts. Data governance programs verify that data input into EHR, clinical, financial, and operational systems are accurate and complete—and that only authorized edits can be made and logged.

Vanderbilt University Medical Center Adopts EHR and Data Governance

Vanderbilt University Medical Center (VUMC) in Nashville, TN, was an early adopter of EHR and implemented data governance in 2009. VUMC's experience provides valuable lessons.

VUMC consists of three hospitals and the Vanderbilt Clinic, which have 918 beds, discharge 53,000 patients each year, and count 1.6 million clinic visits each year. On average, VUMC has an 83 percent occupancy rate and has achieved HIMSS Stage 6 hospital EHR adoption. HIMSS (Healthcare Information and Management Systems Society, himss.org) is a global, nonprofit organization dedicated to better health-care outcomes through IT. There are seven stages of EHR adoption, with Stage 7 being a fully paperless environment. That means all clinical data are part of an electronic medical record and, as a result, can be shared across and outside the enterprise. At Stage 7, the health-care organization is getting full advantage of the *health information exchange (HIE)*. HIE provides interoperability so that information can flow back and forth among physicians, patients, and health networks (Murphy, 2012).

VUMC began collecting data as part of its EHR efforts in 1997. By 2009 the center needed stronger, more disciplined data management. At that time, hospital leaders initiated a project to build a data governance infrastructure.

Data Governance Implementation
VUMC's leadership team had several concerns.

1. IT investments and tools were evolving rapidly, but they were not governed by HIM (Healthcare Information and Management) policies.
2. As medical records became electronic so they might be transmitted and shared easily, they became more vulnerable to hacking.
3. As new uses of electronic information were emerging, the medical center struggled to keep up.

Health Record Executive Committee
Initially, VUMC's leaders assigned data governance to their traditional medical records committee, but that approach failed. Next, they hired consultants to help develop a data governance structure and organized a *health record executive committee* to oversee the project. The committee reports to the medical board and an executive committee to ensure executive involvement and sponsorship. The committee is responsible for developing the strategy for standardizing health record practices, minimizing risk, and maintaining compliance. Members include the chief medical information officer (CMIO), CIO, legal counsel, medical staff, nursing informatics, HIM, administration, risk management, compliance, and accreditation. In addition, a legal medical records team was formed to support additions, corrections, and deletions to the EHR. This team defines procedures for removal of duplicate medical record numbers and policies for data management and compliance.

Costs of Data Failure
Data failures incur the following costs:

- Rework
- Loss of business

- Patient safety errors
- Malpractice lawsuits
- Delays in receiving payments because billing or medical codes data are not available

Measuring the Value of Data Governance
One metric to calculate the value of a data governance program is *confidence in data-dependent assumptions*, or CIDDA. CIDDA is computed by multiplying three confidence estimates as follows:

$$CIDDA = G \times M \times TS$$

where

G = Confidence that data are *good* enough for their intended purpose

M = Confidence that data *mean* what you think they do

TS = Confidence that you know where the data come from and *trust the source*

CIDDA is a subjective metric for which there are no industry benchmarks, yet it can be evaluated over time to gauge any improvement in data quality confidence.

Benefits Achieved from Data Governance
As in other industries, in health care, data are the most valuable asset. The handling of data is the real risk. EHRs are effective only if the data are accurate and useful to support patient care. Effective ongoing data governance has achieved that goal at VUMC.

Sources: Compiled from Murphy (2012), HIMSS.org (2014), HIMSSanalytics.org (2014), Reeves & Bowen (2013).

Questions
1. What might happen when each line of business, division, and department develops its own IT apps?
2. What are the consequences of poorly managed apps?
3. What two risks are posed by data chaos? Explain why.
4. What are the functions of data governance in the health-care sector?
5. Why is it important to have executives involved in data governance projects?
6. List and explain the costs of data failure.
7. Calculate the CIDDA over time:

    Q1: $G = 40\%$, $M = 50\%$, $TS = 20\%$
    Q2: $G = 50\%$, $M = 55\%$, $TS = 30\%$
    Q3: $G = 60\%$, $M = 60\%$, $TS = 40\%$
    Q4: $G = 60\%$, $M = 70\%$, $TS = 45\%$

8. Why are data the most valuable asset in health care?

CASE 2.3
Video Case: Cloud Computing: Three Case Studies

When organizations say they are "using the cloud," they can mean a number of very different things. Using an IaaS service such as Amazon EC2 or Terremark is different from using Google Apps for outsourced e-mail, which is different again from exposing an API in Facebook.

A video shows three cloud computing case studies from Vordel's customers. The cases cover SaaS, IaaS, and PaaS. In first two examples, customers are connecting to the cloud: first to Google Apps (for single sign-on to Google Apps e-mail) and second to Terremark to manage virtual servers. In the third example, the connection is from the cloud using a Facebook app to a company's APIs. You might spot *Animal House* references. Follow these three steps: Visit SOAtoTheCloud.com/2011/10/video-three-cloud-computing-case.html. View the 11-minute video of the three case studies.

Question
1. Explain the value or benefits of each organization's cloud investment.

References

Cloud Standards Customer Council. *Practical Guide to Cloud Service Level Agreements.* Version 1. April 10, 2012. http://www.cloudstandardscustomercouncil.org/2012_Practical_Guide_to_Cloud_SLAs.pdf

De Clerck, J. P. "Optimizing the Digital and Social Customer Experience." *Social Marketing Forum,* February 16, 2013.

Enterprise Architecture Research Forum (EARF). 2012.

First San Francisco Partners. "How McAfee Took Its First Steps to MDM Success." 2009.

GAO (General Accounting Office). "Practical Guide to Federal Enterprise Architecture." Version 2. August 2010.

Hamilton, N. "Choosing Data Governance Battles." *Inside Reference Data,* December 2013.

HIMSS.org (2014)

HIMSSanalytics.org (2014),

Hripscak, G. & D. J. Albers. "Next Generation Phenotyping of Electronic Health Records." *Journal of the American Medical Informatics Association,* Volume 19, Issue 5. September 2012.

IBM Institute for Business Value. "IBM Chief Information Officer Study: The Essential CIO." May 2011.

IDC MarketScape. "U.S. Ambulatory EMR/EHR for Small Practices." 3012 Vendor Assessment. May 2012.

Keitt, T.J. "Demystifying The Mobile Workforce–An Information Workplace Report." *Forrester.com.* June 7, 2011.

mcafee.com. *McAfee Fact Sheet.* 2013.

Miliard, M. "IBM Unveils New Watson-based Analytics." *Healthcare IT News.* October 25, 2011.

Murphy, K. "Health Information Exchange." *EHR Intelligence,* April 9, 2012.

National Institute of Standards and Technology (NIST). Cloud Computing Program. 2012.

Reeves, M. G. & R. Bowen. "Developing a Data Governance Model in Health Care." *Healthcare Finance Management,* February 2013.

Rich, R. "Master Data Management or Data Governance? Yes, Please." *Teradata Magazine* Q3, 2013.

Tech CEO Council Report 2010. *techceocouncil.org/news/reports/*

Data Management, Big Data Analytics, and Records Management

3

Learning Outcomes

1. Describe the functions of database and data warehouse technologies, the differences between centralized and distributed database architecture, how data quality impacts performance, and the role of a master reference file in creating accurate and consistent data across the enterprise.

2. Evaluate the tactical and strategic benefits of big data and analytics.

3. Describe data and text mining, and give examples of mining applications to find patterns, correlations, trends,

   or other meaningful relationships in organizational data stores.

4. Explain the operational benefits and competitive advantages of business intelligence, and how forecasting can be improved.

5. Describe electronic records management and how it helps companies meet their compliance, regulatory, and legal obligations.

Chapter Snapshot

Analytics differentiates business in the 21st century. Transactional, social, mobile, cloud, web, and sensor data offer enormous potential. But without tools to analyze these data types and volumes, there would not be much difference between business in the 20th century and business today—except for mobile access. High-quality data and human expertise are essential to the value of analytics (Figure 3.1).

Human expertise is necessary because analytics alone cannot explain the reasons for trends or relationships;

know what action to take; or provide sufficient context to determine what the numbers represent and how to interpret them.

Database, data warehouse, big data, and business intelligence (BI) technologies interact to create a new biz-tech ecosystem. Big data analytics and BI discover insights or relationships of interest that otherwise might not have been recognized. They make it possible for managers to make decisions and act with clarity, speed, and confidence. Big data analytics is not just about managing more or varied data. Rather, it is about asking new questions, formulating new hypotheses, exploration and discovery, and making data-driven decisions. Ultimately, a big part of big data analytic efforts is the use of new analytics techniques.

Mining data or text taken from day-to-day business operations reveals valuable information, such as customers' desires, products that are most important, or processes that can be made more efficient. These insights expand the ability to take advantage of opportunities, minimize risks, and control costs.

While you might think that physical pieces of paper are a relic of the past, in most offices the opposite is true. Aberdeen Group's survey of 176 organizations worldwide found that the volume of physical documents is growing by up to 30 percent per year. Document management technology archives digital and physical data to meet business needs, as well as regulatory and legal requirements (Rowe, 2012).

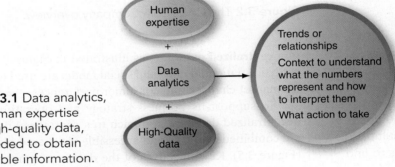

Figure 3.1 Data analytics, and human expertise and high-quality data, are needed to obtain actionable information.

CASE 3.1 OPENING CASE

Coca-Cola Manages at the Point That Makes a Difference

COCA-COLA'S DATA MANAGEMENT CHALLENGES

Petabyte (Pb) = 1,000 Terabytes (Tb) = 1 million Gigabytes (Gb).

The Coca-Cola Company is a Fortune 100 company with over $48 billion in sales revenue and $9 billion in profit (Figure 3.2). The market leader manages and analyzes several **petabytes** (Pb) of data generated or collected from more than 500 brands and consumers in 206 countries. Its bottling partners provide sales and shipment data, while retail customers transmit transaction and merchandising data. Other data sources are listed in Table 3.1. From 2003 to spring 2013, data analysts at Coca-Cola knew there were BI opportunities in the mountains of data its bottlers were storing, but finding and accessing all of that data for analytics proved to be nearly impossible. The disparate data sources caused long delays in getting analytics reports from IT to sales teams. The company decided to replace the legacy software at each bottling facility and standardize them on a new BI system, a combination of MicroStrategy and Microsoft BI products.

Enterprise Data Management Like most global companies, Coca-Cola relies on sophisticated enterprise data management, BI, and analytic technologies to sustain its performance in fiercely competitive markets (Figure 3.3). Data are managed

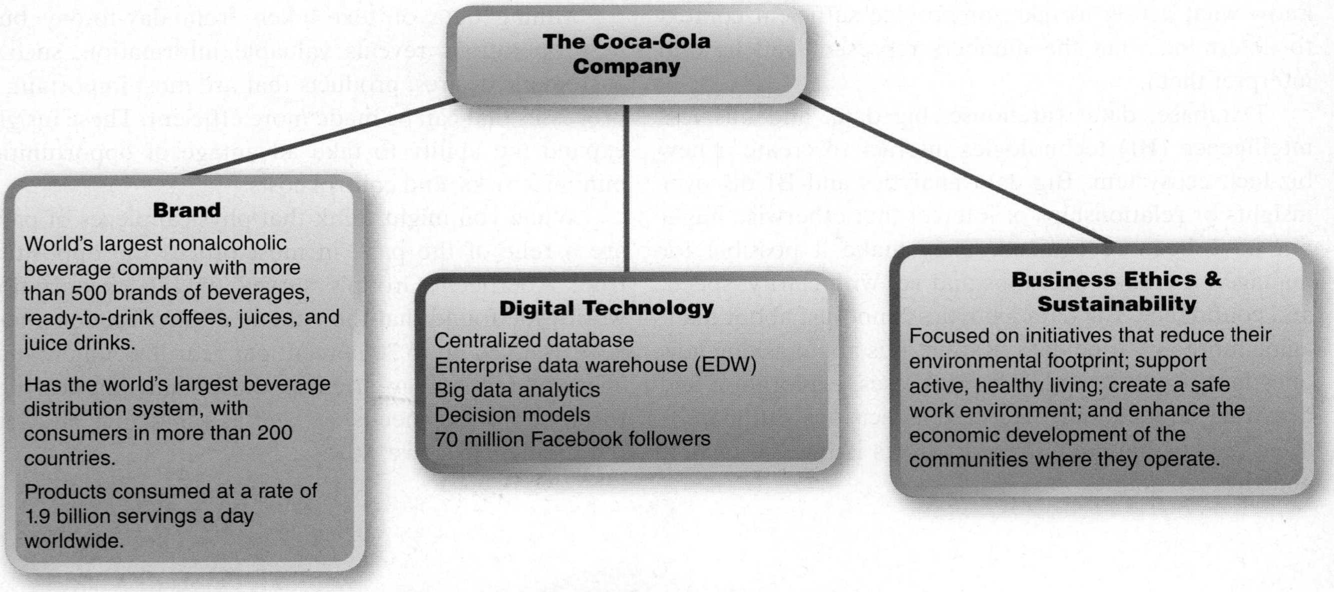

The Coca-Cola Company
Brand
World's largest nonalcoholic beverage company with more than 500 brands of beverages, ready-to-drink coffees, juices, and juice drinks.
Has the world's largest beverage distribution system, with consumers in more than 200 countries.
Products consumed at a rate of 1.9 billion servings a day worldwide.
Digital Technology
Centralized database
Enterprise data warehouse (EDW)
Big data analytics
Decision models
70 million Facebook followers
Business Ethics & Sustainability
Focused on initiatives that reduce their environmental footprint; support active, healthy living; create a safe work environment; and enhance the economic development of the communities where they operate.

Figure 3.2 The Coca-Cola Company overview.

Centralized database stores data at a single location that is accessible from anywhere. Searches can be fast because the search engine does not need to check multiple distributed locations to find responsive data.

Data warehouses that integrate data from databases across an entire enterprise are called enterprise data warehouses (EDW).

in a **centralized database,** as illustrated in Figure 3.4. **Data warehousing,** big data, analytics, data modeling, and social media are used to respond to competitors' activity, market changes, and consumer preferences.

To support its business strategy and operations, Coca-Cola changed from a decentralized database approach to a centralized database approach. Now its data are combined centrally and accessible via shared platforms across the organization (Figure 3.5). Key objectives of the data management strategy are to help its retail customers such as Walmart, which sells $4 billion of Coca-Cola products annually, sell

Coca-Cola
Trade-mark

© Katherine Welles/Shutterstock

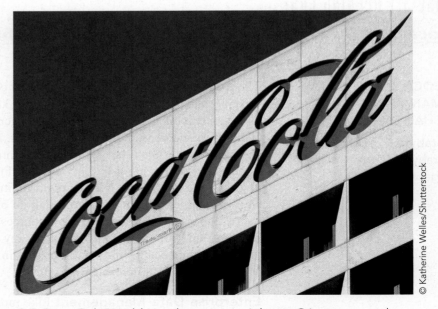

Figure 3.3 Coca-Cola World Headquarters in Atlanta, GA, announced on January 25, 2010, that new packaging material for plastic bottles will be made partially from plants—as part of its sustainability efforts.

TABLE 3.1   Opening Case Overview

Company	• The Coca-Cola Company, coca-cola.com • Sustainability: www.coca-colacompany.com/sustainability • $48 billion in sales revenue and profits of $9 billion, 2013
Industry	• The global company manufactures, sells, and distributes nonalcoholic beverages.
Product lines	• More than 500 brands of still and sparkling beverages, ready-to-drink coffees, juices, and juice drinks.
Digital technology	• Enterprise data warehouse (EDW) • Big data and analytics • Business intelligence • In 2014, moved from a decentralized approach to a centralized approach, where the data are combined centrally and available via the shared platforms across the organization.
Business challenges	• In 2010, Coca-Cola had 74 unique databases, many of them used different software to store and analyze data. Dealing with incompatible databases and reporting systems remained a problem from 2003 to 2013. • Chief Big Data Insights Officer Esat Sezer has stated that Coca-Cola took a strategic approach instead of a tactical approach with big data.
Global data sources	• Transaction and merchandising data • Data from nationwide network of 74 bottlers • Multichannel retail data • Customer profile data from loyalty programs • Social media data • Supply chain data • Competitor data • Sales and shipment data from bottling partners

more Coca-Cola products and to improve the consumer experience. The company has implemented a data governance program to ensure that cultural data sensitivities are respected.

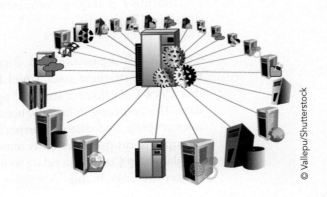

Figure 3.4 Centralized data architecture.

© Vallepu/Shutterstock

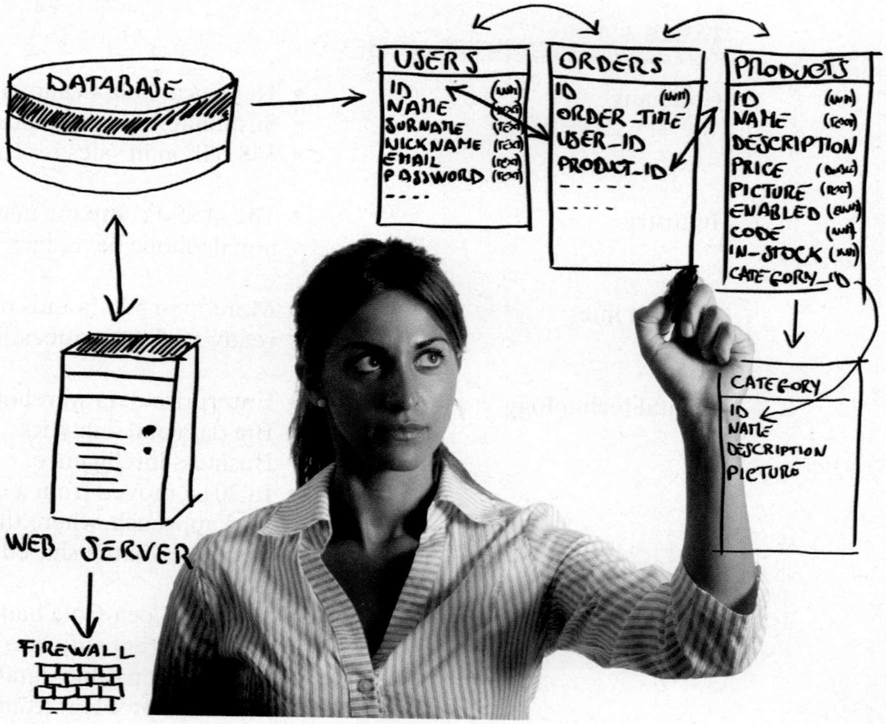

Figure 3.5 Data from online and offline transactions are stored in databases. Data about entities such as customers, products, orders, and employees are stored in an organized way.

SUSTAINING BUSINESS
PERFORMANCE

All data are standardized through a series of master data management (MDM) processes, as discussed in Chapter 2. An enterprise data warehouse (EDW) generates a single view of all multichannel retail data. The EDW creates a trusted view of customers, sales, and transactions, enabling Coca-Cola to respond quickly and accurately to changes in market conditions.

Throughout Coca-Cola's divisions and departments, huge volumes of data are analyzed to make more and better time-sensitive, critical decisions about products, shopper marketing, the supply chain, and production. Point-of-sale (POS) data are captured from retail channels and used to create customer profiles. Those profiles are communicated via a centralized iPad reporting system. POS data are analyzed to support collaborative planning, forecasting, and replenishment processes within its supply chain. (Supply chain management, collaborative planning, forecasting, and replenishment are covered in greater detail in Chapter 10.)

Coca-Cola's Approach to Big Data and Decision Models Big data are treated as a strategic asset. Chief Big Data Insights Officer Esat Sezer has stated that Coca-Cola takes a strategic approach instead of a tactical approach with big data. The company is far advanced in the use of big data to manage its products, sales revenue, and customer experiences in near real time and to reduce costs. For example, it cut overtime costs almost in half by analyzing the service center data. Big data help Coca-Cola relate to its 70 million Facebook followers—many of them bolster the Coke brand.

Big data play a key role in ensuring that its orange juice tastes the same year-round and is readily available anywhere in the world. Oranges used by Coca-Cola have a peak growing season of only three months. Producing orange juice with a consistent taste year-round despite the inconsistent quality of the orange supply is complex. To deal with the complexity, an orange juice decision model was developed, the *Black Book model*. A **decision model** quantifies the relationship between variables, which reduces uncertainty. Black Book combines detailed data on the 600+ flavors that make up an orange, weather, customer preferences, expected crop yields, cost pressures, regional consumer preferences, and acidity or sweetness rate. The model specifies how to blend the orange juice to create a consistent taste. Coke's Black Book juice model is considered to be one of the most complex business analytics apps. It requires analyzing up to 1 quintillion (10E18) decision variables to consistently deliver the optimal blend.

With the power of big data and decision models, Coca-Cola is prepared for disruptions in supply far in advance. According to Doug Bippert, Coca-Cola's vice president of business acceleration, "If we have a hurricane or a freeze, we can quickly re-plan the business in five or 10 minutes just because we've mathematically modeled it" (BusinessIntelligence.com, 2013b).

Questions

1. Why does the Coca-Cola Company have petabytes of data?
2. Why is it important for Coca-Cola to be able to process POS data in near real time?
3. How does Coca-Cola attempt to create favorable customer experiences?
4. What is the importance of having a trusted view of the data?
5. What is the benefit of a decision model?
6. What is the Black Book model?
7. Explain the strategic benefit of the Black Book model.

Sources: Compiled from Burns (2013), Fernandez (2012), BusinessIntelligence.com (2013a, 2013b), CNNMoney (2014), Big Data Startups (2013), and Teradata (2012).

3.1 Database Management Systems

Data are the driving force behind any successful business. Operations, planning, control, and all other management functions rely largely on processed information, not raw data. And, no one wants to wait for business-critical reports or specific answers to their questions. Data management technologies that keep users informed and support the various business demands are the following:

Databases are collections of data sets or records stored in a systematic way.

Volatile refers to data that change frequently.

- **Databases** store data generated by business apps, sensors, operations, and transaction-processing systems (TPS). Data in databases are extremely **volatile**. Medium and large enterprises typically have many databases of various types.

- **Data warehouses** integrate data from multiple databases and data silos, and organize them for complex analysis, knowledge discovery, and to support decision making. For example, data are extracted from a database, processed to standardize their format, and then loaded into data warehouses at specific times, such as weekly. As such, data in data warehouses are nonvolatile—and ready for analysis.

- **Data marts** are small-scale data warehouses that support a single function or one department. Enterprises that cannot afford to invest in data warehousing may start with one or more data marts.
- **Business intelligence (BI)** tools and techniques process data and do statistical analysis for insight and discovery—that is, to discover meaningful relationships in the data, keep informed in real time, detect trends, and identify opportunities and risks.

Data-processing techniques, processing power, and enterprise performance management capabilities have undergone revolutionary advances in recent years for reasons you are already familiar with—big data, mobility, and cloud computing. The last decade, however, has seen the emergence of new approaches, first in data warehousing and, more recently, for transaction processing, as you read in this chapter.

DATABASE MANAGEMENT SYSTEMS AND SQL

Database management systems (DBMSs) are software used to manage the additions, updates, and deletions of data as transactions occur, and to support data queries and reporting. They are OLTP systems.

SQL is a standardized query language for accessing databases.

Database management systems (DBMSs) integrate with data collection systems such as TPS and business applications; store the data in an organized way; and provide facilities for accessing and managing that data. Over the past 25 years, the **relational database** has been the standard database model adopted by most enterprises. Relational databases store data in tables consisting of columns and rows, similar to the format of a spreadsheet, as shown in Figure 3.6.

Relational management systems (RDBMSs) provide access to data using a declarative language—**structured query language (SQL). Declarative languages** simplify data access by requiring that users only specify what data they want to access without defining how access will be achieved. The format of a basic SQL statement is

SELECT column_name(s)

FROM table_name

WHERE condition

An instance of SQL is shown in Figure 3.7.

Figure 3.6 Illustration of structured data format. Numeric and alphanumeric data are arranged into rows and predefined columns similar to those in an Excel spreadsheet.

© Alexander Fediachov/Alamy

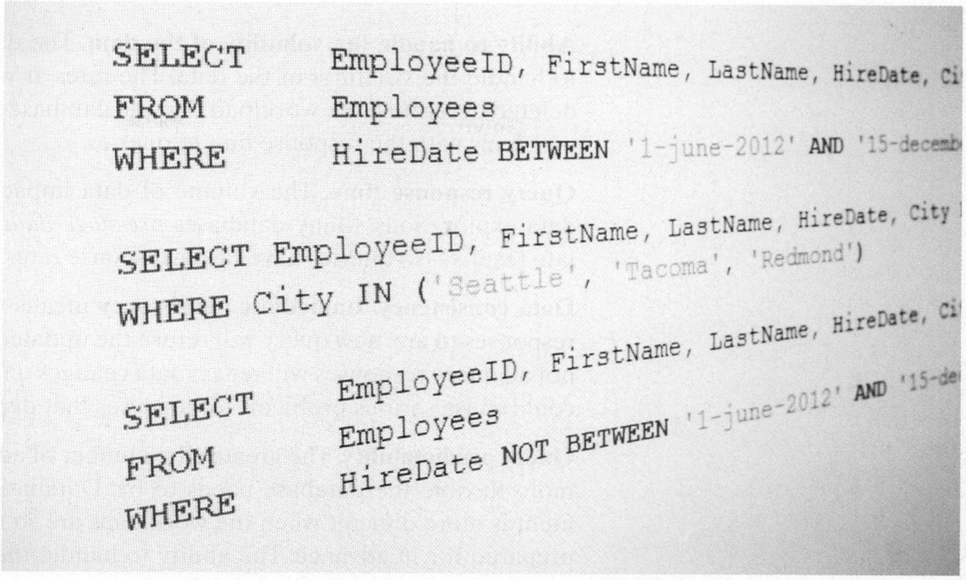

Figure 3.7 An instance of SQL to access employee information based on date of hire.

DBMS Functions

An accurate and consistent view of data throughout the enterprise is needed so one can make informed, actionable decisions that support the business strategy. Functions performed by a DBMS to help create such a view are:

- **Data filtering and profiling:** Process and store data efficiently. Inspect the data for errors, inconsistencies, redundancies, and incomplete information.

- **Data integrity and maintenance:** Correct, standardize, and verify the consistency and integrity of the data.

- **Data synchronization:** Integrate, match, or link data from disparate sources.

- **Data security:** Check and control data integrity over time.

- **Data access:** Provide authorized access to data in both planned and ad hoc ways within acceptable time.

Today's computing hardware is capable of crunching through huge datasets that were impossible to manage a few years back and making them available on-demand via wired or wireless networks (Figure 3.8).

TECH NOTE 3.1 Factors That Determine the Performance of a DBMS

Factors to consider when evaluating the performance of a database are the following.

Queries are ad hoc (unplanned) user requests for specific data.

Data latency. Latency is the elapsed time (or delay) between when data are created and when they are available for a **query** or report. Applications have different tolerances for latency. Database systems tend to have shorter latency than data warehouses. Short latency imposes more restrictions on a system.

Ability to handle the volatility of the data. The database has the processing power to handle the volatility of the data. The rates at which data are added, updated, or deleted determine the workload that the database must be able to control to prevent problems with the response rate to queries.

Query response time. The volume of data impacts response times to queries and data explorations. Many databases *pre-stage data*—that is, summarize or precalculate results—so queries have faster response rates.

Data consistency. Immediate consistency means that as soon as data are updated, responses to any new query will return the updated value. With **eventual consistency,** not all query responses will reflect data changes uniformly. Inconsistent query results could cause serious problems for analyses that depend on accurate data.

Query predictability. The greater the number of ad hoc or unpredictable queries, the more flexible the database needs to be. Database or query performance management is more difficult when the workloads are so unpredictable that they cannot be prepared for in advance. The ability to handle the workload is the most important criterion when choosing a database.

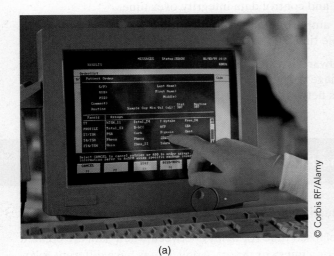

(a)

(b)

Figure 3.8 Database queries are processed in real time (a), and results are transmitted via wired or wireless networks to computer screens or handhelds (b).

Online Transaction Processing and Online Analytics Processing

When most business transactions occur—for instance, an item is sold or returned, an order is sent or cancelled, a payment or deposit is made—changes are made immediately to the database. These online changes are additions, updates, or deletions. DBMSs record and process transactions in the database, and support queries and reporting. Given their functions, DBMSs are referred to as **online transaction-processing (OLTP) systems.** OLTP is a database design that breaks down complex information into simpler data tables to strike a balance between transaction-processing efficiency and query efficiency. OLTP databases process millions of transactions per second. However, databases cannot be optimized for data mining, complex **online analytics-processing (OLAP) systems,** and decision support. These limitations led to the introduction of data warehouse technology. Data warehouses and data marts are optimized for OLAP, data mining, BI, and decision support. OLAP is a term used to describe the analysis of complex data from the data warehouse. In summary, databases are optimized for extremely fast transaction processing and query processing. Data warehouses are optimized for analysis.

Online transaction processing (OLTP) systems are designed to manage transaction data, which are volatile.

DBMS AND DATA WAREHOUSING VENDORS RESPOND TO LATEST DATA DEMANDS

One of the major drivers of change in the data management market is the increased amount of data to be managed. Enterprises need powerful DBMSs and data warehousing solutions, analytics, and reporting. The four vendors that dominate this market—Oracle, IBM, Microsoft, and Teradata—continue to respond to evolving data management needs with more intelligent and advanced software and hardware. Advanced hardware technology enables scaling to much higher data volumes and workloads than previously possible, or it can handle specific workloads. Older general-purpose relational databases DBMSs lack the scalability or flexibility for specialized or very large workloads, but are very good at what they do.

DBMS Vendor Rankings

The highest-ranking enterprise DBMSs in mid-2014 were Oracle's MySQL, Microsoft's SQL Server, PostgreSQL, IBM's DB2, and Teradata Database. Most run on multiple operating systems (OSs).

- MySQL, which was acquired by Oracle in January 2010, powers hundreds of thousands of commercial websites and a huge number of internal enterprise applications.
- SQL Server's ease of use, availability, and Windows operating system integration make it an easy choice for firms that choose Microsoft products for their enterprises.
- PostgreSQL is the most advanced open source database, often used by online gaming applications and Skype, Yahoo!, and MySpace.
- DB2 is widely used in data centers and runs on Linux, UNIX, Windows, and mainframes.

Trend Toward NoSQL Systems

RDBMSs are still the dominant database engines, but the trend toward **NoSQL** (short for "not only SQL") systems is clear. NoSQL systems increased in popularity by 50 percent from 2013 to 2014. Although NoSQL have existed for as long as relational DBMS, the term itself was not introduced until 2009. That was when many new systems were developed in order to cope with the unfolding requirements for DBMS—namely, handling big data, scalability, and fault tolerance for large Web applications. **Scalability** means the system can increase in size to handle data growth or the load of an increasing number of concurrent users. To put it differently, scalable systems efficiently meet the demands of high-performance computing. **Fault tolerance** means that no single failure results in any loss of service.

NoSQL systems are such a heterogeneous group of database systems that attempts to classify them are not very helpful. However, their general advantages are these:

- Higher performance
- Easy distribution of data on different nodes, which enables scalability and fault tolerance
- Greater flexibility
- Simpler administration

Starting in 2010 and continuing through 2014, Microsoft has been working on the first rewrite of SQL Server's query execution since Version 7 was released in 1998. The goal is to offer NoSQL-like speeds without sacrificing the capabilities of a relational database.

With most NoSQL offerings, the bulk of the cost does not lie in acquiring the database, but rather in implementing it. Data need to be selected and migrated (moved) to the new database. Microsoft hopes to reduce these costs by offering migration solutions.

CENTRALIZED AND DISTRIBUTED DATABASE ARCHITECTURE

Databases are centralized or distributed, as shown in Figure 3.9. Both types of databases need one or more backups and should be archived onsite and offsite in case of a crash or security incident.

Centralized Database Architecture

A centralized database stores all related files in a central location—as you read in the opening Coca-Cola case. For decades the main database platform consisted of centralized database files on massive mainframe computers. Benefits of centralized database configurations include:

1. **Better control of data quality.** Data consistency is easier when data are kept in one physical location because data additions, updates, and deletions can be made in a supervised and orderly fashion.
2. **Better IT security.** Data are accessed via the centralized host computer, where they can be protected more easily from unauthorized access or modification.

A major disadvantage of centralized databases, like all centralized systems, is transmission delay when users are geodispersed. More powerful hardware and networks compensate for this disadvantage.

Distributed Database Architecture

A **distributed database system** allows apps on computers and mobiles to access data from both local and remote databases, as diagrammed in Figure 3.10. Distributed databases use client/server architecture to process information requests. Computers and mobile devices accessing the servers are called clients. The databases are stored on servers that reside in the company's data centers, a private cloud, or a public cloud.

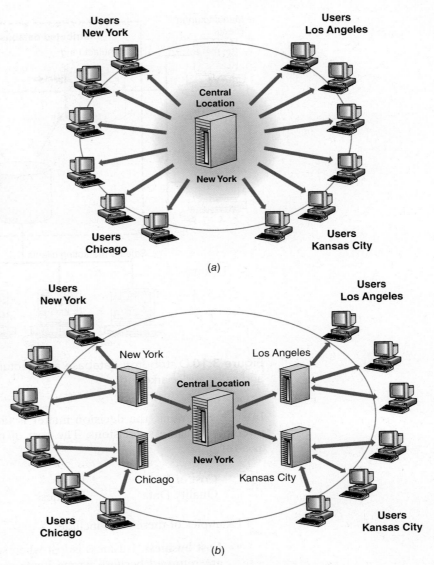

Figure 3.9 Comparison of centralized and distributed databases.

GARBAGE IN,
GARBAGE OUT

Data collection is a highly complex process that can create problems concerning the quality of the data being collected. Therefore, regardless of how the data are collected, they need to be validated so users know they can trust them. Classic expressions that sum up the situation are "garbage in, garbage out" (GIGO) and the potentially riskier "garbage in, gospel out." In the latter case, poor-quality data are trusted and used as the basis for planning. You have encountered data safeguards, such as integrity checks, to help improve data quality when you fill in an online form. For example, the form will not accept an e-mail address that is not formatted correctly.

Dirty Data Costs and Consequences

Dirty data—that is, poor-quality data—lack integrity and cannot be trusted. Too often managers and information workers are actually constrained by data that cannot be trusted because they are incomplete, out of context, outdated, inaccurate, inaccessible, or so overwhelming that they require weeks to analyze.

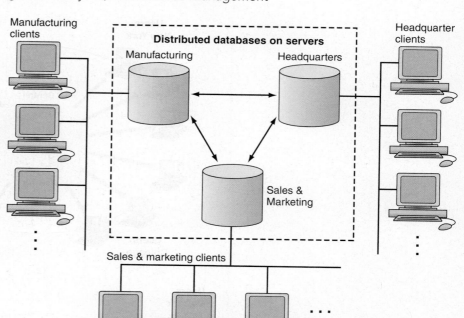

Figure 3.10 Distributed database architecture for headquarters, manufacturing, and sales and marketing.

In such situations, the decision maker is facing too much uncertainty to make intelligent business decisions. The cost of poor-quality data may be expressed as a formula:

$$\text{Cost of Poor-Quality Data} = \text{Lost Business} + \text{Cost to Prevent Errors} + \text{Cost to Correct Errors}$$

Examples of these costs include:

- **Lost business.** Business is lost when sales opportunities are missed, orders are returned because wrong items were delivered, or errors frustrate and drive away customers.

- **Time spent preventing errors.** If data cannot be trusted, then employees need to spend more time and effort trying to verify information in order to avoid mistakes.

- **Time spent correcting errors.** Database staff need to process corrections to the database. For example, the costs of correcting errors at Urent Corporation are estimated as follows:

a) Two database staff members spend 25 percent of their workday processing and verifying data corrections each day:

2 people * 25% of 8 hours/day = 4 hours/day correcting errors

b) Hourly salaries are $50 per hour based on pay rate and benefits:

$50/hour * 4 hours/day = $200/day correcting errors

c) 250 workdays per year:

$200/day * 250 days = $50,000/year to correct errors

The costs of poor-quality data spread throughout a company, affecting systems from shipping and receiving to accounting and customer service. Data errors typically arise from the functions or departments that generate or create the data—and not within the IT department. When all costs are considered, the value of finding and fixing the causes of data errors becomes clear. In a time of decreased budgets, some organizations may not have the resources for such projects and may not even be aware of the problem. Others may be spending most of their time fixing problems, thus leaving them with no time to work on preventing them.

Bad data are costing U.S. businesses hundreds of billions of dollars a year and affecting their ability to ride out the tough economic climate. Incorrect and outdated values, missing data, and inconsistent data formats can cause lost customers, sales, and revenue; misallocation of resources; and flawed pricing strategies.

For a particular company, it is difficult to calculate the full cost of poor data quality and its long-term effects. Part of the difficulty is the time delay between the mistake and when it is detected. Errors can be very difficult to correct, especially when systems extend across the enterprise. Another concern is that the impacts of errors can be unpredictable or serious. For example, the cost of errors due to unreliable and incorrect data alone is estimated to be as high as $40 billion annually in the retail sector (Zynapse, 2010). And, one health-care company whose agents were working with multiple ISs, but were not updating client details in every IS, saw its annual expenses increase by $9 million.

Data Ownership and Organizational Politics

Despite the need for high-quality data, organizational politics and technical issues make that difficult to achieve. The source of the problem is data ownership—that is, who owns or is responsible for the data. Data ownership problems exist when there are no policies defining responsibility and accountability for managing data. Inconsistent data formats of various departments create an additional set of problems as organizations try to combine individual applications into integrated enterprise systems.

The tendency to delegate data-quality responsibilities to the technical teams who have no control over data quality, as opposed to business users who do have such control, is another common pitfall that stands in the way of accumulating high-quality data.

Those who manage a business or part of a business are tasked with trying to improve business performance and retain customers. Compensation is tied to improving profitability, driving revenue growth, and improving the quality of customer service. These key performance indicators (KPIs) are monitored closely by senior managers who want to find and eliminate defects that harm performance. It is strange then that so few managers take the time to understand how performance is impacted by poor-quality data. Two examples make a strong case for investment in high-quality data.

Retail banks: For retail bank executives, risk management is the number-one issue. Disregard for risk contributed to the 2008 financial services meltdown. Despite risk management strategies, many banks still incur huge losses. Part of the problem in many banks is that their ISs enable them to monitor risk only at the product level—mortgages, loans, or credit cards. Product-level risk management ISs monitor a customer's risk exposure for mortgages, or for loans, or for credit cards, and so forth—but not for a customer for all products. With product-level ISs, a bank cannot see the full risk exposure of a customer. The limitations of these siloed product-level risks have serious implications for business performance because bad-risk customers cannot be identified easily, and customer data in the various ISs may differ. For example, consider what happens when each product-level risk management IS feeds data to marketing ISs. Marketing may offer bad-risk customers incentives to take out another credit card or loan that they cannot repay. And since the bank cannot identify its best customers either, they may be ignored and enticed away by better deals offered by competitors. This scenario illustrates how data ownership and data-quality management are critical to risk management. Data defects and incomplete data can quickly trigger inaccurate marketing and mounting losses. One retail bank facing these problems lost 16 percent of its mortgage business within 18 months while losses in its credit card business increased (Ferguson, 2012).

Manufacturing. Many manufacturers are at the mercy of a powerful customer base—large retailers. Manufacturers want to align their processes with those of large retail customers to keep them happy. This alignment makes it possible for a retailer to order centrally for all stores or to order locally from a specific manufacturer. Supporting both central and local ordering makes it difficult to plan production runs. For example, each manufacturing site has to collect order data from central ordering and local ordering systems to get a complete picture of what to manufacture at each site. Without accurate, up-to-date data, orders may go unfilled, or manufacturers may have excess inventory. One manufacturer who tried to keep its key retailer happy by implementing central and local ordering could not process orders correctly at each manufacturing site. No data ownership and lack of control over how order data flowed throughout business operations had negative impacts. Conflicting and duplicate business processes at each manufacturing site caused data errors, leading to mistakes in manufacturing, packing, and shipments. Customers were very dissatisfied.

These two examples represent the consequences of a lack of data ownership and data quality. Understanding the impact of mismanaged data makes data ownership and accurate data a higher priority.

Compliance with numerous federal and state regulations relies on rock-solid data and trusted metrics used for regulatory reporting. Data ownership, data quality, and formally managed data are high on the agenda of CFOs and CEOs who are held personally accountable if their company is found to be in violation of regulations.

DATA LIFE CYCLE AND DATA PRINCIPLES

The data life cycle is a model that illustrates the way data travel through an organization, as shown in Figure 3.11. The data life cycle begins with storage in a database, to being loaded into a data warehouse for analysis, then reported to knowledge workers or used in business apps. Supply chain management (SCM), customer relationship management (CRM), and e-commerce are enterprise applications that require up-to-date, readily accessible data to function properly.

Three general data principles relate to the data life cycle perspective and help to guide IT investment decisions:

1. **Principle of diminishing data value.** The value of data diminishes as they age. This is a simple, yet powerful principle. Most organizations cannot operate at peak performance with blind spots (lack of data availability) of 30 days or longer. Global financial services institutions rely on near real time data for peak performance.

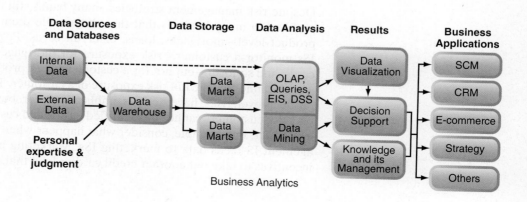

Figure 3.11 Data life cycle.

2. **Principle of 90/90 data use.** According to the 90/90 data-use principle, a majority of stored data, as high as 90 percent, is seldom accessed after 90 days (except for auditing purposes). That is, roughly 90 percent of data lose most of their value after 3 months.

3. **Principle of data in context.** The capability to capture, process, format, and distribute data in near real time or faster requires a huge investment in data architecture (Chapter 2) and infrastructure to link remote POS systems to data storage, data analysis systems, and reporting apps. The investment can be justified on the principle that data must be integrated, processed, analyzed, and formatted into "actionable information."

MASTER DATA AND MASTER DATA MANAGEMENT

As data become more complex and their volumes explode, database performance degrades. One solution is the use of master data and **master data management (MDM),** as introduced in Chapter 2. MDM processes integrate data from various sources or enterprise applications to create a more complete (unified) view of a customer, product, or other entity. Figure 3.12 shows how master data serve as a layer between transactional data in a database and analytical data in a data warehouse. Although vendors may claim that their MDM solution creates "a single version of the truth," this claim is probably not true. In reality, MDM cannot create a single unified version of the data because constructing a completely unified view of all master data is simply not possible.

Master Reference File and Data Entities

Realistically, MDM consolidates data from various data sources into a master reference file, which then feeds data back to the applications, thereby creating accurate and consistent data across the enterprise. In IT at Work 3.1, participants in the health-care supply chain essentially developed a master reference file of its key data entities. A **data entity** is anything real or abstract about which a company wants to collect and store data. Master data entities are the main entities of a company, such as customers, products, suppliers, employees, and assets.

Each department has distinct master data needs. Marketing, for example, is concerned with product pricing, brand, and product packaging, whereas production is concerned with product costs and schedules. A customer master reference file can feed data to all enterprise systems that have a customer relationship component, thereby providing a more unified picture of customers. Similarly, a product master reference file can feed data to all the production systems within the enterprise.

An MDM includes tools for cleaning and auditing the master data elements as well as tools for integrating and synchronizing data to make them more accessible. MDM offers a solution for managers who are frustrated with how fragmented and dispersed their data sources are.

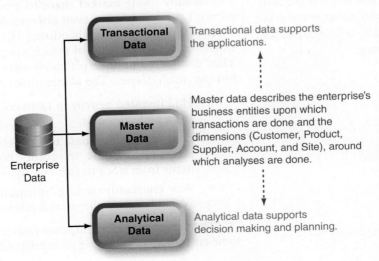

Figure 3.12 An enterprise has transactional, master, and analytical data.

IT at Work 3.1

Data Errors Increase Costs Downstream

At an insurance company, the cost of processing each claim is $1, but the average downstream cost due to errors in a claim is $300. The $300 average downstream costs included manual handling of exceptions, customer support calls initiated due to errors in claims, and reissuing corrected documents for any claims processed incorrectly the first time. In addition, the company faced significant soft costs from regulatory risk, lost revenues due to customer dissatisfaction, and overpayment on claims due to claims-processing errors. These soft costs are not included in the hard cost of $300.

Every day health-care administrators and others throughout the health-care supply chain waste 24 to 30 percent of their time correcting data errors. Each transaction error costs $60 to $80 to correct. In addition, about 60 percent of all invoices among supply chain partners contain errors, and each invoice error costs $40 to $400 to reconcile. Altogether, errors and conflicting data increase supply costs by 3 to 5 percent. In other words, each year billions of dollars are wasted in the health-care supply chain because of supply chain data disconnects, which refer to one organization's IS not understanding data from another's IS.

Questions

1. Why are the downstream costs of data errors so high?
2. What are soft costs?
3. Explain how soft costs might exceed hard costs. Give an example.

Questions

1. Describe a database and a database management system (DBMS).
2. Explain what an online transaction-processing (OLAP) system does.
3. Why are data in databases volatile?
4. Explain what processes DBMSs are optimized to perform.
5. What are the business costs or risks of poor data quality?
6. Describe the data life cycle.
7. What is the function of master data management (MDM)?

3.2 Data Warehouse and Big Data Analytics

Market share is the percentage of total sales in a market captured by a brand, product, or company.

The senior marketing manager of a major U.S. retailer learned that her company was steadily losing **market share** to a competitor in many of their profitable segments. Losses continued even after a sales campaign that combined online promotions with improved merchandizing (Brown, Chui, & Manyika, 2011). To understand the causes, a team of senior managers studied their competitor's practices. They discovered that the problems were not simply due to basic marketing tactics, but ran much deeper. The competitor:

- Had invested heavily in IT to collect, integrate, and analyze data from each store and sales unit.
- Had linked these data to suppliers' databases, making it possible to adjust prices in real time, to reorder hot-selling items automatically, and to shift items from store to store easily.
- Was constantly testing, integrating, and reporting information instantly available across the organization—from the store floor to the CFO's office.

The senior management team realized that their competitor was stealing away their customers because big data analytics enabled them to pinpoint improvement

TABLE 3.2   Four V's of Data Analytics
1.   **Variety:** The analytic environment has expanded from pulling data from enterprise systems to include big data and unstructured sources.
2.   **Volume:** Large volumes of structured and unstructured data are analyzed.
3.   **Velocity:** Speed of access to reports that are drawn from data defines the difference between effective and ineffective analytics.
4.   **Veracity:** Validating data and extracting insights that managers and workers can trust are key factors of successful analytics. Trust in analytics has grown more difficult with the explosion of data sources.

Operating margin is a measure of the percent of a company's revenue left over after paying for its variable costs, such as wages and raw materials. An increasing margin means the company is earning more per dollar of sales. The higher the operating margin, the better.

opportunities across the supply chain—from purchasing to in-store availability management. Specifically, the competitor was able to predict how customers *would behave* and used that knowledge to be prepared to respond quickly. This case is an example of what researchers have learned. According to the McKinsey Global Institute (MGI), big data analytics have helped companies outperform their competitors. MGI estimates that retailers using big data analytics increase their **operating margin** by more than 60 percent. Leading retailers, insurance, and financial services use big data to capture market share away from local competitors (Breuer, Forina, & Moulton, 2013). An IBM study shows that companies with advanced business analytics and optimization can experience 20 times more profit growth and 30 percent higher return on invested capital (ibm.com, 2011).

In this section, you will learn about the value, challenges, and technologies involved in putting data and analytics to use to support decisions and action. The four V's of analytics—variety, volume, velocity, and veracity—are described in Table 3.2.

Big data can have a dramatic impact on the success of any enterprise, or they can be a low-contributing major expense. However, success is not achieved with technology alone. Many companies are collecting and capturing huge amounts of data, but spending very little effort to ensure the veracity and value of data captured at the transactional stage or point of origin. Emphasis in this direction will not only increase confidence in the datasets, but also significantly reduce the efforts for analytics and enhance the quality of decision making. Success depends also on ensuring that you avoid invalid assumptions, which can be done by testing the assumptions during analysis.

CAREER INSIGHT 3.1 JOBS

Managing and Interpreting Big Data Are in Highest Demand

The IT job market is on the rise, and top jobs include anything in big data, mobile, cloud, or IT security. TechRepublic held a roundtable of IT executives and tech recruiters to learn about the latest hiring trends. Here are three forecasts (Hammond, 2014):

- Pete Kazanjy, co-founder of TalentBin, stated there "will be the continued uptick in demand for technical talent, but more broadly across the entire economy, and not just siloed in its own tech sector. Technology is ceasing to be a sector on its

own, and is instead becoming more critical in every industry."

- Tendu Yogurtcu, vice president of engineering at Syncsort, explained: "With the rising popularity of Hadoop, positions are geared towards filling these roles, with lots of interest placed on big data and data mining and analysis. Most of the new hires are recent graduates, since they embody a lot of creativity and forward thinking, both qualities needed in the industry of big data."

- Robert Noble, director of software of engineering at WhitePages, gave an overview of the recruiting issues: "The demand for tech and software talent is exploding. A lot of companies have been aggressive and creative to compete for candidates in these fields. For instance, besides compensation and the technical work of the job role, companies are using culture as a key differentiator. They are not only talking about the company, they are also talking about the perks outside of work, and benefits, like cool team events, providing free haircuts, massages, food and more."

TORTURE DATA LONG ENOUGH AND IT WILL CONFESS . . . BUT MAY NOT TELL THE TRUTH

As someone posted in a *Harvard Business Review* (*HBR*) blog, "If you torture the data long enough, it will confess" (Neill, 2013). That is, analytics will produce results, but those results may be meaningless or misleading. For example, some believe that Super Bowl results in February predict whether the stock market will go up or down that year. If the National Football Conference (NFC) wins, the market goes up; otherwise, stocks take a dive. Looking at results over the past 30 years, most often the NFC has won the Super Bowl and the market has gone up. Does this mean anything? No.

HUMAN EXPERTISE AND JUDGMENT ARE NEEDED

Human expertise and judgment are needed to interpret the output of analytics (refer to Figure 3.1). Data are worthless if you cannot analyze, interpret, understand, and apply the results in context. This brings up several challenges:

- **Data need to be prepared for analysis**. For example, data that are incomplete or duplicated need to be fixed.
- **Dirty data degrade the value of analytics.** The "cleanliness" of data is very important to data mining and analysis projects. Analysts have complained that data analytics is like janitorial work because they spend so much time on manual, error-prone processes to clean the data. Large data volumes and variety mean more data that are dirty and harder to handle.
- **Data must be put into meaningful context.** If the wrong analysis or datasets are used, the output would be nonsense, as in the example of the Super Bowl winners and stock market performance. Stated in reverse, managers need context in order to understand how to interpret traditional and big data.

IT at Work 3.2 describes how big data analytics, collaboration, and human expertise have transformed the new drug development process.

IT at Work 3.2

Researchers Use Genomics and Big Data in Drug Discovery

Drug development is a high-risk business. Almost 90 percent of new drugs ultimately fail. One of the challenges has been the amount, variety, and complexity of the data that need to be systematically analyzed. Big data technologies and private–public partnerships have made biomedical analytics feasible.

New Drug Development Had Been Slow and Expensive

Biotechnology advances have produced massive data on the biological causes of disease. However, analyzing these data and converting discoveries into treatments are much more difficult. Not all biomedical insights lead to effective drug targets, and choosing the wrong target leads to failures late in the drug development process, costing time, money, and lives. Developing a new drug—from early discovery through Food and Drug Administration (FDA) approval—takes over a decade and has a failure rate of more than 95 percent (Figure 3.13). As a consequence, each success ends up costing more than $1 billion.

© anyaivanova/Shutterstock

Figure 3.13 An estimated 90 to 95 percent of new drugs that undergo clinical trials ultimately fail. These costs drive up the prices of drugs that are a success—to an average of $1 billion.

For example, by the time Pfizer Inc., Johnson & Johnson, and Eli Lilly & Co. announced their new drugs had only limited benefit for Alzheimer's patients in late-stage testing, the industry had spent more than $30 billion researching amyloid plaque in the brain.

Cutting Risk of Failure

Drug makers, governments, and academic researchers have partnered to improve the odds of drug success. Partnerships bring together the expertise of scientists from biology, chemistry, bioinformatics, genomics, and big data. They are using big data to identify biological targets for drugs and eliminate failures before they reach the human testing stage.

GlaxoSmithKline, the European Bioinformatics Institute (EBI), and the Wellcome Trust Sanger Institute established the Centre for Therapeutic Target Validation (CTTV) near Cambridge, England. CTTV partners combine cutting-edge genomics with the ability to collect and analyze massive amounts of biological data. By not developing drugs that target the wrong biological pathways, they avoid wasting billions of research dollars.

Janet Thornton, director of the EBI, explained that maximizing "our use of 'big data' in the life sciences is critical for solving some of society's most pressing problems" (Kitamura, 2014). With biology now a data-driven discipline, collaborations such as CTTV are needed to improve efficiencies, cut costs, and provide the best opportunities for success. Other private–public partnerships that had formed to harness drug research and big data include:

- **Accelerating Medicines Partnership and U.S. National Institutes of Health (NIH).** In February 2014 the NIH announced that the agency, 10 pharmaceutical companies, and nonprofit organizations were investing $230 million in the Accelerating Medicines Partnership.

- **Target Discovery Institute and Oxford University.** Oxford University opened the Target Discovery Institute in 2013. Target Discovery helps to identify drug targets and molecular interactions at a critical point in a disease-causing pathway—that is, when those diseases will respond to drug therapy. Researchers try to understand complex biological processes by analyzing image data that have been acquired at the microscopic scale.

"By changing our business model, taking a more open-minded approach to sharing information and forging collaborations like the CTTV, we believe there is an opportunity to accelerate the development of innovative new medicines," said Patrick Vallance, president of Glaxo's pharmaceuticals research and development (Kitamura, 2014).

Sources: Compiled from Kitamura (2014), NIH (2014), and *HealthCanal* (2014).

Questions

1. What are the consequences of new drug development failures?
2. What factors have made biomedical analytics feasible? Why?
3. Large-scale big data analytics are expensive. How can the drug makers justify investments in big data?
4. Why would drug makers such as Glaxo and Pfizer be willing to share data given the fierce competition in their industry?

ENTERPRISE DATA WAREHOUSE AND DATA MART

Data warehouses store data from various source systems and databases across an enterprise in order to run analytical queries against huge datasets collected over long time periods. Warehouses are the primary source of cleansed data for analysis, reporting, and BI. Often the data are summarized in ways that enable quick responses to queries. For instance, query results can reveal changes in customer behavior and drive the decision to redevelop the advertising strategy.

Data warehouses that pull together data from disparate sources and databases across an entire enterprise are called **enterprise data warehouses (EDW)**. Tech Note 3.2 summarizes key characteristics of the two types of data stores.

The high cost of data warehouses can make them too expensive for a company to implement. **Data marts** are lower-cost, scaled-down versions that can be implemented in a much shorter time, for example, in less than 90 days. Data marts serve a specific department or function, such as finance, marketing, or operations. Since they store smaller amounts of data, they are faster, easier to use, and navigate.

TECH NOTE 3.2 Summary of Differences Between Databases and Data Warehouses

Databases are:
- Designed and optimized to ensure that every transaction gets recorded and stored immediately.
- **Volatile** because data are constantly being updated, added, or edited.
- OLTP systems.

Data warehouses are:
- Designed and optimized for analysis and quick response to queries.
- Nonvolatile. This stability is important to being able to analyze the data and make comparisons. When data are stored, they might never be changed or deleted in order to do trend analysis or make comparisons with newer data.
- OLAP systems.
- Subject-oriented, which means that the data captured are organized to have similar data linked together.

Procedures to Prepare EDW Data for Analytics

Consider a bank's database. Every deposit, withdrawal, loan payment, or other transaction adds or changes data. The volatility caused by constant transaction processing makes data analysis difficult—and the demands to process millions of transactions per second consume the database's processing power. In contrast, data in warehouses are relatively stable, as needed for analysis. Therefore, select data are moved from databases to a warehouse. Specifically, data are:

1. *Extracted* from designated databases.
2. *Transformed* by standardizing formats, cleaning the data, integrating them.
3. *Loaded* into a data warehouse.

These three procedures—**extract, transform, and load**—are referred to by their initials **ETL** (Figure 3.14). In a warehouse, data are *read-only*; that is, they do not change until the next ETL.

Three technologies involved in preparing raw data for analytics include ETL, **change data capture (CDC),** and data deduplication ("deduping the data"). CDC processes capture the changes made at data sources and then apply those changes throughout enterprise data stores to keep data synchronized. CDC minimizes the resources required for ETL processes by only dealing with data changes. Deduping processes remove duplicates and standardize data formats, which helps to minimize storage and data synch.

Figure 3.14 Data enter databases from transaction systems. Data of interest are extracted from databases, transformed to clean and standardize them, and then loaded into a data warehouse. These three processes are called ETL.

© Vallepu/Shutterstock

BUILDING A DATA WAREHOUSE

Figure 3.15 diagrams the process of building and using a data warehouse. The organization's data are stored in operational systems (left side of the figure). Not all data are transferred to the data warehouse. Frequently, only summary data are transferred. The warehouse organizes the data in multiple ways—by subject, functional area, vendor, and product. As shown, the data warehouse architecture defines the flow of data that starts when data are captured by transaction systems; the source data are stored in transactional (operational) databases; ETL processes move data from databases into data warehouses or data marts, where the data are available for access, reports, and analysis.

REAL TIME SUPPORT FROM ACTIVE DATA WAREHOUSE

Early data warehouse technology primarily supported strategic applications that did not require instant response time, direct customer interaction, or integration with operational systems. ETL might have been done once per week or once per month. But, demand for information to support real time customer interaction and operations leads to real time data warehousing and analytics—known as an **active data warehouse (ADW).** Massive increases in computing power, processing speeds, and memory made ADW possible. ADW are not designed to support executives'

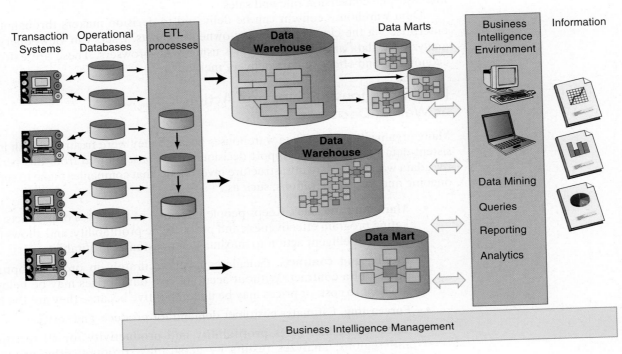

Figure 3.15 Database, data warehouse and marts, and BI architecture.

strategic decision making, but rather to support operations. For example, shipping companies like DHL use huge fleets of trucks to move millions of packages. Every day and all day, operational managers make thousands of decisions that affect the bottom line, such as: "Do we need four trucks for this run?" "With two drivers delayed by bad weather, do we need to bring in extra help?" Traditional data warehousing is not suited for immediate operational support, but active data warehousing is. For example, companies with an ADW are able to:

- Interact with a customer to provide superior customer service.
- Respond to business events in near real time.
- Share up-to-date status data among merchants, vendors, customers, and associates.

Here are some examples of how two companies use ADW:

Capital One. Capital One uses its ADW to track each customer's "profitability score" to determine the level of customer service to provide that person. Higher-cost personalized service is only given to those with high scores. For instance, when a customer calls Capital One, he or she is asked to enter a credit card number, which is linked to a profitability score. Low-profit customers get a voice response unit only; high-profit customers are connected to a live customer service representative (CSR) because the company wants to minimize the risk of losing those customers.

Travelocity. If you use Travelocity, an ADW is finding the best travel deals especially for you. The goal is to use "today's data today" instead of "yesterday's data today." The online travel agency's ADW analyzes your search history and destinations of interest; then predicts travel offers that you would most likely purchase. Offers are both relevant and timely to enhance your experience, which helps close the sale in a very competitive market. For example, when a customer is searching flights and hotels in Las Vegas, Travelocity recognizes the interest—the customer wants to go to Vegas. The ADW searches for the best-priced flights from all carriers, builds a few package deals, and presents them in real time to the customer. When customers see a personalized offer they are already interested in, the ADW helps generate a better customer experience. The real time data-driven experience increases the conversion rate and sales.

Data warehouse content can be delivered to decision makers throughout the enterprise via the cloud or company-owned intranets. Users can view, query, and analyze the data and produce reports using Web browsers. These are extremely economical and effective data delivery methods.

Data Warehousing Supports Action as Well as Decisions

Many organizations built data warehouses because they were frustrated with inconsistent data that could not support decisions or actions. Viewed from this perspective, data warehouses are infrastructure investments that companies make to support ongoing and future operations, such as:

- **Marketing and sales.** Keeps people informed of the status of products, marketing program effectiveness, and product line profitability; and allows them to take intelligent action to maximize per-customer profitability.
- **Pricing and contracts.** Calculates costs accurately in order to optimize pricing of a contract. Without accurate cost data, prices may be below or too near to cost; or prices may be uncompetitive because they are too high.
- **Forecasting.** Estimates customer demand for products and services.
- **Sales.** Calculates sales profitability and productivity for all territories and regions; analyzes results by geography, product, sales group, or individual.

- **Financial.** Provides real time data for optimal credit terms, portfolio analysis, and actions that reduce risk or bad debt expense.

Table 3.3 summarizes several successful applications of data warehouses.

BIG DATA ANALYTICS AND DATA DISCOVERY

Data analytics help users discover insights. These insights combined with human expertise enable people to recognize meaningful relationships more quickly or easily; and furthermore, realize the strategic implications of these situations. Imagine trying to make sense of the fast and vast data generated by social media campaigns on Facebook or by sensors attached to machines or objects. Low-cost sensors make it possible to monitor all types of physical things—while analytics make it possible to understand those data in order to take action in real time. For example, sensors data can be analyzed in real time:

- To monitor and regulate the temperature and climate conditions of perishable foods as they are transported from farm to supermarket.
- To sniff for signs of spoilage of fruits and raw vegetables and detect the risk of *E. coli* contamination.
- To track the condition of operating machinery and predict the probability of failure.
- To track the wear of engines and determine when preventive maintenance is needed.

TABLE 3.3   Data Warehouse Applications by Industry

Industry	Applications
Airline	Crew assignment, aircraft deployment, analysis of route profitability, customer loyalty promotions
Banking and financial	Customer service, trend analysis, product and service services promotions, reduction of IS expenses
Credit card	Customer service, new information service for a fee, fraud detection
Defense contracts	Technology transfer, production of military applications
E-business	Data warehouses with personalization capabilities, marketing/shopping preferences allowing for up-selling and cross-selling
Government	Reporting on crime areas, homeland security
Health care	Reduction of operational expenses
Investment and insurance	Risk management, market movements analysis, customer tendencies analysis, portfolio management
Retail chain	Trend analysis, buying pattern analysis, pricing policy, inventory control, sales promotions, optimal distribution channel decision

Figure 3.16 Machine-generated data from physical objects are becoming a much larger portion of big data and analytics.

Machine-generated sensor data are becoming a larger proportion of big data (Figure 3.16), according to a research report by IDC (Lohr, 2012b). It is predicted that these data will increase to 42 percent of all data by 2020, representing a significant increase from the 11 percent level of 2005.

The value of analyzing machine data was recognized by General Electric (GE) Company, the United States' largest industrial company. Since 2011 GE has been putting sensors on everything from gas turbines to hospital beds. GE's mission is to design the software for gathering data, and the algorithms for analyzing them to optimize cost savings and productivity gains. Across the industries that it covers, GE estimates efficiency opportunities will slash costs by as much as $150 billion (Lohr, 2012a).

Federal health reform efforts have pushed health-care organizations toward big data and analytics. These organizations are planning to use big data analytics to support revenue cycle management, resource utilization, fraud prevention, health management, and quality improvement.

Hadoop and MapReduce

Big data volumes exceed the processing capacity of conventional database infrastructures. A widely used processing platform is Apache **Hadoop** (hadoop. apache.org/). It places no conditions on the structure of the data it can process. Hadoop distributes computing problems across a number of servers. Hadoop implements **MapReduce** in two stages:

1. **Map stage:** MapReduce breaks up the huge dataset into smaller subsets; then distributes the subsets among multiple servers where they are partially processed.

2. **Reduce stage:** The partial results from the map stage are then recombined and made available for analytic tools.

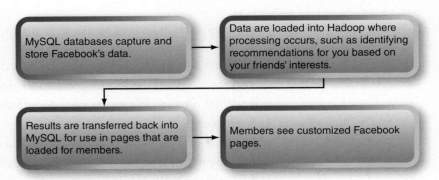

Figure 3.17 Facebook's MySQL database and Hadoop technology provide customized pages for its members.

To store data, Hadoop has its own distributed file system, *HaDoop File Systems* (HDFS), which functions in three stages:

- Loads data into HDFS.
- Performs the MapReduce operations.
- Retrieves results from HDFS.

Figure 3.17 diagrams how Facebook uses database technology and Hadoop. IT at Work 3.3 describes how First Wind has applied big data analytics to improve the operations of its wind farms and to support sustainability of the planet by reducing environmentally damaging carbon emissions.

IT at Work 3.3

Industrial Project Relies on Big Data Analytics

Wind power can play a major role in meeting America's rising demand for electricity—as much as 20 percent by 2030. Using more domestic wind power would reduce the nation's dependence on foreign sources of natural gas and also decrease carbon dioxide (CO_2) emissions that contribute to adverse climate change.

First Wind is an independent North American renewable energy company focused on the development, financing, construction, ownership, and operation of utility-scale power projects in the United States. Based in Boston, First Wind has developed and operates 980 megawatts (MW) of generating capacity at 16 wind energy projects in Maine, New York, Vermont, Utah, Washington, and Hawaii. First Wind has a large network of sensors embedded in the wind turbines, which generate huge volumes of data continuously. The data are transmitted in real time and analyzed on a 24/7 real time basis to understand the performance of each wind turbine.

Sensors collect massive amounts of data on the temperature, wind speeds, location, and pitch of the blades. The data are analyzed to study the operation of each turbine in order to adjust them to maximum efficiency. By analyzing sensor data, highly refined measurements of wind speeds

are possible. In wintry conditions, turbines can detect when they are icing up, and speed up or change pitch to knock off the ice. In the past, when it was extremely windy, turbines in the entire farm had been turned off to prevent damage from rotating too fast. Now First Wind can identify the specific portion of turbines that need to be shut down. Based on certain alerts, decisions often need to be taken within a few seconds.

Upgrades on 123 turbines on two wind farms have improved energy output by 3 percent, or about 120 megawatt hours per turbine per year. That improvement translates to $1.2 million in additional revenue a year from these two farms.

Sources: Compiled from Lohr (2012a), FirstWind.com (2014), and U.S. Department of Energy (2008).

Questions

1. What are the benefits of big data analytics to First Wind?
2. What are the benefits of big data analytics to the environment and the nation?
3. How do big data analytics impact the performance of wind farms?

Questions

1. Why are human expertise and judgment important to data analytics? Give an example.
2. What is the relationship between data quality and the value of analytics?
3. Why do data need to be put into a meaningful context?
4. What are the differences between databases and data warehouses?
5. Explain ETL and CDC.
6. What is an advantage of an active data warehouse (ADW)?
7. Why might a company invest in a data mart?
8. How can manufacturers and health care benefit from data analytics?
9. Explain how Hadoop implements MapReduce in two stages.

3.3 Data and Text Mining

As you read, DBMSs support queries to extract data or get answers from huge databases. But in order to perform queries, you must first know what to ask for or what you want answered. In data mining and text mining, it is the opposite. Data and text mining are used to discover knowledge that you did not know existed in the databases.

Business analytics describes the entire function of applying technologies, algorithms, human expertise, and judgment. Data and text mining are specific analytic techniques.

CREATING BUSINESS VALUE

Enterprises invest in data mining tools to add business value. Business value falls into three categories, as shown in Figure 3.18.

Here are brief cases illustrating the types of business value created by data and text mining.

1. Using pattern analysis, **Argo Corporation,** an agricultural equipment manufacturer based in Georgia, was able to optimize product configuration options for farm machinery and real time customer demand to determine the optimal base configurations for its machines. As a result, Argo reduced product variety by 61 percent and cut days of inventory by 81 percent while still maintaining its service levels.

2. The mega-retailer **Walmart** wanted its online shoppers to find what they were looking for faster. Walmart analyzed clickstream data from its 45 million monthly online shoppers; then combined that data with product and category-related popularity scores. The popularity scores had been generated by text mining the retailer's social media streams. Lessons learned from the analysis were integrated into the Polaris search engine used by customers on the company's website. Polaris has yielded a 10 to 15 percent increase in online shoppers completing a purchase, which equals roughly $1 billion in incremental online sales.

3. **McDonald's** bakery operation replaced manual equipment with high-speed photo analyses to inspect thousands of buns per minute for color, size, and sesame seed distribution. Automatically, ovens and baking processes adjust instantly to create uniform buns and reduce thousands of pounds of waste each year. Another food products company also uses photo analyses to sort every french fry produced in order to optimize quality.

4. **Infinity Insurance** discovered new insights that it applied to improve the performance of its fraud operation. The insurance company text mined years of

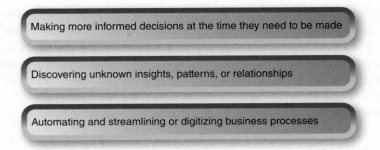

Figure 3.18 Business value falls into three buckets.

Making more informed decisions at the time they need to be made

Discovering unknown insights, patterns, or relationships

Automating and streamlining or digitizing business processes

adjuster reports to look for key drivers of fraudulent claims. As a result, the company reduced fraud by 75 percent, and eliminated marketing to customers with a high likelihood of fraudulent claims.

DATA AND TEXT MINING

Data mining software enables users to analyze data from various dimensions or angles, categorize them, and find correlations or patterns among fields in the data warehouse. Up to 75 percent of an organization's data are nonstructured word-processing documents, social media, text messages, audio, video, images and diagrams, faxes and memos, call center or claims notes, and so on. **Text mining** is a broad category that involves interpreting words and concepts in context. Any customer becomes a brand advocate or adversary by freely expressing opinions and attitudes that reach millions of other current or prospective customers on social media. Text mining helps companies tap into the explosion of customer opinions expressed online. Social commentary and social media are being mined for **sentiment analysis** or to understand consumer intent. Innovative companies know they could be more successful in meeting their customers' needs, if they just understood them better. Tools and techniques for analyzing text, documents, and other nonstructured content are available from several vendors.

Combing Data and Text Mining

Combining data and text mining can create even greater value. Palomäki and Oksanen (2012) pointed out that mining text or nonstructural data enables organizations to forecast the future instead of merely reporting the past. They also noted that forecasting methods using existing structured data and nonstructured text from both internal and external sources provide the best view of what lies ahead.

IT at Work 3.4

U.S. Military Uses Data Mining Spy Machine for Cultural Intelligence

The Defense Advanced Research Projects Agency (DARPA) was established in 1958 to prevent strategic surprise from negatively impacting U.S. national security and to create strategic surprise for U.S. adversaries by maintaining the technological superiority of the U.S. military. One DARPA office is the Information Innovation Office (I2O). I2O aims to ensure U.S. technological superiority in all areas where information can provide a decisive military advantage. This includes intelligence, surveillance, reconnaissance, and operations support.

Figure 3.19 is an example. Nexus 7 is one of DARPA's intelligence systems.

Nexus 7, Data Mining System

Nexus 7 is a massive data mining system put into use by the U.S. military in Afghanistan to understand Afghan society, and to look for signs of weakness or instability. The classified program ties together "everything from spy radars to fruit prices" in order to read the Afghan social situation and help the U.S. military plot its strategy. DARPA describes Nexus 7 as both a breakthrough data analysis tool and an opportunity to move beyond its traditional, long-range research role into a more active wartime mission. Nexus 7 gathers information that can reveal exactly where a town is working and where it is broken; and where the traffic piles up and where it flows free.

Cultural Intelligence

On the military's classified network, DARPA technologists describe Nexus 7 as far-reaching and revolutionary, taking data from many agencies to produce population-centric, cultural intelligence. For example, Nexus 7 searches the vast U.S. spy apparatus to figure out which communities in Afghanistan are falling apart and which are stabilizing, which are loyal to the government in Kabul, and which are falling under the influence of militants.

A small Nexus 7 team is currently working in Afghanistan with military-intelligence officers, while a much larger group

in Virginia with a "large-scale processing capacity" handles the bulk of the data crunching, according to DARPA. "Data in the hands of some of the best computer scientists working side by side with operators provides useful insights in ways that might not have otherwise been realized" (Shachtman, 2011).

Sources: Compiled from DARPA.mil (2012), Shachtman (2011), and *Defense Systems* (2011).

Questions

1. What is Nexus 7?
2. How does data mining help I2O achieve its mission?
3. What are Nexus 7's data sources?
4. According to DARPA, what benefit does Nexus 7 provide that could not be realized without it?

Text Analytics Procedure

With text analytics, information is extracted from large quantities of various types of textual information. The basic steps involved in text analytics include:

1. **Exploration.** First, documents are explored. This might occur in the form of simple word counts in a document collection, or by manually creating topic areas to categorize documents after reading a sample of them. For example, what are the major types of issues (brake or engine failure) that have been identified in recent automobile warranty claims? A challenge of the exploration effort is misspelled or abbreviated words, acronyms, or slang.

2. **Preprocessing.** Before analysis or the automated categorization of content, the text may need to be preprocessed to standardize it to the extent possible. As in traditional analysis, up to 80 percent of preprocessing time can be spent preparing and standardizing the data. Misspelled words, abbreviations, and slang may need to be transformed into consistent terms. For instance, BTW would be standardized to "by the way" and "left voice message" could be tagged as "lvm."

3. **Categorizing and Modeling.** Content is then ready to be categorized. Categorizing messages or documents from information contained within them can be achieved using statistical models and business rules. As with traditional model development, sample documents are examined to train the models. Additional documents are then processed to validate the accuracy and precision of the model, and finally new documents are evaluated using the final model (scored). Models can then be put into production for the automated processing of new documents as they arrive.

Text analytics can help identify the ratio of positive/negative posts relating to the promotion. It can be a powerful validation tool to complement other primary and secondary customer research and feedback management initiatives. Companies that improve their ability to navigate and text mine the boards and blogs relevant to their industry are likely to gain a considerable information advantage over their competitors.

Questions

1. Describe data mining.
2. How does data mining generate or provide value? Give an example.
3. What is text mining?
4. Explain the text mining procedure.

3.4 Business Intelligence

Quicken Loans, Inc. is the largest online mortgage lender and second largest overall retail lender in the United States. The Detroit-based company closed more than $70 billion in home loans in 2012, which was more than double the $30 billion figure in 2011. In 2013 Quicken Loans continued its explosive growth, closing a company record $80 billion in home loan volume. The company also grew its loan servicing capabilities to become the 11th largest mortgage servicer in the nation, with more than $138 billion in home loans in its portfolio.

In 2014 *FORTUNE* Magazine ranked Quicken Loans one of the top 5 places to work nationwide, which marked the 11th consecutive year it ranked in the top 30 of Fortune's benchmark workplace culture study. For the fourth consecutive year, the company was named by J.D. Power as the highest in customer satisfaction among all home loan lenders in America.

One key success factor is BI. At the 2013 Data Warehousing Institute's (TDWI) Best Practices Awards that recognized companies for their world-class BI and data warehousing solutions, Quicken managers explained:

> This growth can be attributed to the success of our online lending platform. Our scalable, technology-driven loan platform has allowed us to handle a large surge in loan applications while keeping closing times for the majority of our loans at 30 days or less. (TDWI, 2013)

Using BI, the company has increased the speed from loan application to close, which allows it to meet client needs as thoroughly and quickly as possible. Over almost a decade, performance management has evolved from a manual process of report generation to BI-driven dashboards and user-defined alerts that allow business leaders to proactively deal with obstacles and identify opportunities for growth and improvement.

The field of BI started in the late 1980s and has been a key to competitive advantage across industries and in enterprises of all sizes. What started as a tool to support sales, marketing, and customer service departments has widely evolved into an enterprisewide strategic platform. While BI systems are used in the operational management of divisions and business processes, they are also used to support strategic corporate decision making. The dramatic change that has taken effect over the last few years is the growth in demand for operational intelligence across multiple systems and businesses—increasing the number of people who need access to increasing amounts of data. Complex and competitive business conditions do not leave much slack for mistakes.

BUSINESS BENEFITS OF BI

BI provides data at the *moment of value* to a decision maker—enabling it to extract crucial facts from enterprise data in real time or near real time. A BI solution with a well-designed dashboard, for example, provides retailers with better visibility into inventory to make better decisions about what to order, how much, and when in order to prevent stock-outs or minimize inventory that sits on warehouse shelves.

Companies use BI solutions to determine what questions to ask and find answers to them. BI tools integrate and consolidate data from various internal and external sources and then process them into information to make smart decisions. BI answers questions such as these: Which products have the highest repeat sales rate in the last six months? Do customer likes on Facebook relate to product purchase? How does the sales trend break down by product group over the last five years? What do daily sales look like in each of my sales regions?

According to TDWI, BI "unites data, technology, analytics, and human knowledge to optimize business decisions and ultimately drive an enterprise's success. BI programs usually combine an enterprise data warehouse and a BI platform or tool set to transform data into usable, actionable business information" (TDWI, 2014). For many years, managers have relied on business analytics to make better-informed decisions. Multiple surveys and studies agree on BI's growing importance in analyzing past performance and identifying opportunities to improve future performance.

COMMON CHALLENGES: DATA SELECTION AND QUALITY

Companies cannot analyze all of their data—and much of them would not add value. Therefore, an unending challenge is how to determine which data to use for BI from what seems like unlimited options (Schroeder, 2013). One purpose of a BI strategy is to provide a framework for selecting the most relevant data without limiting options to integrate new data sources. **Information overload** is a major problem for executives and for employees. Another common challenge is data quality, particularly with regard to online information, because the source and accuracy might not be verifiable.

ALIGNING BUSINESS STRATEGY WITH BI STRATEGY

Reports and dashboards are delivery tools, but they may not be delivering business intelligence. To get the greatest value out of BI, the CIO needs to work with the CFO and other business leaders to create a BI governance program whose mission is to achieve the following (Acebo et al., 2013):

1. Clearly articulate business strategies.
2. Deconstruct the business strategies into a set of specific goals and objectives—the *targets*.
3. Identify the key performance indicators (KPIs) that will be used to measure progress toward each target.
4. Prioritize the list of KPIs.
5. Create a plan to achieve goals and objectives based on the priorities.
6. Estimate the costs needed to implement the BI plan.
7. Assess and update the priorities based on business results and changes in business strategy.

After completing these activities, BI analysts can identify the data to use in BI and the source systems. This is a **business-driven development approach** that starts with a business strategy and work backward to identify data sources and the data that need to be acquired and analyzed.

Businesses want KPIs that can be utilized by both departmental users and management. In addition, users want real time access to these data so that they can monitor processes with the smallest possible latency and take corrective action

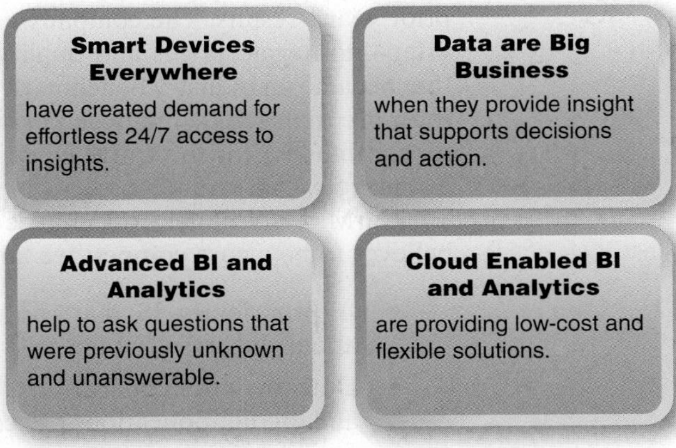

Smart Devices Everywhere	Data are Big Business
have created demand for effortless 24/7 access to insights.	when they provide insight that supports decisions and action.

Advanced BI and Analytics	Cloud Enabled BI and Analytics
help to ask questions that were previously unknown and unanswerable.	are providing low-cost and flexible solutions.

Figure 3.19 Four factors contributing to increased use of BI.

whenever KPIs deviate from their target values. To link strategic and operational perspectives, users must be able to drill down from highly consolidated or summarized figures into the detailed numbers from which they were derived to perform in-depth analyses.

BI ARCHITECTURE AND ANALYTICS

BI architecture is undergoing technological advances in response to big data and the performance demands of end-users (Watson, 2012). BI vendors are facing the challenges of social, sensor, and other newer data types that must be managed and analyzed. One technology advance that can help handle big data is BI in the cloud. Figure 3.19 lists the key factors contributing to the increased use of BI. It can be hosted on a public or private cloud. With a public cloud, a service provider hosts the data and/or software that are accessed via an Internet connection. For private clouds, the company hosts its own data and software, but uses cloud-based technologies.

For cloud-based BI, a popular option offered by a growing number of BI tool vendors is software as a service (SaaS). MicroStrategy offers MicroStrategy Cloud, which provides fast deployment with reduced project risks and costs. This cloud approach appeals to small and midsize companies that have limited IT staff and want to carefully control costs. The potential downsides include slower response times, security risks, and backup risks.

Competitive Analytics in Practice: CarMax

CarMax, Inc. is the nation's largest retailer of used cars and for a decade has remained one of *FORTUNE* Magazine's 100 Best Companies to Work For. CarMax was the fastest retailer in U.S. history to reach $1 billion in revenues. In 2013 the company had $11 billion in revenues, representing a 9.6 percent increase above the

Figure 3.20 CarMax is the United States' largest used-car retailer and a Fortune 500 company.

Bloomberg/Getty Images

prior year's results. The company grew rapidly because of its compelling customer offer—no-haggle prices and quality guarantees backed by a 125-point inspection that became an industry benchmark—and auto financing. In 2014 CarMax recruited for more than 1,200 employee positions in locations across the country in response to continued growth. CarMax currently operates 131 used car superstores in 64 markets.

CarMax continues to enhance and refine its information systems, which it believes to be a core competitive advantage. CarMax's IT includes:

- A proprietary IS that captures, analyzes, interprets, and distributes data about the cars CarMax sells and buys.

- Data analytics applications that track every purchase; number of test drives and credit applications per car; color preferences in every demographic and region.

- Proprietary store technology that provides management with real time data about every aspect of store operations, such as inventory management, pricing, vehicle transfers, wholesale auctions, and sales consultant productivity.

- An advanced inventory management system that helps management anticipate future inventory needs and manage pricing.

Throughout CarMax, analytics are used as a strategic asset and insights gained from analytics are available to everyone who needs them.

Questions

1. How has BI improved performance management at Quicken Loans?
2. What are the business benefits of BI?
3. What are two data-related challenges that must be resolved for BI to produce meaningful insight?
4. What are the steps in a BI governance program?
5. What is a business-driven development approach?
6. What does it mean to drill down, and why is it important?
7. What four factors are contributing to increased use of BI?
8. How did BI help CarMax achieve record-setting revenue growth?

3.5 Electronic Records Management

All organizations create and retain **business records.** A record is documentation of a business event, action, decision, or transaction. Examples are contracts, research and development, accounting source documents, memos, customer/client communications, hiring and promotion decisions, meeting minutes, social posts, texts, e-mails, website content, database records, and paper and electronic files. Business documents such as spreadsheets, e-mail messages, and word-processing documents are a type of record. Most records are kept in electronic format and maintained throughout their life cycle—from creation to final archiving or destruction by an **electronic records management (ERM) system.**

ERM systems consist of hardware and software that manage and archive electronic documents and image paper documents; then index and store them according to company policy. For example, companies may be required by law to retain financial documents for at least seven years, product designs for many decades, and e-mail messages about marketing promotions for a year. The major ERM tools are workflow software, authoring tools, scanners, and databases. ERM systems have query and search capabilities so documents can be identified and accessed like data in a database. These systems range from those designed to support a small workgroup to full-featured, Web-enabled enterprisewide systems.

LEGAL DUTY TO RETAIN BUSINESS RECORDS

Companies need to be prepared to respond to an audit, federal investigation, lawsuit, or any other legal action against them. Types of lawsuits against companies include patent violations, product safety negligence, theft of intellectual property, breach of contract, wrongful termination, harassment, discrimination, and many more.

Because senior management must ensure that their companies comply with legal and regulatory duties, managing electronic records (e-records) is a strategic issue for organizations in both the public and private sectors. The success of ERM depends greatly on a partnership of many key players, namely, senior management, users, records managers, archivists, administrators, and most importantly, IT personnel. Properly managed, records are strategic assets. Improperly managed or destroyed, they become liabilities.

ERM BEST PRACTICES

Effective ERM systems capture all business data and documents at their first touchpoint—data centers, laptops, the mailroom, at customer sites, or remote offices. Records enter the enterprise in multiple ways—from online forms, bar codes, sensors, websites, social sites, copiers, e-mails, and more. In addition to capturing the entire document as a whole, important data from within a document can be captured and stored in a central, searchable repository. In this way, the data are accessible to support informed and timely business decisions.

In recent years, organizations such as the Association for Information and Image Management (AIIM; ww.aiim.org), National Archives and Records Administration (NARA), and ARMA International (formerly the Association of Records Managers and Administrators; www.arma.org) have created and published industry standards for document and records management. Numerous best practices articles, and links to valuable sources of information about document and records management, are available on their websites. IT at Work 3.5 describes ARMA's generally accepted recordkeeping principles.

ERM BENEFITS

Departments or companies whose employees spend most of their day filing or retrieving documents or warehousing paper records can reduce costs significantly with ERM. These systems minimize the inefficiencies and frustration associated with managing paper documents and workflows. However, they do not create a paperless office as had been predicted.

An ERM can help a business to become more efficient and productive by:

- Enabling the company to access and use the content contained in documents.
- Cutting labor costs by automating business processes.
- Reducing the time and effort required to locate information the business needs to support decision making.
- Improving the security of content, thereby reducing the risk of intellectual property theft.
- Minimizing the costs associated with printing, storing, and searching for content.

When workflows are digital, productivity increases, costs decrease, compliance obligations are easier to verify, and green computing becomes possible. Green computing is an initiative to conserve our valuable natural resources by reducing the effects of our computer usage on the environment. You can read about green computing and the related topics of reducing an organization's carbon footprint, sustainability, and ethical and social responsibility in Chapter 14.

IT at Work 3.5

Generally Accepted Recordkeeping Principles

Generally accepted recordkeeping principles are a framework for managing business records to ensure that they support an enterprise's current and future regulatory, legal, risk mitigation, environmental, and operational requirements.

The framework consists of eight principles or best practices, which also support information governance. These principles were created by ARMA International and legal and IT professionals.

- **Principle of Accountability.** An organization will assign a senior executive to oversee a recordkeeping program; adopt policies and procedures to guide personnel; and ensure program audit ability.

- **Principle of Transparency.** The processes and activities of an organization's recordkeeping program will be documented in an understandable manner and available to all personnel and appropriate parties.

- **Principle of Integrity.** A recordkeeping program will be able to reasonably guarantee the authenticity and reliability of records and data.

- **Principle of Protection.** The recordkeeping program will be constructed to ensure a reasonable level of protection to records and information that are private, confidential, privileged, secret, or essential to business continuity.

- **Principle of Compliance.** The recordkeeping program will comply with applicable laws, authorities, and the organization's policies.

- **Principle of Availability.** Records will be maintained in a manner that ensures timely, efficient, and accurate retrieval of needed information.

- **Principle of Retention.** Records and data will be maintained for an appropriate time based on legal, regulatory, fiscal, operational, and historical requirements.

- **Principle of Disposition.** Records will be securely disposed of when they are no longer required to be maintained by laws or organizational policies.

ERM FOR DISASTER RECOVERY, BUSINESS CONTINUITY, AND COMPLIANCE

Businesses also rely on their ERM system for disaster recovery and business continuity, security, knowledge sharing and collaboration, and remote and controlled access to documents. Because ERM systems have multilayered access capabilities, employees can access and change only the documents they are authorized to handle.

When companies select an ERM to meet compliance requirements, they should ask the following questions:

1. Does the software meet the organization's needs? For example, can the DMS be installed on the existing network? Can it be purchased as a service?

2. Is the software easy to use and accessible from Web browsers, office applications, and e-mail applications? If not, people will not use it.

3. Does the software have lightweight, modern Web and graphical user interfaces that effectively support remote users?

4. Before selecting a vendor, it is important to examine workflows and how data, documents, and communications flow throughout the company. For example, know which information on documents is used in business decisions. Once those needs and requirements are identified, they guide the selection of technology that can support the input types—that is, capture and index them so they can be archived consistently and retrieved on-demand.

IT at Work 3.6 describes how several companies currently use ERM. Simply creating backups of records is not sufficient because the content would not be organized and indexed to retrieve them accurately and easily. The requirement to manage records—regardless of whether they are physical or digital—is not new.

IT at Work 3.6

ERM Applications

Here are a few examples of how companies use ERM:

- The Surgery Center of Baltimore stores all medical records electronically, providing instant patient information to doctors and nurses anywhere and at any time. The system also routes charts to the billing department, which can then scan and e-mail any relevant information to insurance providers and patients. The ERM system helps maintain the required audit trail, including the provision of records when they are needed for legal purposes. How valuable has ERM been to the center? Since it was implemented, business processes have been expedited by more than 50 percent, the costs of these processes have been significantly reduced, and the morale of office employees in the center has improved noticeably.

- American Express (AMEX) uses TELEform, developed by Alchemy and Cardiff Software, to collect and process more than 1 million customer satisfaction surveys every year. The data are collected in templates that consist of more than 600 different survey forms in 12 languages and 11 countries. AMEX integrated TELEform with AMEX's legacy system, which enables it to distribute processed results to many managers. Because the survey forms are now readily accessible, AMEX has reduced the number of staff who process these forms from 17 to 1, thereby saving the company more than $500,000 a year.

- The University of Cincinnati provides authorized access to the personnel files of 12,000 active employees and tens of thousands of retirees. The university receives more than 75,000 queries about personnel records every year and then must search more than 3 million records to answer these queries. Using a microfilm system to find answers took days. The solution was an ERM that digitized all paper and microfilm documents, without help from the IT department, making them available via the Internet and the university's intranet. Authorized employees access files using a browser.

Questions

1. What are business records?
2. Why is ERM a strategic issue rather than simply an IT issue?
3. Why might a company have a legal duty to retain records? Give an example.
4. Why is creating backups an insufficient way to manage an organization's documents?
5. What are the benefits of ERM?

Key Terms

active data warehouse (ADW)	database management system (DBMS)	HaDoop	operating margin
business analytics	decision model	information overload	petabyte
business intelligence (BI)	declarative language	immediate consistency	relational database
business record	distributed database system	latency	relational management system (RDBMS)
business-driven development approach	electronic records management (ERM)	MapReduce	sentiment analysis
centralized database	extract, transform, load (ETL)	market share	scalability
change data capture (CDC)	enterprise data warehouse (EDW)	master data management (MDM)	structured query language (SQL)
data entity	eventual consistency	NoSQL	text mining
data mart	fault tolerance	online transaction-processing (OLTP) systems	volatile
data mining		online analytical-processing (OLAP) systems	
data warehouse			
database			

Assuring Your Learning

DISCUSS: Critical Thinking Questions

1. What are the functions of databases and data warehouses?

2. How does data quality impact business performance?

3. List three types of waste or damages that data errors can cause.

4. What is the role of a master reference file?

5. Give three examples of business processes or operations that would benefit significantly from having detailed real time or near real time data and identify the benefits.

6. What are the tactical and strategic benefits of big data analytics?

7. Explain the four V's of data analytics.

8. Select an industry. Explain how an organization in that industry could improve consumer satisfaction through the use of data warehousing.

9. Explain the principle of 90/90 data use.

10. Why is master data management (MDM) important in companies with multiple data sources?

11. Why would a company invest in a data mart instead of a data warehouse?

12. Why is data mining important?

13. What are the operational benefits and competitive advantages of business intelligence?

14. How can ERM decrease operating costs?

EXPLORE: Online and Interactive Exercises

1. Visit YouTube.com and search for SAS Enterprise Miner Software Demo in order to assess the features and benefits of SAS Enterprise Miner. The URL is http://www.youtube.com/watch?v=Nj4L5RFvkMg.

   a. View the SAS Enterprise Miner Software demo, which is about 7 minutes long.

   b. Based on what you learn in the demo, what skills or expertise are needed to build a predictive model?

   c. At the end of the demo, you hear the presenter say that "SAS Enterprise Miner allows end-users to easily develop predictive models and to generate scoring to make better decisions about

   future business events." Do you agree that SAS Enterprise Miner makes it easy to develop such models? Explain.

   d. Do you agree that if an expert develops predictive models, it will help managers make better decisions about future business events? Explain.

   e. Based on your answers to (c), (d), and (e), under what conditions would you recommend SAS Enterprise Miner?

2. Research two electronic records management vendors, such as Iron Mountain.

a. What are the retention recommendations made by the vendors? Why?

b. What services or solutions does each vendor offer?

3. View the "Edgenet Gain Real time Access to Retail Product Data with In-Memory Technology" video on YouTube. Explain the benefit of in-memory technology.

ANALYZE & DECIDE: Apply IT Concepts to Business Decisions

1. Visit Oracle.com. Click the Solutions tab to open the menu; then click Data Warehousing under Technology Solutions.

   a. Select one of the Customer Highlights.

   b. Describe the customer's challenges, why it selected a particular Oracle solution, and how that solution met their challenge.

2. Visit the Microsoft SQL Server website at Microsoft.com/SQLserver.

   a. Click the CloudOS tab and select Customer Stories.

   b. Filter the customer stories by selecting Business Intelligence and Data Discovery.

   c. Summarize each company's business problems or challenges and why it selected a particular solution.

   d. What were the benefits of the BI solution?

3. Visit Teradata.com. Click Resources and review Video News, and select one of the videos related to analytics. Explain the benefits of the solution chosen.

4. Spring Street Company (SSC) wanted to reduce the "hidden costs" associated with its paper-intensive processes. Employees jokingly predicted that if the windows were open on a very windy day, total chaos would ensue as thousands of papers started to fly. If a flood, fire, or windy day occurred, the business would literally grind to a halt. The company's accountant, Sam Spring, decided to calculate the costs of its paper-driven processes to identify their impact on the bottom line. He recognized that several employees spent most of their day filing or retrieving documents. In addition, there were the monthly costs to warehouse old paper records. Sam measured the activities related to the handling of printed reports and paper files. His average estimates were as follows:

   a. Dealing with a file: It takes an employee 12 minutes to walk to the records room, locate a file, act on it, refile it, and return to his or her desk. Employees do this 4 times per day (5 days per week).

   b. Number of employees: 10 full-time employees perform the functions.

   c. Lost document replacement: Once per day, a document gets "lost" (destroyed, misplaced, or covered with massive coffee stains) and must be recreated. The total cost of replacing each lost document is $200.

   d. Warehousing costs: Currently, document storage costs are $75 per month.

   Sam would prefer a system that lets employees find and work with business documents without leaving their desks. He's most concerned about the human resources and accounting departments. These personnel are traditional heavy users of paper files and would greatly benefit from a modern document management system. At the same time, however, Sam is also risk averse. He would rather invest in solutions that would reduce the risk of higher costs in the future. He recognizes that the U.S. PATRIOT Act's requirements that organizations provide immediate government access to records apply to SSC. He has read that manufacturing and government organizations rely on efficient document management to meet these broader regulatory imperatives. Finally, Sam wants to implement a disaster recovery system.

   Prepare a report that provides Sam with the data he needs to evaluate the company's costly paper-intensive approach to managing documents. You will need to conduct research to provide data to prepare this report. Your report should include the following information:

   1. How should SSC prepare for an ERM if it decides to implement one?

   2. Using the data collected by Sam, create a spreadsheet that calculates the costs of handling paper at SSC based on average hourly rates per employee of $28. Add the cost of lost documents to this. Then, add the costs of warehousing the paper, which increases by 10 percent every month due to increases in volume. Present the results showing both monthly totals and a yearly total. Prepare graphs so that Sam can easily identify the projected growth in warehousing costs over the next three years.

   3. How can ERM also serve as a disaster recovery system in case of fire, flood, or break-in?

   4. Submit your recommendation for an ERM solution. Identify two vendors in your recommendation.

CASE 3.2

Business Case: Financial Intelligence Fights Fraud

The Financial Crimes Enforcement Network (FinCEN; fincen.gov) is a bureau of the Treasury Department and the financial intelligence unit of the United States. The bureau reports to the undersecretary for terrorism and financial intelligence. FinCEN's mission is to safeguard the financial system from abuses of financial crimes, to institute anti-money laundering (AML) programs, and to promote national security through the collection, analysis, and dissemination of financial intelligence.

Constrained by Deficient Data Analytics

Prior to 2008, FinCEN was not able to effectively gather data, analyze them, and deliver them to users. Data that financial institutions had to report to FinCEN suffered from inconsistent quality and lack of validation and standardization. When trying to analyze its data, FinCEN was limited to small datasets and simple routines. The bureau could not conduct analysis across massive datasets and lacked capabilities for proactive analysis and trend prediction.

Reporting data to agencies was done using numerous offline systems. Data had to be cleaned and transformed, thus delaying user access. Analytics and reporting deficiencies made it difficult for FinCEN to quickly detect new and emerging threats and aid in disrupting criminal enterprises.

FinCEN Upgrades Data Analytics and Query Capabilities

In 2008 FinCEN launched a major effort to upgrade its analytics capabilities, IT infrastructure, and databases. Upgraded analytics were needed to better collect and analyze data from multiple sources and provide them to federal, state, and local law enforcement and regulatory authorities.

Then in May 2010 FinCEN launched the Bank Secrecy Act (BSA) IT Modernization (IT Mod) program and further improved its IT infrastructure. The IT Mod program has improved data quality and the ability of 9,000 authorized users to access, search, and analyze data. The bureau provides federal, state, and local law enforcement and regulators with

direct access to BSA data. These users make approximately 18,000 queries of the extensive database each day.

Additional milestones achieved by FinCEN were:

- Converted 11 years of data from its legacy system to FinCEN's new System of Record. FinCEN is able to electronically receive, process, and store all FinCEN reports.
- Deployed a new advanced analytics tool that provides FinCEN analysts with improved analytic and examination capabilities.
- Released the FinCEN Query Web-based app, a new search tool accessed by FinCEN analysts, law enforcement, intelligence, and regulatory users as of September 2012. FinCEN Query provides real time access to over 11 years of BSA data.

Predictive Capabilities Attack Crimes

Consulting firm Deloitte helped FinCEN with the massive critical tasks of deploying systems and populating data, providing user access, and ensuring system security. Effective data analytics identify patterns and relationships that reveal potential illicit activity. This intelligence has increased the speed and ability to detect money launderers and terrorist financiers and disrupt their criminal activity.

Sources: Compiled from FinCEN.gov (2014), Fact Sheet Bank Secrecy Act (BSA) IT Modernization (IT Mod) Program (2013), and Deloitte (2014).

Questions

1. Explain FinCEN's mission and responsibilities.
2. What data and IT problems were limiting FinCEN's ability to fight financial crime?
3. Describe the IT upgrades and capabilities needed by FinCEN in order to achieve its mission.
4. On what does financial intelligence depend?
5. Why is the ability to identify patterns and relationships critical to national security?
6. Research recent financial crimes that FinCEN has detected and disrupted. Explain the role of data analytics in crime detection.

CASE 3.3

Video Case: Hertz Finds Gold in Integrated Data

Finding CRM gold after integrating customer data, Hertz is dominating the global rental car market by giving customers unique, real time offers through multiple channels, with upwards of 80,000 during peak times. Visit Teradata.com and search for the video "Hertz: Finding Gold in Integrated Data."

1. Describe Hertz's new strategy and data solution.
2. How did Hertz strengthen customer loyalty?

3. What did Hertz need to do to its data prior to implementing its new solution?
4. Describe the potential short-term and longer-term business benefits of integrated data.

References

Acebo, A., J. Gallo, J. Griffin, & B. Valeyko. "Aligning Business Strategy with BI Capabilities." *Business Intelligence Journal*, 2013.

Breuer, P., F. Forina, & J. Moulton. "Beyond the Hype: Capturing Value from Big Data and Advanced Analytics." McKinsey & Company. April 2013.

MIT Sloan Management Review, Improvisations, February 2, 2012.

Brown, B., M. Chui, & J. Manyika. "Are You Ready for the Era of 'Big Data?'" *McKinsey Quarterly*, October 2011.

Burns, E. "Coca-Cola Overcomes Challenges to Seize BI Opportunities." *TechTarget.com*. August 2013.

BusinessIntelligence.com. "How Coca-Cola Takes a Refreshing Approach on Big Data." July 18, 2013a.

BusinessIntelligence.com. "Coca-Cola's Juicy Approach to Big Data." July 29, 2013b. http://businessintelligence.com/ bi-insights/coca-colas-juicy-approach-to-big-data/

CNNMoney, The Coca-Cola Co (NYSE:KO) 2014.

DARPA.mil, 2012.

Defense Systems. "DARPA Intell Program Sent to Afghanistan to Spy." July 21, 2011.

Deloitte.com. "Case Study: Checkmate—Delivering Next-Gen Financial Intelligence at FinCEN." February 19, 2014.

Fernandez, J. "Big Companies, Big Data." *Research-Live.com*, October 4, 2012.

Ferguson, M. "Data Ownership and Enterprise Data Management: Is Your Data Under Control?" *DataFlux.com*, 2012.

FinCEN.gov, 2014.

FirstWind web site, 2014. Hammond, T. "Top IT Job Skills for 2014: Big Data, Mobile, Cloud, Security." *TechRepublic.com*, January 31, 2014.

HealthCanal. "Where Do You Start When Developing a New Medicine?" March 27, 2014.

ibm.com. "IBM Big Data Success Stories." 2011.

Kitamura, M. "Big Data Partnerships Tackle Drug Development Failures." *Bloomberg News*, March 26, 2014.

Lohr, S. "Looking to Industry for the Next Digital Disruption." *The New York Times*. November 23, 2012a.

Lohr, S. "Big Data: Rise of the Machines." *The New York Times*, December 31, 2012b.

Neill, J. "Big Data Demands Big Context." *HBR Blog Network*, December 3, 2013.

NIH (National Institute of Health). *Accelerating Medicines Partnership*. February 2014. *http://www.nih.gov/science/amp/ index.htm*

Palomäki, P. & M. Oksanen. "Do We Need Homegrown Information Models in Enterprise Architectures?" *Business Intelligence Journal*. Vol. 17, no. 1, March 19, 2012.

Rowe, N. "Handling Paper in a Digital Age: The Impact of Document Management." *Aberdeen Research Report*. February 1, 2012. aberdeen.com/research/7480/ra-document-processing-management/content.aspx

Shachtman, N. "Inside Darpa's Secret Afghan Spy Machine." *Wired*, July 21, 2011.

Schroeder, H. "The Art and Science of Transformation for New Business Intelligence." *Cost Management*, September/October 2013.

The Data Warehousing Institute (TDWI). "Winners: TDWI Best Practices Awards 2013." *Business Intelligence Journal* 18, no. 3, 2013.

The Data Warehousing Institute (TDWI). *tdwi.org/portals/ business-intelligence.aspx*, 2014.

U.S. Department of Energy. "Wind Energy Could Produce 20 Percent of U.S. Electricity By 2030." Energy.gov. May 12, 2008. *energy.gov/articles/wind-energy-could-produce-20-percent-us-electricity-2030* Watson, H. J. "This Isn't Your Mother's BI Architecture." *Business Intelligence Journal*. Vol. 17, no. 1, March, 2012.

Zynapse, "New Strategies for Managing Master Data." *zynapse.com*. September 10, 2010.

Networks for Efficient Operations and Sustainability

Chapter Snapshot

Case 4.1 Opening Case: Sony Builds an IPv6 Network to Fortify Competitive Edge

4.1 Data Networks, IP Addresses, and APIs

4.2 Wireless Networks and Mobile Infrastructure

4.3 Collaboration and Communication Technologies

4.4 Sustainability and Ethical Issues

Key Terms
Assuring Your Learning

- **Discuss:** Critical Thinking Questions
- **Explore:** Online and Interactive Exercises
- **Analyze & Decide:** Apply IT Concepts to Business Decisions

Case 4.2 Business Case: Google Maps API for Business

Case 4.3 Video Case: Fresh Direct Connects for Success

References

Learning Outcomes

1. Describe data networks, their quality-of-service (QOS) issues, and how IP addresses and APIs function. Identify opportunities to apply networked devices to improve operational efficiency and business models.

2. Describe wireless 3G and 4G networks, mobile network infrastructure, and how they support worker productivity, business operations, and strategy.

3. Evaluate performance improvements from virtual collaboration and communication technologies, and explain how they support group work.

4. Describe how companies can contribute to sustainability, and green, social, and ethical challenges related to the use and operations of IT networks.

Chapter Snapshot

The basic technology that makes global communication possible is the **Internet Protocol**, or **IP**. Each device attached to a network has a unique **IP address** that enables it to send and receive files. Files are broken down into blocks known as **packets** in order to be transmitted over a network to their destination, which also has a unique IP address. Most networks use **IP Version 4 (IPv4)**. In April 2014 ARIN, the group that oversees Internet addresses, reported that IPv4

Internet Protocol (IP) is the method by which data are sent from one device to another via a network.

IP address. Every device that communicates with a network must have a unique identifying IP address. An IP address is comparable to a telephone number or home address.

IP Version 4 (IPv4) has been Internet protocol for over three decades, but has reached the limits of its design. It is difficult to configure, it is running out of addressing space, and it provides no features for site renumbering to allow for an easy change of Internet Service Provider (ISP), among other limitations.

Figure 4.1 IPv4 addresses have 4 groups of four alphanumeric characters, which allows for 2^{32} or roughly 4.3 billion unique IP address. IPv6 addresses have 8 groups of alphanumerics, which allows for 2^{128}, or 340 trillion, trillion, trillion addresses. IPv6 offers also enhanced quality of service that is needed by the latest in video, interactive games, and e-commerce.

addresses were running out—making it urgent that enterprises move to the newer IPv6 (Figure 4.1). Enterprises need to prepare for the 128-bit protocol because switching from IPv4 to IPv6 is not trivial.

Networking is undergoing tremendous change. The convergence of access technologies, cloud, advanced 4G networks, multitasking mobile operating systems, and collaboration platforms continues to change the nature of work, the way we do business, how machines interact, and other things not yet imagined. The downsides of such massive use of energy-dependent wired and wireless networks are their carbon footprints and damage to the environment as well as personal privacy. Intelligently planned sustainability efforts can reduce the depletion of the earth's natural resources significantly. Efforts to protect what is left of personal privacy are less successful.

CASE 4.1 OPENING CASE

Sony Builds an IPv6 Network to Fortify Competitive Edge

SONY'S RAPID BUSINESS GROWTH

In the early 2000s, Sony Corporation had been engaged in strategic mergers and acquisitions to strengthen itself against intensifying competition. By 2007 Sony's enterprise network (internal network) had become too complex and incapable

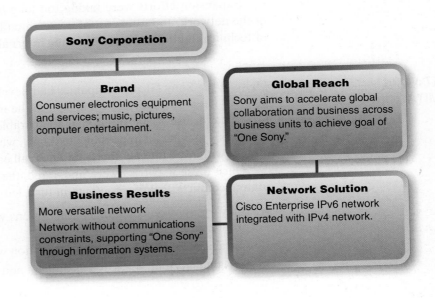

Figure 4.2 Sony Corporation overview.

TABLE 4.1	Opening Case Overview
Company	**Sony Corporation, Sony.com**
Location	Headquartered in Tokyo, Japan. Over 700 total network sites worldwide.
Industries	One of the largest consumer electronics and entertainment companies in the world, including audio/video equipment, semiconductors, computers, and video games. Also engaged in production and distribution of recorded music, motion picture, and video.
Business challenges	• Network expansion required too much time due to complexity of enterprise network. • Networking TCO (total cost of ownership) was continually increasing. • Numerous constraints on networks obstructing communication between companies in Sony Group.
Network technology solution	Integrated its IPv4 networks with new IPv6 solutions from Cisco. The integrated IPv4/IPv6 network has been used by Sony as infrastructure for the development of new products and enterprise-wide collaboration. Sony also upgraded its Cisco switches at the corporate data center, campuses, and remote offices to handle concurrent IPv4 and IPv6 traffic.

of supporting communication, operations, and further business growth. The enterprise network was based on IPv4. A serious limitation was that the IPv4 network could not provide real time collaboration among business units and group companies.

Expansion efforts were taking too long because of the complicated structure of the network, and total cost of ownership (TCO) was increasing. Also, a number of technical limitations were blocking internal communications.

NETWORK LIMITATIONS

Many of the Sony Group companies had developed independently—and had independent networks. Devices connected to the independent networks were using the same IP addresses. That situation is comparable to users having duplicate telephone numbers—making it impossible to know which phone was being called. Also, phones with the same number could not call each other.

Once these networks were integrated, the duplicate IP address caused traffic-routing conflicts. Routing conflicts, in turn, led to the following problems:

1. Sony's employee communication options were severely limited, which harmed productivity.
2. File sharing and real time communication were not possible.
3. Introducing cloud services was difficult and time-consuming.

To eliminate these limitations, Sony decided to invest in IPv6-based networks in 2006; it then launched a full-scale effort in 2008. With its virtually unlimited number of IP addresses, **IPv6** would support Sony's long-term, next-generation **information and communications technology (ICT)** infrastructure strategy and improve collaboration and productivity.

Migrating from IPv4 to IPv6 involved 700 sites, hundreds of thousands of networking devices, and hundreds of thousands of network users spread around the globe. During the transition, Sony realized that it was necessary to support both IP protocols. That is, the IPv6 would supplement and coexist with the existing enterprise IPv4 network, rather than replace it. Running both protocols on the same network at the same time was necessary because Sony's legacy devices and apps only worked on IPv4.

Sony selected Cisco as a key partner in the migration and integration of IPv4 and IPv6 traffic because of the maturity of its IPv6 technology. The integrated network has been used by Sony as infrastructure for product development. Sony also upgraded its Cisco network switches at the corporate data center, campuses, and remote offices to handle concurrent IPv4 and IPv6 traffic.

BUSINESS RESULTS

The use of IPv6 eliminated the issue of conflicting IP addresses, enabling Sony employees in all divisions to take advantage of the productivity benefits of real time collaboration applications. Other business improvements are:

- Flexibility to launch new businesses quickly
- Reduced TCO of enterprise network
- Network without communications constraints, supporting "One Sony" through information systems

Sources: Compiled from Cisco (2014a; 2014b), Khedekar (2012), and AT&T (2012).

Questions

1. Why might IPv6 be a business continuity issue for organizations?
2. Explain how Sony's IPv4 enterprise network was restricting the productivity of its workers.
3. What problems did duplicate IP addresses cause at Sony? Give an analogy.
4. Why did Sony need to run both protocols on its network instead of replacing IPv4 with IPv6?
5. Describe the strategic benefit of Sony's IPv6 implementation.
6. Do research to determine the accuracy of this prediction: "Today, almost everything on the Internet is reachable over IPv4. In a few years, both IPv4 and IPv6 will be required for universal access."

4.1 Data Networks, IP Addresses, and APIs

Managers now need to understand the technical side of networks, IP addressing, and APIs in order to make intelligent investment decisions that impact operations and competitive position. Enterprises run on networks—wired and mobile—and depend upon their ability to interface with other networks and applications.

5G (fifth generation), the next-generation mobile communications network.

Networks are changing significantly with the shift to IPv6 and the build-out of **5G** networks. 5G will offer huge gains in both speed and capacity over existing 4G networks—along with opportunities at the operations and strategic levels. At the 2014 Mobile World Congress in Barcelona, Neelie Kroes, the vice president of the European Commission, discussed how deploying 5G networks could reduce high-level youth unemployment across Europe. In the short term, the 5G infrastructure build-out would create new jobs. In the longer term, 5G would create entirely new markets and economic opportunities driven by superior mobile capabilities in industries ranging from health care to automotive (Basulto, 2014).

FUNDAMENTALS OF DATA NETWORKS

Bandwidth is the capacity or *throughput per second* of a network.

The capacity and capabilities of data networks provide opportunities for more automated operations and new business strategies. M2M communications over wireless and wired networks automate operations, for instance, by triggering action such as sending a message or closing a valve. The speed at which data can be sent depends on the network's **bandwidth**. Bandwidth characteristics are shown in Figure 4.3.

TECH NOTE 4.1 4G and 5G Networks in 2018

More Mobile Network Traffic and Users

Cisco predicts that by 2018, global mobile data traffic will have increased 11 times from current levels. Much of that traffic will be driven by billions of devices talking to other devices wirelessly. This includes a major increase in M2M communications and the number of wearable technology devices. The number of mobile data connections will total more than 10 billion by 2018—8 billion of which will be personal mobile devices and 2 billion M2M connections.

Faster Mobile Network Speeds

Cisco expects that the average global mobile network speed will almost double from 1.4 Mbps in 2013 to 2.5 Mbps by 2018. And 5G networks are promising speeds that will be 100 times faster than mid-2014 speeds.

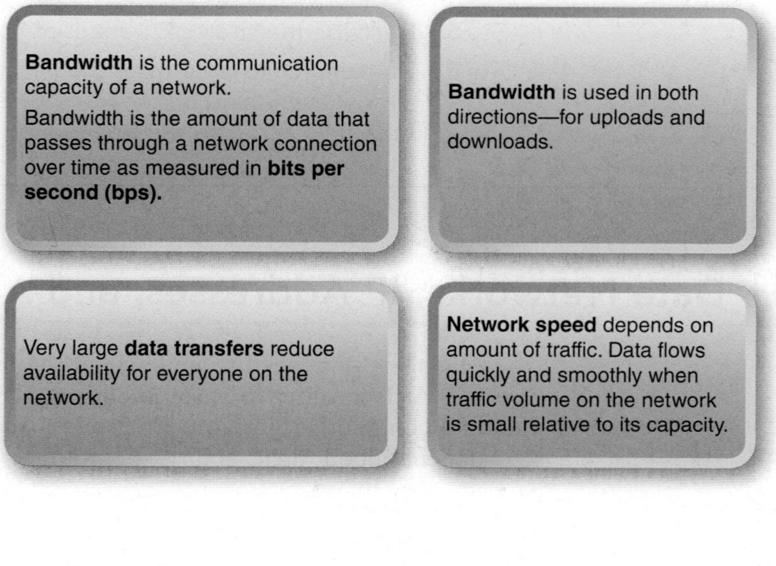

Bandwidth is the communication capacity of a network.
Bandwidth is the amount of data that passes through a network connection over time as measured in **bits per second (bps).**

Bandwidth is used in both directions—for uploads and downloads.

Very large **data transfers** reduce availability for everyone on the network.

Network speed depends on amount of traffic. Data flows quickly and smoothly when traffic volume on the network is small relative to its capacity.

Figure 4.3 Network bandwidth.

By 2018
More Mobile Connections
Over 10 billion
Faster Mobile Speeds
2.5 megabits per second (Mbps)
More Mobile Users
Almost 5 billion
More Mobile Video
70% of mobile traffic

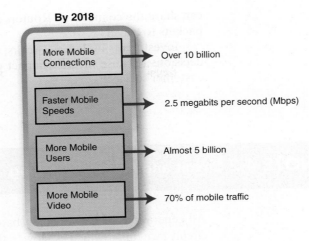

Figure 4.4 Four drivers of global mobile traffic through 2018.

HIGH DEMAND FOR HIGH-CAPACITY NETWORKS

As described in Tech Note 4.1, global mobile data traffic is increasing. The four drivers of that demand are shown in Figure 4.4. Demand for high-capacity networks is growing at unprecedented rates. Examples of high-capacity networks are wireless mobile, satellite, wireless sensor, and VoIP (voice over Internet Protocol) such as Skype. **Voice over IP (VoIP)** networks carry voice calls by converting voice (analog signals) to digital signals that are sent as packets. With VoIP, voice and data transmissions travel in packets over telephone wires. VoIP has grown to become one of the most used and least costly ways to communicate. Improved productivity, flexibility, and advanced features make VoIP an appealing technology.

FUNCTIONS SUPPORTED BY BUSINESS NETWORKS

Figure 4.5 describes the basic functions of business networks: communication, mobility, collaboration, relationships, and search. These functions depend on network **switches** and **routers**—devices that transmit data packets from their source to their destination based on IP addresses. A switch acts as a controller, enabling networked devices to talk to each other efficiently. For example, switches connect computers, printers, and servers within an office building. Switches create a network. Routers connect networks. A router links computers to the Internet, so users

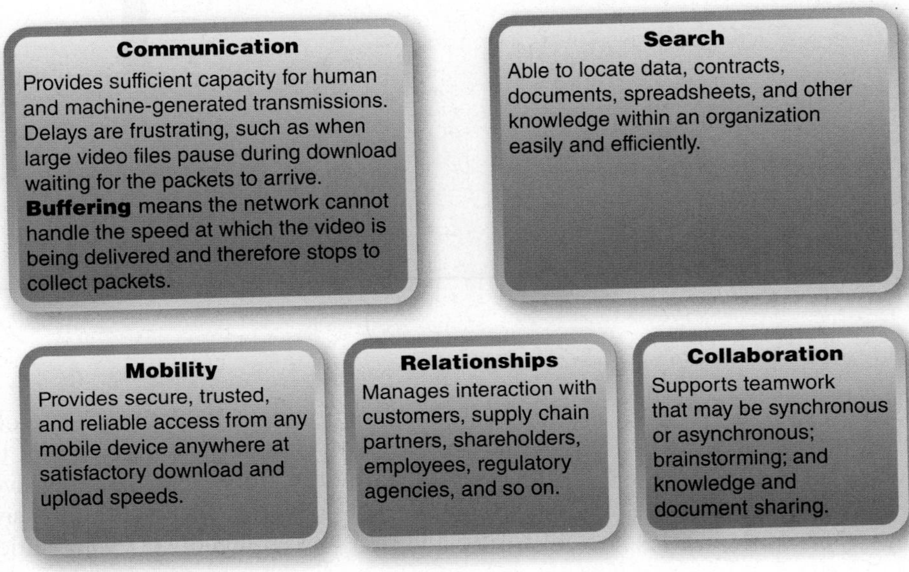

Communication
Provides sufficient capacity for human and machine-generated transmissions. Delays are frustrating, such as when large video files pause during download waiting for the packets to arrive. Buffering means the network cannot handle the speed at which the video is being delivered and therefore stops to collect packets.
Search
Able to locate data, contracts, documents, spreadsheets, and other knowledge within an organization easily and efficiently.
Mobility
Provides secure, trusted, and reliable access from any mobile device anywhere at satisfactory download and upload speeds.
Relationships
Manages interaction with customers, supply chain partners, shareholders, employees, regulatory agencies, and so on.
Collaboration
Supports teamwork that may be synchronous or asynchronous; brainstorming; and knowledge and document sharing.

Figure 4.5 Basic functions of business networks.

can share the connection. Routers act like a dispatcher, choosing the best paths for packets to travel.

Investments in data networks, IP addresses, routers, and switches are business decisions because of their impact on productivity, security, user experiences, and customer service.

TECH NOTE 4.2 Circuit and Packet Switching

All generations of networks are based on switching. Prior to 4G, networks included circuit switching, which is slower than packet switching. 4G was first to be fully packet switched, which significantly improved performance. The two basic types of switching are:

Circuit switching: A circuit is a dedicated connection between a source and destination. In the past, when a call was placed between two landline phones, a circuit or connection was created that remained until one party hung up. Circuit switching is older technology that originated with telephone calls; it is inefficient for digital transmission.

Packet switching: Packet switching transfers data or voice in packets. Files are broken into packets, numbered sequentially, and routed individually to their destination. When received at the destination, the packets are reassembled into their proper sequence.

Wireless networks use packet switching and wireless routers whose antennae transmit and receive packets. At some point, wireless routers are connected by cables to wired networks, as shown in Figure 4.6.

Figure 4.6 Network cables plug into a wireless router. The antennae create wireless access points (WAP).

© Metta digital/Alamy

QUALITY OF SERVICE

An important management decision is the network's **quality of service (QoS)**, especially for delay-sensitive data such as real time voice and high-quality video. The higher the required QoS, the more expensive the technologies needed to manage organizational networks. Bandwidth-intensive apps are important to business processes, but they also strain network capabilities and resources. Regardless of the type of traffic, networks must provide secure, predictable, measurable, and sometimes guaranteed services for certain types of traffic. For example, QoS technologies can be applied to create two tiers of traffic:

- **Prioritize traffic:** Data and apps that are time-delay-sensitive or **latency-sensitive apps**, such as voice and video, are given priority on the network.
- **Throttle traffic:** In order to give latency-sensitive apps priority, other types of traffic need to be held back (throttled).

The ability to prioritize and throttle network traffic is referred to as **traffic shaping** and forms the core of the hotly debated Net neutrality issue, which is discussed in IT at Work 4.1.

IT at Work 4.1

Net Neutrality Debate Intensifies

In 2014 the battle over the complicated issue of net neutrality heated up. **Net neutrality** is a principle that Internet Service Providers (ISPs) and their regulators treat all Internet traffic the same way. On the opposing side of that issue is traffic shaping. Traffic shaping creates a two-tier system for specific purposes such as:

1. Time-sensitive data are given priority over traffic that can be delayed briefly with little-to-no adverse effect. Companies like Comcast argue that Net neutrality rules hurt consumers. Certain applications are more sensitive to delays than others, such as streaming video and Internet phone services. Managing data transfer makes it possible to assure a certain level of performance or QoS.
2. In a corporate environment, business-related traffic may be given priority over other traffic, in effect, by paying a premium price for that service. Proponents of traffic shaping argue that ISPs should be able to charge more to customers who want to pay a premium for priority service.

Specifically, traffic is shaped by delaying the flow of less important network traffic, such as bulk data transfers, P2P file-sharing programs, and BitTorrent traffic.

Traffic shaping is hotly debated by those in favor of Net neutrality. They want a one-tier system in which all Internet data packets are treated the same, regardless of their content, destination, or source. In contrast, those who favor the two-tiered system argue that there have always been different levels of Internet service and that a two-tiered system would enable more freedom of choice and promote Internet-based commerce.

Federal Communications Commission's 2010 Decision

On December 21, 2010, the Federal Communications Commission (FCC) approved a compromise that created two classes of Internet access: one for fixed-line providers and the other for the wireless Net. In effect, the new rules are **Net semi-neutrality**. The FCC banned any outright blocking of and "unreasonable discrimination" against websites or applications by fixed-line broadband providers. But the rules do not explicitly forbid "paid prioritization," which would allow a company to pay an ISP for faster data transmission.

Net Semi-Neutrality Overturned in 2014

In January 2014 an appeals court struck down the FCC's 2010 decision. The court allowed ISPs to create a two-tiered Internet, but promised close supervision to avoid anticompetitive practices, and banned "unreasonable" discrimination against providers.

On April 24 FCC Chairman Tom Wheeler reported that his agency would propose new rules to comply with the court's decision that would be finalized by December 2014. Wheeler stated that these rules "would establish that behavior harmful to consumers or competition by limiting the openness of the Internet will not be permitted" (Wheeler, 2014). But Wheeler's proposal would allow network owners to charge extra fees to content providers. This decision has angered consumer advocates and Net neutrality advocates who view Wheeler with suspicion because of his past work as a lobbyist for the cable industry and wireless phone companies.

Sources: Compiled from Federal Communications Commission (fcc.gov, 2014), Wheeler (2014), and various blog posts.

Questions

1. What is Net neutrality?
2. What tiers are created by traffic shaping?
3. Why did the battle over Net neutrality intensify in 2014?
4. Did the FCC's 2010 ruling favor either side of the debate? Explain.
5. What has been a reaction to the 2014 appeals court decision? Explain.

NETWORK TERMINOLOGY

To be able to evaluate networks and the factors that determine their functionality, you need to be familiar with the following network basics:

- **Bandwidth:** Bandwidth depends on the network protocol. Common wireless protocols are 802.11b. 802.11g, 802.11n, and 802.16. For an analogy to bandwidth, consider a pipe used to transport water. The larger the diameter of the pipe, the greater the throughput (volume) of water that flows through it and the faster water is transferred through it.

- **Protocol:** Protocols are rules and standards that govern how devices on a network exchange data and "talk to each other." An analogy is a country's driving rules—whether to drive on the right or left side of the road.

- **TCP/IP:** Transmission control protocol/Internet protocol (TCP/IP) is the basic communication protocol of the Internet. This protocol is supported by every major network operating system (OS) to ensure that all devices on the Internet can communicate. It is used as a communications protocol in a company's private network for internal uses.

Broadband (short for *broad bandwidth*) means high-capacity or high-speed network.

- **Fixed-line broadband:** Describes either cable or DSL Internet connections.

- **Mobile broadband:** Describes various types of wireless high-speed Internet access through a portable modem, telephone, or other device.

- **3G:** 3G networks support multimedia and broadband services, do so over a wider distance, and at faster speeds than prior 1G and 2G generations. 3G networks have far greater ranges because they use large satellite connections to telecommunication towers.

- **4G:** 4G mobile network standards enable faster data transfer rates. 4G networks are digital, or IP, networks.

Overall, 2G networks were for voice, 3G networks for voice and data, and 4G networks for broadband Internet connectivity.

TECH NOTE 4.3 Origin of the Internet, e-mail, and TCP/IP

The Advanced Research Projects Agency network (ARPAnet) was the first real network to run on packet-switching technology. In October 1969 computers at Stanford University, UCLA, and two other U.S universities connected for the first time—making them the first hosts on what would become the Internet. ARPAnet was designed for research, education, and government agencies. ARPAnet provided a communications network linking the country in the event that a military attack or nuclear war destroyed conventional communications systems.

In 1971 e-mail was developed by Ray Tomlinson, who used the @ symbol to separate the username from the network's name, which became the domain name.

On January 1, 1983, ARPAnet computers switched over to the TCP/IP protocols developed by Vinton Cerf. A few hundred computers were affected by the switch. The original ARPAnet protocol had been limited to 1,000 hosts, but the adoption of the TCP/IP standard made larger numbers of hosts possible. The number of Internet hosts reached nearly 1 billion by 2013.

| 3G AND 4G

4G delivers average *realistic* download rates of 3 Mbps or higher (as opposed to *theoretical* rates, which are much higher). In contrast, today's 3G networks typically deliver average download speeds about one-tenth of that rate. Even though individual networks, ranging from 2G to 3G, started separately with their own purposes, soon they will be converted to the 4G network.

4G is based purely on the packet-based IP—unlike 2G and 3G that have a circuit-switched subsystem. Users can obtain 4G wireless connectivity through one of the following standards:

1. **WiMAX** is based on the IEEE 802.16 standard. IEEE 802.16 specifications are:

   - Range: 30 miles (50 km) from base station
   - Speed: 70 megabits per second (Mbps)
   - Line-of-sight not needed between user and base station

   WiMAX operates on the same basic principles as Wi-Fi in that it transmits data from one device to another via radio signals.

2. **Long-Term Evolution (LTE)** is a GSM-based technology that is deployed by Verizon, AT&T, and T-Mobile. LTE capabilities include:

   - Speed: Downlink data rates of 100 Mbps and uplink data rates of 50 Mbps

Improved network performance, which is measured by its *data transfer capacity*, provides fantastic opportunities for mobility, mobile commerce, collaboration, supply chain management, remote work, and other productivity gains.

| BUSINESS USES
| OF NEAR-FIELD
| COMMUNICATION

Near-field communication (NFC) enables two devices within close proximity to establish a communication channel and transfer data through radio waves. NFC are location-aware technologies that are more secure than other wireless technologies like Bluetooth and Wi-Fi. Unlike RFID, NFC is a two-way communication tool.

Location-aware NFC technology can be used to make purchases in restaurants, resorts, hotels, theme parks and theaters, at gas stations, and on buses and trains. Here are some examples of NFC applications and their potential business value.

- The Apple iWatch wearable device with NFC communication capabilities could be ideal for mobile payments. Instead of a wallet, users utilize their iWatch as a credit card or wave their wrists to pay for their Starbucks coffee. With GPS and location-based e-commerce services, retailers could send a coupon alert to the iWatch when a user passes their store. Consumers would then see the coupon and pay for the product with the iWatch.

- Ticketmaster Spain teamed up with Samsung to offer NFC tickets to a Dum Dum Girls concert in Madrid. Consumers needed to download the NFC Ticketmaster app from the Samsung app store to purchase a ticket, which was then stored in their phone for secure entry at the door.

- International fresh produce distributor Total Produce plans to give consumers access to videos, recipes, and interactive games about the benefits of a healthy diet via NFC tag–equipped SmartStands located in supermarkets and convenience stores. "We can upload a new video to these units instantly to respond to opportunities; a barbecue-themed video on a sunny afternoon, a pumpkin carving video for Halloween or a recipe video to complement an in-store price promotion," says Vince Dolan, European marketing manager at Total Produce. "Similarly, we can update grower videos to reflect changes in product range at any time" (Boden, 2014).

- Passengers on public transportation systems can pay fares by waving an NFC smartphone as they board.

IT at Work 4.2

NFC-Embedded Guitar Picks

Fans attending gigs by The Wild Feathers were given guitar picks embedded with an NFC tag. Warner Music had distributed the guitar picks for fans to enter a competition, share content via social media, and vote at the gig simply by tapping with an NFC phone. NFC-embedded picks were inserted into the band's promotional flyers at six European venues. Each pick was encoded with a unique URL and also printed with a unique code for iPhone users to enable tracking and monitoring.

Marketing Campaign Success Shows an Exciting Future for NFC

The tags generated a high response rate. Over 65 percent of the NFC guitar picks had registered in the competition. And 35 percent of the fans had shared content on social media—spending an average of five minutes on the site.

NFC is being used in marketing campaigns because the technology offers slick one-tap interaction. NFC allows brands to engage with their customers in unique ways and create exciting user experiences. With millions of NFC-equipped smartphones set to reach users over the next few years and the technology's advantages for shoppers and businesses, NFC is emerging as a major technology.

Questions

1. Assume you attended a concert and were given a brochure similar to the one distributed to fans at The Wild Feathers concert. Would you use the guitar pick or comparable NFC-embedded item to participate in a contest? To post on Facebook or tweet about the concert? Explain why or why not.

2. How can NFC be applied to create an interesting user experience at a sporting event? At a retail store or coffee shop?

3. Refer to your answers in Question 2. What valuable information could be collected by the NFC tag in these businesses?

Mashup is a general term referring to the integration of two or more technologies.

Mashup of GPS and Bluetooth

The **mashup** of GPS positioning and short-range wireless technologies, such as **Bluetooth** and **Wi-Fi**, can provide unprecedented intelligence. These technologies create opportunities for companies to develop solutions that make a consumer's life better. They could, for example, revolutionize traffic and road safety. Intelligent transport systems being developed by car manufacturers allow cars to communicate with each other and send alerts about sudden braking. In the event of a collision, the car's system could automatically call emergency services. The technology could also apply the brakes automatically if it was determined that two cars were getting too close to each other.

Advancements in networks, devices, and RFID sensor networks are changing enterprise information infrastructures and business environments dramatically. The preceding examples and network standards illustrate the declining need for a physical computer, as other devices provide access to data, people, or services at any time, anywhere in the world, on high-capacity networks.

Figure 4.7 Common mobile and desktop operating systems. Each computer OS provides an API for programmers. Mobile OSs are designed around touchscreen input.

Common Mobile OS	Common Desktop OS
Android	Windows
iOS	Mac OS X
Windows Phone	Linux

APPLICATION PROGRAM INTERFACES AND OPERATING SYSTEMS

Application program interface (API). An interface is the boundary where two separate systems meet. An API provides a standard way for different things, such as software, content, or websites, to talk to each other in a way that they both understand without extensive programming.

When software developers create applications, they must write and compile the code for a specific operating system (OS). Figure 4.7 lists the common OSs. Each OS communicates with hardware in its own unique way; each OS has a specific API that programmers must use. Video game consoles and other hardware devices also have **APIs** that run software programs.

What Is an API?

An API consists of a set of functions, commands, and protocols used by programmers to build software for an OS. The API allows programmers to use predefined functions or reusable codes to interact with an OS without having to write a software program from scratch. APIs simplify the programmer's job.

APIs are the common method for accessing information, websites, and databases. They were created as gateways to popular apps such as Twitter, Facebook, and Amazon and enterprise apps provided by SAP, Oracle, NetSuite, and many other vendors.

Automated API

The current trend is toward automatically created APIs that are making innovative IT developments possible. Here are two examples of the benefits of automated APIs:

- Websites such as the European Union Patent office have mappings of every one of their pages to both URLs for browser access and URLs for REST APIs. Whenever a new page is published, both access methods are supported.

- The startup SlashDB offers the capability to automatically create an API to access data in a SQL database. This API simplifies many of the details of SQL usage and makes it much easier for developers to get at the data (Woods, 2013a and 2013b).

TECH NOTE 4.4 Spotify Released Its API to Developers

In early 2012 the digital music service Spotify released its API to developers. The developers quickly created hundreds of apps that fans are using to discover and share new music. The most popular new app is Tunigo, which uses its music experts to curate playlists targeted to various moods. The Tunigo service was so successful that Spotify bought it and made it part of *Browse*. Browse is the in-house curation department that searches Spotify's catalog and continuously delivers new playlists (Dean, 2013).

Browse lets you search for specific playlists based on your mood. These playlists are created by other users and selected by Spotify staffers. Users have created over 1 billion playlists, which grow and morph every day.

The power of Spotify was demonstrated in 2013 when it won a challenge with Pink Floyd to gain access to the group's entire music collection: every track from every album the band had ever released. The Pink Floyd collection became part of Spotify's streaming music service when the tracks were officially "unlocked" in June 2013. The challenge was for the song "Wish You Were Here" to be streamed by fans over 1 million times in just a few days. Pink Floyd members fulfilled the deal.

API Value Chain in Business

APIs deliver more than half of all the traffic to major companies like Twitter and eBay. APIs are used to access business assets, such as customer information or a product or service, as shown in Figure 4.8. IT developers use APIs to quickly and easily connect diverse data and services to each other. APIs from Google, Twitter, Amazon, Facebook, Accuweather, Sears, and E*Trade are used to create many thousands of applications. For example, Google Maps API is a collection of APIs used by developers to create customized Google Maps that can be accessed on a Web browser or mobile devices.

The API value chain takes many forms because the organization that owns the business asset may or may not be the same as the organization that builds the APIs. Different people or organizations may build, distribute, and market the applications. At the end of the chain are end-users who benefit from the business asset. Often, many APIs are used to create a new user experience.

The business benefits of APIs are listed in Table 4.2.

TABLE 4.2   Business Benefits of APIs

APIs are channels to new customers and markets: APIs enable partners to use business assets to extend the reach of a company's products or services to customers and markets they might not reach easily.

APIs promote innovation: Through an API, people who are committed to a challenge or problem can solve it themselves.

APIs are a better way to organize IT: APIs promote innovation by allowing everyone in a company to use each other's assets without delay.

APIs create a path to lots of Apps: Apps are going to be a crucial channel in the next 10 years. Apps are powered by APIs. Developers use APIs and combinations of APIs to create new user experiences.

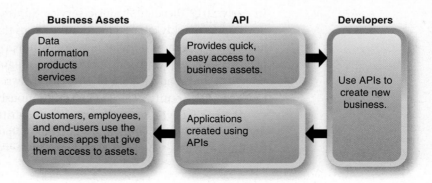

Figure 4.8 API value chain in business.

Questions

1. Why has IPv6 become increasingly important?
2. What is an IP address?
3. What are bandwidth and broadband?
4. Briefly described the basic network functions.
5. What is the difference between circuit switching and packet switching?
6. What is the difference between 3G and 4G?
7. What are the mobile network standards?
8. Explain the Net neutrality debate.
9. What are two applications of NFC?
10. What are the benefits of APIs?

4.2 Wireless Networks and Mobile Infrastructure

In the 21st-century global economy, advanced wireless networks are a foundation on which global economic activity takes place. Current 3G and 4G networks and technologies provide that foundation, moving entire economies. For any nation to stay competitive and prosperous, it is imperative that investment and upgrades in these technologies continue to advance to satisfy demand.

Global mobile data traffic is forecasted to increase nearly 11-fold between 2013 and 2018. Mobile data traffic will grow at a compound annual growth rate (CAGR) of 61 percent from 2013 to 2018, reaching 15.9 exabytes (EB) per month by 2018, according to the *Cisco Visual Networking Index (VNI): Global Mobile Data Traffic Forecast Update, 2013–2018*. Mobile data traffic will reach the following milestones:

1. The average mobile connection speed will surpass 2 Mbps by 2016.
2. Smartphones will reach 66 percent of mobile data traffic by 2018.
3. Monthly mobile tablet traffic will surpass 2.5 EB per month by 2018.
4. Tablets will exceed 15 percent of global mobile data traffic by 2016.
5. 4G traffic will be more than half of total mobile traffic by 2018.
6. There will be more traffic offloaded from cellular networks and onto Wi-Fi networks than remains on cellular networks by 2018.
7. In addition to supporting mobile users, increased bandwidth is needed to support the numerous industrial applications that leverage wireless technologies—primarily the smart grid, or smart energy, and health-care segments.

With a combination of smart meters, wireless technology, sensors, and software, the smart grid allows utilities to accurately track power grids and cut back on energy use when the availability of electricity is stressed. And consumers gain insight into their power consumption to make more intelligent decisions about how to use energy. A fully deployed smart grid has the potential of saving between \$39.69 and \$101.57, and up to 592 pounds of carbon dioxide emissions, per consumer per year in the United States, according to the Smart Grid Consumer Collaborative (SGCC).

Wireless hospitals and remote patient monitoring, for example, are growing trends. Tracking medical equipment and hospital inventory, such as gurneys, is done with RFID tagging at a number of hospitals. Remote monitoring apps are making health care easier and more comfortable for patients while reaching patients in remote areas.

IT at Work 4.3

Smart City or Police State?

In the small city of Santander on Spain's Atlantic coast, Mayor Iñigo de la Serna raised $12 million, mostly from the European Commission, to launch *SmartSantander*. SmartSantander is a smart city experiment that is improving the quality of life, reducing energy consumption, and engaging its citizens in civic duties.

10,000 Sensors Embedded

The city implemented wireless sensor networks and embedded 10,000 sensors in its streets and municipal vehicles to monitor garbage collection, crime, and air quality and manage street lighting for better energy efficiency. Sensors communicate with smartphone apps to inform drivers and commuters on parking availability, bus delays, road closures, and the current pollen count in real time. Parking apps direct drivers to available spaces via cell phone alerts. Drivers benefit from a reduction in the time and annoyance of finding parking spots. Anyone can feed his or her own data into the system by, for example, snapping a smartphone photo of a pothole or broken streetlight to notify the local government that a problem needs to be fixed.

Build-Out of Smart City Applications

This mobile technology can help cities contribute to a greener planet. Municipal landscape sprinklers can send facts to city agencies for analysis to conserve water usage. Sensors can monitor weather and pollen counts as well as water and power leaks.

Police State

The data streams and mobile apps that keep citizens informed also keep the government informed. What is the difference between a smart city and a police state? Consider how data collected from sensors mounted outside a bar to track noise levels might be used.

- Scenario #1. Instances of loud noises and squealing tires are transmitted to local police. The city uses the information to enforce public nuisance laws and make arrests.
- Scenario #2: People who live in the neighborhood show civic leaders what is keeping them up at night and receive help in resolving the problem.
- Scenario #3: Landlords could use data showing less noise and cleaner air to promote their apartments or office buildings.

The Dark Side of Smart

The wireless networks and sensors need to be maintained. Thousands of batteries embedded in roadways could have expensive and disruptive maintenance requirements.

Parking space alerts might create other annoyances. If everyone becomes aware of a parking spot up the street, the rush of cars converging on a few open locations could lead to rage and defeat the purpose of such an alert.

Sources: Compiled from O'Connor (2013) and Edwards (2014).

Questions

1. What are the benefits of a smart city?
2. What are the potential abuses of data collected in this way?
3. Consider the dark side of smart. Are you skeptical of the benefits of a smart city?
4. Would you want to live in a smart city? Explain.
5. How would you prevent Santander from becoming a police state?

STRATEGIC BUILD-OUT OF MOBILE CAPABILITIES	Enterprises are moving away from the ad hoc adoption of mobile devices and network infrastructure to a more strategic planning build-out of their mobile capabilities. As technologies that make up the mobile infrastructure evolve, identifying strategic technologies and avoiding wasted investments require more extensive planning and forecasting. Factors to consider are the network demands of multitasking mobile devices, more robust mobile OSs, and their applications.

Mobile Infrastructure

Mobile infrastructure consists of the integration of technology, software, support, security measures, and devices for the management and delivery of wireless communications.

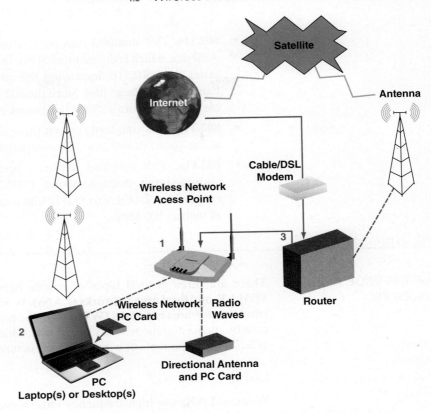

1. Radio-equipped access point connected to the Internet (or via a router). It generates and receives radio waves (up to 400 feet).
2. Several client devices, equipped with PC cards, generate and receive radio waves.
3. Router is connected to the Internet via a cable or DSL modem, or is connected via a satellite.

Figure 4.9 Overview of Wi-Fi.

Wi-Fi and Bluetooth

Bluetooth is a short-range wireless communications technology.

Wi-Fi is the standard way computers connect to wireless networks.

Bluetooth is a short-range—up to 100 meters or 328 feet—wireless communications technology found in billions of devices, such as smartphones, computers, medical devices, and home entertainment products. When two Bluetooth-enabled devices connect to each other, this is called pairing.

Wi-Fi is the standard way computers connect to wireless networks. Nearly all computers have built-in Wi-Fi chips that allow users to find and connect to wireless routers. The router must be connected to the Internet in order to provide Internet access to connected devices.

Wi-Fi technology allows devices to share a network or Internet connection without the need to connect to a commercial network. Wi-Fi networks beam packets over short distances using part of the radio spectrum, or they can extend over larger areas, such as municipal Wi-Fi networks. However, municipal networks are not common because of their huge costs. See Figure 4.9 for an overview of how Wi-Fi works.

TECH NOTE 4.5 Wi-Fi Networking Standards

- **802.11b.** This standard shares spectrum with 2.4-GHz cordless phones, microwave ovens, and many Bluetooth products. Data are transferred at distances up to 100 meters or 328 feet.

- **802.11a.** This standard runs on 12 channels in the 5-GHz spectrum in North America, which reduces interference issues. Data are transferred about 5 times faster than 802.11b, improving the quality of streaming media. It has extra bandwidth for large files. Since the 802.11a and b standards are not interoperable, data sent from an 802.11b network cannot be accessed by 802.11a networks.

- **802.11g.** This standard runs on three channels in the 2.4-GHz spectrum, but at the speed of 802.11a. It is compatible with the 802.11b standard.

- **802.11n.** This standard improves upon prior 802.11 standards by adding multiple-input multiple-output (MIMO) and newer features. Frequency ranges from 2.4 GHz to 5 GHz with a data rate of about 22 Mbps, but perhaps as high as 100 Mbps.

WIRELESS WIDE AREA NETWORKS

There are three general types of mobile networks: **wide area networks (WANs)**, **WiMAX**, and **local area networks (LANs)**. WANs for mobile computing are known as **wireless wide area networks (WWANs)**. The range of a WWAN depends on the transmission media and the wireless generation, which determines which services are available. Two components of wireless infrastructures are wireless LANs and WiMAX.

LANs

Wireless LANs use high-frequency radio waves to communicate between computers, devices, or other nodes on the network. A wireless LAN typically extends an existing wired LAN by attaching a wireless AP to a wired network.

WiMAX

Wireless broadband WiMAX transmits voice, data, and video over high-frequency radio signals to businesses, homes, and mobile devices. It was designed to bypass traditional telephone lines and is an alternative to cable and DSL. WiMAX is based on the IEEE 802.16 set of standards and the metropolitan area network (MAN) access standard. Its range is 20 to 30 miles and it does not require a clear line of sight to function. Figure 4.10 shows the components of a WiMAX/Wi-Fi network.

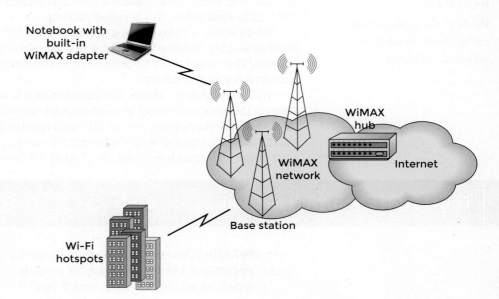

Figure 4.10 WiMAX/Wi-Fi network.

TECH NOTE 4.6 Mobile Network Evaluation Factors

When evaluating mobile network solutions, there are four factors to consider. They are:

1. **Simple:** Easy to deploy, manage, and use.
2. **Connected:** Always makes the best connection possible.
3. **Intelligent:** Works behind the scenes, easily integrating with other systems.
4. **Trusted:** Enables secure and reliable communications.

Questions

1. What factors are contributing to mobility?
2. Why is strategic planning of mobile networks important?
3. How does Wi-Fi work?
4. What is a WLAN?
5. Why is WiMAX important?
6. What factors should be considered when selecting a mobile network?

4.3 Collaboration and Communication Technologies

Now more than ever, business gets done through information sharing and collaborative planning. Business performance depends on broadband data networks for communication, mobility, and collaboration. For example, after Ford Motor Company began relying on UPS Logistics Group's data networks to track millions of cars and trucks and to analyze any potential problems before they occur, Ford realized a $1 billion reduction in vehicle inventory and $125 million reduction in inventory carrying costs annually.

People need to work together and share documents. Teams make most of the complex decisions in organizations. And organizational decision making is difficult when team members are geographically spread out and working in different time zones.

Messaging and collaboration tools include older communications media such as e-mail, videoconferencing, fax, and texts—and blogs, Skype, Web meetings, and social media. Yammer is an enterprise social network that helps employees collaborate across departments, locations, and business apps. These private social sites are used by more than 400,000 enterprises worldwide. Yammer functions as a communication and problem-solving tool and is rapidly replacing e-mail. You will read about Yammer is detail in Chapter 7.

VIRTUAL COLLABORATION

Leading businesses are moving quickly to realize the benefits of virtual collaboration. Several examples appear below.

Information Sharing Between Retailers and Their Suppliers

One of the most publicized examples of information sharing exists between Procter & Gamble (P&G) and Walmart. Walmart provides P&G with access to sales information on every item Walmart buys from P&G. The information is collected by P&G

on a daily basis from every Walmart store, and P&G uses that information to manage the inventory replenishment for Walmart.

Retailer–Supplier Collaboration: Asda Corporation

Supermarket chain Asda (asda.com) has rolled out Web-based electronic data interchange (EDI) technology to 650 suppliers. Web EDI technology is based on the AS2 standard, an internationally accepted HTTP-based protocol used to send real time data in multiple formats securely over the Internet. It promises to improve the efficiency and speed of traditional EDI communications, which route data over third-party, value-added networks (VANs).

Lower Transportation and Inventory Costs and Reduced Stockouts: Unilever

Unilever's 30 contract carriers deliver 250,000 truckloads of shipments annually. Unilever's Web-based database, the Transportation Business Center (TBC), provides these carriers with site specification requirements when they pick up a shipment at a manufacturing or distribution center or when they deliver goods to retailers. TBC gives carriers all of the vital information they need: contact names and phone numbers, operating hours, the number of dock doors at a location, the height of the dock doors, how to make an appointment to deliver or pick up shipments, pallet configuration, and other special requirements. All mission-critical information that Unilever's carriers need to make pickups, shipments, and deliveries is now available electronically 24/7.

Reduction of Product Development Time

Caterpillar, Inc. is a multinational heavy-machinery manufacturer. In the traditional mode of operation, cycle time along the supply chain was long because the process involved paper–document transfers among managers, salespeople, and technical staff. To solve the problem, Caterpillar connected its engineering and manufacturing divisions with its active suppliers, distributors, overseas factories, and customers through an extranet-based global collaboration system. By means of the collaboration system, a request for a customized tractor component, for example, can be transmitted from a customer to a Caterpillar dealer and on to designers and suppliers, all in a very short time. Customers also can use the extranet to retrieve and modify detailed order information while the vehicle is still on the assembly line.

GROUP WORK AND DECISION PROCESSES

Managers and staff continuously make decisions as they develop and manufacture products, plan social media marketing strategies, make financial and IT investments, determine how to meet compliance mandates, design software, and so on. By design or default, group processes emerge, referred to as **group dynamics**, and those processes can be productive or dysfunctional.

Group Work and Dynamics

Group work can be quite complex depending on the following factors:

- Group members may be located in different places or work at different times.
- Group members may work for the same or different organizations.
- Needed data, information, or knowledge may be located in many sources, several of which are external to the organization.

Despite the long history and benefits of collaborative work, groups are not always successful.

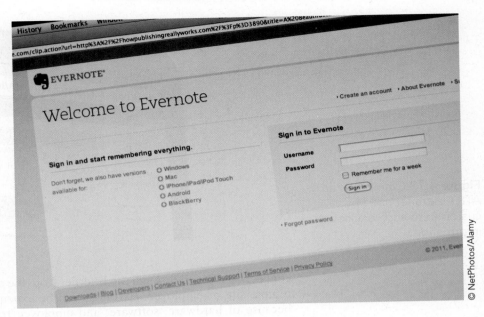

Figure 4.11 Evernote brainstorming, note taking, and archiving software website.

Online Brainstorming in the Cloud

Brainstorming ideas is no longer limited to a room full of people offering their ideas that are written on a whiteboard or posters. Companies are choosing an alternative—online brainstorming applications, many of them cloud-based. An advantage is the avoidance of travel expenses if members are geographically dispersed, which often restricts how many sessions a company can afford to hold. The following are two examples of online brainstorming apps:

- **Evernote** (evernote.com) is a cloud-based tool that helps users gather and share information, and brainstorm ideas. One function is Synch, which keeps Evernote notes up-to-date across a user's computers, phones, devices and the Web. See Figure 4.11. A free version of Evernote is available for download.

- **iMindmap Online**, from UK-based ThinkBuzan (thinkbuzan.com), relies on mind mapping and other well-known structured approaches to brainstorming. iMindmap Online helps streamline work processes, minimize information overload, generate new ideas, and boost innovation.

INTRANETS, EXTRANETS, AND VIRTUAL PRIVATE NETWORKS

Intranets are used within a company for data access, sharing, and collaboration. They are portals or gateways that provide easy and inexpensive browsing and search capabilities. Colleges and universities rely on intranets to provide services to students and faculty. Using screen sharing and other groupware tools, intranets can support team work.

An **extranet** is a private, company-owned network that can be logged into remotely via the Internet. Typical users are suppliers, vendors, partners, or customers (Figure 4.12). Basically, an extranet is a network that connects two or more companies so they can securely share information. Since authorized users remotely access content from a central server, extranets can drastically reduce storage space on individual hard drives.

A major concern is the security of the transmissions that could be intercepted or compromised. One solution is to use **virtual private networks (VPNs)**, which encrypt the packets before they are transferred over the network. VPNs consist of encryption software and hardware that encrypt, send, and decrypt transmissions, as shown in Figure 4.13. In effect, instead of using a leased line to create a dedicated, physical connection, a company can invest in VPN technology to create virtual

Figure 4.12 Example of an AT&T extranet used by a customer to access account information.

© Ian Dagnall/Alamy

connections routed through the Internet from the company's private network to the remote site or employee. Extranets can be expensive to implement and maintain because of hardware, software, and employee training costs if hosted internally rather than by an application service provider (ASP).

Figure 4.13 Virtual private networks (VPNs) create encrypted connections to company networks.

© tungphoto/iStockphoto

Questions

1. Why is group work challenging?
2. What might limit the use of in-person brainstorming?
3. How can online brainstorming tools overcome those limits?
4. What is the difference between an intranet and an extranet?
5. How does a virtual private network (VPN) provide security?

4.4 Sustainability and Ethical Issues

Being profit-motivated without concern for damage to the environment is unacceptable. Society expects companies to generate a profit and to conduct themselves in an ethical, socially responsible, and environmentally sustainable manner. Four factors essential to preserving the environment are shown in Figure 4.14. **Sustainability** grows more urgent every year as carbon emissions contribute to **climate changes** that are threatening quality of life—and possibly life itself.

Figure 4.14 The 4 Rs of environmental sustainability.

GLOBAL TEMPERATURE RISING TOO MUCH TOO FAST

At the United Nations' 2009 climate conference in Copenhagen, climatologists estimated that countries must keep the global mean temperature (GMT) from rising by more than 2°C (3.6°F) above the preindustrial GMT in order to avoid profound damage to life on the earth. Damage includes water and food scarcity, rising sea levels, and greater incidence and severity of disease. Only three years later, GMT had already increased by 0.7°C, or 1.3°F. In 2012 IEA chief economist Faith Birol warned that this trend is perfectly in line with a temperature increase of 6°C by 2050, which would have devastating impacts on the planet. Since 2005 the Prince of Wales' Corporate Leaders Group on Climate Change has lobbied for more aggressive climate legislation within the United Kingdom, the European Union, and internationally. It holds that carbon emission reductions between 50 percent and 85 percent are necessary by 2050 to prevent the global temperature from rising too much too fast because of the greenhouse effect, as shown in Figure 4.15.

TECH NOTE 4.7 NASA's Greenhouse Gas Emission Warnings

According to NASA (climate.nasa.gov), CO_2 and other **greenhouse gases (GHGs)** trap the sun's heat within the earth's atmosphere, warming it and keeping it at habitable temperatures. Scientists have concluded that increases in CO_2 resulting from human activities have thrown the earth's natural carbon cycle off balance, increasing global temperatures and changing the planet's climate.

GHG emissions worldwide hit record highs in 2011, according to the International Energy Agency (IEA). The IEA's preliminary estimates indicate that global emissions of carbon dioxide (CO_2) from fossil-fuel combustion spiked to 31.6 gigatonnes (Gt) in 2011, an increase of 1 Gt or 3.2 percent from the 2010 level (Lemonick, 2012). One Gt equals 1 billion metric tons. GHG is now a serious a global concern. The main international treaty on climate change is the United Nations Framework Convention on Climate Change (UNFCCC).

In 2010 parties to the UNFCCC agreed that future global warming should be limited to below 2°C (3.6°F) relative to the preindustrial level. Analysis suggests that meeting the 2°C target would require annual global emissions of GHG to peak before the year 2020 and decline significantly thereafter, with emissions in 2050 reduced by 30 to 50 percent compared to 1990 levels.

Analyses by the United Nations Environment Programme and International Energy Agency warn that current policies are too weak to achieve the 2°C target.

| GLOBAL WARMING

Figure 4.15 Illustration of the earth's greenhouse effect.

Global warming refers to the upward trend in GMT. It is one of the most complicated issues facing world leaders. Figure 4.16 shows the relationship of fossil fuel, soil, water, atmosphere, and so on in the carbon cycle. Even though the global carbon cycle plays a central role in regulating CO_2 in the atmosphere and thus the earth's climate, scientists' understanding of the interlinked biological processes that drive this cycle is limited. They know that whether an ecosystem will capture, store, or release carbon depends on climate changes and organisms in the earth's biosphere. The biosphere refers to any place that life of any kind can exist on the earth and contains several ecosystems. An ecosystem is a self-sustaining functional unit of the biosphere; it exchanges material and energy between adjoining ecosystems. Global warming occurs because of the greenhouse effect, which is the holding of heat within the earth's atmosphere. GHGs such as CO_2, methane (CH_4), and nitrous oxide (N_2O) absorb infrared radiation (IR), as diagrammed in Figure 4.17.

ICT's Role in Global Warming

The IT industry sector is called the information and communications technology, or ICT, in emission reports. ICT has certainly supported economic growth in developed and developing countries and transformed societies, businesses, and people's lives. But what impacts do our expanding IT and social media dependence have on global warming? How can business processes change or reduce GHGs? And what alternative

Figure 4.16 Carbon cycle. The Orbiting Carbon Observatory-2 was launched in July 2014. The observatory is NASA's first satellite mission dedicated to studying CO_2, which is a critical component of the earth's carbon cycle driving changes in the earth's climate. CO_2 is also the largest human-produced GHG. Courtesy of genomicscience. energy.gov.

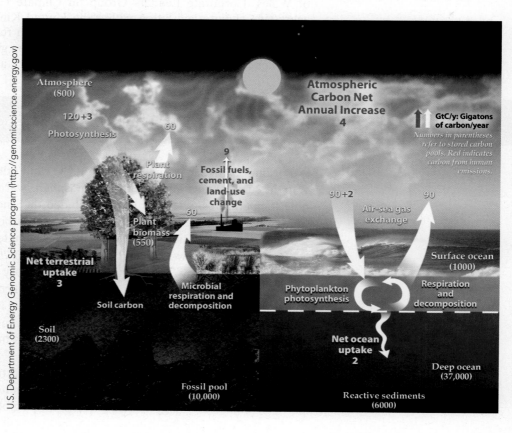

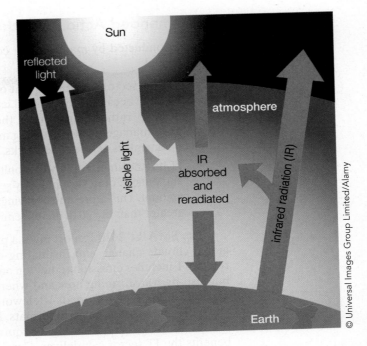

Figure 4.17 Greenhouse gases absorb infrared radiation (IR) emitted from the earth and reradiate it back, thus contributing to the greenhouse effect.

energy sources can be used to power the increasing demands for connectivity? Listed below are several reports and initiatives to help answer these questions.

Global e-Sustainability Initiative and the SMART 2020 Report

The Climate Group's SMART 2020 Report is the world's first comprehensive global study of the IT sector's growing significance for the world's climate. On behalf of the Global e-Sustainability Initiative (GeSI, gesi.org), Climate Group found that ICT plays a key role in reducing global warming. Transforming the way people and businesses use IT could reduce annual human-generated global emissions by 15 percent by 2020 and deliver energy efficiency savings to global businesses of over 500 billion euros, or $800 billion U.S. And using social media, for example, to inform consumers of the grams (g) of carbon emissions associated with the products they buy could change buyer behavior and ultimately have a positive eco-effect. Like food items that display calories and grams of fat to help consumers make healthier food choices, product labels display the CO_2 emissions generated in the production of an item, as shown in Figure 4.18. By 2020 not only will people become more connected, but things will, too—an estimated 50 billion machine-to-machine connections in 2020. A benefit of machine-to-machine connections is that they can relay data about climate changes that make it possible to monitor our emissions.

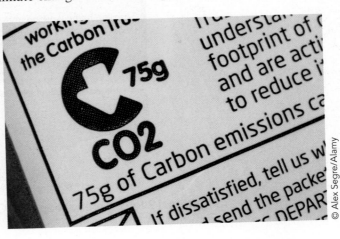

Figure 4.18 Label showing the amount of CO_2 emission generated by the production of an item.

Recommended Actions for the IT Sector

Analysis conducted by management consultants McKinsey & Company concludes the following:

- The IT sector's own footprint of 2 percent of global emissions could double by 2020 because of increased use of tablets, smartphones, apps, and services. To help, rather than worsen, the fight against climate change, the IT sector must manage its own growing impact and continue to reduce emissions from data centers, telecom networks, and the manufacture and use of its products.

- IT has the unique ability to monitor and maximize energy efficiency both within and outside of its own industry sector to cut CO_2 emissions by up to 5 times this amount. This represents a savings of 7.8 Gt of CO_2 per year by 2020, which is greater than the 2010 annual emissions of either the United States or China.

The SMART 2020 Report gives a picture of the IT industry's role in addressing global climate change and facilitating efficient and low-carbon development. The role of IT includes emission reduction and energy savings not only in the sector itself, but also by transforming how and where people work. The most obvious ways are by substituting digital formats—telework, video-conferencing, e-paper, and mobile and e-commerce—for physical formats. Researchers estimate that replacing physical products/services with their digital equivalents would provide 6 percent of the total benefits the IT sector can deliver. Greater benefits are achieved when IT is applied to other industries. Examples of those industries are smart building design and use, smart logistics, smart electricity grids, and smart industrial motor systems.

| SUSTAINABILITY

YouTube reported that 100 hours of video are uploaded every minute in 2014—more than double the 48 hours per minute in 2012. Over 6 billion hours of video are watched each month on YouTube—almost an hour for every person on the earth. Within 5 years, from 2008 through 2013, most U.S. households tripled the number of computing, gaming, consumer electronics, and mobile devices. Statistics about Twitter and other social services also show phenomenal growth. Almost all of these network activities are powered by the burning of fossil fuels. Today's connected lifestyles will further harm the environment unless corrective actions are taken such as those listed in Figure 4.19.

Global Warming: A Hot Debate

Does our society have the capacity to endure in such a way that the 9 billion people expected on the earth by 2050 will all be able to achieve a basic quality of life? The

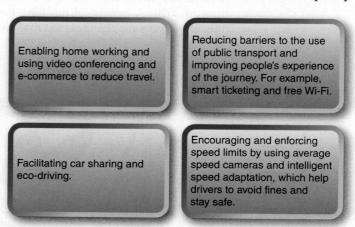

Figure 4.19 Recommendations for ICT from the Sustainable Development Commission (2010).

answer is uncertain—and hotly debated. As you read, many scientists and experts are extremely alarmed by global warming and climate change, but other experts outright deny that they are occurring.

This debate may be resolved to some degree by NASA. A NASA spacecraft was designed to make precise measurements of carbon dioxide (CO_2) in the earth's atmosphere. The Orbiting Carbon Observatory-2 (OCO-2) was launched in July 2014. The observatory is NASA's first satellite mission dedicated to studying CO_2, a critical component of the earth's carbon cycle that is the most prevalent human-produced GHG driving changes in the earth's climate (Figure 4.16).

OCO-2 is a new tool for understanding both the sources of CO_2 emissions and the natural processes that remove CO_2 from the atmosphere, and how they are changing over time. The mission's data will help scientists reduce uncertainties in forecasts of how much carbon dioxide is in the atmosphere and improve the accuracy of global climate change predictions.

According to NASA, since the start of the Industrial Revolution more than 200 years ago, the burning of fossil fuels, as well as other human activities, have led to an unprecedented buildup in this GHG, which in 2014 was at its highest level in at least 800,000 years. Human activities have increased the level of CO_2 by more than 25 percent in just the past half century.

It is possible that we are living far beyond the earth's capacity to support human life. While sustainability is about the future of our society, for businesses, it is also about return on investment (ROI). Businesses need to respect environmental limits, but also need to show an ROI.

Sustainability Through Climate Change Mitigation

There are no easy or convenient solutions to carbon emissions from the fossil fuels burned to power today's tech dependencies. But there are pathways to solutions, and every IT user, enterprise, and nation plays a role in **climate change mitigation**. Climate change mitigation is any action to limit the magnitude of long-term climate change. Examples of mitigation include switching to low-carbon renewable energy sources and reducing the amount of energy consumed by power stations by increasing their efficiency. There have been encouraging successes. For example, investments in research and development (R&D) to reduce the amount of carbon emitted by power stations for mobile networks are paying off. Announced in April 2014, a breakthrough in the design of signal amplifiers for mobile technology will cut 200 megawatts (MW) from the load of power stations, which will reduce CO_2 emissions by 0.5 million tonnes a year (Engineering and Physical Sciences Research Council, 2014).

Mobile, Cloud, and Social Carbon Footprint

No one sees CO_2 being emitted from their Androids or iPhones. But wired and mobile networks enable limitless data creation and consumption—and these activities increase energy consumption. Quite simply, the surge in energy used to power data centers, cell towers, base stations, and recharge devices is damaging the environment and depleting natural resources. It is critical to develop energy systems that power our economy without increasing global temperatures beyond 2°C. To do their part to reduce damaging carbon emissions, some companies have implemented effective sustainability initiatives.

Sustainability Initiatives

Communications technology accounts for approximately 2 percent of global carbon emissions; it is predicted that this figure will double by 2020 as end-user demand for high-bandwidth services with enhanced quality of experience explodes worldwide. Innovative solutions hold the key to curbing these emissions and reducing environmental impact.

Network service providers as well as organizations face the challenges of energy efficiency, a smaller **carbon footprint**, and eco-sustainability. To deal with these challenges, wired and wireless service providers and companies need to upgrade their networks to next-generation, all-IP infrastructures that are optimized and scalable. The network must provide eco-sustainability in traffic transport and deliver services more intelligently, reliably, securely, efficiently and at the lowest cost.

For example, Alcatel-Lucent's High Leverage Network (HLN) can reduce total cost of ownership (TCO) by using fewer devices, creating an eco-sustainable choice for service providers. Fewer devices mean less power and cooling, which reduces the carbon footprint. HLN can also handle large amounts of traffic more efficiently because the networks are intelligent, sending packets at the highest speed and most efficiently.

ETHICAL CONSIDERATIONS OF HYPER-CONNECTED HUMANS

The complexity of a connected life will increase as we move to the new era of nano-sensors and devices, virtual spaces, and 3D social networks exchanging zillions of bytes of data. Managers and workers need to consider ethical and social issues, such as quality of life and working conditions. Individuals will experience both positive and negative impacts from being linked to a 24/7 workplace, working in virtual teams, and being connected to handhelds whose impact on health can be damaging. A 2008 study by Solutions Research Group found that always being connected is a borderline obsession for many people. According to the study, 68 percent of Americans may suffer from *disconnect anxiety*—feelings of disorientation and nervousness when deprived of Internet or wireless access for a period of time. Consider this development and its implications.

Driving while distracted is a crime. Texting while driving is comparable to driving under the influence (DUI), according to safety experts. Several studies indicate that the use of mobile devices is a leading cause of car crashes. At any given moment, more than 10 million U.S. drivers are talking on handheld cell phones, according to the National Highway Traffic Safety Administration. Why is this a problem? Mobiles are a known distraction, and the NHTSA has determined that driver inattention is a primary or contributing factor in as many as 25 percent of all police-reported traffic accidents. This does not include the thousands of accidents not reported to the authorities.

In most or all states, distracted driving is a crime that carries mandatory fines (Figure 4.20). For example, in California and New York State, drivers charged with this crime face fines and have their driving license suspended. If driving while distracted causes injury or death to others, violators face jail time.

The importance of understanding ethical issues has been recognized by the Association to Advance Collegiate Schools of Business (AACSB International, aacsb.edu). For business majors, the AACSB International has defined Assurance

Figure 4.20 Texting while driving is a crime and potentially fatal.

© ZUMA Wire Service/Alamy

of Learning Requirements for ethics at both the undergraduate and graduate levels. In *Standard 15: Management of Curricula* (AACSB, 2006), the association identifies general knowledge and skill learning experiences that include "ethical understanding and reasoning abilities" at the undergraduate level. At the graduate level, *Standard 15* requires learning experiences in management-specific knowledge and skill areas to include "ethical and legal responsibilities in organizations and society" (AACSB, 2006).

Additions and Life Out of Control

The technologies covered in this chapter blur work, social, and personal time. IT keeps people connected with no real off switch. Tools that are meant to improve the productivity and quality of life in general can also intrude on personal time. Managers need to be aware of the huge potential for abuse by expecting a 24/7 response from workers.

The report *Looking Further with Ford—2014 Trends* identifies trends in how the technology explosion will affect consumer choices and behaviors. Sheryl Connelly, Ford global trend and futuring manager, summarized what was learned: "There is no escaping the impact—both positive and negative—of the rapid pace of technology. . . . We are seeing a consumer culture that is increasingly mindful of the need to nurture society's valuable and irreplaceable resources" (Ford Motors, 2013). Four trends were discussed in this report:

1. **Micro Moments:** With so much information at our fingertips, downtime has given way to filling every moment with bite-sized chunks of information, education, and entertainment—seemingly packing our lives with productivity.

2. **Myth of Multitasking:** In an increasingly screen-saturated, multitasking modern world, more and more evidence is emerging to suggest that when we do everything at once, we sacrifice the quality—and often safety—of each thing we do.

3. **Vying for Validation:** In a world of hyper-self-expression, chronic public journaling, and other forms of digital expression, consumers are creating a public self that may need validation even more than their authentic self.

4. **Sustainability:** The world has been fixated on going green, and now attention is shifting beyond recycling and eco-chic living to a growing concern for the power and preciousness of the planet's water.

In our hyper-connected world, people are always on, collaborating, communicating, and creating—and not always aware of how technology impacts them. We need to learn how to harness that energy and connection to develop the next generation of critical, thoughtful thinkers.

Questions

1. Why do some experts warn that carbon emission reductions between 50 percent and 85 percent are necessary by 2050?
2. What contributes to the rise of global mean temperature?
3. What is the greenhouse effect?
4. How does the use of mobile devices contribute to the level of greenhouse gases?
5. What is ICT's role in global warming?
6. Why is global warming hotly debated?
7. Explain the goal of sustainability.
8. Explain the characteristics of a life out of control.

Key Terms

3G
4G
5G
application program
  interface (API)
bandwidth
Bluetooth
carbon footprint
circuit switching
climate change
climate change mitigation
extranet
fixed-line broadband

greenhouse gases
  (GHGs)
group dynamics
information and commu-
  nications technology
  (ICT)
Internet Protocol (IP)
intranet
IP address
IP Version 4 (IPv4)
IP Version 6 (IPv6)
latency-sensitive apps
local area network (LAN)

Long-Term Evolution
  (LTE)
mashup
mobile broadband
near-field communication
  (NFC)
Net neutrality
Net semi-neutrality
packet
packet switching
protocol
quality of service (QoS)
router

sustainability
switch
traffic shaping
transmission control
  protocol/Internet
  protocol (TCP/IP)
virtual private network
  (VPN)
voice over IP (VoIP)
wide area network (WAN)
Wi-Fi
WiMAX

Assuring Your Learning

DISCUSS: Critical Thinking Questions

1. Explain how network capacity is measured.
2. How are devices identified to a network?
3. Explain how digital signals are transmitted.
4. Explain the functions of switches and routers.
5. QoS technologies can be applied to create two tiers of traffic. What are those tiers? Give an example of each type of traffic.
6. Typically, networks are configured so that downloading is faster than uploading. Explain why.
7. What are significant issues about 4G wireless networks?
8. What are two 4G wireless standards?
9. How is network performance measured?
10. Discuss two applications of near-field communication (NFC).
11. What are the benefits of APIs?

12. Describe the components of a mobile communication infrastructure.
13. What is the range of WiMAX? Why does it not need a clear line of sight?
14. Why are VPNs used to secure extranets?
15. How can group dynamics improve group work? How can it disrupt what groups might accomplish?
16. What are the benefits of using software to conduct brainstorming in the cloud (remotely)?
17. How do mobile devices contribute to carbon emissions?
18. Discuss the ethical issues of anytime-anywhere accessibility.
19. What health and quality-of-life issues are associated with social networks and a 24/7 connected lifestyle?
20. Is distracted driving an unsolvable problem? Explain.

EXPLORE: Online and Interactive Exercises

21. Visit the Alcatel-Lucent website (www.alcatel-lucent.com) and search for "eco-sustainability strategy."
    a. Read about Alcatel's eco-sustainability strategy.
    b. Describe how the company is developing eco-sustainable networks. In your opinion, is this an effective strategy? Explain.
    c. Explain how the company is enabling a low-carbon economy. What is its most significant contribution to sustainability?
22. Visit the Google apps website. Identify three types of collaboration support and their value in the workplace.

23. Compare the various features of broadband wireless networks (e.g., 3G, Wi-Fi, and WiMAX). Visit at least three broadband wireless network vendors.
    a. Prepare a list of capabilities for each network.
    b. Prepare a list of actual applications that each network can support.
    c. Comment on the value of such applications to users. How can the benefits be assessed?

ANALYZE & DECIDE: Apply IT Concepts to Business Decisions

24. Visit Youtube.com and search for tutorials on the latest version of iMindMap. Watch a few of the tutorials. As an alternative, watch the video at http://www.youtube.com/watch?v=UVt3Qu6Xcko&list=PLA42C25431E4EA4FF. Describe the potential value of sharing maps online and synching maps with other computers or devices. What is your opinion of the ease or complexity of the iMindMap interface?

25. Visit Google Green at www.google.com/green/bigpicture. Describe Google's efforts to minimize the environmental impact of its services. Do you believe that Google can reduce its carbon footprint beyond zero, as the company claims? Explain your answer.

CASE 4.2

Business Case: Google Maps API for Business

A restaurant owner has a website where customers can place orders for delivery. When a customer inputs a delivery address, a software script verifies whether the address is within the delivery range of the restaurant. If the address is not in the delivery range, the site does not let the customer check out and sends a message informing the customer that he or she is outside of the delivery range. The script requests information from Google Maps via an API to calculate whether or not the address was in the range. The free version, called *Google Maps API*, allows up to 2,500 requests per day from a single IP address and is limited to noncommercial purposes.

The owner needs to purchase a *Google Maps API for Business* license because any requests in excess of 2,500 will be ignored. The Google Maps API for Business provides better resolution, scale, and enhanced features and support to businesses that add maps to their websites, mobile apps, or asset-tracking applications.

Directions and Routing Features

The Google Maps API delivers the full power of Google's routing engine to applications. Among other features, it:

- Generates routes between up to 23 locations for driving, walking, or cycling.
- Generates routes to avoid toll roads or highways.
- Reduces travel time by calculating the optimal order to visit each location.
- Calculates travel time and distance between locations, for example, to offer users a way to filter search results by drive time.

Data Visualization

The Google Maps API lets managers visualize data using heat maps, symbols, and custom styles. For U.S. maps, companies have access to a demographics layer containing up-to-date census data provided by Nielsen and 5-year projections of many data fields. The demographics layer may only be used on intranets or internal websites.

Advanced Analytics

The Google Maps API for Business offers an analytics tool that shows how visitors interact with the maps—for example, how many visitors switched to satellite view, what they zoomed, and which map features were used the most. Using this information, businesses can customize the user experience based on their preferences and better engage with customers.

Automobile Association

Google Maps is the most widely used online mapping service in the world, with more than 800,000 sites using the Google Maps API and over 250 million active users on mobile devices alone. In the United Kingdom, the Automobile Association (AA) provides roadside assistance and directions to motorists. AA invested in the Google Maps API for Business to offer interactive route planning and improve visitors' experiences. The value AA derived from the API was a 12 percent increase in the number of routes downloaded, hitting an average of 4 million downloads per week of its routing or trip-planning service. Approximately 20 percent of site visitors remained on the site for at least five minutes—up from only six percent prior to implementation. The API also cuts the time and cost of IT support for the mapping platform.

Questions

1. Describe Google Maps API.
2. Why do you think Google provides free noncommercial use of its Maps API?
3. How many times have you used a website's mapping feature for directions or to calculate distance? How did having a familiar interface improve your experience?
4. Google claims that its Maps API helps a company's customers and employees make better business and purchasing decisions by visualizing important information on a familiar map. Explain how data visualization provides these benefits. Give two examples in your explanation.

CASE 4.3

Video Case: Fresh Direct Connects for Success

Visit and explore the Fresh Direct website at www.freshdirect. com to learn about the company. Visit the Cisco website at www.cisco.com. Search for the video "Fresh Direct Produce." The URL is www.cisco.com/cisco/web/solutions/small_business/resource_center/index.html. Watch the video to learn how Fresh Direct uses network technology to connect employees, suppliers, and customers. Meet CEO Davis Yung and see how Cisco wireless technology gives his team constant connectivity to meet customer demands (video runs 2:50 minutes).

Questions

1. Describe how network technology enables Fresh Direct's business model.
2. What factors are critical to Fresh Direct's performance?

References

AT&T Enterprise. "Sony Builds an IPv6 Network for the Future." *AT&T VPN Services Case Study.* October 16, 2012. business.att.com/content/customertestimonial/sony-case-study-IP-VPN.pdf

Basulto, D. "Five Reasons to Get Excited About 5G Networks." *The Washington Post,* February 27, 2014.

Boden, R. "Total Produce Pushes Fruit and Veg with NFC in Supermarkets." *NFC World,* April 15, 2014.

Cisco. *Cisco Visual Networking Index (VNI): Global Mobile Data Traffic Forecast Update, 2013–2018.* February 5, 2014a.

Cisco. "Sony Adopts Cisco Solution for Global IPv6 Project." Cisco Public Information, Customer Case Study. 2014b.

Dean, J. "Let a Billion Streams Bloom." *Fast Company,* November 2013.

Edwards, J. "The Connected Life." *Teradata Magazine,* Q1, 2014.

Engineering and Physical Sciences Research Council. "New Design for Mobile Phone Masts Could Cut Carbon Emissions." April 22, 2014.

Ford Motors. "Looking Further with Ford—2014 Trends." 2013.

Khedekar, N. "IPv6 Demystified—What You Should Know." *Tech 2 FirstPost,* June 7, 2012.

O'Connor, M. C. "Santander: Test Bed for Smart Cities and Open Data Policies." *SmartPlanet.com,* May 8, 2013.

Sustainable Development Commission. "Smarter Moves: How Information Communications Technology Can Promote Sustainable Mobility." SDC Report. January 25, 2010.

Wheeler, T. "Setting the Record Straight on the FCC's Open Internet Rules." *FCC blog,* April 24, 2014.

Woods, D. "The Strengths and Limits of Automatically Created APIs." *CITO Research,* September 20, 2013a.

Woods, D. "The Strengths and Limits of Automatically Created APIs." *CITO Research,* October 2, 2013b.

Chapter 5

Cybersecurity and Risk Management

Chapter Snapshot

Case 5.1 Opening Case: BlackPOS Malware Steals Target's Customer Data

5.1 The Face and Future of Cyberthreats

5.2 Cyber Risk Management

5.3 Mobile, App, and Cloud Security

5.4 Defending Against Fraud

5.5 Compliance and Internal Control

Key Terms

Assuring Your Learning

- **Discuss:** Critical Thinking Questions
- **Explore:** Online and Interactive Exercises
- **Analyze & Decide:** Apply IT Concepts to Business Decisions

Case 5.2 Business Case: Lax Security at LinkedIn Exposed

Case 5.3 Video Case: Botnets, Malware Security, and Capturing Cybercriminals

References

Learning Outcomes

1. Describe today's most destructive cyberthreats, data breaches, targeted attacks, malware, and other IT security risks facing organizations and why they are so difficult to defend against.

2. Explain why cyber risk management is a business priority; outline an organizational model for cybersecurity; and describe the cybersecurity process.

3. Explain why mobile devices, apps, and cloud-based services are high-risk attack vectors, the importance of

BYOD (bring your own devices) policies, and the defenses needed to counteract exposure to mobile malware.

4. Describe the characteristics of fraud and how enterprises can defend against and detect fraudulent activities.

5. Explain how internal controls help ensure compliance with industry and federal regulations. Assess the ability to maintain business operations in the event of a network crash, debilitating hacker attack, or other IT disruption.

Chapter Snapshot

Managers no longer question whether their networks will be attacked, but how much damage will be done, how long the investigation will take, and how much the investigation and fines will cost. After detecting a network hack, credit card-processing company Global Payments, Inc. spent 14 months investigating the resulting data breach that exposed 1.5 million U.S. debit and credit card accounts. Global's damages totaled $93 million, broken down as follows: $36 million in fraud losses and fines and $77 million for the investigation, remediation, credit

141

monitoring, and identity theft insurance for affected consumers. In October 2013 a data breach at Adobe exposed the account information of up to 152 million users—the largest data breach in history. No costs have yet been reported, but according to the *Ponemon 2013 Cost of Data Breach Study,* the average cost of a breached account is $188 (Ponemon Institute, 2013). In August 2014, fraudsters targeted customers of JPMorgan Chase, the No. 1 U.S. bank by assets. The massive phishing campaign, called *Smash and Grab,* was unusual because it collected customers' login data and also infected PCs with Dyre, a banking trojan that lifted login data for other institutions. The bank was not able to identify who was behind the *Smash and Grab* attack.

In Chapter 5, you will learn about devastating cyberthreats, data breaches, fraud, damages caused by cybercriminals' aggressive tactics—and how organizations defend against them.

CASE 5.1 OPENING CASE

BlackPOS Malware Steals Target's Customer Data

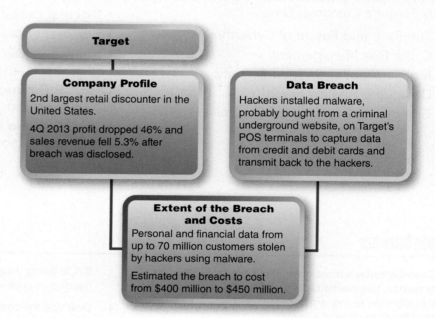

Figure 5.1 Target data breach overview.

Target is a major discount retailer in the United States (Figure 5.1). Target's management admitted that 40 million credit and debit card accounts were exposed between November 27 and December 15, 2013. During that peak holiday shopping season, hackers captured credit card data from the stores' point-of-sale (POS) payment terminals (Figure 5.2).

Target disclosed the breach on December 19, 2013; then on January 10, 2014, the retailer also reported that hackers stole 40 million credit card numbers along with the personal information of another 70 million customers. The incident scared shoppers away, affecting the company's profits throughout 2014.

HOW THE ATTACK WAS CARRIED OUT

Several experts believe that POS malware bought from the criminal underground was responsible. **Malware**, short for *malicious software*, are computer programs whose code causes disruption, destruction, or other devious action. Malware named **BlackPOS** is sold on the black market for $1,800 or more. The malware is advertised on Internet underground forums under the generic name *Dump Memory Grabber by Ree.* BlackPOS is malware designed to be installed on POS devices in

Figure 5.2 POS payment terminal. Malware-infected POS terminals caused Target's data breach.

© Aleph Studio/Shutterstock

order to record data from credit and debit cards swiped through the infected device. Specifically, the malware identifies the process associated with the credit card reader and steals payment card Track 1 and Track 2 data from its memory. These are the data stored on the magnetic strip of payment cards that were used to clone or create counterfeit cards.

More feature-rich versions of BlackPOS selling for roughly $2,300 provide encryption support for stolen data. The BlackPOS creator is not confirmed, but experts tracking the malware suggest that the hacker may be based in Russia or Ukraine. The U.S. Secret Service estimated that the type of malware that led to Target's breach has affected over 1,000 U.S. businesses.

| FINANCIAL IMPACT OF THE DATA BREACH | In February 2014 Target reported that its 2013 fourth-quarter (4Q) profit dropped 46 percent and sales revenue fell 5.3 percent. A few months later, in May 2014, Target estimated that technological changes to harden its IT security would cost more than $100 million in addition to $61 million incurred in breach-related expenses in Q4 2013. These costs and damages harmed the company's profitability. |

Gregg Steinhafel, chairman, president, and CEO of Target, tried to reassure customers and investors, saying, "As we plan for the new fiscal year, we will continue to work tirelessly to win back the confidence of our guests. . . . We are encouraged that sales trends have improved in recent weeks" (D'Innocenzio, 2014).

Six months after the breach, it still was not clear when Target would fully recover. A security analyst at the tech firm Gartner estimated the costs of the breach to range from $400 million to $450 million. That includes the bills associated with fines from credit card companies and services for its customers like free credit card report monitoring. Target also faced at least 70 lawsuits related to privacy invasion and negligence, alleging Target did not take proper steps to protect consumer data.

TARGET BRUSHED OFF WARNINGS

According to financial services firm Cowen Group's note to investors, criminals were able to hack into Target's database due to a lack of security, which might have been a result of underinvestment by senior management.

Target's cybersecurity staff had also warned management to review the security of its payment card system at least two months before the breach. At the time of the warning, Target was updating the payment terminals, which makes them more vulnerable to attack, in preparation for the holiday season. Data security was not a top priority. Months before the attack, the federal government and private research firms were also warning companies about the emergence of new types of malware (malicious computer code) targeting payment terminals. However, because of numerous security warnings that retailers receive every week, it is difficult to identify or decide which ones are the most urgent.

| EXECUTIVE FALLOUT

On May 5, 2014, CEO Steinhafel resigned from all his positions effective immediately, after extensive discussions with the board of directors. Steinhafel had been CEO since 2008 and a Target employee for 35 years. The company stated that Steinhafel and board members had mutually decided that it was time for Target to continue under new leadership. Target shares were down close to 3 percent in morning trading following the news.

Steinhafel's untimely exit was the second significant executive fallout from the data breach. In April 2014 Target's CIO had also been replaced.

Questions

1. Was cybersecurity a priority at Target? Explain.
2. How did lax security impact Target's sales revenue and profit performance?
3. According to experts, how was the data breach executed?
4. In addition to the data theft, what else was damaged by this incident?
5. Was this cybersecurity incident foreseeable? Was it avoidable?
6. Why might management not treat cyberthreats as a top priority?
7. Research recent news concerning this data breach. Has Target recovered from it? Explain.
8. Assuming that the CEO and CIO were forced to resign, what message does that send to senior management at U.S. companies?

Sources: Compiled from D'Innocenzio (2014), Yadron et al. (2014), Krebs on Security (2014), Sharf (2014), O'Connor (2014), and Kratsas (2014).

5.1 The Face and Future of Cyberthreats

Since 2013 the number of data records stolen by hackers has increased at an alarming rate, as shown in Figure 5.3. In fact, 2013 has been dubbed the "Year of the Breach" because there were 2,164 reported data breaches that exposed an estimated 823 million records. Almost half of the 2013 breaches occurred in the United States, where the largest number of records were exposed—more than 540 million data records or 66 percent. Table 5.1 lists the top seven biggest data breaches

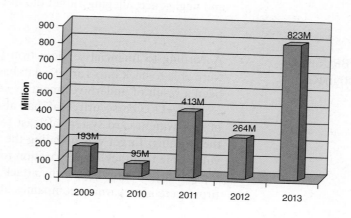

Figure 5.3 Number of reported data records breached worldwide, 2009–2013.

TABLE 5.1	Biggest Data Breaches Worldwide, 2013–2014, in Terms of Number of Data Records Breached	
Company		**Number of Data Records Breached**
eBay **Online auction** Attackers compromised several employees' log-in credentials between February and March 2014 to gain access to the company's network and, through it, compromised a database that contained customer names, encrypted passwords, email addresses, physical addresses, phone numbers, and dates of birth.		Up to 145 million
Michaels Stores **Retail stores** The POS systems at 54 Michaels stores were attacked by criminals using highly sophisticated malware between May 2013 and January 2014.		2.6 million payment card numbers and expiration dates
Adobe **Software vendor** The stolen files contained active and inactive accounts for numerous Adobe products: Acrobat, Photoshop, ColdFusion, and CreativeCloud. The files hold Adobe IDs, e-mail addresses, passwords, credit/debit card numbers, expiration dates, and other PII (Personally Identifiable Information).		150 million
Target 2nd largest discount retailer in the United States		110 million
UbiSoft 3rd largest gaming company in Europe and the United States		58 million
Turkish Government No antivirus software was installed on the hacked system.		54 million
Evernote Online note-taking service		50 million
Living Social Daily deals website		50 million
Cupid Media **Popular dating service** The records of 56 Department of Homeland Security employees were stolen in this breach.		42 million

worldwide in 2013. The consequences of lax cybersecurity include damaged reputations, financial penalties, federal and state government fines, lost market share, falling share prices, and consumer backlash.

The main cause of a data breach is hacking, but the reason hacking is so successful is *negligence*—management not doing enough to defend against cyberthreats. Even high-tech companies and market leaders, as shown in Table 5.1, appear to be detached from the value of the confidential data they store and the threat that highly motivated hackers will try to steal them. As you will read in this section, robust data security is not the responsibility of IT alone, but the ongoing duty of everyone in an organization.

Hacks of high-tech companies like LinkedIn, Google, Amazon, eBay, and Sony, and top security agencies like the CIA and FBI are proof that no one is safe. Cyberwarriors are too well funded and motivated. Countering cyber-threats demands diligence, determination, and investment. IT at Work 5.1 illustrates the self-destructing and encryption features of a secure smartphone in order to protect conversations, transmissions, and stored data effectively.

IT at Work 5.1

Black—the Self-Destructing Smartphone

Boeing Co. is an aerospace and defense contractor known for its fighter planes, jets, and satellites (Figure 5.4). It possesses advanced technology that prevents its products from being hacked. Boeing made the unusual decision to build a smartphone that provides complete security against hacking and spying by governments or well-financed adversaries. The **Black smartphone**, released in 2014, is an Android phone manufactured as a sealed device, with both epoxy around the casing and screws with tamper-proof covering. The phone encrypts voice and data communication and, if tampered with, self-destructs. For instance, any attempt to open the Black's casing deletes all data and software on the device and leaves it inoperable.

Boeing Black's Security Features

Manufactured in the United States, Black uses dual SIM cards to enable it to access multiple cell networks instead of a single network. It can be configured to connect with biometric sensors and to communicate via satellite. Due to the phone's security features, Boeing released few details about the wireless network operators or manufacturer it was working with. The advanced features needed to achieve this level of cybersecurity include:

- Encryption to store sensitive information securely
- Hardware root of trust to ensure software authenticity

Figure 5.4 Boeing Co. is best known as a jet and fighter plane manufacturer. The company expanded into the secure smartphone market with the release of Black.

© Jordan Tan/Shutterstock

- Hardware crypto engine to protect both stored and transmitted data
- Embedded secure components to enable trusted operations
- Trusted platform modules to provide secure key storage
- Secure boot to maintain device image integrity

Boeing applied the *defense-in-depth* model to Black to ensure that if one layer of security was compromised, other layers would continue to secure the device, its data, and transmissions. Multilayered defense-in-depth models are absolutely necessary.

Assessing the Value of Smartphone Security

According to Boeing's filings with the U.S. Federal Communications Commission (FCC), Black is designed for use by government agencies and contractors who need to secure their communication and data. It is also for companies aiming to keep their data away from the prying tactics of the NSA or other spying organizations. Black enables the secure access and exchange of critical data and communications on a trusted mobile device.

It is believed that the use of a secure smartphone like Black might have prevented a recent leaked telephone call that undercut Washington's diplomacy in Ukraine. A senior U.S. State Department officer and ambassador to Ukraine apparently used unencrypted cell phones for a call about political developments in Ukraine that became public—and caused embarrassment. All State Department government-owned BlackBerry devices have data encryption, but not voice encryption.

Sources: Compiled from Hosenball (2014), Westcott (2014), Boeing.com (2014), and Gallagher (2014).

Questions

1. Why do you think government-issued smartphones are a target for data theft and transmission theft?
2. What security precautions is Boeing taking with respect to the manufacture and sale of Black?
3. What security features are built into Black?
4. Why is voice encryption an important digital security measure?
5. Why is a defense-in-depth model vital to a security smartphone such as Black?

BATTLING CYBERTHREATS IS THE COST OF DOING BUSINESS

Cybersecurity experts warn that battling **distributed denial-of-service (DDoS)** and malware attacks has become part of everyday business for all organizations. **Hackers, hactivists**, crime syndicates, the military, militant groups, industrial spies, disgruntled employees, fraudsters, and hostile governments will continue to attack networks for profit, fame, revenge, or an ideology; to wage warfare, terrorism, or an antiterrorism campaign; or to disable their target. For example, the Department of Homeland Security (DHS) Industrial Control Systems Cyber Emergency Response Team (ICS-CERT) warned that attacks against **critical infrastructure** are growing (Figure 5.5). There were more than 200 brute-force cyberattack incidents reported

© Werner Nick/Age Fotostock © alptraum/Age Fotostock

© Zoonar/NREY/ Age Fotostock © Zoonar/unknown/ Age Fotostock © Blakeley/Age Fotostock © Philip Lange/Age Fotostock

Figure 5.5 Six of the 18 national critical infrastructures (from upper left, clockwise): commercial facilities; defense industrial base; transportation systems; national monuments and icons; banking and finance; and agriculture and food.

A **distributed denial-of-service (DDoS)** attack bombards a network or website with traffic (i.e., *requests for service*) to crash it and leave it vulnerable to other threats.

Hactivist is short for hacker-activist or someone who does hacking for a cause. Hacking, regardless of motive, is a crime.

Critical infrastructure is defined as "systems and assets, whether physical or virtual, so vital to the United States that the incapacity or destruction of such systems and assets would have a debilitating impact on security, national economic security, national public health or safety, or any combination of those matters."

between October and May 2013, surpassing the 198 total attacks in all of fiscal year 2012. More than half of the attacks were against the energy sector. Attacks on critical infrastructure could significantly disrupt the functioning of government and business—and trigger cascading effects far beyond the targeted sector and physical location of the incident.

International, federal, and state laws and industry regulations mandate that enterprises invest in cybersecurity defenses, audits, and internal controls to help secure confidential data, prevent attacks, and defend against fraud and unauthorized transactions such as money laundering. To help keep managers updated on the latest cyberthreats and prioritize defenses, KPMG publishes its *Data Loss Barometer*. The annual report describes the latest trends and statistics for data losses worldwide. Key findings and predictions are listed in Table 5.2.

Social Engineering and BYOD

New cyberthreats are emerging and overtaking the familiar threats—viruses, lost disks, and DDoS attacks. Experts believe the greatest cybersecurity dangers over the next few years will involve persistent threats, mobile computing, and the use of social media for social engineering. **Social engineering** is also known as human hacking—tricking users into revealing their credentials and then using them to gain access to networks or accounts. From an IT security perspective, social engineering is a hacker's clever use of deception or manipulation of people's tendency to trust, be helpful, or simply follow their curiosity. Powerful IT security systems cannot defend against what appears to be authorized access.

Humans are easily hacked, making them and their social media posts high-risk attack vectors. For instance, it is often easy to get users to infect their corporate network or mobiles by tricking them into downloading and installing malicious apps or backdoors.

Another more recent vulnerability is **bring your own device (BYOD).** The BYOD trend is driven by employees using their own devices for business purposes because they are more powerful than those the company has provided. Another factor is mobility. More and more people are working from home and on the go—putting an end to the formerly typical 9 to 5 workday. In consequence, employees do not want to juggle multiple devices. With BYOD, companies cut costs by not having to purchase and maintain mobile devices.

Of course, when an employee's device is lost, the company can suffer a data breach if the device is not encrypted. In the past, and before the BYOD push,

---

TABLE 5.2 KPMG Data Loss Barometer

Key findings from *KPMG Data Loss Barometer Report* and its predictions for the next few years:

- Hacking is the number-one cause of data loss.
- Internal threats have reduced significantly, while external threats are increasing significantly.
- The most hacked sectors are technology, financial services, retail, and media.
- Expect increased loss of data from mobile devices.
- Expect a steep rise in automated hacking and botnets.
- Expect less tolerant regulators and greater fines and negative consequences.
- Expect greater visibility and reporting of data loss as a result of less tolerant regulators.

Source: KPMG (2012).

employees would be at their desks on a land line and on a computer plugged into the wall with a network cable. This change in exposure requires greater investment to defend against BYOD risks.

Cybercrime Survey

Respondents to the *2013 U.S. State of Cybercrime Survey* indicated that security incidents increased 33 percent despite implementation of security practices. Current cybersecurity technologies and policies are simply not keeping pace with fast-evolving threats. Many threats and challenges that organizations face today were unimaginable 10 years ago. And longstanding threats such as fraud and identity theft still remain. Cyberthreats will continue to emerge, evolve, and worsen over the next 10 years and beyond. IT at Work 5.2 provides a summary of the *2014 Global State of Information Security Survey*. The results of Survey 2014 show that executives are responding to the need to fund enhanced security activities and have substantially improved technology safeguards, processes, and strategies. Unfortunately, adversaries have done better.

HIGH-VISIBILITY CYBERCRIMINALS AND HACKTIVISTS

Advanced persistent threat (APT) attackers want to remain unnoticed so they can continue to steal data, as described in IT at Work 5.2. Profit-motivated cybercriminals often operate in stealth mode. In contrast, hackers and hacktivists with personal agendas carry out high-profile attacks.

IT at Work 5.2

Global State of Information Security Survey

The *2014 Global State of Information Security Survey* is conducted by the consulting firm PwC US (Pricewaterhouse Coopers, pwc.com) and CIO and CSO magazines (PWC, 2014). According to the annual global survey:

- **Defending yesterday.** While organizations have improved security significantly, they are not keeping pace with today's determined adversaries. Too many rely on yesterday's cybersecurity practices that are ineffective at combating today's threats.

- **Bigger attack surface.** The attack surface—consisting of business partners, suppliers, customers, and others—has expanded due to larger volumes of data flowing through multiple channels. Protecting all data at an equally high level is no longer practical. Cybersecurity strategies need to classify and prioritize defenses.

- **Implementing before securing.** Popular technologies like cloud computing, mobile, and BYOD (bring your own device) are implemented before they are secured.

- **Not ready for next-generation cyberthreats.** Few organizations are prepared to manage future threats. According

to Gary Loveland, a principal in PwC's security practice, "What's needed is a new model of information security, one that is driven by knowledge of threats, assets, and the motives and targets of potential adversaries" (PWC, 2014).

- **Unsafe cloud.** While 47 percent of respondents use cloud computing, only 18 percent include provisions for cloud in their security policy. SaaS is the most widely adopted cloud service, but PaaS shows strong growth.

- **Unprepared for advanced persistent threats (APT).** Among the most dangerous cyberthreats are advanced persistent threats (APT). APT is a stealth network attack in which an unauthorized person gains access to a network and remains undetected for a long time. Skilled hackers launch APT attacks to steal data continuously (e.g., daily) over months or year—rather than to cause damage that would reveal their presence. APTs require a new information-protection model that focuses on continuous monitoring of network activity and high-value information. Most U.S organizations lack these capabilities.

Hacktivists' Motivations and Dangerous Pranks

LulzSec is a hacker group and spin-off of the loosely organized hacking collective.

These types of cybercriminals seemed to take on everyone from Sony and security firm RSA to the CIA (Central Intelligence Agency) and a Mexican drug cartel throughout 2011 and 2012. During the Arab Spring (street revolutions of 2013), hacktivists **LulzSec** and **Anonymous** showed how vulnerable anyone's online presence was, even that of major governments. One of LulzSec's specialties is finding websites with poor security, and then stealing and posting information from them online. Some of their attacks may seem more like Internet pranks than serious cyberwarfare, but they are still illegal.

Hacktivist Attacks and Victims

Hackers committed daring data breaches, compromises, data leaks, thefts, threats, and privacy invasions in 2012. Two cases are listed below.

Combined Systems, Inc. Proudly displaying its hacktivist flag, Anonymous took credit for knocking Combined Systems, Inc. offline and stealing personal data from its clients. Anonymous went after Combined Systems, which sells tear gas and crowd-control devices to law enforcement and military organizations, to protest war profiteers.

CIA. In February 2012, for the second time in less than a year, Anonymous launched a denial of service (DoS) attack that forced the CIA website offline. The CIA takedown followed a busy week for the hacktivists. Within 10 days, the group also went after Chinese electronics manufacturer Foxconn, American Nazi groups, antivirus firm Symantec, and the office of Syria's president.

STEALTH, PROFIT-MOTIVATED CYBERCRIMES

Most hack activities do not become headline-grabbers until after the incidents are detected and reported. However, victimized companies are reluctant to discuss them so statistics are scarce. Most data breaches go unreported, according to cybersecurity experts, because corporate victims fear that disclosure would damage their stock price, or because they never knew they were hacked in the first place.

Theft of Trade Secrets and Other Confidential Information

Theft of trade secrets has always been a threat from corporate moles, disgruntled employees, and other insiders. Of course, now it is easier to steal information remotely, mostly because of smartphones and the BYOD trend. Hackers' preferred modus operandi is to break into employees' mobile devices and leapfrog into employers' networks—stealing secrets without a trace.

U.S. cybersecurity experts and government officials are increasingly concerned about breaches from other countries into corporate networks either through mobile devices or other means. Mike McConnell, former director of the National Security Agency (NSA), warned: "In looking at computer systems of consequence—in government, Congress, at the Department of Defense, aerospace, companies with valuable trade secrets—we've not examined one yet that has not been infected by an advanced persistent threat" (Perlroth, 2012b). In the meantime, companies are leaking critical information, often without realizing it. Scott Aken, a former FBI agent who specializes in counterintelligence and computer intrusion, stated, "In most cases, companies do not realize they've been burned until years later when a foreign competitor puts out their very same product—only they're making it 30 percent cheaper" (Perlroth, 2012b).

Do-Not-Carry Rules

U.S. companies, government agencies, and organizations are now imposing **do-not-carry rules**, which are based on the assumption that devices will inevitably be compromised according to Mike Rogers, current chairman of the House Intelligence Committee. House members can bring only "clean" devices and are forbidden from connecting to the government's network while abroad. Rogers said he travels "electronically naked" to ensure cybersecurity during and after a trip. IT at Work 5.3 describes the reasons for following do-not-carry rules.

IT at Work 5.3

Traveling Electronically Clean

When Kenneth G. Lieberthal, an expert at the Brookings Institution, travels to other countries, he follows a routine that seems straight from a secret agent movie. He leaves his smartphone and laptop at home. Instead, he brings loaner devices, which he erases before he leaves the United States and wipes clean the minute he returns. While traveling, he disables Bluetooth and Wi-Fi and never lets his phone out of his sight. While in meetings, he not only turns off his phone, but also removes the battery for fear his microphone could be turned on remotely.

Lieberthal connects to the Internet only through an encrypted, password-protected channel. He never types in a password directly, but copies and pastes his password from a USB thumb drive. By not typing his password, he eliminates the risk of having it stolen if key-logging software were to be installed on his device.

Questions

1. Many travelers might consider Lieberthal's method too inconvenient. Clearly, his electronically clean methods are time-consuming and expensive. In your opinion, is there a trade-off between cybersecurity and convenience? Explain.

2. Create a list of best cybersecurity practices for travelers based on Lieberthal's methods.

The U.S. Chamber of Commerce did not learn that it and its member organizations were the victims of a cybertheft for months until the FBI informed the Chamber that servers in China were stealing data from four of its Asia policy experts, individuals who frequently travel to Asia (Perlroth, 2012a). Most likely, the experts' mobile devices had been infected with malware that was transmitting information and files back to the hackers. By the time the Chamber hardened (secured) its network, hackers had stolen at least six weeks of e-mails, most of which were communications with the largest U.S. corporations. Even later, the Chamber learned that its office printer and a thermostat in one of its corporate apartments were communicating with an Internet address in China. The Chamber did not disclose how hackers had infiltrated its systems, but its first step was to implement do-not-carry rules.

OBJECTIVES OF CYBERSECURITY

Cybersecurity needs to accomplish the following:

- Make data and documents available and accessible 24/7 while simultaneously restricting access.
- Implement and enforce procedures and acceptable use policies (AUPs) for data, networks, hardware, and software that are company- or employee-owned, as discussed in the opening case.
- Promote secure and legal sharing of information among authorized persons and partners.
- Ensure compliance with government regulations and laws.
- Prevent attacks by having network intrusion defenses in place.
- Detect, diagnose, and respond to incidents and attacks in real time.
- Maintain internal controls to prevent unauthorized alteration of data and records.
- Recover from business disasters and disruptions quickly.

Business policies, procedures, training, and disaster recovery plans as well as hardware and software are critical cybersecurity.

In 2013 cyberthreats were at the top of US intelligence reports for the first time. Cyberthreats are now the number one type of danger facing the United States, according to current U.S. National Intelligence Director James Clapper, who coordinates the CIA, NSA, and many other agencies.

Questions

1. Why was 2013 dubbed the "Year of the Breach"?
2. What causes or contributes to data breaches?
3. Why are cybercriminals so successful?
4. What was the biggest data breach in history?
5. Describe the basic method of a distributed denial-of-service (DDoS) attack.
6. What is a critical infrastructure? List three types of critical infrastructures.
7. What are the motives of hactivists?
8. What is the number-one cause of data loss or breaches?
9. Why is social engineering a technique used by hackers to gain access to a network?
10. What are two BYOD security risks?
11. Explain why APT attacks are difficult to detect.
12. What are the objectives of cybersecurity?

5.2 Cyber Risk Management

Every enterprise has data that profit-motivated criminals want. Customer data, networks, websites, proprietary information systems, and patents are examples of **assets**—things of value that need to be protected. The greater the value of the asset to the company and to criminals, the greater the security needs to be. The smart strategy is to invest more to protect the company's most valuable assets rather than try to protect all assets equally, as discussed in IT at Work 5.2. The IT security field—like sports and law—has its own terminology, which is summarized for quick reference in Table 5.3 and Figure 5.6.

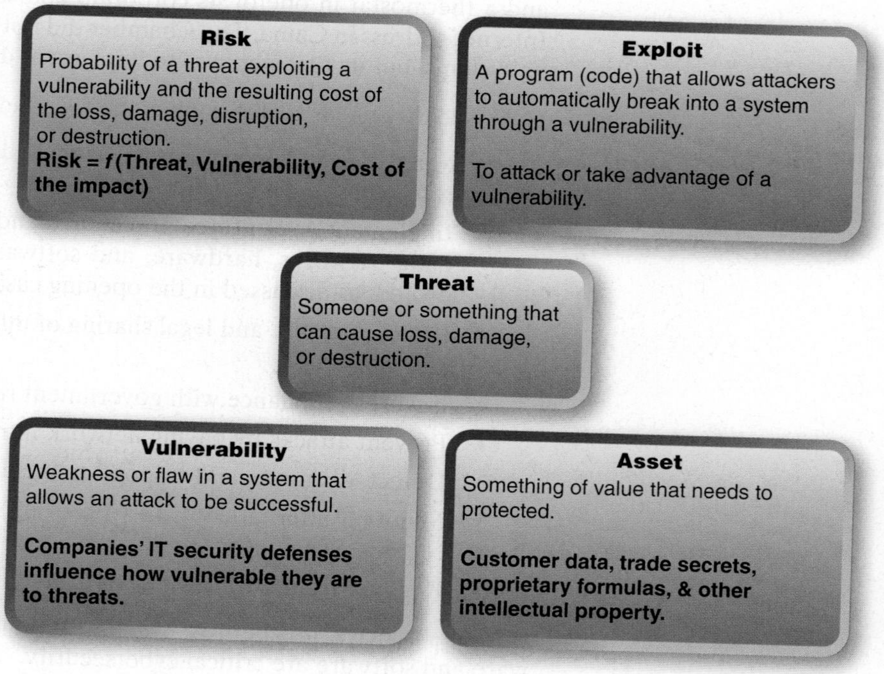

Risk
Probability of a threat exploiting a vulnerability and the resulting cost of the loss, damage, disruption, or destruction.
Risk = f(Threat, Vulnerability, Cost of the impact)

Exploit
A program (code) that allows attackers to automatically break into a system through a vulnerability.

To attack or take advantage of a vulnerability.

Threat
Someone or something that can cause loss, damage, or destruction.

Vulnerability
Weakness or flaw in a system that allows an attack to be successful.

Companies' IT security defenses influence how vulnerable they are to threats.

Asset
Something of value that needs to protected.

Customer data, trade secrets, proprietary formulas, & other intellectual property.

Figure 5.6 Basic IT security concepts.

TABLE 5.3 Definitions of IT Security Terms

Term	Definition
Threat	Something or someone that may result in harm to an asset
Risk	Probability of a threat exploiting a vulnerability
Vulnerability	A weakness that threatens the confidentiality, integrity, or availability (CIA) of an asset
CIA triad (confidentiality, integrity, availability)	Three key cybersecurity principles
Exploit	Tool or technique that takes advantage of a vulnerability
Risk management	Process of identifying, assessing, and reducing risk to an acceptable level
Exposure	Estimated cost, loss, or damage that can result if a threat exploits a vulnerability
Access control	Security feature designed to restrict who has access to a network, IS, or data
Audit	Procedure of generating, recording, and reviewing a chronological record of system events to determine their accuracy
Encryption	Transforming data into scrambled code to protect them from being understood by unauthorized users
Plaintext or clear text	Readable text
Ciphertext	Encrypted text
Authentication	Method (usually based on username and password) by which an IS validates or verifies that a user is really who he or she claims to be
Biometrics	Methods to identify a person based on a biological feature, such as a fingerprint or retina
Firewall	Software or hardware device that controls access to a private network from a public network (Internet) by analyzing data packets entering or exiting it
Intrusion detection system (IDS)	A defense tool used to monitor network traffic (packets) and provide alerts when there is suspicious traffic, or to quarantine suspicious traffic
Fault tolerance	The ability of an IS to continue to operate when a failure occurs, but usually for a limited time or at a reduced level
Botnet (short for Bot network)	A network of hijacked computers that are controlled remotely—typically to launch spam or spyware. Also called software robots. Botnets are linked to a range of malicious activity, including identity theft and spam.

Confidentiality: No unauthorized data disclosure.

Integrity: Data, documents, messages, and other files have not been altered in any unauthorized way.

Availability: Data is accessible when needed by those authorized to do so.

Figure 5.7 Three objectives of data and information systems security.

A **threat** is something or someone that can damage, disrupt, or destroy an asset. **Vulnerabilities** are gaps, holes, weaknesses, or flaws in corporate networks, IT security defenses, user training, policy enforcement, data storage, software, operating systems, apps, or mobile devices that expose an organization to intrusions or other attacks. Vulnerabilities threaten the confidentiality, integrity, or availability (CIA) of data and information systems, as defined in Figure 5.7.

Vulnerabilities exist in networks, operating systems, apps, databases, mobile devices, and cloud environments. These vulnerabilities are **attack vectors** or entry points for malware, hackers, hactivists, and organized crime.

The term **exploit** has more than one meaning. An exploit is a hacker tool or software program used to break into a system, database, or device. An attack or action that takes advantage of a vulnerability is also called an exploit. Criminal and terrorist groups buy exploits from more than 25 underground forums or brokers. Exploits themselves are not against the law, and several legitimate firms also sell them. For example, in 2012 Massachusetts-based Netragard (netragard.com) sold more than 50 exploits to businesses and government agencies in the United States for prices ranging from $20,000 to more than $250,000.

Risk is the probability of a threat successfully exploiting a vulnerability and the estimated cost of the loss or damage. For example, car insurance premiums are based on risk calculations that take into consideration the probability of an accident and the cost of the damage.

TECH NOTE 5.1 Vulnerabilities in Microsoft Sidebar and Gadgets

In July 2012 Microsoft issued a *security advisory* warning of vulnerabilities in Gadgets and Sidebar:

> We've discovered that some Vista and Win7 gadgets don't adhere to secure coding practices and should be regarded as causing risk to the systems on which they're run.

Hackers Exploit Gadget: How Did They Do That?

A vulnerability in Windows Gadgets makes it easy for hackers to gain access and run malware or a malicious app as if the hacker were the real user. That means, if the legitimate user is logged on with administrative (admin) user rights, then those rights give the attacker complete control of the system.

Security Solution: *Fix It*

An automated Fix It solution was posted on Microsoft's support site. Clicking the Fix It button disabled the Windows Sidebar and Gadgets on Windows Vista and Windows 7 platforms, so the vulnerability could not be exploited.

Key Observation

Toolbars, gadgets, and any other add-ons are pieces of code, or software—and can create vulnerabilities or actually be malware. Many free add-ons, apps, and other downloads are trojans. These trojans look and function as you expect them to, but in stealth mode they track everything you do on the Internet and then send that information to the creator of the malware.

| HACKERS: INTERNET UNTOUCHABLES

How big is the threat of malware? IT security researchers discover roughly 70,000 malicious programs every day. Why would so many hackers be spending so much time generating or launching these programs? The simple answers are that hacking is a profitable industry, a big part of underworld cybercrime, and a way for hactivists to protest. Hackers feel untouchable knowing that they face very low risk of capture and punishment.

Inside Look at How the Hacking Industry Operates

Hacking is an industry with its own way of operating, a workforce, and support services. **Contract hackers** are available for hire or complete hack attacks can be bought. Hacking help desks provide 24/7 support—making sophisticated attacks easier to arrange. Hackers use social networks and underground forums to share exploits, usernames, and passwords—the credentials needed to infect users' personal and work accounts.

Organized crime groups quickly learned that cybercrimes have better payoffs than the drug trade and with almost no risk. They become virtually untouchable by law enforcement because no one sees the crime. It is not surprising then that almost every survey reaches the same troubling conclusion—the costs and frequency of cybercrimes are increasing. That means much stronger IT security practices and defenses are obviously needed. One of the greatest weaknesses is users who ignore the dangers of weak passwords. Password management is essential to security.

Users Set Themselves up for Cybermuggings

In July 2012 the hacker group *D33Ds Company* published almost half a million e-mail addresses and passwords on underground sites that allegedly had been stolen from Yahoo. D33Ds claims it hacked into Yahoo's database by exploiting a common vulnerability that had not been patched. Here is a breakdown of the users whose passwords invited a cybermugging:

- 1,600 users used "1234546"
- 800 users used "password"
- 1,400 users used "mypassword" or "password" as the base word, such as "password1"

Weak passwords are clearly dangerous. If any password, such as for Adobe software, becomes known to hackers, they can try that e-mail/password combination at all popular sites like Facebook, Gmail, and so on and compromise not one but many of your accounts. Unfortunately, too many people are lazy and choose passwords that are easily guessable, short, common, or a word in the dictionary. Strong passwords contain a combination of upper- and lowercase letters, numbers, and punctuation marks, and are at least eight characters long.

Internal Threats

Threats from employees, referred to as **internal threats**, are a major challenge largely due to the many ways an employee can carry out malicious activity. Insiders may be able to bypass physical security (e.g., locked doors) and technical security (e.g., passwords) measures that organizations have put in place to prevent unauthorized access. Why? Because defenses such as firewalls, intrusion detection systems (IDS), and locked doors mostly protect against external threats. Despite the challenges, insider incidents can be minimized with a layered defense-in-depth strategy consisting of security procedures, acceptable use policies, and technology controls.

Phishing and Web-based Threats

Companies increasingly adopt external, Web-based applications and employees bring consumer applications into the enterprise. Criminal enterprises are following the money on the Internet, a global market of potential victims.

Phishing is a deceptive method of stealing confidential information by pretending to be a legitimate organization, such as PayPal, a bank, credit card company, or other trusted source. Phishing messages include a link to a fraudulent phish website that looks like the real one. When the user clicks the link to the phish site, he or she is asked for a credit card number, social security number, account number, or password. Phishing remains successful and profitable for criminals.

Criminals use the Internet and private networks to hijack large numbers of PCs to spy on users, spam them, shake down businesses, and steal identities. But why are they so successful? The Information Security Forum (securityforum.org), a self-help organization that includes many Fortune 100 companies, compiled a list of the top information problems and discovered that nine of the top ten incidents were the result of three factors:

1. Mistakes or human error
2. Malfunctioning systems
3. Misunderstanding the effects of adding incompatible software to an existing system

Unfortunately, these factors can too easily defeat cybersecurity technologies that companies and individuals use to protect their information. A fourth factor identified by the Security Forum is motivation, as described in IT at Work 5.4.

IT at Work 5.4

Money Laundering, Organized Crime, and Terrorist Financing

According to the U.S. Department of State (state.gov), organized crime rings rely on money laundering to fund their operations. This practice poses international and national security threats. It undermines free enterprise by crowding out the private sector, and it threatens the financial stability of nations.

Funds used to finance terrorist operations are very difficult to track. Despite this obscurity, by adapting methods used to combat money laundering, such as financial analysis and investigations, authorities can significantly disrupt the financial networks of terrorists and build a paper trail and base of evidence to identify and locate leaders of terrorist organizations and cells.

International organized crime syndicates, al-Qaeda–affiliated groups, and other cybercriminals steal hundreds of billions of dollars every year. Cybercrime is safer and easier than selling drugs, dealing in black market diamonds, or robbing banks. Online gambling offers easy fronts for international money-laundering operations.

GOVERNMENT REGULATIONS

IT defenses must satisfy ever-stricter government and international regulations. Primary regulations are the United States' Sarbanes-Oxley Act (SOX), Gramm-Leach-Bliley Act (GLB), Federal Information Security Management Act (FISMA), and USA PATRIOT Act; Japan's Personal Information Protection Act; Canada's Personal Information Protection and Electronic Document Act (PIPEDA); Australia's Federal Privacy Act; the United Kingdom's Data Protection Act; and global financial services' Basel III. All mandate the protection of personally iden-tifiable information (PII). The director of the Bureau of Consumer Protection at the Federal Trade Commission (FTC) warned that the agency would bring enforce-ment action against small businesses lacking adequate policies and procedures to protect consumer data.

Two accepted models for IT governance are **enterprise risk management (ERM)** and **Control Objectives for Information** and **Related Technology (COBIT)**. ERM is a risk-based approach to managing an enterprise that integrates internal control, the Sarbanes–Oxley Act mandates, and strategic planning. ERM is intended to be part of routine planning processes rather than a separate initiative. The ideal place to start is with buy-in and commitment from the board and senior leadership.

COBIT, which is described in IT at Work 5.5, is an internationally accepted IT governance and control framework for aligning IT with business objectives, deliver-ing value, and managing associated risks. It provides a reference for management, users, and IS audit, control, and security practitioners.

IT at Work 5.5

COBIT and IT Governance Best Practices

IT governance is the supervision, monitoring, and control of an organization's IT assets. The IT Governance Institute (itgi.org) publishes COBIT, which many companies use as their IT governance guide. COBIT can be downloaded from isaca.org.

The Sarbanes-Oxley Act requires that companies pro-vide proof that their financial applications and systems are controlled (secured) to verify that financial reports can be trusted. This requires that IT security managers work with business managers to do a risk assessment to identify which systems depend on technical controls rather than on busi-ness process controls. To meet COBIT, IT systems should be based on the following three principles:

- *Principle of economic use of resources:* This principle acknowledges that the cost of information security needs to be balanced with its benefits. It is the basic cost–benefit principle with which you are familiar. For example, you would not spend more to protect your auto, home, or other asset than they were worth. Because it is possible, for instance, for companies to set a very low value on the confidential data of customers and employers and therefore avoid basic information security defenses, the next two principles try to ensure that this does not happen.

- *Principle of legality:* This principle requires that compa-nies invest in information security to meet minimum legal requirements. This is a basic security principle, just like having hand railings on stairways, fire extinguishers, and alarm systems.

- *Accounting principles:* These principles require that the integrity, availability, and reliability of data and informa-tion systems be maintained.

INDUSTRY STANDARDS

Industry groups imposed their own standards to protect their customers and their members' brand images and revenues. One example is the **Payment Card Industry Data Security Standard (PCI DSS)** created by Visa, MasterCard, American Express, and Discover. PCI is required for all members, merchants, or service pro-viders that store, process, or transmit cardholder data. PCI DSS requires merchants and card payment providers to make certain their Web applications are secure. If done correctly, this could reduce the number of Web-related security breaches.

The purpose of the PCI DSS is to improve customers' trust in e-commerce, especially when it comes to online payments, and to increase the Web security of online merchants. To motivate following these standards, the penalties for noncompliance are severe. The card brands can fine the retailer, and increase transaction fees for each credit or debit card transaction. A finding of noncompliance can be the basis for lawsuits.

IT SECURITY DEFENSE-IN-DEPTH MODEL

Defense-in-depth is a multilayered approach to information security. The basic principle is that when one defense layer fails, another layer provides protection. For example, if a wireless network's security was compromised, then having encrypted data would still protect the data, provided that the thieves could not decrypt it.

The success of any type of IT project depends on the commitment and involvement of executive management, also referred to as the *tone at the top*. The same is true of IT security. This information security tone makes users aware that insecure practices and mistakes will not be tolerated. Therefore, an IT security model begins with senior management commitment and support, as shown in Figure 5.8. The model views information security as a combination of people, processes, and technology.

Step 1: Senior management commitment and support. Senior managers' influence is needed to implement and maintain security, ethical standards, privacy practices, and internal control. IT security is best when it is top-driven. Senior managers decide how stringent infosec policies and practices should be in order to comply with laws and regulations. Financial institutions are subject to strict security and antimoney laundering (AML) rules because they face numerous national and international regulations and have high-value data. Advertising agencies and less regulated firms tend to have more lenient rules. Other factors influencing infosec policies are a corporation's culture and how valuable their data are to criminals.

For instance, management may decide to forbid employees from using company e-mail accounts for nonwork purposes, accessing social media during work hours, or visiting gambling sites. These decisions will then become rules stated in company policy, integrated into procedures, and implemented with technology defenses. Sites that are forbidden, for instance, can be blocked by firewalls.

Step 2: Acceptable use policies and IT security training. Organizations need to put in place strong policies and processes that make responsibilities and accountabilities clear to all employees. An **acceptable use policy (AUP)** explains what management has decided are acceptable and unacceptable activities, and the consequences of noncompliance. Rules about tweets, texting, social media, e-mail, apps, and hardware should be treated as extensions of other corporate policies—such as physical safety, equal opportunity, harassment, and discrimination. No policy can address

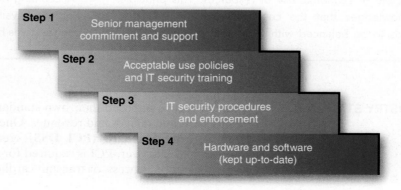

Figure 5.8 IT security defense-in-depth model.

Step 1 — Senior management commitment and support

Step 2 — Acceptable use policies and IT security training

Step 3 — IT security procedures and enforcement

Step 4 — Hardware and software (kept up-to-date)

every future situation, so rules need to be evaluated, updated, or modified. For example, if a company suffers a malware infection traced to an employee using an unprotected smartphone to connect to the company network, policies to restrict or prohibit those connections might be advisable.

Step 3: IT security procedures and enforcement. Secure procedures define how policies will be enforced, how incidents will be prevented, and how to respond to an incident. Here are the basic secure procedures to put in place:

1. **Define enforcement procedures.** Rules that are defined in the AUP must be enforced and enforcement procedures must be applied consistently. Procedures for monitoring employee Internet and network usage are defined at this stage.

2. **Designate and empower an internal incident response team (IRT).** The IRT typically includes the CISO, legal counsel, senior managers, experienced communicators, and key operations staff. Minimizing the team size and bureaucracy can expedite decision making and response. Because there may be significant liability issues, legal counsel needs to be involved in incident response planning and communication.

3. **Define notification procedures.** When a data breach occurs, the local police department, local office of the FBI, Securities and Exchange Commission (SEC), the U.S. Secret Service, or other relevant agency needs to be notified immediately. Federal and state laws or industry regulations may define how and when affected people need to be notified.

4. **Define a breach response communications plan.** Effective incident response communication plans include personnel and processes with lists, channels, and social media needed to execute all communications that might be needed.

5. **Monitor information and social media sources.** Monitor Twitter, social media, and news coverage as a standard procedure to understand how people are responding to the incident and criticizing the company. Damage control procedures may be needed.

When an incident occurs, the organization is ready to respond intelligently—having the correct information to be honest, open, and accountable, and to communicate with consumers and other important audiences as quickly as possible.

Step 4: Hardware and software. The last step in the model is implementation of software and hardware needed to support and enforce the AUP and secure practices. The selection of hardware and software defenses is based on risk, security budget, AUP, and secure procedures. Every device that connects to an organization's network; every online activity and mobile app of employees; and each file sent or received is an access point. Technology defense mechanisms need to be:

- able to provide strong authentication and access control.
- industrial-grade.
- appropriate for the types of networks and operating systems.
- installed and configured correctly.
- tested rigorously.
- maintained regularly.

Keep in mind that security is an ongoing unending process, and not a problem that can be solved with hardware or software. Hardware and software security defenses cannot protect against irresponsible business practices.

One of the biggest mistakes managers make is underestimating IT vulnerabilities and threats. Most workers use their laptops and mobiles for both work and leisure, and in an era of multitasking, they often do both at the same time. Yet offtime or offsite use of devices remains risky because, despite policies, employees continue to engage in dangerous online and communication habits. Those habits make them a weak link in an organization's otherwise solid security efforts. These threats can be classified as *unintentional* or *intentional*.

UNINTENTIONAL THREATS

Unintentional threats fall into three major categories: human error, environmental hazards, and computer system failures.

- **Human error** can occur in the design of the hardware or information system. It can also occur during programming, testing, or data entry. Not changing default passwords on a firewall or failing to manage patches creates security holes. Human errors also include untrained or unaware users responding to phishing scams or ignoring security procedures. Human errors contribute to the majority of internal control and information security problems.

- **Environmental hazards** include volcanoes, earthquakes, blizzards, floods, power failures or strong fluctuations, fires (the most common hazard), defective air conditioning, explosions, radioactive fallout, and water-cooling-system failures. In addition to the primary damage, computer resources can be damaged by side effects, such as smoke and water. Such hazards may disrupt normal computer operations and result in long waiting periods and exorbitant costs while computer programs and data files are recreated.

- **Computer systems failures** can occur as the result of poor manufacturing, defective materials, and outdated or poorly maintained networks. Unintentional malfunctions can also happen for other reasons, ranging from lack of experience to inadequate testing.

INTENTIONAL THREATS

Examples of intentional threats include data theft; inappropriate use of data (e.g., manipulating inputs); theft of mainframe computer time; theft of equipment and/or programs; deliberate manipulation in handling, entering, processing, transferring, or programming data; labor strikes, riots, or sabotage; malicious damage to computer resources; destruction from viruses and similar attacks; and miscellaneous computer abuses and Internet fraud.

TYPES OF MALWARE

Viruses, **worms**, **trojans**, **rootkits**, **backdoors**, **botnets**, and **keyloggers** are types of malware. Technically, malware is a computer program or code that can infect anything attached to the Internet and is able to process the code. Most viruses, trojans, and worms are activated when an attachment is opened or a link is clicked. But when features are automated, they may trigger malware automatically, too. For example:

- If an e-mail client, such as Microsoft Outlook or Gmail, is set to allow scripting, then virus infection occurs by simply opening a message or attachment.

- Viewing e-mail messages in HTML, instead of in plain text, can trigger virus infections.

Remote-access trojans, or **RATS**, create an unprotected backdoor into a system through which a hacker can remotely control that system. As the name implies, a backdoor provides easy access to a system, computer, or account by eliminating the need to authenticate with a username and password. Whenever you store your username and password, you create a backdoor to that account.

A malware's **payload** refers to the actions that occur after a system has been infected. The payload carries out the purpose of the malware. The payload could cause damage that is visible or operate in stealth mode so as to remain undetected. A **vector** is the specific method that malware uses to *propagate,* or spread, to other machines or devices. Malware may also *replicate,* or make copies of itself.

Today's malware is designed for long-term control of infected machines. Advanced malware sets up outbound communication channels in order to upload stolen data, download payloads, or do reconnaissance.

Malware creators use social engineering to maximize the range or impact of their viruses, worms, and so forth. For example, the *ILoveYou* worm used social engineering to entice people to open malware-infected e-mail messages. The ILoveYou worm attacked tens of millions of Windows computers in May 2000 when it was sent as an e-mail attachment with the subject line: ILOVEYOU. Often out of curiosity, people opened the attachment named LOVE-LETTER-FOR-YOU.TXT.vbs—releasing the worm. Within nine days, the worm had spread worldwide, crippling networks, destroying files, and causing an estimated $5.5 billion in damages. Notorious hacker Kevin Mitnick, who served time in jail for hacking, used social engineering as his primary method to gain access to computer networks. In most cases, the criminal never comes face-to-face with the victim, but communicates via the phone or e-mail.

Malware Reinfection, Signatures, Mutations, and Variants

When a host computer is infected, attempts to remove the malware may fail—and the malware may reinfect the host for these two reasons:

1. **Malware is captured in backups or archives.** Restoring the infected backup or archive also restores the malware.
2. **Malware infects removable media.** Months or years after the initial infection, the removable media may be accessed, and the malware could attempt to infect the host.

Most antivirus (AV) software relies on **signatures** to identify and then block malware. According to the Worldwide Malware Signature Counter, at the start of 2013, there were an estimated 19 million malware signatures. Detecting and preventing infections are not always a possibility. **Zero-day exploits**—malware so new their signatures are not yet known—are an example. Malware authors also evade detection by AV software and firewalls by altering malware code to create *variants*, which have new signatures. But not all procedures or AV tools are capable of removing every trace of the malware. Even if the malicious parts of the infection can be cleaned from a system, the remaining pieces of code could make the system unstable or exposed to future infection.

Data tampering is a common means of attack that is overshadowed by other types of attacks. It refers to an attack during which someone enters false or fraudulent data into a computer, or changes or deletes existing data. Data tampering is extremely serious because it may not be detected. This is the method often used by insiders and fraudsters.

TARGETED ATTACKS ON ENTERPRISES

Corporate and government secrets are currently being stolen by APTs. Most APT attacks are launched through phishing. Typically, this type of attack begins with some reconnaissance on the part of attackers. This can include researching publicly available information about the company and its employees, often from social networking sites. This information is then used to create targeted phishing e-mail messages. A successful attack could give the attacker access to the enterprise's network.

APTs are designed for long-term espionage. Once installed on a network, APTs transmit copies of documents, such as Microsoft Office files and PDFs, in stealth mode. APTs collect and store files on the company's network; encrypt them; then send them in bursts to servers often in China or Russia. This type of attack has been observed in other large-scale data breaches that exposed significant numbers of identities.

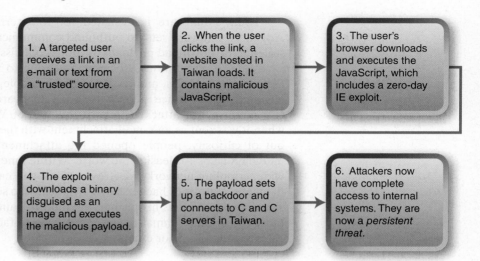

1. A targeted user receives a link in an e-mail or text from a "trusted" source.

2. When the user clicks the link, a website hosted in Taiwan loads. It contains malicious JavaScript.

3. The user's browser downloads and executes the JavaScript, which includes a zero-day IE exploit.

4. The exploit downloads a binary disguised as an image and executes the malicious payload.

5. The payload sets up a backdoor and connects to C and C servers in Taiwan.

6. Attackers now have complete access to internal systems. They are now a *persistent threat.*

Figure 5.9 Overview of the six steps in Operation Aurora APT attack.

APT Example: Operation Aurora

An attack named *Operation Aurora* proved to be very successful at targeting, exploiting, accessing, and stealing valuable intellectual property from its victims' databases. Operation Aurora attacked in six steps, as described in Figure 5.9. Standard IT security technologies failed to prevent these six steps from occurring and users did not know they had been hacked. Once attackers gain access to internal systems (Step 6), they can steal corporate secrets.

Botnets

A botnet is a collection of bots, which are malware-infected computers. Those infected computers, called zombies, can be controlled and organized into a network of zombies on the command of a remote botmaster (also called *bot herder*). *Storm* worm, which is spread via **spam,** is a botnet agent embedded inside over 25 million computers. Storm's combined power has been compared to the processing might of a supercomputer, and Storm-organized attacks are capable of crippling any website. Zombies can be commanded to monitor and steal personal or financial data—acting as spyware. Botnets are used to send spam and phishing e-mails and launch DDoS attacks. Botnets are extremely dangerous because they scan for and compromise other computers, which then can be used for every type of crime and attack against computers, servers, and networks.

Spear Phishing

Spear phishers often target select groups of people with something in common—they work at the same company, bank at the same financial institution, or attend the same university. The scam e-mails appear to be sent from organizations or people the potential victims normally receive e-mails from, making them even more deceptive.

Here is how **spear phishing** works:

1. Spear phish creators gather information about people's companies and jobs from social media or steal it from computers and mobile devices, and then use that same information to customize messages that trick users into opening an infected e-mail.

2. Then they send e-mails that look like the real thing to targeted victims, offering all sorts of urgent and legitimate-sounding explanations as to why they need your personal data.

3. Finally, the victims are asked to click on a link inside the e-mail that takes them to a phony but realistic-looking website, where they are asked to provide passwords, account numbers, user IDs, access codes, PINs, and so on.

IT Defenses

Since malware and botnets use many attack methods and strategies, multiple tools are needed to detect them and/or neutralize their effects. Three essential defenses are the following:

1. **Antivirus Software:** Antimalware tools are designed to detect malicious codes and prevent users from downloading them. They can also scan systems for the presence of worms, trojans, and other types of threats. This technology does not provide complete protection because it cannot defend against zero-day exploits. Antimalware may not be able to detect a previously unknown exploit.

2. **Intrusion Detection Systems (IDSs):** As the name implies, an IDS scans for unusual or suspicious traffic. An IDS can identify the start of a DoS attack by the traffic pattern, alerting the network administrator to take defensive action, such as switching to another IP address and diverting critical servers from the path of the attack.

3. **Intrusion Prevention Systems (IPSs):** An IPS is designed to take immediate action—such as blocking specific IP addresses—whenever a traffic-flow anomaly is detected. An application-specific integrated circuit–based (ASIC) IPS has the power and analysis capabilities to detect and block DDoS attacks, functioning somewhat like an automated circuit breaker.

Questions

1. What are threats, vulnerabilities, and risk?
2. Explain the three components of the CIA triad.
3. What is an attack vector? Give an example.
4. What is an exploit? Give an example.
5. What is a contract hacker?
6. Give an example of a weak password and a strong password.
7. How are phishing attacks done?
8. What are the four steps in the defense-in-depth IT security model?
9. Define and give an example of an unintentional threat.
10. Define and give an example of an intentional threat.
11. List and define three types of malware.
12. What are the risks caused by data tampering?
13. Define botnet and explain its risk.
14. Explain spear phishing.
15. What are the functions of an IDS and IPS?

5.3 Mobile, App, and Cloud Security

With the popularity of e-readers, netbooks, Google's Chrome OS, Facebook, YouTube, Twitter, LinkedIn, and other social networks, IT security dangers are growing worse.

CLOUD COMPUTING AND SOCIAL NETWORK RISKS

Social networks and cloud computing increase vulnerabilities by providing a single point of failure and attack for organized criminal networks. Critical, sensitive, and private information is at risk, and like previous IT trends, such as wireless networks, the goal is connectivity, often with little concern for security. As social networks increase their services, the gap between services and information security also increases. E-mail viruses and malware have been declining for years as e-mail security has improved. This trend continues as communication shifts to social networks and newer smartphones. Unfortunately, malware finds its way to users through security vulnerabilities in these new services and devices. Web filtering, user education, and strict policies are key to preventing widespread outbreaks.

In Twitter and Facebook, users invite in and build relationships with others. Cybercriminals hack into these trusted relationships using stolen logins. Fake antivirus and other attacks that take advantage of user trust are very difficult to detect.

An overriding reason why these networks and services increase exposure to risk is the **time-to-exploitation** of today's sophisticated spyware and mobile viruses. Time-to-exploitation is the elapsed time between when vulnerability is discovered and when it is exploited. That time has shrunk from months to minutes so IT staff have ever-shorter timeframes to find and fix flaws before they are compromised by an attack. Some attacks exist for as little as two hours, which means that enterprise IT security systems must have real time protection.

When new vulnerabilities are found in operating systems, applications, or wired and wireless networks, patches are released by the vendor or security organization. **Patches** are software programs that users download and install to fix a vulnerability. Microsoft, for example, releases patches that it calls **service packs** to update and fix vulnerabilities in its operating systems, including Vista, and applications, including Office 2010. Service packs can be downloaded from Microsoft's website.

Left undetected or unprotected, vulnerabilities provide an open door for IT attacks and business disruptions and their financial damages. Despite even the best technology defenses, information security incidents will occur mostly because of users who do not follow secure computing practices and procedures.

TECH NOTE 5.2 Android Botnet over SMS

A botnet of exploited Android phones was sending massive amounts of spam via Yahoo e-mail servers using the short messaging service (SMS) as the **command and control (C&C) channel**. Infected androids, or bots, log into the owner's Yahoo Mail account to send spam. Most of the devices were located in Chile, Venezuela, Thailand, Indonesia, Lebanon, Philippines, Russia, and Saudi Arabia—that is, in countries where users are less likely to get their Android apps from the Google Play market, which automatically ensures that the apps are safe. Users downloading free phone apps from third-party app stores to avoid paying for legitimate versions were actually downloading the Android malware.

User should only download apps from trusted sources and also check the reviews to verify the apps are legitimate because there are many bogus apps.

| BYOD

Users bringing their personal mobile devices and their own mobile apps to work and connecting them to the corporate network is part of the larger **consumerization of information technology (COIT)** trend. Bring your own device (BYOD) and bring your own apps (BYOA) are practices that move enterprise data and IT assets to employees' mobiles and the cloud, creating a new set of tough IT security challenges. Figure 5.10 summarizes how apps, mobiles, and cloud services put organizations at a greater risk of cyberattack. Widely used apps that are outside of the organization's firewall are Twitter, Google Analytics, Dropbox, WebEx, and Salesforce.com.

Enterprises take risks with BYOD practices that they never would consider taking with conventional computing devices. One possible reason is that new

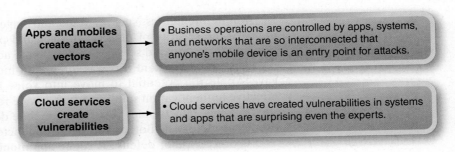

Figure 5.10 Factors that expose companies and users to attack.

devices, apps, and systems, such as the Windows Phone 7 platform, have been rolled out so quickly. As a result, smartphones are not being managed as secure devices, with fewer than 20 percent of users installing antimalware and 50 percent using some type of data encryption. In fact, employees expected instant approval of (or at least no disapproval of) and support for their new iPads within hours of the product's release.

BYOD raises serious and legitimate areas of concern. Hackers break into employees' mobile devices and leapfrog into employers' networks—stealing secrets without a trace. New vulnerabilities are created when personal and business data and communications are mixed together. All cybersecurity controls—authentication, access control, data confidentiality, and intrusion detection—implemented on corporate-owned resources can be rendered useless by an employee-owned device. Also, the corporation's mobile infrastructure may not be able to support the increase in mobile network traffic and data processing, causing unacceptable delays or requiring additional investments.

| NEW ATTACK VECTORS

Mobile devices and apps, social media, and cloud services introduce even more attack vectors for malware, phishing, and hackers. By mid-2012, roughly 75 percent of U.S. organizations had adopted BYOD practices, but many rushed in without considering security. Mobiles rarely have strong authentication, access controls, and encryption even though they connect to mission-critical data and cloud services. Only 20 percent of Androids have a security app installed.

Malicious (Rogue) Mobile Apps

The number of malicious Android apps is growing at an alarming rate. According to the report *Mobile Phone Biometric Security Analysis and Forecasts 2011–2015* (Egan, 2011), at least 5,000 new malicious Android apps were found in the first quarter of 2012 (Q1 2012). During the next quarter (Q2 2012), 10,000 new rogue apps were found within one month—and by the end of the quarter, there were 40,000 rogue apps (TrendMicro TrendLabs, 2012). Almost all of these apps were found in unreliable third-party stores. But 17 rogue apps managed to get into Google Play and they were downloaded over 700,000 times before being removed. Rogue mobile apps can serve up trojan attacks, other malware, or phishing attacks.

Companies offering legitimate apps for online banking, retail shopping, gaming, and other functions might not be aware of threats lurking in their app stores. And despite their best efforts, legitimate app store operators cannot reliably police their own catalogs for rogue apps.

With a single click on a malicious link, users can launch a targeted attack against their organizations.

Minimum Security Defenses for Mobiles

Minimum security defenses for mobile devices are mobile biometrics, rogue app monitoring, remote wipe capability, and encryption. For travelers, do-not-carry rules may be a necessary defense.

Mobile biometrics, such as voice and fingerprint biometrics, can significantly improve the security of physical devices and provide stronger authentication for remote access or cloud services. When Apple acquired Siri, Inc. in 2010, the voice-based personal assistant Siri was integrated into its operating system, **iOS 5**. Siri gave Apple the potential to move into **voice biometrics**. Voice biometrics is an effective authentication solution across a wide range of consumer devices including smartphones, tablets, and TVs. Future mobile devices are expected to have fingerprint sensors to add another authentication factor.

Another type of defense is **rogue app monitoring** to detect and destroy malicious apps in the wild. Several vendors offer 24/7 monitoring and detection services to monitor major app stores and shut down rogue apps to minimize exposure and damage.

In the event of loss or theft of a device, a mobile kill switch or **remote wipe capability** is needed as well as encryption. All major smartphone platforms have some kind of remote erase capability and encryption option.

In response to mobile security threats, many U.S. companies and government agencies are imposing do-not-carry rules on mobiles to prevent compromise. Travelers can bring only "clean" devices and are forbidden from connecting to the government's network while abroad.

Questions

1. How do social networks and cloud computing increase vulnerability?
2. Why are patches and service packs needed?
3. What is consumerization of information technology (COIT)?
4. Why does BYOD raise serious and legitimate areas of concern?
5. What are two types of mobile biometrics?
6. Explain rogue app monitoring.
7. Why is a mobile kill switch or remote wipe capability important?
8. What are the purposes of do-not-carry rules?

5.4 Defending Against Fraud

Crime can be divided into two categories depending on the tactics used to carry out the crime: violent and nonviolent. Fraud is nonviolent crime because instead of a gun or knife, fraudsters use deception, confidence, and trickery. Fraudsters carry out their crime by abusing the power of their position or by taking advantage of the trust, ignorance, or laziness of others.

| FRAUD

Occupational fraud refers to the deliberate misuse of the assets of one's employer for personal gain. Internal audits and internal controls are essential to the prevention and detection of occupation frauds. Several examples are listed in Table 5.4.

High-profile cases of occupational fraud committed by senior executives such as Bernard Madoff have led to increased government regulation. However, increased legislation has not put an end to fraud. IT at Work 5.6 gives some insight into Madoff's multibillion fraud that also led to the investigation of the agency responsible for fraud prevention—the U.S. Securities and Exchange Commission (SEC, sec.gov/).

TABLE 5.4   Types and Characteristics of Organizational Fraud

Type of Fraud	Does This Fraud Impact Financial Statements?	Typical Characteristics
Operating management corruption	No	Occurs *off the books*. Median loss due to corruption: over 6 times greater than median loss due to misappropriation ($530,000 vs. $80,000).
Conflict of interest	No	A breach of confidentiality, such as revealing competitors' bids; often occurs coincident with bribery.
Bribery	No	Uses positional power or money to influence others.
Embezzlement or "misappropriation"		Employee theft: employees' access to company property creates the opportunity for embezzlement.
Senior management financial reporting fraud	Yes	Involves a massive breach of trust and leveraging of positional power.
Accounting cycle fraud	Yes	This fraud is called "earnings management" or earning engineering, which are in violation of generally accepted accounting principles (GAAP) and all other accounting practices. See aicpa.org.

IT at Work 5.6

Madoff Defrauds Investors of $64.8 Billion

Disgraced financier Bernard Madoff is in jail after pleading guilty in 2009 to the biggest fraud in Wall Street history. For four decades, Madoff perpetrated a complex and sinister fraud. Prior to his arrest, Madoff was viewed as a charismatic man and stellar financier with favorable connections to power brokers on Wall Street and in Washington. Since his arrest, federal prosecutors have maintained that Bernard Madoff ran a scheme that bilked wealthy individuals and large nonprofits out of an estimated $64.8 billion.

Social Engineering

Fundamentally, Madoff relied on social engineering and the predictability of human nature to generate income for himself—and not on financial expertise. Madoff would ask people to invest in his funds, which were by invitation only, to create the illusion of exclusivity. Madoff used this tactic to create the illusion that only the elite could invest because of consistent returns and his stellar Wall Street reputation. As he expected, wealthy investors mistook *exclusivity* to mean a secret formula for a *sure thing*.

Unusual steady returns were one of the many well-known red flags indicating fraud that investors and watchdogs chose to disregard. In fact, in hindsight, investors admit they missed several glaring red flags.

The Red Flags

Among others, the following classic red flags would have made this fraud detectable much earlier if they had not been consistently ignored:

- Madoff was trusted because he was a Wall Street fixture, so his work was not given full scrutiny.
- Unbelievable returns defied the market. They were impossible, yet this fact was ignored.
- Madoff used a sense of exclusivity—a hook to play "hard to get." This false sense of exclusivity is a telltale sign of a Ponzi scheme.
- Reports of consistently good but never spectacular gains, so-called steady returns, lulled all kinds of investors into a false sense of security over time.

Madoff and SEC Under Investigation

Not only did this scandal trigger an investigation into Madoff; it also prompted an investigation of the watchdog agency, the SEC. It was investigated by Congress and the agency's inspector general for repeatedly ignoring whistleblowers' warnings about Madoff's operations. Created by Congress in 1934 during the Great Depression, the SEC is charged with ensuring that public companies accurately disclose their financials and business risks to investors, and that brokers who trade securities for clients make their investors' interests a first priority.

Madoff is not the only party at fault. Madoff worked with dozens of feeder funds and other middlemen to lure money into his Ponzi scheme. The investigation into "how-could-this-have-happened?" has involved forensic accounting as well as computer forensics. The latter experts were tasked with uncovering any smoking-gun e-mails and other digital messages that revealed "who knew what" and "who did what." Forensics experts dug deeper into the physical evidence to determine who else was complicit in the fraud.

Regulatory Reaction

In January 2009 the Senate Banking Committee introduced legislation to provide $110 million to hire 500 new FBI agents, 50 new assistant U.S. attorneys, and 100 new SEC enforcement officials to crack down on fraud.

Sources: Compiled from Antilla (2008), Chew (2009), Gold (2008), and Quinn (2009).

Questions

1. How important was trust to Madoff's scheme?
2. What else did Madoff rely upon to carry out his fraud?
3. What is a *red flag*?
4. In your opinion, how were so many red flags ignored given the risk that investors faced?
5. Could such a large investment fraud happen again—or are there internal fraud prevention and detection measures in place that would prevent or stop it from occurring? Explain your answer.

INTERNAL FRAUD PREVENTION AND DETECTION

The single most effective fraud prevention tactic is making employees know that fraud will be detected by IT monitoring systems and punished, with the fraudster possibly turned over to the police or FBI. The fear of being caught and prosecuted is a strong deterrent. IT must play a visible and major role in detecting fraud.

Corporate Governance

IT monitoring and control also demonstrate that the company has implemented effective **corporate governance** and fraud prevention measures. Regulators look favorably on companies that can demonstrate best practices in corporate governance and operational risk management. Management and staff would then spend less time worrying about regulations and more time adding value to their brands and business.

Internal fraud prevention measures are based on the same controls used to prevent external intrusions—perimeter defense technologies, such as firewalls, e-mail scanners, and biometric access. They are also based on human resource (HR) procedures, such as recruitment screening and training.

Intelligent Analysis and Anomaly Detections

Most detection activity can be handled by intelligent analysis engines using advanced data warehousing and analytics techniques. These systems take in audit trails from key systems and personnel records from the HR and finance departments. The data are stored in a data warehouse where they are analyzed to detect anomalous patterns, such as excessive hours worked, deviations in patterns of behavior, copying huge amounts of data, attempts to override controls, unusual transactions, and inadequate documentation about a transaction. Information from investigations is fed back into the detection system so it learns of any anomalous patterns. Since insiders might work in collusion with organized criminals, insider profiling is important to find wider patterns of criminal networks.

An enterprisewide approach that combines risk, security, compliance, and IT specialists greatly increases the prevention and detection of fraud. Prevention is the most cost-effective approach, since detection and prosecution costs are enormous in addition to the direct cost of the loss. It starts with corporate governance culture and ethics at the top levels of the organization.

Identity Theft

One of the worst and most prevalent crimes is identity theft. Such thefts where individuals' Social Security and credit card numbers are stolen and used by thieves are not new. Criminals have always obtained information about other people—by stealing wallets or dumpster diving. But widespread electronic sharing and databases have made the crime worse. Because financial institutions, data processing firms, and retail businesses are reluctant to reveal incidents in which their customers' personal financial information may have been stolen, lost, or compromised, laws continue to be passed that force those notifications.

Questions

1. What are the two categories of crime?
2. Explain fraud and occupational fraud.
3. What defenses help prevent internal fraud?
4. What are two red flags of internal fraud?
5. Explain why data on laptops and computers need to be encrypted.
6. Explain how identity theft can occur.

5.5 Compliance and Internal Control

All enterprises are subject to federal and state laws and regulations. Compliance with regulations always requires internal controls to ensure that sensitive data are protected and accurate.

I INTERNAL CONTROL

The internal control environment is the work atmosphere that a company sets for its employees. **Internal control (IC)** is a process designed to achieve:

- Reliability of financial reporting, to protect investors
- Operational efficiency
- Compliance with laws, regulations, and policies
- Safeguarding of assets

The Sarbanes-Oxley Act (SOX) mandates more accurate business reporting and disclosure of generally accepted accounting principles (GAAP) violations. Section 302 deters corporate and executive fraud by requiring that the CEO and CFO verify that they have reviewed the financial report, and, to the best of their knowledge, the report does not contain an untrue statement or omit any material fact. To motivate honesty, executive management faces criminal penalties including long jail terms for false reports. Section 805 mandates a review of the Sentencing Guidelines to ensure that "the guidelines that apply to organizations . . . are sufficient to deter and punish organizational criminal conduct." The Guidelines also focus on the establishment of "effective compliance and ethics" programs. As indicated in the Guidelines, a precondition to an effective compliance and ethics program is "an organizational culture that encourages ethical conduct and a commitment to compliance with the law."

Among other measures, SOX requires companies to set up comprehensive internal controls. There is no question that SOX, and the complex and costly provisions it requires public companies to follow, have had a major impact on corporate financial accounting. For starters, companies have had to set up comprehensive internal controls over financial reporting to prevent fraud, catching it when it occurs. Since the collapse of Arthur Andersen, following the accounting firm's conviction on criminal charges related to the Enron case, outside accounting firms have gotten tougher with clients they are auditing, particularly with regard to their internal controls.

SOX and the SEC are making it clear that if controls can be ignored, there is no control. Therefore, fraud prevention and detection require an effective monitoring system. If a company shows its employees that it can find out everything that every employee does and use that evidence to prosecute a wrongdoer to the fullest extent possible under the law, then the likelihood of any employee adopting an "I can get away with it" attitude drops drastically.

Approximately 85 percent of occupational fraud could have been prevented if proper IT-based internal controls had been designed, implemented, and followed.

DEFENSE STRATEGY

The objective of IT security management practices is to defend all of the components of an information system, specifically data, software applications, hardware, and networks, so they remain in compliance. Before they make any decisions concerning defenses, the people responsible for security must understand the requirements and operations of the business, which form the basis for a customized defense strategy.

The defense strategy and controls that should be used depend on what needs to be protected and a cost–benefit analysis. That is, companies should neither underinvest nor overinvest. The SEC and FTC impose huge fines for data breaches to deter companies from underinvesting in data protection. The following are the major objectives of defense strategies:

1. **Prevention and deterrence.** Properly designed controls may prevent errors from occurring, deter criminals from attacking the system, and, better yet, deny access to unauthorized people. These are the most desirable controls.

2. **Detection.** Like a fire, the earlier an attack is detected, the easier it is to combat, and the less damage is done. Detection can be performed in many cases by using special diagnostic software, at a minimal cost.

3. **Contain the damage.** This objective involves minimizing or limiting losses once a malfunction has occurred. It is also called damage control. This can be accomplished, for example, by including a *fault-tolerant system* that permits operation in a degraded mode until full recovery is made. If a fault-tolerant system does not exist, a quick and possibly expensive recovery must take place. Users want their systems back in operation as fast as possible.

4. **Recovery.** A recovery plan explains how to fix a damaged information system as quickly as possible. Replacing rather than repairing components is one route to fast recovery.

5. **Correction.** Correcting the causes of damaged systems can prevent a problem from occurring again.

6. **Awareness and compliance.** All organization members must be educated about the hazards and must comply with the security rules and regulations.

A defense strategy is also going to require several controls, as shown in Figure 5.11. **General controls** are established to protect the system regardless of the specific application. For example, protecting hardware and controlling access to the data center are independent of the specific application. **Application controls** are safeguards that are intended to protect specific applications. In the next two sections, we discuss the major types of these two groups of information system controls.

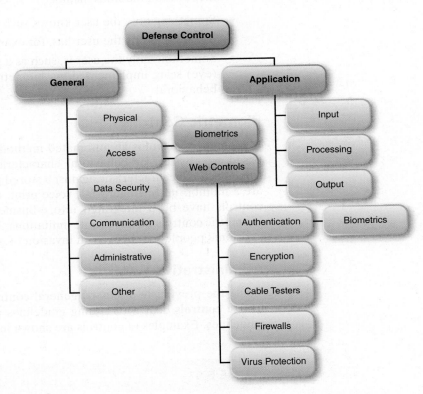

Figure 5.11 Major defense controls.

| GENERAL CONTROLS

The major categories of general controls are physical controls, access controls, data security controls, communication network controls, and administrative controls.

Physical Controls

Physical security refers to the protection of computer facilities and resources. This includes protecting physical property such as computers, data centers, software, manuals, and networks. It provides protection against most natural hazards as well as against some human hazards. Appropriate physical security may include several **physical controls** such as the following:

- Appropriate design of the data center. For example, the data center should be noncombustible and waterproof.
- Shielding against electromagnetic fields.
- Good fire prevention, detection, and extinguishing systems, including a sprinkler system, water pumps, and adequate drainage facilities.

- Emergency power shutoff and backup batteries, which must be maintained in operational condition.
- Properly designed and maintained air-conditioning systems.
- Motion detector alarms that detect physical intrusion.

Access Controls

Access control is the management of who is and is not authorized to use a company's hardware and software. Access control methods, such as firewalls and access control lists, restrict access to a network, database, file, or data. It is the major line of defense against unauthorized insiders as well as outsiders. Access control involves authorization (having the right to access) and authentication, which is also called user identification (proving that the user is who he or she claims to be).

Authentication methods include:

- Something only the user knows, such as a password
- Something only the user has, for example, a smart card or a token
- Something only the user is, such as a signature, voice, fingerprint, or retinal (eye) scan; implemented via biometric controls, which can be physical or behavioral

Biometric Controls

A **biometric control** is an automated method of verifying the identity of a person, based on physical or behavioral characteristics. Most biometric systems match some personal characteristic against a stored profile. The most common biometrics are a thumbprint or fingerprint, voice print, retinal scan, and signature. Biometric controls have been integrated into e-business hardware and software products. Biometric controls do have some limitations: They are not accurate in certain cases, and some people see them as an invasion of privacy.

Administrative Controls

While the previously discussed general controls are technical in nature, **administrative controls** deal with issuing guidelines and monitoring compliance with the guidelines. Examples of controls are shown in Table 5.5.

TABLE 5.5   Representative Administrative Controls

- Appropriately selecting, training, and supervising employees, especially in accounting and information systems
- Fostering company loyalty
- Immediately revoking access privileges of dismissed, resigned, or transferred employees
- Requiring periodic modification of access controls, such as passwords
- Developing programming and documentation standards (to make auditing easier and to use the standards as guides for employees)
- Insisting on security bonds or malfeasance insurance for key employees
- Instituting separation of duties, namely, dividing sensitive computer duties among as many employees as economically feasible in order to decrease the chance of intentional or unintentional damage
- Holding periodic random audits of the system

| BUSINESS CONTINUITY

Risk management is not complete without a **business continuity plan** that has been tested to verify that it works. Business continuity refers to maintaining business functions or restoring them quickly when there is a major disruption. The plan covers business processes, assets, human resources, business partners, and more. Fires, earthquakes, floods, power outages, malicious attacks, and other types of disasters hit data centers. Yet business continuity planning capabilities can be a tough sell because they do not contribute to the bottom line—that is, until it is too late. Compare them to an insurance policy: If and only if a disaster occurs, the money has been well spent. And spending on business continuity preparedness is an ongoing process because there is always more that could be done to better prepare.

The purpose of a business continuity plan is to keep the business running after a disaster occurs. Each function in the business should have a feasible backup plan. For example, if the customer service center or call center was destroyed by a storm or lost all power, would anyone know how the reps would continue to answer customer calls? The backup plan could define how to provide necessary network access to enable business to continue.

| AUDITING
INFORMATION
SYSTEMS

An **audit** is an important part of any control system. Auditing can be viewed as an additional layer of controls or safeguards. It is considered as a deterrent to criminal actions, especially for insiders. Auditors attempt to answer questions such as these:

- Are there sufficient controls in the system? Which areas are not covered by controls?
- Which controls are not necessary?
- Are the controls implemented properly?
- Are the controls effective? That is, do they check the output of the system?
- Is there a clear separation of duties of employees?
- Are there procedures to ensure compliance with the controls?
- Are there procedures to ensure reporting and corrective actions in case of violations of controls?

Auditing a website is a good preventive measure to manage the legal risk. Legal risk is important in any IT system, but in Web systems it is even more important due to the content of the site, which may offend people or be in violation of copyright laws or other regulations (e.g., privacy protection). Auditing e-commerce is also more complex since, in addition to the website, one needs to audit order taking, order fulfillment, and all support systems.

| COST–BENEFIT
ANALYSIS

It is usually not economical to prepare protection against every possible threat. Therefore, an IT security program must provide a process for assessing threats and deciding which ones to prepare for and which ones to ignore or provide reduced protection against. Two methods are risk assessment and business impact analysis.

Risk Assessment

Risk assessments are done using an app or spreadsheet. The basic computations are shown here:

$$\text{Expected loss} = P_1 \times P_2 \times L$$

where

P_1 = probability of attack (estimate, based on judgment)

P_2 = probability of attack being successful (estimate, based on judgment)

L = loss occurring if attack is successful

Example:

$$P_1 = .02, P_2 = .10, L = \$1,000,000$$

Then expected loss from this particular attack is

$$P_1 \times P_2 \times L = 0.02 \times 0.1 \times \$1,000,000 = \$2,000$$

The amount of loss also depends on the duration of a system being out of operation.

Business impact analysis

A **business impact analysis (BIA)** estimates the consequences of disruption of a business function and collects data to develop recovery strategies. Potential loss scenarios are first identified during the risk assessment. Operations may also be interrupted by the failure of a supplier of goods or services or delayed deliveries. There are many possible scenarios that should be considered.

The BIA identifies both operational and financial impacts resulting from a disruption. Several examples of impacts to consider include (Ready.gov, 2014):

- Lost sales and income
- Delayed sales or income
- Increased expenses (e.g., overtime labor, outsourcing, expediting costs, etc.)
- Regulatory fines
- Contractual penalties or loss of contractual bonuses
- Customer dissatisfaction or defection
- Delay of new business plans

These costs and losses should be compared with the costs for possible recovery strategies. The BIA report should prioritize the order of events for restoration of the business, with processes having the greatest operational and financial impacts being restored first.

Questions

1. Why are internal controls needed?
2. What federal law requires effective internal controls?
3. Why do the SEC and FTC impose huge fines for data breaches?
4. What are the two types of controls in a defense strategy?
5. Explain authentication and two methods of authentication.
6. What are biometric controls? Give an example.
7. Why do organizations need a business continuity plan?
8. Why should websites be audited?
9. How is expected loss calculated?
10. Explain business impact analysis.

Key Terms

acceptable use policy (AUP)
access control
administrative controls
advanced persistent threat (APT)

Anonymous
application controls
assets
attack vectors
audit
backdoor

biometric control
BlackPOS
Black smartphone
botnet
bring your own apps (BYOA)

bring your own device (BYOD)
business continuity plan
business impact analysis (BIA)

command and control (C&C) channel

consumerization of information technology (COIT)

contract hacker

Control Objectives for Information and Related Technology (COBIT)

corporate governance

critical infrastructure

data tampering

distributed denial-of-service (DDoS) attack

do-not-carry rules

enterprise risk management (ERM)

exploit

general controls

hacker

hacktivist

internal control (IC)

internal threats

intrusion detection system (IDS)

intrusion prevention system (IPS)

iOS 5

IT governance

LulzSec

malware

mobile biometrics

occupational fraud

patches

payload

Payment Card Industry Data Security Standard (PCI DSS)

phishing

physical controls

programming attacks

remote access trojan (RAT)

remote wipe capability

risk

rogue app monitoring

rootkit

service pack

signature

social engineering

spam

spear phishing

spyware

threat

time-to-exploitation

vector

virus

voice biometrics

vulnerability

worm

zero-day exploit

zombie

Assuring Your Learning

DISCUSS: Critical Thinking Questions

1. Why is cybercrime expanding rapidly? Discuss some possible solutions.

2. In addition to hackers, what kinds of cybercriminals do organizations need to defend against?

3. What are the major motives of cybercriminals?

4. In what ways do users make themselves vulnerable to cybercrimes?

5. Why do malware creators alter their malware?

6. Why should you set a unique password for each website, service, and device that you use?

7. How can malware be stopped from stealing or disclosing data from an organization's network?

8. What impact might huge fines have on how much a company budgets for IT security defenses?

9. Why are BYOD, BYOA, and do-not-carry rules important to IT security? Why might users resist such rules?

10. Why do users refuse to use strong passwords even though they know how dangerous weak passwords are?

11. How can the risk of occupational fraud be decreased?

12. Why should information control and security be of prime concern to management?

13. Explain what firewalls protect and what they do not protect.

14. Why are authentication and authorization important in e-commerce?

15. Some insurance companies will not insure a business unless the firm has a computer disaster recovery plan. Explain why.

16. Explain why risk management should involve the following elements: threats, exposure associated with each threat, risk of each threat occurring, cost of controls, and assessment of their effectiveness.

17. Discuss why the Sarbanes-Oxley Act focuses on internal control. How does that focus influence information security?

EXPLORE: Online and Interactive Exercises

1. *The Wall Street Journal* (WSJ.com) has detailed a cyberattack against the U.S. Chamber of Commerce in which e-mails were stolen. Review *The Wall Street Journal* interactive graphic "China Hackers Hit U.S. Chamber, Attacks Breached Computer System of Business-Lobbying Group; Emails Stolen," dated December 21, 2011. Also view the video. The links are posted in the book's website at www.wiley.com/

college/turban or you can search the WSJ.com website using the video title.

a. Explain the importance and role of social engineering in this intrusion and cybertheft.

b. What can be done to prevent this type of intrusion from occurring again?

c. How serious was the intrusion and when did it occur?

d. What or who did the hackers focus on? Why?

e. What information could the hackers have gleaned from the intrusion of the Chamber?

f. What did the Chamber do to increase cybersecurity after learning of the intrusion and cybertheft?

g. Explain why cars and appliances can be hack targets.

h. What other resources are at risk?

i. Does this incident indicate about how widespread hacking is? Explain your answer.

2. Access the Anti-Phishing Working Group website (antiphishing.org) and download the most recent Phishing Activity Trends Report.

a. Describe the recent trends in phishing attacks.

b. Explain the reasons for these trends.

3. Research a botnet attack. Explain how the botnet works and what damage it causes. What preventive methods are offered by security vendors?

4. Visit cio.com and search for a recent article on security, privacy, or compliance. What three lessons are learned from the article?

5. Research vendors of biometrics. Select one vendor and discuss three of its biometric devices or technologies. Prepare a list of major capabilities. What are the advantages and disadvantages of its biometrics?

ANALYZE & DECIDE: Apply IT Concepts to Business Decisions

1. Many firms concentrate on the wrong questions and end up throwing a great deal of money and time at minimal security risks while ignoring major vulnerabilities. Why?

2. Assessing how much a company is legally obligated to invest in cybersecurity remains a challenge. Since there is no such thing as perfect security (i.e., there is always more that you can do), resolving these questions can significantly affect cost.

a. When are a company's security measures sufficient to comply with its obligations? For example, does installing a firewall and using virus detection software satisfy a company's legal obligations?

b. Is it necessary for an organization to encrypt all of its electronic records?

6. Assume that the daily probability of a major earthquake in Los Angeles is .07 percent. The chance of your computer center being damaged during such a quake is 5 percent. If the center is damaged, the average estimated damage will be $1.6 million.

a. Calculate the expected loss (in dollars).

b. An insurance agent is willing to insure your facility for an annual fee of $15,000. Analyze the offer, and discuss whether to accept it.

7. Should an employer notify employees that their usage of computers is being monitored? Why or why not?

8. Twenty-five thousand messages arrive at an organization each year. Currently, there are no firewalls. On average, 1.2 successful hackings occur each year. Each successful hack attack results in a loss of about $130,000 to the company. A major firewall is proposed at a cost of $66,000. The estimated useful life is 3 years. The chance that an intruder will break through the firewall is 0.0002. In such a case, the damage will be $100,000 (30%), or $200,000 (50%), or no damage. There is an annual maintenance cost of $20,000 for the firewall.

a. Should management buy the firewall?

b. An improved firewall that is 99.9988 percent effective and that costs $84,000, with a life of 3 years and annual maintenance cost of $16,000, is available. Should this firewall be purchased instead of the first one?

CASE 5.2

Business Case: Lax Security at LinkedIn Exposed

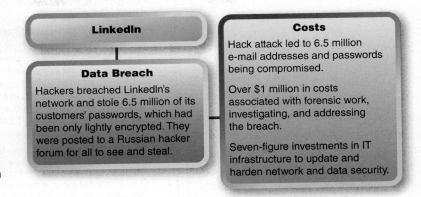

LinkedIn

Data Breach

Hackers breached LinkedIn's network and stole 6.5 million of its customers' passwords, which had been only lightly encrypted. They were posted to a Russian hacker forum for all to see and steal.

Costs

Hack attack led to 6.5 million e-mail addresses and passwords being compromised.

Over $1 million in costs associated with forensic work, investigating, and addressing the breach.

Seven-figure investments in IT infrastructure to update and harden network and data security.

Figure 5.12 LinkedIn data breach overview.

On any social network, most users mistakenly believe that their privacy is only as good as the privacy of their most careless—or temporary—friend. In fact, weak passwords and hackers can deprive users of all privacy.

Business social networking site LinkedIn was hacked in June 2012 (Figure 5.12). Hackers stole 6.5 million passwords and e-mail addresses. This data breach was discovered by IT security experts when they found millions of LinkedIn passwords posted on a Russian underground website (Figure 5.13). Experts also determined that a hacker named Dwdm was asking underground members for help in cracking the stolen passwords. Within only two days, most passwords were cracked. Why were LinkedIn's passwords cracked so quickly? The simple answer is that LinkedIn was using an outdated encryption method instead of up-to-date industry-standard encryption. As a result, members' passwords were really only camouflaged—and crackable.

LinkedIn Criticized for Bad Data Security

What could hackers do to your online accounts if they had your passwords for 48 hours and you did not know? That is what LinkedIn allowed to happen by waiting two days before notifying members that their passwords had been stolen. The company took a lot of criticism for not notifying members via Twitter or Facebook immediately. According to the chief executive of the Public Relations Consultants Association, Francis Ingham, LinkedIn ignored the first rule of crisis management, which is to be first to tell your customers.

What surprised customers and IT security experts was that a company that collects and profits from vast amounts of data had taken a negligent approach to protecting it. Figure 5.14 explains why it was surprising and alarming that LinkedIn's password protection was weak.

E-mail Addresses Are Universal Usernames

At most e-commerce and social sites, usernames are e-mail addresses—making them our universal username for online accounts. If the e-mail is a work account, then everyone also knows where we work and our login name. Therefore, knowing users' usernames and passwords provides authorized access to corporate accounts with almost no risk of being detected. Hackers attacked LinkedIn to gain access to over 161 million members' credentials as a means to gain access to much more valuable business networks and databases.

Figure 5.13 LinkedIn did not discover its own data breach and, when informed of it, delayed notifying members.

© Kevin Britland/Alamy

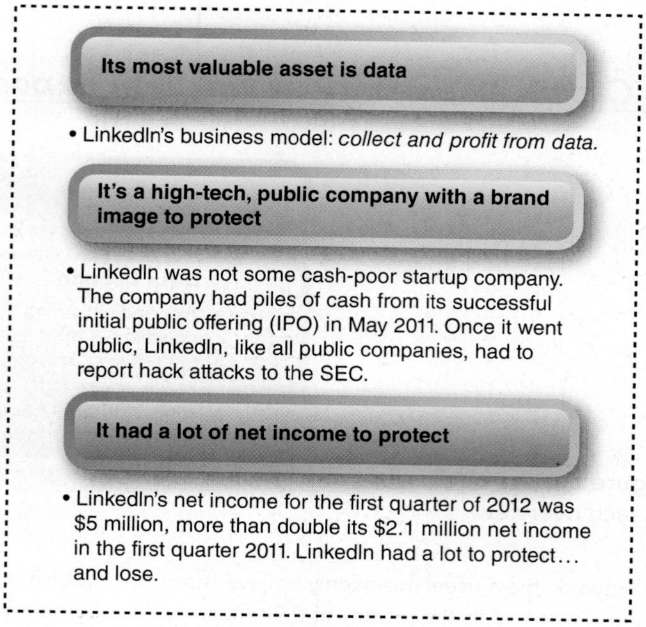

> Its most valuable asset is data
>
> • LinkedIn's business model: *collect and profit from data.*
>
> It's a high-tech, public company with a brand image to protect
>
> • LinkedIn was not some cash-poor startup company. The company had piles of cash from its successful initial public offering (IPO) in May 2011. Once it went public, LinkedIn, like all public companies, had to report hack attacks to the SEC.
>
> It had a lot of net income to protect
>
> • LinkedIn's net income for the first quarter of 2012 was $5 million, more than double its $2.1 million net income in the first quarter 2011. LinkedIn had a lot to protect… and lose.

Figure 5.14 Three reasons why LinkedIn's underinvestment in data security did not make business sense.

Business Risks and Collateral Damage

The hack caused the following business risks and collateral damage.

- **Takeover of members' other accounts by hackers, fraudsters, and other criminals.** Hackers know that people reuse passwords; once their LinkedIn accounts are linked to Facebook and Twitter, far too much information may be revealed. Knowing where people worked and their e-mail accounts allowed hackers to quickly use the stolen LinkedIn passwords to log in to corporate accounts, online bank accounts, and so on to steal more data or transfer funds.

- **Damage to LinkedIn's biggest revenue source—its advertising business.** LinkedIn's financial success is tied to its advertising revenues, which in turn are based on the number of active members and membership growth.

- **Fines for violating privacy laws and regulations.** Any company exposing the confidential data of customers or employees faces steep fines. Regulators impose harsh penalties for breaking privacy laws and not taking reasonable care to defend against data breaches. Strict data privacy laws in states such as Massachusetts and California could keep LinkedIn fighting legal battles for years.

- **Cleanup costs.** The cleanup cost LinkedIn nearly $1 million and another $2 to $3 million in upgrades. Forensic work on the password theft cost another $500,000 to $1 million.

Data Security: A Top Management Concern

Data security is a senior management concern and responsibility. It affects a company's operations, reputation, and customer trust, which ultimately impact revenue, profits, and competitive edge. Yet defenses that could help to prevent breaches are not always implemented.

Some experts argue that senior management continues to skimp on basic protections because computer security is not regulated—that is, until a business suffers a major crisis. After the data breach, LinkedIn implemented improved password storage encryption, hired private security and forensics experts, and called in the Federal Bureau of Investigation (FBI) to help investigate the security breach.

Jeremiah Grossman, chief technology officer of White Hat Security, estimated that it would have cost LinkedIn "a couple hundred thousand dollars" to secure its members' passwords, Web servers, and applications (Perlroth, 2012a).

How This Attack Compares to Others

While 6.5 million leaked passwords represents a serious breach, it affected a relatively small percent of the more than 175 million members LinkedIn had at that time. Overall, the LinkedIn breach, while somewhat costly, did not do as much harm as those experienced by other hacked companies such as Global Payments, Sony, and Certificate Authority DigiNotar, which was literally hacked out of business.

Sources: Compiled from Perlroth (2012a), Ponemon Institute (2013), whitehatsec.com, and prca.org.uk.

Questions

1. LinkedIn does not collect the credit card or other financial account information of its members. Why then would profit-motivated hackers be interested in stealing LinkedIn's stored data? What data would they be most interested in?

2. Companies are often slow to self-detect data breaches so a cyberattack can occur without a company even knowing it has a problem. What effect do you think LinkedIn's failure to self-detect its massive data breach had on its popularity and credibility?

3. Most corporate security incidents are uncovered by a third party, like a security firm, that picks up on evidence of malicious activity. Why do you think IT security experts and not LinkedIn discovered the data breach?

4. LinkedIn's lax approach to members' information security and weak passwords was very surprising to members and information security professionals. Why?

5. Identify and evaluate the actual and potential business risks and damages from LinkedIn's data breach.

6. Why is data encryption an important information security defense?

7. Discuss why information security is a concern of senior managers.

8. Explain why someone who used the same password for several sites would need to change all those passwords. In your opinion, was LinkedIn negligent in protecting its main asset? Explain.

CASE 5.3

Video Case: Botnets, Malware Security, and Capturing Cybercriminals

Gunter Ollmann, vice president of research at Damballa, Inc., explains the Aurora attacks against major companies. Thousands of botnet operators launched targeted botnet campaigns with the help of automated tools. In the video, you learn why it is difficult for law enforcement to track and prosecute cybercriminals and the effectiveness of Microsoft's legal action to shut down the C&C (command and control) network of the Waladec botnet. Visit searchsecurity.techtarget.com/video/Botnets-malware-and-capturing-cybercriminals to view the video and read the transcript of it.

Questions

1. What are botnets used for?
2. What is needed to get started in the botnet industry? Explain why.
3. Given your answers, what should users and organizations do and/or not do to reduce the threat of botnets?

Quiz

1. From research into Operation Aurora and analysis of the botnets, investigators learned all of the following except:
    a. There are about 50 botnet operators.
    b. Botnet operators have increased their range by running multiple botnets and campaigns.
    c. The feature set of modern malware is similar for both the amateur and the professional operator.
    d. Many of the advanced types of malware are available in kit form.

2. What really differs between the professional practice and the amateur operator is the way that they _____.
    a. select their targets.
    b. have hardened their malware.
    c. infect a network.
    d. use proxies.

3. Armoring malware is done to make sure that if researchers obtain a sample of the code, it cannot be automatically used for deconstructing who the command and control chains are. True or false?

4. Many consumers know that a traditional antivirus program has value, but that value is depreciating considerably. True or false?

References

Antilla, S. "Red Flags Were There All Along: Suspicious Activities Largely Unquestioned." *Gazette* (Montreal), December 16, 2008.

Boeing.com. "Overview: Boeing Black Smartphone." 2014.

Chew, R. "A Madoff Whistle-Blower Tells His Story." *Time*, February 4, 2009.

D'Innocenzio, A. "Data-breach Cuts Target Profit." *Timesleader.com*, February 26, 2014.

Egan, S. "New Report Predicts High Growth in Mobile Biometric Security." *SecureIDNews.com*. September 15, 2011.

Gallagher, S. "Update: Boeing's Black—This Android Phone Will Self-Destruct." *Ars Technica*, February 26, 2014.

Gold, L. "Forensic Accounting: Finding the Smoking E-mail: E-discovery Is Now a Critical Part of Forensics—and of Firm Policy." *Accounting Today* 22, no. 8, May 5, 2008.

Hosenball, M. "Leaked Call on Ukraine Made on Unencrypted Cellphones—U.S. Officials." *Reuters,* February 7, 2014.

Kratsas, G. "Reports: Target Warned Before Data Breach." *USA Today*, February 18, 2014.

KPMG. *Data Loss Barometer.* 2012. http://www.kpmg.com/US/en/IssuesAndInsights/ArticlesPublications/Documents/data-loss-barometer.pdf

Krebs on Security. "A First Look at the Target Intrusion, Malware." January 14, 2014.

Mobile Phone Biometric Security Analysis and Forecasts 2011–2015.

O'Connor, C. "Target CEO Gregg Steinhafel Resigns in Data Breach Fallout." *Forbes,* May 5, 2014.

Perlroth, N. "Hacked Chamber of Commerce Opposed Cyber-security Law." *bits.blogs.nytimes.com,* December 21, 2012a.

Perlroth, N. "Traveling Light in a Time of Digital Thievery." *The New York Times,* February 10, 2012b.

Ponemon Institute. "2013 Cost of Data Breach Study: Global Analysis." Ponemon Institute Research Report. May 2013.

PricewaterhouseCoopers (PWC). *2014 Global State of Information Security Survey.* http://www.pwc.com/gx/en/consulting-services/information-security-survey/download.jhtml

Quinn, J. "On the Trail of Madoff's Missing Billions." *The Sunday Telegraph* (London), January 18, 2009.

Ready.gov. "Business Impact Analysis." January 29, 2014.

Sharf, S. "Target Shares Drop After CEO Gregg Steinhafel's Resignation." *Forbes,* May 5, 2014.

TrendMicro TrendLabs, "Repeating History." 2012 http://www.trendmicro.com/cloud-content/us/pdfs/security-intelligence/reports/rpt-repeating-history.pdf

Westcott, L. "Boeing's New Self Destructing Phone Is Ideal for Those Who Need to Keep Secrets." *The Wire,* March 5, 2014.

Yadron, D., P. Ziobro, & D. Barrett. "Target Warned of Vulnerabilities Before Data Breach." *The Wall Street Journal,* February 14, 2014.

Chapter

6

Attracting Buyers with Search, Semantic, and Recommendation Technology

Chapter Snapshot

Case 6.1 Opening Case: Nike Golf Drives Web Traffic with Search Engine Optimization

6.1 Using Search Technology for Business Success

6.2 Organic Search and Search Engine Optimization

6.3 Pay-Per-Click and Paid Search Strategies

6.4 A Search for Meaning—Semantic Technology

6.5 Recommendation Engines

Key Terms

Assuring Your Learning

- **Discuss:** Critical Thinking Questions
- **Explore:** Online and Interactive Exercises
- **Analyze & Decide:** Apply IT Concepts to Business Decisions

Case 6.2 Business Case: Recommending Wine to Online Customers

Case 6.3 Video Case: Power Searching with Google

References

Learning Outcomes

1. Describe how search engines work and identify ways that businesses gain competitive advantage by using search technology effectively.

2. Describe how to improve website ranking on search results pages by optimizing website design and creating useful content.

3. Describe how companies manage paid search advertising campaigns to increase awareness and drive sales volume.

4. Describe how semantic Web technology enhances the accuracy of search engines results and how businesses can optimize their websites to take advantage of this emerging technology.

5. Describe how recommendation engines are used to enhance user experience and increase sales on e-commerce websites.

Chapter Snapshot

Every day, over 1.5 billion people around the world use what seems to be a simple tool to find information online—a search engine. We sometimes take for granted that behind a relatively simple user interface, an increasingly complex set of search engine technologies are at work, helping us find the information we need to do our jobs, conduct research, locate product reviews, or find information about the television shows we watch.

Because most search engine services are free, people are not generally aware that "Search" has become a multibillion-dollar-a-year business. More importantly, the way search engines work and how they rank-order the links displayed when we conduct a search have huge implications for millions of other businesses. Because consumers typically don't look past the first few pages of search results, having your business appear at the top of a search results page can make a big difference in how much traffic your website gets. In this chapter, you will read about how search engines work and how they determine page rankings. You will also read about the strategies companies use to increase their presence on search results pages including search engine optimization (SEO) and pay-per-click (PPC) advertising.

Semantic technologies are increasingly being used by search engines to understand webpage content. In this chapter you will read about the ways that search engines are using semantic technology to improve performance, increasing relevant pages and decreasing the number of irrelevant pages that appear in search results.

Finally, you will read about recommendation engines. These tools attempt to anticipate online information you might be interested in. Netflix uses recommendation engines to suggest movies you might like to watch and news organizations use them to recommend stories you might want to read on their websites. Amazon credits its recommendation technology for increasing sales by suggesting products that customers might want to buy.

Business managers need to understand search and recommendation technologies because their influence in directing potential consumers to business websites is already significant and expected to grow substantially in the future.

CASE 6.1 OPENING CASE

Nike Golf Drives Web Traffic with Search Engine Optimization

Search Engine Results Page (SERP): the list of links and other descriptive information about webpages returned by a search engine in response to a search query.

Keywords: in the context of web search or SEO, words or phrases that describe the content on a webpage. Search engines use keywords to match webpages with user search queries.

According to some estimates, 50 to 75 percent of Web traffic is generated by search engines (Pick, 2012, Safran, 2013, Van Zelst, 2013, Willcocks, 2013). This should not come as a surprise to most of us, considering how often we use search engines like Google, Bing, or Yahoo to find online information. Because businesses compete for our attention, they have a vested interest in maintaining a high degree of visibility on **search engine results pages**, or **SERP**s.

Traffic from search engines comes from two basic sources: organic search results and paid search advertisements. Organic search results are heavily influenced by website content and design features (e.g., the technology used to create the site, webpage coding, etc.). Paid search traffic is the result of ads that appear on SERPs. Companies pay search engines to place these ads on SERPs when certain **keywords** are used in a search query. Search engine users frequently ignore these ads—about 85 percent of website traffic generated by search engines is the result of organic search listings (Downhill & Peggie, 2005).

| COMPANY OVERVIEW

Nike, Inc., based near Beaverton, OR, is one of the world's most recognized brand names in sports apparel and equipment. Revenues in 2013 increased 8 percent from the previous year to $25.3 billion. The company is currently experiencing a period of growth, particularly with its "direct to consumer" (DTC) sales strategy involving a combination of online sales and company stores (Figure 6.1). DTC sales at the company grew 24 percent to $4.3 billion compared to the previous year. This was fueled, in part, by increasing the number of company stores from 557 to 645 worldwide over the past year (Nikeinc.com, 2013).

Nike is frequently associated with what it calls a "big athlete, big ad, big product" marketing strategy (Nikeinc.com, 2014). This involves signing endorsement deals with the most widely recognized athletes in the sporting world, creating

Figure 6.1 Nike is expanding its "direct to consumers" name-brand stores worldwide like this one in Beijing, China. (shutterstock.com.)

© testing/Shutterstock.com

signature products, and supporting them with high-powered advertising campaigns featuring the company's famous tagline, "Just do it." Perhaps the best example of this promotional strategy is Nike's popular campaign for Air Jordans, a line of basketball shoes named for Michael Jordan. Other well-known Nike athletes include golf pro Tiger Woods, Russian tennis star Maria Sharapova, Brazilian soccer phenomenon Ronaldinho, and professional skateboarder Paul Rodriguez, Jr. (Goldman, 2008).

TABLE 6.1	Opening Case Overview
Company	**Nike, Inc., nikeinc.com**
History	Founded in 1964 as Blue Ribbon Sports, the company changed its name to Nike in 1971 and sells products under a variety of brand names, including Nike Golf, Nike Pro, Air Jordan, Nike Vision, Converse, and Nike Skateboarding.
Industry	Athletic apparel, footwear, and equipment
Product lines	The global company manufactures, sells, and distributes athletic footwear, apparel, and sports equipment to retail outlets, colleges and universities, sports clubs, professional sports teams, and directly to consumers.
Digital technology	Nike is a leader in e-commerce innovation, for instance, allowing consumers to design their own individual footwear. Nike+ products integrate traditional sports equipment with digital technology (e.g., mobile apps, wristbands, watches, and software) that allow athletes to monitor and track their performance.
Business challenges	• Placing greater emphasis on digital marketing strategies, including search engine marketing. • Growing its direct to consumer (DTC) sales channels. • Expanding the Nike Digital Sports division.
Taglines	"Just do it."

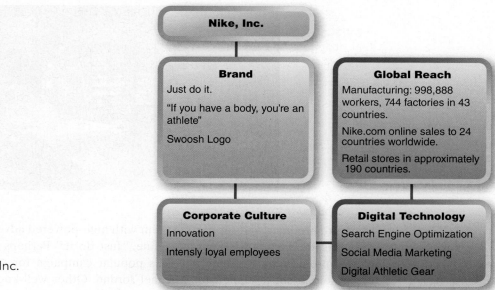

Figure 6.2 Nike, Inc. overview.

More recently, Nike has shifted its marketing and promotion strategy, placing greater emphasis on digital or online channels, attempting to engage consumers in ways not possible via traditional mass media. See Figure 6.2.

NIKE'S BUSINESS CHALLENGES

In order to continue online sales growth, Nike's e-commerce sites need to maintain high levels of visibility on major search engines. This means that when consumers conduct searches for things like "golf shoes," "sports equipment," or "athletic gear," Nike would like to appear at the top of SERP listings. Unfortunately, the Nike website does not appear in the search results of many queries for which you would expect it to.

BUSINESS AND IT STRATEGIES

Despite its well-known brand name and established position as a market leader in sports apparel, footwear, and athletic equipment, Nike has not historically done well in search engine rankings. The company hired SwellPath, a digital marketing agency based in Portland, OR, to help it increase the visibility of its golf brand on popular search engines for the 2011 golf season. Swellpath set out to improve Nike's organic search rankings and provide an analysis of the company's improved performance in search. The strategy involved identifying changes that needed to be made to Nike's golf site (nikegolf.com) and researching keywords that prospective customers were most likely to use when searching for the type of products that Nike sells. Changing the design and content of a website to improve its ranking in SERPs is called **search engine optimization (SEO)**.

Search Engine Optimization (SEO): a collection of strategies and techniques designed to increase the number of visitors to a website as a result of the website's rank on search engine results pages.

SwellPath discovered that Nike had built its website using Java technology, which created attractive and visually compelling webpages, but was practically invisible to the tools (called spiders) that search engines use to crawl webpage content looking for keywords that serve as clues to what the website is about. This was a big problem since search engines rely on matching words in search queries with words in the website content to determine if a page is relevant.

SwellPath also analyzed the keywords that people were likely to use when searching for the kind of products Nike sells. It is not practical or effective to optimize for all possible keywords, so SwellPath set out to identify the words that not only produced traffic to Nike's site, but also attracted customers most likely to "convert" (purchase products). For instance, the company examined the words "golf apparel," "golf clothing," "golf clothes," and "golf sportswear." Research showed that people in the U.S. searched on the words "golf apparel" more frequently, and customers who visited the site when searching those words stayed on the Nike site longer, visited more pages, and were more likely to purchase an item.

SEO SOLUTION

Completely redesigning Nike's Java-based website was not a viable option because of the cost involved. SwellPath recommended an alternative solution—creating a parallel site using HTML, a more basic Web programming language that could be read by search engine spiders. Visitors to the site still saw the original Java-based site with the attractive pages, but search engines could easily read the content on the parallel site. In addition, it turned out that the HTML site displayed better on mobile devices, an added benefit.

Once the site's technology problem was solved, SwellPath optimized the content for "golf apparel" along with other terms and phrases it had identified in its keyword research.

PERFORMANCE RESULTS

Between the 2010 and 2011 golf seasons, Web traffic from organic search increased 169 percent, an impressive gain. However, SwellPath discovered that most of this traffic derived from consumers who included the word "Nike" in their search queries. These are referred to as **branded search queries**. To really judge the impact of SEO, SwellPath evaluated changes in Web traffic from nonbranded searches (such as "golf shoes" vs. "Nike golf shoes"). It discovered that traffic from nonbranded organic searches actually slipped 17 percent. As a result, the SwellPath team redoubled its efforts by continued research on keywords and adding site content around terms and phrases likely to attract customers. The effort paid off. When its plan was fully implemented, nonbranded traffic to the Nike site increased 250 percent between the 2011 and 2012 golf seasons.

More recently, the SwellPath team helped Nike Vision, the company's unit that sells sunglasses and athletic eyewear. Prior to the 2012 Olympic Games in London, Nike signed professional beach volleyball star Misty May-Treanor (see Figure 6.3). Knowing that people would be using search engines to look up information on star athletes during the Olympics, SwellPath optimized the Nike Vision website with blog content about Misty May-Treanor and her Nike-branded sunglasses. As a result, during the six-day period that Misty May-Treanor competed in the London Olympics, organic traffic from search engines to Nikevision.com increased 169 percent. If Nike had failed to update its site with optimized blog posts and other content about Misty May-Treanor prior to

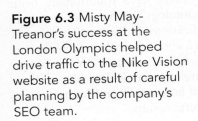

Figure 6.3 Misty May-Treanor's success at the London Olympics helped drive traffic to the Nike Vision website as a result of careful planning by the company's SEO team.

Figure 6.4 Olympic athlete Shawn Johnson (L) and Nike Vice President of Digital Sport Stefan Olander discussing Nike's new digital wristband product at a 2013 NikeFuel Forum in New York City.

Mike Lawrie/Getty Images

the Olympics, it would have missed out on an opportunity to capture the attention of thousands of prospective customers (Arnesen, 2012). This example illustrates how SEO is a constantly evolving strategy, requiring companies to anticipate the interests, search behavior, and needs of the marketplace and to regularly create optimized content that will rank high in organic SERPs.

As Nike expands its product line into digital products (Figure 6.4) that allow athletes to monitor and track their performance, the Nike Digital Sports division will need to optimize its webpages with content that will rank high in search results. What type of content and keywords do you think will help people discover these new digital products on search engines?

Sources: Compiled from Safran (2013), Van Zelst (2013), Pick (2012), Willcocks (2013), Nikeinc.com (2013, 2014), Goldman (2008), Arnesen (2012), SwellPath.com (2012), Downhill & Peggie (2005).

Discussion Questions

1. Why is it important that companies strive to have high rankings on search engine results pages?
2. What is meant by the term "organic search results"?
3. What two basic strategies did SwellPath use to optimize the Nike Golf website?
4. How did Nike take advantage of Olympic star Misty May-Treanor's popularity to increase its search-related Web traffic?
5. Why do organic search results produce more website traffic than PPC or paid search advertisements?

6.1 Using Search Technology for Business Success

Search engines like Google, Bing, Yahoo, and others have traditionally been regarded as a consumer technology. But search technology has become an important business tool with many different uses and applications. In this section, you will read about how search engines work. You will learn about the role search engines play in generating revenue and consumer awareness for organizations. You will also discover how businesses use enterprise search technology to unlock hidden content with their organizations. Finally, you will read about how search and Internet technology is evolving to provide more accurate and useful results.

HOW SEARCH ENGINES WORK

Search engine: an application for locating webpages or other content (e.g., documents, media files) on a computer network. Popular web-based search engines include Google, Bing and Yahoo.

Spiders: also known as **crawlers**, **web bots** or simply **"bots,"** spiders are small computer programs designed to perform automated, repetitive tasks over the Internet. Used by search engines for scanning webpages and returning information to be stored in a page repository.

People use the word **search engine** to refer to many different kinds of information retrieval (IR) services that find content on the World Wide Web. However, these services vary in significant ways. Understanding the nature of these differences is important if you want to get the best results from your search. Listed below is a brief description of different IR services for finding Web content:

- **Crawler search engines** rely on sophisticated computer programs called "**spiders**," "**crawlers**," or "**bots**" that surf the Internet, locating webpages, links, and other content that are then stored in the search engine's page repository. The most popular commercial search engines, Google and Bing, are based on crawler technology.
- **Web directories** are categorized listings of webpages created and maintained by humans. Because websites are only included after being reviewed by a person, it is less likely that search results will contain irrelevant websites. Examples of popular directories include Open Directory Project (dmoz.org), Best of the Web (botw.org), and Looksmart.com.
- **Hybrid search engines** combine the results of a directory created by humans and results from a crawler search engine, with the goal of providing both accuracy and broad coverage of the Internet. Yahoo.com, the third most popular commercial search tool, uses a hybrid approach to information search.
- **Meta-search engines** compile results from other search engines. For instance, Dogpile.com generates listings by combining results from Google and Yandex, two crawler-based search engines, and Yahoo, a hybrid search tool.
- **Semantic search engines** are designed to locate information based on the nature and meaning of Web content, not simple keyword matches. The goal of these search engines is to dramatically increase the accuracy and usefulness of search results. Semantic search engines are described in more detail in Section 6.4

WEB DIRECTORIES

Before crawler search engines became the dominant method for finding Web content, people relied on directories created by human editors to help them find information. Web directories are typically organized by categories (for instance, see the homepage of the popular Web directory dmoz.org). Webpage content is usually reviewed by directory editors prior to its listing in a category to make sure it is appropriate. This reduces the number of irrelevant links generated in a search. The review process, however, is very slow compared to the automated process used by crawlers (described below). As a result, the listings in a Web directory represent a relatively small portion of the Web. Directories are particularly useful when conducting searches on a narrow topic, such as identifying suppliers of a specific type of product or service. Companies who need to identify vendors or suppliers may consult a niche Web directory created for just this purpose. For example, see the Web directory at business.com.

HOW CRAWLER SEARCH ENGINES WORK

The two most popular commercial search engines on the Web, Google and Bing, are based on crawler technology. Behind the relatively simple interfaces of these two powerful search engines, a great deal of complex technology is at work (Figure 6.5). Because modern search engines use proprietary technology in the race to stay ahead of competitors, it is not possible to tell exactly how they decide what websites will appear in a search engine results page (SERP). While they each produce different results, it is possible to describe the basic process shared by most crawler search engines. The following description is based on publications by Grehan (2002) and Oak (2008).

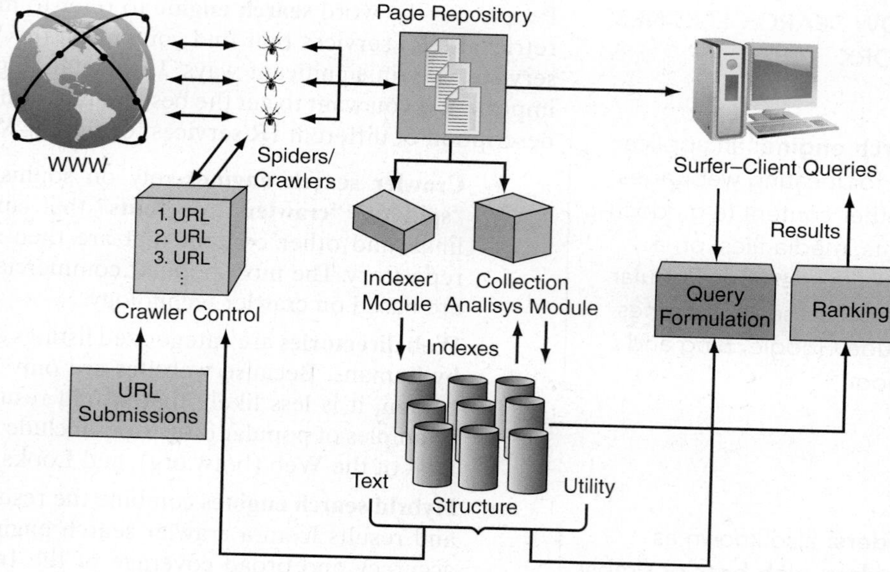

Figure 6.5 Components of crawler search engine (Adapted from Grehan, 2002).

Page repository: a data structure that stores and manages information from a large number of webpages, providing a fast and efficient means for accessing and analyzing the information at a later time.

Crawler control module: a software program that controls a number of "spiders" responsible for scanning or crawling through information on the Web.

1. The crawler control module assigns webpage URLs to programs called spiders or bots. The spider downloads these webpages into a **page repository** and scans them for links. The links are transferred to the **crawler control module** and used to determine where the spiders will be sent in the future. (Most search engines also allow webmasters to submit URLs, requesting that their websites be scanned so they will appear in search results. These requests are added to the crawler control queue.)

2. The **indexer module** creates look-up tables by extracting words from the webpages and recording the URL where they were found. The indexer module also creates an inverted index that helps search engines efficiently locate relevant pages containing keywords used in a search. (See Figure 6.6 for examples of an inverted index.)

3. The **collection analysis module** creates utility indexes that aid in providing search results. The utility indexes contain information about things like how many pages are in a website, the geographic location of the website, number of pictures on a webpage, webpage length, or other site-specific information the search engine may use to determine the relevance of a page.

4. The **retrieval/ranking module** determines the order in which pages are listed in a SERP. The methods by which search engines determine page rank vary and the specific algorithms they use are often carefully guarded trade secrets. In some cases, a search engine may use hundreds of different criteria to determine which pages appear at the top of a SERP. Google, for instance, claims to use over 200 "clues" to determine how it ranks pages (Google.com, 2014). According to Dover and Dafforn (2011), all these factors can be grouped into two categories: relevance and popularity (or "authority").

5. Webpages retrieved by the spiders, along with the indexes and ranking information, are stored on large servers (see IT at Work 6.1).

6. The **query interface** is where users enter words that describe the kind of information they are looking for. The search engine then applies various algorithms to match the query string with information stored in the indexes to determine what pages to display in the SERP.

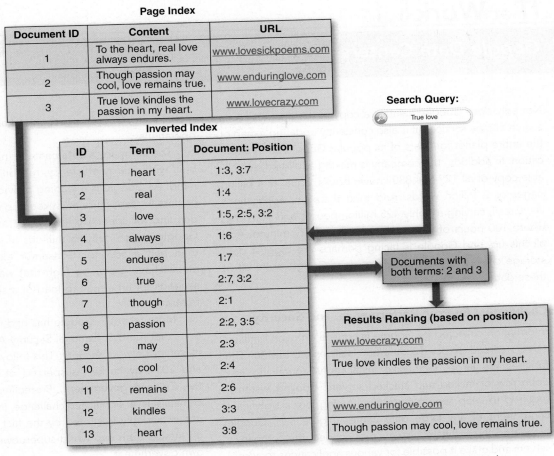

Figure 6.6 Search engines use inverted indexes to efficiently locate Web content based on search query terms.

Each search engine utilizes variations and refinements of the above steps in an attempt to achieve superior results. The Web search industry is highly competitive and the proprietary advances in search technology used by each company are closely guarded secrets. For instance, even the first step in the process, crawling the Web for content, can vary greatly depending on the strategic goals of the search engine. Some search engines limit the number of pages scanned at each website, seeking instead to use limited computing power and resources to cover as many websites as possible. Other search engines, however, program their spiders to scan deep into each website, seeking more complete coverage of the site's content. Still other search engines direct their spiders to seek out websites that contain certain types of content, such as government sites, shopping (e-commerce) sites, and so on. Another decision that search engines make with regard to spiders is the amount of resources directed at searching new websites versus devoting resources to exploring previously indexed pages for updates or changes.

One of the many challenges faced by large commercial search engines is storage. In the simplest sense, the crawler approach to search requires a company to store a copy of the Web in large data centers. In addition to the **petabytes** of storage required to maintain this copy of the Web, the search engine must also store the results of its indexing process and the list of links for future crawls.

Petabyte: a unit of measurement for digital data storage. A petabyte is equal to one million gigabytes.

IT at **Work 6.1**

Google Data Centers

Not only does Google maintain a copy of the Internet for its search engine services, it is also constantly updating a map of the entire planet for users of its popular Google Earth application. In addition, the company is making a full-text, searchable copy of all 129,864,880 known books, equal to 4 billion pages or 2 trillion words. And then there are applications like Gmail, serving roughly 425 million people and YouTube, where 100 hours of video are uploaded every minute! Add all this up, and Google is facing perhaps the biggest data storage challenge ever. So where does Google store all of these data?

Challenges: Energy, Performance, and Security

Information collected by Google is housed on over 1 million servers spread across 12 different facilities worldwide. The facilities are large, factorylike installations containing row upon row of racked and stacked servers. Cooling systems, required to keep servers from overheating, are a significant component of any large data center (Figure 6.7). Google pioneered the software systems that connect the company's servers and make it possible for various applications to access data stored on the machines. Unlike other companies that purchase servers from outside suppliers, Google builds its own. Based on its experience creating the hardware, software, and facilities necessary to power the company on a

global scale, Google is recognized as a leader in data center operations.

The company's data centers, including the servers, are built with energy efficiency, reliability, and performance in mind. As Google is a leading provider of Internet services, its data infrastructure must keep up with growing consumer demand for speedy performance and reliability. A typical Google search delivers millions of pages of results in less than half a second. Consumer expectations for performance have grown so high that waiting more than a few seconds for an e-mail to load or a search to run can cause frustration.

More recently, Google has had to contend with revelations that the U.S. National Security Agency (NSA) breached its server network security. This follows cyberattacks in 2010 and 2011 by hackers suspected of being associated with the Chinese government. Protecting company data from criminals is a significant challenge in itself, but Google is understandably frustrated by the fact that it must now fight off attacks from two world superpowers, one of which is its own government.

Environmental Impact

Industrywide, data centers used 38,000 megawatts of electricity in 2012, representing a tremendous increase of over 63 percent from the previous year. Industrywide, data center energy use and the related environmental impact have become an issue of growing concern. Google is widely recognized as operating some of the most efficient data centers in the world, but many critics are disturbed by the industry's overall level of energy consumption. According to some estimates, data centers account for about 2 percent of the world's energy use and the fast rate of growth is cause for concern (see Figure 6.8). Google has taken an active approach to reducing its environmental footprint by increasing the company's use of renewable energy sources and continuously developing new ways to become more energy-efficient. (For further information, see google.com/about/datacenters.)

Google Data Center Statistics

- **Number of servers worldwide:** Over 1 million
- **Number of data centers:** 6 to 12 in North America, 1 in South America, 2 in Asia, and 3 in Europe
- **2013 capital investment in data centers:** $7.35 billion

Figure 6.7 Pipes pass through the chiller plant at the Google, Inc. data center in Changhua, Taiwan. Google doubled its spending plan for its new data center in Taiwan to $600 million amid surging demand from Asia for its Gmail and YouTube services.

Bloomberg/Getty Images

© asharkyu/Shutterstock

Figure 6.8 New, large-scale data centers being constructed for companies like Google, Microsoft, and Facebook house thousands of servers and are creating concern among environmentalists over increases in energy consumption.

- **Estimated investment in data centers since 2006:** $21 billion

- **Data processing volume:** Over 20 petabytes a day

- **Average energy efficiency:** PUE* = 1.12
- **Energy use:** Continual use of about 260 megawatts of electricity, approximately 0.01 percent of global energy consumption
- **Energy use comparisons:** Owns about 3 percent of servers worldwide, but only uses about 1 percent of data center industry energy
- **Renewable energy:** Claims that approximately 35 percent of its energy use comes from renewable sources

*PUE stands for **Power Usage Effectiveness**. A PUE of 2.0 means that for every watt of power devoted to computing, an additional watt is spent on cooling, power distribution, and overhead. The Data Center Industry average PUE falls between 1.8 and 1.89.

Sources: Anthony (2013), Miller (2013), Glanz (2011, 2012), Venkatraman (2012), Schneider (2011), Gallagher (2012), Grifantini (2011), Newman (2011), Jacobson (2010).

WHY SEARCH IS IMPORTANT FOR BUSINESS

Search engines have become a part of our everyday life. They are free, easy to use, and become more powerful and effective every day. Most of us take them for granted and are generally unaware of the complex technologies that power these tools. For the average Web user, it may not be vitally important to understand how search technology is evolving. But for business managers, understanding the potential power of search technology is crucial and becoming more important every day. It has long been recognized that access to information is a competitive advantage. Search technology impacts business in each of the following ways:

- Enterprise search—finding information within your organization
- Recommendation engines—presenting information to users without requiring them to conduct an active search
- Search engine marketing (SEM)—getting found by consumers on the Web
- Web search—finding crucial business information online

Each of these important search technology applications is described below.

Enterprise Search

Enterprise search tools are used by employees to search for and retrieve information related to their work in a manner that complies with the organization's information-sharing and access control policies. Information can come from a variety of sources, including publicly available information, enterprise information found in databases and intranets, as well as information on individual employee computers (Delgado, Laplanche, & Krishnamurthy, 2005, Smartlogic.com, 2012). An organization's ability to share knowledge among employees is vital to its ability to compete (Bock, Zmud, Kim, & Lee, 2007; Brown & Duguid, 2000; Small & Sage, 2006, Hatala & Lutta, 2009). Enterprise search tools allow companies to leverage the value of internal information by unlocking content that would otherwise remain hidden or "siloed" because of:

- Technology silos—incompatible software or systems (Thomas, 2013)
- Departments operating as individual business units with different priorities and goals (Smith, 2012)

- Concerns about the cost of integrating information (Walker, 2014)
- Organizational structure and culture (Simon, 1998, Hattal & Lutta, 2009)
- Security concerns (Hattal & Lutta, 2009)
- Concerns about diverting or overloading employees' work-related attention (Hattal & Lutta, 2009)

In most organizations today, a large portion of employees are "knowledge workers" (e.g., business analysts, marketing managers, purchasing agents, IT managers, etc.). Almost half of their time is spent on unproductive work—gathering information, unsuccessful searches, converting data to different formats, or recreating information (Google.com, 2008, Feldman & Sherman, 2001).

Enterprise search tools allow businesses, companies, and organizations to extract information from databases, intranets, content management systems, files, contracts, policy manuals, and documents to make timely decisions, adding value to the company and enhancing its competitive advantage.

Structured vs. unstructured data One of the challenges encountered by developers of enterprise search tools is that information is not always in the same format. Data exist in two formats: structured or unstructured. **Structured data** can be defined as "information with a high degree of organization, such that inclusion in a relational database is seamless and readily searchable by simple, straightforward search engine algorithms or other search operations" (Brightplanet.com, 2012). **Unstructured data**, sometimes called messy data, refers to information that is not organized in a systematic or predefined way. Unstructured data files are also more likely to contain inaccuracies or errors. Examples of unstructured data include e-mails, articles, books, and documents. It is estimated that unstructured data accounts for about 80 percent of all the data present on computers today (Kahn, 2012). Originally, enterprise search tools worked only with structured data. Many newer systems claim to work with unstructured information as well, although there is great variability in terms of how well they actually do this.

Security issues in enterprise search Unlike a Web search, enterprise search tools must balance the goal of making information widely available throughout the organization with the need to restrict access based on an employee's job function or security clearance. Limiting access to certain documents or data is referred to as **access control**. Enterprise search tools introduce the potential for a number of security breaches or access of unauthorized information. Most of these can be addressed as long as the organization's IT workers install and maintain the search system's security features, including security integrations with other enterprise programs. An audit of requests logs should be conducted regularly to look for patterns or inconsistencies.

Enterprise search vendors Market analysts Frost and Sullivan (Prnewswire.com, 2013) estimate that the global market for enterprise search tools was over $1.47 billion in 2012; it is predicted that the market will grow to $4.68 billion by 2019. Clearly, organizations around the world recognize the value of this technology. Several different companies make and sell enterprise search systems, Autonomy, Google, Coveo and Perceptive Software being the top contenders (Andrews and Koehler-Kruener, 2014). Vendors can be broken down into the following three categories:

- Specialized search vendors (for instance, Attivio, Endeca, Vivisimo): Software designed to target specific user information needs
- Integrated search vendors (for instance, Autonomy, IBM, Microsoft): Software designed to combine search capabilities with information management tools
- Detached search vendors (for instance, Google, ISYS): Software designed to target flexibility and ease of use

With so many options available for enterprise search, it is important that organizations conduct a careful needs analysis prior to acquisition (Martin, 2012).

Recommendation Engines

Recommendation engines represent an interesting twist on IR technology. Unlike Web search engines that begin with a user query for information, recommendation engines attempt to anticipate information that a user might be interested in. Recommendation engines are used by e-commerce sites to recommend products, news organizations to recommend news articles and videos, Web advertisers to anticipate the ads people might respond to, and so on. They represent a huge potential for businesses and developers. While the use of recommendation engines is widespread, there is still a lot of work to be done to improve the accuracy of these fascinating applications. You can read more about recommendation engines in Section 6.5.

Search Engine Marketing

Most traditional advertising methods target customers who are not actively engaged in shopping for a product. Instead, they are watching television, listening to the radio, reading a magazine, or driving down the road, paying little attention to the billboards they pass. To most people, advertising represents an unwelcome interruption. On the other hand, people using search engines are actively looking for information. As a result, they are much more likely to be interested in product and service information found in SERPs as long as it is related to the topic they are searching for. Efforts to reach this targeted audience are much more likely to produce sales. That's why **search engine marketing (SEM)** has become an important business strategy. Industry experts report that people generally engage in three basic types of searches:

1. **Informational search**—using search engines to conduct research on a topic. This is the most common type of search.

2. **Navigational search**—using a search engine to locate particular websites or webpages.

3. **Transactional search**—using a search engine to determine where to purchase a product or service.

Search Engine Marketing (SEM): a collection of online marketing strategies and tactics that promote brands by increasing their visibility in SERPs through optimization and advertising.

You might think businesses would be primarily interested in transactional searches, but all three types are important and play a key role in the buying process. Say you are interested in purchasing a new tablet computer. Your first step is likely to engage in an informational search, attempting to learn about the product category of mobile tablet devices. Businesses should offer content on their websites and social media sites for consumers seeking general product information. An informational search also represents an opportunity to influence consumers early in the purchasing process.

After researching a product category, you might try finding websites of particular companies to learn more about individual tablet computer brands (navigational search). Companies need to design their websites so that they can be found easily by search engines.

Finally, you might try to determine where to buy your tablet computer by searching on terms like "lowest price," "free shipping," and so on. This is an example of a transactional search.

Search engine marketing (SEM) (Figure 6.9) consists of designing and advertising a webpage, with the goal of increasing its visibility when consumers conduct the three types of searches just described. SEM strategies and tactics produce two different, but complementary outcomes:

1. **Organic search listings** are the result of content and website design features intended to improve a site's ranking on SERPs that result from specific keyword queries. No payments are made to the search engine service for organic search listings.

2. **Paid search listings** are a form of advertising and are purchased from search engine companies. The placement and effectiveness of paid search ads on SERPs

Figure 6.9 Search engine marketing integrates three different strategies: search engine optimization, pay-per-click advertising, and social media optimization.

are a function of several factors in addition to the fees paid by advertisers. You will read more about these factors in Section 6.3 below.

Businesses utilize search engine optimization (SEO) to improve their website's organic listings on SERPs. SEO specialists understand how search engines work and guide companies in designing websites and creating content that will produce higher organic SERP rankings than competitive websites.

Paid search listings are often referred to as **pay-per-click (PPC)** advertising. This is because advertisers pay search engines based on how many people click on the ads. Typically, PPC ads are listed separately from organic search results. Managing an effective PPC ad campaign involves making strategic decisions about what keyword search queries you want to trigger the display of your ad. You will read more about PPC or paid search advertising in Section 6.3.

Social media optimization refers to strategies designed to enhance a company's standing on various social media sites. Increasingly, search engines evaluate a company's presence on social media to determine its reputation, which in turn influences how the company is ranked in SERPs. You will read more about social media strategies in Chapter 7.

Growth of search engine marketing
As companies begin to realize the power of search engine marketing, more money is being spent on this highly effective strategy. Forrester Research estimates that search marketing is the largest segment of the digital marketing category, and will account for over $33 million by 2016, representing an increase of 77.6 percent since 2011 (VanBoskirk, 2011).

Unlike many traditional advertising methods, return on investment (ROI) can be calculated for search engine marketing by tracking **click-through rates (CTRs)**, changes in site traffic, and purchasing behavior.

Click-through rate: the percentage of people who click on a hyperlinked area of a SERP or webpage.

Mobile Search (and Mobile Search SEO)

Mobile devices have become ubiquitous (Figure 6.10). With the emergence of smartphones and tablets like the Apple iPad, mobile devices account for over a quarter of all website traffic (Sterling, 2013). Mobile Web traffic is expected to triple by 2017 due to an annual growth rate of approximately 61 percent (Cisco, 2014).

With the dramatic increase in smartphones, tablets, and other mobile devices, companies need to make sure their websites and content can be found via search engines on mobile devices. This means optimizing mobile websites differently from a desktop site. The two essential issues that need to be addressed are:

1. Properly configuring the technical aspects of the mobile site so that it can be crawled and indexed by search engines.

Figure 6.10 Mobile phone users watch One Direction perform on *Good Morning America* in New York City's Central Park on November 6, 2013.

2. Providing content that is useful to people using mobile devices. Webmasters should consider how people use their mobile devices and adjust content accordingly (see Table 6.2).

When designing a mobile site for e-commerce, Web developers should make sure that information about store location, product reviews, and promotional offers is easily available and optimized so that it is likely to appear in a mobile SERP. Mobile shoppers also use barcode scanning apps as a kind of mobile search engine for locating product reviews and price comparisons while shopping in stores. This practice, called **showrooming**, is becoming increasingly popular with consumers and creating a great deal of frustration and worry on the part of brick-and-mortar retailers.

Web Search for Business

Commercial search engines and Web directories are useful tools for knowledge workers in business. To use search engines effectively, workers should familiarize themselves with all the features available on the search engine they use. Since Google is the most popular search engine, we highlight some of those features below. Many of these features are also available on Bing.com.

- **Focused search:** You can focus your search to information in different formats—webpages, videos, images, maps, and the like—by selecting the appropriate navigation button on the SERP page.

- **Filetype:** If you are looking specifically for information contained in a certain file format, you can use the "filetype:[file extension]" command following your keyword query. For instance, the search "private colleges filetype:xls" will produce links to MSExcel files with information related to private colleges. Use this command to find Adobe files (pdf), MSWord files (doc), PowerPoint files (ppt), and so on.

- **Advanced search:** To narrow your search, go to the Advanced Search panel. From this page, you can set a wide range of parameters for your search, including limiting the search to certain domains (e.g., .gov, .org, .edu), languages, dates, and even reading level. You can also use this to narrow your search to a particular website.

- **Search tools button:** Allows you to narrow your results to listings from specific locations or time frames.

- **Search history:** Have you ever found a page using a search engine, but later had trouble finding it again? If you are logged into your Google account while using the search engine, it's possible to review your search history. It will show you not only your search queries, but also the pages you visited following each query.

TABLE 6.2 How In-Store Shoppers are Use Mobile Devices	
Shopping Behavior	**Percentage**
Use a mobile device to assist with shopping at least once a month	62%
Use a mobile device to assist with shopping at least weekly	17%
Use their smartphones for more than 15 minutes while in a store	~50%
Use a search engine to browse product information while shopping in a store (Search engines dominate store websites, brand websites, store apps, and brand apps as a starting point.)	82%
Use their smartphone for preshopping activities such as finding store locations, finding product reviews, making price comparisons, finding promotional offers, and so on	90%
Top mobile shopping categories include:	
Appliances	97%
Groceries	89%
Baby care	87%
Electronics	87%
Household care	86%
Across all product categories, mobile shoppers report using their smartphones instead of asking for information from store employees	33%
Use smartphones instead of asking for information from store employees when shopping for appliances	55%
Use smartphones instead of asking for information from store employees when shopping for electronics	48%
In-store price comparisons are the most common shopping activity across product categories	
Appliances	74%
Electronics	70%
Baby care	62%
Household care	58%
Mobile shoppers prefer to view mobile websites vs. mobile apps	65% vs. 35%

Source: ThinkWithGoogle.com (2013).

These are just a few of the many features you can use to conduct a power search. While you are in college, take the time to become proficient with using different search engine features. Not only will it help with your immediate research needs, it will help you in your career as well. At the end of this chapter, we include information for a free online Power Search course offered by Google. This is a good way to enhance your ability to find the information you need.

Finding intellectual property Your business may have an interest in protecting certain kinds of intellectual property being used without permission on the Web. This might include confidential reports, images, copyrighted blog posts, creative writing (e.g., poetry, novels, etc.), and so on. You can use search engines to find where someone may have posted your intellectual property on the Web without permission (see Osher, 2014). You can search for text-based work by simply using queries containing strings of text from the material you're looking for. Images can be found by using Google's reverse image search engine (images.google.com). Tin Eye is an alternative reverse image search engine with a number of interesting features (tineye.com).

Real time search Sometimes you need information about things as they happen. For instance, you may be interested in monitoring news stories written about your company or you might need to know what people are saying about your brand or a political candidate on Twitter. For these situations, you'll need a real time search tool.

Say your company wants to explore accepting Bitcoin payments. (Bitcoin is a digital currency that was launched in 2009.) After engaging in a traditional Web search to learn about the currency, you decide you want to learn about public interest in the currency and find news stories about it that have recently been published. You might consider using the following tools:

- **Google Trends**—Trends (google.com/trends) will help you identify current and historical interest in the topic by reporting the volume of search activity over time. Google Trends allows you to view the information for different time periods and geographic regions.
- **Google Alerts**—Alerts (google.com/alerts) is an automated search tool for monitoring new Web content, news stories, videos, and blog posts about some topic. Users set up alerts by specifying a search term (e.g., a company name, product, or topic), how often they want to receive notices, and an e-mail address where the alerts are to be sent. When Google finds content that match the parameters of the search, users are notified via e-mail. Bing has a similar feature called News Alerts.
- **Twitter Search**—You can leverage the crowd of over 650 million Twitter users to find information as well as gauge sentiment on a wide range of topics and issues in real time. Twitter's search tool (twitter.com/search-home) looks similar to other search engines, and includes an advanced search mode.

Social bookmarking search Social bookmarking sites (described in Chapter 7) provide a way for users to save links they want to access at a later time. When saving page links, users tag them with keywords that describe the page's content. In effect, the bookmarked links form a graph of content on the Web that can be used by others. The two largest social bookmarking services are delicious.com and diigo.com. Because the webpages are tagged by humans, search results are often different from and more relevant than what you get from commercial search engines.

Specialty search engines: vertical search As described previously, large commercial search engines use indicators of popularity or reputation to determine website quality. This seems to work well for a generalized Web search, but it might not be effective when users search on very specific topics such as rare disease, which by definition, does not generate a lot of activity on the Web. Crawlers also do not often index pages in the lower levels of less popular websites. **Vertical search**

engines are programmed to focus on webpages related to a particular topic and to drill down by crawling pages that other search engines are likely to ignore. Vertical search engines exist for a variety of industries. Ironically, the best way to find a vertical search engine for a particular industry or topic is to search for it on a commercial search engine like Google or Bing.

Questions

1. What is the primary difference between a Web directory and a crawler-based search engine?
2. What is the purpose of an index in a search engine?
3. Why are companies increasingly interested in enterprise search tools capable of handling unstructured data?
4. What is the difference between search engine optimization and PPC advertising?
5. Describe three different real time search tools.

6.2 Organic Search and Search Engine Optimization

The goal of SEO practitioners is to help organizations increase traffic to their websites. They accomplish this by optimizing websites in an effort to increase visibility and ranking on SERPs. Using Web analytics programs like *Google Analytics*, companies can determine how many people visit their site, what specific pages they visit, how long they spend on the site, and what search engines are producing the most traffic (see Figure 6.11). More sophisticated SEO practitioners will also analyze **keyword conversion rates**, or the likelihood that using a particular keyword to optimize a page will result in conversions (i.e., when a website *visitor* converts to a *buyer*). These are just a few of the many metrics used to measure the effectiveness of SEO strategies.

STRATEGIES FOR SEARCH ENGINE OPTIMIZATION

As mentioned at the beginning of this chapter, all search engines use somewhat different proprietary methods for determining where a website will appear in search results. As a result, it is not possible to tell what specific factors will be used and how much weight they will carry in determining SERP ranking. However, in the section below, we describe three categories of ranking factors (see Brown, 2013) and attempt to illustrate each with a few examples.

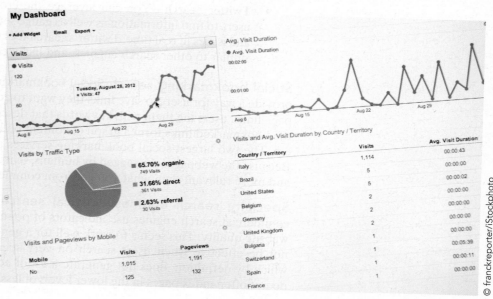

Figure 6.11 Tools like Google Analytics are used to monitor changes in website traffic as a result of search engine optimization practices.

© franckreporter/iStockphoto

Ranking Factors

Ranking factors can be grouped into at least three different categories: reputation or popularity, relevance, and user satisfaction.

Reputation or Popularity: In simple terms, search engines attempt to provide links to good websites—sites that contain high-quality content. But how do they determine this? It is not possible for the search engine to directly evaluate the quality of a website's content. That would require the system to understand the site's content and have expertise in all possible subject matters. Instead, search engines use indirect measures of quality. One way of assessing the quality of a website is to use measures of popularity. This is based on the assumption that websites with good content will be more popular than sites with poor-quality content. Google's **PageRank** algorithm is perhaps one of the most well-known attempts to use popularity to determine website quality. It is based on the assumption that people are more likely to link to high-quality websites than poor-quality sites. Therefore, the algorithm counts **backlinks**—external links that point back to a site. The effectiveness of the PageRank strategy is what initially set Google apart from competing search engines and led to its dominance in the marketplace. SEO practitioners and writers in the field have placed great emphasis on the importance of backlinks over the years. A number of creative strategies have been developed for encouraging others to link to a website (see Zrekat, 2013, Solihin, 2013, Gaiker, 2012, Ward & French, 2013).

Recent changes in Google's ranking methods have led others to speculate that backlinks, while still very important, are not weighted as heavily as they used to be (see Schachinger, 2012). Table 6.3 lists a number of other factors that SEO specialists believe are used by search engines to gauge reputation.

TABLE 6.3   Popularity Factors Used by Search Engines

Social media indicators: Webpages being discussed in social media are more likely to be popular. Examples include comments on Facebook and Google+, shares, Tweets, Likes, and so on.

Site traffic: The more traffic a site gets, the more likely it is to contain quality content.

Listings in quality Web directories: Sites that have been accepted for listing in quality Web directories are more likely to contain quality content because they have been reviewed by human editors.

Reputation on review sites: Sites with high ratings on review sites (such as Yelp.com, Zagat.com, and Epinions.com) are more likely to have quality content.

PageRank of sites containing backlinks: Backlinks from sites with high PageRank scores themselves are thought to be more valuable.

SERP click-through rate (CTR): Google and other search engines monitor how often searchers click through on a SERP listing. People tend to click listings that appear to contain quality content.

Onpage factors: Metadata (e.g., page titles, page descriptions) and descriptive URLs influence how a listing appears on a SERP. This, in turn, can affect the CTR.

Dwell time and bounce rate: Dwell time is the amount of time a user stays on a page before returning to the SERP. Longer dwell times suggest users found content that was worth reading. A "bounce" is an extremely short dwell time—in other words, a user who clicks on a listing and comes right back is said to "bounce." Low **bounce rates** and long dwell times correlate with high content quality.

Relevance: In addition to popularity, search engines attempt to determine if the content on a webpage is relevant to what the searcher is looking for. As with quality, the search engine cannot determine relevance directly, so algorithms have been developed to look for clues that suggest a site might be relevant. The factors listed in Table 6.4 have been identified by SEO specialists as likely clues used by search engines to determine relevance scores. Note that some of these are the same or similar to factors used to evaluate popularity, but are interpreted to evaluate relevance.

User Satisfaction: Like all successful businesses, search engines want their customers to be satisfied. As a result, SERP ranking is influenced by factors that impact user satisfaction. Table 6.5 lists factors that are likely to influence a search engine's user satisfaction rating.

CONTENT AND INBOUND MARKETING

The ultimate goal of a search engine is to help users find the information or content that they are searching for. Sometimes it seems that SEO practitioners lose sight of this and spend too much time chasing down hundreds of factors they think are being used by search engine ranking algorithms. At worst, SEO can represent an attempt to "game the system" or trick search engines into ranking a site higher than its content deserves (see the discussion of black hat SEO in the next section).

Inbound marketing: an approach to marketing that emphasizes SEO, content marketing and social media strategies to attract customers. Often viewed as an alternative to traditional marketing strategies based on advertising and personal selling.

Perhaps the most important action an organization can take to improve its website's ranking and satisfy website visitors is provide helpful content that is current and updated regularly. When SEO practices are combined with valuable content, websites become easier to find in search engines but, more importantly, contribute to building brand awareness, positive attitudes toward the brand, and brand loyalty.

Inbound marketing represents an alternative approach to traditional outbound marketing strategies (e.g., mass media advertising) that have been used by companies historically (see Figure 6.12).

TABLE 6.4 Factors That Affect Relevance Scores

Keywords related to the search topic suggest relevant content.

Page titles: Words in the page title that are related to the topic suggest relevant content.

Relevant phrases in text: In addition to keywords, search engines look at the words and phrases on the page to determine relevance.

Amount of text on page that appears relevant: The proportion of relevant text to nonrelevant text can influence relevance.

Backlinks from relevant sites and Web directories: Webpages that are listed in relevant categories of Web directories are more likely to be relevant because they were reviewed by human editors.

SERP click-through rate (CTR): Searchers are more likely to click on listings that contain relevant content.

Onpage factor: Metadata (such as page titles, page descriptions) and descriptive URLs should reflect the page content. People use the information in search listings to determine if a link contains relevant information. This affects CTR.

Dwell time and bounce rate are impacted by how relevant a website's content is. Long dwell times and short bounce rates suggest relevant content related to the search.

TABLE 6.5 Factors Affecting User Satisfaction

Dwell time: Users who stay on a site longer are probably more satisfied.

Site speed: Slow page loading time on websites reduces satisfaction.

Reading level: Reading levels that are too high or too low frustrate users.

Hacked sites, malware, spam reduce user satisfaction significantly.

Website satisfaction surveys: Google created user satisfaction surveys that webmasters can embed in their websites. Positive responses to these surveys can improve ranking.

Barriers to content: Making people register, provide names, or fill out forms to get to content has a negative impact on user satisfaction.

Other factors: Too many ads, page-not-found errors, duplicate content/pages, content copied from other websites, and spam in comment sections all detract from user satisfaction.

Inbound marketers attract customers to their websites with content that is informative, useful, or entertaining. Inbound marketing campaigns are based on strategies that integrate content generation, SEO, and social media tactics. In Chapter 7, you will read more about how inbound marketers integrate content, SEO, and social media strategies into powerful marketing campaigns that deliver sales and profits to companies that use this new approach to marketing.

BLACK HAT vs. WHITE HAT SEO: ETHICAL ISSUES IN SEARCH ENGINE OPTIMIZATION

Search engines regularly update their algorithms to improve results. Two well-known Google updates called Panda (released in 2011) and Penguin (released in 2012) were designed to improve the ranking of websites with quality content and downgrade poor-quality sites. Both updates are designed to defeat what are commonly referred to as **black hat SEO** tactics. People who employ black hat SEO

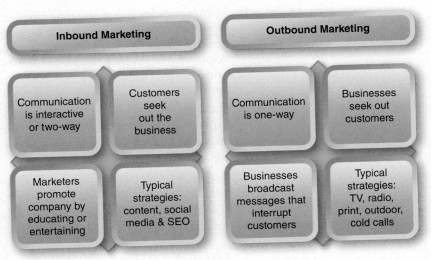

Figure 6.12 Inbound marketers use valuable content, SEO, and social media to attract customers.

tactics try to trick the search engine into thinking a website has high-quality content, when in fact it does not. Some examples of obvious black hat techniques are listed below. With stronger detection systems now in place, websites that use these tactics (or even appear to use them) will be severely downgraded in Google's ranking system.

Link spamming—generating backlinks for the primary purpose of SEO, not adding value to the user. Black hat SEOs use tricks to create backlinks. Some examples include adding a link to a page in the comments section of an unrelated blog post, or building sites called **link farms** solely for the purpose of linking back to the promoted page.

Keyword tricks—Black hat SEOs will embed several high-value keywords on pages with unrelated content to drive up traffic statistics. For instance, an e-commerce site might embed words like "amazon" (a word that frequently shows up in search queries) in an attempt to get listed on SERPs of people looking for amazon.com.

Ghost text—This tactic involves adding text on a page that will affect page ranking. The text may not have anything to do with the real content of the page, or it may simply repeat certain words to increase the content density. The text is then hidden, usually by making it the same color as the background.

Shadow pages—Also called **ghost pages** or **cloaked pages**, this black hat tactic involves creating pages that are optimized to attract lots of people. The pages, however, contain a redirect command so that users are sent to another page to increase traffic on that page.

These particular tactics are no longer effective as a result of updates Google has made to its ranking system. Most likely, other major search engines have adopted similar measures. However, there will always be people who attempt to take shortcuts to achieve higher SERP rankings. Businesses need to be very careful when hiring SEO consultants or agencies to make sure they do not use inappropriate SEO techniques because when they are discovered, Google and other search engines will usually punish the business by dramatically lowering the website's rank so that it does not show up on SERPs at all.

Questions

1. Search engines use many different "clues" about the quality of a website's content to determine how a page should be ranked in search results. These clues fall into three primary categories: Reputation or Popularity, Relevance, and User Satisfaction. Explain the rationale for using each of these three categories as an indicator of a website's content quality.

2. Backlinks were a key factor in Google's original PageRank algorithm. Explain what a backlink is and why Google has reduced its emphasis on backlinks and instead uses many other additional factors in its ranking algorithm.

3. Explain why so-called black hat SEO tactics are ultimately short-sighted and can lead to significant consequences for businesses that use them.

4. How do organizations evaluate the effectiveness of their search engine optimization (SEO) strategies and tactics?

5. Explain why providing high quality, regularly updated content is the most important aspect of any SEO strategy.

6.3 Pay-Per-Click and Paid Search Strategies

In addition to organic listings, most search engines display paid or sponsored listings on their SERPs. These advertisements provide revenue for the search engine and allow it to offer Web search services to the general public for free. They also provide a way for smaller organizations or businesses with new websites to gain visibility on SERPs while waiting for their SEO strategies to produce results. Most major search engines differentiate organic search results from paid ad listings on SERPs with labels, shading, and placing the ads in a different place on the page. Some critics have complained that paid advertisements receive preferential page placement and are not clearly distinguished from organic listings. However, at the time of this publication, it is easy to distinguish ads from organic results on Google and Bing SERPs. Defenders of the search engine companies argue that since the paid ads make it possible for everyone to use search services for free, the preferential page placement is justified.

**CREATING A PPC
ADVERTISING
CAMPAIGN**

There are four steps to creating a PPC advertising campaign on search engines.

1. Set an overall budget for the campaign.
2. Create ads—most search engine ads are text only.
3. Select keywords associated with the campaign.
4. Set up billing account information.

Search advertising allows businesses to target customers who are likely to purchase their products. They do this by selecting keywords that correspond to search queries that potentially identify someone as a customer. For instance, a company that sells women's purses may want to appear on a SERP when someone conducts a search using any of the following terms or phrases:

- Purse
- Handbag
- Women's purses
- Ladies' purses
- Designer purses
- Designer handbags

Google and other search engines provide advertisers with tools for evaluating the impact of different keywords or phrases. These tools typically display information about how often people use the word in a search and also recommend alternative words the advertiser may want to consider including in the campaign. Advertisers "bid" on having their ads appear when someone searches on one of their keywords. Higher bids result in a greater probability that the ad will be selected to appear when someone searches on a particular keyword, but also deplete the advertiser's budget more quickly. If a bid is too low, the ad might not appear very often or not at all. The keyword tools usually provide information about typical bid prices for each keyword or phrase. Smart advertisers will typically start with a modest bid and increase it over time to achieve the ad placement rate they desire.

The likelihood of ad placement can also influenced by a **quality score** determined by factors related to the user's experience. Ads that are considered to be more relevant (and therefore more likely to be clicked on) will cost less and more likely run in a top position. According to Google, quality scores are determined by several factors:

- Expected keyword CTR
- The past CTR of your URL

- Past effectiveness (overall CTR of ads and keywords in the account)
- Landing page quality (relevance, transparency, ease of navigation, etc.)
- Relevance of keywords to ads
- Relevance of keywords to customer search query
- Geographic performance—account success in geographic regions being targeted.
- How well ads perform on different devices (quality scores are calculated for mobile, desktop/laptop, and tablets).

Relevant ads are good for all parties—the search engine makes more money from clicked ads, the advertiser experiences more customers visiting its site, and the customer is more likely to find what he or she is looking for.

In addition to selecting keywords and setting bid prices, advertisers also set parameters for the geographic location they want their ad to appear in and the time of day. These factors allow for additional customer targeting designed to help advertisers reach the consumers most likely to purchase their products.

In their review of paid search advertising, Jansen and Mullen (2008) point out that the effectiveness of PPC ads is heavily influenced by factors on the webpages that ads are linked to. For instance, sometimes companies create product-oriented ads, but then link to the main page of their website instead of a page with information about the product in the ad. Other factors include landing page design, effectiveness of the call to action, and the quality of the shopping cart application. It does not make sense to spend a lot of money on a PPC campaign if the website is not attractive to consumers once they reach it.

You can learn more about advertising on the major commercial search engines by visiting the following websites:

- **Google**: adwords.google.com
- **Bing:** advertise.bingads.microsoft.com
- **Yahoo:** advertising.yahoo.com

METRICS FOR PAID SEARCH ADVERTISING

In addition to more effective targeting, one of the key benefits of online advertising is the ability to evaluate its contribution to sales revenue more effectively. PPC advertisers use the following metrics to gauge the effectiveness of their campaigns:

Click-through rates (CTRs)—By themselves, CTRs do not measure the financial performance of an ad campaign. But they are useful for evaluating many of the decisions that go into a campaign, such as keyword selection and ad copy.

Keyword conversion—High CTRs are not always good if they do not lead to sales. Since the cost of the campaign is based on how many people click an ad, you want to select keywords that lead to sales (conversions), not just site visits. PPC advertisers monitor which keywords lead to sales and focus on those in future campaigns.

Cost of customer acquisition (CoCA)—This metric represents the amount of money spent to attract a paying customer. To calculate CoCA for a PPC campaign, you divide the total budget of the campaign by the number of customers who purchased something from your site. For instance, if you spent $1,000 on a campaign that yielded 40 customers, your CoCA would be $1,000/40 = $25 per customer.

Return on advertising spend (ROAS)—The campaign's overall financial effectiveness is evaluated with ROAS (revenue/cost). For example, if $1,000 was spent on a campaign that led to $6,000 in sales, ROAS would be $6,000/$1,000 = $6. In other words, for every dollar spent on PPC ads, $6 was earned.

Questions

1. What would most people say is the fundamental difference between organic listings and PPC listings on a search engine?
2. What are the four primary steps to creating a PPC advertising campaign on search engines?
3. In addition to the "bid price" for a particular keyword, what other factor(s) influence the likelihood that an advertisement will appear on a search results page? Why don't search engines just rely on the advertisers bid when deciding what ads will appear on the search results page?
4. How do webpage factors influence the effectiveness of PPC advertisements?
5. Describe four metrics that can be used to evaluate the effectiveness of a PPC advertising campaign.

6.4 A Search for Meaning—Semantic Technology

If there is one thing history has taught us, it is that the future is hard to predict. It might seem silly to predict what the future Internet will look like when it's clear so many people are having trouble understanding all the implications of the Internet that now exists. However, forward-thinking businesses and individuals are beginning to plan for the next evolution, which is sometimes called Web 3.0.

The current Web is disjointed, requiring us to visit different websites to get content, engage in commerce, and interact with our social networks (community). The future Web will use context, personalization, and vertical search to make content, commerce, and community more relevant and easier to access (Mitra, 2007). With the addition of mobile technology, this Web will be always accessible.

- Context defines the intent of the user; for example, trying to purchase music, to find a job, to share memories with friends and family.
- Personalization refers to the user's personal characteristics that impact how relevant the content, commerce, and community are to an individual.
- Vertical search, as you have read, focuses on finding information in a particular content area, such as travel, finance, legal, and medical.

Many technologies are being developed that will create a new, richer experience for Web users of the future. Semantic technology is one of those growth areas.

WHAT IS THE SEMANTIC WEB?

Metadata: data that describe and provide information about other data.

Semantic refers to the meaning of words or language. The **semantic Web** is one in which computers can interpret the meaning of content (data) by using **metadata**:

> "Semantics (in an IT setting) is meaningful computing: the application of natural language processing (NLP) to support information retrieval, analytics, and data-integration that compass both numerical and "unstructured" information." (Grimes, 2010)

Tim Berners-Lee, creator of the technology that made the World Wide Web possible is the director of the *World Wide Web Consortium (W3C)*. This group develops programming standards designed to make it possible for data, information, and knowledge to be shared even more widely across the Internet. The result of these standards is a metadata language, or ways of describing digital information so that it can be used by a wide variety of applications. Much of the world's digital information is stored in files structured so that they can only be read by the programs that created them. With metadata, the content of these files can be labeled with tags describing the nature of the information, where it came from, or how it is arranged, essentially making the Web one large database that can be read and used by a wide variety of applications.

It is helpful to think about the semantic Web against the background of earlier Internet functionality (see Table 6.6). The early Internet allowed programmers and users to access information and communicate with one another without worrying about the details associated with the machines they used to connect to the network and store the information. The semantic Web continues this evolution, by making it possible to access information about real things (people, places, contracts, books, chemicals, etc.) without worrying about the details associated with the nature or structure of the data files, pages, and databases where these things are described or contained (Hendler and Berners-Lee, 2010). This will increase the amount of information available on the Web and enhance our ability to search for and find useful information.

TABLE 6.6 Evolution of the Web	
Web 1.0 (The Initial Web) A Web of Pages	Pages or documents are "hyperlinked," making it easier than ever before to access connected information.
Web 2.0 (The Social Web) A Web of Applications	Applications are created that allow people to easily create, share, and organize information.
Web 3.0 (The Semantic Web) A Web of Data	Information within documents or pages is tagged with metadata, allowing users to access specific information across platforms, regardless of the original structure of the file, page, or document that contains it. It turns the Web into one giant database.

THE LANGUAGE(S) OF WEB 3.0

The early Web was built using hypertext markup language (HTML). Web 2.0 was made possible, in part, by the development of languages like XML and JavaScript. The semantic Web utilizes additional languages that have been developed by the W3C. These include **resource description framework (RDF), Web ontology language (OWL)**, and **SPARQL protocol and RDF query language (SPARQL)**. RDF is a language used to represent information about resources on the Internet. It will describe these resources using metadata **uniform resource identifiers (URIs)** like "title," "author," "copyright and license information." It is one of the features that allow data to be used by multiple applications.

As the acronym SPARQL implies, it is used to write programs that can retrieve and manipulate data stored in RDF format. OWL is the W3C language used to categorize and accurately identify the nature of things found on the Internet. These three languages, used together, will enhance the element of context on the Web, producing more fruitful and accurate information searches. The W3C continues its work, with input by programmers and the broader Internet community to improve the power and functionality of these languages.

SEMANTIC WEB AND SEMANTIC SEARCH

As you have read, the semantic Web is (or will be) described by metadata, making it easier for a broad range of applications to identify and utilize data. One of the barriers to creating the semantic Web, however, is the tagging process. Who will tag all of the data that currently exist on the Web? How can we be sure that such data will be tagged correctly? Will people purposely tag data incorrectly to gain some kind of advantage in the same way that black hat SEO tactics are used to mislead search engines?

Semantic search engines could be programmed to take advantage of metadata tags, but their usefulness would be very limited if they could only identify Web content that had been tagged with metadata:

> "Semantic search is the process of typing something into a search engine and getting more results than just those that feature the exact keyword you typed into the search box. Semantic search will take into account the context and meaning of your search terms. It's about understanding the assumptions that the searcher is making when typing in that search query." (DiSilvestro, 2013)

Instead of relying solely on metadata tags, current semantic search engines use alternative approaches to understanding the meaning of content on the Web. Semantic search engines use natural language processing, contextual cues, synonyms, word variations, concept matching, specialized queries, and other strategies to generate search results that are superior to those created by simple keyword-matching algorithms. Understanding the context or intent of users is particularly important. If a search engine understood the proper context of a search query containing the word "Disneyworld," it would know if the search engine should return information that would be of interest to people

- planning a vacation, or
- looking for a job at the theme park, or
- interested in the history of Disneyworld.

Simple keyword matching is likely to produce a wide assortment of information, much of which will not be of interest to users with a specific goal in mind.

Semantic Search Features and Benefits

So what can semantic search engines do that is superior to search engines that work solely on keyword matching? Grimes (2010) provides a list of practical benefits that could result from semantic search technology:

Related searches/queries. The engine suggests alternative search queries that may produce information related to the original query. Search engines may also ask you, "Did you mean: [search term]?" if it detects a misspelling.

Reference results. The search engine suggests reference material related to the query, such as a dictionary definition, Wikipedia pages, maps, reviews, or stock quotes.

Semantically annotated results. Returned pages contain highlighting of search terms, but also related words or phrases that may not have appeared in the original query. These can be used in future searches simply by clicking on them.

Full-text similarity search. Users can submit a block of text or even a full document to find similar content.

Search on semantic/syntactic annotations. This approach would allow a user to indicate the "syntactic role the term plays—for instance, the part-of-speech (noun, verb, etc.)—or its semantic meaning—whether it's a company name, location, or event." For instance, a keyword search on the word "center" would produce too many results. Instead, a search query could be written using a syntax such as the following:

<organization> center </organization>

This would only return documents where the word "center" was part of an organization's name (e.g., Johnson Research Center or Millard Youth Center). Google currently allows you to do something similar to specify the kind of files you are looking for (e.g., filetype:pdf).

Concept search. Search engines could return results with related concepts. For instance, if the original query was "Tarantino films," documents would be returned that contain the word "movies" even if not the word "films."

Ontology-based search. Ontologies define the relationships between data. An ontology is based on the concept of "triples": subject, predicate, and object. This would allow the search engine to answer questions such as "What vegetables are green?" The search engine would return results about "broccoli," "spinach," "peas," "asparagus," "Brussels sprouts," and so on.

Semantic Web search. This approach would take advantage of content tagged with metadata as previously described in this section. Search results are likely to be more accurate than keyword matching.

Faceted search. Faceted search provides a means of refining results based on predefined categories called facets. For instance, a search on "colleges" might result in options to "refine this search by. . ." location, size, degrees offered, private or public, and so on. Faceted search tools available today tend to focus on a specific domain, such as Wikipedia or Semidico, a search tool for biomedical literature.

Clustered search. This is similar to a faceted search, but without the predefined categories. Visit Carrot2.org to better understand this concept. After conducting a search, click on the "foamtree" option to see how you can refine your search. The refining options are extracted from the content in pages of the initial search.

Natural language search. Natural language search tools attempt to extract words from questions such as "How many countries are there in Europe?" and create a semantic representation of the query. Initially, this is what people hoped search engines would evolve toward, but Grimes wonders if we have become so accustomed to typing just one or two words into our queries that writing out a whole question may seem like too much work.

You may recognize some of these search enhancements when using popular commercial search engines like Google or Bing. That is because they have begun to build semantic technologies into their systems. You are encouraged to explore other search engines that are developing semantic search features: DuckDuckGo.com, Hakia.com, and Swoogle (swoogle.umbc.edu).

SEMANTIC WEB FOR BUSINESS

What opportunities and challenges does the semantic Web hold for businesses? Perhaps the most immediate challenge faced by businesses is the need to optimize their websites for semantic search. Because search engines are responsible for directing so much traffic to business websites, it will be important that companies take advantage of semantic technologies to ensure they continue to remain visible to prospective customers who use search engines. While the details of semantic SEO are beyond the scope of this book, we can illustrate one important benefit of semantic website optimization. Websites optimized for semantic technology with metadata produce richer, more attractive listings on SERPs. Google calls these **rich snippets** (see Figure 6.13).

Note how detailed the organic search listing in Figure 6.13 is compared to a basic listing. These enhanced search listings are more visually attractive and produce greater CTRs.

Businesses need to stay up-to-date with advances in semantic search so that they can continuously optimize their sites to increase traffic from major search engines.

Questions

1. List five different practical ways that semantic technology is enhancing the search experience of users.

2. How do metadata tags facilitate more accurate search results?

3. Briefly describe the three evolutionary stages of the Internet?

4. Define the words "context," "personalization," and "vertical search" and explain how they make for more powerful and accurate search results.

5. What are the three languages developed by the W3C and associated with the semantic Web?

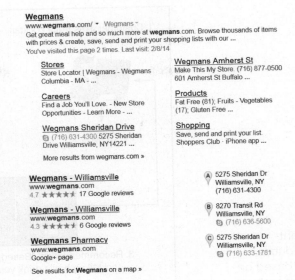

Figure 6.13 The Google search listing for this New York–based grocery chain is more attractive because it uses metadata from the business's website. (Google and the Google logo are registered trademarks of Google, Inc., used with permission.)

6.5 Recommendation Engines

> A lot of times, people don't know what they want until you show it to them.
> —Steve Jobs (quoted in *Business Week,* May 12, 1998)

Think about the challenge faced by large e-commerce websites like Amazon or Netflix. Brick-and-mortar retailers can capture people's attention in the store with eye-catching point-of-purchase displays or suggestive selling by store employees. However, these are not options for retail websites. They need an effective way of recommending their vast array of products to customers. Most e-commerce sites provide website search tools based on the technologies previously discussed in this chapter. Relying on customers to find products through an active search, however, assumes customers know what they want and how to describe it when forming their search query. For these reasons, many e-commerce sites rely on recommendation engines (sometimes called recommender systems). Recommendation engines proactively identify products that have a high probability of being something the consumer might want to buy. Amazon has long been recognized as having one of the best recommendation engines. Each time customers log into the site, they are presented with an assortment of products based on their purchase history, browsing history, product reviews, ratings, and many other factors. In effect, Amazon customizes their e-commerce site for each individual, leading to increased sales. According to Amazon employees, click-through and conversion rates "vastly exceed those of untargeted content such as banner advertisements and top-seller lists" (Linden, Smith & York, 2003).

RECOMMENDATION FILTERS

There are three widely used approaches to creating useful recommendations: content-based filtering, collaborative filtering, and hybrid strategies (Burke, 2007).

Content-Based Filtering

Content-based filtering recommends products based on the product features of items the customer has interacted with in the past (Figure 6.14). Interactions can include viewing an item, "liking" an item, purchasing an item, saving an item to a wish list,

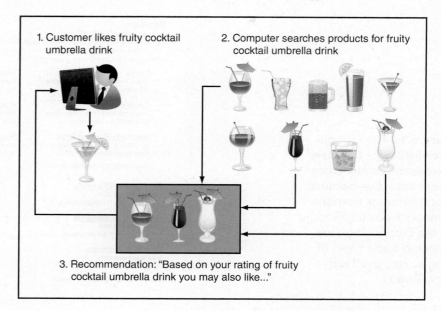

1. Customer likes fruity cocktail umbrella drink

2. Computer searches products for fruity cocktail umbrella drink

3. Recommendation: "Based on your rating of fruity cocktail umbrella drink you may also like..."

Figure 6.14 Content-based filtering produces recommendations based on similarity of product features.

and so on. In the simplest sense, content-based filtering uses item similarity to make recommendations. For instance, the Netflix recommendation engine attempts to recommend movies that are similar to movies you already watched (see IT at Work 6.2). Music-streaming site Pandora creates its recommendations or playlists based on the Music Genome Project©, a system that uses approximately 400 different attributes to describe songs (Glaser et al., 2006). These detailed systems for describing movies and songs enhance Netflix's and Pandora's positions in highly competitive industries because of their ability to offer superior recommendations to their customers.

IT at Work 6.2

Violent Nightmare-Vacation Movies and Other Fun Movie Genres at Netflix

Alexis Madrigal (2014) reverse-engineered Netflix's list of movie genres and was surprised to learn the company uses approximately 76,897 different ways to describe movies, creating the potential for some unusually specific movie recommendations. Christian Brown (2012) compiled a list of possible humorous and sometimes disturbing movie categories, a few of which are listed below:

10. Cerebral Con-Game Thrillers
9. Visually Striking Father-Son Movies
8. Violent Nightmare-Vacation Movies
7. Understated Independent Workplace Movies

6. Feel-Good Opposites-Attract Movies
5. Witty Dysfunctional-Family TV Animated Comedies
4. Period Pieces About Royalty Based on Real Life
3. Campy Mad-Scientist Movies
2. Mind-Bending Foreign Movies
1. More like *Arrested Development*

The fact that Netflix went to the trouble of creating so many detailed and descriptive labels suggests that a content-based filtering strategy is at use in the company's recommendation system.

Collaborative Filtering

Collaborative filtering makes recommendations based on a user's similarity to other people. For instance, when a customer gives a product a high rating, he or

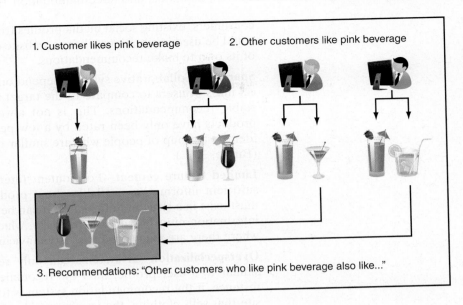

1. Customer likes pink beverage   2. Other customers like pink beverage

3. Recommendations: "Other customers who like pink beverage also like..."

Figure 6.15 Collaborative filtering bases recommendations on similarity to other customers.

she may receive recommendations based on the purchases of other people who also gave the same product a high rating. Sometimes websites will explain the reason for the recommendations with the message, "Other people who liked this product also bought. . ." Many collaborative filtering systems use purchase history to identify similarities among customers. In principle, however, any customer characteristic that improves the quality of recommendations could be used (see Figure 6.15).

In an effort to develop increasingly better recommendation engines, developers are exploring a number of creative ways to predict what consumers might like based on patterns of consumer behavior, interests, ratings, reviews, social media contacts and conversations, media use, financial information, and so on.

In addition to content filtering and collaborative filtering, two other approaches to recommendation engines are mentioned in the literature: knowledge-based systems and demographic systems (Burke, 2007). Knowledge-based systems use information about a user's needs to recommend products. This kind of system is useful for developing recommendations for products that consumers do not shop for very often. For instance, an insurance company may ask a customer a series of questions about his or her needs, and then use that information to recommend policy options. Demographic systems base recommendations on demographic factors corresponding to a potential customer (i.e., age, gender, race, income, etc.). While similarity to other customers might play a role in developing these recommendations, such systems are different from collaborative filtering systems that typically rely on information about a person's behavior (i.e., purchase, product ratings, etc.).

Systems are being developed that leverage big data streams from multiple sources to refine and enhance the performance of current systems.

Limitations of Recommendation Engines

While recommendation engines have proven valuable and are widely used, there are still challenges that must be overcome. Four commonly cited limitations are described below:

Cold start or new user—Making recommendations for a user who has not provided any information to the system is a challenge for most systems since they require a starting point or information about the user (Burke, 2007, Adomavicius & Alexander, 2005). Tiroshi and colleagues (2011) have suggested consumers' existing social media profiles from sites like Facebook and Twitter could be used in situations where a website did not have sufficient information of its own to make recommendations.

Sparsity—Collaborative systems depend on having information about a critical mass of users to compare to the target user in order to create reliable or stable recommendations. This is not always available in situations where products have only been rated by a few people or when it is not possible to identify a group of people who are similar to a user with unusual preferences (Burke, 2007).

Limited feature content—For content filter systems to work, there must be sufficient information available about product features and the information must exist in a structured format so it can be read by computers. Often feature information must be entered manually, which can be prohibitive in situations where there are many products (Adomavicius & Alexander, 2005).

Overspecialization—If systems can only recommend items that are highly similar to a user profile, then the recommendations may not be useful. For instance, if the recommendation system is too narrowly configured on a website that sells clothing, the user may only see recommendations for the same clothing item he or she liked, but in different sizes or colors (Adomavicius & Alexander, 2005).

Hybrid Recommendation Engines

Hybrid recommendation engines develop recommendations based on some combination of the methodologies described above (content-based filtering, collaboration filtering, knowledge-based and demographic systems). Hybrid systems are used to increase the quality of recommendations and address shortcomings of systems that only use a single methodology. Burke (2007) identified various ways that hybrid recommendation engines combine results from different recommender systems. To illustrate the potential complexity and variation in hybrid systems, four approaches are listed below:

- **Weighted hybrid:** Results from different recommenders are assigned a weight and combined numerically to determine a final set of recommendations. Relative weights are determined by system tests to identify the levels that produce the best recommendations.

- **Mixed hybrid:** Results from different recommenders are presented alongside of each other.

- **Cascade hybrid:** Recommenders are assigned a rank or priority. If a tie occurs (with two products assigned the same recommendation value), results from the lower-ranked systems are used to break ties from the higher-ranked systems.

- **Compound hybrid:** This approach combines results from two recommender systems from the same technique category (e.g., two collaborative filters), but uses different algorithms or calculation procedures.

Recommendation engines are now used by many companies with deep content (e.g., large product inventory) that might otherwise go undiscovered if the companies depended on customers to engage in an active search.

To simplify our description of recommendation engines, most of the examples above have been based on the e-commerce sites recommending products to customers. However, this technology is used by many different kinds of business organizations, as illustrated in Table 6.7.

TABLE 6.7 Examples of Recommendation Engine Applications

Company	How It Uses Recommendation Engines. . .
Amazon	Recommends products using multiple filtering methods.
Netflix	Approximately 75 percent of Netflix movies are selected as a result of its recommendation system.
Pandora	This streaming-music site creates playlists based on similarity to initial songs or artists selected by the user.
CNN, Time, Fast Company, Rolling Stone, NBCNews.com, Reuters, Us Weekly	These news and entertainment companies all use a recommendation engine (or "content discovery system") created by Outbrain.com to suggest additional articles related to the one site visitors initially viewed.
YouTube	YouTube uses a variation of Amazon's recommendation engine to suggest additional videos people might like to watch (Linden, 2011).
Goodreads	This social website for readers recommends books based on user ratings of books they have read.
Samsung	Uses recommendation engines built into its "smart TVs" to suggest television programming to viewers.
Facebook and LinkedIn	These social networking services use recommendation engines to suggest people that users may want to connect with.
Apple	Helps users find mobile apps they might enjoy.
Microsoft Xbox 360	Suggests new games based on what users have previously shown an interest in.
Tripadvisor	Recommends travel destinations and services based on destinations people have viewed or rated.
Stitch Fix	This fashion start-up uses a recommender system in conjunction with human stylists to select and ship clothing products to customers, before customers viewed or ordered them!
Fashioning Change	This online clothing retailer lets customers select what their recommendations are based on: style preferences, personality, causes, and "likes."

Questions

1. How is a recommendation engine different from a search engine?
2. Besides e-commerce websites that sell products, what are some other ways that recommendation engines are being used on the Web today?
3. What are some examples of user information required by recommendation engines that use collaborative filtering?
4. Before implementing a content-based recommendation engine, what kind of information would website operators need to collect about their products?
5. What are the four distinct methodologies used by recommender systems to create recommendations?
6. What is a recommendation engine called that combines different methodologies to create recommendations? What are three ways these systems combine methodologies?

Key Terms

access control
backlinks
black hat SEO
bounce rates
click-through rate (CTRs)
collaborative filtering
collection analysis module
content-based filtering
crawler control module
crawler search engines
dwell time
enterprise search
ghost pages
hybrid recommendation
    engines
hybrid search engines

inbound marketing
indexer module
informational search
keyword conversion rates
keywords
link farms
link spamming
metadata
meta-search engines
navigational search
organic search listings
page repository
PageRank
paid search listings
pay-per-click (PPC)
petabyte

quality score
query interface
recommendation engines
resource description
    framework (RDF)
retrieval/ranking module
rich snippets
search engine
search engine marketing
    (SEM)
search engine optimization
    (SEO)
search engine results page
    (SERP)
semantic search engines
semantic web

shadow pages
showrooming
social media optimization
SPARQL protocol and
    RDF query language
    (SPARQL)
spiders
structured data
transactional search
uniform resource
    identifiers (URIs)
unstructured data
vertical search engines
Web directories
Web ontology language
    (OWL)

Assuring Your Learning

DISCUSS: Critical Thinking Questions

1. Why is it important that businesses maintain a high level of visibility on search engine results pages?

2. Why are organic search listings more valuable than paid search listings for most companies over the long term? Even though organic search listings are more valuable, what are some reasons that companies should consider using PPC advertising as part of their search marketing strategies?

3. Why is relevant and frequently updated content a significant factor for companies concerned about their visibility on popular search engines? Does the quality of content impact organic results, paid results, or both? Explain.

4. Explain the differences between Web directories, crawler search engines, and hybrid search engines.

5. Why do search engines consider their page-ranking algorithms to be trade secrets? What would be the consequences of providing detailed information about how a search engine ranks SERP listings?

6. Why do consumer search engines like Google and Bing require vast amounts of data storage? What actions do they take to address this need?

7. Explain why enterprise search technology is becoming increasingly important to organizations. Describe how enterprise search applications are

different from consumer search engines in terms of their functionality, purpose, and the special challenges they must overcome.

8. Explain why people are much more likely to view and pay attention to product and service information in SERPs compared to traditional mass media advertising? What strategies are businesses adopting to take advantage of this trend?

9. Why is it easier to measure the return-on-investment of resources spent on search engine marketing compared to mass media advertising?

10. How are consumers using mobile devices to search for information about goods and services? How can businesses respond to this trend to gain a competitive advantage?

11. Identify at least five ways that Google has changed its page-ranking algorithms in recent years to encourage website developers to do more than simply list keywords in an attempt to improve their ranking on search results.

12. The ultimate goal of Google, Bing, and other consumer search engines is to provide users with search listings that contain useful information on the topic of their search. What recommendations would you make to a website owner with regard to website content that will improve its rank on search result listings over time?

13. Why are "black hat" SEO techniques (see Section 6.2) considered unethical? Who is harmed by the use of such techniques? What are the consequences of using these questionable SEO tactics?

14. Explain how search engines determine if websites contain relevant information or content.

15. Identify and describe the four steps to creating a pay-per-click (PPC) ad campaign.

16. How does an advertiser's bid and quality score determine the frequency of PPC ad placement on SERPs? What are the factors that Google uses to determine an advertiser's quality score? Why does Google use the quality score instead of relying solely on the advertiser's bid?

17. Describe three metrics used by PPC advertisers to evaluate the effectiveness of their search ad campaign.

18. Describe the difference between the semantic Web and semantic search.

19. Describe five ways that semantic search engines will enhance functionality for users. How will businesses benefit from the development of semantic search functions?

20. Recommender systems use different approaches to generating recommendations. Explain the difference between content-based filtering and collaborative filtering. Describe the kind of information required for each approach to work.

21. What are the alternatives to content-based filtering and collaborative filtering recommender systems? When is it most useful to use these alternatives?

22. Hybrid recommendation engines utilize two or more filtering strategies to create recommendations. Describe the four different approaches to creating a hybrid system.

EXPLORE: Online and Interactive Exercises

1. Select a search query term or phrase based on a class assignment, a product you plan to purchase, or some area of personal interest. Use the query at each of the following search engines:
    a. Google.com
    b. Bing.com
    c. Yahoo.com
    d. Hakia.com
    For each site, make the following observations:
    a. How relevant or useful are the websites listed on the first two pages of search results?
    b. What differences do you observe in terms of how the search engines list websites on the search results page?
    c. Do you see any indication that the search engine is using semantic technology to generate results (see "Semantic Search Features and Benefits" in Section 6.4)?

2. Visit the Nike website for its Fuelband product here: nike.com/us/en_us/c/nikeplus-fuelband.
    a. Make a list of nonbranded keywords that you would recommend Nike use to optimize pages so that they would show up in organic search listings.
    b. Make a list of recommendations for content (i.e., articles, blog posts, information, etc.) that Nike should add to its website for this product to increase the chances that it will show up in organic search results. What keywords should be emphasized in the content you recommend?

3. Use an existing account, or sign up for an account, at one of the websites listed in Table 6.7. Make a list of the ways that the website recommends its content, goods, or services to you. Based on your observations, are you able to determine what kind of recommendation system is in use by the website?

4. Pretend you are going to purchase an expensive item like a large flat-screen television or a major appliance

from a national retailer like Best Buy or Sears. Using your mobile phone, attempt to find store locations, product information, and customer reviews. Next, install one of the popular shopping and price comparison apps listed below on your phone:

- Red Laser
- Amazon Price Check, or Flow (also by Amazon)
- Google Shopper
- Barcode Scanner
- Or, find a similar price-checking app at your mobile app store.

Now, go shopping (visit the store). While shopping, use your mobile app to find product reviews and make price comparisons of the products you find. Briefly describe your mobile shopping experience.

How did the mobile technology help or hinder your shopping experience? What challenges does mobile technology pose for traditional retailers?

5. Pretend you are an SEO consultant for a local business or not-for-profit organization. Visit the organization's website to familiarize yourself with the brand, mission, products, services, and so on. Next, make a list of keywords or phrases that you think should be used to optimize the site for search engines. Rank-order the list based on how frequently you think the words are used in searches. Finally, go to google.com/trends/explore and enter your keywords or phrases, creating a graph that illustrates how often they have been used in search queries. Based on what you learn, what keywords or phrases would you recommend the organization use to optimize its site?

ANALYZE & DECIDE: Apply IT Concepts to Business Decisions

1. Perform a search engine query using the terms "data center" + "environmental impact". Describe the environmental concerns that large-scale data centers are creating around the globe and steps that companies are taking to address these concerns. Read about Google's efforts at google.com/green. In your opinion, is Google making a satisfactory effort to minimize its negative impact on the environment? Explain your answer.

2. Review the information in Section 6.1 about the three types of searches (informational, navigational, and transactional) that people conduct on search engines. Put yourself in the role of an SEO consultant for your college or university. Create a set of content and/or keyword strategies that you would recommend to your institution's leaders to increase the chances of appearing on SERPs resulting from prospective students conducting each kind of search.

3. Review Table 6.3, Popularity Factors Used by Search Engines. Select three factors that search engines use to evaluate a website's reputation. Next, generate a list of strategies or ways that a website owner could use the factors to improve its ranking on a search engine. For instance, if one of your factors is "site traffic," you might recommend that the website owner post links to the website on the company Facebook page to increase traffic. Or, you might recommend the website run a contest that requires people to visit the site to enter. This would increase traffic during the contest. Come up with as many creative ideas as you can for each popularity factor.

4. Traditional brick-and-mortar stores are increasingly frustrated by competition with online retailers. Online websites often have a cost advantage because they

do not have to maintain physical storefronts or pay salespeople, and can use more efficient logistical and operational strategies. This sometimes allows them to offer better prices to consumers. With the emergence of recommendation engines, they appear to be gaining another advantage—the ability to suggest products to customers based on their past shopping history and personal characteristics. Pretend you are a senior manager for a national retail chain. How could your company make use of recommendation systems to suggest products to customers shopping in your store? Outline a creative approach to this problem that identifies the information you would need to collect, the in-store technology required, and the manner in which you would inform customers about the personalized recommendations generated by your system.

5. Select a consumer product or service for which there are at least three popular brand names. For example, you might choose the category "cell phone carriers" which includes Verizon, AT&T, Sprint and T-Mobile. On the Google.com/trends page, type the brand names, separated by commas, into the search field at the top of the screen (e.g. Verizon, AT&T, Sprint, T-Mobile). The resulting chart will display the search query volume by brand, an indicator of how much interest each brand has received over time. Using the Google Trends data, answer the following questions.

Tip: Before answering the questions below, use Google's search engine to find articles on "how to interpret Google trends". This will help you better understand the Google trends report and make it easier to answer the questions below.

a. Using the date setting at the top of the *Google Trends* page, explore different periods of time.

Briefly summarize how interest in each brand has changed over the last four years.

b. In the *Regional Interest* section, you can see how interest in each brand varies by country or city. In which countries and cities is each brand most popular?

c. In the *Related Searches* section, you will see a list of topics and query terms of interest to people who used one of the brand names in a search. How does the list of related topics change from one brand name to another? Do the topic and query term lists give you any insight into what kind of information people may be interested in relative to each brand?

d. Using a search engine, see if you can find market share data for the product or industry you researched on Google Trends. If you find this information, does there seem to be any relationship between search volume and market share for the brand names you explored?

CASE 6.2

Business Case: Recommending Wine to Online Customers

Wine.com, headquartered in San Francisco, CA, is the world's largest online wine retailer, selling over 2 million bottles a year. The company maintains an inventory of over 13,000 different wines and ships its product throughout the United States. The company also operates wineshopper.com, a members-only site for customers interested in special sales and discounts on wine products.

While online retailers in other product categories have enjoyed considerable success over the years, online wine sellers have to work harder because of several political and regulatory factors. Chief among these challenges is complying with a number of federal laws controlling the sale of alcohol as well as state-level regulations that vary across the country. Wine.com had to create seven different distribution centers around the country to comply with varying state regulations, raising its cost of doing business. Wine is also a potentially perishable product, which means the company must take factors like weather into consideration when shipping during the hot summer months.

A quick look at the Wine.com website will give you some insight into how hard the company works to maintain its top spot in online wine sales. The website features an extensive community section where customers provide product reviews and create wish lists of wines they would like to try. A blog on the site keeps customers informed about the latest wine news and the company engages its customers through social media using Facebook and Twitter.

When consumers purchase wine at a local retailer, they often rely on the expertise and recommendations of a knowledgeable salesperson. This benefit can be difficult to replicate on a website. Historically, Wine.com placed information for alternative wine selections on product pages, but these recommendations were not customized to individual users. These "static" recommendations were sometimes based on wines the company wanted to promote, or the price category and type of wine the customer was viewing at the time. For instance, a product page for a particular type of Chardonnay might display recommendations for three alternative brands of Chardonnay in the same price category. All customers viewing that page would see the same three recommendations.

In an effort to provide more attractive and relevant recommendations, Wine.com contracted with RichRelevance, a San Francisco–based company, to create a system capable of providing personalized recommendations. The new system uses customer purchases, product search history, and information about the wine purchases of similar customers to create pages containing unique, personalized recommendations. Customers are encouraged to create profile pages on the site to aid in identifying shoppers who are similar to one another. As well, customers can write product reviews that provide additional information about consumer preferences to the recommendation system. According to Wine.com Director of Business Development Cam Fortin, "By analyzing the data pulled from each purchase and then personalizing the product recommendations, we can enable customers to discover great new wines that fit with their tastes and lifestyle" (Wine.com, 2012).

The new system allows wine.com to deliver several different types of recommendations:

- Customers With Similar Interests Also Viewed. . .
- Customer Lists Including This Wine. . .
- Customers Who Bought This Item Also Bought. . .
- Customers Who Viewed This Item Also Viewed. . .
- Top Sellers Of This Varietal/Region/Price Range
- Other products (similar to the one being viewed)

Recommendations appear on search results pages, homepages, product detail pages, and on the site's Gift Center page. In addition to this automated recommender system, wine.com sales representatives sometimes appear in chat windows offering to assist customers with making a product selection.

When Wine.com launched its personalized recommendation engine in 2009, the company did not have to wait long to see impressive results (marketingsherpa.com, 2009):

- Unit sales and revenue on gift baskets increased.
- Sales from recommendations increased to 10 percent of the company's total volume.
- Orders that included products from recommendations had a value that was 15 percent higher than the site's overall average.
- Conversions, or sales resulting from recommendations, were 52 percent higher than the site's overall average.

Since the initial launch of its recommendation system, Wine.com has continued to work with RichRelvance to improve and expand system capabilities as well as implementing other customer-centric features on its site. Today, Wine.com represents a good example of how online retailers can utilize a wide variety of technological features to overcome challenges and provide a personalized and positive shopping experience that inspires customer loyalty and growth for the company.

Sources: Compiled from Bensinger (2012), wine.com (2012), marketingsherpa.com (2009), dmnews.com (2009).

Questions

1. Based on the information in this case, would you categorize the Wine.com recommendation system as content filtering, collaborative filtering, or hybrid?
2. Why does Wine.com have to work harder to succeed than other online retailers?
3. Visit the Wine.com website. Identify website features the company has created to enhance the consumer's shopping experience.
4. Why do you think the recommendations provided by the new recommendation system are likely to have a greater influence on consumer behavior than the company's earlier attempt to make recommendations?
5. What impact has the new recommendation system had on Wine.com's business performance?

CASE 6.3

Video Case: Power Searching with Google

This video case is a bit different from what you have seen in other chapters. Google has created two easy-to-follow video courses designed to teach you how to use search engines more effectively: Power Searching and Advanced Power Searching. Each course contains a series of videos that you can view at your own pace. Following each video, you are shown a set of activities and small quizzes that you can use to test your knowledge. Start with the Power Searching course. Once you have mastered the basic skills discussed in that course, move on to the Advanced Power Searching course.

Visit Google's Search Education Page for Power Searching. Go to powersearchingwithgoogle.com. On this page, you will see links for the two self-guided courses: Power Searching and Advanced Power Searching. Select the Power Searching link, and begin viewing the course videos. After each video, do the related activities and test your knowledge with any online quizzes or tests that are provided. After you have completed the Power Searching course, go back and take the Advanced Power Searching course.

While it may take several days to complete both courses, we encourage you to do so. The time you invest in learning these power search techniques will pay off next time you need to use a search engine for a class or work-related research project.

Question

1. Describe two or three search techniques you learned from these tutorial videos that you think will be particularly helpful.

References

Adomavicius, G. & T. Alexander. "Toward the Next Generation of Recommender Systems: A Survey of the State-of-the-Art and Possible Extensions." *IEEE Transactions on Knowledge and Data Engineering* 17, no. 6, 2005, 734–749.

Andrews, W. & H. Koehler-Kruener. "Magic Quadrant for Enterprise Search." *gartner.com*, July 16, 2014.

Anthony, S. "Microsoft Now Has One Million Servers— Less than Google, But More than Amazon, Says Ballmer." *extremetech.com*, July 19, 2013.

Arnesen, M. "Olympic-sized Traffic Spikes for Misty May-Treanor Sunglasses or, the Online Effect of Offline Wins." *SwellPath.com*, August 1, 2012.

Bensinger, G. "Wine: The Web's Final Frontier." *Wall Street Journal,* October 26, 2012.

Bock, G. W., R. W. Zmud, Y. G. Kim, & J. N. Lee. "Behavioral Intention Formation in Knowledge Sharing: Examining the Roles of Extrinsic Motivators, Social-Psychological Forces, and Organizational Climate." *Management Information Systems Quarterly* 29, no. 1, March 30, 2007, 87–111.

Brightplanet.com. "Structured vs. Unstructured Data." June 28, 2012.

Brown, C. "43 Increasingly Precise Netflix Custom Genre Recommendations." *TheAwl.com*, March 16, 2012.

Brown, M. "5 Questions About Semantic SEO." The Moz Blog (*moz.com*), June 25, 2013.

Brown, J. S. & P. Duguid. *The Social Life of Information.* Cambridge, MA: Harvard Business School Press, 2000.

Burke, R. "Hybrid Recommender Systems." In Brusilovsky, P., A. Kobsa, & W. Nejdl (eds.), *The Adaptive Web*, pp. 377–408. Heidelberg: Springer-Verlag Berlin, 2007.

Cisco. "Cisco Visual Networking Index: Global Mobile Data Traffic Forecast Update 2013–2018." February 5, 2014.

Delgado, J., L. Renaud, & V. Krishnamurthy. "The New Face of Enterprise Search: Bridging Structured and Unstructured Information." *Information Management Journal* 39, no. 6, 2005, 40–46. Business Source Premier. Web. February 28, 2014.

DiSilvestro, A. "The Difference Between Semantic Search and Semantic Web." *Search Engine Journal,* July 10, 2013.

dmnews.com. "DMNews Chats with Amy Kennedy, VP of Marketing at Wine.com." *Direct Marketing News,* October 26, 2009.

Dover, D. & E. Dafforn. *Search Engine Optimization (SEO) Secrets.* Indianapolis, IN: John Wiley & Sons, 2011.

Downhill, D. & J. Peggie. "SEO: The Secret Weapon in the E-Commerce Wars." *Sempo.org*, 2005.

Feldman, S. & C. Sherman. "The High Cost of Not Finding Information." White paper, IDC, June 2001.

Gaikar, V. "Effective Backlink Strategies for SEO." *tricksmachine.com,* October 20, 2012.

Gallagher, S. "The Great Disk Drive in the Sky: How Web Giants Store Big—and We Mean Big—Data." *Arstechnica.com,* January 26, 2012.

Glanz, J. "The Cloud Factories: Power, Pollution and the Internet." *The New York Times,* September 22, 2012.

Glanz, J. "Google Details, and Defends, Its Use of Electricity." *The New York Times,* September 8, 2011.

Glaser, W., T. Westergren, J. Stearns, & J. Kraft. "Music Genome Project US Patent: No. 7,003,515." Filed May 16, 2002; issued February 21, 2006.

Goldman, L. "Nike's Superstar Endorsers." *Forbes.com,* January 24, 2008.

Google.com. "Algorithms." Google.com, accessed March 24, 2014.

Google.com. "Custom Search: Overview." September 26, 2013.

Google.com. "Enterprise Findability Without the Complexity." 2008.

Grehan, M. "How Search Engines Work." Excerpted from *Search Engine Marketing: The Essential Best Practice Guide,* New York: Incisive Media, 2002.

Grifantini, K. "What It Takes to Power Google." *MIT Technology Review,* September 9, 2011.

Grimes, S. "Breakthrough Analysis: Two + Nine Types of Semantic Search." *InformationWeek.com,* January 1, 2010.

Hatala, J. & J. G. Lutta. "Managing Information Sharing Within an Organizational Setting: A Social Network Perspective." *Performance Improvement Quarterly* 21, no. 4, 2009, 5–33. ERIC. Web. February 28, 2014.

Hendler, J. & T. Berners-Lee. "From the Semantic Web to Social Machines: A Research Challenge for AI on the World Wide Web." *Artificial Intelligence* 174, 2010.

Jacobson, J. "Google: 129 Million Different Books Have Been Published." *PCWorld.com,* August 6, 2010.

Jansen, B. J. & T. Mullen. "Sponsored Search: An Overview of the Concept, History, and Technology." *International Journal of Electronic Business* 6, no. 2, 2008, 114–131.

Kahn, K. "Structuring the Unstructured: Why Big Data Is Suddenly Interested in Enterprise Search." *cmswire.com,* December 6, 2012.

Linden, G. "YouTube Uses Amazon's Recommendation Algorithm." *glinden.blogspot.com,* February 1, 2011.

Linden, G., B. Smith, & J. York. "Amazon.com Recommendations: Item-to-Item Collaborative Filtering." *IEEE Internet Computing,* 7, no. 1, January–February 2003, 76–80.

Madrigal, A. "How Netflix Reverse Engineered Hollywood." *The Atlantic,* January 2, 2014.

marketingsherpa.com. "Revamped Recommendations Lift Order Value 15%: 5 Steps to More Relevant Suggestions." November 18, 2009.

Martin, J. "How to Choose an Enterprise Search Solution." *computerworkduk.com,* February 8, 2012.

Miller, R. "Google Has Spent $21 Billion on Data Centers." *Datacenterknowledge.com,* September 17, 2013.

Mitra, S. "Web 3.0 = (4C + P + VS)." *Sramanamitra.com,* February 14, 2007.

Newman, J. "6 Things You'd Never Guess About Google's Energy Use." *Techland.time.com* September 9, 2011.

Nikeinc.com. "History and Heritage." 2014.

Nikeinc.com. "Nike, Inc. Reports Fiscal 2013 Fourth Quarter and Full Year Results." Press release, June 27, 2013.

Oak, M. "How Does a Search Engine Work?" *buzzle.com,* June 5, 2008.

oracle.com. "Oracle Secure Enterprise Search 11g R1." July 2011.

Osher, M. "Finding Copyright Infringements of Your Artwork on the Internet." *MarianOsher.com,* February 9, 2014.

Pick, T. "How Much of Your Traffic 'Should' Come from Search?" *SocialMediaToday.com,* July 3, 2012.

Prnewswire.com. "Growth of Big Data in Businesses Intensifies Global Demand for Enterprise Search Solutions, Finds Frost & Sullivan." January 24, 2013.

Reinhardt, A. "Steve Jobs on Apple's Resurgence: Not a One Man Show", Business Week, May 12, 1998.

Safran, N. "310 Million Visits: Nearly Half of All Web Site Traffic Comes From Natural Search [Data]." *Conductor.com,* June 25, 2013.

Schachinger, K. "10 Website Quality Indicators That Can Sink Your SEO Battleship." *SearchEngineWatch.com,* November 29, 2012.

Schneider, D. "Under the Hood at Google and Facebook." *spectrum.ieee.org,* May 31, 2011.

Simon, N. "Barriers to an Information Sharing Culture." *Competitive Intelligence Magazine* 1, no. 3, October–December 1998.

Small, C. T. & A. P. Sage. "Knowledge Management and Knowledge Sharing: A Review." *Information Knowledge Systems Management* 5, no. 3, 2006, 153–169.

Smartlogic.com. "Enterprise Search." 2012.

Smith, N. "To Build Your Business, Smash Your Silos." *Fastcompany.com,* June 5, 2012.

Solihin, N. "Search Engine Optimization: A Survey of Current Best Practices." Garden Valley State University Technical Library, Paper 151, 2013.

Sterling, G. "Mobile Now 28 Percent of Total Web Traffic— Report." *Marketingland.com,* November 6, 2013.

SwellPath.com. "SEO Case Study: How SwellPath Grew Nike Golf's Organic Traffic by 250%+." 2012.

ThinkwithGoogle.com. "Mobile In-Store Research: How In-store Shoppers Are Using Mobile Devices." Google Shopper Marketing Council and M/A/R/C Research. April 2013.

Thomas, V. "Six Reasons to Break Out of Your Organization's Silos." *mangoapps.com,* September 24, 2013.

Tiroshi, A., T. Kuflik, J. Kay, & B. Kummerfeld. "Recommender Systems and the Social Web." In *Proceedings of the International Workshop on Augmenting User Models with Real World Experiences to Enhance Personalization and Adaptation (AUM),* Girona, Spain, July 15, 2011. Ardissono, L., and Kuflik, T. (Eds.), Springer-Verlag Berlin, Heidelberg, 2012.

Van Boskirk, S. "U.S. Interactive Marketing Forecast, 2011–2016." Forester Research. August 24, 2011.

Van Zelst, P. "What Is the Average Percentage of Traffic from Search Engines That a Website Receives?" *Moz.com,* October 18, 2013.

Venkatraman, A. "Global Census Shows Data Centre Power Demand Grew 63% in 2012." *Computerweekly.com,* October 8, 2012.

Walker, M. "Data Silos Obstruct Quest for Competitive Advantage." *datasciencecentral.com,* February 11, 2014.

Ward, E. & G. French. "Ultimate Guide to Link Building." Irvine, California: Entrepreneur Press, 2013.

Willcocks, R. "E-commerce Marketing: Where Your Website Traffic Will Come From & How." *ScreenPages.com,* 2013.

wine.com. "Wine.com Launches Advanced Personalized Recommendations to Enhance Shopping Experience." *pr.wine.com,* May 16, 2012.

Zreikat, L. "Effective Link Building Strategies." *laithzreikat.com,* April 5, 2013.

7 Social Networking, Engagement, and Social Metrics

Learning Outcomes

1. Understand the key technologies that made Web 2.0 possible, and appreciate the opportunities and challenges that social media represents for business organizations.

2. Describe the features and capabilities of large social networking services.

3. Explain how blogs and microblogs facilitate communication on a global scale.

4. Describe how mashups, RSS technology, and monitoring tools are valuable to business organizations and individual users.

5. Describe how organizations and groups make use of new Web 2.0 collaboration tools and services.

Chapter Snapshot

Everyone is talking about social media. Chances are you and your friends connect on **social networking services** or other forms of social media frequently. Every day, people discover new ways to share things with their network of friends through messaging, photographs, videos, and blogs. The digital-savvy connected generation or millenials—teens and those in their early twenties—"get" social media,

but might not be able to accurately define it or how companies use social technology to influence brand attitudes and consumer behavior. After you venture past the big brand names—Facebook, Twitter, YouTube, and LinkedIn—awareness of social media tools drops off quickly. Most social media use among Millennials is for recreational or entertainment purposes. There is little understanding of how social media can be used for marketing, recruiting, research, collaboration on projects, or personal branding.

Facebook has caught the attention of business organizations because the number of people who use the site is huge (and continues to grow!). Businesses are also exploring promotional opportunities on sites like Twitter, Pinterest, Tumblr, and YouTube. Companies get 24/7 advertising, live interaction with customers and prospects, and targeted ads. Organizations are working feverishly to prompt consumers to engage—to like, tweet, comment, and share their brand experiences with others. And they are spending a lot of time doing just that. According to media consulting firm BIA/Kelsey, companies will spend $8 billion promoting goods and services through social media by 2015.

In this chapter, you will learn what makes social media *social*. You will also learn about social media applications that have both personal and professional uses, and you will learn how business organizations make use of social media to gain competitive advantages in the marketplace.

CASE 7.1 OPENING CASE

The Connected Generation Influences Banking Strategy

THREE KEY OBSERVATIONS	

1. Banks, even the biggest ones, need to think in terms of the consumer because social media has given them a powerful voice.
2. The two most effective mechanisms for banks dealing with *connected customers* is to provide great service and to listen to them when they are not happy. The process can be brutal because it demands that banks be transparent. Bad surprises and "hidden fees" will be exposed in negative tweets and posts.
3. Unless you honestly engage customers and get rid of outdated processes that harm customer service, you risk negatively impacting your brand image or revenues.

BACKGROUND ON THE BANKING INDUSTRY

During the 2010s, the banking industry worldwide was in serious trouble. In the United States, mortgage foreclosures, a soft economy, high unemployment, and distrust of large corporations stirred by Occupy Wall Street protests against "big money" were just some of the problems facing retail banks.

BIG BANKS FACING CUSTOMER DISTRUST AND PROTEST

In late 2011 big retail banks were losing huge numbers of customers to credit unions (CU) and small community banks. According to an October 2011 survey by *Intuit Financial Services,* more than 36 percent of long-time banking customers said they had already moved or planned to move their accounts to a CU or other financial institution largely because of the high checking account and debit card fees their banks had imposed.

The seriousness of the situation led to an event called Bank Transfer Day, a Facebook-organized protest against "ridiculous fees and poor customer service" originally aimed at Bank of America (BoA), but expanded to include large banks in general. It is an example of a groundswell-organized group that came into existence via the shared opinions of a large number of people on social media.

People were urged to close accounts at multinational banks and encouraged to "move your money" to a neighborhood bank or CU by November 5, 2011. Even though BoA reversed its initial fees after mass outrage, the response was too late. In less than two months, over 650,000 customers had opened accounts at nonprofit CUs in the U.S., taking away an estimated $4.5 billion from big banks.

ADAPTING TO CUSTOMERS AND THE POWER OF SOCIAL MEDIA

Consumers today have a voice that can reward organizations that listen to them, and punish those that do not. Social media can provide that powerful voice. "Social media is rewriting the rules and increasing the speed with which banks have to respond," says Mark Schwanhausser, a senior analyst for Javelin Strategy and Research (Quittner, 2011). Troubled banks (those that had angered customers) needed a turnaround strategy to restore customers' trust and satisfaction, while also holding down costs and complying with many regulations. Citigroup is a large, global banking and financial services enterprise (see Figure 7.1). The strategies employed by its Citibank division are a good example of how some banks have chosen to respond to new consumer needs.

Figure 7.1 Citigroup, Inc. overview.

ACTION STEP: CITIBANK RESPONDS TO THE CONNECTED GENERATION WITH A SOCIAL STRATEGY

Citibank's turnaround strategies involve using *social outreach* to better solve customer issues in real time, engage them for marketing purposes, and monitor *online comments* to know what to fix. Citi is reaching out to tech-savvy customers, dubbed the *Connected Generation*, or *Gen C*, using YouTube, Facebook, and other social platforms. Gen C typically offers the most long-term value to big banks, which make investments in social networks worthwhile. Citi's ultimate goal is to attract Gen C customers who remain loyal by building their trust through increased interactivity and involvement.

Citi worked extensively with three companies to support its social media strategy: CoTweet Inc. (now part of salesforce.com), Hearsay Social, and Socialware, Inc. On August 16, 2011, Citibank used the front page of the *Wall Street Journal* to promote its Facebook page. On the Facebook site for Citibank US (facebook.com/citibank), visitors were prompted to hit "Like" to learn how to get special access to Beyonce tickets. The payoff was this: By midnight, Citi had acquired an additional 2,000 fans or likes.

Sources: Compiled from Fiorenza (2011), Quittner (2011), Skinner (2011), White (2011).

TABLE 7.1	Opening Case Overview
Company	Citigroup, Inc.
Location	Headquartered in Manhattan, New York City, Citigroup is a publicly held U.S. firm with customers and markets around the world.
Industries	Citigroup is a banking and financial services firm that offers a wide range of products and services including retail, corporate, and investment banking; credit cards; global wealth management; financial analysis; and private equity services.
Business challenges	Federal regulations place severe limits and substantial disclosure requirements on communications with customers. Banks have traditionally responded to these regulations by carefully screening all promotional messages (i.e., ads, direct mail, brochures, etc.) for regulatory compliance before distribution to the marketplace. The emergence of social media as a communications channel represents significant challenges because of the real time, individual, and public nature of "conversations" on social media. Banks do not have the ability to manage social media communications to ensure that their employees will comply with all regulations in each and every interaction that takes place.
Technology solution	Citigroup has created a presence on major social media sites—Facebook, Twitter, YouTube—and added a blog to its website (new.citi.com).
	Hired Frank Eliason, who pioneered social customer service at Comcast, to oversee its social media strategy.
	Employees who interact with customers via social media are trained to express concern for customers' issues, but move conversations to more secure channels (i.e., direct message or phone) to protect customer privacy.
	Citigroup uses Facebook and YouTube to provide timely and accurate information to investors.
	The company created a private social network for homeowners called homeowner-support.com. This online community for homeowners offers homeowner support forums, information about mortgage options, a homeowner support blog, and links for talking to mortgage counselors.

Questions

1. Technology can greatly influence businesses. How has social media changed retail banking?

2. Imagine having to live the next 24 hours without your smartphone, tablet, or any other mobile computing or communication device—and without any access to social media, texting, or tweets. What would be your biggest challenges? List two changes you would have to make to survive.

3. Think over what you expect from companies, such as airlines, banks, voice and data service providers, and online retailers. Select two companies. How have your "customer service" expectations for each of these companies changed in the past three years?

4. Have you used social media to let others know of great or bad service or product problems? Explain what you did or did not do, and why.

7.1 Web 2.0—The Social Web

In your lifetime, there have been dramatic changes in the way people use the Internet. In the early 1990s, many people did not have regular access to the Internet, and those who did typically "dialed up" their network from a home or office telephone. Dial-up access meant long waits as content from webpages "downloaded" onto the screen. Some users joked that the letters "www" in a Web address stood for "world wide wait." E-mail was the primary mechanism for social interaction. Online communities were often like public bulletin boards where all members of the community could read the messages that others posted. Websites were static, essentially online billboards for the businesses that created them. Online purchasing (e-commerce) was rare and risky because there were few safeguards in place to protect your credit card information. But all that has changed.

THE CONSTANTLY CHANGING WEB

Today, most of us access the Internet using wired or wireless broadband technology, consuming bandwidth that was unheard of a few years ago. We expect to be able to stream audio and video files, and watch feature-length films over wireless connections and mobile devices. We surf webpages that constantly change their appearance in response to how we interact with them. While e-mail is still a common form of communication in business, young people tend to view it with disdain in favor of tweets, texts, or social networking sites like Facebook. We keep track of our world, interests, and hobbies by reading blogs and online newspapers, and use a variety of tools and services for sharing them with others. In addition to consuming content, we add comments or reviews and signal our appreciation for the content by clicking a "Like" or "+1" button.

Increasingly, Internet users are becoming content creators—they write their own blogs, post videos on YouTube, and share pictures using sites like Flickr or Photobucket. E-commerce continues to grow and evolve, in some cases changing entire industries. E-books are now more popular than print books on sites like Amazon. More people purchase music from sites like iTunes or use streaming-music sites like Pandora or Spotify than purchase music on CDs. Sites like Travelocity and Orbitz have almost completely replaced traditional travel agencies and agents. Many people are more likely to use sites like eBay and Craigslist to get rid of unwanted household items instead of holding garage sales or placing classified ads in a local paper. One of the biggest changes in online retail is the use of social features by e-commerce sites. Most online retailers make use of customer reviews, customer ratings, and information sharing on social networks.

Web 2.0: a term used to describe a phase of World Wide Web evolution characterized by dynamic webpages, social media, mashup applications, broadband connectivity and user-generated content.

While there are many exciting examples of companies that have embraced the potential of **Web 2.0** technologies (Figure 7.2) and the emerging social culture that characterizes our modern online experience, many businesses, agencies, and individuals have been slow to understand both the challenges and opportunities created

Figure 7.2 Web 2.0 is also referred to as the social Web.

by the social Web. Smart managers are constantly evaluating how changes in social media and related technologies affect their business and industry. Businesses and business professionals must devote time and resources to consistently monitoring technological innovation and related changes in consumer behavior in order to remain relevant, taking advantage of potential opportunities to create competitive advantages when they arise.

INVENTION OF THE WORLD WIDE WEB

World Wide Web: a network of documents on the Internet, called webpages, constructed with HTML markup language that supports links to other documents and media (e.g. graphics, video, audio, etc.).

The **World Wide Web (WWW)** was invented by Tim Berners-Lee and launched in 1991. Its use outside of scientific and academic circles was uncommon until the mid-1990s. Web access from homes was mostly via telephone lines, slow 56-kbps (kilobits per second) dial-up modems, and paid subscription network services such as CompuServe and America Online (AOL). Websites were primitive static designs that served as online billboards or postcards. You can view archived websites using the *WayBackMachine* at www.archive.org. During that time, e-mail was viewed as a sophisticated communications tool that most people accessed at work or college campuses, but not from home.

As the above description suggests, communication was primarily uni-directional. There were no easy-to-use conduits for widespread social interaction. The average user was the target or recipient of communications, not a creator.

WWW AS A PLATFORM FOR SERVICES AND SOCIAL INTERACTION

Broadband: refers to wide bandwidth technologies that create fast, high volume connections to the Internet and World Wide Web.

Social media: a collection of Web applications, based on Web 2.0 technology and culture, that allows people to connect and collaborate with others by creating and sharing digital content.

Now the Web is a platform for all kinds of activity—shopping, entertainment, news, education, research, and business processes like logistics and electronic funds transfer (EFT). Homes maintain **broadband** wireless networks to connect multiple users simultaneously to the Internet from computers, tablets, video game systems, and video-streaming devices like the Roku box. In addition to the activities listed above, new Web technologies gave rise to websites with features and services that make it easy for people to interact with one another. As a result, these services collectively are referred to as **social media**. While the applications that are labeled as Web 2.0 may simply be an extension of earlier advances, it is the change in user behavior that matters most to business organizations around the world. The new technologies dramatically increase the ability of people to interact with businesses and each other, sharing and finding information, and forming relationships. This perspective explains why Web 2.0 is often called the **social Web**.

TABLE 7.2 Web 1.0 vs. Web 2.0

Web 1.0—The Early Web	Web 2.0—The Social Web
Static pages, HTML	Dynamic pages, XML, and Java
Author-controlled content	User-controlled content
Computers	Computers, cell phones, televisions, PDAs, game systems, car dashboards
Users view content	Users create content
Individual users	User communities
Marketing goal: *influence*	Marketing goal: *relationships*
Data: single source	Data: multiple sources, e.g., mashups

EMERGENCE OF SOCIAL APPLICATIONS, NETWORKS, AND SERVICES

Starting in 2000, a series of developments in the technology and business environment occurred that set the stage (infrastructure) for Web 2.0.

1. **Broad bandwidth (broadband).** Internet access became faster and more widely available due to large-scale adoption of broadband technology. Website load times shrank from a minute to instantaneous. Huge bandwidth is required to support byte-intensive music downloads and streaming video and movie services. Figure 7.3 shows the increase in the number of broadband connections in people's homes. Speed increased the overall attractiveness and accessibility of the Internet—laying the foundation for interactivity and the social Web.

2. **Sustainable business models.** After the dot.com bust in the late 1990s when many badly conceived Internet businesses failed, a new breed of business emerged. These businesses had realistic revenue models. Companies like Amazon, Google, eBay, and others began to demonstrate that it was possible to create e-commerce and consumer service sites that could generate revenue and become not only self-sustaining, but also profitable.

3. **New Web programming technologies.** New Web programming languages and technologies were developed that made it possible for programmers to create dynamic and feature-rich websites. In some cases, these new features and website capabilities created new business opportunities, which in turn led to increased demand for Web access. Increased Web usage then led to larger potential markets for businesses with successful revenue models. The businesses frequently reinvested earnings into expanding their technological capabilities in an effort to attract even more customers. This cycle of enhanced technological features leading to greater value for the consumer/Web user and then to more people using the Web continues today. Some of these new Web technologies are described in more detail in Tech Note 7.1.

4. **Application programming interface (API).** APIs facilitate the transfer of data from one website app to another. APIs can be either proprietary or open source. Use of a proprietary API requires the developer to pay a fee to gain access to data.

Fortunately, many popular APIs are **open source**, which means that anyone can use them for free, although there may be other terms and conditions placed on their use. Not surprisingly, the most popular API on the Web is the Google Maps API, which is used by over 30 percent of the mashups on the Web today. Visit programmableWeb.com/apis for a listing of popular APIs. The Google Maps API allows developers to create apps where information like store locations can be displayed on a map that comes from Google.

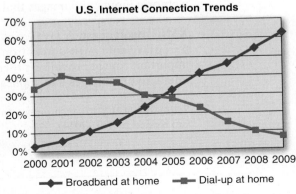

Figure 7.3 The increased number of broadband at-home connections was a critical driver of online interactivity. (Horrigan, 2009.)

TECH NOTE 7.1 AJAX Technologies and APIs

AJAX technologies, or **asynchronous JavaScript** and **XML**, is a term referring to a group of technologies and programming languages that make it possible for webpages to respond to users' actions without requiring the entire page to reload. AJAX makes it possible for Web developers to create small apps that run on a page instead of a server. This capability makes programs run much faster, eliminating a key source of frustration with the early Web. Another important programming development is the application programming interface (API), which acts as a software gateway programmers can use to pass data back and forth between two or more applications, platforms, or websites (see IT at Work 7.1). With AJAX and APIs, website programmers can import data from other sources to create new functions and features that we have come to associate with social media applications (see the discussion of mashups later in this chapter).

AJAX technologies include **JavaScript**, extendable markup language **(XML)**, document object model **(DOM)**, hypertext markup language **(HTML)**, **XMLHttpRequest**, and cascading style sheets **(CSS)**, all of which are defined in Table 7.3.

TABLE 7.3 AJAX Technologies for Web 2.0

HTML: The predominant language for webpages; it is used, along with CSS, to describe how things will appear on a webpage.

CSS: A language used to enhance the appearance of webpages written in a markup language.

DOM: A programming API for documents. Programmers use it to manipulate (e.g., build, add, modify, delete, etc.) HTML documents.

XML: A set of rules and guidelines for describing data that can be used by other programming languages. It makes it possible for data to be shared across the Web.

JavaScript: An object-oriented language used to create apps and functionality on websites. Examples of JavaScript apps include pop-up windows, validation of webform inputs, and images that change when a cursor passes over them.

XMLHttpRequest: A JavaScript object that serves as an API used by programs to retrieve data or resources from a URL without requiring a page load. It plays an important role in providing programmers with the ability to create dynamic and interactive webpages and applications.

Sources: W3C (2010); techterms.com (2014); Hegaret, Wood, & Robie (2000); van Kesteren et al. (2014).

IT at Work 7.1

American Express – Feeling the Love

APIs also make it possible for businesses to create apps for interacting with users. Taking advantage of Facebook's Social Graph API, American Express recently created the Link, Like, Love app that allows users to link their American Express card to their Facebook profile. This makes it possible for American Express to deliver customized deals and offers to users that are based on things they do on Facebook (Kim, 2011). For instance, card members who discuss vacation and travel plans with friends on Facebook may receive special offers for hotel and airline tickets.

Sources: Kim (2011), American Express (2011).

WHY MANAGERS SHOULD UNDERSTAND WEB TECHNOLOGY

You might ask yourself why business managers who are not directly involved in managing an organization's website should be concerned about the underlying technology of Web 2.0 and social media. The answer is that these technologies determine website features and capabilities. In other words, they determine what is possible on the Web. Understanding how Web technology is evolving helps managers identify strategic opportunities and threats as well as the ways in which a company might develop sustainable competitive advantages in the marketplace. Therefore, it is important to monitor the ongoing development of APIs, Web development languages, and other technologies that affect the functioning of the Web.

APIs: For instance, APIs associated with Facebook determine the nature of apps that can be written to interact with core Facebook features. Major changes to the Facebook APIs are often rolled out to much fanfare because they define opportunities for developing new ways for users to create and share content on Facebook and across the Web, as described in IT at Work 7.1.

At Facebook's annual developer conferences in 2010 and 2011, founder Mark Zuckerberg made announcements about changes in Facebook APIs that would extend the social networking giant's presence across the Web through the use of social **plug-ins**, which are listed in Table 7.4. See the discussion of Open Graph in Section 7.2.

Plug-Ins: Plug-ins are buttons or features on non-Facebook sites that interact with Facebook in some way. For instance, CNN.com might include a Recommend button on all its news articles. When a Facebook user presses the button, a link to the story is automatically created on the user's Facebook page. You don't have to be a Web programmer to follow and understand public announcements about API updates from Facebook, Google Maps, YouTube, Twitter, and other popular social media platforms. Using the monitoring tools discussed later in this chapter, you can stay informed about these changes and begin to assess how they will impact you as an individual, website developer, or business manager.

COMMUNICATING ON THE WEB

Collectively, social media apps have shifted the locus of control for mass communications from large organizations to one shared with individual users. Now people as well as organizations control both the message and the medium. Instead of an organization broadcasting a single message to a mass audience, a massive number of conversations take place among any number of people and organizations.

No one has complete control over the message or the medium, yet everyone can play a part. The challenge for businesses today is to change mindsets and

TABLE 7.4	Facebook Social Plug-Ins Used Across the Web
Like button	Shares pages from a website back to a user's Facebook profile with a single click.
Send button	Allows users to send content from a website to their Facebook friends.
Comments	This plug-in allows users to comment on a webpage's content using their Facebook profile and shows the activity to the user's friends in a newsfeed.
Embedded posts	Places content from any public Facebook post on to your website or blog.
Facepile	This feature displays the profile photos of the people who have connected with your Facebook page or app.
Login button	Shows profile pictures of the user's friends who have already signed up for your site in addition to a login button.

Source: Facebook (2014).

develop strategies that take advantage of social media. Instead of a focus on developing sophisticated ways of getting their message heard, companies must now develop sophisticated strategies for listening and responding to what their consumers are saying.

Because of the relatively low cost and ease of use, social media is a powerful force for democratization; the network structure enables communication and collaboration on a massive scale. Figure 7.4 shows the emergence of mass social

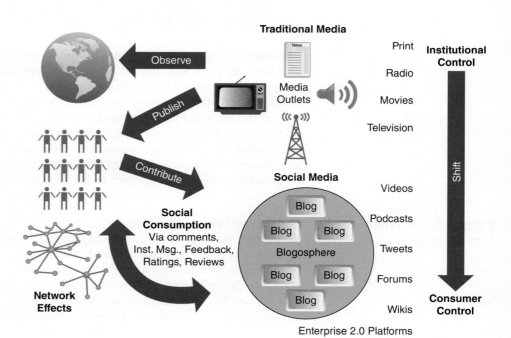

Figure 7.4 The emergence and rise of mass social media.

media. The figure compares traditional and social media and illustrates the new tools of social media, for example, blogs and **video blogs (vlogs)**, as being in the consumer's control. With traditional media, content is tightly controlled and brand messages are "pushed" out to users, often in the form of an ad interruption. With social media, users are frequently attracted or "pulled" to content that is interesting to them and they have greater freedom to decide if, when, and how they want to interact with such content.

Notice that traditional media content goes from the technology to the people, whereas in social media, people create and control the content.

SOCIAL MEDIA APPLICATIONS AND SERVICES

Social networking service (SNS): an online platform or website that allows subscribers to interact and form communities or networks based on real-life relationships, shared interests, activities and so on.

Early descriptions of Web 2.0 would often identify the apps listed in Table 7.5 as typical of social media. You will read more about each of these applications later in the chapter.

Few apps fit neatly into these categories anymore because of feature convergence. For instance, Facebook started as a **social networking service**, but now has features that span almost all of the categories in Table 7.5. It is a sharing site used by many to distribute photos. It is increasingly common for people to tag or label photos with the names of people in the picture, making it easy to find and display photos of individuals that have been saved in multiple locations on Facebook. Users can maintain blogs on their Facebook page and Facebook hosts thousands of apps that pull data from sources outside of the social network, making it a huge mashup app.

Likewise, YouTube (see Figure 7.5) started as a sharing site, making it easy for people to share video clips with others. However, YouTube now contains many features that make it difficult to distinguish from a social networking service. The same is true of Flickr, a photo-sharing site that has really become a community platform for people interested in photography.

While some original social media apps are still present on the Web today, thousands of newer apps have sprung up that continue to blur the lines of the original social media app categories.

TABLE 7.5	Web 2.0 Applications
Apps	**Descriptions**
Social networking services (SNSs)	Online communities
Blogs	Online journals
Mashups/ widgets/RSS	Web apps that pull data from various sources and display on another page to create new functionality
Social bookmarking/tags	An app for tagging or labeling online content for later retrieval
Wikis	A collaborative app that allows multiple people to create and edit online content
Sharing sites	Websites that make it easy for users to upload and share digital content like photos, videos, or music

Figure 7.5 YouTube, a video-sharing site, is the third most popular site on the Internet.

SOCIAL MEDIA IS MORE THAN FACEBOOK, YOUTUBE, AND TWITTER

Many people think that social media is limited to a few iconic companies or brand names: Facebook, Twitter, YouTube, and LinkedIn. While those companies have certainly capitalized on the new technology, in fact, social media is a term describing a range of technologies that are used across the cloud (Internet) and are, in some way, part of most websites you use today.

While you may be familiar with using social media for recreational purposes or communicating with friends and family, businesses use social technologies for a wide variety of other benefits:

- Collaboration
- Communication and Engagement with Customers (Marketing)
- Image and Reputation Management (Public Relations)
- Communication and Engagement with Employees and Partners (Management)
- Talent Acquisition and Recruiting (Human Resources)
- Research and Knowledge Management
- Productivity and Information Utilities
- Fund Raising

The following section lists some of the key elements of social media that distinguish it from other types of media.

Elements of Social Media: What Makes it Different?

In order to understand what makes the modern Web so much different from its earlier incarnation, it is helpful to understand the differentiating features and benefits made possible by XML, Java Script, APIs, and related technologies.

User-generated content (UGC). In contrast to traditional media–TV, radio, and magazines—social media make it possible for users to create and share their own content. Using various social technologies, people share photographs, music, and video with the world. They express themselves using the written word in stories, articles, and opinion pieces that they publish on their own websites or other platforms. They rate products and write reviews.

Content control. Most of this content creation and sharing is done without editorial review—users thus decide for themselves what they want to create and share. Social technologies have shifted control of online content to a broad base of users. It is users who determine what content "goes viral" or becomes highly popular through sharing, not advertising agencies or companies with large advertising budgets.

Conversation. With the advent of social media a paradigm shift occurred in marketing communications, from a broadcast (one-way) communications model to a conversation (two-way) communications model. Dialogue takes place in the form of one-to-one, one-to-many, and many-to-one formats. Social media websites contain features that allow people to talk back in a variety of ways.

Community (common values, culture). Many social media technologies ultimately result in the creation of communities. Like their offline counterparts, these online communities are made up of people who share a bond of common interests, values, norms, and even sanctions. Some communities are highly structured, whereas others may be more fluid and informal. As businesses learn to communicate on Web 2.0, some will attempt to create communities made up of consumers who have a strong interest in a particular brand. Social networking services lend themselves to this type of strategy, but brand communities can be developed around blogs, wikis, sharing sites, and other types of social media applications.

Categorization by users (tagging). Newer Web technologies have begun to allow users to decide for themselves how to categorize and label information they find online. This has created the potential for powerful forms of collaboration and information sharing as well as alternative forms of information search (see the discussion of social bookmarking later in the chapter).

Real people (profiles, usernames, and the human voice vs. the corporate "we"). Social media technologies allow people to express their individuality through the creation of online identities. In traditional media, communication and expression come from celebrities or corporate spokespersons. Web 2.0 provides people with the tools to create personal brands that characterize their personal, professional, or creative identity.

Connections (followers, friends, members, etc.). There are many ways to establish additional levels of connection and reflect some level of a relationship. You can become someone's friend on Facebook. Follow someone on Twitter. Subscribe to a person's blog. Perhaps just as important, these connections can be severed when one party wants to end the relationship (see Table 7.6).

TABLE 7.6   Things That Will Get You Un-Friended on Facebook

Posting unimportant and annoying stuff—Enough with the stupid quizzes already!

Too many religious and political posts—If we really want to know, we'll ask, thank you.

Posting inappropriate stuff—Porn, sexist humor, racist stuff, etc. Remember: Your friends' moms or kids are all part of the extended network.

You're just too boring—You aren't Beyonce. People don't care that you just made a PB&J for lunch.

Too many posts—Watch how often your friends post to Facebook and avoid being the person who shares twice as much as most other people.

Source: Based on Sibona & Walczak (2011).

Constant updating (real time, dynamic). Unlike the static Web of the 1990s, social technologies reflect our constantly evolving relationships, opinions, political views, religious beliefs, and values. The social Web is a constant stream of communications that never turns off and can sometimes be overwhelming.

Content separated from form. Data from one source can be used or exported to other platforms. This allows users to organize and display content in ways they find most helpful. For instance, with an RSS aggregator, users pull content from a number of sources into a single location, making it easier to follow news stories and blog posts from multiple sites. Someone writing about local restaurants can pull content from food critics, customer comments, and map location information from a variety of sources and aggregate this information into a single site, making it easier for users to get a complete picture of a restaurant without having to surf around to different sites.

Equipment independence. Increasingly, people access the Web and social media from a variety of computers and mobile devices, including laptops, tablets, smartphones, video game systems, DVD players, and televisions. In the near future, you might access the Web from such home appliances as your refrigerator or even a kitchen countertop. (Check out the amazing new technology featured on videos by Corning Glass. Go to YouTube and search for "A Day Made of Glass" using the YouTube search engine.)

WEB 2.0 ATTITUDE

As you have read, the availability of Web 2.0 applications is changing not only how people behave, but also the way they think about things. This new way of thinking is captured in a provocative list of 95 statements called the **Cluetrain Manifesto** (Levine et al., 2000). Perhaps the fundamental principle of the Manifesto is described by its first thesis: *Markets are conversations.* Other excerpts from the Manifesto are listed in Table 7.7. Over time, successful companies will learn to engage customers in conversations as an alternative to the unidirectional or broadcast method of communication. While the Cluetrain Manifesto seemed idealistic, impractical, and revolutionary when it was first written in 2000, we are starting to see more examples of individuals and companies finding ways of turning those principles into action.

While most companies still struggle with the concept of *conversation*, Forrester researchers Charlene Li and Josh Bernoff describe a number of companies who recognize the power of what they call the **groundswell**, "a spontaneous movement of people using online tools to connect, take charge of their own experience and get what they need—information, support, ideas, products, and bargaining

---

TABLE 7.7   Excerpts from the Cluetrain Manifesto

Select Cluetrain Theses

- "Markets are conversations."
- These conversations enable powerful forms of social organization and knowledge exchange.
- People have figured out they obtain better information and support from one another than from vendors. So much for corporate rhetoric about adding value to commoditized products.
- Companies should realize their markets are often laughing. At them.

Source: Levine et al. (2000).

power—from each other" (2008). Li and Bernoff identify five key strategic priorities that companies should focus on to leverage the groundswell:

1. **Listening**—Monitoring what your customers say on social media. By listening to what customers say to your company and what they say to each other, organizations can gain valuable insights.

2. **Talking**—While listening is perhaps the most important priority, businesses still need to develop their message and communicate to their target audience(s).

3. **Energizing**—Using a variety of tactics, companies can create and maintain relationships with brand advocates who will support and promote the brand to their friends and followers on the Web. Energizing brand advocates is analogous to generating word-of-mouth communications in traditional marketing.

4. **Supporting**—Using social media to deliver effective and convenient customer service is one way to support your customers. Some businesses create communities where customers can help each other with product-related issues and questions.

5. **Embracing**—Many companies are utilizing social media to solicit new product ideas and suggestions for improving customer satisfaction from current customers. Managers are often surprised to learn that customers have great ideas for how the company can do better.

These groundswell strategies identify the most significant activities that companies should focus on with regard to using social media.

In the rest of this chapter, we describe a variety of social media apps that are growing in popularity. We highlight some of the most attractive features, and encourage you to explore them firsthand. Most are free, so they are easy to try. You are also encouraged to stay on top of new trends and applications by following online sources like Mashable, Social Media Today, and Social Media Examiner. The only way to truly understand the social media environment is to immerse yourself in it, experiencing it directly. We think it is both fascinating and fun, and hope you will too.

Questions

1. How has Web 2.0 changed the behavior of Internet users?
2. What are the basic tools or applications that characterize Web 2.0?
3. Why is Web 2.0 referred to as the social Web?
4. What are some of the benefits or advantages that Web developers gain from using AJAX technologies?
5. What are some of the most important messages for business organizations in the Cluetrain Manifesto?
6. What is feature convergence? Give some examples of this trend with regard to social media apps.

7.2 Social Networking Services and Communities

Online or **virtual communities** parallel typical physical communities, such as neighborhoods, clubs, and associations, except that they are not bound by political or geographic boundaries. These communities offer several ways for members to interact, collaborate, and trade. Virtual or online communities have been around for a long time and pre-date the World Wide Web. The **Usenet** provided the initial platform for online communities by making it possible for users to exchange messages on various topics in public **newsgroups**, which are similar in many ways to online bulletin board systems. While the Usenet is technically not part of the Internet, much of its content can be accessed from Internet sites like Google Groups or subscription-based news server services like Giganews and Astraweb. (For additional information about online communities during the early phases of the Internet, see Leiner et al., 2009.)

Online communities can take a number of forms. For instance, some people view the blogosphere (all the blogs on the Web) as a community. YouTube is a community of people who post, view, and comment on videos. Epinions is a community of people who share their experiences and opinions about products and companies. Flickr, Photobucket, Webshots, and similar sites are photo-sharing communities. Wikipedia is a community of people who create, edit, and maintain an online knowledge base. Twitter is a community, or perhaps several communities, of people who frequently share short, 140-character messages with one another about a variety of topics. Obviously, social networking sites like Facebook and LinkedIn are communities and have seen tremendous growth in recent years. The mass adoption of social networking websites points to an evolution in human social interaction (Weaver & Morrison, 2008).

Social network analysis (SNA) is the mapping and measuring of relationships and flows between people, groups, organizations, computers, or other information- or knowledge-processing entities. The nodes in the network are the people and the groups, whereas the links show relationships or flows between the nodes. SNA provides both a visual and a mathematical analysis of relationships. In its corporate communications, Facebook has begun using the term **social graph** to refer to the global social network reflecting how we are all connected to one another through relationships (Figure 7.6). Facebook users can access a social graph application that visually represents the connections among all the people in their network. Berners-Lee (2007) extended this concept even further when he coined the term **giant global graph**. This concept is intended to illustrate the connections between people and/ or documents and pages online. Connecting all points on the Giant Global Graph is the ultimate goal for creators of the **semantic Web**, which you read about in Chapter 6.

Online communities have received increasing attention from the business community. Online communities can be used as a platform for:

- Selling goods and services
- Promoting products to prospective customers; for example, advertising
- Prospecting for customers
- Building relationships with customers and prospective customers
- Identifying customer perceptions by "listening" to conversations

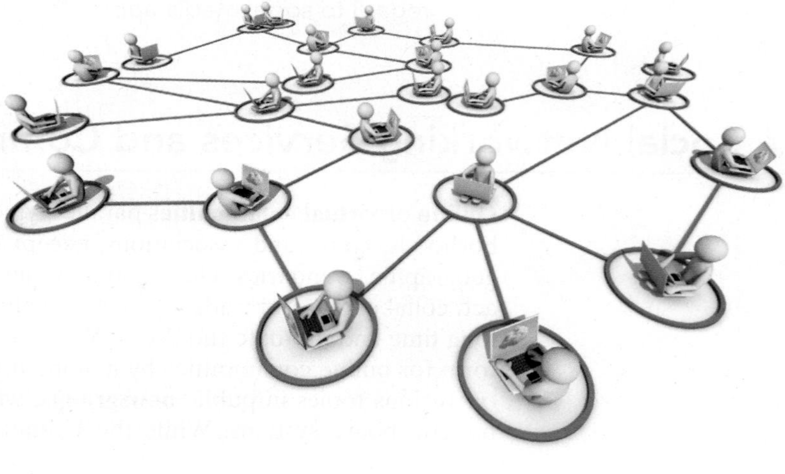

Semantic Web: An extension of the World Wide Web that utilizes a variety of conventions and technologies that allow machines to understand the meaning of Web content.

Figure 7.6 A social graph uses nodes and ties to illustrate relationships between individuals and groups of people.

© Tom De Spiegelaere/Alamy

- Soliciting ideas for new products and services from customers
- Providing support services to customers by answering questions, providing information, and so on
- Encouraging customers to share their positive perceptions with others; for example, via word of mouth
- Gathering information about competitors and marketplace perceptions of competitors
- Identifying and interacting with prospective suppliers, partners, and collaborators (See the discussion of Enterprise 2.0 in the next section.)

LEVERAGING THE POWER OF THE CROWD

In recent years, several companies have created online communities for the purpose of identifying market opportunities through crowdsourcing. **Crowdsourcing** is a model of problem solving and idea generation that marshals the collective talents of a large group of people. Using Web 2.0 tools, companies solicit, refine, and evaluate ideas for new products and services based on input from their customers. Business organizations that have implemented this approach include Fiat, Sara Lee, BMW, Kraft, Procter & Gamble, and Starbucks. See Openinnovators.net for a list of other examples.

CROWDFUNDING

More recently, businesses and entrepreneurs have turned to the crowdsourcing model to raise money for business start-ups or projects. A number of **crowdfunding** sites have become popular in recent years, including Kickstarter, GoFundMe, and Indiegogo (see crowdfunding.com). The crowdfunding sites are each governed by different rules that establish the kinds of projects or organizations that can use them to raise money as well as the types of crowdfunding allowed on the site (Table 7.8).

TABLE 7.8   Types of Crowdfunding

Donations	Often used by charities and political campaigns, contributors do not receive anything tangible in exchange for their donation, just the knowledge that they are supporting a cause they like or believe in. (In some cases, contributors may be eligible for a tax write-off.)
Rewards	Contributors receive some kind of "perk" or thank-you gift. Often it is something related to the project. For instance, people who contribute to a filmmaker's project may receive a copy of the finished work on DVD.
Credit	Contributors essentially make microloans to fund projects and expect to be repaid with interest.
Equity	With this approach, contributors make "micro-investments" and receive a proportional ownership stake in the company. It is likely that regulatory agencies that oversee equities markets in the U.S. and other countries will establish rules governing or even restricting this type of crowdfunding.
Royalties	Contributors receive a percentage of the sales revenue generated by a project. For instance, people who contribute to a musician's recording project might receive royalties from the sale of the artist's music.

Sources: Outlaw (2013), Wikipedia (2014).

The crowdfunding sites typically collect a percentage of the money raised. The fee can vary significantly depending on the site and the crowdfunding model used, so it is important to read the **terms of service** carefully before selecting a particular site to raise money on.

SOCIAL NETWORKING SERVICES

Social networking services (SNSs) represent a special type of virtual community and are now the dominant form of online community. With social networking, individual users maintain an identity through their profile and can be selective about which members of the larger community they choose to interact with. Over time, users build their network by adding contacts or friends. On some social network platforms, organizations create an identity by establishing discussion forums, group pages, or some other presence. Social networking has increased substantially in recent years. Research company comScore reported that people in the U.S. spent an average of 6 hours and 54 minutes a month on social networking sites in 2011, up from only 2 hours and 13 minutes in 2008. Figure 7.7 illustrates the growth rate of time spent on social networking sites.

Terms of Service (TOS) Agreement: a formal listing of the policies, liability limits, fees and user rights and responsibilities associated with using a particular service. Users are typically required to acknowledge they have read, understand and agree to the TOS before they are allowed to use the service.

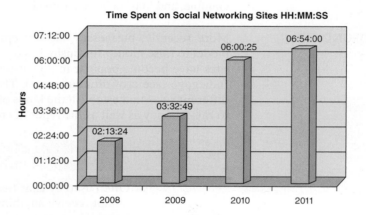

Figure 7.7 Average time spent per month on social networking services, 2008–2011. (Nielsen, 2010, comScore, 2011.)

The number of social networking services has grown tremendously in recent years. It is expected that the social networking sector will segment and consolidate in the future just like other industries. Among the general-purpose SNS platforms, Facebook is the clear leader with over 1.2 billion active users (Statista, 2014). Facebook is the second most visited site on the Internet after Google, according to alexa.com (2014), and it has publicly stated its intention to become number one (Vogelstein, 2009, Harvey, 2010). If Facebook were a country, it would be the second or third largest in the world. In the first quarter of 2014, Facebook's active user population appears to have grown slightly larger than the population of India, the

Figure 7.8 LinkedIn is used as a primary recruiting tool by a majority of companies.

second largest country in the world behind China. For an up-to-date list of popular social networking sites around the world, see en.wikipedia.org/wiki/List_of_social_networking_sites.

While SNS sites share some common features, they are not all alike. As the category matures, sites are differentiating themselves in a variety of ways. For instance, the SNS services in Wikipedia's list differ in terms of:

- Target age group
- Geographic location of users
- Language
- Area of interest; for example, music, photography, gaming, travel
- Social vs. professional networking (see IT at Work 7.2)
- Interface; for example, profile page, microblog, virtual world, emphasis on graphic vs. text content

IT at Work 7.2

Recruiters Use Professional Networking Sites

Susan Heathfield, a human resources (HR) expert at About.com, maintains that it is no longer sufficient to post job openings on monster.com, Careerbuilder.com, and Craigslist.com. Job postings on these large sites often generate hundreds of applications from unqualified candidates. This can be overwhelming for recruiters and very inefficient. Instead, many have turned to professional networking sites like LinkedIn. In a blog post, Heathfield identified a number of specific ways that businesses can use LinkedIn to increase the effectiveness of their recruiting:

- Identify potential candidates among your existing network of professionals.
- Ask your network to identify or recommend candidates for a position.
- Evaluate potential employees based on references and referrals from your existing network.
- Actively search for candidates among LinkedIn users using keywords or qualifications from their profiles.
- Ask current employees to search among their LinkedIn networks for potential candidates.

- For a fee, you can post job openings on LinkedIn.
- Request introductions to potential candidates through your existing network of professionals.
- Use Inmail (the internal LinkedIn e-mail system) to contact potentially qualified individuals.

It is clear that recruiters have come to embrace LinkedIn as an effective and cost-efficient way of generating qualified candidates. As LinkedIn's global presence grows, this will provide an important benefit to companies who need to fill positions internationally.

Source: Heathfield (2012).

Questions

1. Why have monster.com, Careerbuilder.com, and Craigslist.com lost their effectiveness?
2. Why have HR departments turned to professional networking sites like LinkedIn?
3. Why is it so essential for career-minded workers to build a professional social network? What can this network do for you?

FACEBOOK DOMINATES SOCIAL NETWORKING

Facebook is the largest social networking service the world. (The next largest social network is China's Qzone with 848 million users.) Facebook was launched in 2004 by a former Harvard student, Mark Zuckerberg. Photos, groups, events, marketplace, posted items, and notes are the basic applications already installed in

Figure 7.9 People are increasingly using mobile devices like tablets and smartphones to access Facebook and other social media sites.

© incamerastock/Alamy

Facebook. Apart from these basic applications, users can develop their own apps or add any of the millions of Facebook apps that have been developed by other users. Increasingly, people are accessing Facebook (and other social media sites) using mobile devices instead of computers (Figure 7.9).

Facebook was responsible for originating a unique feature called Newsfeed. This app featured a constantly updated stream of status updates from a user's friends. In late 2011 Facebook introduced another major revision to its site called Timeline. The Timeline app is designed to show the chronological progression of key events in a person's life as illustrated by his or her Facebook status updates, photos, the songs that person is listening to, bad haircuts, as well as changes in occupations, locations, relationships, and the like. Facebook says it wants to make it easier for people to tell their life stories by curating all the content they have shared on the social networking service. Many users, however, were surprised by the radical interface change and are uncomfortable with how easy it became for others to access old, long forgotten posts and status updates. According to many news reports, the new app has encouraged many to tighten their privacy settings even further to limit the content that is shared with others.

When Zuckerberg created Facebook, he had very strong social ambitions aimed at helping people connect to others on the Web. Facebook was initially an online social space for college and high school students. It started by connecting students to all others at the same school. In 2006 Facebook expanded to anyone 13 years or older with a valid e-mail address. The lack of privacy controls (e.g., tools that restrict who sees your profile) was among the biggest reasons why many businesspeople resisted joining Facebook.

In 2008 Facebook introduced new controls that allow users to set different levels of access to information about themselves for each of their groups; for example, family, friends from school, friends from work, and so on. For instance, close friends might see your mobile phone number, music favorites, e-mail address, and so forth, while other friends might see only the basics of your résumé (Abram & Pearlman, 2008). Facebook is regularly criticized for its approach to user privacy, highlighting an ongoing tension between the corporate goals of Facebook, which depends on a high level of access to user data, and the desire of individual users to control access to their personal information. See IT at Work 7.3 for additional information about social media privacy issues.

Facebook has expanded to the rest of the world with the help of its foreign-language members: Engineers first collected thousands of English words and phrases throughout the site and invited members to translate those bits of text into another language. Members then rated translations until a consensus was reached. The Spanish version was done by about 1,500 volunteers in less than a month.

The German version was done by 2,000 volunteers in less than two weeks. In early March 2008 Facebook invited French members to help out. They completed the translations in a few days. Facebook exists in over 70 different languages and approximately 81 percent of their members reside outside of the U.S. In May 2012 Facebook went public with its Initial Public Offering (IPO), selling company shares on the NASDAQ stock exchange. It raised over $16 billion, making it the third largest ever IPO in U.S. history. While founder Mark Zuckerberg sold some 30 million shares during the offering (for $1.15 billion), he continues to own approximately 22 percent of the company. His net worth of over $27.7 billion places him among the 30 most wealthy people on the planet.

The Open Graph Initiative

Network effect: From the field of economics, the network effect explains how the perceived value of a product or service is affected by the number of people using the product or service.

A primary reason that Facebook expands is the **network effect:** More users mean more value. In April 2010 Zuckerberg announced Facebook's new initiative called **Open Graph**. The goal was to connect all the different relationships that exist on the Internet by linking websites to Facebook. Programmers at external websites were encouraged to include a Facebook "Like" button on their websites. That way, when a Facebook member visits the website, they can click "Like" and their relationship with that website will be reflected back on their Facebook page for friends to see.

Facebook also encourages other websites to allow people to use their Facebook username and password to sign in or create accounts. For instance, if you are a Facebook member and you visit Pandora.com (a music service) or Yelp.com (a local directory service), you can sign into the sites using your Facebook username and password. Facebook will then share your profile information with those sites. This new initiative is exciting for its potential to enhance the social richness and ease of use of the Internet. On the other hand, this is just one more example of how Facebook creates concerns about how it shares users' information with others.

GOOGLE TAKES ON FACEBOOK WITH G+

Launched in June 2011, Google+, or G+ as some like to call it, is the latest entrant to the SNS market and some believe it is capable of becoming a formidable competitor to Facebook (see Figure 7.10). By March 2012 Google+ had over 100 million users.

Like Facebook, Google+ offers building and sharing features, including Google Hangouts, a popular and easy to use video conferencing feature.

It is clear that Mark Zuckerberg is not taking Google+ lightly. Facebook continues to launch new features and apps it hopes will help maintain its dominant status. Search "Google+ vs. Facebook" for current news and information.

Figure 7.10 With the launch of Google+, the search engine giant hopes to create a social network that is fully integrated with all of its other services.

© Zoonat/D Vasileva/Age Fotostock

Figure 7.11 Second Life residents participate in a virtual world beauty contest sponsored by cosmetics manufacturer L'Oreal.

AND NOW FOR SOMETHING DIFFERENT: SECOND LIFE

Avatar: an icon, figure or visual representation of a person in computer games, simulations, virtual worlds or online discussion forms.

Second Life is a social network service unlike most others. What makes it unique is that it uses a 3D virtual world interface in which users, called *Residents*, are represented by **avatars**, or cyberbodies that they create (Figure 7.11).

Developed by Linden Research in 2003, Second Life lets residents communicate with others in the virtual world through chat or voice communications. Residents can create and trade things they make in Second Life, including virtual clothes, art, vehicles, houses, and other architectural structures. They can also earn money by providing services such as instruction in a foreign language or serving as a DJ in a virtual club. This has led to the evolution of a Second Life economy with its own currency, the Linden dollar (L$). While most of the economic activity remains in the Second Life world, there are news reports of a few entrepreneurs who have made considerable sums of real money. Residents who make a lot of Linden dollars can exchange them at a rate of about 250 L$ for every U.S. dollar.

Between 2006 and 2008, there was a big spike in interest on the part of businesses that saw great potential in using Second Life. For example, IBM used it as a location for meetings, training, and recruitment. American Apparel was the first major retailer to set up shop in Second Life. Starwood Hotels used Second Life as a relatively low-cost market research experiment in which avatars visit Starwood's virtual Aloft hotel. The endeavor created publicity for the company and feedback on the design of the hotel was solicited from visiting avatars. This information was used in the creation of the first real-world Aloft hotel, which opened in 2008 (Carr, 2007). Starwood subsequently donated its Second Life property to a not-for-profit educational organization. Fashion and clothing manufacturers like Reebok, American Apparel, Adidas, and others used Second Life as a place to feature new clothing designs, setting up virtual stores where Second Life citizens could purchase digital clothing for their avatars. The hope was that awareness of fashion products on Second Life would spur interest and eventual purchase of real-world products. But efforts by these and other businesses, like 1-800-flowers, to get Second Life citizens to purchase real-world products through the virtual community have proven disappointing. Many businesses that were quick to become part of the early excitement around Second Life have left the virtual world community.

Will Second Life eventually replace Facebook and other 2D SNS platforms? Probably not, in spite of its impressive interface. While Second Life is visually compelling, it requires users to master a much larger range of controls and technology to become fully functional. Its aesthetic similarity to video games may cause some to underestimate its potential for more serious applications. Also, avatars interact in real time, so users need to be online at the same time as their friends and acquaintances in order to interact. That said, there are some niche applications that show promise. Using speakers and microphones, groups of people can conduct meetings in Second Life. Teachers can interact with their students in Second Life. How would you like it if your professor held offices hours on a virtual beach? Linden Labs has revamped the special browser that residents use to participate in the virtual world and is actively promoting its use for interesting business applications, but it is unlikely to achieve the same level of attention as Facebook in its present form. We believe, however, that Second Life will continue to provide benefit as a fascinating niche player in the overall SNS marketplace.

PRIVATE SOCIAL NETWORKS

The ultimate niche community is the **private social networking service (SNS)**. Private SNSs use social technology to create a community restricted to members selected by the SNS' owner. Private SNSs allow a greater degree of control over the network. Companies can easily monitor activity on their own SNS platforms and track conversations taking place about their brands and products. However, managing a private SNS requires considerably more time, attention, and resources than maintaining a presence on a general SNS. Organizations need to understand up-front that they are making a substantial commitment with this strategy.

Most colleges and universities have Facebook pages. In addition, many institutions have set up private SNSs to engage students even before they have started school there. Students typically gain access to these private SNSs when they are admitted to the institution. On the system, they can interact with admissions counselors, current students, and other admitted students. Interactions that occur on these networks set the stage for relationships and engagement that are simply not possible with e-mail and phone calls.

In 2008 Mercedes-Benz created two private SNSs designed to increase engagement with current and potential customers. The Mercedes Advisor network is for current Mercedes-Benz owners. GenerationBenz.com is a private network for prospective Mercedes owners. Membership in the network is limited to those who fit Mercedes' profile for younger luxury car buyers. Both of these communities provide the company with an opportunity to engage their target audiences directly. Members participate in market surveys and polls, provide feedback on prospective ad campaigns and product features, and participate in discussion groups with company managers. This provides valuable feedback to Mercedes as well as creating strong advocates for the company's luxury car brand.

While engaging customers on a private SNS can be time-consuming and potentially require significant staffing resources, the technological challenges associated with setting up a private SNS are relatively small. A number of companies offer a combination of free and subscription-based pricing for individuals or organizations wishing to create a private social network. Basic SNS sites can be set up fairly quickly for free. Search on "private social network services" for the latest information.

FUTURE OF SOCIAL NETWORKING SYSTEMS

Social networking services are perhaps the most feature-rich applications of Web 2.0. It is expected that growth and innovation in this sector will continue as individual users and business organizations discover its power for building networks and relationships. We expect that Facebook will continue to dominate the field, but that smaller SNSs will stake out strong positions in niche markets using traditional market segmentation strategies—focusing on the needs of specific geographic, cultural, age, or special interest segments.

IT at Work 7.3

Addressing Social Media Privacy Concerns

Privacy rights are too easily abused. Governments and industry associations are trying to control these abuses through legislation and professional standards, but they frequently fail to provide adequate protection. One of the most effective deterrents is fear of backlash from abuses that become public and cause outrage. So it is important to identify privacy issues that pertain to social media and specifically social networking services. Examples of privacy violations include:

- Posting pictures of people on social networking sites without their permission
- Tricking people into disclosing credit or bank account information or investing in "work at home" scams
- Sharing information about members with advertisers without the users' knowledge or consent
- Disclosing an employer's proprietary information or trade secrets on social networking sites
- Posting information on social networking sites that could compromise people's safety or make them targets for blackmail

Taking Control of Your Privacy

The most important thing that users can do to protect themselves is to understand that they are responsible for protecting their own information. The basic solution is common sense. Unfortunately, most social networking sites create the illusion of privacy and control. This sometimes can lull even the most vigilant users into making mistakes. Sites like Facebook make us feel like our information is only going to be seen by those we have allowed to become part of our network. Wrong. Listed below are commonsense guidelines:

- Do not post private data. Nothing, absolutely nothing you put on a social networking site is private. You should avoid posting personal information including full birth date, home address, phone number, and the like. This information can be used for identity theft.
- Be smart about who you allow to become part of your network. It is not uncommon for teenagers to "friend" hundreds of individuals on their Facebook accounts. With this many contacts, there is no way to protect profile or other information.
- Do not rely on current privacy policies or **terms of service (TOS) agreements**. Social networking sites change their privacy policies regularly. Many have accused Facebook of doing this specifically to wear down user vigilance with regard to maintaining desired privacy settings. Regularly review your social network service privacy policies explained in the TOS. Set your privacy settings at the level offering maximum protection—operating as if you have no privacy whatsoever.
- Minimize your use of applications, games, and third-party programs on social networking sites until you have carefully investigated them. They can expose you to malicious programs or viruses. Do not automatically click on links that look as if they were sent to you by members of your network.

Questions

1. Which of these guidelines is the easiest to follow? Which is the toughest? Explain why.
2. Why is it recommended that you not post private data on a social network, even those with privacy settings?

Questions

1. What are the major differences between social networking services and older online communities?
2. What is the basic difference between the social graph and Berners-Lee's concept of the Giant Global Graph?
3. Explain Facebook's Open Graph initiative and how it plans to expand its influence across the World Wide Web.
4. What are some potential ways that business organizations can take advantage of Second Life's unique virtual world interface?
5. Why would a business want to create a private SNS? What are some of the challenges associated with doing this?

7.3 Engaging Consumers with Blogs and Microblogs

One of the problems with traditional media, like newspapers and magazines, is that editors and publishers decide what you should read. Often their decisions are based on what the masses will buy at the newsstands. Space is limited and barriers to getting published are high. News services frequently fail to devote sufficient space to complex issues or viewpoints that might challenge the financial or business interests of the publication's owners or advertisers. But with social media, anyone can write a column or article and publish it online for the world to read (see IT at Work 7.4, "How to Create a Blog").

Of course, this creates another potential problem: clutter. Blogging is so easy that even people who do not have much to say can publish their thoughts, opinions, and ideas. Readers need to be prepared to look at online content with a skeptical eye and find ways to judge the credibility of the material they find on social media.

In their simplest form, blogs are websites where people regularly post content. Some personal blogs are simply online diaries or journals where people share their thoughts, reflections, or an account of their life. Other blogs are more sophisticated and professional in format, resembling online newspapers or magazines. Because blogging technology has become so commonplace, you may not always realize you are reading a blog when accessing online content. Many organizations have integrated one of the blogging platforms discussed later with their website. Blogging tools make it easy for organizations to provide website visitors with frequently updated content on pages with titles such as "What's New," "Company News," or "Product Updates." As a result, you may be a frequent blog reader without realizing it!

Blogs contain content in a variety of digital formats including text, photographs, video, and music. People who create and maintain blogs are referred to as bloggers.

Internet users increasingly use blogs as a source for information about topics of interest. Technorati.com, an advertising network of blog publishers, listed approximately 1.3 million blogs as of February 22, 2014. The site also reports that it receives 138 million unique visitors each month, which suggests there is a sizable audience for blogging sites.

WHAT IS THE PURPOSE OF A BLOG?

Many professionals now blog as a way to establish their reputation and promote their business interests, or because they enjoy writing and sharing their viewpoints with others. Corporate bloggers use the medium to tell stories about their brands and connect with customers.

On the surface, blogging appears to be a broadcast (one-to-many) communication tool. However, it can also be an effective tool for interactive dialogue. Many blogs utilize comment features, allowing readers to respond to blog posts, interacting with the blogger and other readers. Successful bloggers tend to comment on and link to other blogs in their posts, in effect maintaining a dialogue or conversation with other bloggers. These connections between blogs create what some refer to as the **blogosphere**, or a network of blogs. IT at Work 7.5 lists a number of ways that organizations use blogs for marketing.

BLOGGING AND PUBLIC RELATIONS

Some bloggers have become highly successful and have developed a large audience for their material. Many people approach blogging like a business and consider themselves "publishers," with the goal of generating enough readers or subscribers that they can make money from advertisers and ad agencies who will pay to display their ads on an individual blogger's site (see technorati.com). Earlier in this chapter, you read about a set of groundswell social media strategies described by Charlene Li and Josh Bernhoff. One of those strategies, *Energizing,* is accomplished when a business identifies a blogger whose audience matches its target market and persuades that person to write about the company's product. This is similar to a public relations manager sending a press release to a journalist, hoping he or she will write a news story about the company in the local paper. When a highly credible and influential blogger writes a positive story about your company, it can have a very positive impact on your brand's image. Bloggers can also have a negative impact if they write unfavorable posts about the company or its products. As a result, public relations professionals are learning how to identify and form positive relationships with influential bloggers with the goal of generating favorable coverage of the company and its products. Frequently, this will involve doing things like providing the blogger with information in advance of it being released to the public, providing access to company executives for interviews, sending the blogger samples of the company's product so that he or she can write about it from firsthand experience, and so on. For some companies, particularly those in the technology industry, building relationships with influential bloggers has become an important public relations strategy.

READING AND SUBSCRIBING TO BLOGS

The best way to gain an understanding of the blogging phenomenon is to simply start reading blogs. You can use search engines like Google or Yahoo to find blogs on all kinds of topics. Most blogs make it easy to subscribe using an RSS reader (see Section 7.4 later on in this chapter). Reading blogs is a great way to stay current on rapidly evolving topics related to technology and business.

IT at Work 7.4

How to Create a Blog

Setting up a blog is relatively easy. Making the effort to regularly write and post content that others will find interesting is more challenging. The following steps outline the process of setting up a blog.

1. Create a plan. Successful blogging requires a certain degree of organization and discipline. You can address this part of the project by developing a plan at the outset. The plan should answer questions like these:

    a. What are you going to blog about? What will be the focus or topic of your blog?

    b. Identify your target audience. For whom are you writing?

    c. How often do you intend to update your blog? Some bloggers post new material daily, some weekly, and some just a few times a month. How often you blog is, of course, up to you, but readers are more likely to follow blogs that are updated regularly. Avoid sporadic updates or only blogging when you feel like it. Successful bloggers frequently set up a publication schedule outlining topics and posting dates to keep themselves on track.

    d. Who else is blogging about the same topic? Identify bloggers you can interact with through your posts and comments on their blogs.

2. Determine if you will self-host your blog by purchasing a hosting plan and domain name (URL), or if your blog will use a free blogging service. Free services allow you to get up and running quickly and do not require any

long-term commitments. This provides an easy, low-risk way to get started. While this might be the most convenient approach, you do not actually own your blog or the content you post there because it is on a domain owned by someone else. Your domain name in these situations is usually in the form of "myblogname.blogspot.com," which can appear less professional to some readers. Purchasing a hosting plan and domain name, however, is the better long-term strategy since it creates a unique identity for your blog.

3. Select a blogging platform (see the section below). This is the software that will provide the look and feel of your site and give you myriad features you can employ to build a successful blog. Standard features in most blog platforms include a comment section, RSS buttons so readers can subscribe to your blog, and share buttons so readers can post links to your blog on other social media sites (e.g., Twitter, Facebook, Digg, etc.).

4. Set up your blog. Once you've set up your hosting and platform arrangements, you will need to create the aesthetic design for your site. Most platforms make this easy with a multitude of template options that you can further customize to give your blog a unique look.

5. Get started. Now comes the challenging part, writing your posts and regularly updating your blog to attract readers. You can read blogs about blogging to get great tips and advice.

Figure 7.12 WordPress is one of the leading platforms for online blogs.

BLOGGING PLATFORMS

Blogging Platform: a software application used to create, edit, and add features to a blog. *WordPress* and *Blogger* are two of the most popular blogging platforms.

Selecting a **blogging platform** is an important decision when setting up a blog. Installing a platform when you are creating a blog is relatively easy. Converting to a new blogging platform after using another one for a while is not. According to a study by Technorati (2011), the two most popular platforms are WordPress (51 percent) followed by Google's Blogger platform (21 percent). Other blog platforms include TypePad, Moveable Type, LiveJournal, and Tumblr. The Tumblr platform is significantly different from traditional platforms in that it emphasizes easy posting of photos and light copy. As such, it is considered to be a microblogging platform and is discussed later in this chapter.

When choosing between WordPress and Blogger, WordPress is a feature-rich platform and offers greater control over site appearance (Figure 7.12). Blogger is simpler and easier to use, making it a more desirable choice for beginning bloggers who want to get up and running without becoming bogged down in technological issues. Blogger's affiliation with Google might also be attractive because of the potential for integration with other Google services. For instance, Blogger comes with a built-in analytics program that appears to share many similarities with Google Analytics, a stand-alone Web traffic–monitoring tool.

For now, begin by reading blogs about social media, information technology, and other topics that are of personal interest. Note how these blogs vary in terms of style, length, and appearance. Identify the features they offer readers for commenting on and sharing content. After you get a feel for how people blog, try setting up your own blog using Google's free platform and hosting service at www.google.com/blogger.

MICROBLOGS

Microblog: a blog that consists of frequent, but very brief posts containing text, pictures or videos. Twitter is perhaps the most well-known example of a microblog.

You may be a microblogger and not even know it! Microblogging is a way of sharing content with people by the regular, often frequent posting of short messages. Although people don't usually call it microblogging, perhaps the most common form of this social media activity occurs when you update your status message on Facebook. More often, however, the term is used to describe popular microblogging services like Twitter and Tumblr.

Most **microblog** content consists of text-based messages, although there appears to be an increase in people who are microblogging photos and video on Twitter and Tumblr. Tumblr has increased in popularity recently among younger Internet users because of its multimedia capabilities and ease of use.

IT at Work 7.5

How Marketers Use Blogs and Microblogs

Blogs and microblogs provide individuals and organizations with a means to accomplish a variety of communications objectives. Marketers use blogs and microblogs to:

- Develop relationships with independent bloggers, encouraging them to write positive stories about the brand, product, and company.

- Engage members of the blogging community, via corporate blogs, by providing helpful and interesting information.

- Tell the company's "story," position a product, create brand identity, and differentiate from the competition.

- Engage customers and readers by soliciting comments and feedback about information provided in blog posts.

- Drive traffic to the company website by using Twitter to announce recent updates to the company blog.

- Inform current or prospective customers about positive blog posts featuring your product or company that were written by independent, third-party bloggers.

- Encourage repeat visits to the company website through regular updates or new posts to the blog.

- Have a celebrity or influential expert send a tweet with a promotional message about your brand using Twitter's new advertising program.

| TWITTER

Tweet: a brief 140-character message or post broadcast on Twitter, a microblogging service.

Figure 7.13 Twitter is a microblogging SNS that limits users to messages of 140 characters or less.

© 2020WEB/Alamy

Twitter has grown in popularity over the last few years, becoming one of the world's largest communication platforms. According to Twitter, approximately 5 million messages, or **tweets**, are sent each day by over 255 million active users (see Figure 7.13).

Twitter has played a significant role in both global and domestic events (Lee, 2013). In countries where the media is largely dominated by government control, Twitter has proven to be a valuable tool for activists engaged in organizing protests, debating political viewpoints, and broadcasting real time information about significant events that might otherwise be ignored by the mainstream media. Twitter has been credited by many with playing a key role in the Arab Spring revolutions that took place across the Middle East during the early 2010s. In the United States presidential election of 2012, Twitter was used heavily by both candidates. The winner, Barak Obama, is largely regarded as having out-performed his opponent, Mitt Romney, on Twitter and other social media platforms. Because of Twitter's reach, most federal and state political leaders now use Twitter as a regular channel for communicating with their followers. For the same reason, most advocacy groups engage in what some call **hashtag activism**, using the service to maintain awareness levels about their cause as well as influence people's beliefs and attitudes on key issues. Twitter has even begun to influence investment decisions made on Wall Street. Financial research analysts have created algorithms that use the volume and sentiment of Twitter traffic to predict the future stock value of a company.

Twitter is attractive to individuals, groups, and organizations because it provides a direct link to the public, bypassing traditional mass media which often acts as an information gatekeeper. Ironically, Twitter frequently influences what we see on traditional media. Journalists regularly use Twitter to broadcast breaking news stories. **Hashtag journalists** increasingly monitor Twitter to identify newsworthy events being tweeted (reported) by eyewitnesses and to gauge the public's interest in an event or issue by monitoring **trending topics**. Using Twitter to monitor public sentiment as well as influence public opinion has become an important skill for public relations professionals working for business and not-for-profit organizations. Organizations can no longer afford to ignore the conversations that take place on

Twitter about their brands, products, and executives. Furthermore, public relations professionals must understand how to actively participate in these conversations or risk appearing aloof and out-of-touch.

Twitter is often used by consumers to complain about frustrations they are having with a company or its products. In response, some companies have adopted Twitter as a customer service channel, along with email and telephone call centers. When customer service representatives find people complaining about their brand or product, they can use the service to empathize with the customer's frustration and offer solutions for resolving the problem. Because conversations on Twitter are public, other customers can watch or "listen in" on interactions between an unhappy customer and a customer service representative and judge how effective the company is at solving problems. This can be a benefit or liability for organizations depending on how adept they are at communicating and resolving customer problems on Twitter.

While many businesses seem to intuitively understand the desirability of maintaining a presence on an SNS like Facebook, many businesspeople freely admit to being somewhat confounded by the success of Twitter, and the role that Twitter should play in a company's marketing strategy.

Twittersphere: the universe of people who use Twitter, a microblogging service.

Like other social media tools, the best way to gain an understanding of Twitter is to use it. The official Twitter interface is simple and efficient, but a large segment of the **Twittersphere** uses third-party apps that have been developed to enhance the site's functionality and user experience. Some are considered essential tools in the life of the power Twitter user:

- **TweetDeck** is an advanced, split-screen app that allows users to view messages streaming from followers, people being followed, and people the user might wish to follow. It also makes it easy to quickly reply to incoming tweets, increasing the frequency of Twitter conversations. The TweetDeck interface makes it easy to participate in Twitter forums or online discussion groups similar to what takes place in a chat room. In 2011, this popular Twitter application was acquired by Twitter and continues to be a popular interface application for people accessing the service from a computer.

- **Twitpic** allows users to add photos to their tweets.

- **Twitterfeed** automatically tweets posts published on a blog using RSS technology.

- **Twitterholic** is a service that ranks users by number of followers, friends, and updates.

Many users believe Twitter is best suited for mobile devices like smartphones or tablets, which enable users to post spontaneous messages and updates regardless of their location. There are literally hundreds of third-party Twitter apps for computers and mobile devices, with more being written every day. You can find the most popular mobile apps by using an Internet search engine or searching your phone's app store.

How Do People and Businesses Use Twitter?

Think of Twitter as a social network where the dominant focus is on status updates. People tweet messages to their followers that they think will be of interest. While some businesses still struggle with ways to use Twitter effectively, many have adopted strategies that engage consumers, enhance brand image and improve revenue. Examples include:

- Celebrities use Twitter to update loyal fans about their day-to-day activities.
- Social media experts like Jeremiah Owyang and Brian Solis use Twitter to share links to online material that people in their profession will find interesting.

- Companies use Twitter to update customers about new products and special offers.
- Mobile food service trucks in large cities use Twitter to update customers about their current and future locations.
- News services like CNN and Mashable use Twitter as a "headline news" stream, sending links to news stories on their websites.
- Coupon and shopping services use Twitter to send daily deals and special offers to their followers.
- People use Twitter to send status updates to their friends, keeping others informed about their activities, sharing stories and links to online material they find interesting.
- Politicians use Twitter to communicate with their constituents, often linking to stories or material on their website that they believe will help support their positions on issues.

When users receive a tweet from someone they follow, they can "Reply" to the message, or **retweet** it by forwarding the message to everyone in their network. In this way, users engage in a dialogue of sorts with people they are connected to on the service. Tweets that are retweeted among many different users can go viral. People frequently attach descriptive keywords or **hashtags**, designated by the # sign, to their tweets to make it easier for others to find (e.g., #news, #politics, #fail).

| TUMBLR BLOGS

Tumblr is often described as a microblogging service because it makes the posting of multimedia content easy for users, and allows them to update their blogs frequently. However, Tumblr blogs can include just as much text as a regular blog, although most who use the service emphasize photographs and video as the primary content. This emphasis on multimedia makes the Tumblr blogs more visually compelling. Tumblr is particularly popular among those who are blogging about things like fashion, entertainment, and the arts.

Questions

1. What is the difference between a blog and a microblog?
2. What is a blogging platform?
3. Why do marketers use blogs and microblogs?
4. What makes Twitter a more attractive communication channel than traditional media for many individuals and organizations?
5. How is Tumblr different from other types of blogging platforms?

7.4 Mashups, Social Metrics, and Monitoring Tools

A mashup is a Web application that combines information from two or more sources and presents this information in a way that creates some new benefit or service. Using AJAX technologies and APIs, websites and applications can pull information from a variety of sources. See IT at Work 7.6.

One of the most common examples of a consumer mashup that you are likely to encounter involves the integration of map data (from companies such as Google or Mapquest) with information like store names, locations, phone numbers, and consumer reviews from other websites.

By combining this information in a single location or application, users enjoy a powerful and visually compelling service. ProgrammableWeb maintains a directory of mashups at programmableweb.com/mashups/directory.

Enterprise mashups combine data from internal business sources (e.g., sales records, customer information, etc.) and/or information from external sources for enhanced usefulness and productivity. For instance, a bank may utilize an enterprise mashup to display a mortgage application from its own records, the property location on a Google map, and information from county government property tax records.

WHAT MAKES A MASHUP APP SOCIAL?

To begin with, many of the most popular APIs used in mashup apps are from social media sites. That means the data involved in the mashup are likely to be user-generated social information. The other reason mashups are considered social media is that they represent the power to separate content from form—allowing Web developers (and sometimes users) greater control over how information is displayed and used on the Web.

Mashups also represent a change in philosophy for content creators. Traditionally, a business that created content operated a closed system where it maintained almost complete control over the "product." On the social Web, content creators enjoy greater distribution by allowing others access to their digital information through an API. For instance, the Google brand name appears on thousands of websites due to its open source API. If Twitter did not have an open source API, awareness and use of the service would be far less than they are today because users would have to go to the Twitter site in order to use it. By giving up some control, these content creators enjoy much wider distribution and market penetration.

So while the ability to create powerful mashup applications has not yet reached most individual Web users, it has decentralized control over how content is displayed and used, which is a key principle of social technologies (Section 7.1). We anticipate that it will not be long before someone develops a technology that will make it easier for the average user to create his or her own custom mashup applications (for instance, see Yahoo Pipes).

Mashup technology also represents a tremendous opportunity for new Web-based businesses with limited start-up capital. For example, the online directory and business review service, Yelp.com, uses the Google Maps API to make it easier for users to locate restaurants and bars in their area. In turn, Yelp has an API that allows sites like Zillow.com to use Yelp's information when displaying information about homes and neighborhoods to prospective real estate customers.

RSS TECHNOLOGY

Another technology that extends control of Web content beyond the creator is really simple syndication (RSS) (Figure 7.14). Traditionally, users had to visit multiple sites in order to view content at each location. This is potentially time-consuming and difficult for users who are interested in following several sources. RSS technology allows users to subscribe to multiple sources (e.g., blogs, news headlines, video) and have the content displayed in a single application, called an **RSS reader** or **RSS aggregator**. Depending on the features of the aggregator, users can personalize how they want information from their news sources organized and displayed.

© AKP Photos/Alamy

Figure 7.14 Users can subscribe to online content using RSS technology.

IT at Work 7.6

How Businesses Use Mashups and RSS

Businesses use mashups and RSS technology in a variety of ways. Examples include:

- Integrating Google Maps with information about company store or office locations, so that they appear together on a store locator webpage, making it easier for customers to locate the business.

- Use the Twitter API to add a Twitter stream box to an organization's website, displaying a consistent stream of tweets about the company, product, or brand.

- Create a desktop widget program that imports and displays useful information like sports scores, weather, or stock prices on a user's computer desktop or company website. Branded widgets display the sponsor's name so that every time the user checks for updates, he or she sees the brand name.

- Using RSS technology so customers and partners can subscribe to your blog, newsletter, product reviews, and articles. People are more likely to read content that is easy to access.

Most RSS readers are available online for free. You can find articles that provide reviews, descriptions, and recommendations about which one to use by utilizing a search engine. If you do not have time to research all the options, any of the following will probably provide a good initial experience with the technology: feedly.com, theoldreader.com, Digg.com Reader, and Bloglines.com. All provide the essential functionality of allowing you to subscribe to RSS content. The readers tend to differ in terms of available social features and the aesthetics of the interface. Feedly.com offers attractive displays that are visually compelling and contains social features allowing people to share what they are reading with their network. Some users, however, prefer a more rudimentary and basic interface, similar to what you will find on the Digg Reader.

| MONITORING SERVICES

A fast-growing sector in the social technology field involves **social monitoring services**. Monitoring applications allow users to track conversations taking place on social media sites. The initial impetus for the growth of monitoring tools was the need for business organizations to better understand what people were saying about their brands, products, and executives (the "listening" part of the groundswell strategy model). Monitoring services can be used to identify industry experts, commentators and opinion leaders who post regularly to social media sites. Once identified, public relations professionals can build relationships with these individuals and encourage them to become **brand advocates** who regularly portray the brand or company positively in their online writing and social media posts. See IT at Work 7.7.

In the next section, we describe two categories of social monitoring tools: subscription-based services and free monitoring services.

Subscription Monitoring Services

The most comprehensive social media monitoring tools require the user to pay a subscription or licensing fee. These tools not only monitor the social media environment for mentions of your brand or company name, but also provide analytics and tools for measuring trends in the amount of conversation occurring, the tone or sentiment (e.g., positive, negative, neutral) of the conversation, and other important aspects of the social interactions occurring online. Some of these tools are actually social media management platforms that help companies administer social media marketing campaigns and inbound marketing programs. The monitoring tools are just one of several features available in these enterprise-level applications.

Most high-end monitoring tools report information using a dashboard interface, which graphically represents the data it collects. Some of the most popular among these paid services include Radian 6, Alterian SM2, Hubspot, Biz 360 Community, and Nielsen Buzz Metrics. While prices for these high-end monitoring services can vary widely (typically, hundreds of dollars a month), they are usually beyond the budget of individual users.

IT at Work 7.7

Businesses Monitor Social Activity. . .

- To identify brand advocates—people who repeatedly discuss a particular topic.
- To find experts talking about technical or business topics.
- To assess reputation or sentiment in the online community about a brand, person, or issue.
- To understand customers by listening—identifying topics of interest to the online community.

- To track trends in the volume or nature of online conversations.
- To assess the relationship between marketing actions (e.g., product launch) and online conversations.
- To identify potential problems with your brand's reputation before things get out of control.

Free Monitoring Services

Fortunately, there are number of free monitoring tools that can be used by anyone. Some of these tools, like Twitter Search, are designed to monitor conversations on a single social media platform, while others, like Social Mention, are designed to provide feedback on activity across a number of social media platforms including Facebook, Twitter, and blogs. The following list provides a brief description of some free social monitoring services.

Social mention Our favorite free monitoring tool can be found at socialmention.com. This tool aggregates content from over 80 different social media sites including Facebook, YouTube, and Twitter. The best thing about Social Mention is that it provides users with four metrics that give insight into the nature of conversations taking place on the Web.

Users can generate these statistics daily for a particular topic (e.g., brand name, public figure, current event) and record them in a spreadsheet. Over a period of time, it becomes easy to see trends developing with regard to factors such as how many people are talking about a topic or how they feel about a topic. This is useful information for the social media marketer.

Social mention metrics

- **Strength**—The likelihood that a particular topic is being discussed on social media platforms
- **Passion**—A measure of the degree to which people who are talking about your brand will do so repeatedly

- **Sentiment**—A measure of the tone of the conversation, which helps you understand if people are feeling positive, negative, or neutral about the topic
- **Reach**—A measure of the range of people discussing a particular topic

Go to socialmention.com and explore what people are talking about with regard to current events, celebrities, popular products, or any other issue you are interested in. See what you can learn from the four metrics listed by the site.

Twitter search This tool on the Twitter website generates a list of recent tweets containing a specific word or phrase. You can use the search engine to generate a list of tweets containing keywords related to an issue, a brand name, a company name, elected official, and so on. If your goal is to measure the sentiment of the conversation about a particular topic or brand, you can accomplish this informally by simply scrolling through the messages to get a feel for what people are saying (see twitter.com/search).

If you want to do a more formal analysis, randomly sample, say, 100 tweets and manually categorize each as positive, negative, or neutral. Repeat this on a daily basis and you will be able to identify trends in the sentiment of online conversations over time. Companies can use Twitter search to identify users who are having problems or complaining about their product and take corrective action by responding to specific tweets.

Klout Klout claims to measure a user's influence across a number of social media sites including Facebook, Twitter, and more recently, LinkedIn, YouTube, and Foursquare. Klout reports a user's influence using a score from 0 to 100. Klout's formula for determining the influence score has been criticized (Clough, 2011, Walker, 2011). In fact, some believe that it is almost impossible to create a formula that truly measures influence (Masnick, 2011, Singer, 2011). That said, Klout does quantify aspects of a person's potential to influence, which could be helpful to understand. As Klout continues to build and improve on its influence algorithm, this tool could prove increasingly valuable.

Google alerts Unlike the other tools listed above, Google alerts do not provide much in the way of metrics that describe social media activity. However, it is an extremely useful monitoring tool that conducts automated Google searches for new Web content. Searches can be general or specific to social content on blogs and discussion forums. Users receive regular e-mail updates with search results (see google.com/alerts). This tool is particularly useful for managers who need to be aware of any news stories, blog posts, and discussion forums where a particular product, brand name, company, or person is mentioned. It is great for monitoring competitive organizations. It is easy to use, and because the searches are automated, it is very convenient.

Social monitoring tools play an essential role in helping social media marketers gain insight into the conversations taking place on the Web. They represent a set of powerful tools in the arsenal of firms that seek to understand consumers, what they are interested in, what they are talking about, and what they are thinking. As such, it is important that you become familiar with these tools, their strengths and weaknesses.

Questions

1. Why are mashups considered part of social media?
2. Describe a typical consumer mashup.
3. What is an RSS reader?
4. Describe the ways in which businesses can benefit from using social media monitoring tools.

7.5 Knowledge Sharing in the Social Workplace

Face it: Working in groups can sometimes be a real pain. Whether you are working with a group of fellow students on a class project, or a team of employees charged with developing a marketing plan, there are all kinds of factors that can interfere with success.

However, in today's competitive environment, businesses must be agile, able to respond quickly to a rapidly evolving marketplace. Employees must be able to work collaboratively, communicate effectively, and work together to make decisions and take action. Many businesses use Intranets to deploy tools that employees use for collaboration and productivity. An Intranet is a password-protected computer network that uses Web-based technologies (e.g., browsers, webpages). Think of it as a private or internal Web. Unfortunately, many Intranets are based on older Web technologies that do not include the social features we have become comfortable with on the modern Web. Some companies, however, are updating their Intranets to take advantage of advanced social features and technology. This trend is sometimes referred to as **Enterprise 2.0**.

In this section, we review a number of social tools for collaboration that are available to everyone. Small businesses, startups, and nonprofits that lack resources to deploy modern Intranets can use these tools for increased productivity. Larger companies will use similar tools, but as part of their enhanced (Enterprise 2.0) Intranets.

TOOLS FOR MEETINGS AND DISCUSSIONS

Synchronous communication: dialogue or conversation that takes place in real time, without the long delays between exchanges that occur, for instance, in email or discussion board conversations.

Dialogue or **synchronous communication** is an important part of the collaborative process. This can pose a challenge, however, for teams that cannot meet face to face. In the last few years, services like Skype and ooVoo have become popular in the marketplace for offering the possibility of reasonably good-quality video calls between at least two people.

Both services now make it possible to conduct video calls among small groups, making it easier to hold meetings. Google+ Hangouts is the latest entrant to this field of services, allowing up to 10 people to participate in a video chat on the Google+ social network (see Figure 7.15).

For something really unique, check out VenueGen.com. This service makes it possible for users to conduct meetings in a virtual world where users are represented by avatars. Similar in appearance to the role-playing platform Second Life, VenueGen is focused on the business organization's need for online meetings, and has created virtual environments for a variety of group sizes. Small meetings between two people can take place in an office environment or a coffee shop. Larger groups can use

Figure 7.15 On January 30, 2012, President Barack Obama participated in an online interview held through a Google+ Hangout, making it the first completely virtual interview from the White House.

© White House Photo/Alamy

boardroom environments, and very large groups can use auditorium or theater-size rooms. Within the virtual world, users can talk, make gestures, and display content from documents, PowerPoint presentations, and spreadsheets, just as they would in a face-to-face meeting.

TOOLS FOR RESEARCH AND KNOWLEDGE SHARING

A common step in many collaborative projects involves the identification and sharing of information relevant to the project topic. Search engines like Google, Yahoo, Bing, and others are among the most frequently used tools on the Web. Some of these large search engines are beginning to incorporate social features into their tools. Google makes it easy for users to share links on its SNS by placing a "+1" button next to each of the links in a search result. Yahoo includes a list of trending topics on its start page, featuring the topics that most people are searching on at the moment.

Searching the Web for information is not a particularly social activity, although there are social tools that can be used, in addition to search engines, to acquire information needed for a project. **Discussion groups** on SNSs can provide a forum for asking questions to groups of people. For instance, the American Marketing Association maintains a discussion group on LinkedIn that has over 6,500 members. Participants can ask questions and solicit input from other members of the group. Members can also monitor discussion groups, receiving periodic digests of group activity that can be scanned for material of interest. In a similar fashion, people frequently use Twitter as a way of asking questions and soliciting advice from their network.

Finally, as you learned in the previous section, social media monitoring tools can be used to search the Web for blog posts, tweets and other social activity by industry experts and commentators that might prove to be sources of valuable information. It is often possible to engage these experts on social media by commenting on blog posts, interacting on social networks or services like Twitter.

SOCIAL BOOKMARKING TOOLS

Most Web browsers allow users to store links to online content by saving them to a list of favorites or bookmarks. This approach becomes cumbersome as more information is saved because lists grow long and difficult to use. Organizing bookmarks into folders helps a bit, but the folders tend to hide information and users can forget what folder they have stored information in.

Diigo and Delicious

Social bookmarking tools allow users to tag Web content with keywords of their choosing. Users can retrieve links by searching on these keywords. Delicious.com is the most well-known social bookmarking tool. In addition to retrieving links tagged with keywords, users can search for Web content tagged by others. This is what makes the bookmarking system "social." Delicious can serve as an alternative search engine when seeking information. Searches on Delicious are based on a **folksonomy** (folk taxonomy) producing results different from traditional search engines because they are based on the way human beings tag content, not a computer algorithm.

Folksonomy: a system of classifying and organizing online content into categories by the use of user-generated metadata such as keywords.

Diigo.com is a newer social bookmarking service and contains additional features that make it an even more powerful collaboration tool. In Diigo, users can form open or private groups for sharing links to Web content. Social tools on Diigo allow users in these groups to comment on and discuss links as well as indicate their approval of a link using a "Like" button. Diigo also has a highlight tool that allows users to feature excerpts from webpages for other members of the group. Because of these extra social features, Diigo is a powerful tool for collaboration. Public groups on Diigo can take on the feel of an online community, with potentially large groups of people contributing, liking, and commenting on links related to a particular topic.

CONTENT CREATION AND SHARING

Sometimes, groups find it necessary to share documents and files as part of their collaborative efforts. In the past, e-mail was perhaps the easiest way for working teams to share documents. This approach has several drawbacks, perhaps the most obvious being the challenge of keeping different versions of the work organized.

Dropbox

Dropbox.com is a **cloud storage service** that makes it easy to access your documents from any of the devices you work on. Think of it as a shared hard drive for your computer, phone, and tablet computer. Dropbox also allows you to share files and folders with others, making it a great tool for document sharing. There are two features of Dropbox that make it a great tool. First, saving files to Dropbox is just as easy as saving a file to your hard drive. Other services require you to manually upload and download files. Dropbox also maintains a version history for documents, making it easy to see changes made to a document and undo them if necessary. This is a great feature for teams working on collaborative writing projects.

Box.net

Like Dropbox, box.net is a cloud storage service but places greater emphasis on social tools and features, which make it a great choice for collaborating teams. Users can edit files stored on box.net without downloading to their hard drives. Like many other social companies, box.net has created an open source API, allowing third-party developers to write applications for box.net users that offer additional sharing and collaboration features. Over 60 such apps have been developed so far.

Wikis

While Dropbox and box.net allow teams to collaborate on the creation of documents, a Wiki allows teams to collaborate on the creation of webpages. A wiki is a website that allows many people to add or update information found on the site. Wikis can be used as a work space for collaborative teams or they can become public websites built by groups of collaborators. The most popular wiki project is Wikipedia, the online encyclopedia (alexa.com, 2014). Businesses can create wikis for a particular product and allow employees and even customers to contribute information that will form a knowledge base resource for those who need information about the product.

There are many different sites like wikispaces.com and wikidot.com that offer free, basic wiki services to users.

Questions

1. How can working teams use social media as an alternative to face-to-face meetings?
2. Why are social bookmarking services superior to the traditional method of saving "favorites" or "bookmarks" in a browser?
3. What are some ways you can use social media to solicit knowledge, information, and advice from experts on the Web?
4. What advantages do sites like Dropbox and box.net have over e-mail as a way of sharing and collaborating on creating documents?

Key Terms

application programming interface (API)

asynchronous JavaScript and XML (AJAX)

blog

cascading style sheets (CSS)

cloud storage service

crowdfunding

crowdsourcing

document object model (DOM)

enterprise mashups

extendable markup language (XML)

Giant Global Graph

hashtags

hypertext markup language (HTML)

JavaScript

mashup

microblog

network effect

Really Simple Syndication (RSS)

RSS aggregator

RSS reader

semantic Web

sharing sites

social bookmarking

social media

social monitoring service

social network analysis (SNA)

social networking service (SNS)

social Web

synchronous communication

terms of service (TOS) agreement

twittersphere

Usenet

Web 2.0

widget

wiki

XMLHttpRequest

Assuring Your Learning

DISCUSS: Critical Thinking Questions

1. Explain the fundamental differences between Web 1.0 and Web 2.0.

2. Define social media and explain why these technologies are different from earlier manifestations of the Web.

3. Compare the methods that companies chose to communicate with their customers using the broadcast model vs. the ways that companies can have conversations with their customers using Web 2.0 tools.

4. What are the four primary factors described in the text that set the stage for Web 2.0 or the social Web that we enjoy today?

5. What is an API? Why should marketing professionals monitor changes in the kind of APIs available to Web developers?

6. Explain Facebook's Open Graph Initiative. How do Facebook's social plug-ins play a role in the Open Graph program?

7. Briefly describe each of the following kinds of social media:

    a. social networking service

    b. blog

    c. microblogging service

    d. social bookmarking service

    e. RSS reader

    f. sharing communities

    g. mashup

    h. wiki

8. Explain what is meant by "feature convergence" and how it is blurring the distinction between different types of social media tools.

9. Each of the following was listed as an element of social media. Describe each and explain its role in shaping and defining the social Web.

    a. user-generated content (UGC)

    b. content control

    c. conversation

    d. community (common values, culture)

    e. categorization by users (tagging)

    f. real people

    g. connections

    h. constant updating

    i. content separated from form

    j. equipment independence

10. If you were looking for a job or wanted to build your reputation as an expert in some area related to marketing, what social media tools would you use for personal branding and why?

11. How can companies utilize social media collaboration tools to become more competitive?

12. Describe how mashups create new benefits and functionality from existing data or information.

13. Describe some common ways that marketers can benefit by using social media monitoring tools.

14. How will concern for individual privacy affect the growth and expansion of social networking services and other social Web applications?

EXPLORE: Online and Interactive Exercises

1. Using online sources, research Facebook's Open Graph initiative. Make a list of "pros" and "cons" regarding these changes from the viewpoint of a Facebook user.

2. Using Google's blog search tool, identify some active blogs on a topic of interest to you and read a few posts. Leave comments in the response section (if available). See if the blog author or other readers reply.

3. Set up an account on two different RSS readers (e.g., Digg Reader and Feedly.com) and use them to subscribe to some blogs that are of interest to you. Prepare a report or presentation comparing the strengths and weakness of each application.

4. Using articles you can find online, prepare a report on the economic activity that takes place on Second Life. Describe how people make money in the virtual world and identify the opportunities and challenges associated with making a living via Second Life.

5. If you have an account on Twitter, download Tweetdeck, an alternative interface for Twitter. Use Tweetdeck and prepare a brief report on the advantages or disadvantages of using this program.

6. Visit the LinkedIn page for college students: students. linkedin.com. Using the information on this page, create a LinkedIn account and begin building your professional network. Search the Internet for additional tips on using LinkedIn to find jobs and prepare a brief report on your findings.

7. Using a search engine, find four examples of mashup applications. Prepare a report describing each one. If possible, identify the website(s) where data are pulled from to create the application.

8. Create an account on diigo.com, the social book-marking site. Actively use it to tag and categorize webpages that you want to remember for future viewing. Use the search engine on diigo.com to find pages that other users have tagged. Compare the effectiveness of your searches to similar searches using Google and Yahoo.

ANALYZE & DECIDE: Apply IT Concepts to Business Decisions

1. Use socialmention.com to evaluate the nature of conversations people are having about three telecommunications companies: AT&T, Verizon, and Sprint. Based on the four metrics provided by Social Mention, decide which company is viewed most favorably and least favorably by the marketplace. Using Twitter search, read a sample of tweets where people discuss the companies. Can you draw any conclusions as to specific reasons why the companies are viewed favorably or unfavorably?

2. Your boss would like you to recommend a free service for storing and sharing documents in the cloud. Create accounts at box.net and dropbox.net. Explore each service so that you understand how it works. Make a recommendation and provide your reasons for the service you select.

3. The supervisor of your department recently read a story about companies that used Second Life to conduct virtual meetings on the service. Create an account on Second Life and spend a few hours learning how to use it. With a handful of other students, arrange to meet in Second Life for a brief discussion. Based on your experience, prepare a recommendation for your supervisor stating whether or not you think using Second Life for meetings would be a good idea. Justify your recommendation.

4. After reading Video Case 7.3 below, get together with two or three other students and brainstorm some ideas for how your college or university could create a viral video campaign. Use the success factors listed in the case to evaluate your ideas. Write up a brief recommendation for your best idea, describing how it performs on each factor.

CASE 7.2

Business Case: Social Customer Service

In 2008 a little-known musician by the name of Dave Carroll initiated a social media firestorm of bad publicity for United Airlines, Inc. (UAL) after the company refused to pay for damaging his expensive Taylor guitar during a layover at Chicago's O'Hare Airport. After a frustrating year of negotiations with UAL, Carroll became convinced the company had created a system designed to simply wear down customers to avoid paying claims. As a result, he launched what would become a legendary social media attack on UAL's alleged corporate stonewalling by producing three YouTube videos that went viral, attracting millions of viewers and generating countless news stories, blog posts, and even a Harvard Business School (2010) business case. (Read the full story and watch the videos at davecarrollmusic.com.)

While Carroll ultimately embarrassed the company into settling his claim, it is clear that United Airlines continues to struggle with not only its customer satisfaction levels, but also its ability to manage the airline's online reputation effectively. That is not the case, however, at several other large companies that are increasingly learning to use social media to engage customers, correct problems, and enhance their brand image through social customer service.

Turning Complaints into Happy Customers

While business organizations were initially interested in social media because of its potential for branding and public relations, many organizations have begun to realize its potential for customer service and product support functions. In fact, a recent study by Forrester Research (2010) shows that customer service activities are the second most common application of social technologies by business organizations (marketing was first). Even excellent companies sometimes make mistakes or fail to completely satisfy customers. Because the cost of retaining a customer is often less than the cost of acquiring a new customer, many organizations invest in customer service operations to assist customers when problems occur. Traditional customer service channels consist of phone (call centers), mail, and in-store support. Today, customers may also use e-mail for such exchanges, and a wide range of social channels including Facebook, Twitter, and YouTube. Furthermore, customers may not complain directly to the company on its official Facebook or Twitter pages. Companies need to be able to identify unhappy customers that share negative comments outside of "official" channels. Traditional wisdom suggests that when consumers have a negative experience with a company, they share it with as many as 10 people. But now, unhappy customers can potentially share their experience with hundreds of people using a single message on social media. Or, as David Carroll learned, the message might reach tens of millions.

The WOW Factor at Zappos

At online shoe retailer Zappos, customer service through all channels is designed to "WOW" customers (Figure 7.16). A 10-person team of social customer service agents is trained and empowered to go the extra mile for customers who contact them through Zappos' official Twitter channel, @zappos_service. Agents have even gone as far as helping customers find the shoes they want at a competing retailer. Zappos agents strive to personalize their service by talking to customers in a normal "voice," sharing their names, and taking whatever time is necessary to address customer concerns. The company does not use scripted responses or policy documents restricting what agents can or cannot say to customers on the company's Twitter customer service channel. The only objective is to WOW the customer. This helps customers feel as if they are dealing with a real person who cares about their needs. The absence of scripted guidelines for assisting customers does not mean Zappos takes customer service lightly. After a lengthy and careful screening process, prospective Zappos agents receive weeks of training and become immersed in its customer-focused culture during their initial stages of employment. Once the agent passes the training program, he or she is actually offered money to quit the company! This is done to ensure that only those agents who truly want to excel at Zappos remain with the company. This approach to customer service is one that extends throughout the company, and reflects Zappos' corporate culture of happiness (see Figure 7.16). As a result, Zappos has earned one of the best reputations for its ability to please its customers, even when mistakes happen.

Comcast Makes a Turnaround with Social Media

Like United Airlines, cable giant Comcast was once the target of many social media public relations disasters. YouTube videos of service technicians falling asleep while on hold with their own customer service call center were embarrassing for

Figure 7.16 Zappos CEOs and co-founders Tony Hsieh and Jenn Lim (shown here) have worked hard to create a culture of happiness across the company, including the customer service team.

© Scott Harrison./Retna Ltd./Corbis

the company. Now, Comcast is considered a pioneer in the area of using social technologies for customer service. Under the leadership of Frank Eliason (now senior vice president of social media at Citibank), Comcast was one of the first corporations to recognize the potential of using Twitter for customer service. Twitter allowed the company to respond more quickly to customer complaints than with traditional channels. In fact, because of the public nature of Twitter messages, Eliason and his team were able to identify upset customers even when they were not directly communicating with the company. By monitoring Twitter for all messages that mentioned Comcast, agents are able to offer assistance to sometimes surprised customers who do not realize the company is interested in helping them solve their problems. Despite Comcast's innovations in social customer service, a quick scan of the Internet will produce evidence that lots of people still grow frustrated with Comcast's inability to deliver cable and Internet service that meets their expectations. But by using social tools to engage customers on the major social platforms, Comcast has made great strides in helping to solve customers' problems when they arise.

Cisco Systems Creates Social Tools for Customer Service

Cisco Systems, Inc. is an American multinational corporation and a market leader in the design and manufacture of computer networking equipment. Cisco not only uses social channels for

customer service, but also leverages its expertise in networking and software development to create applications that other companies can use to provide multiple channel support services to customers. Cisco has developed a social customer service app called SocialMiner. This app makes it possible for companies to take a pro-active approach to social customer service, monitoring conversations on Twitter, Facebook, blogs, and other social media platforms. This makes it possible for service agents to identify and resolve issues as they emerge. The app also stores conversations in a database for later analysis, allowing companies to identify systematic problems and take corrective action to prevent problems from happening in the first place.

Sources: Compiled from March (2011), Reisner (2009), Forrester Research (2010), davecarrollmusic.com.

Questions

1. How does social media represent a threat to companies who limit their customer support services to traditional channels?
2. When customers have a negative experience with a company, what are the various ways they can use social media to tell others about their experience?
3. Explain why companies can no longer afford to limit their customer service to traditional channels (e.g., call centers).
4. What are some of the frustrations customers encounter when seeking customer service support from a company?

CASE 7.3

Video Case: Viral Marketing: Will It Blend?

Founded in 1975, Blendtec is a Utah-based manufacturer of high-quality blenders that typically sell for between $300 to over $1,000. While the company's products are perhaps the most expensive on the market, they enjoy a reputation for being among the strongest, most durable blenders available. Part of the reason for Blendtec's reputation is the success of a promotional campaign that *Advertising Age* calls the "the number one viral campaign of all time" (Learmonth, 2010). The campaign has generated more views than any other viral marketing campaign in history.

You can watch the videos at the campaign website: willitblend.com. Or, you can initiate a search on the "Will It Blend" campaign at YouTube, or visit Blendtec's YouTube channel: youtube.com/user/blendteconsumer.

The "Will It Blend?" Campaign

Prior to 2006, Blendtec was relatively unknown outside of the commercial food service equipment industry. That year the company's new marketing director, George Wright, came up with the idea to make videos demonstrating the strength and durability of the blender by grinding up all sorts of unusual things: marbles, a McDonald's Happy Meal, and even a garden rake. The videos, featuring company founder

Tom Dickson in a white lab coat and goggles, were posted to YouTube and quickly generated millions of views as people shared them with others in their social network. The success of the early videos inspired the company to make additional episodes, resulting in over 130 videos. Some of the more outrageous episodes show Dickson grinding up iPhones, hockey pucks, a video recorder, an iPad, Bic lighters, and even a stun gun.

The Will It Blend? viral video campaign was effective because it did well on success factors that experts have identified as essential for viral marketing campaigns.

Create Content that Appeals to a Wide Audience

By definition, viral campaigns involve millions of people viewing and sharing content. Therefore, successful campaigns are based on content that has mass appeal, as opposed to narrow or niche market segments. Even though Blendtec's products are a specialty item with a price point that most consumers would find prohibitive, the videos are of interest to a larger audience. Many of the products that are "blended" in the videos (i.e., iPhones, iPads, Barbie dolls, and Nike sneakers) have broad-based appeal.

Create Content that People Want to Share with Friends and Family

Viral marketing experts report that viral content tends to be entertaining, emotional, novel or unexpected, humorous or offers something free. Blendtec's videos are both entertaining and novel because they use the blender in a completely unusual and unexpected way. Many of the videos are also funny, depending on the item being destroyed.

Make Use of Large Social Media Platforms for Easy Sharing

From the beginning, the Will It Blend? videos were posted to both YouTube and a company website created specifically for the campaign. Later, the company integrated Facebook, Twitter, Google+, and Pinterest into the campaign, which expanded sharing across these large social sites.

Keep Fans Engaged

The problem with many viral campaigns is that they fizzle out after viewers tire of the original content. Great campaigns find ways of building on initial successes. The Blendtec campaign has managed to maintain people's interest since 2006 by creating sequels to the initial episodes. The company actively solicited suggestions from fans about what they wanted to see blended. The most popular episode, added in 2010, blended an Apple iPad and generated over 16.9 million views.

Employ Tactics to Generate Initial Interest and Traffic

Successful viral campaigns create the impression that all the traffic generated is organic, resulting purely from wide-scale sharing by Internet users. However, in many cases, the campaign creators employ a number of strategies at the beginning of the campaign to jumpstart initial interest and awareness. Examples of such strategies include e-mail campaigns, promoting content to influential bloggers, SEO, optimizing your YouTube page and/or channel (if the content is in video format), promoting your content using PPC and/or paid promotion of a video on YouTube. At the beginning of the Will It Blend? campaign, Blendtec encouraged its employees to share the videos with their friends and family. The company promoted its videos using Google's Adwords and early videos were featured on YouTube's homepage, which

helped generate initial interest (Mendelson, 2013). Additional traffic was generated later in the campaign as a result of public relations efforts that led to widespread news coverage and appearances on NBC's *The Tonight Show* and the History Channel series *Modern Marvels*.

Campaign Results

The Will It Blend? campaign has generated over 294 million views across its 130+ video episodes on YouTube since 2006 (McDonald & Horan, 2014). The company continues to build on the brand awareness created by the campaign. Blendtec has over 702,000 YouTube subscribers, 53,806 "likes" on Facebook, and 24,700 followers on Twitter. While the company has clearly achieved its original objective of building awareness for its brand, Blendtec also experienced a 700 percent increase in retail sales between 2006 and 2008, about two years after the beginning of the campaign (Briggs, 2009). The videos are so popular that the company even makes approximately $50,000 a month from advertising that YouTube places around the videos (Akman, 2012).

Sources: Compiled from Mendelson (2013), Learmonth (2010), McDonald & Horan (2014), Briggs (2009), Akman (2012).

Questions

1. Why do you think Blendtec's video campaign was more appealing to viewers than a traditional product advertisement?
2. In addition to the success factors listed throughout this case, what other aspects of the Will It Blend? campaign contributed to its success?
3. On Blendtec's YouTube channel, take a look at a handful of the most recent videos that have been added to the campaign. Does it appear that interest in the videos is declining or growing stronger?
4. Based on the number of views (listed just below each video on YouTube), what kinds of items seem to generate the greatest interest when featured in a Will It Blend? video? Based on this observation, what suggestions would you give the company for items to feature in future videos?
5. Why do you think the campaign had such a significant impact on retail sales as opposed to commercial sales (e.g., sales to food service businesses)?

References

Abram, C. & L. Pearlman. *Facebook for Dummies.* Hoboken, NJ: John Wiley & Sons, 2008.

Akman, M. " 'Will It Blend?': An Early Social Media Success Case Study." *Delightwave.com*, April 27, 2012.

alexa.com. "Alexa Topsites." June 5, 2014.

American Express. "American Express Launches 'Link, Like, Love' on Facebook—First-Ever Platform to Deliver Deals,

Access and Experiences Based on Cardmember 'Likes' and Interests." Press release, *about.americanexpress.com*, July 19, 2011.

Berners-Lee, T. "Giant Global Graph." *Timbl's blog*, Decentralized Information Group, November 2007.

Briggs, C. "BlendTec Will It Blend? Viral Video Case Study." *socialens.com*, January 2009.

Carr, D. "Is Business Ready for Second Life?" *Baselinemag.com,* March 2007.

Clough, A. "Klout's Peer Index Score Is 40, Peer Index's Klout Score Is 57. Do They Care?" *LewisPR360,* October 27, 2011.

comScore.com. "It's a Social World: Top 10 Need-to-Knows About Social Networking and Where It's Headed." December 21, 2011.

Deighton, J. and Kornfeld, L. "United Breaks Guitars", Harvard Business School Case 510-057, hbr.org, January 6, 2010.

Facebook. "Social Plugins." *developers.facebook.com,* June 10, 2014.

Fiorenza, P. "Daily Dose: More Trouble for Banking Industry." *GovLoop.com,* October 6, 2011.

Forrester Research. "Social Networking in The Enterprise: Benefits and Inhibitors." June 2010.

Harvey, M. "Facebook Sets Up Google War with Vast Expansion through Open Graph." *thetimes.co.uk, April 22,* 2010.

Heathfield, S. "Use LinkedIn for Recruiting Employees." *Humanresources.com,* (Accessed, August 12, 2012.

Hegaret, P., L. Wood, & J. Robie (eds.). "What Is the Document Object Model?" World Wide Web Consorium, *W3.org,* November 2000.

Horrigan, J. "Home Broadband Adoption 2009." Pew Internet & American Life Project, June 2009.

Kim, R. "American Express Delivers Deals via Facebook's Social Graph." *GigaOm.com,* July 19, 2011.

Learmonth, M. "The Top 10 Viral Ads of All Time." *Advertising Age* (Adage.com), September 2010.

Lee, D. "How Twitter changed the world, hashtag-by-hashtag," bbc.com, November 7, 2013.

Leiner, B., V. Cerf, D. Clark . . . S., D., Kahn, R., Kleinrock, L., Lynch, D., Postel, J., Roberts, L., Wolff. "A Brief History of the Internet." *ACM SIGCOMM Computer Communication Review* 39, no. 5, October 2009.

Levine, R., C. Locke, D. Searls, & D. Weinberger. *The Cluetrain Manifesto: The End of Business as Usual.* Cambridge, MA: Perseus, 2000.

Li, C. & J. Bernoff. *Groundswell: Winning in a World Transformed by Social Technologies.* Cambridge, MA: Harvard Business Press, 2008.

March, J. "Zappos: Delivering WOW Customer Service through Twitter." *The Social Customer,* November 25, 2011.

Masnick, M. "Is Influence a Number. . . And Is It Based on Twitter?" *TechDirt.com,* May 25, 2011.

McDonald, C. & M. Horan. "Will It Blend?" *knowyourmeme. com,* March 2014.

Mendelson, B. J. "Why Does Blendtec Lie About Their Viral Marketing Success?" *bjmendelson.com,* December 2013.

Nielsen Company. "Facebook and Twitter Post Large Year over Year Gains in Unique Users." May 2010.

Outlaw, S. "What Type of Crowdfunding Is Best for You?" *Entrepreneur.com,* October 3, 2013.

Quittner, J. "For Banks, There's More Tech Behind Tweets." *AmercianBanker.com,* June 24, 2011.

Reisner, R. "Comcast's Twitter Man." *Bloomberg Business-week,* January 2009.

Sibona, C. & S. Walczak. "Unfriending on Facebook: Friend Request and Online/Offline Behavior Analysis." Paper presented at 44th International Conference on System Sciences, Hawaii, January 2011.

Singer, A. "Obsessed With Your Klout Score? You're Doing It Wrong." *thefuturebuzz.com,* June 21, 2011.

Skinner, C. "Banks Have Bigger Development Shops than Microsoft." *Financial Services Club Blog,* September 9, 2011.

Statista.com. "Number of Monthly Active Facebook Users Worldwide as of 1st Quarter 2014." 2014.

technorati.com. "State of the Blogosphere 2011." November 4, 2011.

techterms.com. "Javascript." June 10, 2014.

van Kesteren, A., J. Aubourg, J. Song, & H. Steen (eds.). "XML Http Request Level 1: W3C Working Draft 30 January 2014." World Wide Web Consortium, *W3.org,* January 2014.

Vogelstein, F. "Great Wall of Facebook: The Social Network's Plan to Dominate the Internet—And Keep Google Out." *Wired Magazine,* June 2009.

W3C. "XML Essentials." World Wide Web Consortium, *W3.org,* June 10, 2014.

Walker, L. "What to Do If Your Klout Score Drops." *LauraleeWalker.com,* October 27, 2011.

Weaver, A. & B. Morrison. "Social Networking." *Computer,* February 2008.

White, M. C. "Bank Transfer Day, the Day After." *Time Moneyland,* November 7, 2011.

Wikipedia. "Ajax (Programming)." June 10, 2014.

Wikipedia. "Crowdfunding." June 10, 2014.

Retail, E-commerce, and Mobile Commerce Technology

Chapter Snapshot

Case 8.1 Opening Case: Macy's Races Ahead with Mobile Retail Strategies

8.1 Retailing Technology

8.2 Business to Consumer (B2C) E-commerce

8.3 Business to Business (B2B) E-commerce and E-procurement

8.4 Mobile Commerce

8.5 Mobile Transactions and Financial Services

Key Terms

Assuring Your Learning

- **Discuss:** Critical Thinking Questions
- **Explore:** Online and Interactive Exercises
- **Analyze & Decide:** Apply IT Concepts to Business Decisions

Case 8.2 Business Case: Chegg's Mobile Strategy

Case 8.3 Video Case: Searching with Pictures Using MVS

References

Learning Outcomes

1. Describe how the concept of omni-channel retailing is changing the nature of shopping for consumers.

2. Identify five key challenges faced by online retail businesses in the Business to Consumer (B2C) marketplace.

3. Identify various ways that e-businesses are facilitating trade between buyers and sellers in the Business to Business (B2B) marketplace.

4. Understand how mobile technologies are creating opportunities for new forms of commerce in established industries.

5. Recognize how mobile payment methods benefit both consumers and retailers.

Chapter Snapshot

This is both an exciting and challenging time to be a retailer. Traditional brick-and-mortar stores face increasingly intense competition from other traditional retailers as well as competitors in the online and mobile retail channels. Consumers, armed with mobile devices, have more information than ever before about products, prices, and alternative places to buy products. A particular source of frustration for traditional retailers is the practice of show-rooming, where consumers visit a store to look at merchandise, seek information and advice from salespeople, maybe even try on clothes, and then leave the store to make their purchases online from a company that offers lower prices.

Online retailers also face significant challenges. Maintaining an e-commerce website requires ongoing investment in new technologies designed to enhance the online shopping experience, increase operational and logistical efficiency, as well as maintain high levels of customer satisfaction. Thanks to social media, dissatisfied customers now have numerous forums for informing others about frustrating experiences they might have with a company. It can be difficult meeting customer expectations that seem to grow more and more demanding everyday.

Companies that are branching out into mobile commerce face challenges as well. For years, industry pundits have said that mobile commerce, or m-commerce, is going to be huge. But those predictions have failed to materialize for a number of reasons, leaving some to question their investments in mobile technology. However, there are signs that mobile devices have finally begun to make an impact on retailing in noticeable ways. Nevertheless, the question still remains whether or not this emerging channel will become as big a force as some have predicted for years. In this chapter, you will read about the forces that are shaping consumer shopping behavior, and the ways that traditional, online, and mobile retailers are using technology to address the many challenges they face.

CASE 8.1 OPENING CASE

Macy's Races Ahead with Mobile Retail Strategies

Barcode: A machine-readable code consisting of numbers and a pattern of thick and thin lines that can be scanned to identify the object on which the code appears.

Showrooming: The practice of examining products in a traditional retail store, sometimes with the help of a salesperson, and then purchasing the product online.

Mobile devices, particularly smartphones, have become a key tool in the arsenal of modern-day shoppers. Using **barcode** scanner apps, customers in brick-and-mortar retail stores can quickly compare prices with other stores and online retailers. They can access product information, check expert and consumer product reviews, and even purchase products from online retailers. This practice, called **showrooming**, represents a significant threat to many traditional retailers who continue to ignore the impact of mobile consumer behavior.

Showrooming is frustrating to retailers who bear the costs of providing sales support, product inventory and maintaining a store front, only to see customers

TABLE 8.1	Opening Case Overview
Company	**Macy's, Inc.**
The business	Macy's is a premier department store retailer with a significant online e-commerce website and mobile shopping app.
Product lines	Macy's department stores offers a range of products, including fashionable clothing, jewelry, footwear, furniture, bedding, small kitchen appliances, cookware, and other household goods.
Business challenges	Implementation of an omni-channel retail concept that allows consumers to freely and seamlessly engage with Macy's through a traditional storefront, e-commerce website, or mobile technology.
Digital technology	Macy's embraces technology to enhance the shopping experience through the use of QR codes and SMS text messaging, mobile videos to provide information about merchandise, and an SMS database for distribution of mobile coupons and marketing communications.
Taglines	"The Magic of Macy's," "Macy's, way to shop!"

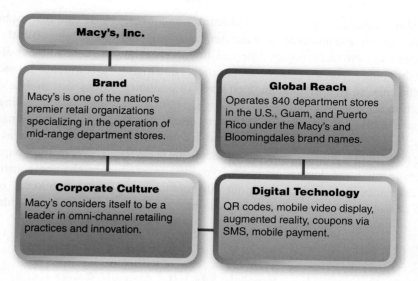

Macy's, Inc.

Brand
Macy's is one of the nation's premier retail organizations specializing in the operation of mid-range department stores.

Global Reach
Operates 840 department stores in the U.S., Guam, and Puerto Rico under the Macy's and Bloomingdales brand names.

Corporate Culture
Macy's considers itself to be a leader in omni-channel retailing practices and innovation.

Digital Technology
QR codes, mobile video display, augmented reality, coupons via SMS, mobile payment.

Figure 8.1 Macy's, Inc. overview.

Quick response (QR) codes:
A machine readable code typically used to store a link to a URL or web address that can be read by a mobile device.

Short message service (SMS): A technology used to send and receive text messages on mobile devices via a telecommunications network.

purchase products at a lower price from an online retailer with lower overhead costs. Target recently wrote to several of its vendors asking them to create special products, only sold in Target stores, in an attempt to stifle consumer comparison shopping via mobile devices (Zimmerman, 2012). But other retailers, recognizing the pervasive nature of mobile shopping trends, are developing strategies to embrace and engage the mobile shopper.

Department store giant Macy's (Figure 8.1) is recognized as a pioneer when it comes to using mobile technologies to enhance the shopping experience of its customers (Figure 8.2). Macy's uses in-store displays to encourage customers to use mobile devices while shopping. The *Backstage Pass Program* is designed to enhance the in-store shopping experience at Macy's. Using **quick response (QR) codes** and **short message service (SMS)** technology, customers can easily access fun and informative 30-second videos that highlight the retailer's celebrity designers and fashion experts (see related videos at youtube.com/Macys). Mobile shoppers can access the videos by scanning the QR codes posted on displays in each department. Shoppers who do not have a QR code scanner can access the videos by texting a special keyword to Macy's using codes supplied on the displays. Backstage Pass is an example of what marketers call a **mobile display strategy**. It is supported by

Figure 8.2 Macy's encourages shoppers to use mobile technology in its stores through a variety of strategies, including mobile videos that describe merchandise, benefits from mobile check-in, and fun augmented-reality apps.

© gpointstudio/Shutterstock

an integrated communications campaign involving traditional television and print media advertising. Macy's can measure customer interest in the program by tracking the number of times customers watch the videos. Based on the initial success of the program, Macy's has increased spending on mobile display strategies by 70 percent (Kats, 2012).

Another key mobile strategy used by Macy's is the **SMS database strategy**, growing its list of customers who have opted-in to receive discounts and special offers via text message. According to Martine Reardon, executive vice president of national marketing at Macy's, New York, the retailer is including SMS short codes in most of its printed coupons to encourage customers to opt-in to receive coupons and other offers via text message. Macy's customers have responded well to these kinds of promotions, so growing the list of people who opt-in to this program should be easy.

With its **mobile check-in strategy**, Macys has partnered with Foursquare and Shopkick to create check-in programs that reinforce shopping behavior at retail outlets. Mobile customers using the Shopkick app on their phones receive points on their account just for visiting a Macy's store. They may also receive special offers from Macy's via the Shopkick app when they visit particular departments or scan featured merchandise. The points can be redeemed for restaurant vouchers, iTunes gift cards, and gift cards from a variety of participating retailers. Macy's partnered with Foursquare and a charitable foundation created by insurance company Aflac. For every consumer who checks-in at Macy's via the Foursquare app, Aflac donates $1 to its charity, The Aflac Cancer Center and Blood Disorders Service of Children's Healthcare of Atlanta. Aflac made the same offer to customers who checked-in while watching Macy's famous Thanksgiving Day Parade, using an entertainment check-in service called GetGlue.com (now called tvtag.com). These kinds of partnerships and programs not only reinforce store shopping behavior, but also enhance Macy's positive brand reputation among target consumers.

Via the **mobile payment** strategy, customers can pay for products at Macy's using Google Wallet, a mobile payment app (Figure 8.3). At the register, customers simply tap their phones on a Near-Field Communications (NFC) device in order to transfer funds to Macy's. Google Wallet is one of several approaches to mobile payment competing to become the dominant alternative to traditional credit cards. Mobile payment is expected to become widespread in the near future as banks, retailers, and telecommunications companies gain experience with the technology. (Read more about mobile payment in Section 8.5.)

Figure 8.3 Customers at Macy's can pay for purchases with their smartphones by using a mobile wallet app.

© LDProd/iStockphoto

Augmented reality: A technology that superimposes a computer-generated image onto an image of the real world to provide information or entertainment.

In an **augmented reality** strategy, during the Thanksgiving and Christmas holiday season, Macy's runs a program to benefit the Make-A-Wish Foundation. Over the past few years, Macy's has donated $1 for every customer who visits a store and "mails" a letter to Santa. In 2011 Macy's made that visit even more fun, inviting customers to take pictures of their children in special holiday displays using augmented reality apps that inserted one of the animated characters associated with the campaign into the picture. Pictures could then be uploaded into a holiday card template, shared by e-mail, or posted to the customer's Facebook page.

While other retailers are still trying to understand mobile consumer behavior, Macy's is already adapting to a new retail environment where increasing numbers of consumers are using handheld devices. It has shown that traditional brick-and-mortar retailers can enhance the in-store shopping experience using mobile technologies in a variety of ways.

Sources: Compiled from Zimmerman (2012), Tsirulnik (2011), Macy's (2011), Johnson (2011), Kats (2012).

Questions

1. Describe how each of Macy's mobile retail strategies enhances the in-store shopping experience for customers.
2. What will most customers think about Target's attempt to make mobile price comparison more difficult?
3. How does Macy's benefit from the use of location-based apps like Foursquare and Shopkick?
4. Why is it important that Macy's get customers to "opt-in" to its program before sending promotional text messages?
5. Does Macy's Backstage Pass Program really add value to the customer, or is it just a "gimmick" with short-term benefits?
6. Traditional retailers spend a considerable amount of money to maintain an inventory of products and provide salespeople to service in-store customers. Explain whether or not the practice of showrooming is unethical. What can retailers do to respond to the showrooming trend?

8.1 Retailing Technology

Life is not easy for managers in the retail sector these days. The challenges faced by retailers have never been more complex, frustrating, and fraught with peril. Consumers are demanding, price-conscious, and easily swayed by competitors. Technology is both a blessing and a curse. Countless new and innovative technology "solutions" to retailing problems are offered by a dizzying array of both established and new vendors. Many of the newest technologies promise to give retailers a competitive edge in the marketplace, but are unproven. Budgets for technology are limited, and making the wrong decision can lead to financial consequences, operational failures, and lost customers. However, because of intense competition, retailers cannot afford to be too conservative, or they risk losing out to competitors with technologies that enhance the shopping experience, reduce costs, integrate sales channels, and improve record keeping, data collection, and analysis of key performance indicators (KPIs).

KEEPING UP WITH CONSUMER DEMANDS AND BEHAVIOR

Understanding and responding to consumer needs and behavior is the key to survival for the modern retailer. The challenge, however, is increasingly complex as retailers are confronted with a number of difficult industrywide trends and changing consumer behavior (Galgey & Pattinson, 2013).

Empowered Price Sensitivity. Consumers have always been concerned about price. In today's retail environment, the consumer is more empowered than ever to find the lowest price available for a product. Using the Web and mobile technology, consumers can look up information about alternative products and prices from a variety of local and online retailers using a mobile device. Retailers need clear strategies to respond to the empowered consumer by price-matching or finding ways to offer greater value.

Nonlinear Search and Influence Patterns. The path by which consumers pursue purchases today is often varied and unpredictable. In simpler times, consumers were largely influenced by mass media advertising that drove them to brick-and-mortar stores for purchase. While things were perhaps never quite that simple, consumers today are influenced by a range of new communications channels including social media, mobile ads, e-mail, search marketing, and other digital communications.

Channel Hopping. Just as consumers are influenced by a greater number of communications channels, their options for purchasing products have increased. Consumers can now purchase products through traditional retailers, online, and via mobile devices and apps. Some experts are beginning to view social media as a potential retail channel called **social commerce**. For instance, Dell reportedly sells millions of dollars of refurbished computer equipment each year through its @delloutlet Twitter account (Leslie, Chawla, Aaker, 2010). The manner in which consumers use each channel varies. Some consumers will use a brick-and-mortar store to gather information about a product, but purchase it online. Others will do their research online, but prefer to purchase the product through a traditional retailer. Some may plan to purchase the product at a store, but if they find the product they want is not available they will buy it from their mobile device while in the store. The many combinations of shopping channel, communications channel, and stage of the shopping process are enormous and make strategic planning a challenge. Modern retailers will increasingly rely on data analytics to distinguish patterns or trends in consumer shopping behavior across channels to identify the best ways to satisfy customer needs.

Digital Immigrants, Natives, and Dependents. Retailers have long been aware of the difference between digital immigrants and digital natives. **Digital natives** are the first generation to have grown up surrounded by digital devices (i.e., computers, smartphones, digital cameras, video recorders, etc.) and Internet connectivity. They are comfortable using technology to move easily between various retail channels to optimize their purchasing on price, convenience, and desire for instant gratification. **Digital immigrants**, however, are older, and although they are increasingly comfortable with technology, they fundamentally view retail channels as separate and distinct. They are much less likely than natives to incorporate mobile technology into their shopping behavior. **Digital dependents** represent the emerging generation of young people who are growing up in a world of broadband connections, constant connectivity, and related technology and become uncomfortable if they do not have access to it. This generation will place even greater demands on retailers, expecting to use technology to accomplish all facets of the shopping experience. Brick-and-mortar retailers will continue to play an important role in the lives of this generation, but they will expect in-store shopping to be fully integrated with the technology they have come to depend on.

Need for Convenience. As economic and social factors lead to more stressful lives, consumers will be looking for products and shopping channels that reduce the impact on their time and financial resources, while satisfying their demand for immediate gratification and desirable goods and services.

THE OMNI-CHANNEL RETAILING CONCEPT

As the retailing world began to evolve as a result of digital technology and the Internet, new channels emerged that were initially thought to be separate and distinct. Most retailers and a fairly large segment of the consumer market still view online shopping (**e-commerce**) and **mobile commerce** (**m-commerce**) channels as competing with traditional brick-and-mortar stores.

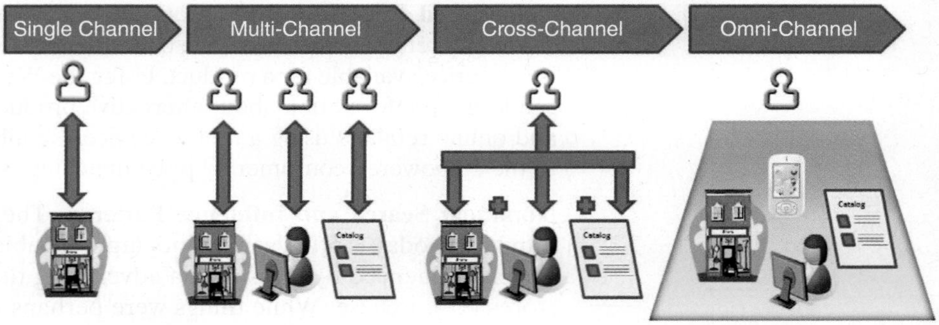

The Legacy	The Reality	The Aspiration	Nirvana
Consumer contact with retailers limited to single channel.	Customers see multiple retail channels available for acquiring goods and services.	Customers see multiple but separate channels with which they can interact with the same brand.	Customers enjoy an integrated, value-added experience with brand across multiple channels.
Retailers only had a single "touch point" with which to connect with consumers.	Retailers operate separate channels as independent "silos" that sometimes compete for consumer attention.	Retailers have a single view of the consumer, but continue to operate separate channels as silos.	Retailers leverage the functionality of each channel as well as their single view of the customer to provide optimal overall experience.

Figure 8.4 Retail strategy is evolving toward an omni-channel approach (adapted from National Retail Federation, 2011).

As you read in the opening case, Target feels threatened by customers who showroom its stores using mobile devices. However, as businesses learn about the full potential of mobile and other digital technologies, the distinction between the newer channels and in-store retailing is beginning to blur. While most businesses currently operate their e-commerce and mobile channels separately from the traditional retail channel, it is expected that strategies integrating the customer experience across channels will emerge, resulting in what the National Retail Federation (2011) refers to as the **omni-channel retailing** approach.

As illustrated in Figure 8.4, many businesses operate separate retail channels. For instance, in-store product prices may be different from those the customer finds on the company's e-commerce website and direct mail catalog. Records of customer purchases from the e-commerce site may not be available to service personnel assisting the customer at the store level. But retail strategy is evolving. The ultimate goal is to offer consumers multiple brand–based "touchpoints" that leverage the strengths of each channel. For instance, a company with a truly integrated or omni-channel strategy might spark a customer's interest using mobile advertising or direct mail catalogs. The customer then visits a brick-and-mortar store to examine the product firsthand and speak to a salesperson. In-store purchases might be made using one of the mobile payment methods discussed later in this chapter. If the store does not have the particular size or color of the product desired, the customer might order it by accessing the store's e-commerce site with his or her smartphone by scanning a QR code placed strategically on an in-store display. The product would then be delivered through the mail. Product returns could be handled through the mail or returned to the store, depending on what is most convenient for the customer. Customer service reps in a call center would have a record of the customer's purchase regardless of which channel the transaction had been completed through. The omni-channel strategy will also take into consideration the potential impact of social media, whereby customers interact with the brand on sites like Facebook or Twitter and share brand experiences with others in their social network.

Questions

1. Describe the factors that influence consumer shopping behavior today.
2. What does the concept of digital native, digital immigrant, and digital dependent help us to understand about people's use of technology during shopping activities?

3. Why are retailers likely to view technology as both a blessing and a curse?

4. Describe how an omni-channel retailer is likely to be different from a traditional, single-channel retailer?

8.2 Business to Consumer (B2C) E-commerce

Electronic wallet (e-wallet): A software application that can store encrypted information about a user's credit cards, bank accounts, and other information necessary to complete electronic transactions, eliminating the need to re-enter the information during the transaction.

During the late 1990s, the idea of purchasing things online was still a novel concept. People who purchased books and other low-priced items from websites were seen as innovators. Nowadays, shopping for things online and finding the best deal by comparing online prices with those in brick-and-mortar stores are common consumer behaviors. In the past decade, the variety of goods and services available through e-commerce sites has skyrocketed. If you look through older textbooks in the IT field, you will find authors predicting that e-commerce will only be successful with low-priced consumer goods. But we now know that this is simply not the case. People today purchase everything from toothpaste to cars and diamond rings online. E-commerce in the B2B sector is even larger than it is in the B2C marketplace.

Retail sales via online channels, financial services, travel services, and digital products (e.g., music- and movie-streaming services) are widely popular forms of B2C commerce. The most well-known B2C site is Amazon.com, whose IT developments received U.S. patents that keep it ahead of competition. Many of these are described in IT at Work 8.1.

IT at Work 8.1

Amazon.com's IT Patents Create Competitive Edge

Entrepreneur and e-commerce pioneer Jeff Bezos envisioned the huge potential for retail sales over the Internet and selected books for his e-commerce venture. In July 1995 Bezos started Amazon.com, offering books via an electronic catalog from its website. Key features offered by Amazon.com were broad selection, low prices, easy searching and ordering, useful product information and personalization, secure payment systems, and efficient order fulfillment. Early on, recognizing the importance of order fulfillment, Amazon.com invested hundreds of millions of dollars in building physical warehouses designed for shipping small packages to hundreds of thousands of customers.

Amazon has continually revised its business model by improving the customer's experience. For example, customers can personalize their Amazon accounts and manage orders online with the patented One-Click order feature. This personalized service includes an **electronic wallet (e-wallet)**, which enables shoppers to place an order in a secure manner without the need to enter their address, credit card number, and so forth, each time they shop. One-Click also allows customers to view their order status and make changes on orders that have not yet entered the shipping process. To emphasize its large inventory of books, Amazon obtained registered trademarks for its retail slogans: "Earth's Biggest Selection" and "If It's in Print, It's in Stock."

In addition, Amazon added services and alliances to attract more customers and increase sales. In January 2002 Amazon.com declared its first-ever profit during the 2001 fourth quarter; 2003 was the first year it cleared a profit in each quarter.

Amazon has invested heavily in its IT infrastructure and obtained patents for much of the technology that powers its website. The select list of patents below gives a glimpse into the legal side of the e-commerce giant, and explains why numerous major retailers, such as Sears and Sony, have used Amazon.com as its sales portal.

- 6,525,747: Method and system for conducting a discussion relating to an item

- 6,029,141: Internet-based customer referral system, also known as the Affiliate program
- 5,999,924: Method for producing sequenced queries
- 5,963,949: Method for data gathering around forms and search barriers
- 5,960,411: Method and system for placing a purchase order via a communications network (One-Click purchase)
- 5,826,258: Method and apparatus for structuring the querying and interpretation of semi-structured information
- 5,727,163: Secure method for communicating credit card data when placing an order on a nonsecure network
- 5,715,399: Secure method and system for communicating a list of credit card numbers over a nonsecure network

Amazon launched the Kindle e-reader in 2007. Its success demonstrated the viability of the e-book market and led to the entry of numerous competitors, such as Barnes & Noble's Nook and the Apple iPad. E-books now account for about 30 percent of all books sold, and Amazon's share of the e-book market is 65 percent (Bercovici, 2014). Since 2011 Amazon has sold more e-books than print books (Miller and Bosman, 2011). See Figure 8.5.

In mid-2010 Amazon started rolling out a software upgrade for Kindle, adding the ability for users to share e-book passages with others on Facebook and Twitter. The new social networking feature in Version 2.5 adds another Web link to the standard Kindle and the larger Kindle DX, as Amazon finds itself in an increasingly competitive market because of the iPad's features. The iPad is designed for reading digital books, watching online video, listening to music, and Web browsing, making it more of a tablet device than simply an e-reader.

Finally, as you read in Chapter 6, Amazon has been a pioneer in the development of recommendation engines

© nicolamargaret/iStockphoto

Figure 8.5 Amazon now sells more e-books than print books and is considered the dominant e-book retailer.

designed to suggest products to customers based on their purchase history and shopping behavior. Amazon's recommendation system is considered among the best in the industry.

Sources: Compiled from Gonsalves (2010), Rappa (2010), Bercovici (2014), Miller & Bosman (2011).

Questions

1. Why is order fulfillment critical to Amazon's success?
2. Why did Amazon patent One-Click and other IT infrastructure developments?
3. How has Amazon adapted the Kindle to new technologies?
4. Why would other retailers form an alliance with Amazon.com?

Several of the leading online service industries are banking, trading of securities (stocks, bonds), and employment, travel, and real estate services.

| ONLINE BANKING

Online banking includes various banking activities conducted via the Internet instead of at a physical bank location. Online banking, also called direct banking, offers capabilities ranging from paying bills to applying for a loan. Customers can check balances and transfer funds at any time of day. For banks, it offers an inexpensive alternative to branch banking. Transaction costs are about 2 cents per transaction versus $1.07 at a physical branch.

Most brick-and-mortar conventional banks provide online banking services and use e-commerce as a major competitive strategy. Customers are aware that if they bank exclusively with a brick-and-mortar institution, they may be missing out on high-paying investment options or competitive loan rates that easily undercut those of many traditional banking entities.

IT at Work 8.2

Ally Bank – Building Trust and Confidence Online

A Crisis of Confidence in Consumer Banking

While the first Internet-only bank, or direct bank, appeared in the mid-1980s, it wasn't until around 2010 that these online institutions became mainstream. Some have attributed general consumer frustration resulting from the 2008 economic crisis with generating consumer interest in new, agile banking institutions that appear to be more responsive to consumer needs for convenience and customer support.

Banks have historically built their reputations on trust and consumer confidence that they would act ethically, protect consumers' money, and make customer interests a priority. However, the financial crisis of 2008 led to wide-scale consumer mistrust and frustration with traditional banks and financial services companies. Banking is now considered one of the least trustworthy industries by consumers (Edleman, 2013, O'Connell, 2013). Consumers also believe that irresponsible behavior by banking organizations was a primary cause of the economic meltdown that led to high levels of unemployment and fiscal uncertainty in the U.S. and across the globe (The Financial Brand, 2013).

Many banks only made matters worse during this period when they instituted a number of business practices that further alienated consumers (O'Connell, 2013). During a time when consumers were already frustrated with financial institutions because of the economic crisis, many banks hiked interest rates on loans, reduced the interest rate they paid on consumer savings and checking accounts, made it more difficult for consumers to open credit accounts, imposed new types of fees on consumer services, and oftentimes failed to transparently disclose information about fees and interest rates in promotional messages and other forms of communication with consumers. As a result, consumer confidence in the banking industry dropped to an all-time low following the 2008 financial crisis (Gallup, 2014). See Figure 8.6.

In an effort to take advantage of widespread consumer frustration and dissatisfaction with traditional banking companies, a number of new, smaller, and more agile banks are moving to offer alternative approaches to consumer banking services. Ally Bank is a popular Internet-only bank that is widely recognized for its success in developing a business model with significant appeal to retail banking customers.

Overview of Ally Bank

Ally Bank, based in Midvale, Utah, is a subsidiary of Ally Financial, formerly GMAC, the financial unit of General Motors Corporation. Since its launch in 2009, Ally Bank has worked hard to create a public image that differentiates itself from business practices that caused consumers to mistrust and grow frustrated with traditional banks and financial service corporations. Ally's marketing communications messages emphasize that it:

- Puts customer needs first.
- Offers consumers smart banking alternatives with no hidden fees and higher interest rates on savings and investment accounts.

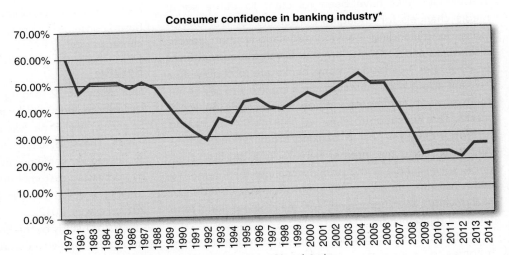

Figure 8.6 Consumer confidence in the banking industry from 1979 to 2014. *Source:* Gallup, 2014

*percent of consumers who indicated a "great deal" or "quite a lot" of confidence in banks

- Is friendly, transparent, and easy to work with, unlike large, fee-happy banks.
- Is new, innovative, fun and offers an attractive alternative to traditional banking corporations.

What Makes Ally Bank Different?

Apart from a brand image that differentiates Ally Bank from its competitors, the company uses technology to distinguish itself in three important ways:

1. The company is part of a growing group of Internet-only, or direct banks. Instead of brick-and-mortar bank branches, Ally Bank's customers use the Web to access their accounts, make transactions, and monitor their funds.
2. Unlike other banks that have been slow to embrace social media, Ally Bank is recognized as a leader in the banking industry for its use of social media to engage consumers.
3. Ally Bank offers customers mobile banking apps to make doing business with the company even more convenient.

Internet banks provide customers with the convenience of 24/7 banking services through the Web. Consumers access their account information using a computer, tablet or smartphone. Deposits are made by scanning or photographing checks and transferring the image to the bank. Checks can also be mailed to the bank. Internet banks typically offer savings and checking accounts, certificates of deposit, retirement accounts, and various types of loans and mortgages. Because Internet banks do not bear the cost of maintaining physical branch offices, they often offer customers better interest rates and lower fees than traditional banks. To retrieve cash, customers use ATM machines. Many Internet banks reimburse customers for fees they incur when using the ATM machines of other banks.

Social Media

Traditional banks have been reluctant to utilize social media channels for engaging consumers for fear of violating long-standing banking regulations that govern disclosures and consumer privacy. Given the current level of consumer frustration, many banks are probably also hesitant about what their customers are likely to say about them through comments, ratings, and reviews on social media. This hesitation to embrace new media has created an opportunity for upstart banking organizations such as Ally Bank. Since the Internet bank lacks a physical presence, social media is the primary channel for interacting with customers in ways that promote trust, confidence, and loyalty, key ingredients for maintaining long-term financial relationships.

Ally Bank is recognized as an industry leader when it comes to its innovative use of social media. According to Smith (2014), Ally Bank excels in three areas of social media:

- Communicating the brand via social channels
- Using data to drive social marketing decisions
- Cross-platform integration of marketing strategies

Examples of Ally's social media marketing include using Twitter to offer personal finance advice. Ally has also teamed up with Bankrate.com to sponsor a monthly, hour-long TweetChat (discussion group) called #AllyBRchat, where participants discuss a range of personal finance issues. The firm's Facebook page is used to engage consumers with links to Ally's "Straight Talk Blog," opinion polls, and educational videos. On Ally Bank's YouTube channel, visitors will find installments of financial advice programs with titles such as "Ally Bank Financial Etiquette," "Discovering Retirement," and "Behind the Scenes with Kiplinger." Across all of these social platforms, Ally Bank offers consumers information, advice, and tools by posting over 1,500 pieces of content every month (Tejwani, 2012).

Ally Bank's Mobile Strategy

Ally Bank's adoption of mobile technology follows the bank's philosophy of putting the customer first and creating the most convenient ways for them to access and manage their money. According to Carrie Sumlin, a Digital Deposits Executive at Ally Bank, the company's goal with both mobile and Web technology is to make sure that all applications live up to the promise of transparency, simplicity, and ease of use (Yurcan, 2014). First introduced in April 2012, Ally's mobile apps offer a wide range of functionality including account management, bill payment, fund transfers to external banks, and a tool for finding ATM and cash-back locations. Managers at Ally Bank are constantly evaluating customer reaction to the mobile apps by monitoring how the apps are used, which devices are being used, and customer feedback collected through social media, Web-based consumer surveys, and calls to their customer service center.

Results

In a study of 22 leading banks, credit unions, and financial service firms conducted by the research firm Change Sciences, Ally Bank was ranked #1 for its use of social media. The study cited the importance of "authenticity" in social media communications—going beyond advertising by addressing customer needs and communicating in a personal tone or real voice instead of a corporate tone (Yurcan, 2012, Tejwani, 2012).

A 2011 study by the Ponemon Institute ranked Ally Bank among the top five most-trusted banks in the industry based on a survey of 5,571 consumers.

Ally Bank was rated among the best in the nation by the Pew Charitable Trusts for its use of best disclosure practices, evidence that the company is succeeding in its goal to be transparent about fees and other information important to consumers (Malone, 2014).

Ally Bank is regularly recognized by organizations and publications like Money Magazine, Kiplinger, Forester Research, and Bank Tracker as being among the best banks in the industry, providing the best banking website, and providing an excellent customer experience. For an extensive list of awards and recognitions, see the Media Center—Awards and Recognitions page on the Allybank.com website.

Conclusion

Ally Bank is clearly an innovator and a disruptive competitor in an otherwise tradition-bound industry that has not always been responsive to consumer needs. The company has distinguished itself by its innovative, technology-driven approach to providing financial services, a provocative and engaging marketing and branding strategy, and an ability to communicate with consumers through social media channels. In the short time that Ally Bank has been in business, it has attracted over 825,000 customers, manages $45 billion in retail deposits, and achieves customer satisfaction levels of over 90 percent (Ally Financial, 2014). It is recognized as a leader in the direct banking segment of the consumer banking industry.

Questions

1. Visit Ally Bank's Facebook page. Identify examples of how the company speaks in an authentic or real voice to its customers.
2. How has Ally Bank attempted to take advantage of negative consumer sentiment toward traditional banks in the industry?
3. As Ally Bank develops its mobile banking service, what guides the company's development of the necessary technological applications?
4. Visit Ally Bank's YouTube channel. After reviewing video clips of Ally's past advertising campaigns, how would you describe its brand image?
5. Visit Allybank.com and review the information about its banking services. Do you think that Internet-only banks will eventually attract a significant number of customers away from traditional banks?

INTERNATIONAL AND MULTIPLE-CURRENCY BANKING

International banking and the ability to handle trading in multiple currencies are critical for international trade. **Electronic fund transfer (EFT)** and electronic letters of credit are important services in international banking. An example of support for e-commerce global trade is provided by TradeCard (tradecard.com). TradeCard offers a *software-as-a-service (SaaS)* model that provides supply chain collaboration and a trade finance compliance platform.

Electronic fund transfer (EFT): A transfer of funds from one bank account to another over a computerized network.

Although some international retail purchasing can be done by giving a credit card number, other transactions may require cross-border banking support. For example, Hong Kong and Shanghai Bank (hsbc.com.hk) has developed a special system, HSBCnet, to provide online banking in 60 countries. Using this system, the bank has leveraged its reputation and infrastructure in the developing economies of Asia to rapidly become a major international bank without developing an extensive new branch network.

ONLINE JOB MARKET

Most companies and government agencies advertise job openings, accept résumés, and take applications via the Internet. The online job market is especially effective and active for technology-oriented jobs. While sites like dice.com and monster.com can still be helpful, job seekers nowadays are employing a variety of social media tools, including the use of LinkedIn.com, to develop a network of contacts and establish a personal, online reputation. In many countries, governments must advertise job openings on the Internet. In addition, hundreds of job-placement brokers and related services are active on the Web.

ISSUES IN ONLINE RETAILING

Despite the tremendous growth of online retailers, many face challenges that can interfere with business growth. Major issues include:

1. **Resolving channel conflict**. Sellers that are click-and-mortar companies, such as Levi's or GM, face a conflict with their regular wholesale and retail

Channel conflict:
Competition between a manufacturer's distribution partners who sell through different channels. Channel conflict can occur at the wholesale, retail, or internal sales department level.

distributors when they circumvent those distributors by selling online directly to customers. (These distributors are other businesses that carry the company's product.) This situation is called **channel conflict** because it is a conflict between an online selling channel and physical selling channels. Channel conflict has forced some companies to limit their B2C efforts, or not to sell direct online. An alternative approach is to try to collaborate in some way with the existing distributors whose services may be restructured. For example, an auto company could allow customers to configure a car online, but require that the car be picked up from a dealer, where customers could also arrange financing, warranties, and service.

2. **Resolving conflicts within click-and-mortar organizations.** When an established company sells online directly to customers, it creates conflict with its own offline operations. Conflicts may arise in areas such as pricing of products and services, allocation of resources (e.g., advertising budget), and logistics services provided by the offline activities to the online activities (e.g., handling of returns of items bought online). To minimize this type of conflict, companies may separate the online division from the traditional division. The downside is that separation can increase expenses and reduce the synergy between the two organizational parts.

3. **Managing order fulfillment and logistics.** Online retailers face tough order fulfillment and **logistics** problems when selling online because of the need to design systems to accept and process a huge volume of small orders, to physically pick items from warehouse shelves and put them into boxes, to be sure that the correct labels are applied, and to accept returns. The return process is referred to as reverse logistics.

4. **Determining viability and risk of online retailers.** Many pure online retailers went bankrupt in the dot.com era, the result of problems with cash flow, customer acquisition, order fulfillment, and demand forecasting. Online competition, especially in commodity-type products such as CDs, toys, books, or groceries, became very fierce due to the ease of entry into the marketplace. As Porter's (2008) five competitive forces model explains, low entry barriers intensify competition in an industry. So a problem most new and established online retailers face is to determine how long to operate while you are still losing money and how to finance those losses.

5. **Identifying appropriate revenue (business) models.** One early dot.com model was to generate enough revenue from advertising to keep the business afloat until the customer base reached critical mass. This model did not always work. Too many dot.coms were competing for too few advertising dollars, which went mainly to a small number of well-known sites such as AOL, MSN, Google, and Yahoo. In addition, there was a "chicken-and-egg" problem: Sites could not get advertisers to come if they did not have enough visitors. To succeed in e-commerce, it is necessary to identify appropriate revenue models and modify those models as the market changes.

ONLINE BUSINESS AND MARKETING PLANNING

Online marketing planning is very similar to any other marketing plan. It is not a best practice, though, and somewhat strange, to devise separate online and offline plans because that is not how customers perceive a business. Here are several online business and planning recommendations:

1. Build the marketing plan around the customer, rather than on products.

2. Monitor progress toward the one-year vision for the business in order to identify when adjustments are needed, and then be agile enough to respond.

3. Identify all key assumptions in the marketing plan. When there is evidence that those assumptions are wrong, identify the new assumptions and adjust the plan.

4. Make data-driven, fact-based plans.

Questions

1. Describe how digital content and services can lead to significantly lower costs.
2. Why does channel conflict sometimes occur when companies sell their products through both traditional and online channels?
3. How has Amazon maintained its competitive edge?
4. Describe some of the ways that Ally Bank has become one of the most successful direct banks in the industry today.
5. Explain why retail banking has become one of the least trusted industries by consumers since the early 2000s.
6. List three online marketing planning recommendations.

8.3 Business to Business (B2B) E-commerce and E-procurement

In **business-to-business (B2B)** markets, the buyers, sellers, and transactions involve only organizations. B2B comprises about 85 percent of e-commerce dollar volume. It covers applications that enable an enterprise to form electronic relationships with its distributors, resellers, suppliers, customers, and other partners. By using B2B, organizations can restructure their supply chains and partner relationships.

There are several business models for B2B applications. The major ones are sell-side marketplaces and e-sourcing (the buy-side marketplace).

SELL-SIDE MARKETPLACES

In the **sell-side marketplace** model, organizations sell their products or services to other organizations from their own private website or from a third-party site. This model is similar to the B2C model in which the buyer is expected to come to the seller's site, view catalogs, and place an order. In the B2B sell-side marketplace, however, the buyer is an organization. The two key mechanisms in the sell-side model are forward auctions and online catalogs, which can be customized for each buyer.

Sellers such as Dell Computer (dellauction.com) use auctions extensively. In addition to auctions from their own websites, organizations can use third-party auction sites, such as eBay, to liquidate items. Companies such as Overstock.com help organizations to auction obsolete and excess assets and inventories.

The sell-side model is used by hundreds of thousands of companies and is especially powerful for companies with superb reputations. The seller can be either a manufacturer (e.g., IBM), a distributor (e.g., avnet.com is an example of a large distributor in IT), or a retailer (e.g., Walmart.com). The seller uses e-commerce to increase sales, reduce selling and advertising expenditures, increase delivery speed, and reduce administrative costs. The sell-side model is especially suitable to customization. For example, organizational customers can configure their orders online at cisco.com and other sites. Self-configuration of orders results in fewer misunderstandings about what customers want and much faster order fulfillment.

E-SOURCING

E-sourcing refers to many different procurement methods that make use of an electronic venue for identifying, evaluating, selecting, negotiating and collaborating with suppliers. The primary methods are online auctions, RFQ (request for quote) processing, and private exchanges. E-sourcing also applies to many other secondary activities, which add to the cycle time and transaction costs when performed using traditional methods. Secondary activities include trading partner collaboration, contract negotiation, and supplier selection.

| E-PROCUREMENT

Corporate procurement, also called **corporate purchasing**, deals with the transactional elements of buying products and services by an organization for its operational and functional needs. Organizations procure materials to produce finished goods, which is referred to as **direct procurement**, and products for daily operational needs, which is referred to as **indirect procurement**. **E-procurement** refers to the reengineered procurement process using e-business technologies and strategies. Strategies and solutions linked to e-procurement have two basic goals:

- **Control costs:** The first goal is to control corporate spending. Organizations want to spend intelligently for procurement activities to maximize the value of their spending, that is, to ensure that money spent to procure items results in procuring the right products at the best value. Corporate e-procurement constitutes a substantial portion of an organization's operational spending. For example, it is common for large manufacturing organizations to spend millions of U.S. dollars procuring products and services. Organizations thus design e-procurement systems to facilitate and control overall procurement spending.

- **Simplify processes:** The second goal is to streamline the procurement process to make it efficient. Inefficiencies in the procurement process introduce delays in ordering and receiving items and tax internal resources.

The two goals of cost control and streamlining can be met in three ways:

1. Streamline the e-procurement process within an organization's value chain. Doing so reduces the number of employees needed to process purchasing, reduces the procurement cycle time to order and receive items, and empowers an organization's staff with enough information about the products and services to enable them to make intelligent decisions when procuring items.

2. Align the organization's procurement process with those of other trading partners, which belong to the organization's virtual supply chain. Alignment can be achieved by automating the process from end-to-end, including trading partner's systems, and simplifies the buying process. This enables suppliers to react efficiently to buyers' needs.

3. Use appropriate e-procurement strategies and solutions. Organizations analyze spending patterns in an effort to improve spending decisions and outcomes.

| PUBLIC AND PRIVATE
| EXCHANGES

Exchanges are sites where many buyers and sellers conduct business transactions. They may be public or private, depending on whether or not they are open to the public.

Vertical exchanges serve one industry (e.g., automotive, chemical), along the entire supply chain. **Horizontal exchanges** serve many industries that use the same products or services (e.g., office supplies, cleaning materials). Four types of exchanges are:

1. **Vertical exchanges for direct materials.** These are B2B marketplaces where *direct materials*—materials that are inputs to manufacturing—are traded, usually in *large quantities* in an environment of long-term relationship known as **systematic sourcing**. An example is PlasticsNet.com, a vertical marketplace for industry professionals.

2. Indirect materials in *one industry* are purchased as needed using a practice called **spot sourcing**. Buyers and sellers may not even know each other. In vertical exchanges, prices change continuously (like a stock exchange), based on the matching of supply and demand. Auctions are typically used in this kind of B2B marketplace. Some question exists as to how viable the market is for this type of exchange. Several companies that have been previously cited as successful indirect material vertical exchanges have gone out of business: paperexchange.com, chemconnect.com, esteel.com, and Altra Energy Technologies.

3. **Horizontal exchanges.** These are many-to-many e-marketplaces for indirect materials, such as office supplies, light bulbs, and cleaning materials used by *any industry*. Because these products are used for maintenance, repair, and operations (and not resold to generate revenue), these indirect supplies are called **MRO supplies**. Prices are fixed or negotiated in this systematic exchange. Examples are Worldbid.com, Globalsources.com, and Alibaba.com.

American Express applied its own experience in indirect purchasing to develop tools that improve compliance with established procurement rules on indirect purchases, or MRO supplies. Instead of a pile of catalogs or personal supplier preferences, the system relies on a master catalog that lists only approved products from authorized vendors. One of the big gains is the elimination of **maverick buying**. Maverick buying is outside the established system. If the procurement process is too complicated, people will go outside the system, and buy from a local vendor. Maverick buying can prove costly not only because that vendor's prices may be high, but it can also keep the company from achieving volume levels that could trigger a new tier of discounts.

Since catalog purchases have high transaction costs, American Express put catalogs from multiple suppliers and from various categories of spending into its master catalog, CatalogPro. This catalog makes it easier for users to find the right items and purchase at contract rates.

4. **Functional exchanges.** Needed services such as temporary help or extra space are traded on an as-needed basis. For example, Employease.com (recently purchased by ADP) can find temporary labor using employers in its Employease Network (eease.com). Prices are dynamic, and vary depending on supply and demand.

Another important facet of managing procurement is **demand management**—knowing or predicting what to buy, when, and how much. The best procurement cost is zero, when people are not buying what they do not need.

Questions

1. Briefly differentiate between the sell-side marketplace and e-sourcing.
2. What are the two basic goals of e-procurement? How can those goals be met?
3. What is the role of exchanges in B2B?
4. Explain why maverick buying might take place and its impact on procurement costs.

8.4 Mobile Commerce

In 1997 two Coca-Cola vending machines that accepted payment via SMS text message were installed in Helsinki, Finland. Ever since, industry experts and pundits have been predicting that mobile commerce was about to become "the next big thing" in marketing and the sale of consumer goods. Before we explore how mobile commerce has evolved since 1997, let us define some terms related to this topic:

Mobile commerce, or m-commerce: The buying or selling of goods and services using a wireless, handheld device such as a cell phone or tablet (slate) computer.

Mobile e-commerce: The use of a wireless handheld devices to order and/or pay for goods and services from online vendors. *Example: Ordering a pair of shoes from Zappos.com using a mobile app, or purchasing music from iTunes from your iPod.*

Mobile retailing: The use of mobile technology to promote, enhance, and add value to the in-store shopping experience. *Example: Using a coupon on your cell phone when checking out at the Hard Rock Café, or "checking-in" to a retail location using a mobile app from ShopKick.com or Foursquare.com.*

Mobile marketing: A variety of activities used by organizations to engage, communicate, and interact over Wi-Fi and telecommunications networks with consumers using wireless, handheld devices. *Example: Sending special offers to customers who have opted-in to receive discounts via SMS text message or advertising a brand on a popular mobile game app like Angry Birds.* For additional illustrations of mobile marketing, see IT at Work 8.3.

These four terms are not mutually exclusive. Mobile e-commerce, mobile retailing, and mobile marketing are all forms of mobile commerce. Mobile e-commerce emphasizes the use of mobile apps and mobile websites for carrying out transactions and does not necessarily involve interaction with a traditional retail store. Mobile retailing, on the other hand, emphasizes in-store shopping using a mobile device, but could include situations where the customer ultimately orders from a website or mobile app. Mobile marketing is the term used to describe promotional strategies and tactics that encourage both mobile e-commerce and mobile retail. This overlap is a reflection of the evolution toward the omni-channel retail concept discussed earlier in the chapter (see Figure 8.4).

Although there have been some interesting and even successful examples of m-commerce since 1997, predictions about mobile technology becoming a pervasive force in consumer retailing have proven overly optimistic. There are several reasons why consumers and businesses have been slow to embrace m-commerce:

- Relatively primitive mobile devices (compared to modern smartphones and tablets)
- Concerns about privacy and security
- Slow network connection speeds
- Limited market size
- Limited and inconvenient mobile payment options
- Lack of technological standardization (devices, OSs, browsers, etc.)

However, many of these barriers have been reduced or eliminated. As you read in the previous section, the number of people who now own mobile devices, particularly smartphones, has grown dramatically. According to one widely quoted statistic, more people own cell phones today than own toothbrushes! Telecommunications carriers have expanded their coverage of populated areas using high-speed networks. Modern smartphones and tablet devices have features that make shopping via bright colorful screens fun and easy. While security will always be an evolving concern, consumer comfort with completing transactions on mobile devices continues to grow. A number of mobile payment methods are emerging that are more convenient than traditional transaction methods. So after years of waiting, it appears the stage is finally set for earlier predictions about m-commerce to come true. In this section, we will describe some of the many ways businesses and consumers are using mobile technologies to buy and sell goods and services.

INFORMATION: COMPETITIVE ADVANTAGE IN MOBILE COMMERCE

Integrating mobile technology with a brand's retail and e-commerce strategy provides another important benefit to business: customer information and identification. When customers interact with a brand using a mobile device, information is collected about the customer that can be used to optimize the interaction. For instance, when customers use a brand's mobile app to shop for products, their shopping experience can be customized based on the company's knowledge of previous purchases, payment methods, product preferences, and even location.

In-Store Tracking. In-store shopping experiences can be optimized through mobile technology that can track a customer's movement through a retail store. This is analogous to e-commerce sites that track the pages a customer looks at in order to better understand consumer interests and to make decisions about website design. Tracking how a customer moves through a store, noting what displays the customer looks at, or what departments the customer spends the most time in can be extremely helpful for understanding individual consumer preferences as well as creating optimal store layout. Systems for tracking customers based on signals emitted from cell phones and other mobile devices are under development. It is expected that they will be available on a commercial basis in the near future.

Although the goal of in-store tracking is to provide an enhanced shopping experience for the consumer, most people are likely to find this kind of monitoring a violation of privacy. In plain language, many will find it creepy. Businesses that are not careful about how they implement these programs will experience customer backlash and may even run afoul of new privacy laws and regulations. Therefore, it is important that brands involved in mobile e-commerce and mobil retailing have clear privacy statements and use an opt-in system to obtain permission from customers before tracking their online and offline shopping behaviors. Customers are generally willing to give up some degree of privacy as long as companies explain how collecting the information will benefit them and identify the safeguards used to protect customers' information. Companies often reward customers for providing information and opting-in to monitoring programs. This is generally accomplished through loyalty programs that offer discounts and special premiums to customers who opt-in.

Few businesses fully utilize mobile tracking and monitoring systems at present. But as brands become more sophisticated with mobile technology, it is expected they will strive to gain a competitive advantage by using this information to provide better service, convenience, and a more enjoyable shopping experience, both online and in traditional stores.

Quick Response (QR) Codes. In Japan, many products are tagged with QR codes. Consumers in that country frequently scan QR codes to access product information from a mobile device. Using a barcode scanner app and the camera feature of a mobile device, customers scan the QR code containing a link to an Internet webpage. You read in the case at the beginning of this chapter how Macy's uses QR codes on in-store displays to direct customers to promotional videos that feature its products. The QR code is supposed to be an easier alternative to typing a URL address into a **mobile browser** (see Figure 8.7). While QR codes have not been as popular in the U.S. as they are in Asia, marketers have used them in print advertising and direct mail ads with some success. Charitable organizations use QR codes on the outside of direct mail solicitations. Scanning the code takes the user to a video explaining the mission of the organization and typically makes a more compelling request for a donation than is possible through print media.

Mobile browser: A Web browser that is optimized to display Web content effectively on a small mobile device such as a smart phone.

Figure 8.7 Smartphone users can scan QR codes that help them easily access product information on the Internet without the hassle of typing a URL code into a mobile browser.

© pressureUA/iStockphoto

Additionally, responses to the QR code promotions can be tracked and used to evaluate program effectiveness.

Some experts believe, however, that QR code technology is never going to be as popular in the U.S. as it is in Asia. They cite studies that report many smartphone users simply do not know what to do with a QR code. Other research suggests that users think the scanning process is either inconvenient or that QR codes frequently direct users to pages that do not really contain anything of interest. For QR codes to become something American consumers use frequently, businesses will have to prove that they help mobile users find content that is interesting and valuable. **Mobile visual search** technology is emerging as an alternative to QR codes. See Video Case 8.3 at the end of this chapter for additional information.

Mobile visual search engine: A search engine that uses an image instead of a text-based query to search for information on the Web.

IT at **Work** 8.3

Angry Birds Make Mobile Game Developers Happy

Have you ever played popular mobile games like Angry Birds (Figure 8.8), Candy Crush, or the highly addictive Flappy Bird? Media research firm Nielsen (2011) reports that games are the most popular mobile apps in the U.S. While many apps in this category are free, 93 percent of app downloaders are willing to pay for game apps, compared to 76 percent for news apps, another popular category. Mobile gamers spend an average of 7.8 hours a month playing games, but smartphone users appear to be heavier users of this category, with iPhone owners playing 14.7 hours/month and Android owners playing 9.3 hours/month. Reports of market size and growth rates differ on the exact amounts, but agree this category is sizable and growing rapidly. Estimates of 2013 mobile game revenue range from approximately $12 billion to $17 billion and analysts predict the market could grow to as much as $22 billion by 2015.

To put this in perspective, in 2009, iOS and Android mobile gaming apps accounted for just 11 percent of the portable (handheld) gaming market dominated by Sony and Nintendo. By 2013, mobile games accounted for 27 percent of the gaming market and are projected to rise to 35 percent by 2017. Clearly, mobile gaming apps have become a disruptive force in the marketplace, displacing two historically strong companies. Even more impressive is the fact that the above statistics are based on revenues produced by paid downloads and don't reflect the millions of free games downloaded every year. Many mobile games are available as free apps supported by advertising revenues. Some analysts estimate that ad revenue produced by mobile games was approximately $297 million in 2013 (eMarketer, 2013).

Sources: Compiled from Dotson (2012), Nielsen (2011), Asante (2012), eMarketer (2013).

Questions

1. Why did established companies like Nintendo and Sony fail to gain an early position in the growing mobile gaming market?
2. How are mobile games different from traditional video games? What advantages do mobile game apps have over traditional video games?
3. Gaming and social media are among the most popular mobile app categories in the U.S. What do you think this says about the role of mobile devices in the lives of U.S. consumers?
4. Since many gaming apps are free, how do developers make money in this category?

© Ian Dagnall/Alamy

Figure 8.8 Angry Birds is such a popular mobile game that it generates additional revenue from sales of clothing, plush toys, posters, lunch boxes, and even bed linens.

MOBILE ENTERTAINMENT

Mobile entertainment is expanding on wireless devices. Most notable are music, movies, videos, games, adult entertainment, sports, and gambling apps. For more information about the most popular mobile app category, mobile gaming, see IT at Work 8.3.

Sports enthusiasts enjoy a large number of apps and services on their mobile devices. Apps exist to check game scores; track news about specific athletes, teams, or sports; take part in fantasy team contests like fantasy football; and participate in sports-oriented social networking services. A number of sports-related games like mobile golf and sports trivia apps are widely available. There are even apps designed to provide tips and information for improving your own athletic performance. Apps are available to record workout times, schedule training exercises, record heart rates and a variety of other information related to athletic training. The iPhone even has an app that analyzes a person's golf swing and provides advice for improving performance.

ESPN is widely acknowledged as a leader in mobile marketing to the sports fan. It offers a number of popular branded mobile apps that deliver information and entertainment to its target audience. It also utilizes well-designed mobile websites and has a large database of fans that have opted-in to receive sports-related news alerts sent to their phones via text messages.

Industry analysts predict that recent improvements in mobile devices will lead to an even bigger increase in the number of people who watch video clips, movies, and television programming on their mobile devices. The screen size of devices like Apple's iPad makes watching video programming more attractive than on a smartphone. However, the number of people viewing video on smartphones seems to be increasing as well (Google, IPSOS OTX MediaCT, 2011). Companies like theChanner.com offer television programming to mobile device users. Popular streaming services such as Netflix and Hulu now offer mobile apps for iOS and Android devices.

The iTunes Store continues to be a leading in distributor of digital music, movies, TV shows, e-books, and podcasts available to consumers for a fee. While most iTunes content is available to be purchased, there are frequently e-books, movies, and other digital content available for free. Mobile users can also access music from digital streaming sites like Pandora.com and Grooveshark.com. Both of these services offer free streaming music. Users can upgrade their accounts by paying a subscription fee, which then reduces the amount of advertising they are exposed to.

While still relatively small, the mobile gambling industry is expected to grow substantially over the next few years. Some predict this type of mobile commerce could generate as much as $20 billion in the near future. Primary growth of this market is expected to take place in Japan and other Asian countries, such as horse racing in Hong Kong. Current laws in the U.S. prohibit most forms of online gambling; consequently, gambling via mobile devices is largely unavailable in the U.S.

Many mobile apps are available for consumers interested in home-based entertainment activities. The Food Network offers an app with tips and recipes for fine dining and entertaining. Martha Stewart's Digital Magazines publishes a number of home entertainment and lifestyle mobile apps (see marthastewart.com/apps). Mobatech is the maker of a mobile bartending app with numerous recipes for cocktails and party drinks.

HOTEL SERVICES AND TRAVEL GO WIRELESS

In recent years, smartphones and other mobile devices have become essential travel aids. Most major airlines, hotel chains, and Internet travel agencies have developed mobile apps to help travelers manage their arrangements. Airlines frequently give passengers the option of receiving up-to-date information about their flights via SMS text messaging. Google Maps is perhaps one of the most

© Aleksandra Gigowska/Shutterstock

Figure 8.9 Travelers use mobile apps to book reservations, find directions, and locate reviews and recommendations for a wide range of travel and hospitality services.

popular apps used by travelers, particularly those traveling by automobile. Even AAA, the automobile club, has a mobile app that helps drivers plan their trips and an app for drivers who need roadside assistance. Other interesting mobile travel tools include apps that translate text when traveling abroad, apps for finding nearby Wi-Fi hotspots, and apps created by a number of popular travel guides.

Most large hotels chains and many independent hotels and inns offer guests in-room, wireless high-speed Internet connections, although this is not always a free service. Some of these same hotels offer Wi-Fi Internet access in public areas like the lobby and meeting rooms. Larger hotel chains have apps that allow guests to make reservations, check their bills, and locate hotel services using a mobile app. Starwood, Hilton and other hotels are experimenting with mobile check-in programs whereby guests use their mobile devices to gain access to their rooms using NFC or SMS text message technology. This makes it possible to check-in to the hotel without having to stop first at the front desk. Many airlines now offer travelers the option of loading a boarding pass onto their mobile devices (see Figure 8.9).

MOBILE SOCIAL NETWORKING

People are increasingly using mobile devices to connect with social networking sites such as Facebook and Twitter. According to Nielsen (2011), social media apps are the third most popular kind of mobile app (after games and weather apps). Much like Web-based social networking, mobile social networking occurs in virtual communities. All of the most popular social networking sites offer apps that allow users to access their accounts from a smartphone or other mobile device. Some experts predict that mobile social media will continue to be a primary driving force in the growth of the mobile market.

IT at Work 8.4

Wireless Marketing and Advertising in Action

Industry analysts expect advertising in the mobile channel to heat up. Increasing numbers of smartphones, better browsers, enhanced GPS capabilities, and better ways of measuring advertising effectiveness are all factors powering this growth. The following are a few examples of wireless advertising in action.

Mobile location-based marketing: a marketing strategy that uses information from a mobile device's GPS or customer's mobile check-in on a social network to determine the content of marketing communications they receive on the device (e.g., advertisements, coupons, special offers).

Figure 8.10 The NBC Universal store at Rockefeller Center in New York City encourages customers to check-in to the store using the popular Foursquare app.

Location-Based Marketing. Foursquare.com is one of the most popular apps in the growing field of **mobile location-based marketing** and mobile advertising. The Foursquare app makes use of the mobile device's GPS system to determine the user's location. Part of Foursquare's success is the fact that most users do not view it as an advertising program. Structured as a mobile social media game, users "check-in" from their phones when they visit retail shops and restaurants. Users provide information and ratings based on their reaction to these outlets. This information is shared with advertisers and friends who are also part of the Foursquare network. Foursquare develops a profile of users based on the kinds of businesses they frequent and can use this information to better target consumers with advertising messages. Foursquare reinforces member use of the service by awarding *badges* to members for various types and levels of usage. Members who are the most frequent shoppers at a particular location are awarded the title of *Mayor* and may receive special attention and discounts from the retailer. The company provides advertisers with information about target customers that they usually do not have: their location. This helps advertisers deliver timely messages that can be more relevant and meaningful to consumers, increasing the chances that the ads will lead to a purchase transaction. See Figure 8.10.

Another popular location-based mobile marketing app is Shopkick. When the Shopkick app is activated, users receive points when they visit a participating retailer. Retailers use the app to encourage and reward specific kinds of shopper behavior. Shopkick points are used to reward consumers for visiting specific locations in a store, purchasing products, scanning featured products, and even participating in brief surveys. Shoppers often receive targeted discounts and promotional offers when they are in a store. Shopkick users can trade in their points for restaurant vouchers, iTunes cards, or gift cards from participating retailers.

Augmented Reality (AR). These apps utilize a special technology that will become more commonplace in the future. Augmented reality involves computer-generated graphic images that are superimposed on pictures of real things (e.g., people, rooms, buildings, roads, etc.). This technology can be used by advertisers in several ways. For instance, a mobile phone user might point his or her phone camera at an office building and activate an AR app that generates the logos of all food-service outlets (e.g., Starbucks, Subway, McDonalds) inside the building. Furniture retailer IKEA offers shoppers an AR app that allows them to project images of its products onto pictures of the rooms in their homes so they can "visualize" how the products will look (MobiAdNews. com, 2009). Industry experts expect that AR advertising will grow as smartphone users become more familiar with the concept (see Figure 8.11).

Figure 8.11 IBM's augmented reality shopping app automatically delivers personalized coupons, customer reviews, and hidden product details (such as whether packaging is biodegradable) to smartphones as consumers browse store shelves. The app transforms marketing promotions from intrusions into services that customers welcome.

Mobile Directories. Companies like Signal Mind, Mobile Marketing Studio, and Mowbi Mobile Directories sell mobile directory software to businesses and organizations that want to create local mobile directories. Businesses that purchase these apps can generate revenue by selling listings in their directory and offering a variety of marketing promotions, like mobile coupons, to companies that pay to be listed in the directory. Another popular directory service, Yellow Pages, uses augmented reality as part of its mobile strategy. You can find several interesting examples of augmented reality applications on YouTube. Simply go to YouTube and enter "augmented reality" in the search engine.

Sources: Compiled from Moore (2010) and Whitfield (2010).

Questions

1. Although the benefits of location-based apps for business are perhaps obvious, many previous attempts to get people to use apps that identify their location have met with limited results. Why do you think consumers are less enthusiastic about location apps and what would it take to prompt people to use a location-based app regularly?

2. Review the Foursquare and Shopkick apps and explain which one you think people will be most likely to use. Explain your answer.

3. At present, augmented reality apps are still relatively new and have not enjoyed high levels of adoption. What do you predict will happen with this technology? What applications of augmented reality seem most interesting to you? What barriers will have to be overcome to get people to use this technology?

Questions

1. Describe some of the ways that people are using mobile devices to shop for products and services.

2. What are some ways in which traditional brick-and-mortar retailers can use mobile technology to enhance a customer's in-store shopping experience?

3. List the types of mobile entertainment available to consumers.

4. List some ways that travelers and travel-related businesses are using mobile technology.

5. How are companies using QR codes to promote products and services to mobile consumers? Why are QR codes not as popular in the U.S. as they are in Asia and other parts of the world?

6. Explain why the mobile gaming market represents such a lucrative market opportunity.

8.5 Mobile Transactions and Financial Services

MOBILE PAYMENT SYSTEMS

Consumers use mobile devices for a wide range of shopping or commercial activities. As discussed in the case at the beginning of this chapter, shoppers are using mobile devices to compare prices, research products prior to purchase, and identify alternative product options and alternative retailers. Increasingly, mobile devices are becoming an attractive way to pay for products. According to comScore's Mobile "Future in Focus" report (2012), mobile payment activity during the holiday shopping season (October–December) increased over 80 percent from 2010 to 2011. Other industry reports, such as the "World Payments Report" (Capgemini et al., 2011), suggest that the overall use of mobile payment systems will continue to increase at least 50 percent a year for the next three years. Some forms of mobile payment represent an attractive option for consumers who do not have credit cards.

Additionally, retailers may benefit from new payment options that carry lower transaction costs compared to what banks charge when credit cards are used.

As mobile commerce grows, a greater demand exists for payment systems that make transactions from smartphones and other mobile devices convenient, safe, and secure. A number of businesses have attempted to meet this demand using a variety of technologies. There are two basic transaction types of interest: using a mobile device for the online purchase of goods and services (e.g., ordering a book from Amazon.com) and for payment of goods and services in a traditional brick-and-mortar store. Here are examples of some approaches under development:

Charge to Phone Bill with SMS Confirmation (see zong.com and boku.com). This e-commerce payment solution is a lot easier than entering credit card and other information on a small mobile handheld device. It requires users to set up an account with a payment company like zong.com. When completing an online transaction, users click the "ZONG–Buy with Mobile" button and enter their phone number. They receive an SMS text message with a secure PIN number that they enter on the e-commerce website to complete the transaction. The amount of the charge is then added to the payer's phone bill and the telecom carrier remits this amount to the payee. Telecom companies may deduct a service charge from the amount paid. (Zong was recently purchased by PayPal.)

Near-Field Communications (NFC) (see Google Wallet *and* Isis Mobile Wallet). Another approach to mobile payment is designed for payments in traditional retail stores. At check-out, the mobile user simply passes or taps his or her phone on a merchant terminal and payment is transferred. Users receive an SMS text message confirmation. While Google Wallet has received considerable attention in the technology press, in part because of Google's power and influence in the industry, relatively few consumers can use this option. Only a small number of phones have the required NFC feature. Additionally, the program is only available to people with Citi MasterCard with PayPass or Google's prepaid credit card. To be successful, the program will have to expand beyond these limitations.

Phone-Displayed Barcode That Retailer Scans. A number of companies are developing mobile payment systems that generate a QR code on the user's phone, which is, in turn, scanned by the retailer. Starbucks uses this approach with its mobile payment system (Tsirulnik, 2011). Customers create an account with Starbucks as part of the retailer's loyalty program and transfer money to a prepaid account. Upon check-out, a user activates the Starbucks app, which creates a barcode that can be scanned at check-out. The funds are then deducted from the user's account. Other companies are working on programs that could be used at a variety of retailers, much as you currently use a credit card.

Credit Card + Webform. Using a mobile Web browser, the buyer makes online purchases by entering his or her credit card number and other identifying information just the way that person would if using a personal computer. This process can be cumbersome given the smaller screens and keyboards on most mobile devices, but it is an option.

Transfer of Funds from Payment Account Using SMS (see obopay.com and paypal.com). Using this approach, the user creates an account at a company like obopay.com and transfers money into it from a bank or credit card account. Using a mobile phone and SMS, the user can then transfer money to anyone else with a mobile phone number. The receiver must create an account at the payment company in order to retrieve the funds.

Mobile Phone Card Reader (see Square.com and Paypal.com). This novel approach requires mobile phone users to insert a small card reader into the

Figure 8.12 With a small card reader plugged into a mobile device, merchants and individuals can accept credit card payments.

© PhotoInc/iStockphoto

audio jack of their mobile device. The card reader, which resembles a small cube (Square) or pyramid (PayPal), allows those with accounts at Square or PayPal to make or receive credit card payments without a merchant account. See Figure 8.12.

User Scan of 2D Tags Generated by Retailer (see Cimbal.com). This payment system uses QR codes or **2D tags** (a barcode-like image) to identify the merchant or payee. The buyer scans the merchant's tag using a special smartphone app and then approves a funds transfer when it shows up on the device. Person-to-person transfers are also possible since the app can generate custom QR tags that individuals may scan from one another's mobile devices.

Almost all of the payment systems described above are illustrated by videos on Youtube.com. Interested readers are encouraged to view these video resources for a more complete explanation of how the different mobile payment systems work.

Wireless payment systems transform mobile phones into secure, self-contained purchasing tools capable of instantly authorizing payments over the cellular network. One advantage of many mobile payment systems over traditional credit card systems is the ability to handle **micropayments**, or transactions involving relatively small sums of money. The ability to make micropayments allows individuals to use their mobile devices to do things like purchase a beverage from a vending machine or make a payment to a municipal parking meter. Many cities in Europe, and a growing number in the U.S., have adopted mobile phone payment systems for parking and report dramatic increases in revenue because of the reduction in loss due to theft and broken meters, and the reduced expense associated with collecting cash from traditional meters.

Mobile Bill Payments. In addition to paying bills through wireline banking or from ATMs, a number of companies are now providing their customers with the option of paying bills directly from a cell phone. Western Union, HDFC Bank in India, Citibank, and several other institutions worldwide currently offer mobile bill payment services. This trend is proving particularly attractive to mobile users in developing countries where many people do not have bank accounts.

MOBILE BANKING AND FINANCIAL SERVICES

Mobile banking is generally defined as carrying out banking transactions and other related activities via mobile devices (Figure 8.13). The services offered include bill payments and money transfers, account administration and checkbook requests, balance inquiries and statements on an account, interest and exchange rates, and so on.

Figure 8.13 Mobile banking, stock trading, and payment services have increased in recent years.

© bloomua/Shutterstock

Banks and other financial institutions allow customers to use mobile devices for a wide range of services (see Table 8.2).

People access financial services using a combination of mobile media channels including short message service (SMS), mobile Web browsers, and customized apps. Mobile banking is a natural extension of online banking services, which have grown in popularity over the last decade.

Throughout Europe, the U.S., and Asia, an increasing percentage of banks offer mobile access to financial and account information. In 2009 ABI Research evaluated 29 U.S. banks on accessibility of their mobile banking services. Six of the banks received top marks: BB&T, Eastern Bank, Fifth Third Bank, Northeast Bank, USAA, and Wells Fargo. Bank of America and Chase also received positive evaluations.

In Sweden, Merita Bank has pioneered many services and the Royal Bank of Scotland offers mobile payment services. Banamex, one of Mexico's largest banks, is a strong provider of wireless services to customers. Many banks in Japan allow all banking transactions to be done via cell phone. Experts predict that growth in the mobile banking services sector could reach between 894 million and 1.5 billion customers globally by 2015. The Asia-Pacific region is expected to emerge as the predominant market for mobile banking services (berginsight.com, 2010, Global Industry Analysts, 2010).

TABLE 8.2 Most Common Mobile Banking Services
Account alerts, security alerts, and reminders
Account balances, updates, and history
Customer service via mobile
Branch or ATM location information
Bill-pay (e.g., utility bills) and delivery of online payments by secure agents and mobile phone client apps
Funds transfers
Transaction verification
Source: Mobile Marketing Association (2009).

TABLE 8.3	Mobile Banking Security Risks

Cloning Duplicating the electronic serial number (ESM) of one phone and using it in second phone, the clone. This allows the perpetrator to have calls and other transactions billed to the original phone.

Phishing Using a fraudulent communication, such as an e-mail, to trick the receiver into divulging critical information such as account numbers, passwords, or other identifying information.

Smishing Similar to phishing, but the fraudulent communication comes in the form of an SMS message.

Vishing Again, similar to phishing, but the fraudulent communication comes in the form of a voice or voicemail message encouraging the victim to divulge secure information.

Lost or stolen phone Lost or stolen cell phones can be used to conduct financial transactions without the owner's permission.

Sources: Compiled from Howard (2009), McGee (2008), and Mobile Marketing Association (2009).

SHORT CODES

Banks and financial service organizations have two basic options for providing mobile services. Smartphone users can download dedicated apps to conduct banking transactions. The other option is to provide service through SMS (text message) technology. As you know, text messaging is still widely popular, even with people who use smartphones. Many mobile financial services make use of short codes for sending SMS texts. A **short code** works like a telephone number, except that it is only five or six characters long and easier to remember. Businesses lease short codes from the Common Short Code Association (CSCA) for $500 to $1,000 a month. The lower price is for randomly assigned codes, whereas companies that want a specific short code pay a higher monthly rate. Once a company has leased its short code, it can begin using that code in promotions and interactive exchanges with customers.

Short codes are used for a wide variety of SMS text services, not just financial services. For example, voting on the popular television show *American Idol* is done with short codes. Each contestant is assigned a specific short code and viewers are encouraged to send text messages indicating which performer they like the best. The annual MTV Movie Awards also uses short code voting, which allows viewers to pick the winning entry in certain prize categories. On some telecommunications networks, ring tones are sold using short codes and SMS texts.

SECURITY ISSUES

At present, the benefits associated with mobile banking seem to outweigh potential security threats. However, as the number of people who engage in mobile banking increases, the likelihood that criminals will target mobile financial activity is sure to grow as well. What kinds of threats exist to mobile banking? Table 8.3 lists the most common mobile banking risks.

Questions

1. What are the two basic technologies used for mobile banking and financial services?
2. Why have e-wallets not been widely adopted and what will makers of e-wallets need to do to make this payment method more attractive to consumers?

3. What are the most common types of mobile banking activities consumers perform?

4. What are the most common security risks associated with online retailers?

5. Research some of the mobile payment systems currently available to merchants and consumers.

6. What is a micropayment and why is it beneficial to consumers and businesses that mobile payment systems can process these types of transactions?

Key Terms

2D tags	e-procurement	mobile location-based	quick response (QR)
augmented reality	e-sourcing	marketing	codes
barcode	horizontal exchanges	mobile marketing	short code
digital dependents	in-store tracking	mobile payment	short message service
digital immigrants	micropayments	mobile retailing	(SMS)
digital natives	mobile check-in strategy	mobile visual search	showrooming
disruptive innovation	mobile commerce,	engine	SMS database strategy
electronic fund transfer	m-commerce	omni-channel retailing	social commerce
(EFT)	mobile display strategy		
electronic wallet (e-wallet)			

Assuring Your Learning

DISCUSS: Critical Thinking Questions

1. What is showrooming? Are customers who engage in it acting ethically? Provide reasons for your answer.

2. What are some creative and constructive ways for traditional retailers to respond to showrooming?

3. Describe the ways in which online retailer Amazon.com has acted strategically to maintain its position as a leading e-commerce site. What does this suggest about what it takes to be successful in e-commerce today?

4. How is Amazon's investment in the Kindle and e-books consistent with other trends in consumer behavior today?

5. Why is mobile technology potentially important to the banking industry? What consumer needs does it fulfill?

6. Identify and describe five key challenges faced by online retailers in the market today.

7. Why is the online B2B market so much larger than the online B2C market?

8. Explain the fundamental difference between buy-side and sell-side exchanges in the online B2B market.

9. What is the difference between direct procurement and indirect procurement? Why do you think this distinction is important?

10. What are the two primary goals of companies who engage in e-procurement and what strategies do they use to achieve those goals?

11. Discuss the benefits of a B2B exchange to sellers and buyers.

12. Discuss the various ways to pay online in B2C.

13. Why do you think that company employees engage in maverick buying? What can companies do to limit maverick buying?

14. Explain how mobile computing technology is being used by brick-and-mortar retailers to enhance the in-store shopping experience.

15. QR codes are very popular in Japan and other parts of Asia. Manufacturers place QR codes on product packages and advertisements, making it easy for consumers to access information about the products using a mobile device. Why do you think QR codes are not popular with U.S. consumers? Do you think QR codes will eventually become accepted by U.S. consumers? Why or Why not?

16. How are people using mobile devices to conduct banking and other financial services?

17. Evaluate the various mobile electronic payment processes described in this chapter. Which do you think are likely to emerge as the dominant method for mobile payment? Explain your answer.

18. What are some of the risks faced by consumers who use mobile devices for banking and other financial transactions?

19. What are the key benefits of using a mobile wallet? Do you think new improvements to this mobile application will make it more attractive to end-users?

20. How has mobile computing changed the retail shopping behavior of consumers?

21. Describe the mobile entertainment market and the ways people can use their mobile devices to have fun.

22. Why is mobile social networking expected to grow dramatically in the next few years?

23. How is mobile computing creating an attractive opportunity for advertisers? Will consumers be receptive to this type of communication? Why or why not?

24. List some location-based services and explain their value to both businesses and mobile device users.

EXPLORE: Online and Interactive Exercises

1. Assume you are interested in buying a car. You can find information about financing and insurance for cars at autos.msn.com or autobytel.com. Decide what car you want to buy. Configure your car by going to the car manufacturer's website. Finally, try to find the car at autobytel.com. What information is most supportive of your decision-making process? Was the experience pleasant or frustrating?

2. Visit amazon.com and identify at least three specific elements of its personalization and customization features. Browse specific books on one particular subject, leave the site, and then go back and revisit the site. What do you observe? Are these features likely to encourage you to purchase more books in the future from Amazon.com? How does the "One-Click" feature encourage sales from mobile devices?

3. Read Google's new privacy policy at www.google.com/policies/privacy. What types of information does Google collect about people who use its services? How can people either restrict or avoid having Google collect information about them? How does Google say it uses the information it collects about people who utilize its services?

4. Conduct a study on selling diamonds and gems online. Each group member investigates one company such as bluenile.com, diamond.com, thaigem.com, tiffany.com, or jewelryexchange.com.

   a. What features are used in these sites to educate buyers about gemstones?

   b. How do the sites attract buyers?

   c. How do the sites increase trust in online purchasing?

   d. What customer service features are provided?

   e. Would you buy a $5,000 diamond ring online? Why or why not?

5. If you have a smartphone, download the shopping app Shopkick.com. Use the app for a few weeks and then prepare a report or presentation about your experience. Describe how Shopkick uses behavioral reinforcement to encourage specific kinds of shopping behaviors (e.g., store visits, looking for promotional products, participating in marketing surveys, etc.). Explain whether or not you think you will continue using this application.

ANALYZE & DECIDE: Apply IT Concepts to Business Decisions

1. Go to nacha.org. What is the National Automated Clearing House Association (NACHA)? What is its role? What is the Automated Clearing House (ACH)? Who are the key participants in an ACH e-payment? Describe the "pilot" projects currently under way at ACH.

2. Visit IBM's "Many Eyes" website at www.ibm.com/manyeyes. Select visualizations from the left-side menu bar. Generate two visualizations. How does visualization improve understanding of the datasets?

3. Have each team study a major bank with extensive e-commerce offerings. For example, Wells Fargo Bank is well on its way to being a cyberbank. Hundreds of brick-and-mortar branch offices are being closed. In the spring of 2003, the bank served more than 1.2 million cyberaccounts (see wellsfargo.com). Other banks to consider are Citicorp, Netbank, and HSBC (Hong Kong). Each team should attempt to convince the class that its e-bank activities are the best.

4. As an independent IT contract worker, you must often arrange travel to and from your clients' places of business. You do not typically have time to always explore every travel website when planning travel, so you wish to identify the one that over time will work the best for you. Working in a small group of three to four people, use the Internet to explore the following travel sites: orbitz.com, travelocity.com, kayak.com, concierge.com, and expedia.com (search "online travel sites" for additional options). Select a handful of travel destinations and see how helpful each site is in terms of:

a. Finding the lowest airfare.

b. Identifying hotels for business travel.

c. Recommendations for dining and other location-based services.

d. Evaluate the site for its ability to aid in international travel arrangements.

e. Availability and usefulness of travel tips, advisories, and other helpful information.

Prepare a report comparing how each site performed in terms of its ease of use, helpfulness, and best overall deal. Which site would you recommend?

5. Using Youtube.com or any other video-sharing site, watch examples of augmented reality handhelds and promotional campaigns. Write a brief report describing your reaction to this new technology and predict if it will become more commonplace in the future.

CASE 8.2

Business Case: Chegg's Mobile Strategy

Mobile technologies are considered a **disruptive innovation** because they have the capability of transforming traditional business practices by creating new value networks, spawning new markets, and eventually displacing earlier technologies. Popular examples of disruptive innovation include Apple's iTunes service that replaced music CDs with downloadable digital mp3 files. Netflix and other movie-streaming services disrupted the previous model of distributing movies on DVDs through brick-and-mortar retail outlets. Several companies are now exploring the use of mobile technologies as a disruptive innovation in the college textbook market.

End-users (college students) have traditionally had very little power in the college textbook market. Textbook publishers promoted their products to college professors who decided what books to require for their courses. Competition at the retail level was for the most part nonexistent—students almost always had to purchase textbooks from a college bookstore or a used textbook from another student.

All that began to change, however, with the emergence of e-commerce. Nowadays, students have a range of options for purchasing new and used textbooks, renting textbooks, reading books online, or purchasing textbooks in an e-book format. Publishers and booksellers who once held fairly secure positions in the distribution channel now face competition from a variety of nonconventional sources, including online retailers (e.g., Amazon), C2C e-commerce sites (e.g., Craigslist, eBay, half.com), and publishers who sell directly to students (e.g., Flatworld Knowledge).

Chegg.com

As part of this industry restructuring, Chegg.com began renting textbooks to students in 2007, creating an alternative to purchasing from college bookstores and online booksellers like Amazon.com. While renting textbooks was an innovative approach at the time, Chegg managers realized that to remain competitive, they needed to position their company in a way that was not focused on a particular product form (e.g., printed textbook) or distribution method (e.g., retail bookstore). Instead, Chegg set out to create a learning network for students, offering a range of products and services through various channels that enhance students' educational experience. See Table 8.4.

Mobile technology has been a key component of Chegg's value strategy from the beginning. In 2009, just two years after entering the rental market, Chegg created a mobile website and an SMS-based service that made it possible for students to check rental prices for textbooks by texting the ISBN number of the book they were interested in. The following year, Chegg launched an app for iPhone and iPad users. Android users can still access services from the company's well-designed mobile site. In 2012 Chegg launched a cloud-based e-textbook reader designed to give students access to their textbooks from a wide range of mobile devices. While Chegg is not the first company to make textbooks available online, the e-textbook reader provides powerful features for highlighting text, taking notes, and checking word definitions. Users can view *Key Highlights*, or material crowdsourced from the highlighting activities of other students using the reader. Finally, readers can access Chegg's *Always on Q&A Service*, where students ask questions about various academic subjects and often receive an answer back from subject matter experts within hours.

Despite Chegg's innovative and customer-oriented strategy, it faces an increasingly competitive marketplace.

TABLE 8.4	The Chegg Learning Network

Purchase New/Used Textbooks
Online, mobile app, or mobile website

Renting Textbooks
Online, mobile app, mobile website, and bookstores and rental stands at select colleges

Homework Help Q&A
Online and mobile website

e-Textbooks
Cloud-based mobile textbook reader

Course Reviews, Grade Distributions, and Schedule Planning Tools
Online and mobile website

Source: Chegg.com (2012).

Well-funded competitors such as Amazon.com and Barnes & Noble now offer textbook rentals and e-textbooks with some of the same features as Chegg's reader. CourseSmart is another online vendor offering digital content from major publishers such as Pearson, Cengage, McGraw Hill, and John Wiley & Sons (the publisher of this textbook). CourseSmart provides a number of mobile apps for various devices as well as the capability to read texts through mobile browsers (no app download necessary). Finally, Apple has announced its desire to transform the textbook market in much the same way it changed the music business. However, the existing list of companies that are already practicing disruptive innovation may make it more difficult for Apple to have quite the same impact as it did in the music business.

Questions

1. Evaluate the mobile features of Chegg's textbook program. Does it offer services that are truly helpful to college students or are they just a gimmick?

2. Go to Chegg.com to view a demo of its e-textbook reader. After reviewing the service, evaluate whether the reader will motivate students to obtain their textbooks from Chegg instead of using alternative textbook suppliers.

3. How does Chegg's mobile price comparison service provide a benefit to college students? Do you think it helps to increase rentals and purchases from Chegg?

4. What other ways could Chegg use mobile technologies to provide further value to college students?

5. Using a mobile device, check the purchase and/or rental prices of the textbooks you are using this semester. Compare these with prices from alternative vendors (e.g., your college bookstore, Amazon.com, half.com, etc.). Prepare a table comparing your overall cost from each supplier. Based on your findings, do you plan to change the way you obtain textbooks in the future?

Sources: Chegg.com (2010), Conneally (2012), Wired Academic (2012), Crook (2009), Eldon (2012).

CASE 8.3

Video Case: Searching with Pictures Using MVS

Earlier in the chapter, you read that U.S. consumers were not responding to QR code marketing with the same enthusiasm as Asian consumers. In response, some companies are experimenting with an alternative to QR codes called **mobile visual search (MVS)** technology. MVS is an image recognition technology that proponents claim will be more attractive to consumers.

With an MVS app, users scan the pictures they find on product labels, catalogs, or advertisements. This initiates a search function that returns information to the user. Depending on the MVS app used, the search information might be general in nature, similar to what you get when conducting a search on Google. Or, the app may return specific information, for instance, a page where the user can order the product.

© Gregory R. Wood

Figure 8.14 Mobile visual search using Google's Goggle app.

This technology has spawned a new industry of mobile visual search services that include companies like Snaptell (now owned by Amazon), PixlinQ (LTU Mobile), BuzzAR, Mobile Acuity, and, of course, Google (see Figure 8.14).

Find and watch videos of three different MVS applications on YouTube or other video-sharing sites:

MVS Application/ Developer	Videos at YouTube.com
Goggles/Google	Search for "Google Goggles Experiment Video"
PixlinQ/LTU Mobile	Search for "Shopgate—Mobile Shopping"
Buzzar	Search for "buzzAR-mobile visual search platform"

Get the latest news and information about MVS by searching on the phrase "mobile visual search" using Google or some other search engine. Compare and contrast MVS with marketing strategies using QR codes.

Questions

1. If consumers begin to use MVS on a wide-scale basis, how should businesses adjust their marketing practices to take advantage of this technology?
2. Based on the videos and additional research, how do the MVS services differ from one another?

References

Ally Financial. "Company Overview – CEO Letter." *media. ally.com*, May, 2014.

Asante, J. "Mobile Gaming Powers Up: '99 Cents Is the New Quarter.'" *NPR.org*, April 3, 2012.

Bercovici, J. "Amazon vs. Book Publishers, by the Numbers." *Forbes.com*, February 20, 2014.

Berginsight.com. "Berg Insight Predicts 894 Million Mobile Banking Users by 2015." April 2010.

Capgemini, the Royal Bank of Scotland plc (RBS), and Efma. "World Payments Report." *capgemini.com*, 2011.

Chegg.com. "Chegg.com Introduces Two New Ways for College Students to Easily Rent Their Textbooks." *PRNewswire*, August 11, 2010.

comScore, Inc. "Mobile Future in Focus." *comscore.com*, February 2012.

Conneally, T. "Everything You Need to Know about e-Textbooks before Apple Gets Involved." *Betanews.com*, January 17, 2012.

Crook, J. "Chegg Adds Mobile Components to Textbook Rental Service." *Mobile Marketer*, August 31, 2009.

Dotson, C. "How Mobile Games Leapt from Cult to Cultural Phenomenon." *Mashable.com*, January 20, 2012.

Eldon, E. "Chegg Launches Mobile Reader for Online Textbooks." *Techcrunch.com*, January 18, 2012.

Edelman. "2013 Edelman Trust Barometer Reports Financial Services Is Least Trusted Industry Globally." *Edelman.com*, April 9, 2013.

eMarketer. "Half of Mobile Users to Play Games in 2013." *eMarketer.com*, May 30, 2013

Galgey, W. & S. Pattinson. "The Future Shopper: How Changing Shopper Attitudes and Technology Are Reshaping Retail." White paper, the Futures Company/Kanter Retail, 2013.

Gallup, Inc. "Confidence in Institutions 1973–2014", *Gallup.com*, Sept. 18, 2014.

Global Industry Analysts. "Global Mobile Banking Customer Base to Reach 1.1 Billion by 2015." February 2010.

Gonsalves, A. "Amazon Kindle 2.5 Adds Social Networking." *InformationWeek*, May 3, 2010.

Google, IPSOS OTX MediaCT. "The Mobile Movement: Understanding Smartphone Users." April 2011.

Howard, N. "Is It Safe to Bank by Cell Phone?" *MSN Money*, July 2009.

Johnson, L. "Macy's, Aflac Partner for Holiday Donation Campaign." *Mobile Commerce Daily*, November 29, 2011.

Kats, R. "Macy's Mobile Spend Up 70pc: FirstLook Keynote." *Mobile Marketer*, January 20, 2012.

Leslie, S., R. Chawla, & J. Aaker. "Deals @Delloutlet: How Dell Clears Inventory Through Twitter." Stanford Graduate School of Business, Case M-334, May 10, 2010.

Macy's. "Macy's Backstage Pass." Press release, February 2011.

Malone, C. "The Loyalty Storm Brewing for Banks, Wireless and Cable Companies." *Business2community.com*, September 15, 2014.

McGee, B. "Mobile Banking Security—Phishing for Answers?" *Netbanker.com*, January 2008.

Miller, C. & J. Bosman. "E-Books Outsell Print Books at Amazon." *New York Times*, May 19, 2011.

MobiAdNews.com. "IKEA Uses Mobile Augmented Reality to Engage Shoppers' Imagination." August 2009.

Mobile Marketing Association. "Mobile Banking Overview (NA)." January 2009.

Moore, G. "Foursquare Leads New Mobile Advertising Model." *Masshightech.com*, April 2010.

National Retail Federation. "Mobile Retailing Blueprint: A Comprehensive Guide for Navigating the Mobile Landscape." January 4, 2011.

Nielsen. "Play Before Work: Games Most Popular Mobile App Category in US." *NielsenWire*, July 7, 2011.

O'Connell, B. "Consumer Frustration Threatens Billions in Revenue at 10 Banks This Year." *TheStreet.com*, July 23, 2013.

Porter, M. "The Five Competitive Forces That Shape Strategy." *Harvard Business Review*, 86, no. 1 January 2008, pp. 86–104.

Rappa, M. "Case Study: Amazon.com." *DigitalEnterprise.com*, 2010.

Smith, C. "Trio of Online Banks Dominate Social Media Channels." *Thefinancialbrand.com*, April 28, 2014.

Tejwani, A. "One Bank that Got Social Media right – Ally Bank (Case Study)." *Sociallycharged.com*, Sept. 17, 2012.

The Financial Brand. "Majority of Americans Still Hold a Grudge Against Banks." *thefinancialbrand.com*, April 8, 2013.

Tsirulnik G. "Macy's Is 2011 Mobile Marketer of the Year." *Mobile Marketer*, December 9, 2011.

Whitfield, T. "Augmented Reality for Mobile Advertising." *Econsultancy.com*, February 2010.

Wired Academic. "Chegg Trots Out Its HTML5 E-Textbook Reader, Challenging Inkling, Cengage, Kno, et al." January 28, 2012.

Yurcan, B. "Ally, USAA Top Bank Social Media Study." *Banktech.com*, March 15, 2012.

Yurcan, B. "Ally Bank's Mobile Strategy." *Banktech.com*, April 18, 2014.

Zimmerman, A. "Showdown Over 'Showrooming': Target Asks Vendors for Help Keeping Comparison Shoppers." *Wall Street Journal*, January, 23, 2012.

Chapter 9

Effective and Efficient Business Functions

Chapter Snapshot

Case 9.1 Opening Case: Ducati Redesigns Its Operations

9.1 Solving Business Challenges at All Management Levels

9.2 Manufacturing, Production, and Transportation Management Systems

9.3 Sales and Marketing Systems

9.4 Accounting, Finance, and Regulatory Systems

9.5 Human Resource Systems, Compliance, and Ethics

Key Terms

Assuring Your Learning

- **Discuss:** Critical Thinking Questions
- **Explore:** Online and Interactive Exercises
- **Analyze & Decide:** Apply IT Concepts to Business Decisions

Case 9.2 Business Case: HSBC Combats Fraud in Split-Second Decisions

Case 9.3 Video Case: United Rentals Optimizes Its Workforce with Human Capital Management

References

Learning Outcomes

1. Describe various types of functional systems and how they support managers and workers at the operational level.

2. Define how manufacturing, production, and transportation information systems enable organizational processes and support supply chain operations and logistics.

3. Explain how sales and marketing information systems support advertising, market research, intelligence gathering, getting products and services to customers, and responding quickly and efficiently to customers' needs.

4. Describe how accounting, auditing, and finance application systems meet compliance mandates, help deter fraud, and facilitate capital budgeting and forecasting.

5. Analyze how human resources information systems (HRIS) improve business-to-employee (B2E) communications, workforce productivity, and compliance with federal employment laws; and discuss ethical issues related to the use of HRIS data.

Chapter Snapshot

Every business is managed through multiple business functions, each responsible for managing certain aspects of the business. Consider an electronics company. The finance function is responsible for acquiring capital needed for research and development (R&D) and other investment processes. The marketing function is responsible for product promotion and pricing, identifying target customers, and improving the customer experience (CX). The operations function plans and coordinates all the resources needed to design, manufacture, and

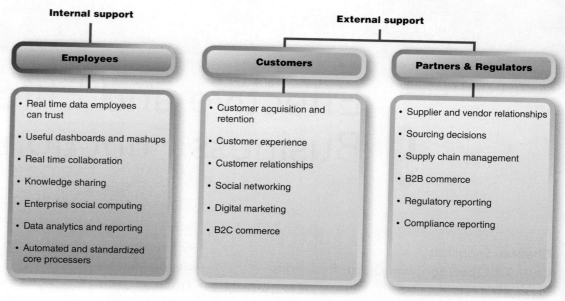

Internal support

Employees

- Real time data employees can trust
- Useful dashboards and mashups
- Real time collaboration
- Knowledge sharing
- Enterprise social computing
- Data analytics and reporting
- Automated and standardized core processers

External support

Customers

- Customer acquisition and retention
- Customer experience
- Customer relationships
- Social networking
- Digital marketing
- B2C commerce

Partners & Regulators

- Supplier and vendor relationships
- Sourcing decisions
- Supply chain management
- B2B commerce
- Regulatory reporting
- Compliance reporting

Figure 9.1 Comparison of the IT capabilities that enterprises provide to employees, consumers, business partners, and regulators.

transport products. The IT function is responsible for the technology infrastructure, data management, and social, mobile, and cloud services. Accounting manages assets and meet compliance mandates. Human resource (HR) recruits, trains, and develops a talented workforce. These business functions involve complex processes that depend on access to data, collaboration, communication, and data analysis to pinpoint what must be done—and employees' workflows to make that happen.

While most attention is on external interests—customers, competitors, and partners—they are only part of the solution. Business success also depends on internal factors—the efficiency and effectiveness of managers, employees, core business processes and functions. A wide

range of specialized technology, such as Salesforce.com and eXtensible Business Reporting Language (XBRL) for financial reporting, supports problem solving, decision making, and compliance (Figure 9.1).

Business is messy, sometimes chaotic. Resolving those situations requires human creativity, critical thinking, and judgment—all of which relate back to corporate culture, training, and empowerment of employees. These topics are covered in Chapter 9.

Ultimately, data from functional systems are used by enterprise applications, including business intelligence (BI), e-commerce, customer relationship management (CRM), and supply chain management (SCM), as shown in Figure 9.2.

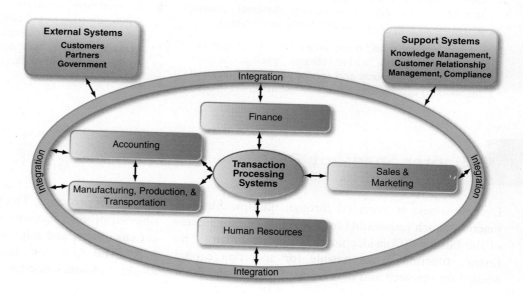

Figure 9.2 Data from functional area ISs support enterprise apps.

CASE 9.1 OPENING CASE

Ducati Redesigns Its Operations

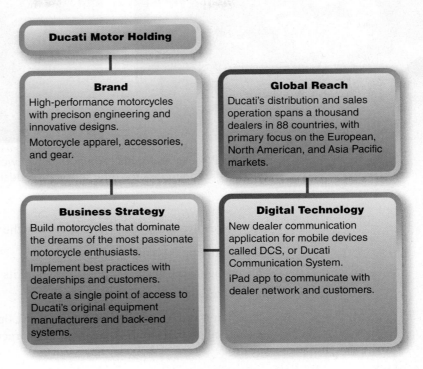

Figure 9.3 Ducati Motor Holding overview.

Ducati Motor Holding

Brand
High-performance motorcycles with precison engineering and innovative designs.
Motorcycle apparel, accessories, and gear.

Global Reach
Ducati's distribution and sales operation spans a thousand dealers in 88 countries, with primary focus on the European, North American, and Asia Pacific markets.

Business Strategy
Build motorcycles that dominate the dreams of the most passionate motorcycle enthusiasts.
Implement best practices with dealerships and customers.
Create a single point of access to Ducati's original equipment manufacturers and back-end systems.

Digital Technology
New dealer communication application for mobile devices called DCS, or Ducati Communication System.
iPad app to communicate with dealer network and customers.

| COMPANY OVERVIEW

Ducati Motor Holding manufactures motorcycles known worldwide for their precision engineering, lightning speed, and sleek design and for customers who are passionate about their motorcycles. Six models make up the product lines, with prices starting at $15,000 to the $90,000 Superleggera Superbike, which produces up to 200 HP at the crankshaft. Ducati is owned by Audi through its Italian subsidiary Lamborghini. Its 2013 net sales were $518 million.

Awards

In March 2014 Ducati received five awards at the annual Motorrad des Jahres (Motorcycle of the Year) event in Stuttgart, Germany. Ducati's Multistrada and Diavel were awarded Motorcycle of the Year in the Allrounder and Cruiser categories, respectively (Figure 9.4). Ducati's models are benchmarks in innovative design and technology.

Product Lines

In addition to six motorcycle brands, the company sells parts, apparel, accessories, and other items to create the Ducati experience. Dealers need to be familiar with thousands of products and customization options for their customers.

| BUSINESS CHALLENGES

Companies worldwide were faced with tougher competition and economic conditions after the financial meltdown in 2008. And as global manufacturers, geography was a marketing challenge.

Internally, its sales staff struggled with conflicting or outdated data on product inventory, availability, and ordering time schedules. The source of the problem was multiple communication systems and data silos that were not coordinated.

Figure 9.4 Ducati Multistrada and Diavel were awarded Motorcycle of the Year in 2014 in their class for their innovative design and technology.

To resolve these challenges and grow the business, Ducati focused on:

1. improving the sales process
2. engaging the customer in the design of its motorcycles, and
3. decreasing the cost of operations

The plan was to redesign dealer operations, business processes, and communication tools to align them with leading industry practices.

TABLE 9.1	Opening Case Overview
Company	Ducatiusa.com and Ducati.com Founded in 1926. Has 911 employees. Ducati's main factory site and headquarters are located in Bologna, Italy, with an additional assembly factory in Thailand.
Industry	Racing-inspired motorcycles characterized by "Desmodromic" performance engines, and innovative design and technology.
Product lines	Six models: Diavel, Hypermotard, Monster, Multistrada, Streetfighter, and Superbike.
Digital technology	New dealer communication application for mobile devices called DCS, or Ducati Communication System. The interface lets dealers easily find, send, and receive all the information they need to place orders and track them through production and delivery. The high-performance global communication system serves more than 5,500 users worldwide in seven languages.
Business challenges	Because of competition and tough economic conditions worldwide, motorcycle dealerships had to offer customers better value and after-sales services.

Partnership with Accenture and Apple

Ducati selected Accenture to help redesign operations and processes; and to roll out a new integrated communication application for its dealers worldwide. Ducati equipped its sales network with iPads and developed a custom in-house app called DCS, or Ducati Communication System. The DCS app gives dealers a single point of access to Ducati's back-end systems. The DCS is an SAP-based interface used by dealers to easily find, send, and receive data necessary to place orders through a point-of-sale (POS) device; and then to track orders through the production and delivery processes.

Authorized dealers receive updates directly through the Apple App Store. They also have access to a configurator app on their iPads to configure a customer's dream motorcycle. An e-mail detailing the customized motorcycle and accessories is then sent to the customer. Dealers communicate in real time with colleagues and complete the sale without delay.

Intuitive User Experience

The familiar user experience was designed to be the same for desktop computers, iPads, and iPhones.

Cristiano Silei, vice president of Global Sales at Ducati, said: "It was clear from the start that iPad was the right device. It's the simplicity, the immediate usability. Everyone understands how it works in just a few minutes."

Visiting a dealership is a very emotional experience for customers. Dealers want to make the experience unforgettable. According to Silei, the iPad helps gives the future Ducati owner a richer experience.

In addition to providing real time sales support, the DCS app on iPad acts as a training interface to keep dealers updated on Ducati's evolving product line. A change management program helped dealers transition smoothly from the old solution to DCS. DCS was quickly embraced by Ducati dealers, whose positive feedback included comments like "It's a game changer" and "a great time saver."

PERFORMANCE IMPROVEMENTS

Ducati's high-performance global DCS was deployed to 88 countries across four continents. DCS serves more than 5,500 users worldwide in seven languages. By leveraging dealer communication, Ducati is able to capture and consolidate local and global sales activity, spare parts, warranty, and service activity. As a result:

- Ducati is able to capture and consolidate local and global sales activity, spare parts, warranty, and service activity, improving the company's ability to respond daily to changing consumer demand.
- Dealers run all parts of their business and have a robust tool to execute their operational, growth, and customer objectives.
- Dealers respond more quickly to customer demands and market conditions, making each dealership easier for customers to do business with.
- Dealers are equipped with leading practices for their processes to help them better serve customers in a simple, streamlined fashion.

The dealer system is one of the most innovative and effective user experiences in the industry. It is user-friendly and sleek, and reinforces Ducati's brand.

Sources: Compiled from Ducati websites (2014), LexisNexis company profiles (2014), Apple.com (2014), Accenture.com (2014).

Questions

1. What pressured or motivated Ducati to implement new digital technology?
2. What costs could Ducati cut? What costs could it not cut? For example, could Ducati cut its research and development (R&D) budget? Explain your answers.
3. Why did Ducati need to improve communications with dealers?
4. Explain the capabilities and benefits of the DCS.
5. Why was it important to implement a change management program?
6. What other factors contributed to the success of DCS? Explain their contributions.
7. Visit the Apple iPad store at apple.com/ipad and search for "ducati." Review the Ducati Communication System app. Explain how the DCS app gives the future Ducati owner a richer experience.

9.1 Solving Business Challenges at All Management Levels

The three major organizational levels are modeled as a pyramid in Figure 9.5. Starting at the base of the pyramid the levels are operational, managerial or administrative, and strategic. The timeframe transitions from in the moment to long term, and the perspective changes from daily to a few years.

The organizational levels correspond to the three major types of managers: operational, tactical, and strategic managers. To be fully effective, operational, tactical, and strategic goals and plans must be aligned. That is, they must be consistent, mutually supportive, and focused on achieving the enterprise's **mission**.

Mission is a set of outcomes an enterprise wants to achieve.

MANAGEMENT LEVELS

Strategic plan is a document used to communicate the company's goals and the actions needed to achieve them.

Strategic planning is a top management activity that sets priorities, focuses energy and human and technology resources, strengthens operations, and ensures that employees and business partners work toward common goals. **Strategic plans** are

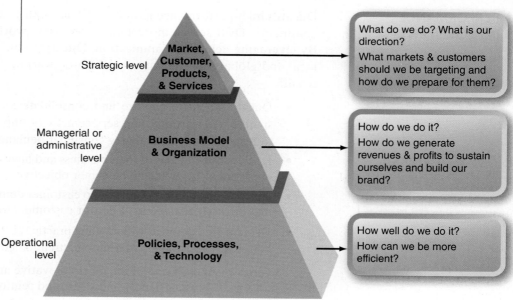

Figure 9.5 Three organizational levels, their concerns, and strategic and tactical questions, planning, and control.

visionary and future-oriented. Data from external sources—the economy, markets, competitors, and business trends—are essential to their SWOT (strengths, weaknesses, opportunities, and threats) analysis, planning, and decisions. As the environment changes, strategic plans are reexamined and adjusted.

At the **tactical level**, middle-level managers design business processes, procedures, and policies to implement strategic plans.

Operational-level managers and supervisors work most closely with the workforce and customers and play a more interpersonal role than any of the other levels of management. They depend on detailed data in real time or near real time to do their jobs, get work done, and close the deal. They need to track inventory levels, sales activity, marketing campaigns, production; meet or expedite delivery schedules; and resolve disruptions. The Ducati dealers and their DCS and iPad apps are examples of the work and data requirements. Decision making is mostly immediate or short-term because decisions are made to close the deal or control ongoing activities and operations. Feedback and control are vital to identify deviations from goals as soon as possible in order to take corrective action. Data captured or created within the company are most important at this level.

BUSINESS FUNCTIONS VS. CROSS-FUNCTIONAL BUSINESS PROCESSES

Originally, information systems were designed to support the accounting function. Systems for other functions were rolled out later. The consequences of this fragmented roll-out approach were data silos that supported various business functions, but that could not support cross-functional business processes. For example, taking customers' orders for contact lenses is a relatively easy process, but the **order fulfillment process** to move products from those orders to the customers includes checking credit and collecting payment, picking shipping departments to pack the product, printing the mailing label, preparing for shipping, and notifying customers that their orders are on the way. Work flows and data flows between departments that are not coordinated result in delays, errors, poor customer service, and higher costs.

Departments or functions interact by passing data from one to the other. In the process, files are generated to record the details of such activity.

Standard operating procedures (SOPs) are a set of written instructions on how to perform a function or activity. SOPs provide the framework for complex processes to be managed more effectively.

Data requirements of the operational-level units are extensive and relatively routine because they have fixed sources of input and tasks follow **standard operating procedures (SOPs)**. SOPs are easily automated or supported by functional area information systems.

SOPs are an integral part of a quality control system because they provide individuals with information to perform jobs properly. A key benefit of SOPs is that they minimize variation and promote quality through consistent implementation of a process or procedure within the organization, even if there are temporary or permanent personnel changes. SOPs are written, for example, for handling purchase orders, order fulfillment, customer complaints, recruitment and hiring, emergency response, and disaster recovery. Data that are lost or compromised have financial implications. As such, it is critical that businesses have SOPs to ensure that data are secure and accurate, and that their integrity is maintained. Tech Note 9.1 gives an outline of SOPs to secure transaction data.

TECH NOTE 9.1 Standard Operating Procedures

Data security: Data must be protected from malicious or unintentional corruption, unauthorized modification, theft, or natural causes such as floods.

Data accuracy: Data validation is used to detect and correct data entry errors, such as address data and customer names.

Data integrity: Data integrity with real time systems involves the ACID test, which is short for atomicity, consistency, isolation, and durability:

- *Atomicity:* If all steps in a transaction are not completed, then the entire transaction is canceled.

- *Consistency:* Only operations that meet data validity standards are allowed. For instance, systems that record checking accounts only allow unique check numbers for each transaction. Any operation that repeated a check number would fail to ensure that the data in the database are correct and accurate. Network failures can also cause data consistency problems.

- *Isolation:* Transactions must be isolated from each other. For example, bank deposits must be isolated from a concurrent transaction involving a withdrawal from the same account. Only when the withdrawal transaction is successfully completed will the new account balance be reported.

- *Durability:* Backups by themselves do not provide durability. A system crash or other failure must not cause any loss of data in the database. Durability is achieved through separate transaction logs that can be used to re-create all transactions from a known checkpoint. Other ways include database mirrors that replicate the database on another server.

BASIC FUNCTIONAL AREA SYSTEMS

The basic functional area information systems and examples of their apps are the following.

- **Manufacturing and production:** materials purchasing, quality control, scheduling, shipping, receiving. For example, to produce small appliances, a manufacturer needs to order materials and parts, pay for labor and electricity, create shipment orders, and bill customers.

- **Accounting:** accounts receivable, accounts payable, general ledger, budgeting. Accounting systems keep account balances up to date, disburse funds, and post statements.

- **Finance:** cash management, asset management, credit management, financial statement reporting to comply with federal and industry-specific regulations and government agencies.

- **IT:** cloud computing services, service-level agreement (SLA) management, software license management, user accounts management, information and network security.

- **Sales and marketing:** pricing, social media promotions, market research, demand forecasts, sales campaign management, order tracking, and online and mobile order processing and sales (see Figure 9.6).

- **HR:** payroll, recruitment and hiring, succession planning, employee benefits, training, compensation, performance appraisal, compliance with federal and state employment regulations.

In **online transaction processing (OLTP)**, events or transactions are processed as soon as they occur. Data are accessed directly from the database, and reports can be generated automatically (Figure 9.7). IT at Work 9.1 describes a real time sales and reporting system.

These functions are supported by TPSs that monitor, collect, store, process, and distribute data for all financial and nonfinancial transactions, such as hiring and managing business contracts.

Figure 9.6 A billboard in New York City's Times Square advertises the services of SquareUp, a credit card reader system for Apple and Android mobile devices.

© Richard Levine/Alamy

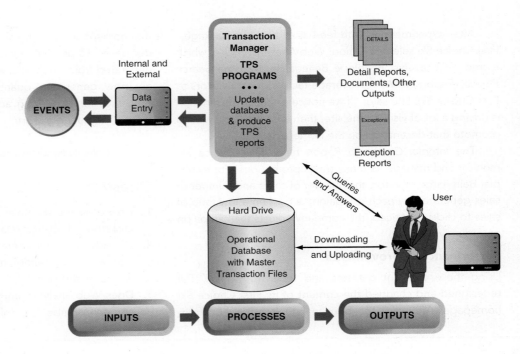

Figure 9.7 Information flows triggered by a transaction or event.

IT at Work 9.1

Tracking Customer Behavior

First Choice Ski holds a 14 percent market share of the online UK ski vacation industry. TUI Travel, its parent company, is an international leisure travel group, which operates in 180 countries and serves more than 30 million customers. In the highly competitive tour operator industry, profit margins are tight. Being lean and responsive is essential to maintaining profitability. By using Yahoo! Web Analytics and real time reporting, First Choice Ski was able to monitor and quickly respond to the behaviors of visitors on its travel website. Figure 9.8 is an example of a Web analytics interface.

First Choice Ski Tracks Customers' Behavior

At First Choice Ski, customers spend a lot of time researching and selecting their vacations. Simon Rigglesworth, e-commerce manager, explained: "We see users return multiple times from multiple sources such as paid search, e-mail and even social networking as they try to find the vacation that suits them the best. Capturing as much information as possible allows us to identify the best way to complete the sale and optimize for it."

Figure 9.8 Example of a Web analytics interface.

© NAN/Alamy

After experimenting with fee-based analytics packages, First Choice Ski selected Yahoo! Web Analytics (YWA), which is free. Web analyst Penelope Bellegarde used the *Search Phrases Report* in YWA to leverage factors driving visitors to First Choice Ski. She said: "If we notice a specific destination is driving a lot of visits to the site, then it is very likely we will promote that destination on the homepage."

The *Internal Campaign Report* helps First Choice Ski monitor and manage its many travel promotions. For example, Bellegarde monitors the number of clicks and number of sales generated by each campaign, and when a low ratio of sales to clicks is noticed, the company adjusts the campaign accordingly.

Performance Improvements

Using these different datasets and tools from YWA, TUI redesigned and changed the content of its First Choice Ski homepage. Afterward the bounce rate (transfer out) from the homepage decreased 18 percent, and the exit rate decreased 13 percent. Most important, the number of sales generated from the homepage increased 266 percent. "We are now generating quantifiable, actionable, data-driven processes for prioritizing and reviewing web site developments," says Rigglesworth.

Sources: Compiled from firstchoice-ski.co.uk and Yahoo.com.

Questions

1. How does the ski travel site's quick response to visitors' clickstream behavior relate to its profit margin?
2. Consider this measurement principle: You cannot manage what you cannot measure. Explain how the case illustrates this principle.
3. Does Web analytics impact barriers to entry and rivalry among incumbents in this industry?

Questions

1. Explain the core concerns and time horizons of each level of management.
2. Define what a standard operating procedure (SOP) is and give an example.
3. Explain each component of the ACID test.
4. Explain the differences between batch and online processing.
5. Describe the flow of information in transaction processing.

9.2 Manufacturing, Production, and Transportation Management Systems

Day-to-day operations are connected by data and processes that they share. Decisions made in sales departments, for example, cause ripple effects in other functional departments—accounting, finance, IT, manufacturing/production, and HR.

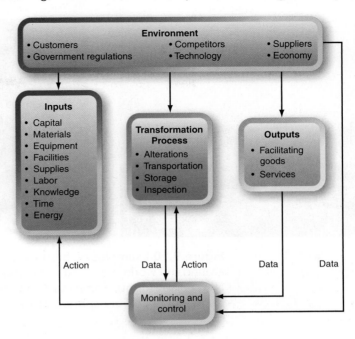

Figure 9.9 Production operations management (POM) systems process and transform inputs into outputs.

Likewise, financial decisions, such as stricter credit requirements, impact sales and production. Ideally, functional systems enable:

- **Transparency:** being able to access current data to learn what is needed in order to make informed decisions without delay.
- **Quick response:** being able to respond appropriately to changes in conditions, demand, or new opportunities.

MANUFACTURING AND PRODUCTION SYSTEMS

The **production and operations management (POM)** function is responsible for processes that transform inputs into value-added outputs, as shown in Figure 9.9. These inputs include human resources, such as workers, staff, and managers; facilities and processes, such as buildings and equipment; they also include materials, IT, and information. Outputs are the goods and services a company produces.

POM is responsible for decisions and activities, including product design and delivery problems. The design and management of operations strongly influence material costs, inventory availability, and quality control. For these reasons, POM is a function management resorts to in order to improve performance and the bottom line.

TRANSPORTATION MANAGEMENT SYSTEMS

Transportation management systems (TMSs) are relied on to handle transportation planning, which includes shipping consolidation, load and trip planning, route planning, fleet and driver planning, and carrier selection. TMSs also support vehicle management and accounting transactions.

Four trend factors contributing to the growth of TMS include:

1. **Outdated transportation systems need to be upgraded or replaced.** Many systems were installed over 10 years ago—before tablet computers and mobile technologies had become widespread in business. Similar to most legacy (old) systems, they are inflexible, difficult to integrate with other newer systems, and expensive to maintain.

2. **Growth of intermodal transport.** Intermodal transportation refers to the use of two or more transport modes, such as container ship, air, truck, and rail, to move products from source to destination. See Figure 9.10 for examples. Many more companies are shipping via intermodals and their older TMSs cannot support or deal with intermodal movement, according to Dwight Klappich, a research vice president for Gartner.

Figure 9.10 Examples of intermodal transportation ports. Container ships from around the world are unloaded in the Brooklyn, New York (left), and Bayonne, New Jersey (right), shipyards. Containers are tracked as they are loaded onto trucks or rail and transported across the country.

When brick-and-mortar manufacturers began selling online, for example, they learned that their existing TMSs were inadequate for handling the new line of business. Shippers that expand globally face similar challenges when they try to manage multiple rail, truck, and ocean shipments. Thus, there is a growing need for more robust TMSs to handle multidimensional shipping arrangements.

3. **TMS vendors add capabilities.** The basic functions performed by a TMS include gathering data on a load to be transported and matching those data to a historical routing guide. Then the TMS is used to manage the communication process with the various carriers. New feature-rich TMSs are able to access information services to help the shipper identify optimal routes given all current conditions. For example, the latest TMSs can interact directly with market-data benchmarking services. An automated, real time market monitoring function saves shippers time and errors, and cuts costs significantly.

4. **TMSs handle big data.** Transportation tends to generate a high volume of transactional data. Managing the data is not easy. TMS vendors are developing systems that make valuable use of the big data that are collected and stored. By drilling down into specific regions or focusing on particular market trends, for example, shippers can use their big data to make better decisions.

IT at Work 9.2 describes a cloud-based software-as-a-service (SaaS) TMS.

IT at Work 9.2

Total Visibility, a SaaS Transportation System

Agistix introduced Total Visibility, a new cloud-based SaaS transportation management system (TMS). Using the cloud, shippers have access from any location at any time. The leased nature of the SaaS makes it affordable to more shippers.

Total Visibility provides shippers with real time visibility to eliminate blind spots. Visibility is achieved by capturing shipment estimates, so clients can better forecast spend (costs) and meet compliance reporting requirements. Real time data allow customers to know what is happening and to analyze big data to ensure their supply chain is functioning as designed.

Total Visibility aggregates and standardizes a company's shipping activities and provides shippers with a comprehensive view into every shipment they have paid for anywhere in the world. The key benefits of Total Visibility for shippers are real time visibility to all shipments in transit across all carriers, all service levels, all modes, international and domestic, inbound and outbound.

LOGISTICS MANAGEMENT

Inbound logistics refers to receiving.

Outbound logistics refers to shipping.

Inventory control systems are stock control or inventory management systems.

Logistics management deals with the coordination of several complex processes, namely ordering, purchasing or procurement, **inbound logistics**, and **outbound logistics** activities. Logistics management systems:

- Optimize transportation operations.
- Coordinate with all suppliers.
- Integrate supply chain technologies.
- Synchronize inbound and outbound flows of materials or goods.
- Manage distribution or transport networks.

These systems enable real time monitoring and tracking of supply chain shipments, schedules, and orders. You will read about supply chain management in more detail in Chapter 10.

INVENTORY CONTROL SYSTEMS

Safety stock is extra inventory used as a buffer to reduce the risk of stockout. Also called **buffer stock**.

Stockout: inventory shortage.

Figure 9.11 Inventory holding and managing costs can significantly increase cost of goods sold (CGS).

Inventory control systems are important because they minimize the total cost of inventory while maintaining optimal inventory levels. Inventory levels are maintained by reordering the quantity needed at the right times in order to meet demand. POM departments keep **safety stock** as a hedge against **stockouts**. Safety stock is needed in case of unexpected events, such as spikes in demand or longer delivery times.

Managing inventory is important to profit margins because of numerous costs associated with inventory, in addition to the cost of the inventory. Inventory control systems minimize the following three cost categories:

1. **Inventory holding costs:** warehousing costs (see Figure 9.11), security costs, insurance, losses due to theft or obsolescence, and inventory financing costs based on the interest rate
2. **Ordering and shipping costs:** employees' time spent ordering, receiving, or processing deliveries; and shipping fees
3. **Cost of shortages:** production delays and missed sales revenues because of stockouts

To minimize the sum of these three costs, the POM department has to decide when to order and how much to order. One inventory model that is used to answer both questions is the **economic order quantity (EOQ)** model. The EOQ model takes all costs into consideration.

Just-in-Time Inventory Management Systems

Just-in-time (JIT) and lean manufacturing are two widely used methods or models to minimize waste and deal with the complexity of inventory management. Minimizing inventory costs remains a major objective of supply chain management.

JIT inventory management attempts to minimize holding costs by not taking possession of inventory until it is needed in the production process. With JIT, costs associated with carrying large inventories at any given point in time are eliminated. However, the trade-off is higher ordering costs because of more frequent orders.

© Huntstock, Inc /Alamy

Because of the higher risk of stockouts, JIT requires accurate and timely monitoring of materials' usage in production.

Everything in the JIT chain is interdependent, so coordination and good relationships with suppliers are critical for JIT to work well. Any delay can be very costly to all companies linked in the chain. Delays can be caused by labor strikes, interrupted supply lines, bad weather, market demand fluctuations, stockouts, lack of communication upstream and downstream in the supply chain, and unforeseen production interruptions. In addition inventory or material quality is critical. Poor quality causes delays, for example, fixing products or scrapping what cannot be fixed and waiting for delivery of the reorder.

JIT was developed by Toyota because of high real estate costs in Tokyo, Japan, that made warehousing expensive. It is used extensively in the auto manufacturing industry. For example, if parts and subassemblies arrive at a workstation exactly when needed, holding inventory is not required. There are no delays in production, and there are no idle production facilities or underutilized workers, provided that parts and subassemblies arrive on schedule and in usable condition. Many JIT systems need to be supported by software. JIT vendors include HP, IBM, CA, and Steven Engineering.

Despite potential cost-saving benefits, JIT is likely to fail in companies that have:

- Uncooperative supply chain partners, vendors, workers, or management.
- Custom or nonrepetitive production.

Lean Manufacturing Systems

In a **lean manufacturing system**, suppliers deliver small lots on a daily or frequent basis, and production machines are not necessarily run at full capacity. One objective of lean manufacturing is to eliminate waste of any kind; that is, to eliminate anything that does not add value to the final product. Holding inventory that is not needed very soon is seen as waste, which adds cost but not value. A second objective of lean manufacturing is to empower workers so that production decisions can be made by those who are closest to the production processes.

Oracle, Siemens, and other vendors offer demand-driven lean manufacturing systems. Like any IS, JIT needs to be justified with a cost–benefit analysis. And all JIT success factors apply to lean manufacturing. For example, JIT requires that inventory arrive on schedule and be the right quality. For companies subject to bad weather or labor strikes, lean manufacturing may not be suitable.

Quality Control Systems

Manufacturing quality control (QC) systems can be stand-alone systems or part of an enterprisewide **total quality management (TQM)** effort. QC systems provide data about the quality of incoming materials and parts, as well as the quality of in-process semifinished and finished products. These systems record the results of all inspections and compare actual results to expected results.

QC data may be collected by sensors or RFID (radio frequency identification) systems and interpreted in real time, or they can be stored in a database for future analysis. Reports on the percentage of defects or percentage of rework needed can keep managers informed of performance among departments. KIA Motors introduced an intelligent QC system to analyze customer complaints, so it could more quickly investigate and make corrections.

Other POM Technologies

Many other areas of POM are improved by information systems and tools. Production planning optimization tools, product routing and tracking systems, order management, factory layout planning and design, and other tasks can be supported by POM subsystems. For example, a Web-based system at Office Depot matches employee scheduling with store traffic patterns to increase customer satisfaction and reduce costs. Schurman Fine Papers, a manufacturer/retailer of greeting cards and specialty products, uses special warehouse management software to improve demand forecasting and inventory processes. Its two warehouses efficiently distribute products to over 30,000 retail stores.

COMPUTER-INTEGRATED MANUFACTURING AND MANUFACTURING EXECUTION SYSTEMS

Computer-integrated manufacturing (CIM) systems control day-to-day shop floor activities. In the early 1980s, companies invested greatly in CIM solutions even though they were complex, difficult to implement, and costly to maintain. They had required the integration of many products and vendors.

Prior to CIM, production managers were given many pieces of information such as time, attendance, receiving reports, inspection reports, and so on to figure out how to accomplish production tasks. The information was frequently late, rarely current or reliable, voluminous, and extremely difficult to assimilate. CIM helps production managers better use information to execute manufacturing plans.

Manufacturing execution systems (MESs) manage operations on the shop floors of factories. Some MESs schedule a few critical machines, while others manage all operations on the shop floor. Functions of MES programs include: compiling a bill of materials, resource management and scheduling, preparing and dispatching production orders, preparing work-in-progress (WIP) reports, and tracking production lots. For instance, an MES can schedule and track each step of the production phase of a particular job, and then print out the bill of materials for the operator and the production steps to complete at each phase. It repeats this process for each operator and each step until a particular job is complete.

CIM and MES are very similar concepts, but there are differences. MES typically refers to a broader infrastructure than CIM. MES is based much more on standard reusable application software, instead of custom-designed software programs on a contract-by-contract basis. MES tries to eliminate the time and information gap of early years on the shop floor by providing the plant with information in real time. Corporate business functions are given timely plant information to support business planning decisions. For the most part, the term CIM is more commonly used, and will be used in the rest of this section.

Today's CIM systems provide scheduling and real time production monitoring and reporting. CIM data-driven automation affects all systems or subsystems within the manufacturing environment: design and development, production, marketing and sales, and field support and service. CIM systems can perform production monitoring, scheduling and planning, statistical process monitoring, quality analysis, personnel monitoring, order status reporting, and production lot tracking. The manufacturer BAE has implemented CIM.

MESs are generally installed on-premises, but cloud-based solutions are becoming available. MES is a subset of enterprise resource planning (ERP) systems, which you will read about in Chapter 10.

BAE Systems uses CIM in Its Combat Aircraft Facility

BAE Systems is a global company headquartered in London, England, engaged in the development, delivery, and support of advanced defense, security, and aerospace systems. BAE is among the world's largest military contractors.

In September 2010 BAE opened a titanium-machining facility to manufacture components for the F-35 Lightning II combat aircraft. It took 10 months to complete the facility, during which time engineers at BAE considered a number of ways to ensure that it would be able to accommodate the high throughput of titanium military aircraft parts cost-effectively. According to Jon Warburton, BAE's F-35 program manager, after conducting a thorough examination of numerous potential manufacturing solutions, the BAE team finally decided to deploy a highly auto-mated CIM system (Wilson, 2011). The CIM system ensures that titanium parts for the aircraft can be manufactured on a JIT basis. To do so, it coordinates the orders received at the plant, as well as the movement of raw materials and tooling, and optimizes the use of the machine tools.

A key element of the CIM strategy was the deployment of two **flexible manu-facturing systems (FMSs)** that can accommodate the manufacture of different parts at different volumes. When an order for a part is received, the data relating to it are passed to the FMSs, which schedule the manufacture of a part in the most expedient way by examining the current workload across each of eight machine tools. Each FMS can store up to 1,000 cutting tools in a racking system ready to be loaded into the machine tools. A series of twin robot systems deliver the stored cutting tools into each machine, as well as replenishing any worn tools. The biggest challenge faced by the team in the development of the facility was to ensure that the FMS and the machine tools communicated effectively with one another and with BAE's CIM system.

Reasons Why Companies Invest in CIM

The benefits of CIM are as follows: (1) It simplifies manufacturing technologies and techniques, (2) automates as many of the manufacturing processes as pos-sible, and (3) integrates and coordinates all aspects of design, manufacturing, and related functions. CIM is comprehensive and flexible, which is especially important in the redesign or elimination of business processes. Without CIM, it may become necessary to make large investments to change existing ISs to fit new processes.

Questions

1. What is the function of POM in an organization?
2. What trends are contributing to the growing use of TMS?
3. Define logistics management.
4. What are the three categories of inventory costs?
5. What are the objectives of JIT?
6. Explain the difference between EOQ and JIT inventory models.
7. What is the goal of lean manufacturing?
8. What is CIM?

9.3 Sales and Marketing Systems

Sales and marketing information systems can expand the capacity to create new products, services, channels, and market opportunities that lead to new revenue streams. IT at Work 9.3 describes such an example. In general, sales and marketing systems support advertising, market research, intelligence gathering, getting prod-ucts and services to customers, and responding to customers' needs. Many of these systems are depicted in Figure 9.12.

Chapters 7, 8, and 10 covered or will discuss sales and marketing systems and strategies, including ecommerce and customer relationship management (CRM). This chapter, specifically this section, focuses on data-driven marketing and the capabilities of sales and marketing ISs.

Figure 9.12 Sales and marketing systems and subsystems.

IT at Work 9.3

Google Customer Surveys

Google Customer Surveys is a service publishers can use to generate revenues from their online content. The service is an alternative to having a paywall for online news content. For example, when users visit the websites of partners like the *New York Daily News* and *Texas Tribune*, they find several articles partially blocked. To continue reading the full article, they have to answer a question or microsurvey provided by Google.

Adweek

Adweek's editors, reporters, and designers spend a lot of time analyzing how digital technology transforms businesses and the people they cover. They needed to monetize their digital assets to keep the brand profitable. To that end, *Adweek* partnered with Google on a new Web-based revenue play. By answering a single marketing question per day, readers receive full access to Adweek.com and reporting, analysis, and video.

Market Research

One or two market research multiple-choice questions are asked, for instance, 'Which types of candy do you usually buy for your household?" Possible answers: none, chocolate, hard candies, gummies, toffees. Advertisers pay Google to host the surveys, and the sites receive 5 cents per response from Google. To minimize the possibility that people select untruthful answers leading to poor-quality data, Google makes the questions as engaging as possible. And if users start to just answer the first question on each page, or answer too quickly, the program notices that behavior and forces readers to answer new questions.

| DATA-DRIVEN MARKETING | Data-driven, fact-based decision making increasingly relies on data that are *hot*—impacting the business or potential customer right now, or in real time. One use of hot data is *push-through* pay-per-click (PPC) marketing, which refers to online advertising that "appears" on the screens of consumers' devices based on their location, behavior, interests, or demographic information. Unlike *pull-through* ads that appear based on the user's keyword searches, push-through ads use data about the person to determine whether the ad should appear. This capability creates opportunities for highly targeted advertising programs. For example, Facebook members self-report data about their location, age, interests, and so on. Based on these data, advertisers can request that their ad be pushed to Facebook members who fit a specific profile based on demographic, geographic, or behavioral factors.

SALES AND DISTRIBUTION CHANNELS

Marketers need to determine the optimal ways to distribute their products and services through a combination of electronic, mobile, and physical channels. For example, integrating a PPC advertising campaign with other online and offline advertising initiatives generally provides the best overall results.

Here are representative topics relating to sales and distribution channels:

- In Macy's stores and many other retailers, customers can check current sale prices on digital screens with barcode readers.
- Customers use Exxon Mobil Speedpass to fill their tanks by waving a token, embedded with an RFID device, at a gas-pump sensor. Then the RFID starts an authorization process, and the purchase is charged to the debit or credit card linked to the account.
- Home Depot and many supermarkets installed self-check-out machines. Self-service kiosks cut labor costs for retailers, and can reduce customers' check-out times, as shown in Figure 9.13.

MARKETING MANAGEMENT

The following are some representative examples of how marketing management is being accomplished.

Pricing of Products or Services

Sales volumes as well as profits are determined by the prices of products or services. Pricing is a difficult decision, particularly during economic recessions. Prices can be changed frequently, as you read in IT at Work 9.1. Flash sales engage fans or customers and trigger quick sales. Flash sales work by offering customers an incredible deal for a very short time. This sales method lends itself perfectly to the immediacy of social media.

Salesperson Productivity

The performance of salespeople is collected in the sales and marketing TPS and used to compare performance along several dimensions, such as time, product, region, and even the time of day. Actual current sales can be compared to historical data and to expectations. Multidimensional spreadsheet software facilitates this type of analysis.

© Marmaduke St. John/Alamy

Figure 9.13 Self-check-out kiosks reduce labor costs.

Sales productivity can be boosted by Web-based call centers. When a customer calls a sales rep, the rep can look at the customer's history of purchases, demographics, services available where the customer lives, and more. This information enables reps to provide better customer service.

Sales automation software is especially helpful to small businesses, enabling them to rapidly increase sales and growth. One leading software is Salesforce.com, which is a CRM application that is offered as a software as a service (SaaS). You will read about Salesforce.com in detail in the CRM section of Chapter 10.

Profitability Analysis

In deciding on advertising and other marketing efforts, managers need to know the profit contribution or profit margin (profit margin = sale price minus cost of good) of certain products and services. Profitability metrics for products and services can be derived from the cost accounting system. For example, profit performance analysis software available from IBM, Oracle, SAS, and Microstrategy is designed to help managers assess and improve the profit performance of their line of business, products, distribution channels, sales regions, and other dimensions critical to managing the enterprise. Several airlines, for example, use automated decision systems to set prices based on profitability.

Marketing activities conclude the primary activities of the value chain. Next we look at the functional systems that are *support activities,* also called *secondary activities,* in the value chain: accounting, finance, and human resources management.

Questions

1. Explain push-through marketing and pull-through marketing.
2. List two sales and distribution channels.
3. Describe profitability analysis.

9.4 Accounting, Finance, and Regulatory Systems

Income statement summarizes a company's revenue and expenses for one quarter of a fiscal year or the entire fiscal year. Also known as a P&L (profit and los) or earnings statement.

FASB develops accounting standards and principles.

Accounting and finance departments control and manage cash flows, assets, liabilities, and net income (profit). Financial accounting is a specialized branch of accounting that keeps track of a company's financial transactions and prepares financial statements, such as balance sheets and **income statements**. Investors, regulators, and others rely on the integrity and accuracy of external financial statements. Accounting must comply with generally accepted accounting principles (GAAP) and the **Financial Accounting Standards Board (FASB)**.

Corporations whose stock is publicly traded must also comply with the reporting requirements of the Securities and Exchange Commission (SEC), a regulatory agency of the U.S. government. Using standardized guidelines, the transactions are recorded, summarized, and presented in a financial report or financial statement such as an income statement or a balance sheet. However, the objective of financial accounting is not simply to report the value of a company. Rather, its purpose is to provide sufficient and accurate information for others to assess the value of a company for investment or other purposes.

FINANCIAL DISCLOSURE: REPORTING AND COMPLIANCE

As part of an organization's compliance obligations, the accounting function must attest (verify) that there are no material weaknesses in internal controls. A weakness in an internal control is a major cause of fraud, which is also known as white collar crime. The prevention, detection, and investigation of financial fraud are needed to reduce the risk of publicly reporting inaccurate information.

TABLE 9.2	Three of the Worst Accounting Scandals of All Time		
Company and Fraudsters	**Damages**	**How They Did It**	**Penalties**
Bernie Madoff Investment Securities LLC (2008) Bernie Madoff, his accountant David Friehling, and CFO Frank DiPascalli	Tricked investors out of $64.8 billion through the largest Ponzi scheme in history.	Investors were paid returns out of their own money or money from other investors—rather than from profits.	150 years in prison for Madoff + $170 billion restitution. Prison time for Friehling and DiPascalli.
Lehman Brothers (2008) Lehman executives and the company's auditors, Ernst & Young	Hid over $50 billion in loans disguised as sales.	Allegedly sold toxic assets to Cayman Island banks with the understanding that they would be bought back eventually. Created the impression Lehman had $50 billion more in cash and $50 billion less in toxic assets than it actually had.	Forced into the largest bankruptcy in U.S. history.
Enron (2001) CEO Jeffrey Skilling and former CEO Ken Lay	Shareholders lost $74 billion, thousands of employees and investors lost their retirement accounts, and many employees lost their jobs.	Kept huge debts off its balance sheets.	Lay died before serving time; Skilling received 24 years in prison. The company filed for bankruptcy. Arthur Andersen was found guilty of fudging Enron's accounts.

Financial misrepresentation occurs when a company has intentionally deceived one or more other parties.

High-profile examples of **financial misrepresentations** are Bernard L. Madoff Investment Securities (2008), Lehman Brothers (2008), Enron (2001), and many related to the subprime mortgage crisis. Table 9.2 describes three of the worst accounting fraud cases of all time. The FBI investigates white collar crime and reports on the subject at its website FBI.gov.

Accounting Software Packages

Accounting software is a foundational technology for many companies, and as a business grows, powerful, effective accounting solutions are critical. Most accounting software packages offer the same basic features necessary for managing finances: accounts receivable (A/R), accounts payable (A/P), general ledger, billing and invoicing, purchase and sales orders, and reporting. In addition to basic functionality, the top accounting solutions offer additional features to give users more power, flexibility, and customization. Often accounting solutions are closely integrated with enterprise systems, such as ERP systems that include an extensive accounting module.

Many providers offer cloud-based solutions. SaaS accounting software solutions include the features of traditional systems, with the added benefit of anytime, anywhere accessibility and updating.

Financial Disclosure

The SEC's financial disclosure system is central to its mission of protecting investors and maintaining fair, orderly, and efficient markets. Since 1934 the SEC has required financial disclosure in forms and documents. In 1984 the SEC began collecting electronic documents to help investors obtain information, but those documents made it difficult to search for and find specific data items. To eliminate that difficulty and improve how investors find and use information, the SEC sought a new disclosure system that required **data disclosure**, whereby data items are tagged to make them easily searchable. The reporting (disclosure) system was based on electronic data tagging, or **eXtensible Business Reporting Language (XBRL)**. Beginning in 2012, the SEC mandated new interactive data reporting requirements as described in IT at Work 9.4.

XBRL Tagging

XBRL is a language for the electronic communication of business data. Each item, such as cash or depreciation expense, is tagged with information about various attributes, such as calendar year, audited/unaudited status, currency, and so on. XBRL-tagged data can be read by any software that includes an XBRL processor, which makes them easy to transfer among computers. Creating XBRL documents does not require XML computer programming. Software is available to tag data, submit tagged data to various recipients, and receive and analyze tagged data from other sources. Figure 9.14 shows how XBRL documents are created. XBRL helps companies:

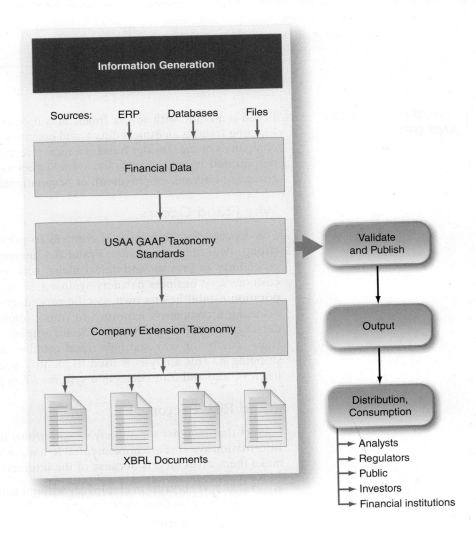

Figure 9.14 Overview of the creation of XBRL documents.

- Generate cleaner data, including written explanations and supporting notes.
- Produce more accurate data with fewer errors that require follow-up by regulators.
- Transmit data more quickly to regulators and meet deadlines.
- Increase the number of cases and amount of information that staffers can handle.

IT at **Work** 9.4

XBRL Reporting Compliance

The SEC requires data reporting using XBRL tags, and those reports require XBRL software.

In March 2012 the SEC adopted the U.S. GAAP Financial Reporting Taxonomy, which is based on XBRL. Public companies, called filers, registered with the SEC must submit their financial reports as *tagged interactive data files* (FASB.org, 2012). Interactive data make it easier for investors to analyze and compare the financial performance of public companies. Prior to XBRL, reports were noninteractive. Investors who wanted specific data had to manually search lengthy

corporate annual reports or mutual fund documents. As more companies use interactive data, sophisticated analysis tools used by financial professionals are now available to average investors.

Interactive data increase the efficiency of reporting processes, including the ability to consolidate financial data from different operating systems. Banks also submit their *call reports* to the Federal Deposit Insurance Corporation (FDIC) in XBRL format.

| **FRAUD PREVENTION AND DETECTION** | Fraud is a crime with severe financial consequences, as you observed in Table 9.2. Fighting fraud is an ethical duty—and essential to public trust and the integrity of a company's brand. **Insider fraud** is a term referring to a variety of criminal behaviors perpetrated by an organization's employees or contractors. Other terms for this crime are **internal, employment, or occupational fraud**. |

Why Fraud Occurs

Fraud occurs because internal controls to prevent insider fraud—no matter how strong—will fail on occasion. **Fraud risk management** is a system of policies and procedures to prevent and detect illegal acts committed by managers, employees, customers, or business partners against a company's interests. Although each corporation establishes its own specific procedures, fraud risk management involves assessing a company's exposure to fraud; implementing defenses to prevent and detect fraud; defining procedures to investigate, prosecute, and recover losses from fraud. Analyzing why and how fraud could occur is as important as detecting and stopping it. This analysis is used to identify necessary corporate policies to deter insider fraud and fraud detection systems when prevention fails.

Fraud Risk Factors

Factors that increase a company's exposure to fraud are illustrated in Figure 9.15. Information systems are implemented to harden it against these factors. Companies make themselves targets because of the interaction of these four factors:

1. A high level of trust in employees without sufficient oversight to verify that they are not stealing from the company
2. Relying on informal processes of control

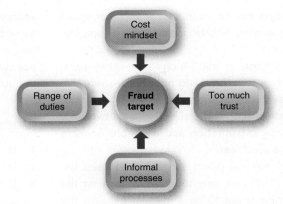

Figure 9.15 Factors that make companies targets for fraud.

3. A mindset (belief) that internal controls and fraud prevention systems are too expensive to implement

4. Assigning a wide range of duties for each employee, giving them opportunities to commit fraud

When a small manufacturer was the victim of theft of intellectual property, the computer network logs identified the computer that had been used to commit the alleged crime. But there was no way to connect that computer to one specific individual. A manager's conviction that he knew who had perpetrated the crime was not sufficient evidence. The lesson learned was that the internal control—*separation of duties*—is not only important to fraud prevention, but also to fraud prosecution and recovery of losses. At the company, employees had shared computer accounts, so they were not able to link the fraud to the person who committed it. Designing effective fraud response and litigation-readiness strategies (post-incident strategies) is crucial to be able to:

- recover financial losses.
- punish perpetrators through lawsuits, criminal charges, and/or forfeited gains.
- stop fraudsters from victimizing other organizations.

History has shown that if the punishment for committing fraud is not severe, the fraudster's next employer will be the next victim, as described in IT at Work 9.5.

Trying to keep fraud hidden can mean either *doing nothing* or simply firing the employee. These approaches to dealing with fraud are not sustainable because they erode the effectiveness of fraud prevention measures and produce **moral hazard**—that is, they take the risk out of insider fraud.

One of the most effective fraud prevention techniques is the perception of detection and punishment. If a company shows its employees that it can find out everything that every employee does and will prosecute to the fullest extent anyone who commits fraud, then the feeling that "I can get away with it" drops drastically (Johnson et al., 2011). The Catch-22 is that companies may have limited resources that hinder a proper fraud diagnosis or forensic accounting investigation, even though they cannot afford unrecoverable losses either.

IT at Work 9.5

Serial Fraudster

A dental practice with $4 million in annual revenues had fired its bookkeeper after a tax audit revealed to the owners that she had been stealing over $100,000 per year for at least four years. The bookkeeper was responsible for all accounting duties and financial reporting for tax purposes. Her work was not inspected closely by external auditors or the owners.

No internal control systems, for example, controls that would prevent checks being written to bogus vendors or employees, were implemented.

The classic **red flags**, or fraud indicators—lavish vacations, jewelry, and cars that she could not afford—were evident, but ignored by the owners/managers. The bookkeeper was a "serial fraudster," having defrauded at least two prior employers: a religious organization and a nonprofit where she had worked as a volunteer.

The defrauded medical practice decided to keep the incident quiet, so it did not take legal action against the bookkeeper. That turned out to be a mistake because the bookkeeper used that situation to her advantage. She filed a wrongful termination lawsuit. For several reasons, including not being able to collect evidence (lax internal controls enabled the bookkeeper to destroy evidence), the practice settled the lawsuit by paying her over $5,000. In effect, the fraudster had turned to extortion, knowing that the practice was unprepared to fight back. Inarguably, she must be defrauding her current employer.

Questions

1. How was the fraud detected?
2. How long had it been going on?
3. What were the red flags that suggested the bookkeeper was living beyond her means?
4. What mistakes were made in the handling of the fraud?
5. In your opinion, did the dental practice have an ethical responsibility to prosecute the fraudster?

Financial Meltdowns Triggered by Fraud

In the early 2000s, the U.S. business economy was significantly impacted by fraud scandals that involved senior executives at a number of major corporations. Lawmakers believed that the scope of the crimes destroyed the public's confidence in the country's financial systems and markets. A number of laws were passed that heightened the legal responsibilities of corporate management to actively guard against fraud by employees, established stricter management and reporting requirements, and introduced severe penalties for failure to comply. As a result, fraud management became a necessary functional process. These frauds played a role in the SEC's rule for XBRL data reporting.

Internal Controls

In companies with lax accounting systems, it is too easy for employees to misdirect purchase orders and payments, bribe a supplier, or manipulate accounting data. When senior managers are involved in a fraud, preventing fraud is extremely tough. Consider Bernie Madoff, who committed a record-setting fraud scheme for many years even after Sarbanes-Oxley was passed in 2002 to help prevent financial fraud.

In a much smaller but still serious fraud case involving a New York–based nonprofit, a volunteer was responsible for counting cash receipts at the annual fundraiser. The volunteer had performed this task for 30 years. One year, an accountant was assigned to assist the volunteer with the count. The volunteer offered the accountant a "cut" of the cash in exchange for her silence about the theft.

Strong internal controls, which depend on IT for their effectiveness, consist of the following:

- **Segregation of duties** tops the list of best practices in control procedures. When handling a company's assets, the work of managers and employees needs to be subject to approval or authorization. For example, any attempt to issue a check to a vendor not in the database of approved vendors will be prevented by the accounting information system.
- **Job rotation.** More than one person should be familiar with each transaction cycle in the business wherever possible. Rotation of jobs helps prevent over-reliance on a single individual—and is a way to expose fraudulent activities.

- **Oversight.** Management—whether a single owner or a team of individuals—must monitor what is actually happening in the business. Auditing information systems are part of a strong oversight function. Unannounced periodic walk-throughs of a process or review of how things are really being done can reveal existing or potential problem areas.

- **Safeguarding of assets** is essential to a fraud prevention program. Access to networks, financial systems, and databases must be controlled with strong passwords and other security measures. Similarly, bank checks, petty cash funds, and company credit cards need to be locked up when not in use.

- **IT policies.** Understand your information system. Heavy reliance on IT staff can open up opportunities for fraud. Establish a computer use policy and educate employees on the importance of securing information. Strictly enforce the use of separate logins and keep passwords confidential.

AUDITING INFORMATION SYSTEMS

Fraud can be easy to commit and hard to detect. Just ask any auditor. The problem is worse in government and nonprofit entities that have inadequate accounting and internal control systems. The problem is so bad at the federal level that auditors have been unable to express an opinion on the fairness of the consolidated financial statements of the United States. For example, space agency NASA had been unable to explain $565 billion in year-end adjustments to its books. It could be bad accounting, fraud, waste, or abuse. Without adequate records, no one really knows. This amount is astounding, especially when one considers that the combined cost of fraud at Enron and WorldCom was less than $100 billion in shareholder equity.

Because the physical possession of stolen property is no longer required and it is just as easy to program a computer to misdirect $100,000 as it is $1,000, the size and number of frauds have increased tremendously. See IT at Work 9.6, which describes a real case, but one that occurs nonetheless throughout all types of organizations.

IT at Work 9.6

Lax Accounting Controls Invite Fraud

Chris was a compulsive gambler, and she hid it well. Her problem began innocently at work when one day a casino website popped up on her computer as she surfed the Internet during lunch. She placed a few bets using the free credits offered by the site to entice first-time players. She won, and that gave her a thrilling feeling, she would later explain to fraud investigators.

Two years later, as the payroll manager of a medium-sized manufacturing firm, Chris had defrauded her employer of over $750,000. Why did she do it? To pay off her gambling losses that were costing her an average of $7,000 a week. How did she do it? She took advantage of the lack of controls in her company's payroll and accounting information systems and controls.

Chris's Employment History and Deception

Chris had worked at the company for a decade. Her performance reviews described her as hardworking, reliable, and loyal, but did not mention she felt underpaid. Chris was bitter, thinking her employer did not treat her fairly. When her gambling began to spiral out of control, she turned to fraud. "As far as I was concerned, they owed me," she told the forensic accountants.

The company's HR manager and comptroller were supposed to review Chris's work. But, the HR manager focused on providing her with the correct data for employees' wages and benefits. The comptroller appeared not to have exercised control over payroll processing, which Chris knew.

Chris created two phony employees on the company's hourly payroll system as a new and separate cost center. As she processed and received the records sent to and from an external payroll provider (EPP) without effective oversight, she was able to control the scheme without detection. The phantom employees' checks were drawn up manually by EPP, sent to Chris, and deposited into an account she maintained in a bank near her home. Near year-end, she also had EPP make adjustments to the payroll register to eliminate the amounts paid to the phony employees. When she went on vacation, she deactivated the two phony names from the payroll.

Fraud Scheme Based on Lack of Oversight

Chris started paying herself for unauthorized overtime. This plan proved to be a great success—she paid herself for 1,500 hours overtime over two years as opposed to the actual 50 she did work. Chris falsified records and increased the size of her theft until the HR manager finally noticed. When confronted with the evidence, she confessed that she had gambled away the money and could not repay it.

Questions

1. What role did trust play in Chris's ability to commit fraud for so long (i.e., the employer's trust in Chris)?
2. What role did weak accounting ISs play in her ability to commit fraud?
3. In your opinion, if Chris knew that strong accounting ISs were in place would that have deterred her from trying to steal from her employer?

FINANCIAL PLANNING AND BUDGETING

The management of financial assets is a major task in financial planning and budgeting. Financial planning, like any other functional planning, is tied to the overall organizational planning and to other functional areas. It is divided into short-, medium-, and long-term horizons, much like activities planning.

Knowing the availability and cost of money is a key ingredient for successful financial planning. Especially important is projecting cash flows, which tells organizations what funds they need and when, and how they will acquire them. In today's tough economic conditions with tight credit and limited availability of funds, this function has become critical to most companies' survival.

Inaccurate cash flow projection is the #1 reason why many small businesses go bankrupt. The inability to access credit led to the bankruptcy of investment bank Lehman Brothers in September 2008.

Budgeting

The best-known part of financial planning is the annual budget, which allocates the financial resources of an organization among participants, activities, and projects. The budget is the financial expression of the enterprise's plans. Management allocates resources in the way that best supports the mission. IT enables the introduction of financial logic and efficiency into the budgeting process. Several software packages, many of which are Web-based, are available to support budget preparation and control.

Capital budgeting is the process of analyzing and selecting investments with the highest ROI for the company. The process may include comparing alternative investments; for example, evaluating private cloud vs. public cloud computing options.

The major benefits of using budgeting software are that it can reduce the time and effort involved in the budget process, explore and analyze the implications of organizational and environmental changes, facilitate the integration of corporate strategic objectives with operational plans, make planning an ongoing continuous process, and automatically monitor exceptions for patterns and trends.

Forecasting

As you read, a major reason organizations fail is their inability to forecast and/or secure sufficient cash flow. Underestimated expenses, overspending, financial mismanagement, and fraud can lead to disaster. Good planning is necessary, but not sufficient, and must be supplemented by skillful control. Control activities in organizations take many forms, including control and **auditing** of the information systems themselves. Information systems play an extremely important role in supporting organizational control, as we show throughout the text. Specific forms of financial control are discussed in the next section.

Financial Ratio Analysis

A major task of the accounting/finance department is to watch the financial health of the company by monitoring and assessing a set of financial ratios. These ratios are also used by external parties when they decide whether to invest in an organization, extend credit, or buy it.

The collection of data for ratio analysis is done by the TPS, and computation of the ratios completed through financial analysis models. Interpretation of ratios and the ability to forecast their future behavior require expertise, which is supported by DSSs (decision support systems).

Profitability Analysis and Cost Control

Companies are concerned with the profitability of individual products or services, product lines, divisions, or the financial health of the entire organization. Profitability analysis DSS software allows accurate computation of profitability and allocation of overhead costs. One way to control cost is by properly estimating it. This is done by using special software. For example, Oracle Hyperion Profitability and Cost Management software is a performance management app that provides insights into costs and profitability. This app helps managers evaluate business performance by discovering the drivers of cost and profitability and improving resource alignment. Sophisticated business rules are stored in one place, enabling analyses and strategies to be shared easily across an enterprise.

Questions

1. What is eXtensible Business Reporting Language (XBRL)?
2. Why does the SEC mandate data disclosure, whereby data items are tagged to make them easily searchable?
3. What is insider fraud? What are some other terms for insider fraud?
4. What is fraud risk management?
5. What four factors increase the risk of fraud?
6. Explain how accounting ISs can help deter fraud.
7. Define capital budgeting.
8. What is the purpose of auditing?

9.5 Human Resource Systems, Compliance, and Ethics

Companies cannot simply hire a great workforce. They have to find, recruit, motivate, and train employees to succeed in their workplace. Retaining high-performance people requires monitoring how people feel about the workplace, their compensation, value to the company, and chances for advancement—and maintaining workplace health and safety.

HR is a field that deals with employment policies, procedures, communications, and compliance requirements. Effective HR compliance programs are a necessity for all organizations in today's legal environment. HR needs to monitor workplace and employment practices to ensure compliance with the Fair Labor Standards Act (FLSA), Occupational Health & Safety Agencies (OSHA), and the antidiscrimination and sexual harassment laws. Seven other employment laws to protect against discrimination are listed in Table 9.3.

TABLE 9.3	HR Monitors Compliance with Antidiscrimination Employment Laws
Title VII of the Civil Rights Act of 1964	Prohibits discrimination on the basis of race, color, religion, national origin, and sex. It also prohibits sex discrimination on the basis of pregnancy and sexual harassment.
Civil Rights Act of 1966	Prohibits discrimination based on race or ethnic origin.
Equal Pay Act of 1963	Prohibits employers from paying different wages to men and women who perform essentially the same work under similar working conditions.
Bankruptcy Act	Prohibits discrimination against anyone who has declared bankruptcy.
Americans with Disabilities Act	Prohibits discrimination against persons with disabilities.
Equal Employment Opportunity Act	Prohibits discrimination against minorities based on poor credit ratings.
Age Discrimination in Employment Act (ADEA)	Prohibits discrimination against individuals who are age 40 or above.

CAREER INSIGHT 9.1

Compliance Is Good Business

While carrying out day-to-day operations or trying to hit targets, managers may lose sight of the big picture. A narrow focus can lead to serious compliance and regulatory violations, which can do permanent damage to the brand and expose managers to criminal charges. Crossing the line is a crime.

According to the U.S. Department of Justice (DOJ) *Federal Prosecution of Corporations (1999)*:

Corporations are "legal persons," capable of suing and being sued, and capable of committing crimes.

Under the doctrine of *respondeat superior,* a corporation may be held criminally liable for the illegal acts of its employees, directors, officers, and agents.

In all cases involving wrongdoing by corporate agents, prosecutors should consider the corporation, as well as the responsible individuals, as potential criminal targets.

Source: justice.gov.

HR INFORMATION SYSTEMS

Effective human resource information systems (HRISs) reduce the workload of the HR department. PeopleSoft Human Capital Management, which is one of the market-leading HRISs, provides a global foundation for HR data and improved business processes.

HRISs have been moved to intranets and clouds—wherein HR apps are leased in SaaS arrangements. Using intranets, HR apps have shifted many routine tasks to employees who log in to manage their benefits, deductions, direct deposits, health care, and the like. When employees manage their own HR services, HR professionals can focus on legal and compliance responsibilities, employee development, talent management, hiring, and succession planning.

Benefits of SaaS for HR

Three real-world examples illustrate the benefits of tying SaaS to global HR transformation efforts:

- A global medical device manufacturer needed to create an independent HR system as it divested from its parent company. Cloud computing was at the core of its new global HR delivery model, which reduced the demand on internal business and IT resources. The company was able to establish fully independent HR operations within 10 months.

- A national nonprofit foundation with a fast-growing employee population wanted to improve the effectiveness of HR operations. The organization selected a cloud-based solution, which dramatically improved time to value without overstretching internal IT resources. Because little front-end investment was required, the foundation hit its budget target.

- A global entertainment company needed a learning management system that could deliver content varying from instructor-based training to 30-second video how-to snippets. It chose to deploy a new learning management system in the cloud. With this approach, it quickly got the new system up and running.

Figure 9.16 illustrates how IT facilitates the work of the HR department. The figure summarizes the role HR plays in acquiring and developing talented people in organizations.

Recruitment

Recruitment is the process of finding potential employees with the skills and talent needed by the company, testing them, and deciding which ones to hire. Most companies are flooded with applicants, but might still have difficulty finding the right people. LinkedIn is a primary social media site for recruitment and headhunters.

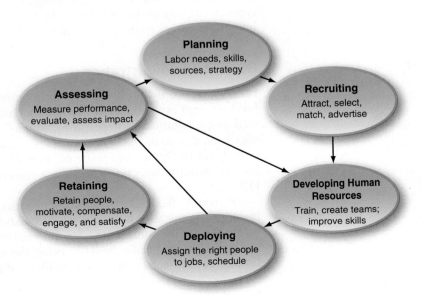

Figure 9.16 HR management activities.

Once recruited, employees become part of the corporate HR talent pool, which needs to be maintained and developed. Several activities supported by IT include the following.

Performance Evaluation

Employees are evaluated periodically by their immediate supervisors. Peers or subordinates may also evaluate others. Evaluations are usually recorded on paper or electronic forms. Using such information manually is a tedious and error-prone job. Once digitized, evaluations can be used to support many decisions, ranging from rewards to transfers to layoffs. For example, Cisco Systems is known for developing an IT-based human capital strategy. Many universities evaluate professors online. The evaluation form appears on the screen, and the students fill it in. Results can be tabulated in minutes. Corporate managers can analyze employees' performances with the help of intelligent systems, which provide systematic interpretation of performance over time. Several vendors provide software for performance evaluation, such as HalogenSoftware.com and Capterra.com.

Training and Human Resources Development

Employee training and retraining are mportant activities of the human resources department. Major issues are planning of classes and tailoring specific training programs to meet the needs of the organization and employees. Sophisticated HR departments build a career development plan for each employee. IT can support the planning, monitoring, and control of these activities by using workflow applications.

HR PLANNING,
CONTROL, AND
MANAGEMENT

In some industries, labor negotiation is an important aspect of HR planning and it may be facilitated by IT. For most companies, administering employee benefits is also a significant part of the human resources function. Here are several examples of how IT can help.

Personnel Planning and HR Strategies

The HR department forecasts requirements for people and skills. In some geographical areas and for overseas assignments, it may be difficult to find particular types of employees. In such cases, the HR department plans how to locate sufficient human resources or develop them from within.

Benefits Administration

Employees' contributions to their organizations are rewarded by salary/wage, bonuses, and other benefits. Benefits include those for health and dental care as well as contributions for pensions. Managing the benefits system can be a complex task, due to its many components and the tendency of organizations to allow employees to choose and trade off benefits. In large companies, using computers for self-benefits selection can save a tremendous amount of labor and time for HR staff.

Providing flexibility in selecting benefits is viewed as a competitive advantage in large organizations. It can be successfully implemented when supported by computers. Some companies have automated benefits enrollments. Employees can self-register for specific benefits using the corporate portal or voice technology. Employees self-select desired benefits from a menu. Payroll pay cards are now in use in numerous companies, such as Payless Shoes, which has 30,000 employees in 5,000 stores. The system specifies the value of each benefit and the available benefits balance of each employee. Some companies use intelligent agents to assist employees and monitor their actions.

Employee Relationship Management

In their effort to better manage employees, companies are developing human capital management, facilitated by the Web, to streamline the HR process. These Web applications are more commonly referred to as employee relationship management. For example, self-services such as tracking personal information and online training are very popular in ERM. Improved relationships with employees result in better retention and higher productivity.

Ethical Challenges and Considerations

HRIS apps raise ethical and legal challenges. For example, training activities that are part of HRM may involve ethical issues in recruiting and selecting employees and in evaluating performance. Likewise, TPS data processing and storage deal with private information about people, their performance, and so forth. Care should be taken to protect this information and the privacy of employees and customers.

The federal law related to workplace substance abuse, the Drug-Free Workplace Act of 1990, requires employers with federal government contracts or grants to ensure a drug-free workplace by documenting and certifying that they have taken a number of steps. Dealing with alcoholism and drugs at work entails legal risks because employees have sued for invasion of privacy, wrongful discharge, defamation, and illegal searches. Employment laws make securing HR information necessary for the protection of employees and the organization.

Questions

1. What are the key HR functions?
2. What are the benefits of moving HRISs to intranets or the cloud?
3. Why have companies implemented SaaS HR?
4. What concerns have deterred companies from implementing SaaS HR?
5. How can companies reduce the cost of recruiting qualified employees?
6. Describe IT support for HR planning and control.
7. What are ethical issues related to HRM apps?

Key Terms

auditing
capital budgeting
computer-integrated
   manufacturing (CIM)
economic order quantity
   (EOQ)
eXtensible Business
   Reporting Language
   (XBRL)

Financial Accounting
   Standards Board
   (FASB)
financial
   misrepresentation
fraud risk management
inbound logistics
income statement
insider fraud

inventory control systems
just-in-time (JIT)
manufacturing quality
   control (QC) systems
mission
moral hazard
online transaction
   processing (OLTP)
outbound logistics

red flag
safety stock
standard operating
   procedures (SOPs)
strategic plan
total quality management
   (TQM)
transparency

Assuring Your Learning

DISCUSS: Critical Thinking Questions

1. Discuss the need for sharing data among functional areas.
2. How does waste increase costs? Give three examples.
3. What is the value of lean manufacturing?
4. What is the objective of EOQ?
5. What are the risks of JIT?
6. Explain the value of being able to respond to hot data.
7. Push-through ads use data about a person to determine whether the ad should appear. What marketing opportunities does this capability create?
8. Explain why the SEC requires that filers use XBRL.
9. How can internal controls help to prevent fraud?
10. How do companies allow themselves to become targets for insider fraud?
11. What are the benefits of prosecuting an employee who has committed fraud against the company?
12. Why might a company not want to prosecute a fraudster?
13. Explain moral hazard. Give a fraud-related example.
14. Fraudsters typically spend the money they steal on luxury items and vacations. Explain why these items are red flags of fraud.
15. What are three examples of strong internal controls?
16. Discuss how IT facilitates the capital budgeting process.
17. Discuss the role IT plays in auditing.
18. Explain the role and benefits of SaaS in HR management.
19. How does digital technology improve the recruitment process?

EXPLORE: Online and Interactive Exercises

1. Visit the Oracle website at www.oracle.com.
   a. Search for "Peoplesoft."
   b. Select *Human Capital Management* and review the HR applications. Describe three benefits of PeopleSoft Human Capital Management.
   c. Return to the Peoplesoft site. Select *Financial Management*. Describe how PeopleSoft Financial Management reduces costs.
2. Search for a video or demo that explains EOQ. Explain the formula.
3. Finding a job on the Internet is challenging; there are almost too many places to look. Visit two recruiting sites, for example, careerbuilder.com and LinkedIn.com. What benefits do these sites provide to you as a job seeker?
4. Examine the capabilities of two financial software packages: Prepare a table that clearly compares and contrasts their capabilities.
5. Review Salesforce.com. What functional support does the software provide?

ANALYZE & DECIDE: Apply IT Concepts to Business Decisions

6. Research and analyze a major corporate fraud.
   a. Identify the company and explain when and how the fraud occurred, who was involved, and damages.
   b. How was the fraud detected?
   c. Describe any red flags associated with the fraud.
   d. Visit SAS.com and search "SAS fraud management." Explain how SAS fraud management could have helped prevent the fraud.

CASE 9.2

Business Case: HSBC Combats Fraud in Split-second Decisions

With billions of dollars, corporate reputations, customer loyalty, and criminal penalties for noncompliance at stake, financial firms must outsmart fraudsters. Detecting and preventing fraudulent transactions across many lines of business (checking, savings, credit cards, loans, etc.) and online channels require comprehensive real time data analytics to assess and score transactions. That is, each transaction has to be analyzed within a split second to calculate the probability that it is fraudulent or legitimate.

A big part of a bank's relationship with customers is giving them confidence that they are protected against fraud, and balancing that protection with their need to have access to your services.

HSCB Overview

HSBC is a commercial bank known by many as the "world's local bank." HSBC is a United Kingdom–based company that provides a wide range of banking and related financial services. The bank reported a pre-tax profit of $6.8 billion in the first quarter of 2014 (1Q 2014). It has 6,300 offices in 75 countries and over 54 million customers.

Fighting Fraudulent Transactions

HSBC was able to reduce the incidence of fraud across tens of millions of debit and credit card accounts. The bank implemented the latest Fraud Management software from SAS. The software includes an application programming interface (API) and a real time transaction scoring system based on advanced data analytics. Using the Fraud Management app, HSBC has reduced its losses from fraudulent transactions worldwide and its exposure to increasingly aggressive threats. The antifraud solution is live in the United States, Europe, and Asia, where it protects 100 percent of credit card transactions in real time.

Scenario

Consider this scenario. A credit card transaction request comes in for the purchase of $6,000 in home appliances. The bank has a moment to decide to approve the transaction, or reject it as potentially fraudulent. Two outcomes are possible:

- **Legitimate purchase rejected:** When a legitimate purchase is rejected, the customer might pay with another card. The bank loses the fee income from the purchase and the interest fee. Risk of account churn increases.

- **Fraudulent purchase accepted:** When a fraudulent purchase is accepted, a legitimate customer becomes a victim of a crime. The bank incurs the $6,000 loss, the cost of the fraud investigation, potential regulatory scrutiny, and bad publicity. Chances of recovering any losses are almost zero.

With trillions of dollars in assets, HSBC Holdings plc is a prime target for fraud. Fighting all forms of fraud—unauthorized use of cards for payment and online transactions, and even customer fraud—has risen to the top of the corporate agenda. Fraud losses are operating costs that damage the bottom line.

As required by regulations, HSBC has implemented policies to segregate duties, create dual controls, and establish strong audit trails to detect anomalies. In addition, the bank has antifraud technology, which includes SAS Fraud Management, to monitor and score the millions of daily transactions. It is the cornerstone of these efforts.

Fraud Management

In 2007 HSBC's first SAS implementation went live in the United States, which was their largest portfolio with 30 million cards issued there. All transactions were scored in real time. Detection rates on debit ATM transactions have been very effective. HSBC has updated its Fraud Management solution multiple times as newer technology and threats emerged.

Of course, financial fraud morphs to avoid new detection methods so antifraud models have a very short shelf life. Once HSBC closes up one loophole, thieves devise new threats to exploit other potential vulnerabilities. To counteract threats, fraud-monitoring algorithms and scoring models require constant refreshing.

Sources: BusinessWire (2011), SAS.com (2014), Reuters (2014), YouTube video "HSBC Relies on SAS for Comprehensive Fraud Detection."

Questions

1. Analyze the reasons to invest millions of dollars to detect and prevent fraudulent transactions. In your evaluation, do a cost–benefit analysis to show why the investment cost is worthwhile.
2. Review the two outcomes of the fraud scenario. Assess the business implications of each of the following two goals. Explain why these goals are conflicting.
   a. To minimize rejecting legitimate purchases by authorized customers
   b. To minimize the risk of making customers victims of fraud
3. The Fraud Management solution is based on a scoring model. For example, assume the scores range from 1 to 10, with 10 being the highest probability that the transaction is fraudulent. What cutoff score would you use to decide to approve a purchase? What cutoff score would you use to decide not to approve a purchase? If those cutoff scores are not the same, how do you suggest those falling between scores be treated?
4. Why are approval decisions made in a split second? Would customers tolerate a brief delay in the approval process if it reduced their risk of identity theft? Explain your answer.
5. Research ATM or other banking transaction fraud. How has a financial firm been defrauded or harmed?

CASE 9.3

Video Case: United Rentals Optimizes Its Workforce with Human Capital Management

Visit Oracle.com and search "United Rentals Optimizes Workforce." Click on the video link to "United Rentals Optimizes Its Workforce with Oracle HCM." Watch the video. Describe the key benefits of its HR software. Visit Forbes.com and search for the article "10 Trends Driving the Mandate for Modern HCM" posted on February 7, 2014.

Questions

1. Typically, the importance of the HR function is overlooked, or at least overshadowed by accounting and finance, which manage cash and other financial assets. In your opinion, is HCM software as important as accounting software? Explain your answer.

2. Briefly describe three of the key trends driving HCM and how they relate to the HR software benefits at United Rentals.

References

Accenture.com. "Ducati Motor Holding S.p.A: SAP Dealer Communication System." 2014.

Apple.com. "Ducati." 2014.

BusinessWire. "SAS Fraud Management Speeds Real time Processing, Boosts Detection and Prevention." June 15, 2011.

Ducati Motor Holding S.p.A. 2014. http://www.ducatiusa.com/index.do

fasb.org. "US GAAP Financial Reporting Taxonomy." 2012.

Johnson, P., L. Volonino, & I. Redpath. "Fraud Response and Litigation-Readiness Strategies for Small and Medium Businesses: A Handbook on How to Prepare for Litigation, Prosecution & Loss Recovery in Response to Insider Fraud." *IFP.org*, November 2011.

Justice.com, 2014.

Oracle.com. 2014.

Reuters. "HSBC Holdings plc Company Profile." 2014. http://www.reuters.com

Salesforce.com. 2014.

SAP.com. 2014.

SAS.com. "Reduce Losses from Fraudulent Transactions." http://www.sas.com

sec.gov. 2014

Wilson, D. "Manufacturing Technology: Hard Work." *The Engineer* 33, April 25, 2011.

xbrl.sec.gov. 2014.

Strategic Technology and Enterprise Systems

Chapter Snapshot

Case 10.1 Opening Case: Strategic Technology Trend—3D Printing

Key Terms
Assuring Your Learning

- **Discuss:** Critical Thinking Questions
- **Explore:** Online and Interactive Exercises
- **Analyze & Decide:** Apply IT Concepts to Business Decisions

Case 10.2 Business Case: Avon's Failed SAP Implementation: Enterprise System Gone Wrong

Case 10.3 Video Case: Procter & Gamble: Creating Conversations in the Cloud with 4.8 Billion Consumers

References

Learning Outcomes

1. Explain the potential executive, managerial, and operational support of enterprise systems, their success factors, and reasons for failure.

2. Identify the leading enterprise social platforms and their capabilities.

3. Describe the functions of enterprise resource planning (ERP) systems, implementation risks, and how ERP investments are justified.

4. Explain the planning and forecasting, sourcing and purchasing, and distribution support provided by supply chain management (SCM) systems.

5. Describe customer relationship management (CRM) systems and their role in customer acquisition, retention, and customer lifetime value.

Chapter Snapshot

Many enterprises in business for over 25 years have mission-critical information systems that run on mainframe computers and software implemented in the 1980s or 1990s. These **legacy systems** run core business processes that may handle tens of millions of transactions. Disadvantages of a legacy core are that they are

Figure 10.1 Integration of enterprise systems is achieved via access to shared data.

© vaeenma/iStockphoto

difficult and expensive to maintain, update, and **interface** securely with leading-edge business apps. When companies decide to update, they invest in enterprise systems. **Enterprise systems**—ERP, SCM, and CSM—are integrated by their connection to central data repositories that enable them to synch and share the latest data, as illustrated in Figure 10.1.

In Chapter 10, you will learn the benefits, limitations, and implementation risks of cross-functional enterprise systems and business apps that support business strategy, managers, and employees—and relationships with suppliers and customers.

CASE 10.1 OPENING CASE

Strategic Technology Trend—3D Printing

3D PRINTING, ADDITIVE MANUFACTURING

With **3D printing**, computer-created digital models are used to create real-world objects. 3D printing, which is also called **additive manufacturing**, has produced toys, jewelry, food, spare parts, and more.

According to global investment management firm **Goldman Sachs**:
3D printing is 1 of 8 technologies that are going to creatively destroy how we do business.

IT research firm **Gartner** predicted:
3D printing of nonliving medical devices such as prosthetic limbs, combined with fast population growth and insufficient health care in emerging markets, is likely to cause an explosion in demand for the technology.

Global research firm **McKinsey** forecasted:
3D printing is 1 of 12 disruptive technologies that could deliver major economic impact to the global economy by 2025.

Figure 10.2 Strong forecasts for 3D printing made by leading research and investment management firms—Goldman Sachs, Gartner, and McKinsey.

TABLE 10.1   Overview of 3D Printing

What is 3D printing? How does it work?	3D printing, also known as additive manufacturing, builds objects layer by layer. Traditional manufacturing typically uses a subtractive process, whereby materials are cut, ground, or molded to create an object.
What enterprise systems are impacted by 3D printing?	The potential for 3D printing to revolutionize ERP (enterprise resource planning) and SCM (supply chain management) means business and IT professionals must develop a framework for evaluating its impact.
Where is 3D print technology used?	3D technology is being used by consumer-product designers, automotive manufacturing engineers, and dental labs for building prototypes, replacement parts, and customized products on demand. Retailers and manufacturers are evaluating applications of 3D printing.
What factors are limiting widespread use?	3D printing has not yet reached the point where its cost, speed, and scalability can compete with traditional manufacturing.

For several decades, 3D printing has been used by manufacturers to reduce research and development (R&D) costs. 3D printing builds products layer by layer, a process that has less overhead costs and allows for more complex designs. Using this technology, engineers rapidly created a physical prototype of a new design. The prototype was used to test the quality of the design and to check for defects. Until recently, 3D printers were expensive. Prices dropped significantly from more than $100,000 to models that cost a few hundred dollars, as shown in Figure 10.3. Figure 10.4 shows Urbee, the first 3D-printed car. Not only is Urbee designed to be highly energy-efficient, the manufacturing processes to build it are clean and energy-efficient.

Figure 10.3 3D printers displayed at the Robot and Makers Milano Show.

© Stefano Tinti/Shutterstock

Figure 10.4 Urbee is the world's first 3D-printed car. The entire car body was 3D-printed using Stratasys printers. Urbee is designed to be highly energy-efficient, including manufacturing processes.

© Piero Cruciatti/Alamy

CREATIVE DESTRUCTION: 3D PRINTING'S IMPACT ON MANUFACTURING AND RETAIL

Creative destroyer is a term coined by Joseph Schumpeter in 1942 to warn that innovation can disrupt industries in capitalistic societies; and force established companies and business models to either adapt or fail.

Supply chain starts with the acquisition of raw materials or the procurement (purchase) of products and proceeds through manufacture, transport, and delivery—and the disposal or recycling of products.

3D bioprinting is the medical application of 3D printing to produce living tissue and organs.

Compared to traditional manufacturing and prototyping methods, 3D printing offers high levels of customization, reduced costs for complex designs, and lower overhead costs for short-run parts and products. A **creative destroyer** is how Goldman Sachs describes 3D printing technology because its ability to build cheaper, better, and more customizable products will, to some extent, destroy traditional manufacturing methods. Capabilities of 3D printing hardware are expanding and costs have dropped dramatically. They will be able to build larger components with greater precision or resolution at higher speeds and lower costs. Forecasts indicate that 3D printing is becoming a viable alternative to traditional manufacturing processes in a growing number of applications.

According to McKinsey, 3D printing will have an impact on consumer sectors that place a premium on highly customizable products, for example, footwear, toys, and jewelry. McKinsey estimates that by 2025 sales of 3D-printed products in these three industries alone may reach $550 billion per year.

The following examples show the potential of 3D printing.

Hardware Stores

When customers shop for replacement parts, the store could use a 3D printer with all the pattern specifications to print onsite and on-demand. Hardware stores could slash their inventory and store sizes, and improve customer service.

Defense

Troops in the field and their equipment require regular maintenance. Having a 3D printer at small supply post in the field rather than at a larger base far away alters the ability to complete maintenance and repair, and provide a **supply chain** in combat.

Health Care

Hospitals use expensive equipment, such as magnetic resonance imaging (MRI) scanners. Downtime spent waiting for onsite repair is expensive. A technician who was guided remotely by the manufacturer could diagnose and fix the problem immediately by 3D-printing the MRI scanner replacement part onsite.

Hip surgery done with a 3D-printed titanium implant and bone stem cell graft has been conducted in the U.K. The hip part was designed using the patient's CT scan, thereby matching the patient's exact specifications and measurements. Even more radical is the potential for complex and controversial **3D bioprinting** of human tissue and organs. Scientists are already 3D-printing tiny strips of organ tissue. Although printing whole human organs for surgical transplants is still years away, the technology is rapidly developing. The ethical arguments and challenges of bioprinting will be discussed in Chapter 14.

Dental Work

Stratasys Ltd., a leader in 3D printing and additive manufacturing solutions, introduced the highest-precision wax 3D printers available to the dental industry in mid-2014. The Stratasys CrownWorx and FrameWorx 3D Printers allow dental labs to create wax molds for crowns, bridges, and denture frameworks.

Reproduction of Vintage Car Components

In 1969 Ferrari introduced one of its most masterful race cars—the 312P, shown in Figure 10.5. But parts for that vintage car do not exist. To rebuild an engine, a special aluminum alloy was poured into a cast, which was created by 3D printing. The new engine block and engine rebuild were completed in record time. 3D printing is by far the most efficient method for reproducing components that are no longer available. Often, it is the only way to reproduce certain components quickly and at reasonable cost.

Aerospace Manufacturing

GE is using additive manufacturing to make fuel nozzles for its next-generation Leap engines that will power the new Boeing 737 and Airbus A320 jets. The fuel nozzles will be 25 percent lighter and 5 times more durable. Since there are 20 nozzles in each engine, the weight savings for each aircraft are significant.

Industrial Design

Large industrial group Siemens explains that 3D printing allows its designers to imagine shapes that would be impossible to create through older techniques. The use of additive manufacturing has radically speeded up prototyping of Siemens's gas turbine blades, from 20 weeks to 48 hours. Additive manufacturing has also cut the cost of tooling and materials. For example, a piece can have all of its holes incorporated into it with precision because it is built up from powder rather than being expensively drilled afterward. Siemens hopes to cut the cost of some parts by 30 percent.

Figure 10.5 Parts to rebuild the Ferrari 312P have vanished, so the engine was rebuilt using 3D printing to create the engine's cast form.

© BG Motorsports/Alamy

Manufacturing On-Demand

The ability to manufacture replacement parts on-demand using 3D printers is expected to transform after-market services and restructure industries. Smaller facilities with 3D printers onsite could replace large regional warehouses. The supply of service parts might even be outsourced: Small fabricators located, for example, at airports, hospitals, or major manufacturing venues could make these parts for much of the equipment used onsite, with data supplied directly by the manufacturers.

Makeup 3D Printer

Harvard Business School graduate Grace Choi unveiled her Mink makeup 3D printer at the 2014 TechCrunch Disrupt conference. With Mink, users create lipstick, blush, eyeshadow, and other makeup in any color and print it. The printer uses the same substrates found in factory-made makeup, which means the printed cosmetics are the same quality as those sold by retailers. At its 2015 debut, the Mink 3D printer cost $200, making it affordable for the target 13 to 21 age demographic. How this will impact the multibillion dollar makeup industry remains to be seen.

3D PRINTING WITHIN AN ERP SYSTEM

stock-keeping unit (SKU) is a code number, typically a machine-readable bar code, assigned to a single item of inventory.

The process of creating a product in traditional manufacturing is widely different from 3D printing. Most parts are built by removing layers of material (cutting, drilling, sanding, etc.), which results in the part's final form. But with 3D printing, layers of materials are added to each other by applying heat or chemicals to create a finished product.

Manufacturers using 3D printing will need software in their ERP system that understands and manages the 3D process. Figure 10.6 presents a simplified view of the key role of ERP. For example, in order to combine specific materials or alloys, the 3D printing process may involve heat or chemical reactions in order to create something new. It will be more important than ever to maintain records of chemical components that each **stock-keeping unit (SKU)** or part is made of. Since the

© designdepot_ltd/Shutterstock

Figure 10.6 ERP systems act as the hub for managing inventory, order management, HR, manufacturing, and other enterprise systems. Any change to these systems impacts ERM.

inventory of spare parts is much lower, the need for raw materials increases. ERP systems will need accurate forecasting models to determine how much raw materials to hold and the availability of 3D printers.

Just like any new technology that gains traction in business, 3D printers will impact more parts of the business. This technology will transform industries—some in unexpected ways.

Sources: Compiled from Fine (2014), Bourne (2014), goldmansachs.com (2014), Gartner.com (2014), *The Engineer* (2014), Cole (2014), and Cohen et al. (2014).

Questions

1. What do the leading research and investment firms forecast for 3D printing?
2. Why is 3D printing more appropriately called additive manufacturing?
3. Is 3D printing better suited for high or low volumes of production? Explain your answer.
4. In what situations is 3D printing most valuable?
5. How would you benefit from 3D printing?
6. How can 3D printing make some types of traditional manufacturing obsolete?
7. Do you consider 3D printing an important technology? Explain.

10.1 Enterprise Systems

Core business processes include accounting, finance, sales, marketing, human resources, inventory, productions, and manufacturing.

Customer lifetime value (CLV) is a formula for estimating the dollar value, or worth, of a long-term relationship with a customer.

A **Value-added reseller (VAR)** customizes or adds features to a vendor's software or equipment and resells the enhanced product.

Enterprise systems refer to a category of information systems that run an enterprise's operations and integrate **core business processes**. Enterprise systems link the enterprise with suppliers, business partners, and customers. Primary enterprise systems are:

- **Enterprise resource planning (ERP)**
- **Supply chain management (SCM)**
- **Customer relationship management (CRM)**

The major enterprise systems are described in Table 10.2. Companies implement most or all of these systems.

For maximum benefit, these systems are integrated to share data. For example, the integration of ERP and SCM improves inventory management and supply chain performance; and by integrating CRM and KM, companies can capitalize on their data by calculating **customer lifetime value (CLV)**. Another advantage of enterprise systems is that processes can be automated for consistency and efficiency.

IMPLEMENTATION CHALLENGES OF ENTERPRISE SYSTEMS

Interface means to connect to and exchange data with apps and systems.

Implementing an enterprise system is complex, time-consuming, and typically requires the help of a consulting firm, vendor, or **value-added reseller (VAR)**. Integrating legacy systems with cloud-based applications is complex, as described in Tech Note 10.1. Much of the complexity is due to getting new apps or system modules to **interface** with existing or legacy systems that are several generations older.

TABLE 10.2 Enterprise Systems and Their Functions

Name	Abbreviation	Description
Enterprise resource planning	ERP	ERP is the software infrastructure that integrates an enterprise's internal applications, supports its external business processes, and links to its external business partners. ERP systems are commercial software packages that integrate business processes, including supply chains, manufacturing, financial, human resources, budgeting, sales, and customer service.
Supply chain management	SCM	SCM software supports the steps in the supply chain—procurement, sourcing, manufacturing, storage, inventory control, scheduling, order fulfillment, and distribution. SCM improves decision making, forecasting, optimization, and analysis.
Customer relationship management	CRM	CRM systems help create a total view of customers to maximize share-of-wallet and profitability. CRM is also a business strategy to segment and manage customers to optimize customer lifetime value (CLV).

TECH NOTE 10.1 Data Transfers to Mainframes

Enterprise systems are cross-functional and interorganizational systems that support the business strategy.

Enterprise systems require data transfers—often to mainframes. Designing enterprise-level systems involves a variety of components that had been implemented on mainframes, midrange computers, networks, or cloud environments. In most large enterprises, mainframes are the workhorse systems that run the majority of business transactions. In contrast, customer interfaces through customer service; ERP, CRM, and SCM apps; websites; and B2B interactions are usually on distributed systems or in the cloud. Many times seemingly well-planned projects fail and require extensive reworking because integration issues had not been properly planned.

Legacy systems are older information systems that have been maintained over several decades because they fulfill critical needs.

Some enterprises choose to avoid the challenges of integration by creating a new system that replaces the full functionality of the old one. This option is the most costly, difficult, and risky. An advantage is that this option offers a longer-term solution that is agile to respond to changing business needs. Despite that potential payoff, complete replacement requires a large up-front investment for development, poses difficulties in duplicating behavior of the **legacy system**, and increases the risk of complete software project failure.

WHY COMPANIES INVEST IN ENTERPRISE SYSTEMS

Companies tend to migrate to an enterprise solution when they need to consolidate their disparate systems, such as when limitations caused by their existing legacy systems interfere with performance or the ability to compete. IT at Work 10.1 is an example. Here are major reasons why companies replace parts of their legacy systems or supplement them with enterprise systems. It is important to realize that many companies do not have the resources to replace all their legacy systems.

- **High maintenance costs.** Maintaining and upgrading legacy systems are some of the most difficult challenges facing CIOs (chief information officers) and IT departments.
- **Inflexibility.** Legacy architectures were not designed for flexibility. These huge systems cannot be easily redesigned to share data with newer systems, unlike modern architectures.
- **Integration obstacles.** Legacy systems execute business processes that are hardwired by rigid, predefined process flows. Their hardwiring makes integration with other systems such as CRM and Web-based applications difficult and sometimes impossible.
- **Lack of staff.** IT departments find it increasingly difficult to hire staff who are qualified to work on mainframes and applications written in languages no longer used by the latest technologies.
- **Cloud.** The cloud has lowered up-front costs. Cloud-based enterprise systems can be a good fit for companies facing upgrades to their legacy ERP and other enterprise systems.

IT at Work 10.1

Organic Valley Does Business Better with Enterprise System

Organic Valley Family of Farms is the largest U.S. cooperative (co-op) of organic farmers and one of the nation's leading organic brands. The co-op represents over 1,300 family farms in 34 states and Canada. Its mission is to keep small and mid-sized farmers farming. Organic Valley produces over 200 organic foods, including organic milk, soy, cheese, butter, eggs, produce, juice, and meats, which are sold in supermarkets, natural foods stores, and food co-ops, and as ingredients for other organic food manufacturers nationwide. One of the biggest challenges for Organic Valley had been managing growth in the face of increasing competition from larger companies.

Need to Consolidate Disparate Systems

Organic Valley needed to consolidate its disparate systems into one enterprise solution to improve operating efficiencies and maintain the high quality of its line of perishable food products. The company had been doing planning using spreadsheets; separately, it completed its financials, order management, and inventory on an enterprise system designed for discrete manufacturing. As operations expanded, it needed to make a major leap in business systems.

Organic Valley also needed a solution with enough flexibility and versatility to manage the company's dairy, produce, meat, and egg lines of business, all of which have different and unique requirements.

Use of a Consultant and Vendor

Organic Valley hired a consultant during the selection process to help identify the most important functions and features, such as shelf-life management and expiration date management. Based on these requirements, three possible vendors were identified. Organic Valley and its consultant agreed that the solutions offered by the vendor Infor best fit its business.

Doing Business Better

The company now has one integrated system to support all business processes across all of its lines of business. With the Infor enterprise solution, Organic Valley is much more agile on the technical side, and this has given it the ability to support rapid business growth. The company projects savings of $2 million per year through improved supply chain planning and other operational efficiencies.

Questions

1. Why did Organic Valley need an enterprise system?
2. What factors contributed to the successful implementation and outcomes? Explain their importance.
3. Enterprise systems are expensive. What factor helped justify the investment?
4. Using spreadsheets for planning is rather common. Why do you think companies use stand-alone spreadsheets for planning?

IMPLEMENTATION BEST PRACTICES

Implementing best practices involves changes in the management of processes, people, and existing systems. Three required changes are as follows:

1. **Redesign of business processes.** Processes need to be simplified and redesigned so that they can be automated, either totally or partially. Tasks that are no longer necessary are removed from the processes.
2. **Changes in how people perform their jobs.** Jobs and how they are performed will change to accommodate the new processes. Enterprise systems require retraining users whose productivity will drop initially as they adjust to a new way of doing their jobs.
3. **Integration of many types of information systems.** Integrating information systems is necessary so that data can flow seamlessly among departments and business partners. Automated data flows are essential to productivity improvements.

A best practice is to examine the inefficiencies in existing processes to find ways to improve on or significantly simplify the process. For example, manual document-intensive processes such as order entry and billing create major headaches for workers. These processes require users to manually review documents for approval, enter data from those documents into a back-office system, and then make decisions. Automated order entry systems track customer orders from the time of initial order placement through the completion of those orders, and perform backorder processing, analysis, invoicing, and billing.

Common ways to overcome implementation complexity are to lease or license from vendors. The trend toward ERP SaaS (software as a service) continues to increase. In fact, the term ERP commonly refers to commercially available software systems.

ENTERPRISE SYSTEMS INSIGHTS

Here are three other insights related to enterprise systems to better understand the current state of enterprise systems and their potential.

1. One of the IT department's most important roles is to provide and support applications that enable workers to access, use, and understand data. These applications need to be tightly aligned with well-defined and well-designed business processes—a standard that few enterprises are able to achieve.
2. Customer loyalty helps drive profits, but only for customers who are profitable to the company. Many companies do not know how to recognize or encourage the kind of customer loyalty that is worth having. Using data about buying behaviors (e.g., amount spent per month; purchase of high-margin products; return activity; and demands for customer service) helps a company identify its loyal customers and which ones are profitable.
3. Companies worldwide spend billions of dollars in the design and implementation of enterprise systems. Huge investments are made in ERP systems from vendors such as SAP, Oracle JD Edwards, Sage ERP, EVO~ERP, Infor, and NetSuite to create an integrated global supply chain. Interorganizational ISs play a major role in improving communication and integration among firms in a global supply chain.

Questions

1. Explain the purpose of an enterprise system.
2. Describe three types of enterprise systems.
3. What is customer lifetime value (CLV)?
4. What is a value-added reseller (VAR)?
5. What are two challenges of legacy systems?
6. Why do companies migrate to enterprise systems?
7. Explain the challenges of enterprise system implementation.
8. Explain the three types of changes needed when an enterprise system is implemented.

10.2 Enterprise Social Platforms

Social media has rewired the way we connect with people, information, breaking news, work, entertainment, and things. **Enterprise social** refers to private (company-owned) social media, software, platforms, or apps specially designed for use by business leaders and employees to fulfill the strategic mission. As of 2014, enterprise social technology had made it easier for employees to connect and collaborate with others, stay informed, build relationships, and share documents and data.

GROWTH OF ENTERPRISE SOCIAL INVESTMENTS AND MARKETS

In 2011 Forrester conducted its first-ever evaluation of enterprise social platform vendors. According to the report *The Forrester Wave: Enterprise Social Platforms, Q3 2011* (Koplowitz, 2011), there was a noticeable change in IT investments. Specifically, 25 percent had planned to invest in enterprise systems, while 37 percent had planned investments in enterprise social platforms and collaboration tools. There were three main reasons for greater interest in enterprise social:

1. **Knowledge management:** To capture and reuse knowledge within the enterprise
2. **Collaboration:** Maintain human connections across a disparate workforce
3. **Employee pressure:** Pressure from workers to use the social technologies they preferred to use

The trend is toward more informal communication methods in organizations. Companies seek to integrate and embed social into primary enterprise solutions to support business-critical decisions and more social workflows as an alternative to existing communication channels.

Yammer is a social network geared toward enterprises. Employees collaborate across departments, locations, and business apps.

SharePoint is a collaborative and social platform from Microsoft.

Vendors in the enterprise social market have been responding to growing demand. In 2012 Microsoft acquired the four-year-old company Yammer for $1.2 billion. The Yammer deal put Microsoft further into the market of developing social media services specifically for enterprises, an area in which companies such as Oracle, Salesforce, and IBM have actively invested. Microsoft's General Manager Jared Spataro told the audience at the SharePoint Conference that "Microsoft is all in on Yammer and SharePoint." **Yammer** is the social collaboration tool of choice for **SharePoint** going forward (Ryan, 2014). Employees can interact socially while doing work at the same time. Figure 10.7 shows the landing page for Yammer.

| SHAREPOINT

SharePoint was initially released by Microsoft in 2001, and by 2015, 75 percent of Fortune 500 firms were using it. SharePoint is difficult to define because it is not a single software program, but rather a platform for multiple kinds of programs and apps. The platform is a back-end system that links employees' computers and mobile devices to make it easy to communicate and to synchronize their efforts. At

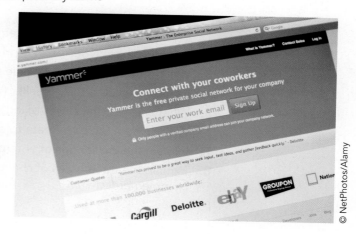

© NetPhotos/Alamy

Figure 10.7 Yammer enterprise social network website. Over 400,000 companies worldwide have integrated enterprise social into the way people already work.

Microsoft Cloud provides a hybrid infrastructure and capabilities to manage enterprise apps and data.

companies that have their SharePoint on-premises, they are now considered legacy systems. SharePoint in the **Microsoft Cloud** is the later version. Microsoft continues to enhance the Office 365 version of SharePoint and Yammer at a much faster pace than SharePoint 2013 on-premises.

SharePoint has the following social capabilities.

Intranet and Extranet

Intranets are the internal-facing sites everyone in a company logs into to find news, announcements, scheduled tasks, and access to files and data. Dashboards are customized by department and role to control access. SharePoint also provides tools for setting up employee social network platforms and company wikis. SharePoint can be used to set up a secure, access-controlled extranet site to share with external partners in the supply chain, contractors, and so on.

Documents

SharePoint provides a shared space to store documents, so they are not siloed on any one person's hard drive or device. Documents stored on SharePoint can be accessed by anyone in the company—unless the administrator has limited access. SharePoint enables coworkers to work simultaneously on a single document, save previous versions, and track updates.

Collaboration and Business Intelligence

The platform makes it easy for users to stay up-to-date and to coordinate their efforts on projects from any desktop or mobile device; and to discover patterns and insights in enterprise data.

Yammer

Yammer is "Facebook for business." The platform has features similar to Facebook likes, newsfeeds, threaded conversation, and direct messaging. This private social channel helps employees, partners, and customers communicate; exchange information; and collaborate across departments, locations, and business apps.

Smart companies connect their employees' desire to contribute and interact with peers with their own need to get timely feedback from the trenches. Red Robin, discussed in IT at Work 10.2, learned the benefits of Yammer for entry-level employees. Six recommendations for realizing business value from enterprise social networking are listed in Table 10.3.

TABLE 10.3 Recommendations to Realize Business Value from Enterprise Social

1. **Make sure management is listening.** Leaders and decision makers need to monitor social chatter to keep informed and respond promptly.

2. **Provide visible feedback and rewards.** Employee participation is largely driven by the desire to be recognized by peers and managers.

3. **Brand the social network.** Employees want to feel the company is behind the initiative. At Red Robin, for example, renaming Yammer to Yummer connected employees to the brand.

4. **Identify and leverage change agents.** Start with those employees most eager to participate, especially Millennials who are looking for recognition and purpose.

5. **Introduce competitions and games.** Experience shows that people are more likely to engage when they are having fun.

6. **Make the rules of engagement simple.** Do not overengineer or control the social network. Make it easy to enroll and participate.

At the first ever YamJam Conference in 2012, Yammer's CEO and founder introduced the new platform **Enterprise Graph**—calling it an enhanced way for business to be more social. Enterprise Graph tries to show how users are related to one another. It enables developers and customers to seamlessly connect people, conversations, and data across all their business services. With Enterprise Graph, Yammer solves the **social network sprawl** problem, which is when businesses end up interacting with multiple social networks inside their own company. The objective is to develop a standard that brings everything together and works off the same database.

Office Graph and Oslo App

Microsoft's newer project, code-named Oslo, builds on the concept of the Enterprise Graph. One of the significant features of Yammer is how it maps the relationships between people and information by simply recording likes, posts, replies, shares, and uploads. Microsoft applied these capabilities to Office with **Office Graph.** Office Graph uses signals from e-mail, social conversations, documents, sites, instant messages, meetings, and more to map the relationships between people and concepts. By tapping into Office Graph, Oslo provides a natural way for users to navigate, discover, and search people, information, and knowledge across the enterprise.

IT at Work 10.2

Red Robin Transforms Its Business with Yammer

Red Robin Gourmet Burgers, Inc. is a casual dining restaurant chain serving an innovative selection of high-quality gourmet burgers in a family-friendly atmosphere. In Q1 2014, revenues were $340.5 million, representing an increase of 11.1 percent over Q1 2013. Revenue at comparable restaurants had increased only 5.4 percent. The restaurant's operating profit, as a percent of restaurant revenue, increased to 22.4 percent in 2014 from 21.5 percent in 2013.

FRONT-LINE STAFF KNOW CUSTOMERS BEST

In retail and restaurants, front-line employees understand the customer experience far better than managers in remote corporate offices. Yet companies often do not pay close attention to their front-line staff. Corporate culture is part of the reason, but a lot has to do with the absence of a channel for employees to be heard. With over 20,000 employees working in 355 restaurants in 42 states, Red Robin's new management team decided to give front-line employees a voice. In 2010 the company invested in enterprise social networking, in part, to reduce the high cost of employee turnover that is common in the restaurant business.

ENGAGING EMPLOYEES WITH YAMMER

Millennials were born between the early 1980s and the early 2000s.

Newly hired Senior VP of Business Transformation and CIO Chris Laping believed that the company's workers—87 percent are **Millennials**—were searching for meaning. So engaging these workers in a meaningful way would create the atmosphere that strengthened employee loyalty.

Laping selected Yammer as the private social channel for employees, partners, and customers. The free version of Yammer was initially rolled out as a social experiment, to see if employees would engage. A few employees were invited to join Yammer. After they were urged to invite colleagues, membership spread quickly. Eventually, two Yammer networks emerged at Red Robin: namely *Yummer*, a network for restaurant managers, regional managers, and corporate office members to exchange information and answer questions from field staff, and *Yummversity*, a network for training employees. Yummer gave a voice to the silent front-line workers at Red Robin. Prior to Yammer, these employees would pass information up the company management chain, but they rarely received feedback on the information or what was done in response to it.

Better Burgers Through Yummer and Yummversity

In 2012 Red Robin introduced a new menu item, the Tavern Double burger. It did not receive customer feedback via Facebook, as expected. However, restaurant servers and regional managers posted what they heard from customers on Yammer. Managers at headquarters monitor Yammer so they immediately knew the burger recipe needed to be adjusted.

They were able to respond with an updated menu within four weeks at much lower cost. Prior to Yammer, this feedback loop took 6 to 12 months, and involved running expensive focus groups and surveys, hiring outside consultants, scheduling review sessions, and generating reports.

MINING EMPLOYEES' IDEAS

"Blueprint Project" was a CEO-led initiative to uncover the best employee idea to cut expenses and not negatively impact customer experience. A $1,000 prize was announced and thousands of employees contributed ideas. The winning entry was submitted by a Seattle location manager who proposed replacing disposable kid beverage cups with reusable ones. According to Laping, this minor change was "a six figure savings for the organization."

Sources: Compiled from Red Robin website (2014) and Lavenda (2014).

Questions

1. Why are employees a source of valuable information? In your opinion, why are employees an untapped resource at many companies?
2. How does Yammer capture BI from employees?
3. Explain Yummer and Yummversity. Why would employees want to use them?

4. What is the expected benefit of naming the enterprise social platform, as Red Robin had done?
5. How did Red Robin motivate its employees to contribute to the enterprise social net?
6. How did the restaurant reduce employee turnover?

ORACLE'S SOCIAL NETWORK

Oracle's social enterprise network connects processes, professionals, and enterprise apps in one place. Users can update CRM leads, communicate in real time, and search for key experts on the network. The social net also makes sharing files and information easy with sales teams and company members. Employees can work on documents together in real time, while having the option to access them anytime. Conversations and CRM data on the network can be accessed through Microsoft Outlook and mobile devices.

JIVE

Jive's enterprise social platform provides tools for communication, sharing, and content creation to make social media monitoring and engagement easier. The platform features activity streams that keep employees updated and a text editor for users to create, review, and edit documents as a team.

Jive also has an enterprise search engine that offers social graph analytics and insight into make searching easier. Users can search across their customer network and SharePoint as well. Employees can also create blogs and custom attention streams to track specific people, projects, or groups.

CHATTER

Chatter is an add-on to Saleforce.com, a CRM tool. As with all other enterprise social platforms, Chatter offers companies their own private network while pushing updates and news in real time to user feeds. The software offers smart search, which places items an employee frequently uses higher in the search list.

Like many enterprises, if someone was trying to solve a problem or get feedback on a presentation, he or she would send out a global e-mail. Some people would reply to everyone, some would just reply to the sender, the e-mail thread gets jumbled—and quickly becomes a mess. With Chatter, the problem-solving process becomes a conversation rather than a series of disjointed e-mails. People can interact and spark new ideas. There is no confusion over which is the latest version of a document. Other employees can be brought into the conversation using the @ function. The whole process is just a much smarter way of working.

Chatter customer groups let users work with external customers, vendors, and partners, with the option of limiting what they can see and access. Private groups can also be set up when employees need to work on sensitive projects with certain colleagues.

Business processes can be approved from within a Chatter feed along with vacation requests or hiring decisions.

The features of enterprise social will continue to evolve and disrupt existing applications and the future of work.

Questions

1. What are the basic functions of an enterprise social platform?
2. What are the capabilities of SharePoint?
3. In what ways can enterprises realize value from Yammer or other enterprise social?
4. How do Office Graph and Enterprise Graph support collaboration?
5. How does Chatter enable workers to solve problems?

10.3 Enterprise Resource Planning Systems

ERP originated in the 1990s as a means to integrate accounting, finance, HR, marketing, and other critical business functions. ERPs were devised to help managers run a business. Ideally, each business function would access a centralized database instead of data silos. In many cases, the ERP was bought, installed, and configured by a vendor who supplied the entire suite of applications, or modules, for manufacturing, distribution, retail, and service organizations. Early ERPs ran on client–server architectures and custom-designed apps that accessed the shared database servers.

Then, like most modern business software, ERP systems migrated to a Web-based architecture. Users accessed the ERP via a Web browser from within the company or accessed it externally via the Internet using a secured encrypted virtual private network (VPN).

ERP Today

ERP is now a mature technology, whose core components have not changed much. What has changed are the way ERPs are deployed—on-premises, in the cloud, or as a managed service—and users' expectations. The latest ERP solutions are designed with a focus on social collaboration, deployment flexibility, faster response, and accessibility from mobile devices. They have touch-enabled user interfaces designed to work with all touch-screen devices. New apps and mobile add-ons enable:

- sales associates to process orders, take payments, and collect signatures with an iPad app.
- field technicians to provide customer service from anywhere.
- marketing to manage every aspect of ongoing customer relationships using a smartphone app.
- production to access to the real time information needed to reduce stock-outs and excess inventory.
- customers to access, pay, and view invoices online.

The worldwide ERP software market grew almost 4 percent in 2013 and 2.2 percent in 2012 (Cole, 2014). SAP remained the ERP market leader, with ERP sales of $6.1 billion in 2013. Next in the market are Oracle with sales of $3.1 billion; Sage with $1.5 billion in sales; Infor with $1.5 billion; and Microsoft with $1.2 billion.

From a technology perspective, ERP is the software infrastructure that links an enterprise's internal applications and supports its external business processes. Departments stay informed about what is ongoing in other departments that impact its operations or performance. Knowing about problem situations and being able to work around them saves time and expense, and preserves good customer relations. For example, using ERP, a manufacturer shares the database of parts, products, production capacities, schedules, backorders, and trouble spots. Responding quickly and correctly to materials shortages, spikes in customer demand, or other contingencies means that small initial problems are solved instead of allowing them to be amplified down the line. Another example of the value of ERP is described in IT at Work 10.3.

In Figure 10.8, you see how an ERP fits into an enterprise's IT infrastructure. The core ERP functions are integrated with other systems or modules, such as SCM and CRM. An **enterprise application integration (EAI)** layer enables the ERP to interface with legacy apps. EAI is middleware that connects and acts as a go-between for applications and their business processes.

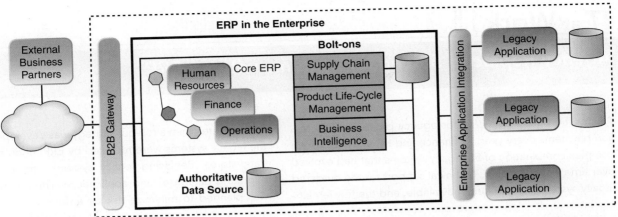

Figure 10.8 Overview of the complexity of ERP and its interfaces with other enterprise systems (U.S. Army Business Transformation Knowledge Center, 2009).

Acquisition

ERPs are not built in-house or built using proprietary software because the costs and time to do so would be staggering. Typically, ERP systems are acquired by purchasing or leasing in a SaaS arrangement. (You will read about IS acquisition and contracts in Chapter 11.) All ERPs must be customized to the company's specifications. Here are two examples:

- Boers & Co Fine Metalworking in the Netherlands has been manufacturing fine mechanical parts, high-precision assembly, and sheet metal products for over 100 years. The company implemented Epicor ERP to access real time data for everything from the shop floor to finance. All business operations from the front office through production, receiving and shipping, to order entry and cash receipts are handled by the ERP.

- Peters Ice Cream in Australia had been under the ownership of food giant Nestlé and was working under its ERP. That ERP was not tailored for the specific needs of an ice cream company and did not interface well with Peters's legacy systems. Peters's network of freezers extends throughout Australia, and to get the ice cream flavors where they were needed when they are needed, it was essential that information on stock levels and deliveries be accurate and in real time. Peters selected Infor's M3 QuickStep for Food and Beverage ERP solution because 70 percent of the necessary business processes were already preconfigured within it. With preconfigured business processes, Peters was able to implement its new ERP system in 8 months.

CAREER INSIGHT 10.1

ERP Consultant: One of the Best Jobs in America

CNNMoney and PayScale publish a "Best Jobs in America" listing of the top 100 careers with big growth, great pay, and satisfying work (CNNMoney, 2013). ERP consultant was ranked #30, with a median pay of $103,000 and top income of $172,000. It was projected that ERP consultants would experience 10-year job growth of 22 percent and over 700,000 total jobs.

What do ERP consultants do all day? They advise companies on which systems best meet their current and future business needs, help with vendor selection and implementation of the system, and support the ERP and users after it has been installed.

IT at Work 10.3

Agency Replaced 50 Legacy Systems with an ERP

A large European public-sector agency processes 200 million payments every year. Its finance and HR systems were a complex combination of 50 legacy systems that had evolved over time without a plan. Technical support for the outdated legacy systems was no longer available, and the few remaining internal developers were near retirement. The agency had to replace this legacy architecture with an ERP system that could process the hundreds of millions of payments and support more than 70,000 users.

In the first phase of the ERP implementation project, the scope and budget of the ERP were approved, vendor proposals were evaluated, and a contract with the selected vendor was negotiated. These activities took almost a year to complete. Then a roll-out strategy was developed wherein the legacy systems were replaced by ERP modules and new data stores. Replacing legacy systems with ERP requires migrating databases and applications. The roll-out strategy was planned to minimize risk by ensuring that the agency met its strict legal requirements of having one leading accounting system at all times.

Implementing the ERP system across the agency took 2.5 years, and was delivered on time and budget, and at the desired quality level. Extensive planning, executive support, experienced consultants, and ERP-informed vendor selection were key success factors.

MANUFACTURING ERP SYSTEMS AND LEAN PRINCIPLES

Manufacturers know that their success depends on lower costs, shorter cycle times, and maximum production throughput. A key factor in lowering costs is inventory management—such as minimizing inventory errors and maintaining the optimal inventory level. An optimal level has enough inventory to keep production running while minimizing inventory-on-hand to control holding costs. ERP demand forecasting modules help manufacturers avoid material shortages, manage production, and coordinate distribution channels, which improves on-time delivery. Engineers, production floor workers, and those in the purchasing, finance, and delivery departments can access and share plans, production status, quality control, inventory, and other data in real time.

TECH NOTE 10.2 ERP and Vendor Selection

The website top10erp.org/ provides comparisons of top ERP vendors' products and their monthly costs.

To simplify and reduce the cost of the ERP software selection process, an annual event called the ERP Vendor Shootout (erpshootout.com) is held and geared toward ERP selection teams and decision makers for companies with manufacturing, distribution, or project-oriented requirements.

Four Rules for Selecting an ERP

ERPs are complex, but they are becoming more user-friendly. Other options are hosted ERP solutions, such as ERP Software-as-a-Service (SaaS), and cloud-based ERP. Still, ERPs are expensive, time-consuming implementations that require a lot of planning. Four rules to consider when selecting an ERP solution or software package are:

1. **Select an ERP solution that targets the company's requirements.** ERP packages are tailored for organizations based on their size and industry. Midmarket solutions have more sophisticated capabilities than packages for small businesses; large enterprise packages are the most complex. It is important to choose an ERP that can support critical functions of the organization, such as accounting or inventory management.

2. **Evaluate potential ERP vendors' strengths and weaknesses.** Check how many customers each vendor has, its financial health (you do not want to select a vendor on the brink of bankruptcy), and whether it has experience in the specific industry, and how the ERP can scale as the company grows.

3. **Meet with each vendor and get a hands-on demo of its ERP solutions.** Demos allow employees to experience the usability of each ERP module and how well the ERP would support business processes.

4. **Calculate the ERP's total cost of ownership (TCO).** The cost of the ERP or the monthly SaaS fee is only the beginning of the calculation. The TCO also includes implementation, customization, management services, training, additional hardware and networks, additional bandwidth for a Web-based product, and IT staff.

ERP IMPLEMENTATIONS MAY NOT BE INITIALLY SUCCESSFUL

Managers and other decision makers tend to think that if an enterprise system works for leading companies, it will work for them, too. But that is not true. In fact, as you read in Table 10.3, several of the best companies have suffered devastating consequences that led to multimillion dollar losses, bankruptcy, or lawsuits. Most often, the ERP is eventually fixed and remains in use, which gives the false impression that the ERP was successful from the start.

The success of an ERP depends on organizational and technological factors that occur prior to, during, and after its implementation. Knowing what to do and what not to do are important. Both the successes and failures teach valuable lessons, too, as you will learn in this section.

Be aware that reading vendor white papers and viewing webcasts or demos may give you a biased view of the benefits of ERP software. You need to conduct your own research to learn the full story behind an enterprise system implementation. Problems may be skipped over or ignored. While blogs and YouTube posts may be good sources of objective data, many vendors have blogs and YouTube videos that are designed to appear neutral, when in fact they are not.

ERP Disasters and Failures

ERP implementations are complex—and risky. Planning, deploying, or fine-tuning these complex business software systems for your company is such a large undertaking that such projects fail more than 50 to 70 percent of the time. Those are not encouraging statistics. ERP failures have made it impossible to ship products and, at the extreme, have led to bankruptcy. Many ERP projects have ended up in litigation, the headlines, and out-of-court settlements. Dell canceled an ERP system after spending two years and $200 million on its implementation. Hershey Food Corp. filed highly publicized lawsuits against its ERP vendors for a failed implementation. Table 10.4 describes recent ERP failures that have led to lawsuits against vendors or consulting firms. Of course, lawsuits do not result in a working ERP.

TABLE 10.4 ERP Failures, Lawsuits, and Damages

Companies Filing the Lawsuit and Companies Sued	Description of ERP Disasters, Charges, and Outcomes
Distributor **ScanSource** filed a lawsuit in 2013 against **Avanade**, the joint venture between Accenture and Microsoft, for "bait-and-switch" tactics.	A half-million lines of custom code were not enough to produce a viable Microsoft Dynamics AX ERP system for point-of-sale and RFID products distributor ScanSource, according to a lawsuit ScanSource has filed against Avanade. AX is one of four ERP products sold under the Dynamics brand, and is aimed at larger companies. The lawsuit alleges: • The project was supposed to cost $17 million and take 11 months, but the cost estimate grew to $66 million and it had failed to go live after 3 years. • Avanade misrepresented the skills of its consultants in order to win the contract; then sent in a continually changing cast of consultants without the expertise to do the job or familiarity with AX. ScanSource terminated the contact with Avanade in September 2012 and hired another company to fix the problems at an additional cost of $58 to $72 million.
Dillard's, Inc. filed a suit against **JDA Software Group**.	Dillard's alleged that i2 failed to meet obligations regarding two software-license agreements for which the department store had paid $8 million. In June 2010 JDA Software Group Inc. reported that its i2 Technologies unit lost the case and was ordered to pay $246 million in damages.
FoxMeyer Drugs was a $5 billion company and the nation's fourth largest distributor of pharmaceuticals before the ERP failure.	FoxMeyer's ERP could not process the transactions needed to supply its customers with their orders. FoxMeyer had been processing 425,000 invoice lines per day on its legacy software. The company's ERP was limited to 10,000 invoice lines per day. This quickly decreased order processing capability, sent the company into bankruptcy protection, and ultimately shut down the business.
FoxMeyer sued **SAP**, the ERP vendor, and **Andersen Consulting**, its SAP integrator, for $500 million each in 1998.	Implementation was troubled almost from the start. Despite warnings from Woltz Consulting, during the early stages of the project, that a schedule for the entire implementation to be completed in 18 months was totally unrealistic, FoxMeyer went ahead with the vendor's planned implementation.

ERP Success Factors

What factors increase the likelihood of ERP success and minimize the risk of problems? Many managers assume that success or failure depends on the software and, furthermore, that a failure is the fault of the software that is purchased or licensed. In reality, 95 percent of a project's success or failure lies in the hands of the company implementing the software, not the software vendor.

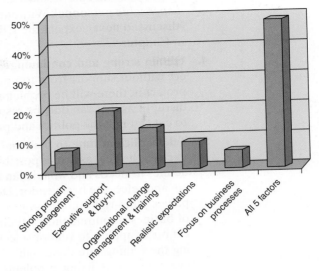

Survey responses to the question:
What is most important to successful ERP projects?

Figure 10.9 Experts identify the combination of factors needed for ERP success.

The results of a survey to identify what ERP experts had found to be most important to successful ERP projects are shown in Figure 10.9. ERP experts were given the following six options and asked to select only one of them as "most important":

1. Strong program management: 6 percent
2. Executive support and buy-in: 19 percent
3. Organizational change management and training :13 percent
4. Realistic expectations: 8 percent
5. Focus on business processes: 5 percent
6. Interaction of all five factors: 49 percent

Nearly half of the experts indicated that the failure of any one of the five factors significantly increases the risk of ERP failure.

The following recommendations explain why ERP success depends on several key factors being met:

1. **Focus on business processes and requirements.** Too often, companies get caught up in technical capabilities or platforms on which the ERP runs. But compared to business processes, none of this really matters. What matters is how managers want business operations to run and what the key business requirements are. Once management and IT have defined them, they can intelligently choose the software, modules, and vendor that fit their unique business needs.

2. **Focus on achieving a measurable ROI.** Developing a business case to get approval from upper management or the board of directors is essential, but not sufficient. Establish key performance measures, set baselines and targets for those measures, and then track performance after going live. The performance results are proof of how well the ERP meets the expectations that had been listed in the business case.

3. **Use a strong project management approach and secure commitment of resources.** An ERP project depends on how it is managed. Responsibility for the management of the ERP implementation project cannot be transferred to vendors or consulting firms. Because of the business disruption and cost involved, ERP projects require the full-time attention and support of high-profile champions on the key functions for a long period of time, from 6 to

12 months on average. It is also known that ERP projects cannot be managed by people who *can be spared*. They must be managed by people who are *indispensable* personnel. Without powerful champions and an adequate budget (discussed next), expect the ERP to fail. Project management will be covered in Chapter 13.

4. **Obtain strong and continuing commitment from senior executives.** Any project without support from top management will fail. No matter how well run a project is, there will be problems such as conflicting business needs or business disruptions that can only be resolved by someone with the power and authority to cut through the politics and personal agendas.

5. **Take sufficient time to plan and prepare up-front.** An ERP vendor's motive is to close the deal as fast as possible. The company needs to make sure it correctly defines its needs and what it can afford to achieve in order to intelligently evaluate and select the best vendor. Do not be rushed into a decision. Too often, companies jump right into a project without validating the vendor's understanding of business requirements or their project plan. The principle of "measure twice, cut once" applies to vendor selection. The more time the company spends ensuring these things are done right at the start, the lower the risk of failure and the less time spent fixing problems later. Filing a lawsuit against a vendor (see Table 10.4) is not a fix. Lawsuits are both expensive and risky, and contribute nothing to the company's performance.

6. **Provide thorough training and change management.** Another key principle to understand is that when you design an ERP, you redesign the organization. ERP systems involve dramatic change for workers. ERPs lose value if people do not understand how to use them effectively. Investing in training, change management, and job design are crucial to the outcome of any large-scale IT project.

Questions

1. What are three ways ERP can be deployed?
2. Briefly describe the latest ERP features and add-ons.
3. Describe ERP from a technology perspective.
4. Explain manufacturing ERP systems and lean principles.
5. List and briefly describe three ERP implementation success factors.
6. Describe causes or factors that contribute to ERP failure.

10.4 Supply Chain Management Systems

Supply chain starts with the acquisition of raw materials or the procurement (purchase) of products and proceeds through manufacture, transport, and delivery—and the disposal or recycling of products.

The journey that a product travels, as shown in Figure 10.10, starting with raw material suppliers and then to manufacturers or assemblers, distributors and retail shelves, and ultimately to customers, is its **supply chain**. The supply chain is like a pipeline composed of multiple suppliers, distributors, manufacturers, retailers, and logistics providers.

Supply chains vary significantly depending on the type, complexity, and perishability of the product. For example, in a simplified sense, the food supply chain begins with the livestock or farm, moves to the manufacturer, then through the distribution centers and wholesalers to the retailer and final customer. In IT at Work 10.4, you read about the benefits of tracking food along the supply chain.

© arka38/Shutterstock

Supply chain management (SCM) is the efficient management of the flows of material, data, and payments along the companies in the supply chain, from suppliers to consumers. SCM systems are configured to achieve the following business goals:

- To reduce uncertainty and variability in order to improve the accuracy of forecasting.
- To increase control over processes in order to achieve optimal inventory levels, cycle time, and customer service.

An example of these goals is discussed in IT at Work 10.5.

Figure 10.10 Model of the supply chain.

IT at Work 10.4

Got Contaminated Food? How Do You Know?

The Food and Drug Administration (FDA) posts Recalls, Market Withdrawals, & Safety Alerts on its website FDA.gov. Almost every day, a recall or alert is posted for human or pet food, drugs, and life-saving devices. A few food contamination alerts posted by the FDA were: listeria in shelled walnuts from California Grown and hummus dips from Trader Joe's, and salmonella in Dragonfly's crushed chili powder and Owl Canyon's eggs—both are potentially fatal. When food contaminations are detected, being able to trace those foods to their sources or track them to retailers or end-consumers takes on a sense of urgency.

Track and Trace to Identify the Scope Accurately and with Confidence

Track-and-trace technologies follow food products "from farm to fork" throughout their supply chain, primarily using barcodes and radio frequency identification (RFID). Without the capability to identify the scope of the contamination and contain it, the food recall is much more extensive than necessary as a safety precaution. For example, when *E. coli*–tainted spinach was discovered in 2007, using the bar code on a bag of bad spinach, investigators traced its origin to California's Salinas Valley. But then they had to do an intense and expensive search for the specific grower in that valley. Because of the uncertainty during the investigation, all spinach products were pulled from grocery stores, distribution

and processing plants, and restaurants and then destroyed. One growers' organization estimates that the recall cost the spinach industry $74 million. It would have been much faster to track the contaminated leaves to the grower if spinach bags and containers had carried RFID tags with complete histories of the contents' origins.

Value of Tracking Capability in the Supply Chain

With tracking information, companies can streamline the distribution chain and lower spoilage and contamination rates. Reducing the rates of spoilage and contamination is important for reasons related to safety and costs. Consumer product and retail industries lose about $40 billion annually, or 3.5 percent of their sales, due to supply chain inefficiencies.

Questions

1. Visit the FDA's website and select "recalls." What do you learn?
2. Select three food recalls. How could those products be tracked and traced?
3. Consider a food that is an ingredient, such as chili pepper, and perishable food, such as beef patties. Which would be more difficult to track and trace? Explain.
4. What costs are reduced during a contaminated food recall if the food has RFID tags?

IT at Work 1 0 . 5

Managing the U.S. Munitions Supply Chain

Munitions Supply Chain Management

The Joint Munitions Command (JMC) is a major part of the U.S. Army Materiel Command (AMC). **Munitions** are the weaponry hardware, vehicles, and equipment and their ammunition. JMC supports U.S. warfighters by managing the *munitions supply chain* to get the right munitions at the right place at the right time. JMC manufactures, procures, stores, and transports tanks, weaponry, howitzers, and other munitions (see Figure 10.11) as well as bullets, artillery shells, and other ammunition to locations worldwide.

Supply Chain Challenges

JMC provides bombs and bullets to America's fighting forces—all services, all types of conventional ammunition from 500-pound bombs to rifle rounds. JMC manages plants that produce more than 1.6 billion rounds of ammunition annually and the depots that store the nation's ammunition for training and combat.

Clearly, managing the munitions supply chain is extremely complex and critical. Like other supply chains, it depends on good relationships among suppliers in the network, the quality of supplier information, and communication channels.

JMC Improves Battle Readiness at Reduced Cost

JMC's project began with a focus on efficiency, but has resulted in increased warfighting readiness at reduced cost.

After transforming operations, integrating its supply chain, and improving data management, JMC is now better able to rapidly supply U.S. forces with the highest-quality munitions when they need them and to cut transportation costs up to 50 percent—a significant savings per year. These improvements were made possible as a result of greater asset visibility (tracking and monitoring), better forecasting and decision-making capabilities, communication, and collaboration along the supply chain.

Sources: Compiled from Schwerin (2012), Accenture (2010), and jmc.army.mil (2012).

Questions

1. Explain the role of the munitions supply chain.
2. Discuss how JMC ensures that soldiers receive the highest-quality ammunition, on time, and where needed.
3. Why would improvements in munitions supply chain management also improve warfighting readiness?
4. What factors impact the ability to manage the munitions supply chain?
5. For the JMC, where does the munitions supply chain start and where does it end?
6. Is munitions supply chain management unique, and if so, why? Or, is it similar to the management of any supply chains? Explain your position.

(a)   (b)

Photo by Josh Hamilton/DVIDS Media

Photo by Spc. Latoya Wiggins/DVIDS Media

Figure 10.11 JMC manages the supply chain of materials used in war (tanks, howitzers, weaponry) and ammunition (bullets, artillery shells).

MANAGING THE FLOW OF MATERIALS, DATA, AND MONEY

Supply chains involve the flow of materials, data, and money. Descriptions of these three main flows are as follows:

1. **Material or product flow:** This is the movement of materials and goods from a supplier to its consumer. For example, Ford supplies dealerships that, in turn, sell to end-users. Products that are returned make up what is called the **reverse supply chain** because goods are moving in the reverse direction.

2. **Information flow:** This is the movement of detailed data among members of the supply chain, for example, order information, customer information, order fulfillment, delivery status, and proof-of-delivery confirmation. Most information flows are done electronically, although paper invoices or receipts are still common for noncommercial customers.

3. **Financial flow:** This is the transfer of payments and financial arrangements, for example, billing payment schedules, credit terms, and payment via **electronic funds transfer (EFT).** EFT provides for electronic payments and collections. It is safe, secure, efficient, and less expensive than paper check payments and collections.

Supply chain links are managed. Think of the chain in terms of its links because the entire chain is not managed as a single unit. A company can only manage the links it actually touches. That is, a company will manage only partners who are one-back and one-up because that is the extent of what a company can manage.

ORDER FULFILLMENT AND LOGISTICS

Order fulfillment is the set of complex processes involved in providing customers with what they have ordered on time and all related customer services.

Back-office operations support the fulfillment of orders.

Order fulfillment depends on the type of product/service and purchase method (online, in-store, catalog, etc.). For example, a customer who has ordered a new appliance via the Sears.com wesite needs to receive it as scheduled, with assembly and operating instructions, and warranty and return information. The customer can receive a paper manual with the product or download the instructions from Sears' website.

Order fulfillment is a part of **back-office operations,** such as accounting, inventory management, and shipping, and is closely related to **front-office operations** or customer-facing activities. The key aspects of order fulfillment are the delivery of materials or products at the right time, to the right place, and at the right cost.

Logistics entails all the processes and information needed to move products from origin to destination efficiently. The order fulfillment process is part of logistics.

STEPS IN THE ORDER FULFILLMENT PROCESS

Front-office operations such as sales and advertising that are visible to customers.

The order fulfillment process starts when an order is received, and includes the following nine activities that are supported by SCM software or are automated:

Step 1: Make sure the customer will pay. Depending on the payment method and prior arrangements with the customer, verify that the customer can and will pay, and agrees to the payment terms. This activity is done by the finance department for B2B sales or an external company, such as PayPal or a credit card issuer such as Visa for B2C sales. Any holdup in payment may cause a shipment to be delayed, resulting in a loss of goodwill or a customer. In B2C, the customers usually pay by credit card, but with major credit card data theft at Target and other retailers, the buyer may be using a stolen card.

Step 2: Check in-stock availability and reorder as necessary. As soon as an order is received, the stock is checked to determine the availability of the product or materials. If there is not enough stock, the ordering system places an order, typically automatically using EDI (electronic data interchange). To perform these operations, the ordering system needs to interface with the inventory system.

Step 3: Arrange shipments. When the product is available, shipment to the customer is arranged (otherwise, go to Step 5). Products can be digital or physical. If the item is physical and available, packaging and shipment arrangements are made. Both the packaging/shipping department and internal shippers or outside transporters may be involved. Digital items are usually available because their "inventory" is not depleted. However, a digital product, such as software, may be under revision, and thus unavailable for delivery at certain times. In either case, information needs to flow among several partners.

Step 4: Insurance. The contents of a shipment may need to be insured. Both the finance department and an insurance company could be involved, and again, information needs to be exchanged with the customer and insurance agent.

Step 5: Replenishment. Customized orders will always trigger a need for some manufacturing or assembly operation. Similarly, if standard items are out of stock, they need to be produced or procured. Production is done in-house or outsourced.

Step 6: In-house production. In-house production needs to be planned and actual production needs to be scheduled. Production planning involves people, materials, components, machines, financial resources, and possibly suppliers and subcontractors. In the case of assembly and/or manufacturing, several plant services may be needed, including collaboration with business partners. Production facilities may be located in a different country than the company's headquarters or retailers. This may further complicate the flow of information.

Step 7: Use suppliers. A manufacturer may opt to buy products or subassemblies from suppliers. Similarly, if the seller is a retailer, such as in the case of Amazon.com or Walmart.com, the retailer must purchase products from its manufacturers. In this case, appropriate receiving and quality assurance of incoming materials and products must take place.

Once production (Step 6) or purchasing from suppliers (Step 7) is completed, shipments to the customers (Step 3) are arranged.

Step 8: Contacts with customers. Sales representatives keep in contact with customers, especially in B2B, starting with the notification of orders received and ending with notification of a shipment or change in delivery date. These contacts are frequently generated automatically.

Step 9: Returns. In some cases, customers want to exchange or return items. The movement of returns from customers back to vendors is *reverse logistics*. Such returns can be a major problem, especially when they occur in large volumes.

INNOVATIONS DRIVING SUPPLY CHAIN STRATEGIC PRIORITIES

MHI is an international trade association that has influenced materials handling and logistics within the supply chain industry.

Supply chain executives are leveraging digital technologies and business innovations to manage the increasing complexity of today's global supply chains. In the past, companies tackled supply chain challenges primarily by focusing on internal cost reduction and improved operational efficiency. But traditional approaches are less effective as supply chains become longer and more interconnected, and there are higher stakeholder expectations and more sources of risk. Companies are examining their approach to supply chain improvement.

Recently, **MHI** and Deloitte Consulting released their first joint research report, "Innovations That Drive Supply Chains—The 2014 MHI Annual Industry Report." More than 450 respondents from large and small companies across a wide range of sectors participated in the survey. Key study findings are:

- The top two strategic priorities of executives are supply chain analytics and multichannel fulfillment.

- The two major barriers preventing innovation in the supply chain are a talent shortage and a continuing focus on cost reduction.

- Sustainability, mobility/machine-to-machine (M2) technology and 3D printing are emerging innovations that are not yet top-of-mind for executives, but may soon be.

Supply Chain Analytics

As global supply chains become more complex and expansive, companies want to leverage analytics that produce insights to improve customer service and reduce costs and risk.

The speed of business is outpacing the level of insight into the supply chain, regardless of industry. Algorithms and SCM models based on past demand, supply, and business cycles are inadequate to effectively manage the supply chain. Companies need updated models to predict the future.

Multichannel Fulfillment

Today's consumers are demanding. They expect 24/7 shopping and then to have their purchases delivered quickly, the next day or even the same day. Although most retailers are good at the front-end handling orders through their multiple channels, they tend to struggle to adapt their back-end order fulfillment processes. Retailers plan to make significant investments to build their multichannel fulfillment capabilities.

Talent Shortage Remains the Biggest Barrier to Innovation

Companies need supply chain talent with the appropriate skills, experience, and mindset to harness the value of supply chain innovations. The right kind of supply chain talent is extremely difficult to find.

Cost Reduction Chokes Off Essential Investments in Innovation

Cost reduction is still the number one priority for many supply chain executives, according to the MHI and Deloitte survey. More than 70 percent of respondents across industries asserted that controlling costs is a top priority for their companies and their customers.

Sustainability

The focus on cost-cutting in the supply chain is squeezing out innovations in sustainability, even though executives believe these investments are important. More than 60 percent of respondents indicated that significant capability gaps exist in their companies and clients that may prevent them from effectively implementing sustainability programs.

Mobility and M2M Technology

Mobility and M2M technologies can improve responsiveness and customer service by providing supply chain workers with the information they need—whenever and wherever they need it.

3D Printing

Additive manufacturing could revolutionize production processes and have far-reaching future implications for product supply chains. But supply chain executives in the MHI and Deloitte study did not see immediate potential for the innovation.

Questions

1. What is a supply chain?
2. List four functions carried out by companies in a supply chain.
3. List and describe the three main flows being managed in a supply chain.
4. Describe SCM.
5. What are steps in the order fulfillment?
6. Explain logistics.
7. What are the top two strategic priorities of SCM executives?
8. What are the two major barriers preventing innovation in the supply chain?
9. What are the top innovative digital technologies impacting SCM?

10.5 Customer Relationship Management Systems

Like ERP and SCM systems, CRM is a widely used and mature technology that can be deployed on-premises or on-demand as a service, or SaaS. The fierce competition among the big four CRM vendors—Salesforce.com, SAP, Oracle, and Microsoft—motivates innovation. Numerous successful CRM implementations have helped transform the business, increased profit, and strengthened customer loyalty. CRM can provide managers with a 360-degree view of the customer relationship, enable real time responses, and improve sales productivity and predictability. However, CRM technology cannot transform or improve anything on its own.

As Figure 10.12 shows, CRM and data are necessary, but insufficient. Business performance improvement actually depends to a greater extent on people and processes. The Avon business case at the end of this chapter is a high-profile example of a $125 million enterprise system failure because people and processes were ignored. Changes in people's behavior, their commitment, attitude toward the mandatory change as well as process improvements make the difference between better bottom lines or a hundred million dollar write-off, as in the case of Avon. Buying the most suitable CRM is like buying a Ferrari or Porsche. You will not win any races or become a better driver simply because you bought the sports car. Your effort and changes in how you drive determine your wins.

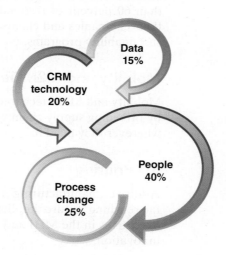

Figure 10.12 Four CRM critical success factors and their importance.

HOW ARE CRM APPS
DIFFERENT FROM
ERP? WHY ARE THEY
DIFFERENT?

ERP and CRM have to interface and share data. They are similar from a technology perspective—sold in modules, offered on site or in the cloud, and must share data. ERPs often requires tight business rules and user practices—that those in accounting, finance, and HR tend to be accustomed to by their professions. For example, they must comply with generally accepted accounting principles (GAAP), the SEC, labor laws, or legal requirements. But sales and marketing are the primary users of CRM—and they tend not to be accustomed to inflexible rules of conduct. They are accustomed to creativity and closing the deal, for instance. If the CRM does not support them their way, they can reject it—and cause total system failure.

Why Does CRM Matter?

CRM systems play the major role in customer experience (CX), and good CX helps to retain customers. However, not all customers are worth retaining. Customers can be unprofitable. Imagine having 20,000 customers. How would you determine the CLV of each customer and continue to recompute their value? The point is that data analytics, sophisticated predictive analytics, and BI are needed to determine CLV; then business rules need to specify how to treat or manage customers based on their value score.

Intelligently managing relationships with customers can increase revenues and net profits significantly. Similar to managing inventory and supplier relationships, effective CRM is data-driven, complex, and continuously changing. The growth of mobile sales channels and social networking makes recognizing customers across multiple touchpoints complex. In addition, many companies have customer data in multiple, disparate systems that are not integrated—until they implement CRM systems.

TECHNOLOGY
PERSPECTIVE

From a technology perspective, CRM refers to the methodologies and software tools to leverage customer data in order to achieve the following:

- Identify the appropriate CX for customers.
- Predict and prevent attrition (loss) of a customer, unless he or she is not worth retaining.
- Acquire new customers who are most likely to become profitable.
- Up-sell (sell more profitable products/services) or cross-sell (sell additional products/services) to unprofitable customers to move them to a profit position.
- Reduce inefficiencies that waste advertising dollars.

CUSTOMER
ACQUISITION AND
RETENTION

CRM technologies help marketing managers run effective campaigns, promotions, commercials, and advertisements to attract new customers, or to increase sales to existing customers, or to do both. Attracting and acquiring new customers are expensive activities: for example, it costs banks roughly $100 to acquire a new customer. Newly acquired customers are unprofitable until they have purchased enough products or services to exceed the cost to acquire and service them. Therefore, retaining customers that generate revenues in excess of the costs (e.g., customer service, returns, promotional items, and the like) is critical. The purpose of loyalty or frequent purchase programs offered by online retailers, coffee shops, airlines, supermarkets, credit card issuers, casinos, and other companies is to track customers for CRM purposes and build customer loyalty to improve financial performance. Loyalty programs rely on data warehouses and data analytics to recognize and reward customers who repeatedly use services or products. The 1-800-Flowers loyalty program is described in IT at Work 10.6.

IT at Work 10.6

1-800-Flowers.com Uses Data Mining for CRM

1-800-Flowers.com is an Internet pioneer. Online sales are a major marketing channel in addition to telephone and fax orders. Competition is very strong in this industry. The company's success was based on operational efficiency, convenience (24/7 accessibility), and reliability. However, all major competitors provide the same features today. To maintain its competitive edge, the company transformed itself into a customer-centric organization, caring for more than 15 million customers.

The company decided to cultivate brand loyalty through customer relationships based on detailed knowledge of customers. How is this accomplished? SAS software spans the entire decision-support process for managing customer relationships. Collecting data at all customer touchpoints, the company turns those data into knowledge for understanding and anticipating customer behavior, meeting customer needs, building more profitable customer relationships, and gaining a holistic view of a customer's lifetime value. Using SAS Enterprise Miner, 1-800-Flowers.com sifts through purchasing data to discover trends, explain outcomes, and predict results so that the company can increase response rates and identify profitable customers. In addition to selling and campaign management, the ultimate goal is to make sure that when a customer wants to buy, he or she continues to buy from 1-800-Flowers.com and cannot be captured by a competitor's marketing. Their objective is not just about getting customers to buy more. It is about making sure that when they decide to purchase a gift online or by phone, they do not even think of going to the competition.

Data mining software helps the company identify the many different types of customers and how each would like to be treated. Customer retention has increased by over 15 percent since this approach was adopted.

Questions

1. Why is being number one in operation efficiency not enough to keep 1-800-FLOWERS.COM at the top of its industry?
2. What is the role of data mining?
3. How is the one-to-one relationship achieved in such systems?

CRM FOR A COMPETITIVE EDGE

According to management guru Peter Drucker, "Those companies who know their customers, understand their needs, and communicate intelligently with them will always have a competitive advantage over those that don't" (Drucker, 1969). For most types of companies, marketing effectiveness depends on how well they know their customers: specifically, knowing what their customers want, how best to contact them, and what types of offers they are likely to respond to positively. According to the *loyalty effect*, a 5 percent reduction in customer attrition can improve profits by as much as 20 percent. Customer-centric business strategies strive to provide products and services that customers want to buy. One of the best examples is the Apple iPhone and iPod—devices that customers were willing to camp out on sidewalks to buy to guarantee getting one on the day of their release. In contrast, companies with product-centric strategies need to create demand for their products, which is more expensive and may fail.

COMMON CRM MISTAKES: HOW TO AVOID THEM

According to Gartner, the CRM market reached $24 billion in 2014 after several years of strong growth. Given that level of investment, companies obviously want to get as much value as possible out of their systems. It is unfortunate, then, that so many of them make mistakes in selecting and implementing CRM software. The editor of *Enterprise Apps Today*, Ann All (2014), described common CRM mistakes and how to avoid them. Five of these CRM mistakes are explained in Table 10.5.

TABLE 10.5 CRM Mistakes and Avoiding Them

CRM Mistakes	How to Avoid The Mistakes
Putting IT department in charge of the CRM project instead of the business users	The hands-on business users need to champion and lead the project initiative, with IT playing a supporting role. **Explanation:** CRM is a software project whose success relies on users' input, which helps ensure they actually will use it. Unlike other apps, salespeople do not have to use CRM. If the system is underused, companies will see only limited improvements.
Not getting the CRM requirements right by not involving key business stakeholders from the outset	CRM implementations need buy-in from the users and other business stakeholders, who can spread enthusiasm. Frequent communication about the project is important to engaging them in a meaningful way.
Making mobile CRM strategy an afterthought	Consider mobility a priority in the CRM project from the outset. Putting an existing CRM on mobile devices is a bad plan.
Taking wrong approach to CRM training	Make sure the interface is intuitive enough that most users will not need hands-on training. When people sit in a classroom for an hour, they will only retain 5 minutes of what they hear. A learning program during lunch that focuses on one or two lessons is a much more effective adoption strategy.
Underestimating users' resistance to change	Users will not tolerate poorly designed systems. Frustrating users is a fast track to failure, or at a minimum, suboptimal results.

Example of a Failure

Citizen National Bank's experience is an example of a failure that then replaced its CRM vendors and became a success. The lessons learned, at a cost of $500,000, were:

- Be absolutely clear on how the CRM application will add value to the sales process.
- Determine if and why salespeople are avoiding CRM.
- Provide incentives for the sales team to adopt CRM.
- Find ways to simplify the use of the CRM application.
- Adjust the CRM system as business needs change.

| JUSTIFYING CRM

One of the biggest problems in CRM implementation is the difficulty of defining and measuring success. In addition, many companies say that when it comes to determining value, intangible benefits are more significant than tangible cost savings.

Yet companies often fail to establish quantitative or even qualitative measures in order to judge these intangible benefits.

A formal business plan must be in place before the CRM project begins—one that quantifies the expected costs, tangible financial benefits, and intangible strategic benefits, as well as the risks. The plan should include an assessment of the following:

- **Tangible net benefits.** The plan must include a clear and precise cost–benefit analysis that lists all the planned project costs and tangible benefits. This portion of the plan should also contain a strategy for assessing key financial metrics, such as ROI, net present value (NPV), or other justification methods.
- **Intangible benefits.** The plan should detail the expected intangible benefits, and it should list the measured successes and shortfalls. Often, an improvement in customer satisfaction is the primary goal of the CRM solution, but in many cases this key value is not measured.
- **Risk assessment.** The risk assessment is a list of all of the potential pitfalls related to the people, processes, and technology that are involved in the CRM project. Having such a list helps to lessen the probability that problems will occur. And, if they do happen, a company may find that, by having listed and considered the problems in advance, the problems are more manageable than they would have been otherwise.

Tangible and Intangible Benefits

Benefits typically include increases in staff productivity (e.g., more deals closed), cost avoidance, revenues, and margin increases, as well as reductions in inventory costs (e.g., due to the elimination of errors). Other benefits include increased customer satisfaction, loyalty, and retention.

Questions

1. Explain the four critical success factors for CRM.
2. Why does CRM matter?
3. Discuss how CRM impacts customer acquisition and retention.
4. According to Peter Drucker, what does marketing effectiveness depend on?
5. Give three reasons why CRM fails.
6. How can CRM be justified?

Key Terms

3D bioprinting
3D printing (additive manufacturing)
back-office operations
core business processes
creative destroyer
customer lifetime value (CLV)
customer relationship management (CRM)

enterprise application integration (EAI)
enterprise resource planning (ERP)
enterprise systems
front-office operations
interface
legacy systems
logistics

Microsoft Cloud
millennials
MHI
order fulfillment
reverse supply chain
SharePoint
social network sprawl
stock keeping unit (SKU)

supply chain
supply chain management (SCM)
value-added reseller (VAR)
Yammer

Assuring Your Learning

DISCUSS: Critical Thinking Questions

1. *Consider the following scenario:* In the 1990s, hard disk drive (HDD) makers were among the first industries to move production to lower-cost countries. Beginning in Singapore, these companies shifted manufacturing operations to China and Thailand, in search of ever-lower labor costs. Since then, Thailand has become the second-largest maker of hard drives and a major supplier of parts to the industry worldwide. With the catastrophic Thai floods in the fall of 2011, the industry faced shortages of over 30 million drives per quarter. Some executives at HDD companies were forced to explain a glaring oversight: Why had they had relied so heavily on a supplier in a country located in a high-flood risk area?

    Also consider that: By the end of the 1990s, most supply chains had become lean by minimizing their inventories and reducing waste, and could schedule deliveries across the globe with incredible precision. Supply chain speed and flexibility were impressive. Products that should take months to procure and manufacture were promised within days of customer requests.

    a. What supply chain management lessons can be learned from the experiences of HDD makers?

    b. What are the risks of highly efficient and lean supply chains?

    c. Could one catastrophic supply chain event wipe out years of profits or market share? Explain your answer.

    d. In your opinion, when do cost savings outweigh the risks?

    e. In your opinion, when are cost savings outweighed by the risks?

Questions for Discussion & Review

1. According to "New Study on Collaborative Execution Finds Supply Chain Collaboration Can Improve Operational Metrics by 50 Percent or More" (Bloomberg, 2012),

    By a ratio of nearly two to one, supply chain professionals agreed that one of the biggest barriers to successful collaboration is a slow *issue resolution* process. This was identified as a systemic problem related to quality of information flow, in terms of both the granularity (level of detail) and timeliness of data shared.

    And 92 percent of respondents agreed that rapid problem resolution was part of good collaboration. True collaboration can be defined in terms of speed, both in problem solving and in organizational learning. More than half of the responses indicated that speed of response in truly collaborative relationships was twice as fast or faster, with learning curve improvements more than 50 percent greater than in non-collaborative trading partner relationships.

    a. Discuss why supply chain partners may not be able to resolve issues quickly. Consider *information flows* in your discussion.

    b. What impacts might slow problem (issue) resolution have on the supply chain?

    c. Based on your answer to (a), discuss which enterprise systems could speed up problem resolution.

    d. What is meant by learning curve improvements?

2. In your opinion, what might limit the growth of 3D printing?

3. Distinguish between ERP and SCM software. In what ways do they complement each other? Why should they be integrated?

4. State the business value of enterprise systems and how they can be used to manage the supply chain more effectively.

5. What problems are encountered in implementing ERP systems?

6. Find examples of how two of the following organizations improve their supply chains: manufacturing, hospitals, retailing, education, construction, agribusiness, and shipping. Discuss the benefits to the organizations.

7. It is claimed that supply chains are essentially "a series of linked suppliers and customers; every customer is in turn a supplier to the next downstream organization, until the ultimate end-user." Explain this statement. Use a diagram.

8. Discuss why it is difficult to justify CRM.

9. A supply chain is much more powerful in the Internet marketplace. Discuss how Internet technologies can be used to manage the supply chain.

EXPLORE: Online and Interactive Exercises

Visit each of the following enterprise vendor websites. Write a brief report on the latest features of their enterprise systems, platforms, apps, or solutions.

1. SharePoint
2. Yammer
3. Oracle
4. Salesforce.com
5. SAP

ANALYZE & DECIDE: Apply IT Concepts to Business Decisions

1. Select an enterprise system vendor. Search and read a case study of one of the vendor's customers. Summarize the case and identify the benefits of the implementation.

2. Assess the costs and benefits of a cloud CRM. A large food-processing company would like to determine the cost–benefit of installing a CRM app in a private cloud. Create a report that contains these analyses:

   a. Calculate the tangible costs and benefits in a spreadsheet using the data provided.

   b. List two intangible benefits of moving to the cloud.

   c. Estimate the value of those two benefits and include them in your spreadsheet prepared for Question 1.

   d. List two risks associated with the CRM app if it were moved to a public cloud.

DATA

Tangible Costs

- CRM in private cloud: $35 per user per month

- Technical support and maintenance: $250 per month
- Total number of users: 100 (90 salespeople and 10 supervisors)
- Training of 90 salespeople for five days: productivity loss $200 per day per person
- Training of five supervisors: productivity loss $300 per day per person
- Additional hardware, networks, and bandwidth: $15,000 per month

Tangible Benefits

- Increase in average sales revenues = $6,000 per month per salesperson
- Increase in sales revenues from an improvement in customer retention = $5,000 per month
- Gross profit from sales revenues = 20 percent

CASE 10.2

Business Case: Avon's Failed SAP Implementation: Enterprise System Gone Wrong

Avon is one of the world's leading direct-selling companies. It uses independent sales representatives (reps) who, in effect, run its cosmetic business as entrepreneurs selling directly to customers. The career is attractive during slow economic times and presents an opportunity for those who need flexibility.

Avon's success depends on retaining independent sales reps, recruiting new ones, and increasing the size and frequency of orders received from their sales representatives. In 2009 Avon CEO Andrea Jung launched the company's most massive recruiting campaign. Avon doubled its investment in recruiting advertising and doubled the number of countries in which recruiting ads were run.

Legacy Order Management System

Avon's selling process is based on a series of campaigns that last 2 to 4 weeks. Sales reps solicit orders from customers, and compile them into larger orders placed with Avon. Order fulfillment takes place at an Avon distribution center, which ships orders to sales reps who then distribute the products to customers and collect payment. The order management system was based on legacy systems and a cumbersome interface, and was so outdated that sales reps could not guarantee product availability for their customers.

Big Bang Approach Was the Wrong Approach

Avon tried to correct its IT challenges using a big bang approach—lots of changes in too short a time. In 2010 Avon launched its Service Model Transformation (SMT) program based on SAP. SMT was intended to improve the way reps interacted with the company, including orders, product returns, and order fulfillment. The SMT and big bang approach failed. Three years and $125 million later, Avon ended the SMT program.

CEO McCoy admitted that a big bang approach to the roll-out was too disruptive to the nature of Avon's business. The nature of direct selling where our 6 million representatives are independent entrepreneurs is one of personal relationships, and motivating change with incentives. Change needed to be introduced slowly and thoughtfully—and not abruptly.

Why Was SMT Halted?

Avon's new management order system was piloted in Canada and later rolled out globally. From the outset, the system seriously disrupted operations in Canada. Sales reps complained the system did not work as promised. They could not log on, orders were not always accepted when submitted, and inventory that was needed to fulfill orders was not regularly reserved. As many as 16,000 Canadian sales reps quit. The departure of large numbers of Canadian sales representatives, in turn, disrupted Avon's ability to do business—and attract new representatives.

Other factors contributed to the failure. The order management system did not interface well with other systems, such as IBM's WebSphere. And Avon put the system into production before the platform was ready. At the end of 2013, in a financial report, Avon indicated that the cost of the project, $125 million, would be taken as a write-down.

SAP's Public Comment

In response to the massive failure, SAP released this public comment—as damage control:

> Traditional enterprise business is failing to offer the easy user experience that modern software customers need. SAP has done a lot of work in 2013 on the user experience aspects of software including the introduction of Fiori and Screen personas. They have also put together a Design and Co-innovation center. (Kepes, 2013).

SAP points out the crucial importance of the user experience in enterprise success—and that it had invested in apps and interfaces to help ensure success.

Sources: Compiled from Avon Annual Reports, Kepes (2013), Saran (2013), Henschen (2013a, 2013b) and Fitzgerald (2013).

Questions

1. How did the older order fulfillment system harm an Avon rep's sales and relationships with her customers?
2. Why do you think the big bang approach was risky at Avon?
3. How would the age of the sales reps impact success or failure?
4. What was Avon trying to accomplish with the Service Model Transformation (SMT)?
5. Why do you think so many sales reps left Avon instead of waiting for it to correct the problems?
6. This case demonstrates the relationship between different functional areas in a company. What do you think should have been done to avoid the problems that happened in the pilot study?

CASE 10.3

Video Case: Procter & Gamble: Creating Conversations in the Cloud with 4.8 Billion Consumers

The decline of traditional marketing channels forced changes in CRM transformation at Procter & Gamble (P&G). P&G's cloud environment allows for all consumer data to be in one location for fresh, relevant relationships with 4.8 billion consumers as they transition from one product to the next over the course of their lifetimes.

Visit Teradata.com and search for the video entitled "Procter & Gamble: Creating Conversations in the Cloud with 4.8 Billion Consumers." Watch the video (time: 5:14).

Questions

1. How does P&G maintain an ongoing dialogue with a customer?
2. What were P&G's data challenges?
3. What is 1, Consumer Place? Where is it?
4. In your opinion, how does P&G try to maximize customer lifetime value (CLV)?

References

Accenture. "Joint Munitions Command Calls on Accenture for Integrated Logistics and High Performance Guidance." *accenture.com*, 2010.

All, A. "8 Common CRM Mistakes, and How to Avoid Them." *Enterprise Apps Today,* February 20, 2014.

Bloomberg. "New Study on Collaborative Execution Finds Supply Chain Collaboration Can Improve Operational Metrics by 50 Percent or More." March 27, 2012. http://www.bloomberg.com

Bourne, A. "What Does 3D Printing Mean for ERP?" *Manufacturing.net,* January 29, 2014.

Cohen, D., M. Sargeant, & K. Somers. "3-D Printing Takes Shape." *McKinsey Quarterly*, January 2014. *www.mckinsey.com*

CNNMoney. "Best Jobs in America." *CNN.com,* November 12, 2013.

Cole, B. "Gartner Report Finds Slow Growth in Global ERP Market." *SearchManufacturingERP.com,* May 16, 2014.

Drucker, P.F. *The Age of Discontinuity*. New York: Harper & Row. 1969.

Fine, R. "What Role Does 3D Printing Play in an ERP-Managed Manufacturing Process?" *Toolbox.com,* May 21, 2014.

Fitzgerald, D. "Avon to Halt Rollout of New Order Management System." *The Wall Street Journal*, December 11, 2013.

Gartner.com. "Gartner Says Uses of 3D Printing Will Ignite Major Debate on Ethics and Regulation." January 29, 2014. *Gartner.com.*

goldmansachs.com. "The Search for Creative Destruction." March 24, 2014. *goldmansachs.com.*

Henschen, D. "Avon Pulls Plug on $125 million SAP Project." *InformationWeek,* December 12, 2013a.

Henschen, D. "Inside Avon's Failed Order-Management Project." *InformationWeek,* December 16, 2013b.

Kepes, B. "UPDATED—Avon's Failed SAP Implementation a Perfect Example of the Enterprise IT Revolution." *Forbes,* December 17, 2013.

Koplowitz, R. "The Forrester Wave: Enterprise Social Platforms, Q3 2011." August 24, 2011.

Lavenda, D. "How Red Robin Transformed Its Business with Yammer." *Fast Company,* February 6, 2014.

MHI and Deloitte. "Innovations That Drive Supply Chains—The 2014 MHI Annual Industry Report." 2014. https://www.mhi.org/publications/report

Ryan, B. "Integrating Yammer with SharePoint 2013: Navigating the Options." *CMS Wire,* May 22, 2014.

Schwerin, C. "Army Gears Up for Next Network Integration Evaluation." U.S. Army, *army.mil,* April 2, 2012.

Saran, C. "Avon Drops SAP Big Bang Transformation." *ComputerWeekly,com,* December 13, 2013.

The Engineer. "Patient Receives 3D Printed Titanium Hip." May 19, 2014.

U.S. Army Business Transformation Knowledge Center, 2009 army.mil/armyBTKC.

Data Visualization and Geographic Information Systems

Chapter Snapshot

Case 11.1 Opening Case: Safeway and PepsiCo Apply Data Visualization to Supply Chain

11.1 Data Visualization and Learning

11.2 Enterprise Data Mashups

11.3 Digital Dashboards

11.4 Geospatial Data and Geographic Information Systems

Key Terms

Assuring Your Learning

- **Discuss:** Critical Thinking Questions
- **Explore:** Online and Interactive Exercises
- **Analyze & Decide:** Apply IT Concepts to Business Decisions

Case 11.2 Visualization Case: Are You Ready for Football?

Case 11.3 Video Case: The Beauty of Data Visualization—Data Detective

References

Learning Outcomes

1. Describe how data visualization applications and interactive reports support learning and business functions.

2. Explain how data mashup applications streamline the process of integrating diverse data sources and information feeds to support data needs that cannot be anticipated.

3. Describe how companies optimize operations with the help of dashboards. Explain how enterprise dashboards are built and how they leverage real time data and people's natural ability to think visually.

4. Assess the business applications and benefits of geospatial data and geographic information systems.

Chapter Snapshot

Analytics has historically been done by statisticians, programmers, and data scientists (the "big guys") who rarely interacted directly with the business. However, this experts-only approach has changed because of easier-to-use data visualization, dashboard, and mashup technologies.

Data analytics are being pushed out into the business by advances that make it possible for most employees to use analytics themselves. Vendors of enterprise-level analytics are also upgrading their visualization and reporting platforms that are designed for use by the big guys.

Several tools discussed in this chapter enable you to be self-sufficient. Drag-and-drop, automation, "show me" wizards, and easy-to-use dashboards enable you to develop your own interactive data visualization (viz), apps, and dashboards. Reducing dependency on IT staff has a long history. For example, at one time, managers did not analyze data with spreadsheets, but now Excel expertise is expected. Vendors offer academic alliances to enable universities to teach their software in MBA and undergraduate business courses. Tableau Desktop, QlikView, TIBCO Spotfire, and IBM's SPSS Analytic Catalyst enable business users to conduct the kind of advanced analysis that could only have been used by expert users of statistical software a few years ago.

In Chapter 3, you read about big data analytics, data mining, and business intelligence (BI). Chapter 11 expands on these topics with the latest in data viz, visual discovery, dashboards, mashups, and geographic information systems (GISs). Companies are incorporating **geospatial data** and GISs into their CRM, SCM, BI, and other enterprise apps. GM, Verizon, Walmart, Starbucks, and Nike use GISs to view their businesses spatially. Maps can tell a more compelling story than words or numbers, as shown in Figure 11.1, by effective use of visual cues.

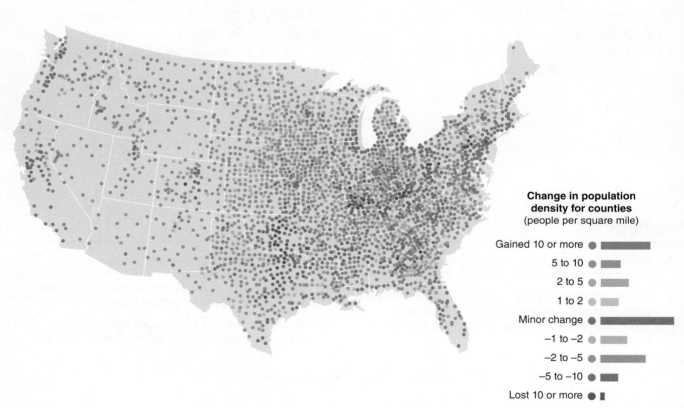

Figure 11.1 U.S. Census Bureau map shows changes in population density for counties using the colors green (gain) and purple (loss) to represent direction of change and color intensity to represent magnitude of change. Source: www.census.gov/

Safeway and PepsiCo Apply Data Visualization to Supply Chain

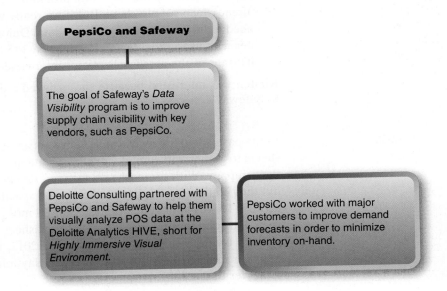

Figure 11.2 Deloitte Consulting partnered with PepsiCo and Safeway to help analyze huge amounts of point-of-sale (POS) data at its state-of-the-art visualization center called HIVE.

TABLE 11.1	Opening Case Overview
Companies	• Safeway, Inc., a $44.2 billion grocery chain incorporated in Pleasanton, CA. • PepsiCo, a major food and beverage company headquartered in Purchase, NY, with 274,000 employees and 2013 revenue of $66.4 billion.
Locations and Industries	• Safeway is a food and drug retailer in North America with 1,335 stores in California, Hawaii, Oregon, Washington, and the Mid-Atlantic region. • PepsiCo is a food and beverage manufacturer whose products are marketed in more than 200 countries and territories.
Deloitte Consulting's HIVE	HIVE is a physical environment where people can examine the latest analytics approaches themselves using their own data.
Business challenges	Inventory management is crucial to retail operations—and a challenge throughout the supply chain.

Supply chain visibility is the awareness and sharing of POS data and data about product orders, inventory levels, demand forecasts, transportation, and logistics by trading partners from raw material to delivery to end customer.

| SUPPLY CHAIN
| VISIBILITY

In an effort to improve **supply chain visibility**, Safeway implemented data-sharing programs with PepsiCo and other key vendors (Figure 11.1 and Table 11.1). Benefits of improved visibility are increased sales and millions of dollars in reduced costs along the entire supply chain.

In 2012, Clay Broussard, Director of Customer Supply Chain & Logistics at PepsiCo, contacted Safeway's Kirsten Curtis, Director of Demand Planning & BI. Clay explained (Curtis, 2013):

> Safeway's Data Visibility program is very forward thinking. Paired with PepsiCo's 360° Retail execution program, our teams are equipped to improve an already lean supply chain. But if we really want to take it to the next level, we need a different way to view the data. Deloitte Consulting has offered to partner with us to provide an effective way to interpret massive amounts of data at its state-of-the-art visualization center called the HIVE . . . are you interested?

Kirsten was interested because she believed a data visualization strategy was vital to Safeway's success.

EXCEL-BASED ANALYTICS

In the past, when Safeway wanted answers about stockouts, managers used spreadsheets to gather and compile inventory data and see how stockouts trended across the company. With spreadsheets, managers could discover general trends over time, but they could not identify trends across a specific brand or universal product code (UPC). Trends about each brand required more data than could be represented in rows and columns of a spreadsheet. Spreadsheet limitations ultimately led the company to try data visualization. In August 2012, representatives from Safeway and PepsiCo came to Deloitte's HIVE for a day-long design session to analyze many terabytes of data.

HIVE

Deloitte hosts meetings with business leaders who want to understand business analytics better. These sessions are tailored to address their business challenges. At the HIVE, executives get help with analytics tools using their own data.

The HIVE gathers together a wide range of the latest analytics technologies from all over the world. In a very short amount of time, executives can learn what might otherwise have taken months of meetings, demonstrations, and business pitches.

Data Visualization Process at the Hive

PepsiCo and Safeway participants collaborated to understand how to reduce the "number of days of supply" from their supply chain while maintaining service levels. This project would save PepsiCo and Safeway millions of dollars each year. During their session, data visualizations were built to explore questions about stockouts. The data included brands, UPC barcodes, costs, districts, store numbers, out-of-stock scans, and out-of-stock reason codes. After Safeway and PepsiCo decided on the visualization technique that best represented their supply chain, they needed to design three processes to operationalize it. The three processes to be designed were:

1. How to feed the huge datasets into the visualization software
2. The best ways to display the data visually
3. How to gather feedback

Within 40 days, Pepsico and Safeway implemented their initial data visualization with dashboards and drill-down capabilities, then spent another 20 days refining it.

What They Learned From Data Visualization and Dashboards

Safeway identified the stores experiencing the most stockouts and their root causes. For example, it learned a disproportionate number of stockouts were occurring at a store on Catalina Island. The store is in a resort area where the tourist traffic causes uneven demand. Safeway adjusted its supply chain strategy to address uneven demand patterns.

Safeway also discovered that they were sending multiple and conflicting forecasts to their vendors from various departments. Safeway changed the way the company creates and communicates forecasts with its suppliers.

Two significant operational improvements at Safeway from discoveries made through data visualization are:

1. Improved forecast accuracy by 35 percent.
2. Reduced on-hand warehouse inventory, which cut inventory carrying costs significantly.

PepsiCo is also benefitting because now it has incredible near real time access to the movement of every PepsiCo item, at every Safeway store, every day.

Sources: Compiled from Deloitte CIO Journal (2013), Curtis (2013), and Sommer and Lovelock (2013).

Questions

1. What is a potential benefit of supply chain visibility?
2. What was the limitation of Excel-based data analytics at Safeway?
3. What is Deloitte's HIVE?
4. What steps did Safeway and PepsiCo undertake to arrive at their data visualization solution?
5. What did Safeway learn from its data visualization dashboards?
6. What were the two operational improvements at Safeway?

11.1 Data Visualization and Learning

Geospatial data identify the geographic location and characteristics of natural or constructed features and boundaries on the earth, typically represented by points, lines, or polygons.

Visuals are the single best way our brain processes information. We rely on visual cues to grasp and process huge amounts of information. Data visualization harnesses the power of analytics and adds a visual display to capitalize on how our brains work. Interactive displays, charts with drill-down capability, and **geospatial data** analysis are a few examples of the many ways to work with data. Data visualization software can be extremely powerful and complex, such as Deloitte's HIVE platform. At the other continuum are tools with simple, point-and-click interfaces that do not require any particular coding knowledge or significant training. Most non-data-scientist-friendly tools have interactive elements and can pull data from Google Docs, Excel spreadsheets, Access databases, and other sources that most business people work with already.

In the first section of this chapter, the focus is on the technologies that fall into the data analytics category, as shown in Figure 11.3. Later sections discuss information delivery and data integration. Vendor packages usually offer tools in more than

Figure 11.3 Tools and technologies in this chapter fall into three related categories.

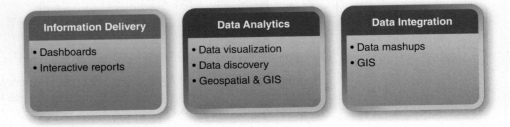

Information Delivery	Data Analytics	Data Integration
• Dashboards • Interactive reports	• Data visualization • Data discovery • Geospatial & GIS	• Data mashups • GIS

one category. In general, **reporting tools** show what has already happened in a business. **Analytical tools** show what might or could happen in the future.

LEARNING, EXPLORING, AND DISCOVERY

When companies, political parties, sports teams, or fund-raising agencies invest in campaigns, promotions, special events, or other projects, they want to learn something from them. Learning is the basis for continuous improvement, such as improved earnings as you read in the opening case. Visualization is also used as a data explorer or for **data discovery**—discovering hidden relationships. Like Safeway and PepsiCo, companies across industries are discovering new relationships and learning how to improve performance using data visualization. Enterprise visualization apps for Androids, Apple iPads, and Blackberry Playbooks are replacing static business reports with real time data, analytics, and interactive reporting tools.

Visuals

Examples of visualizations are dials, charts, graphs, timelines, geospatial maps (refer to Figure 11.1), and heat maps. The tricolor heat map in Figure 11.4 instantly alerts the viewer to critical areas most in need of attention. Visual displays make it easier for individuals to understand data and identify patterns that offer answers to business questions like "Which product lines have the highest and lowest profit margins in each region?" Interactivity and drill-down capabilities are standard features. In Figure 11.5 are two other types of heat maps, both based on the same dataset and created with Tableau Desktop. Notice how visual display depends on what you want to learn or convey.

As you read in Chapter 3 and Figure 3.1, human expertise is an essential component of data visualization. A common mistake is to invest in the analytics foundation—tools, quality data, data integration, touch screens—but overlook the most crucial component—namely, users' ability to interpret the visual reports and analyses correctly.

DATA DISCOVERY MARKET SEPARATES FROM THE BI MARKET

According to Gartner's research, in 2014 the data analytics market split into two segments: the traditional BI market and the new data discovery market. Data discovery software had been viewed as a supplement to traditional BI platforms. Now it is a stand-alone alternative to BI. This split occurred because today's data

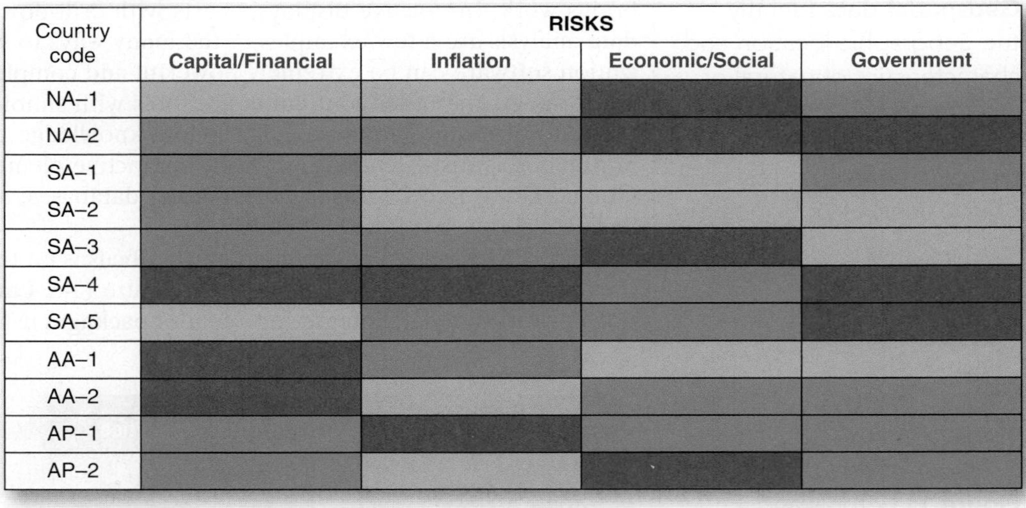

Country code	RISKS			
	Capital/Financial	Inflation	Economic/Social	Government
NA–1				
NA–2				
SA–1				
SA–2				
SA–3				
SA–4				
SA–5				
AA–1				
AA–2				
AP–1				
AP–2				

Figure 11.4 This heat map uses three colors to convey information at a glance. The heat map is like a spreadsheet whose cells are formatted with colors instead of numbers. (Moody's.)

Product Cate...	Product Sub-Category	Region			
		Central	East	South	West
Furniture	Bookcases	73	−10,151	−22,417	−676
	Chairs & Chairmats	37,920	33,583	34,026	44,409
	Office Furnishings	26,293	14,523	25,121	30,941
	Tables	−19,777	−50,677	26,172	−16,990
Office Supplies	Appliances	22,950	16,812	26,986	31,276
	Binders and Binder Accessories	73,951	71,420	69,530	92,273
	Envelopes	10,825	7,482	19,182	11,222
	Labels	2,429	4,041	3,479	3,740
	Paper	11,047	13,510	10,997	10,433
	Pens & Art Supplies	2,781	2,856	1,397	518
	Rubber Bands	−174	−238	156	178
	Scissors, Rulers and Trimmers	−1,765	−1,179	−2,903	−1,953
	Storage & Organization	−68	−7,233	11,836	−2,018
Technology	Computer Peripherals	11,971	14,808	30,475	37,280
	Copiers and Fax	513	67,254	63,598	35,997
	Office Machines	38,876	47,277	129,060	61,377
	Telephones and Communication	79,393	73,715	78,985	84,860

(a)

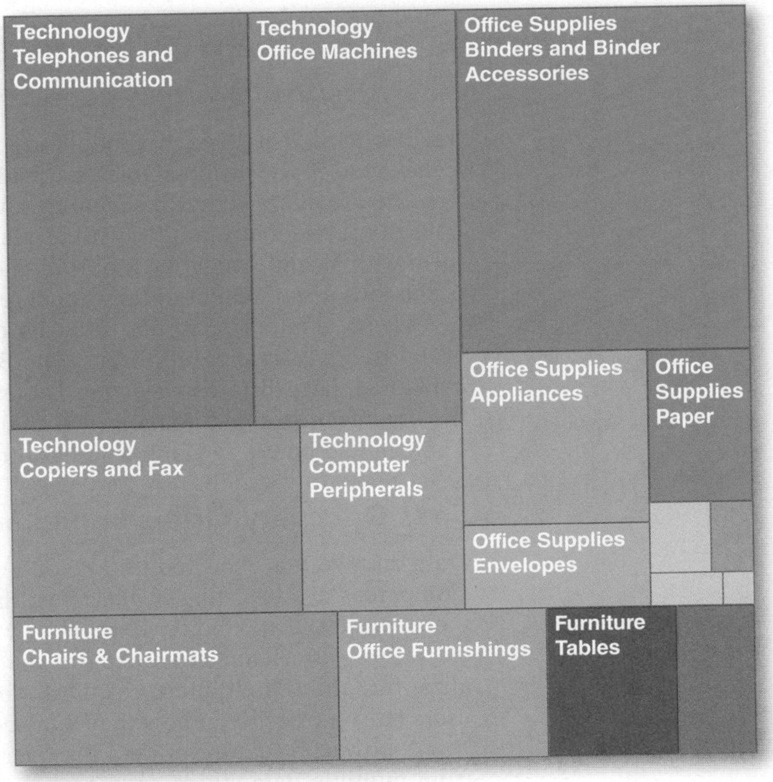

(b)

Figure 11.5 These heat maps represent the same dataset using red and green and color intensity to show the profitability of three product categories and their subcategories. In (a), data labels show detailed profit, while in (b) the area of each segment is used to make comparisons.

discovery technologies provide greater data exploration and ease of use to help users find answers to "why" and "what if" questions through self-service analytic apps. The split is another example of pushing analytics onto the computers of business workers. IT at Work 11.1 describes the trend at eBay.

IT at **Work** 11.1

Do-Your-Own Data Discovery at eBay

At eBay, the trend is toward everyone doing their own data discovery. David Stone, Senior Manager Analytics Platform at eBay, described the importance of offering data analytics tools to members of the eBay team. Stone explained that when limited to Excel and its million-row limit, it caused them:

> "to look at the top three categories instead of the top 40,000 categories and there's so much less data. At eBay that's important because there is more action out in the long tail accumulated than there is in the top three categories." (Groenfeldt, 2013)

Using data discovery software, employees can dig deep into items in the top 40,000 categories because they no longer face row limits. Employees can interact and visualize data and can do data discovery on their own to better manage performance.

Questions

1. In what way is data discovery more critical to online retailers than to retailers with physical stores?
2. How did Excel limit eBay's data analysis?
3. Discuss the impacts of self-service data discovery on eBay.
4. Why do you think eBay employees were willing to do their own data visualizations?

Analytics/Visualization Vendors Responding to Demand

Smaller data visualization vendors are competing head-on with BI megavendors Oracle and SAP BusinessObjects. Vendors QlikView, Birst, Tableau, and TIBCO Spotfire are adding enterprise features with each new release. SAS made one of the boldest moves of any vendor with its plans to replace its current enterprise BI platform with Visual Analytics, a new data discovery environment. SAS is also adding dashboard development to traditional reporting in the same user-friendly platform.

These vendors continue to focus on business users of all levels and backgrounds. For example, Jeff Strauss, the BI architect at Allstate Insurance Company, explained that Allstate invested in Tableau data discovery tools so users throughout the organization could do their own analysis rather than rely on the IT department. Tableau had built a fan club with easy-to-access dashboards.

Data Discovery Offers Speed and Flexibility

Data discovery is expected to take on a greater role in corporate decision making. Companies are investing in the latest data discovery solutions largely because of their speed and flexibility. Experts and nonexperts can collect data quickly from disparate sources and then explore the dataset with easy-to-use interactive visualizations and search interfaces. Drill-down paths are not predefined, which gives users more flexibility in how they view detailed data.

A powerful feature of data discovery systems is their ability to integrate data from multiple data stores and identify data types and roles. See Tech Note 11.1. While data are being loaded into the program, the software automatically extracts and organizes them by data type. Software may also extract and organize terms from unstructured content, such as texts, e-mail, and PDFs and create tag clouds. Figure 11.6 is an example. Tag clouds give users a quick way to size up a situation and start to make discoveries.

TECH NOTE 11.1 Understanding Data Types and Roles

Data types and roles are fundamental components that affect how visualizations behave. Each field in any data source has an associated data type. For example, a field that contains customer names has a string (text) data type, and a field that contains price information usually has a numeric data type. To visualize data QlikView, Tableau—or in any analytics or BI tool, for that matter—you need to understand dimensions and measures.

- **Dimensions.** Dimensions contain discrete or categorical data, such as a region (e.g., Northeast, Southwest), product category, product subcategory, product name, supplier, size, date, and zip code. Dimensions often become labels in the data visualization.

- **Measures.** A measure is a calculation based on numeric data, such as profit, margin, quantity sold, speed, and miles. The calculation always returns one single value that summarizes all relevant records. The calculation is called an **aggregation**. As in spreadsheets, there are several aggregation functions: Sum(), Count(), Average (), Min(), Max(), and so on. Typically, KPIs are measures—revenue, number of orders, quantity, and cost. A measure is always based on an aggregation.

REAL-WORLD EXAMPLES OF DATA VISUALIZATION

The ultimate goal of data analytics is to drive profits, and often that depends on learning how to manage assets, such as inventory, or engage customers in a smarter way. Collecting data is relatively easy. Making sense of that data is not. Here are examples of how companies and/or entire industries are using data visualization and interactivity to improve decision speed and performance often with mobile displays.

Quick Detection and Decisions in Stock Markets

Wall Street firms, traders, wealth managers, risk analysts, and regulators rely on their ability to process and capitalize on market anomalies in real time. Because of the demanding pace of their decisions, capital markets professionals use visualization for risk analysis, pre-trade and post-trade checks, compliance monitoring, fraud detection, client profitability analysis, research and sales, and portfolio

Figure 11.6 Tag clouds represent the relative frequency of words and terms by their sizes.

performance. Vendor Aqumin provides real time visual interpretation solutions for the financial services industry. Aqumin's OptionVision enables traders, risk managers, and market participants to spot opportunities, risk, and market changes. AlphaVision for Excel enables visual interpretation capabilities directly within the Microsoft Excel platform, and AlphaVision for Bloomberg is developed for professional portfolio managers, traders, and risk analysts and is connected directly to the Bloomberg Terminal to leverage data provided by Bloomberg.

The Chicago Board Options Exchange (CBOE), Gain Capital, JP Morgan, hedge funds, and other asset management firms not only need data visualization but their executives and investors expect the quality and excitement of visuals to make sense of dry financial data.

Improving the HR Function

ADP Corporation is one of the largest payroll service providers in the world, with data on 33 million workers. In 2014, payroll processing company ADP rolled out data visualizations with predictive analytics to improve its human resource (HR) function. After organizing the information and funneling it through an analysis program, the HR department found that ADP would soon face a serious retirement problem. To mitigate its foreseeable future talent gaps, ADP constructed new training programs to prepare the next generation of workers.

Prompt Disaster Response by the Insurance Industry

The effectiveness of an insurer's response to a devastating hurricane or other catastrophic event depends on its ability to combine large amounts of data to fully understand the impact. Leading insurers are using Web-based data visualization and analysis technologies to better manage their responses to major disasters. In the days and weeks after a disaster, insurers face analysis and reporting bottlenecks. Analysts capable of creating maps and reports work frantically to respond to requests for information. Because new data continue being generated even after the event, the data have a short life span and reports need to be regenerated and redistributed.

For example, when an earthquake occurs, workers throughout an insurance company access a Web-based (cloud) data app to visualize and analyze the impact. Users quickly determine which properties were subject to specific shake intensities and can visually build analyses on their own, rather than waiting for a report.

LEADING AND LATEST DATA VISUALIZATION TOOLS

IBM SPSS Analytic Catalyst has made sophisticated analytics accessible. Analytic Catalyst enables business users to conduct the kind of advanced analysis that had been designed for experts in statistical software. The software fast tracks analytics by identifying key drivers, selecting an appropriate model, testing it, and then explaining the results in plain English. See the YouTube video titled "IBM SPSS Analytic Catalyst" for an overview. The tool condenses the analytic process into three steps: data upload, selection of the target variable (the dependent variable or outcome variable), and data exploration. Once the data are uploaded, the system selects target variables and automatically correlates and associates the data. Based on characteristics of the data, Analytic Catalyst chooses the appropriate method and returns summary data rather than statistical data. On the initial screen, it communicates so-called top insights in plain text and presents visuals, such as a decision tree in a churn analysis. Once the user has absorbed the top-level information, he or she can drill down into top key drivers. This enables users to see interactivity between attributes.

Tableau is one of the easier data discovery tools to implement, requiring just basic database information to connect it to the target data sources. With a new in-memory database engine such tools are developing the power to perform big data analytics. Despite data viz advancement, data integration between data sources can still be very challenging.

Roambi Analytics is a leading mobile reporting and data visualization app designed for iPads and iPhones. The app can take data from most sources, including Box, Google Docs, spreadsheets, BI systems, databases, and Salesforce.com, and transform them into interactive data visualizations. Roambi has a worldwide customer base of Global 500 companies and small and medium businesses across industries, including: telecommunications, biotechnology, pharmaceuticals, consumer technology, and packaged goods.

Questions

1. How does data visualization contribute to learning?
2. How do heat maps and tag clouds convey information?
3. Why are data visualization and discovery usage increasing?
4. Give two examples of data visualization for performance management.

11.2 Enterprise Data Mashups

Enterprise mashups combine business data and applications from multiple sources—typically a mix of internal data and applications with externally sourced data, SaaS (software as a service) and Web content—to create an integrated experience. Mashups, in general, became popular because of social and mobile technology. Although most early mashups were consumer focused, the ability of enterprise mashups to quickly and easily consolidate on a single webpage or mobile device screen data and functionality that is normally spread across several applications offers real business opportunities for companies of all shapes and sizes around the world.

Enterprises use mashups as quick, cost-effective solutions to a range of issues. Because mashups use preexisting technology, they do not require a huge investment and can be developed in hours rather than days or weeks.

MASHUP ARCHITECTURE

Technically, a mashup is a technique for building applications that combine data from multiple sources to create an integrated experience. As techniques for creating mashups became easier, companies started using them to build enterprise mashups that supported their business models. Tech-savvy managers realize that they can use mashup apps with their existing data and external services to provide new and interesting views on the data.

Figure 11.7 shows the general architecture of an enterprise mashup app. Data from operational data stores, business systems, external data (economic data, suppliers;

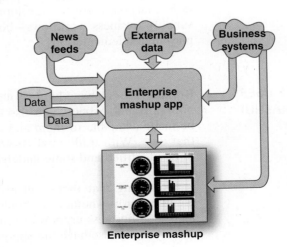

Figure 11.7 Architecture of enterprise mashup application.

information, competitors' activities), and real time news feeds are integrated to generate an enterprise mashup.

TECH NOTE 11.2 Adaptive Discovery Dashboard Software

Software vendor Adaptive Insights offers *Adaptive Discovery,* next-generation dashboard software. The software is widely used by businesses, nonprofits, government, and universities. Several users are Coca-Cola, Siemens, Bridgestone, Nikon, AAA, Toyota, and NBC News.

Users can create dashboards, drill down to understand root causes, and perform what-if scenarios without any programming expertise. In 2014, it was the only cloud-based data visualization and dashboard software designed for use by executives, line-of-business managers, and finance without relying on IT.

One of the features of Adaptive Discovery is Visual Designer for Dashboards. With minimal training in Visual Designer, business users can:

- Use drag and drop to create and edit personalized dashboards
- Leverage predefined chart formats
- Create private dashboards or share them with others

The vendor offers free 30-day trials and demos from AdaptiveInsights.com.

ENTERPRISE DATA MASHUPS

Enterprise data mashups are combinations of data from various business systems and external sources, often in real time, without necessarily relying on a middle step of ETL (extract, transform, and load) from a data warehouse. While combining disparate data sources is common for a data mashup, even if there is only a single data source, a mashup can be made by combining data in a way that is not anticipated. End users and analysts who rely on dashboards and drill-down capabilities benefit from greater access to data, but the mashups remain behind the scene and invisible. Interactive dashboards and drillable reports can be rapidly built based on mashed-up data. Tech Note 11.2 discusses dashboard software. Heat maps and tree maps can be created as data visualizations in mashups.

For organizations, mashup apps decrease IT implementation costs over traditional, custom software development (discussed in Chapter 12) and significantly simplify business workflows—both increase the ROI (return on investment) of mashup implementations.

WHY BUSINESS USERS NEED DATA MASHUP TECHNOLOGY

Business users have a hard enough time identifying their current data needs. It is not realistic to expect them also to consider all the new sources of data that might be made available to them and the analyses they might do if they had access to that data. With traditional BI and data warehousing systems, data sources have to be identified and some understanding of data requirements and data models is needed.

Realizing that there will always be data needs that cannot be anticipated, the question is whether IT should be in the middle of supporting those requests? Providing business users with self-service enables them to meet their needs more quickly. They also have the opportunity to explore and experiment.

TABLE 11.2 Enterprise Mashups Benefits
Summary of benefits of mashup technology to an enterprise: • Dramatically reduces time and effort needed to combine disparate data sources. • Users can define their own data mashups by combining fields from different data sources that were not previously modeled. • Users can import external data sources, e.g., spreadsheets and competitor data, to create new dashboards. • Enables the building of complex queries by nonexperts with a drag-and-drop query building tool. • Enables *agile BI* because new data sources can be added to a BI system quickly via direct links to operational data sources, bypassing the need to load them to a data warehouse. • Provides a mechanism to easily customize and share knowledge throughout the company.

Enterprise mashups improve operational efficiency, optimize the sales pipeline, enhance customer satisfaction, and drive profitability. Within government, mashups have positively impacted strategic areas such as citizen engagement and satisfaction, financial transparency, project oversight, regulatory compliance, and legislated reporting. A summary of enterprise mashup benefits is given in Table 11.2.

ENTERPRISE MASHUP TECHNOLOGY

Mashup technology leverages investments in both BI tools and interactive technologies. BI systems are very good at filtering and aggregating huge data volumes into information. With mashup technology, for example, users can filter down the data based on their needs so that only the information needed is provided by the available data services. Tech Note 11.3 describes mashup self-service.

TECH NOTE 11.3 Mashup Self-Service

Many BI systems are designed by the IT department and based on inflexible data sources. The result is a bottleneck of end-user change requests as business needs and data sources change. The solution is self-service mashup capabilities.

Using data mashup apps, nontechnical users can easily and quickly access, integrate, and display BI data from a variety of operational data sources, including those that are not integrated into the existing data warehouse, without having to understand the intricacies of the underlying data infrastructures or schemas.

In an enterprise environment, mashups can be used to solve a wide variety of business problems and day-to-day situations. Examples of these types of mashups are:

1. **Customer.** A customer data mashup that provides a quick view of customer data for a sales person in preparation for a customer site visit. Data can be pulled from internal data stores and Web sources, such as contact information, links to related websites, recent customer orders, lists of critical situations, and more.

2. **Logistics.** A logistics mashup that displays inventory for a group of department stores based on specific criteria. For example, you can mash current storm information onto a map of store locations and then wire the map to inventory data to show which stores located in the path of storms are low on generators.

3. **Human resource.** An HR mashup that provides a quick glance at employee data such as profiles, salary, ratings, benefits status, and activities. Data can be filtered to show custom views, for example, products whose average quarterly sales are lower than last quarter.

Enterprise Mashup Vendors

Several vendors offer mashup capabilities, but not all of them offer enterprise-grade mashup software. Vendors offering enterprise mashups are Magic Software and JackBe with Presto. Point-and-click dashboard building is a common feature. These mashup technologies provide visually rich and secure enterprise apps created from live data. They provide the flexibility to combine data from any enterprise app and the cloud regardless of its location. Users can build apps and dashboards that can be displayed on the Web and mobile devices.

Questions

1. Sketch or describe the architecture of an enterprise mashup application.
2. What is an enterprise data mashup?
3. What are the functions and uses of enterprise mashups?
4. Explain why business workers may need data mashup technology.
5. What are three benefits of mashup technology to the organization?

11.3 Digital Dashboards

Dashboards are a style of reporting that depicts KPIs, operational or strategic information with intuitive and interactive displays. Table 11.3 lists typical metrics displayed on dashboards by function. An executive dashboard displays a company's performance metrics, which are automatically updated in real time (every 15 minutes) based on custom programming and connectivity with existing business systems. Dashboards improve the information synthesis process by bringing in multiple, disparate data feeds and sources, extracting features of interest, and manipulating the data so the information is in a more accessible format. Users no longer need to log into multiple applications to see how the business is performing.

Components of dashboards are:

- **Design.** The visualization techniques and descriptive captions to convey information so that they are correctly understood. Infographics are widely used because they convey information in interesting and informative designs.

- **Performance metrics.** KPIs and other real time content displayed on the dashboard. All dashboard data should reflect the current value of each metric.

- **API.** APIs (application programming interfaces) connect disparate data sources and feeds to display on the dashboard. The alternative is for users or IT to manually enter data to the dashboard. Dashboards created in this manner tend to fail because of the risk of incomplete, outdated, or wrong data, which users learn not to trust.

- **Access.** Preferred access is via a secure Web browser from a mobile device.

TABLE 11.3   Metrics Displayed on Dashboards by Function

DASHBOARDS	METRICS
Financial performance	• Net income • Cash balance, actual vs. expected • Profit, current month projection • Changes in A/R and A/P
E-commerce	• Daily website visitors by traffic source • Trend of mobile vs. tablet traffic • Location where visitors are located • Top referring websites • Top keywords referring traffic • Revenue per website visitor
Revenue	• Sales per day per channel • How revenue is trending • Days with strongest sales, weakest sales • Products selling the best, worst
Sales team	• Sales by lead source; which leads are most and least effective • Number of leads and proposals per salesperson • Proposal close percentage, • Salesperson closing percentages • Where in the conversion funnel customers are being lost. Conversion funnels are paths that prospective customers take before they become paying clients
Advertising	• Number of leads generated by advertising; which advertising is most and least effective • Cost per lead, by advertising source • Advertising expense, as a percent of sales • Which advertising sources directly lead to sales
Order fulfillment	• Number of products manufactured, reworked • On-time completion percent • Changes in inventory levels • Percent of on-time delivery per week, month

DASHBOARDS ARE REAL TIME

Dashboards are often mistakenly thought of as reports consisting of various gauges, charts, and dials, but the purpose of business dashboards is much more specific and directed. The purpose of dashboards is to give users a clear view of the *current* state of KPIs, real time alerts, and other metrics about operations. Dashboard design is a critical factor because business users need to be able to understand the significance of the dashboard information at a glance and have the capability to drill down to one or more levels of detail. Having real time, or near real time, data is essential to keep users aware of any meaningful changes in the metrics as they occur and to provide information for making decisions in real time. Users can take corrective actions promptly.

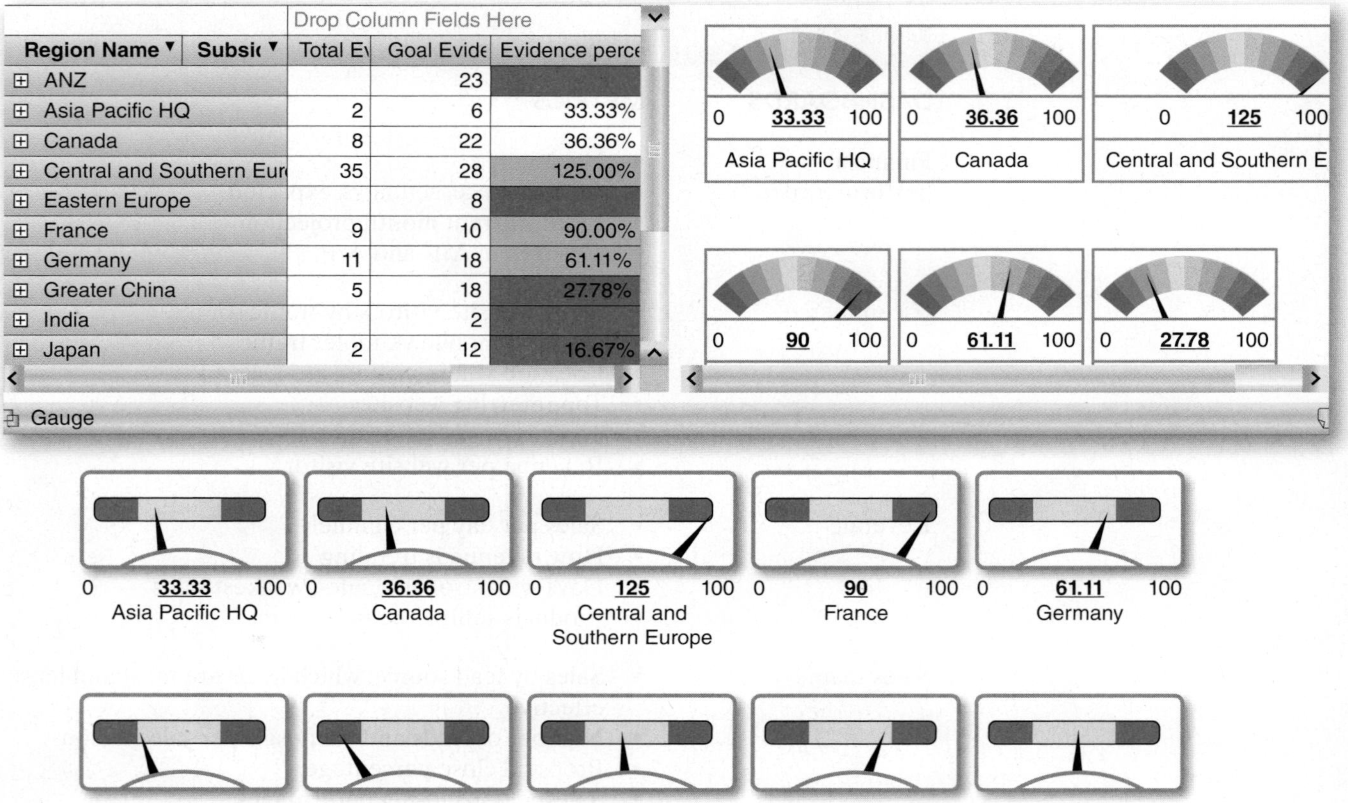

Drop Column Fields Here
Region Name
Subsic
Total E\
Goal Evide
Evidence perce
ANZ 23
Asia Pacific HQ 2 6 33.33%
Canada 8 22 36.36%
Central and Southern Eur 35 28 125.00%
Eastern Europe 8
France 9 10 90.00%
Germany 11 18 61.11%
Greater China 5 18 27.78%
India 2
Japan 2 12 16.67%
Gauge
0 33.33 100 Asia Pacific HQ
0 36.36 100 Canada
0 125 100 Central and Southern E
0 90 100
0 61.11 100
0 27.78 100
0 33.33 100 Asia Pacific HQ
0 36.36 100 Canada
0 125 100 Central and Southern Europe
0 90 100 France
0 61.11 100 Germany

Figure 11.8 Dashboards are designed to meet the information needs of their users.

By looking at the dashboard in Figure 11.8, you notice how color-coded displays can quickly inform the user of the status of KPIs.

HOW OPERATIONAL AND STRATEGIC DASHBOARDS WORK

Dashboards are custom programmed to automatically and securely pull, analyze, and display data from enterprise systems, cloud apps, data feeds, and external sources (Figure 11.9). They work by connecting to business systems, such as accounting

30%
55%
75%
100%
75%
55%
30%
Statistics
Analytics
56%
81%

© Media Mates Oy/iStockphoto

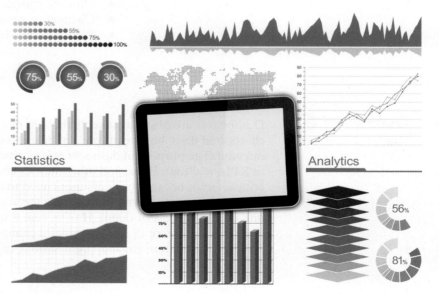

Figure 11.9 Dashboards pull data from disparate data sources and feeds, manipulate the data, and then display the metrics.

software, ERP, CRM, SCM, e-mail systems, website analytics programs, and project management software via APIs. IT at Work 11.2 describes dashboards in action at Hartford Hospital. Tech Note 11.4 lists vendors that offer free trials of dashboard software.

TECH NOTE 11.4 Free Trial Dashboards

A few vendors that offer free trials to build your own dashboards are:

- Dundas.com
- GrowThink.com
- MicroStrategy.com
- SAP Crystal Dashboard Design
- Sisense.com

| BENEFITS

The interrelated benefits of business dashboards are:

1. **Visibility.** Blind spots are minimized or eliminated. Threats and opportunities are detected as soon as possible.
2. **Continuous improvement.** A famous warning from Peter Drucker was "if you can't measure it, you can't improve it." Executive dashboards are custom designed to display the user's critical metrics and measures.
3. **Single sign on.** Managers can spend a lot of time logging into various business systems and running reports. Single-sign-on dashboards save time and effort.
4. **Deviations from what was budgeted or planned.** Any metrics, such as those listed in Table 11.3, can be programmed to display deviations from targets, such as comparisons of actual and planned or budgeted.
5. **Accountability.** When employees know their performance is tracked in near real time and can see their results, they tend to be motivated to improve their performance.

IT at **Work** 11.2

Dashboards in Action at Hartford Hospital

Health-care providers at Hartford Hospital, a 700-bed teaching hospital in Connecticut, were challenged by the shortage of real time data in usable form, according to Michael Lindberg M.D., chairman of the Department of Medicine (Baldwin, 2011). Hartford Hospital implemented dashboard technology from CareFx.

Dr. Lindberg uses the dashboard to track data in three key areas that impact the hospital's performance:

1. **Patient data.** Data on patients' length of stay and percentage of early morning discharges.

2. **Bed availability.** Data on types of beds open, percentage of beds not available for patients such as those being cleaned, or beds in a room with a patient in isolation.
3. **Remission rate.** Data about patients who return to the hospital within 30 days of their discharge date.

The dashboard data helps Dr. Lindberg fulfill Joint Commission requirements for ongoing physician evaluations. He can identify trends and compare current to past performance. According to Dr. Lindberg, "We need to have a handle on what physicians are doing. Having a database to drill down to the individual physician goes a long way toward satisfying those requirements." Purely financial data are not yet available on the CareFx dashboard, but Lindberg plans to add indicators such as cost per hospitalization broken down by physician and department to identify doctors who are outliers for test ordering.

Questions

1. What KPIs are displayed on Dr. Lindberg's dashboard?
2. What KPIs will be added to the dashboard?

Questions

1. Describe business dashboards and their functions.
2. Why do you think dashboards must be in real time and customized for the executive or manager?
3. How do business dashboards differ from other types of visual reports?
4. Explain the components of dashboards.
5. What are benefits of dashboards?

11.4 Geospatial Data and Geographic Information Systems

A **geographic information system (GIS)** captures, manages, analyzes, and displays multidimensional geographic data, also called geospatial data. GIS can connect to location-tracking devices and apps. GIS software can link geospatial data—*where things or people are and where they are going*—with descriptive data—*what things are like or what customers are doing.* GIS's ability to track customers' movement and behavior in real space enables new strategies for marketing, retail, and entrepreneurship. Their ability to track products along the supply chain also offers opportunities in logistics and order fulfillment.

Collecting home and work addresses only paints a static picture of consumers' locations. Their movements over time are not tracked. Data that are organized by zip code only cannot reveal customers' habits. By integrating geographic information systems, businesses can more effectively solve problems like organizing sales territories, pinpointing optimal locations, finding customers, managing campaigns, and delivering services. Geospatial data can also map competitors' actions.

GEOCODING

In many cases, locations are already in existing data stores, but not in a format suitable for analytics. A simple process called **geocoding** can convert postal addresses to geospatial data that can then be measured and analyzed. By tapping into this resource, decision makers can use the geographic or spatial context to detect and respond to opportunities.

Case in Point: GM

General Motors (GM) spends a staggering $2 billion a year on marketing. In the past, it shotgunned its ads at the general public. Now, it maps out which types of households will buy new cars, more accurately determines locations where people buy certain models, and channels its ads specifically to those areas. As a result, GM spends less money to generate higher sales.

GM managers use ESRI's ArcGIS software to view local demographics, location characteristics, regional differences, and the competitive brand environment to determine how a given dealership should be performing compared to actual results. The GIS makes it possible for GM to isolate demand, target its marketing efforts to local preferences, and position its dealerships to improve sales. With the intelligence provided by the GIS, GM has increased sales despite cutting the advertising budget.

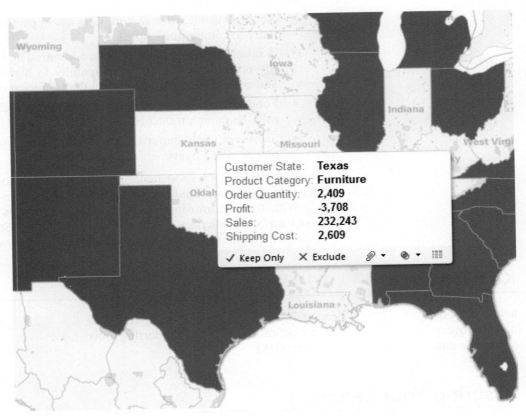

Figure 11.10 GIS can create maps with multiple layers of data.

GIS IS NOT A MAP

On a map, if you looked at retail store #50, you would see the name of the store and a point denoting where it is located. However, if you view a GIS map on your tablet, you can click on retail store #50 and see its location, name, weekly or monthly revenue, product categories, a photo of the storefront, and a virtual tour.

Unlike a flat map, a GIS-generated map has many layers of information for many ways of thinking about a geographic space. Figure 11.10 shows an example. By hovering over a state, such as Texas, another layer of data about sales and financial data appears.

INFRASTRUCTURE AND LOCATION-AWARE COLLECTION OF GEOSPATIAL DATA

The infrastructure needed to collect geospatial data continues to expand. Cellular and Internet service providers, sensors, Google Earth, GPS, and RFID systems know the location of each connected user or object. Foursquare, Google Maps, and other mobile apps rely on GPS locations. With the Shopkick app, Macy's can track a shopper's every move within one of its stores and send the shopper notifications about deals and items of interest. iBeacon is a feature available in iOS 7 devices that uses a low-power Bluetooth transmission to broadcast a user's location. iBeacon allows Apple, or app developers leveraging Apple technology, to track users inside buildings where satellite transmissions may not reach.

Like Macy's, businesses can motivate customers to download a location-tracking app. Using GIS can help businesses target their customer markets more effectively and dynamically by engaging with them in real time.

INTEGRATING GIS INTO BUSINESS APPLICATIONS

GIS tools have made significant contributions to decision making in finance, accounting, marketing, and BI. Business applications include:

- Analysts can pinpoint the average income in areas where the highest performing stores are established.

- Retailers can learn how store sales are impacted by population or the proximity to competitors' stores.
- A retail chain with plans to open a hundred new stores can use GIS to identify relevant demographics, proximity to highways, public transportation, and competitors' stores to select the best location options.
- Food and consumer products companies can chart locations of complaint calls, enabling product traceability in the event of a crisis or recall.
- Sales reps might better target their customer visits by analyzing the geography of sales targets.

With current GIS, geospatial, and geocoding technologies and platforms, GISs can be easily incorporated and managed within data analytics and visualization software.

With the GIS moving into the cloud, developers of enterprise applications based on SAP, Microsoft Office, SharePoint, MicroStrategy, IBM Cognos, and Microsoft Dynamics CRM are using it to create a wide range of mobile applications.

Key Terms

analytical tools	geocoding	geospatial data	supply chain visibility
data discovery	geographic information	reporting tools	
enterprise data mashup	system (GIS)		

Assuring Your Learning

DISCUSS: Critical Thinking Questions

1. How people use, access, and discover data in business is being actively disrupted by tablets, which had been designed for consumers. Users have higher expectations for data displays and capabilities. Boring, static graphs and pie charts are unacceptable. Discuss how performance management—the monitoring of KPIs, for example—may be improved by providing managers with data visualizations. Now consider the opposite. In your opinion, would lack of data visualization hurt the ability to manage performance?

2. Lots of data are available to retailers to make good decisions—loyalty programs, Web analytics, and point-of-sale data. However, there is a big gap between having data and being able to leverage them for real time decision making. How can enterprise mashups close this gap?

3. Visit SAS.com and search for Visual Data Discovery.
   a. Review the screenshots, features, and benefits.
   b. In your opinion, what are the two most important benefits of this data discovery tool?
   c. Would you recommend this tool? Explain your answer.

4. Explain how executive dashboards can lead to better business insights. What are the limitations of dashboards?

EXPLORE: Online and Interactive Exercises

5. Periscopic (http://periscopic.com/) is a socially conscious data visualization firm that specializes in using IT to help companies and organizations facilitate information transparency and public awareness. From endangered species, to politics, to social justice, it is the goal of Periscopic to engage the public and deliver a message of responsibility and action. Its philosophy and tagline are "do good with data."
   a. Visit http://periscopic.com/ and explore its recent work.
   b. Discuss how data are used to do good.
   c. How effective is Periscopic's approach to public awareness and social justice?

6. Visit spotfire.tibco.com and click Demos.
   a. Select and watch one of the featured demos.
   b. Describe the data visualizations features in the demo.
   c. Explain the benefits of the application or analytics.

7. Visit the Analysis Factory at www.analysisfactory.com.
   a. Click Gallery and then select Custom Solutions.
   b. View one demo, such as Performance Trends, Fusion Charts, Manufacturing Performance, and Sales Map Dashboard.
   c. Create a table listing all of the customer solutions for which you tried the demo in the first column. In the second column, list the departments or functions each customer solution supports. In the third column, list the types of visualizations used in each solution.
   d. In the team report, discuss how dashboards can impact the quality of business decisions.

ANALYZE & DECIDE: Apply IT Concepts to Business Decisions

8. Visit www.TableauSoftware.com. Click Learning and Visual Gallery from the drop-down menu.
   a. Review three interactive visualizations and dashboards. How do they convey information at a glance?
   b. Click Free Trial. Download the Tableau Public and create your own data visualization. Print or publish it on a website or blog.
9. Visit www.itdashboard.gov/data_feeds. Use this tool to design your own snapshots of IT dashboard data. Follow the steps to create, save, and publish your IT dashboard.
10. Visit microstrategy.com.
   a. Click Training and Events and select Webcasts from the drop-down menu.
   b. Select the On-Demand tab. Then select and watch a webcast about dashboards or data discovery.
   c. Write a report describing what you learned.

CASE 11.2

Visualization Case: Are You Ready for Football?

Nothing inspires passionate comments among sports fans like preseason predictions. Brett McMurphy's data visualization looks at how teams ranked in different polls.

Visit www.tableausoftware.com and search using "ready for football." You will see the Preseason Polls & Returning Starters visualization. (a) Interact with the Preseason Polls & Returning Starters visualization. (b) Select various filters and observe the changes. (c) Download the workbook by clicking the Download button at the lower right corner of the display. View and interact with two other sports-related visualizations, for example, CBS Sports Defensive Matchup Tracker, Fantasy Closers, and Premier League Points Leaders. Download each. Click the Business and Real Estate Gallery. View and interact with two data visualizations in the gallery. Download each.

Questions
1. Which visualization was the easiest to understand at a glance? Explain.
2. Which visualization was the most difficult or complicated to understand easily? Explain.
3. What are the benefits and potential drawbacks of interactive visualizations?

CASE 11.3

Video Case: The Beauty of Data Visualization

TED stands for technology, entertainment, and design. Visit TED.com and search "data visualization." Select "David McCandless: The beauty of data visualization." The video and transcript are available. In his TED talk, The Beauty of Data Visualization, David McCandless says that data visualization gives us a second language—the language of the eye.

Questions
1. Explain what he means by language of the eye.
2. What are examples of language of the mind?
3. What happens when language of the eye and language of the mind combine?
4. What did David McCandless say about information design?

References

Baldwin, G. "Dashboards in Action." *Health Data Management.* October 20, 2011.

Curtis, K. "Deloitte Hosts PepsiCo and Safeway at the HIVE (Highly Immersive Visual Environment)." *GMAOnline.Org.* 2013. gmaonline.org

Deloitte CIO Journal. "Data Visualization Helps Safeway Keep Shelves Stocked." *The Wall Street Journal.* December 3, 2013.

Groenfeldt, T., "A Tableau Solution To Those Excel Blues." *Forbes.* February 22, 2013. forbes.com/sites/tomgroenfeldt

Henschen, D. "Data Visualization for the Masses?" *InformationWeek,* March 26, 2012.

Sommer, D. & J. D. Lovelock. "Market Trends: The Collision of Data Discovery and Business Intelligence Will Cause Destruction." *Gartner Inc.,* April 16, 2013.

Part 4

Managing Business Relationships, Projects, and Codes of Ethics

IT Strategy and Balanced Scorecard

Chapter Snapshot

Case 12.1 Opening Case: Intel's IT Strategic Planning Process

12.1 IT Strategy and Strategic Planning Process
12.2 Aligning IT with Business Strategy
12.3 Balanced Scorecard
12.4 IT Sourcing and Cloud Strategy

Key Terms
Assuring Your Learning

- **Discuss:** Critical Thinking Questions
- **Explore:** Online and Interactive Exercises
- **Analyze & Decide:** Apply IT Concepts to Business Decisions

Case 12.2 Business Case: AstraZeneca Terminates $1.4B Outsourcing Contract with IBM

Case 12.3 Data Analysis: Third-Party versus Company-Owned Offshoring

References

Learning Outcomes

1. Describe the steps in the IT strategic planning process, how to evaluate the IT strategy, and the role of IT steering committees.

2. Explain the value of aligning the IT and business strategies and how this alignment can be achieved.

3. Describe the balanced scorecard methodology, its four performance metrics, and its function as a road map for strategy execution and making strategy a continual process.

4. Describe how sourcing strategies can improve performance and the risk and challenges of sourcing and off-shore relationships. Explain the IT vendor selection and management processes and how to improve successful relationships through the use of contracts and service level agreements.

Chapter Snapshot

As you have read throughout this book, what a company can do depends on what its IT infrastructure and information systems can do. **IT strategy** shapes the direction of IT investments over the next one to five years to maximize business value and shareholder wealth. Like all strategies, IT strategy defines priorities, a road map, budget, and investment plan—and must align with and support the **business strategy**. Deciding on a strategy entails making decisions about a future that can only be guessed at. According to Roger L. Martin's article in *Harvard Business Review*: "True strategy is about placing bets and making hard choices. The objective is not to eliminate risk but to increase the odds of success" (Martin, 2014). Strategy making is uncomfortable because it is about taking risks and facing the unknown.

In the mid-2010s, this process takes into consideration social, mobile, analytics, cloud, software as a service (SaaS), and methods to measure how well the IT plan is working. IT strategic plans include an operating plan for acquiring or providing new technology and services. The **operating plan** defines how to execute the IT strategic plan; for example, deciding on in-house development or sourcing options such as managed services, cloud computing, or SaaS. Strategies are measured and evaluated continuously and revised annually during the strategic planning process. **Balanced scorecard** is a methodology for evaluating performance based on financial and nonfinancial metrics.

CASE 12.1 OPENING CASE

Intel's IT Strategic Planning Process

INTEL'S IT ENVIRONMENT

Intel operates in 65 countries with almost 100,000 employees in 168 sites, and has 59 IT sites with 6,300 IT employees. In 2013, 94 percent of all new services were deployed to the cloud. IT provides 14,000 Ultrabook touch devices and 43,200 mobile handheld devices.

IT STRATEGIC PLANNING PROCESS

Strategic planning is the process of formulating the direction of a business in terms of how it intends to achieve its mission, goals, and objectives.

IT–business alignment means how closely an organization's IT strategy is interwoven with and driving its overall business strategy.

Intel designed its **strategic planning** process to closely align IT investments and solutions to strategic planning at the corporate level. Close **IT–business alignment** is achieved by bringing together a variety of perspectives from senior management, IT, and business groups in the planning stage—steps 1 through 4 in Figure 12.1. To minimize time demands, the strategic planning team engages subject matter experts at critical points instead of involving them at every step of the process.

The planning, decision-making, measuring, and evaluation activities flow naturally from one step to the next. The business and IT strategic plans are evaluated and adjusted annually to keep pace with rapid changes in the industry. Performance is measured and evaluated using the **balanced scorecard** methodology to ensure that limited resources are invested to achieve the highest possible ROI. Characteristics of the planning process are summarized in Table 12.1.

BALANCED SCORECARD

Balanced scorecard is a methodology—and a tool—for measuring performance using financial and non-financial metrics.

The balanced scorecard translates mission and vision statements into a comprehensive set of objectives and performance measures that can be quantified and appraised. **Objectives** are the building blocks of strategy. Objectives set out what the business is trying to achieve. They are action-oriented statements, for instance, achieve a ROI of at least 10 percent in 201x, that define the continuous improvement activities that must be done to be successful. Objectives have the following "SMART" criteria:

- *Specific*: Define what is to be achieved.
- *Measurable:* Are stated in measurable terms.
- *Achievable:* Are realistic given available resources and conditions.
- *Relevant:* Are relevant to the people who are responsible for achieving them.
- *Time frame:* Include a time dimension.

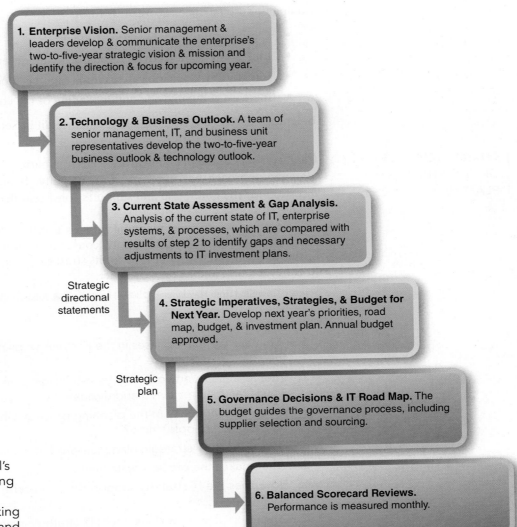

Figure 12.1 Model of Intel's six-step IT strategic planning process. Planning phase: steps 1 to 4. Decision-making phase: step 5. Measuring and evaluation phase: step 6.

The image shows six connected boxes in a cascading flow:

1. **Enterprise Vision.** Senior management & leaders develop & communicate the enterprise's two-to-five-year strategic vision & mission and identify the direction & focus for upcoming year.

2. **Technology & Business Outlook.** A team of senior management, IT, and business unit representatives develop the two-to-five-year business outlook & technology outlook.

3. **Current State Assessment & Gap Analysis.** Analysis of the current state of IT, enterprise systems, & processes, which are compared with results of step 2 to identify gaps and necessary adjustments to IT investment plans.

Strategic directional statements

4. **Strategic Imperatives, Strategies, & Budget for Next Year.** Develop next year's priorities, road map, budget, & investment plan. Annual budget approved.

Strategic plan

5. **Governance Decisions & IT Road Map.** The budget guides the governance process, including supplier selection and sourcing.

6. **Balanced Scorecard Reviews.** Performance is measured monthly.

TABLE 12.1	Characteristics of Intel's Corporate and IT Strategic Planning Process
Integrated	Intel IT activities are synchronized with the company's strategic direction. By tightly linking Intel IT to the corporate planning process, the IT function has strengthened its credibility throughout Intel and earned the position of a trusted partner.
Holistic	The strategic planning process aligns IT investments with Intel's business direction and consolidates expertise and ideas from across Intel IT.
Sustainable	As new strategies are implemented, a common practice is to "look up" every two or three years and ask, "What's next?" Instead of replacing the plan every two to three years, Intel uses a different approach. To keep pace with changes in the environment, the team looks at the plan every year to determine if anything shifted in its environment. If a shift has occurred and affected its business, the IT plan is updated as needed.

Companies use balanced scorecards to:

- Clarify or update a business strategy
- Link strategic objectives to long-term targets and annual budgets
- Integrate strategic objectives into resource allocation processes
- Increase companywide understanding of the corporate vision and strategy

Balanced scorecard is discussed in greater detail in Section 12.4.

CHARACTERISTICS OF THE STRATEGIC PLANNING PROCESS

Characteristics of the planning process are summarized in Table 12.1. Intel's strategic planning approach has improved Intel's agility. It provides a clear and credible direction for the enterprise and supports consistent decision making at all levels of the business.

An effective strategic planning process is critical to an enterprise's long-term success and health. The plan supports consistent decision making at all levels of the business. Each enterprise must adapt its strategic planning process and approach to fit is own culture and leadership style.

Sources: Compiled from Haydamack (2008), Haydamack & Johnson (2008), and Krishnapura et al (2014) .

Questions

1. What are the three phases in the IT strategic planning process? Describe the steps in each phase.
2. Intel formulates a two-to-five-year strategic plan. Given this time frame, why is the plan reviewed and evaluated every year?
3. Given the frequency of the planning process, what is done to minimize demands on people's time?
4. How is Intel's IT strategic plan measured and evaluated?
5. What makes the process sustainable?
6. How does the IT strategy support the short-term (one-year) business strategy?
7. In your opinion, how does Intel's IT strategic planning process impact the company's survival?

12.1 IT Strategy and the Strategic Planning Process

Long-term business planning starts with a clear understanding of the factors that create significant value and that work together with other factors to drive future revenue and profit at or above their current rates. These factors are **value drivers**.

VALUE DRIVERS

Value drivers enhance the value of a product or service to consumers, creating value for the company. Advanced IT, reliability, and brand reputation are examples.

In order to create business value, you must identify value drivers and then link them to daily activities. For example, it is not enough to identify *cost* as a key value drive. Cost is almost always a value driver, but for this factor to be useful, you need to drill down to the activities that impact cost. The general types of business value drivers are explained in Table 12.2.

Drivers can have a limited life span. Their value can diminish due to chances in the economy or industry, at which time they are replaced with relevant ones.

Value drivers are considered in the strategic planning process and the balanced scorecard methodology.

TABLE 12.2 Three General Types of Business Value Drivers

Type of Business Value Drivers	Definitions	Examples
Operational Shorter-term factors	Factors that impact cash flow and the cash generation ability through increased efficiency or growth.	Cost of raw materials, cost of providing service, cost per mile, sales volume, sales revenue
Financial Medium-term factors	Factors that minimize the cost of capital incurred by the company to finance operations	Debt level, working capital, capital expenditures, day's receivables, bad debt expense
Sustainability Long-term factors	Survival factors; factors that enable a business to continue functioning consistently and optimally for a long time	Government regulations, industry standards, federal and state environmental laws, privacy and security regulations

IT STRATEGY

IT strategy directs investments in social, mobile, analytics, cloud, and other digital technology resources. It focuses on the value drivers in core process areas in order to make targeted improvements.

IT strategic planning is a systematic process for determining what a business should become and how it can best achieve that goal, as you read in Opening Case 12.1. It evaluates the full potential of a business often using SWOT analysis (strengths, weaknesses, opportunities, and threats) and then decides how to allocate resources to develop critical capabilities. In practice, competing agendas, tight budgets, poor interdepartmental communication, and politics can turn strategic planning discussions into bar room brawls—if they are not well managed.

Reactive Approach to IT Investments Will Fail

Few companies today could realize their full potential business value without updated IT infrastructures and services. Yet many companies still struggle to make the right IT decisions and investments in order to leverage relatively new IT trends—cloud computing and SaaS, big data, analytics, social, and mobile. Making IT investments on the basis of an immediate need or threat—rather than according to IT strategy—might be necessary at times, but reactive approaches result in incompatible, redundant, expensive to maintain, or failed systems. These IT investments tend to be patches that rarely align with the business strategy.

Two of the biggest risks and concerns of top management are (1) failing to align IT to real business needs and, as a result, (2) failing to deliver value to the business. Since IT has a dramatic effect on business performance and competitiveness, the failure to manage IT effectively seriously impacts the business.

IT Strategies Support the Business Strategy

The four objectives of IT strategic plans are to:

1. Improve management's understanding of IT opportunities and limitations
2. Assess current performance
3. Identify capacity and human resource requirements
4. Clarify the level of investment required

Various functions in the organization—such as manufacturing, R&D (research and development), and IT—are most successful when their strategies are forward looking. Forward looking means that they do SWOT analysis to create their future rather than react to challenges or crises. Additionally, IT implementations that require new infrastructure or the merging of disparate information systems can take years. Long lead times and lack of expertise have prompted companies to explore a variety of IT strategies.

IT Deployment Strategies: In-House and Sourcing

IT strategy guides investment decisions and decisions on how ISs will be developed, acquired, and/or implemented. IT strategies fall into two broad categories:

1. **In-house development**, in which systems are developed or other IT work is done in-house, possibly with the help of consulting companies or vendors. Typically, ITs that provide competitive advantages or that contain proprietary or confidential data are developed and maintained by the organization's own in-house IT function.

2. **Sourcing**, in which systems are developed or IT work is done by a third party or vendor. There are many versions of sourcing, which had been called *outsourcing*. Work or development can be sourced to consulting companies or vendors that are within the same country, which is referred to as **onshore sourcing**. Or the work can be sourced offshore to other countries. Sourcing that is done offshore is also called **offshoring**. Other options are to lease or to purchase ITs as services. Cloud computing and SaaS have expanded sourcing options significantly. Tech Note 12.1 discusses a sourcing challenge and solution.

TECH NOTE 12.1 Managing Sourcing Arrangements and SLA

Sourcing creates its own set of challenges. Companies that have multiple outsourcers face the challenge of managing all of these relationships. As companies increase outsourcing activities, a gap is created in their organizational structures, management methods, and software tools. At that point, companies turn for help to an **outsource relationship management (ORM) company**. ORMs provide automated tools to monitor and manage the outsourcing relationships. ORMs monitor and manage service level agreements (SLAs). The SLA must be managed because it serves as both the blueprint and warranty for the outsourced arrangement.

This example shows the importance of managing SLAs. A U.S. transportation company needed to make cuts immediately to its IT operating budget to reverse cost overruns. The company had a long-standing outsourcing agreement with a top-tier service provider, but it had not implemented effective SLAs to control costs. As a result, it had outsourced 750 terabytes of data at an annual cost of more than $20,000 per terabyte, an overinvestment that contributed to runaway IT outsourcing expenditures of $225 million a year. A companywide budget shortfall forced the IT division to cut $36 million from its 2012 budget—without harming quality of service. The chief information officer (CIO) had to re-examine its data and infrastructure needs and take a more informed, proactive role in managing the relationship with its service provider.

In the mid-2010s, the critical question is no longer whether cloud computing will be a fundamental deployment model for enterprise systems, such as ERP and

SCM. Rather, the question is how companies can profit from the capabilities that cloud computing offers.

Organizations use combinations of these IT strategies—in-house, onshore, or domestic sourcing, offshoring, cloud computing, and SaaS.

IT and Business Strategy Disconnects

According to a survey of business leaders by PwC Advisory, 87 percent of business leaders believe that IT is critical to their companies' strategic success, but not all of them work with IT to achieve that success. Less than 50 percent of business leaders reported that the IT function was very involved in the strategic planning process. When the IT strategy was not aligned with the business strategies, there was a higher risk that the IT project would be abandoned before completion. About 75 percent of companies abandoned at least one IT project and 30 percent abandoned more than 10 percent of IT projects for this reason. There are several possible reasons why a high percentage of IT projects are abandoned—the business strategy changed, technology changed, the project was not going to be completed on time or budget, the project sponsors responsible did not work well together, or the IT strategy was changed to cloud or SaaS.

The fundamental principle to be learned is that when enterprise strategies change, the IT strategies need to change with them. Both strategies are dynamic—to adapt to opportunities and threats.

Governance

Business and IT strategies depend on shared IT ownership and shared IT governance among all senior managers. When an IT or any type of failure causes harm to customers, business partners, employees, or the environment, then regulatory agencies will hold the chief executive officer (CEO) accountable—and the public will too. A high-profile example is BP CEO Tony Hayward, who was held accountable to Congress for "The Role of BP in the Deepwater Horizon Explosion and Oil Spill," the rig explosion that killed 11 workers and caused the subsea oil gusher that released 60,000+ barrels per day into the Gulf of Mexico. Hayward's attempts to claim ignorance of the risks and use the SODDI defense ("some other dude did it") does not get him or any CEOs off the hook. *A company can outsource the work, but not the responsibility for it.*

Because of the interrelationship between IT and business strategies, IT and other business managers share responsibility in developing IT strategic plans. Therefore, a governance structure needs to be in place that crosses organizational lines and makes senior management responsible for the success of key IT initiatives.

| IT STRATEGIC
PLANNING PROCESS | CIOs undertake IT strategic planning on a yearly, quarterly, or monthly basis. A good IT planning process helps ensure that IT aligns, and stays aligned, within an organization's business strategy. Because organizational goals change over time, it is not sufficient to develop a long-term IT strategy and not reexamine the strategy on a regular basis. For this reason, IT planning is an ongoing process. The IT planning process results in a formal IT strategy or a reassessment each year or each quarter of the existing portfolio of IT resources.

Recall that the focus of IT strategy is on how IT creates business value. Typically, annual planning cycles are established to identify potentially beneficial IT services, to perform cost–benefit analyses, and to subject the list of potential projects to resource allocation analysis. Often the entire process is conducted by an IT steering committee. |

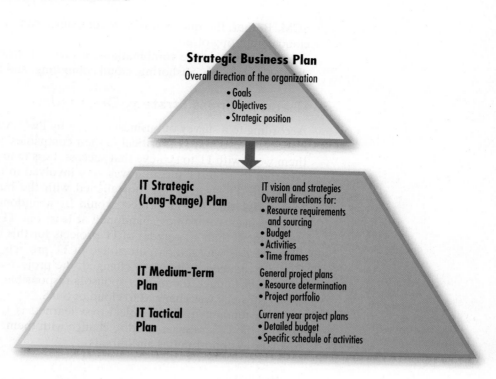

Strategic Business Plan
Overall direction of the organization
• Goals
• Objectives
• Strategic position

IT Strategic (Long-Range) Plan	IT vision and strategies Overall directions for: • Resource requirements and sourcing • Budget • Activities • Time frames
IT Medium-Term Plan	General project plans • Resource determination • Project portfolio
IT Tactical Plan	Current year project plans • Detailed budget • Specific schedule of activities

Figure 12.2 IT strategic planning process.

IT Steering Committees

The steering committee is a team of managers and staff representing various business units that establish IT priorities and ensure the IT department is meeting the needs of the enterprise. The steering committee's major tasks are:

- **Set the direction.** In linking the corporate strategy with the IT strategy, planning is the key activity.

- **Allocate scarce resources.** The committee approves the allocation of resources for and within the information systems organization. This includes outsourcing policy.

- **Make staffing decisions.** Key IT personnel decisions involve a consultation-and-approval process made by the committee, including outsourcing decisions.

- **Communicate and provide feedback.** Information regarding IT activities should flow freely.

- **Set and evaluate performance metrics.** The committee should establish performance measures for the IT department and see that they are met. This includes the initiation of SLAs.

The success of steering committees largely depends on the establishment of IT *governance*, formally established statements that direct the policies regarding IT alignment with organizational goals and allocation of resources.

Figure 12.2 shows the IT strategic planning process. The planning process begins with the creation of a strategic business plan. The *long-range IT plan*, sometimes referred to as the *strategic IT plan*, is then based on the strategic business plan. The IT strategic plan starts with the IT vision and strategy, which defines the future concept of what IT should do to achieve the goals, objectives, and strategic position of the firm and how this will be achieved. The overall direction, requirements, and sourcing—either outsourcing or insourcing—of resources, such as infrastructure, application services, data services, security services, IT governance, and management architecture; budget; activities; and time frames are set for three to five years into the future. The planning process continues by addressing lower level activities with a shorter time frame.

The next level down is a *medium-term IT plan*, which identifies general project plans in terms of the specific requirements and sourcing of resources as well as the **project portfolio**. The project portfolio lists major resource projects, including infrastructure, application services, data services, and security services, that are consistent with the long-range plan. Some companies may define their portfolio in terms of applications. The **applications portfolio** is a list of major, approved information system projects that are also consistent with the long-range plan. Expectations for sourcing of resources in the project or applications portfolio should be driven by the business strategy. Since some of these projects will take more than a year to complete and others will not start in the current year, this plan extends over several years.

The third level is a *tactical plan*, which details budgets and schedules for current-year projects and activities. In reality, because of the rapid pace of change in technology and the environment, short-term plans may include major items not anticipated in the other plans.

The planning process just described is currently practiced by many organizations. Specifics of the IT planning process, of course, vary among organizations. For example, not all organizations have a high-level IT steering committee. Project priorities may be determined by the IT director, by his or her superior, by company politics, or even on a first-come, first-served basis.

The deliverables from the IT planning process should include the following: an evaluation of the strategic goals and directions of the organization and how IT is aligned; a new or revised IT vision and assessment of the state of the IT division; a statement of the strategies, objectives, and policies for the IT division; and the overall direction, requirements, and sourcing of resources.

Questions

1. What are value drivers?
2. What are the three categories of value drivers?
3. Why do reactive approaches to IT investments fail?
4. What is onshore sourcing?
5. What is the goal of IT–business alignment?
6. Why is IT strategic planning revisited on a regular basis?
7. What are the functions of a steering committee?
8. Describe the IT strategic planning process.

12.2 Aligning IT with Business Strategy

Today, all roads lead to digital. From business strategy to execution, digital technology has become the foundation for everything enterprises do. Naturally, IT strategy needs to keep pace with business strategy.

Alignment is a complex management activity, and its complexity increases as the pace of global competition and technological change increases. IT–business alignment can be improved by focusing on the following activities:

1. **Commitment to IT planning by senior management.** Senior management commitment to IT planning is essential to success. See IT at Work 12.1.

2. **CIO is a member of senior management.** The key to achieving IT-business alignment is for the CIO to attain strategic influence. Rather than being narrow technologists, CIOs must be both business and technology savvy. The skill set of CIOs is outlined in Table 12.3.

3. **Understanding IT and corporate planning.** A prerequisite for effective IT–business alignment for the CIO is to understand business planning and for the CEO and business planners to understand their company's IT planning.

4. **Shared culture and good communication.** The CIO must understand and buy into the corporate culture so that IS planning does not occur in isolation. Frequent, open, and effective communication is essential to ensure a shared culture and keep everyone aware of planning activities and business dynamics.

5. **Multilevel links.** Links between business and IT plans should be made at the strategic, tactical, and operational levels.

IT at Work 12.1

PwC's 5th Annual Digital IQ Survey

PwC's 5th annual Digital IQ global survey included 1,108 respondents from 12 countries across a variety of industries. Respondents were divided evenly between IT and business leaders. More than 75 percent of respondents work in corporations with revenues of $1 billion+ (Curran, DeGarmo, & Sviokla, 2013).

Strength of CIO & C-Suite Relationship Influences Performance

Companies were categorized based on the strength of the relationship between the CIO and other C-suite members— the CEO, CFO (chief financial officer), CMO (chief marketing officer), CRO (chief risk officer), and CISO (chief information security officer) and business unit leaders as follows:

- **Strong collaborators.** The CIO has a strong relationship across all relationship pairs with C-suite members. Strong collaborators had scores of at least 4.5 out of 5. Companies with collaborative C-suites link business strategy and IT.

- **Less collaborative.** Companies with scores of 4.5 or less across CIO and C-suite relationships.

Top performers are defined as those in the top quartile (25 percent) of revenue growth and innovation and with annual growth of at least 5 percent.

What Was Learned from the Global Survey

According to the survey, compared to less collaborative companies, strong collaborators:

- **Achieve better results.** They are four times more likely to be top performers than those with less collaborative teams. IT initiatives are more likely to be on time, on budget, and within project scope.

- **Adapt quickly.** They adapt quickly to market changes to maintain an advantage over competitors.

- **Think together.** IT and business leaders share the same understanding of the corporate strategy and the costs needed to implement the strategic road map. They view their CEO as a champion of IT and understand IT risks that may impact the business.

- **Act together.** They have explicit processes in place to link the IT road map to the corporate strategy. They invest more aggressively in social, mobile, cloud, and analytics and map IT to strategic initiatives like new product and service development and market share growth.

- **More aligned on strategy.** In a majority of strong collaborators (82 percent), the CEO is a champion of IT and actively involves IT in the strategic and operational plans, compared with 54 percent for less collaborative companies.

In addition, strong relationships support more frequent and frank conversations about problems and collaborative problem solving. Too many IT projects fail because foundational issues are not dealt with candidly and fast enough. The Digital IQ study clearly shows that strong executive leadership and collaboration are crucial to building lasting value from IT.

TABLE 12.3   Skill Set of the CIO

Skills of CIOs needed to improve IT–business alignment and governance include:

- *Political savvy.* Effectively understand managers, workers, and their priorities and use that knowledge to influence others to support organizational objectives.
- *Influence, leadership, and power.* Inspire a shared vision and influence subordinates and superiors.
- *Relationship management.* Build and maintain working relationships with co-workers and those external to the organization. Negotiate problem solutions without alienating those impacted. Understand others and get their cooperation in nonauthority relationships.
- *Resourcefulness.* Think strategically and make good decisions under pressure. Can set up complex work systems and engage in flexible problem resolution.
- *Strategic planning.* Capable of developing long-term objectives and strategies and translating vision into realistic business strategies.
- *Doing what it takes.* Persevering in the face of obstacles.
- *Leading employees.* Delegating work to employees effectively; broadening employee opportunities; and interacting fairly with employees.

A Perfect IT/Business Alignment Case Study

The Commonwealth Bank of Australia (CBA) launched its Kaching mobile, social, and NFC payments apps in October 2011. (Kaching is pronounced *ka-ching*—the sound of a cash register long ago.) The mobile/social banking apps were criticized by many who claimed that customers would not be interested in mobile payments and banking services; that Facebook and social networks were not good platforms for banking and users would not like the bulky case that added NFC capabilities to the iPhone. They were wrong. By mid-2013, the Kaching app, iPhone NFC case, and Facebook app had been downloaded more than 1 million times across the Android and iOS platforms. The apps had handled over AU$9 billion in transactions (Duckett, 2013).

Kaching is an excellent example of what happens when the CIO has the mandate to drive business change through the use of the latest digital technology. With the success of Kaching, CBA's CIO Michael Harte had not just supported business activities, he had introduced a profitable new line of business (LeMay, 2013). What is also remarkable is that CBA was considered an old, traditional, slow-moving company. By leading with mobile, social, NFC technology, it has become an innovative financial institution.

Questions

1. How can IT–business alignment be improved?
2. How does strong collaboration among the CIO and other chief-level officers influence performance?
3. What skills are important to a CIO's success?
4. How did the CIO of CBA contribute to the bank's competitiveness?

12.3 Balanced Scorecard

The balanced scorecard (BSC) is a strategic measurement and management methodology—and a tool. Robert Kaplan and David Norton introduced it in their 1992 *Harvard Business Review* (HBR) article, "The Balanced Scorecard—Measures that Drive Performance." The BSC methodology is widely used in all industry sectors for strategic planning and for evaluating how well objectives are being achieved. HBR editors consider the BSC as one of the most influential management ideas of the past 75 years.

The BSC method is "balanced" because it does not rely solely on traditional financial measures. Instead, it balances financial measures with three forward-looking nonfinancial measures, as shown in Figure 12.3.

PRIOR TO BALANCED SCORECARD CONCEPT

Lagging indicators confirm what has happened. They evaluate outcomes and achievements.

Leading indicators predict future events to identify opportunities.

Prior to the BSC concept, the typical business objective could be summed up simply as *to make a profit.* Performance metrics were based on:

- P&L (profit and loss) reports: revenue, expenses, net profit
- Cash flow statements: enough cash to pay its current liabilities
- Balance sheets that reflected the overall status of finances at a certain date

These financial metrics are **lagging indicators** because they quantify past performance. As such, they represent historical information and are not ideal tools for managing day-to-day operations and planning.

What was novel about BSC in the 1990s was that it measured a company's performance using a multidimensional approach of **leading indicators** as well as lagging indicators.

HOW IS THE BALANCED SCORECARD APPLIED?

BSC can be used to translate strategic plans and mission statements into a set of objectives and performance metrics that can be quantified and measured. For example, answers to these questions are used to define value drivers.

1. **Financial.** To succeed financially, how should we appear to our investors and shareholders?
2. **Customer.** To achieve our vision, how should we provide value to our customers?
3. **Business processes.** To satisfy our shareholders and customers, what business processes must we focus on and excel at?
4. **Innovation, learning, and growth.** To achieve our vision, how will we sustain our ability to innovate, learn, change, and improve?

Table 12.4 lists examples of measurement criteria.

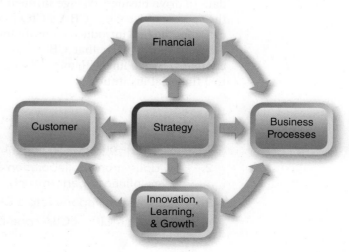

Figure 12.3 Balanced Scorecard (BSC) uses four metrics to measure performance—one financial metric and three nonfinancial metrics.

TABLE 12.4	Examples of Balanced Scorecard (BSC) Measurement Criteria

Metric or Indicator	Examples of Measurement Criteria
Financial	<ul><li>Revenue and revenue growth rates</li><li>Earnings and cash flow</li><li>Asset utilization</li></ul>
Customer	<ul><li>Market share</li><li>Customer acquisition, retention, loyalty</li><li>Customer relationships, satisfaction, likes, recommendations, loyalty</li><li>Brand image, reputation</li><li>Price–value relationship</li></ul>
Business processes	<ul><li>Cycle times, defect rate</li><li>Production throughput, productivity rates</li><li>Cost per process</li><li>Cost per transaction</li></ul>
Innovation, learning and growth	<ul><li>Employee skills, morale, turnover, capacity for change</li><li>IT capabilities</li><li>Employee motivation</li><li>R&D</li><li>Percentage of revenue from new products/services</li></ul>

Application of BSC

BSC converts senior management's priorities into visible, actionable objectives by identifying ways to measure progress against agreed-upon targets.

Assume that a low-cost airline bases its profitability on the following inter-related factors: lower costs, increased revenue, percent of flights departing and arriving on time, competitive pricing, maximum fly time or minimal time jets are on the ground, and the ability of the ground crew to learn to do their jobs faster. Objectives, measures, and targets are diagrammed and detailed in Figure 12.4.

Using the results of the BSC methodology, management teams have an agreed-upon set of objectives and measures that are used to identify and set targets and the actions to achieve them that are appropriate for the company's business model.

Consider JetBlue and Southwest Airlines—both compete to a large extent on price. Yet JetBlue allows one free checked bag while Southwest allows two free checked bags. Now consider the value drivers—time the jet sits on the ground and on-time arrivals. The time it takes to board passengers impacts the ability to take off, which in turn impacts on-ground time and arrival time. Since JetBlue has assigned seats, the terminal crew can control boarding starting at the back of the plane to minimize bottlenecks in the aisle. In contrast, Southwest has open seating, which typically occurs from the front of the jet and can clog the aisle. Now the differing free-baggage policies make sense because the more baggage brought on board, the longer boarding tends to take. By allowing two free checked bags, Southwest attempts to reduce carry-on bags in order to offset the extra time needed for the open-seating boarding process.

By measuring how well targets for on-ground times and arrival times are achieved, both airlines can determine if their actions are optimal or need to be

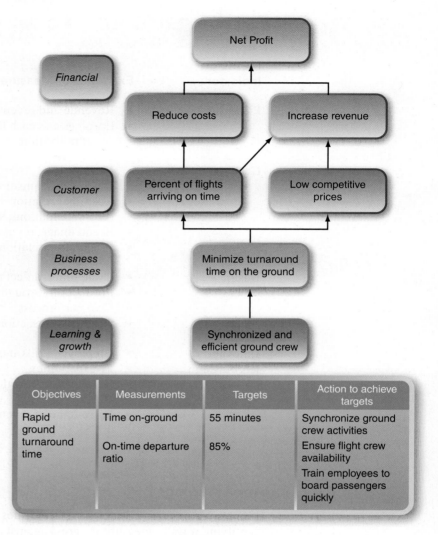

Figure 12.4 Overview of a low-cost airline's BSC objectives, measures, targets, and actions to achieve targets.

revised. Based on these examples, it is easier to understand the processes involved in the BSC methodology, which start with the business vision and strategy. The general steps include:

1. Identify performance metrics (as in Table 12.4) that link vision and strategy to results—financial performance, operations, innovation, employee performance.
2. Select meaningful objectives (Figure 12.4).
3. Select effective measures and targets (Figure 12.4).
4. Determine the actions needed to achieve the targets (Figure 12.4).
5. Implement necessary tracking, analytics, communication, and reporting systems, including sensors, data visualization, mashups, and dashboards via social and mobile channels.
6. Collect, analyze, and compare performance data with targets.
7. Revise actions to improve performance gaps and take advantage of new opportunities.

BSC is used to clarify and update the strategy, align the IT strategy with the business strategy, and link strategic objectives to long-term goals and annual budgets.

Questions

1. How did the BSC approach differ from previous measurement approaches?
2. How does the BSC approach "balance" performance measurements?
3. What are the four BSC metrics?
4. Give an example of each BSC metric.
5. How does BSC align IT strategy with business strategy?

12.4 IT Sourcing and Cloud Strategy

When legacy systems could no longer provide the functionality needed to solve the businesses' problems, companies migrated to the cloud or SaaS to connect core systems and apps. At most companies today, one or more types of outsourcing arrangements are part of their IT strategy. Cloud computing, SaaS, and other types of "as services" were discussed in prior chapters. They are discussed in this chapter as examples of IT outsourcing strategies.

CLOUD STRATEGY AND SERVICES

As you have read, in its simplest form, cloud computing is a way for companies to procure technology *as a service (XaaS)*, including infrastructure (IaaS), applications (AaaS), platforms (PaaS), and business processes, via the Internet. IT resources no longer depend on capital investments and IT developers to own that resource. IT capabilities can be sourced, scaled on, and delivered on demand without physical location, labor, or capital restrictions. As a result, an enterprise's cloud strategy plays a role in its strategy and business growth.

Integrating Cloud With On-Premises Systems

Cloud strategy is short for *cloud computing IT strategy.*

Edge service is a term that refers to a cloud service.

While the concept of cloud is simple, an enterprise's **cloud strategy** tends to be quite complex. Cloud is being adopted across more of the enterprise, but mostly in addition to on-premises systems—not as full replacements for them. Hybrid solutions create integration challenges. Cloud services—also referred to as **edge services**—have to integrate back to core internal systems. That is, edge services have to connect and share data with enterprise systems such as order and inventory management, ERP, CRM, SCM, legacy financial, and HR systems and on mobile and social platforms.

Tactical Adoption Versus Coordinated Cloud Strategy

Deploying cloud services incrementally results in apps and services that are patched together to create end-to-end business processes. This is a short-sighted **tactical adoption approach**. While this approach may have been sufficient in the recent past, cloud services are increasingly more sophisticated and numerous. Tactical approaches will cause difficult integration problems—as occurred with adoption of ERP, mobile, social, and big data systems. Cloud adoption needs to occur according to a coordinated strategy. Given the ever-changing cloud services, it will be tough to know how to design a sustainable cloud strategy. For example, a new class of cloud offerings is being built around business outcomes instead of as point solutions. In effect, this would be business outcomes as a service.

Determining cloud strategies and lease agreements that best support business needs may require hiring cloud consultants, such as Accenture, Booz Allen, Deloitte, Gartner, HP, IBM, or others.

Cloud Strategy Challenges

From the outset, the top challenges about migrating to the cloud revolved around cybersecurity, privacy, data availability, and the accessibility of the service. The newer challenges relate to cloud strategy, including integration of cloud with on-premises resources, extensibility, and reliability of the cloud service. **Extensibility** is the ability to get data into and out of the cloud service. These cloud service challenges need to be addressed before deciding on sourcing solutions.

Cloud Case Examples

Social network LinkedIn has three enterprise lines of business: talent, marketing, and sales solutions. When LinkedIn migrated to cloud services to support sales and CRM, it began by using noncustomized, out-of-the-box capabilities (Main & Peto, 2013). As the company grew rapidly, the standard cloud services could no longer support the lines of business. Business processes increasingly needed to be integrated with ERP and proprietary systems to generate sales leads. LinkedIn switched to a cloud-based integration platform that is able to connect its lead generation, financial, and CRM systems and its proprietary apps and data warehouse. Integrating cloud and on-premises systems gives salespeople a single view of the data they need to do their jobs.

Nestlé Nespresso S. A. transitioned from a traditional coffee shop to an online distributor in the single-serving coffee machine category. Faced with growing global demand, Nespresso needed to replace its complex ERP. By deploying a cloud integration platform, Nespresso has integrated its ERP, warehouse management systems, and ordering tool. Nespresso now leverages its cloud and traditional IT solutions.

IT at Work 12.2

eBay's Outsourcing Lessons Learned

Since its 1998 IPO, eBay has gone from an online experiment in consumer-to-consumer e-commerce to a Fortune 500 enterprise. It supports almost 100 million individual buyers and sellers and small businesses. Exploding demand for eBay's services created enviable but staggering challenges. By 2004, eBay's annual revenues had exceeded $3 billion. At that time, its accounts payable (AP) function was no longer able to support the growing workload. In addition, eBay's acquisition of several companies with incompatible AP processes added to integration challenges. eBay's solution was to outsource. In early 2005, eBay migrated its AP operations to Genpact, a global leader in business process and IT management.

The Solution Had Challenges

The migration was far from perfect at first and hard lessons learned early helped achieve impressive results eventually. Six lessons that eBay learned are the following:

1. **Manage change** by securing the commitment of senior leaders in an overt fashion and by recognizing subtle cultural differences that can undermine initial transition efforts.

2. **Assess organizational readiness** for a transition from a mental and technical standpoint and set realistic expectations and manage them actively.

3. **Anticipate risks and formulate a plan for mitigating them**, beginning with a strategy for dealing with "loss-of-control" threats, both real and imagined.

4. **Build project management infrastructure** that recognizes the "process of transition" needs to be managed as carefully as processes being transitioned. Mapping how the AP process should look posttransition and how it will be managed end to end and by whom is important.

5. **Create a governance mechanism** that can discreetly collect feedback from the transition project manager and provide formal executive oversight and guidance. Form an executive steering committee that includes two senior managers from each organization and representation from all business units impacted by the outsourcing.

6. **Properly define how success will be measured**, both qualitatively and quantitatively. Identifying the right benchmarks for success and vigilantly measuring efforts against them over time are critical. eBay continued to outsource—transitioning its global vendor/supplier maintenance and general ledger activities.

Sources: Compiled from Spears (2010) and Genpact (2014).

Questions

1. Why is the ability to process AP a critical success factor for eBay?
2. Why do you think eBay selected outsourcing at its IT strategy instead of in-house development?
3. What outsourcing challenges did eBay face? In your opinion, what were the reasons for these challenges?

FACTORS DRIVING SOURCING AS AN IT STRATEGY

Enterprises choose outsourcing for several reasons:

- To generate revenue
- To increase efficiency
- To be agile enough to respond to changes in the marketplace
- To focus on core competency
- To cut operational costs
- Because offshoring has become a more accepted IT strategy
- Because cloud computing and SaaS have proven to be effective IT strategies
- To move IT investment from a capital expenditure to a recurring operational expenditure
- To differentiate from competitors—while reducing the burden on the IT organization

IT at Work 12.2 describes eBay's IT sourcing and cloud strategy.

RISK CONCERNS AND HIDDEN COSTS

As companies find their business strategy is increasingly tied to IT solutions, the concerns about outsourcing risks increase. Risks associated with outsourcing are:

- **Shirking.** The vendor deliberately underperforms while claiming full payment, for example, billing for more hours than were worked and/or providing excellent staff at first and later replacing them with less qualified ones.
- **Poaching.** The vendor develops a strategic application for a client and then uses it for other clients.
- **Opportunistic repricing.** When a client enters into a long-term contract with a vendor, the vendor changes financial terms at some point or overcharges for unanticipated enhancements and contract extensions.

Other risks are possible breach of contract by the vendor or its inability to deliver, vendor lock-in, loss of control over data, and loss of employee morale.

Depending on what is outsourced and to whom, an organization might end up spending 10 percent above the budgeted amount to set up the relationship and manage it over time. The budgeted amount may increase anywhere from 15 to 65 percent when outsourcing is sent offshore and the costs of travel and cultural differences are added in.

OFFSHORING

Offshoring of software development has become a common practice due to global markets, lower costs, and increased access to skilled labor. About one-third of Fortune 500 companies outsource software development to software companies in India. It is not only the cost and the technical capabilities that matter. Several other factors to consider are the business and political climates in the selected country, the quality of the infrastructure, and risks such as IT competency, human capital, the economy, the legal environment, and cultural differences.

Duke University's *Center for International Business Education and Research* studied actual offshoring results. According to their study, Fortune 500 companies reduced costs by offshoring—63 percent of the companies achieved over 30 percent annual savings and 14 percent of them achieved savings over 50 percent. The respondents were overwhelmingly satisfied with their offshore operations. Three-quarters (72 percent) said their offshore implementations met or exceeded their expected cost savings. Almost one-third of the respondents (31 percent) achieved their service level goals within the first 5 months of their contracts while 75 percent did so within 12 months. The study concluded that "offshoring delivers faster results than average domestic improvement efforts." Even though these are very general results, offshoring success stories ease the fears about the risks of offshoring.

Based on case studies, the types of work that are not readily offshored include the following:

- Work that has not been routinized.

- Work that if offshored would result in the client company losing too much control over critical operations.

- Situations in which offshoring would place the client company at too great a risk to its data security, data privacy, or intellectual property and proprietary information.

- Business activities that rely on an uncommon combination of specific application domain knowledge and IT knowledge in order to do the work properly.

OUTSOURCING LIFE CYCLE

Strategy sets the overall direction by defining what the business desires to be, within a specified timeframe, and the path to get there.

The International Association of Outsourcing Professionals (IAOP) has defined nine critical stages in the outsourcing life cycle that managers need to understand prior to outsourcing (IAOP, 2009):

1. **Strategy.** Outsourcing is a strategic decision that is typically developed at senior levels within a business. It may be part of a larger strategy to move the company to a leveraged business model and to focus on core competencies. Or it may be to save net costs or due to a lack of internal resources. Outsourcing may act as a key differentiator that will give a business a competitive advantage over its competitors. Too few businesses consider taking legal counsel at this stage, but they should. For example, difficulties about licensing, intellectual property rights, or a preexisting contractual or leasing arrangement require legal expertise.

2. **Reassessment.** This stage is not given enough consideration: Organizations should look again at their business processes, IT capabilities, internal supply, or other problems to see if they could be reengineered to meet the requirements so that outsourcing is not needed.

3. **Selection.** This stage involves identifying and defining the work to be outsourced as well as the selection of the vendors using RFI (request for information) or RFP (request for proposal) processes. The best value outsourcer is selected.

4. **Negotiation.** In this phase, contracts, schedules, and agreements are negotiated by someone experienced in these issues. Then the final contract is reviewed extensively before signing. This negotiation process must involve adequate resources and senior executives from both sides—the key issues in a long-term relationship, such as outsourcing, are too important not to justify executive engagement from the supplier and customer.

5. **Implementation.** This phase involves the start-up activities of planning the transition and the implementation of the outsourced agreement as well as establishing the detailed budget and administrative functions needed for its management and formal launching of the program.

6. **Oversight management.** This phase encompasses all ongoing activities required to manage the program and achieve the contracted results. Specifically, this includes providing a liaison between the customers and the supplier, performance

monitoring, contract administration, vendor/partnership management, delivery integration, and vendor transition. Inevitably stresses will develop in a contract, and it is important for both sides to take an adult approach to contract interpretation. Remember that these are long-term relationships that need to flex with time.

7. **Build completion.** This phase covers all completion activities of the build phase, including any development program and then acceptance, and the introduction of new services.

8. **Change.** All complex outsourcing contracts will be subject to change and alteration. These are run as either minor changes to the outsourcing contract or major changes, which might involve a retendering process. Your contract will—or should—have built into it a contract change procedure to deal with changes that are in the broad scope of the original procurement.

9. **Exit.** All outsourcing relationships end because the contract has expired, by mutual agreement, or because the outsourcing relationship has failed. The terms of the contract become very important at this time.

IT VENDOR RELATIONSHIPS

The starting point in building a positive and strong vendor relationship is vendor selection. If a company makes a bad selection or enters into a vaguely worded service contract, most likely the software, app, or implementation will fail and the vendor will not be able to resolve the problems fast enough, if at all. Failures are usually followed by lawsuits.

Vendor Research and Selection

To minimize interpersonal or technical conflicts with IT vendors, businesses need to thoroughly research the vendor. It is very important to ask questions about the services and products the vendor will provide and get as many specifics as possible. Also take the time to verify the vendor's claims about its products and check all references to make sure that the vendor has a proven track record of success. When selecting a vendor, two criteria to assess first are experience and stability:

*   Experience with very similar systems of similar size, scope, and requirements. Experience with the ITs that are needed, integrating those ITs into the existing infrastructure and the customer's industry.

*   Financial and qualified personnel stability. A vendor's reputation impacts its stability.

Of course, for innovative IT implementations, vendors will not have experience and one major failure—and the lawsuit that follows—can create instability. If those criteria are not met, there is no reason to further consider the vendor.

Research by McKinsey indicates that a majority of technology executives want to have stronger relationships with their IT suppliers, but they often act in ways that undermine that goal. In fact, many corporate customers lose out on the potential benefit of close relationships by an overemphasis on costs instead of value. Ideally, a customer/vendor relationship is a mutually beneficial partnership, and both sides are best served by treating it as such.

Vendors often buy hardware or software from other vendors. In order to avoid problems with the primary IT vendor, check secondary suppliers as well. Ask the primary vendor how they will deliver on their promises if the secondary vendors go out of business or otherwise end their relationship.

Do A Trial Run

Vendors may offer the option to test their products or services in a pilot study or a small portion of the business to verify that it fits the company's needs. If the vendor relationship adds value on a small scale, then the system can be rolled out on a larger scale. If the vendor cannot meet the requirements, then the company avoids a failure.

CONTRACTS: GET EVERYTHING IN WRITING

SLAs are designed to protect the service provider, not the customer, unless the customer takes an informed and active role in the provisions and parameters.

By making both parties aware of their responsibilities and when they may be held liable for failing to live up to those responsibilities, a strong SLA can help prevent many of the disruptions and dangers that can come with sourcing or migrating to the cloud. The provisions and parameters of the contract are the only protections a company has when terms are not met or the arrangement is terminated. No contract should be signed without a thorough legal review.

There is no template SLA and each cloud solution vendor is unique. Certainly, if a vendor's SLA is light on details, that alone may be an indicator that the vendor is light on accountability. Additionally, if a sourcing or cloud vendor refuses to improve its SLAs or negotiate vital points, then that vendor should not be considered.

Questions

1. What contributes to the complexity of a cloud strategy?
2. How does tactical adoption of cloud services differ from a coordinated cloud strategy?
3. What are the major reasons for sourcing?
4. What types of work are not readily outsourced offshore?
5. When selecting a vendor, what two criteria need to be assessed?
6. What is the risk of an overemphasis on cost when selecting or dealing with an IT vendor?
7. What needs to be done before signing a contract with an IT vendor?

Key Terms

applications portfolio	IT–business alignment	onshore sourcing	strategy
balanced scorecard	IT strategic planning	operating plan	tactical adoption approach
business strategy	IT strategy	project portfolio	value driver
edge service	lagging indicators	sourcing	vision statement
extensibility	leading indicators	strategic planning	
in-house development	offshoring		

Assuring Your Learning

DISCUSS: Critical Thinking Questions

1. What are three value drivers for a major retail store, such as Macy's or Sears? Do any of them have a limited life span? Explain.

2. What directs investments in social, mobile, analytics, cloud, and other digital technology resources?

3. What are the four objectives of IT strategic plans?

4. What might be some reasons why companies use sourcing instead of in-house development?

5. In your opinion, what are the benefits of onshore sourcing?

6. What are the benefits and disadvantages of offshoring work/jobs to other countries, for example, to China or India?

7. Describe the IT strategic planning process.

8. If there are conflicting priorities and disagreements among members of the IT steering committee, how might they be resolved?

9. Review IT at Work 12.1. Why do you think strong collaborators achieved better results?

10. Why is the balanced scorecard methodology "balanced"?

11. Why are financial metrics lagging indicators?

12. Why has tactical adoption of IT become a risky approach compared to a coordinated cloud strategy?

13. Why is an SLA a legal document?

14. Who do SLAs typically protect? Explain why.

EXPLORE: Online and Interactive Exercises

1. Visit Accenture.com and search for "outsourcing." Describe the IT outsourcing services offered by Accenture. Do the same for Deloitte at deloitte.com, Ernst & Young at ey.com, KPMG at kpmg.com, or PricewaterhouseCoopers at pwc.com. Create a table that compares the outsourcing services of two of these consulting firms.

2. Visit the Government Technology website at govtech.com. *S*earch for "managing successful vendor relationships." Prepare a list of recommendations based on what you learn.

3. Visit the IBM website and search for "balanced scorecard." Identify and describe its balanced scorecard software product.

4. Search for a YouTube video featuring Harvard Business School's Robert Kaplan and the balanced scorecard. List three lessons learned from Kaplan, the title of the video, and its URL.

ANALYZE & DECIDE: Apply IT Concepts to Business Decisions

1. Vinay Gupta, President and CEO of Janeeva, which sells software to help companies manage outsourcing relationships, gave this advice (Bloomberg Businessweek, 2013):

   "I would strongly encourage business owners to visit the vendor's facilities. There are a lot of fly-by-night operators, so you want to make sure you have touched and seen the facility before you hand them your business—I would do at least a 30-day free pilot with the provider. You want to see if it is a good fit and find out who you will be interacting with on a day-to-day basis."

   Not all companies follow this advice.

   a. Discuss why companies would take these precautions when setting up an outsourcing relationship.

   b. Discuss why companies would not take these precautions when setting up an outsourcing relationship.

2. Research legal websites discussing SLAs. Compile a list of recommendations, including what to do and what to avoid.

3. In 2007, AstraZeneca entered a 10-year outsourcing agreement with IBM. By 2011, AstraZeneca decided to exit the arrangement, resulting in a tough court case with IBM. Research the failed outsourcing agreement between AstraZeneca and IBM. Explain the reasons for the failure. How did AstraZeneca change its subsequent outsourcing arrangements?

4. Netflix streams videos on TVs, personal computers, and smartphones using cloud services from Amazon Web Services (AWS). Its model is a direct challenge to traditional content distributors, which are limited by physical distribution and network broadcasting. In contrast, Netflix capitalizes on low cost and virtually unlimited cloud capacity to deliver content on demand almost anywhere. In 2011, Netflix's subscriber base surpassed that of Comcast, the largest cable provider in terms of subscribers, to become one of the largest video content distributors in the nation. Research Netflix to learn more about its use of the cloud to create business value. Explain its cloud strategy. Then research another company in the media and entertainment space—for example, HBO or Apple. Compare the cloud strategies of the competitor to Netflix.

CASE 12.2

Business Case: AstraZeneca Terminates $1.4B Outsourcing Contract with IBM

AstraZeneca is one of the world's leading biopharmaceutical companies. The company focuses on the discovery, development, and commercialization of prescription medicines for six health care areas. AstraZeneca has also been one of the most prolific users of information technology in the pharma world.

In July 2007, AstraZeneca signed a $1.4 billion, seven-year global strategic outsourcing agreement with IBM. The extensive SLA included 90 clauses and 32 schedules governing the provision of IT infrastructure services to 60 countries. Yet it was still imprecise about the exit obligations on IBM if the contract was terminated.

On April 8, 2011, AstraZeneca terminated the SLA. In the legal battle, the court sided with AstraZeneca.

Here are the details and timeline.

2007

AstraZeneca depends on its IT capabilities as much as it depends on its R&D—both are crucial. In 2007, AstraZeneca had signed a seven-year global outsourcing agreement with IBM. The contract includes server hosting and storage for scientific, network and communications, commercial, and supply chain operations.

Richard Williams, CIO of AstraZeneca, said the outsourcing deal enabled the company a consistent infrastructure across all its global sites. The consistent infrastructure enabled it to roll out new technologies, reporting systems, and apps more quickly and efficiently.

2011

By 2011, AstraZeneca decided to exit the arrangement with IBM, resulting in a tough court case with IBM. One reason why the AstraZeneca–IBM deal failed was the use of *outcome-based specifications*. These specifications in the contract were commonly used to encourage innovation among vendors. In fact, in 2007, the contract was considered a ground-breaking model, but that model failed because AstraZeneca's business was changing very rapidly and the contract was not designed for that pace. Although very popular in the 2000s, like other IT trends from that decade, companies would do things much differently now.

Problems with Large Outsource Contracts

Very large and long-term IT outsourcing contracts are difficult to change because of the way the vendor accrues profit from the deal. With huge outsource deals, vendors make major investment in the first two years as the service is set up and customized. Then the vendor expects to make its profit margin in the last two or three years, which is why large deals are five or more years.

2012

After the failure of its IT outsourcing contract with IBM, AstraZeneca has taken on a new strategy for working with IT vendors that stresses rapid action on technical problems under a cooperative structure.

New Outsourcing Model

AstraZeneca created a new IT outsourcing model to replace the services provided by IBM. Now the company uses multiple contracts with Computacenter, HCL, AT&T, and Wipro. Contracts cover the standard provisions of IT service deals, namely SLAs and pricing, and also a cooperation policy. That policy includes 13 principles that specify the terms of collaboration. One principle is "fix first, pay later." That means when an urgent IT problem occurs, vendors and AstraZeneca cooperate to fix it fast without asking questions about cost. Previously, a vendor might have examined the contracts to confirm its responsibilities and, to protect profit margins, delay the fix. In return for fast solutions, AstraZeneca agreed to faster payment to the vendor. In the event of a contract conflict, both parties can appeal to an independent arbiter who oversees the cooperation policy.

Lesson Learned

This IT and legal case illustrates the importance of considering thoroughly what will happen when an outsourcing relationship comes to an end. This is often overlooked in the dash to close the deal and will be an expensive oversight.

Sources: Compiled from Barton (2011), Boyle (2010), Clark (2013), Lomas (2007), and Pagnamenta (2007).

Questions

1. What mistakes did AstraZeneca make?
2. What mistakes did IBM make?
3. Why are outsourcing contracts for five or more years?
4. Why do you think two major corporations could make such mistakes?
5. Do you think the 2007 SLA was doomed to fail? Explain your answer.
6. What provisions in the 2001 SLAs protect AstraZeneca and the vendors?
7. Why would parties prefer to use an arbitrator instead of filing a lawsuit in court?

CASE 12.3

Data Analysis: Third-Party versus Company-Owned Offshoring

Major companies, such as Citigroup, had wholly owned offshore service centers. Those types of company-owned offshore centers are called captive models. Captive offshoring models reduce the risk of offshoring. A recent study from the Everest Research Institute estimated the costs of third-party offshoring and captive offshoring. The estimates are below.

Create a spreadsheet that totals the average cost of each model for each cost item. For example, average the annual salary based on the range for third parties and also the captives. Then calculate the total cost of ownership (TCO) of each model. The difference is the cost of risk.

Full-time equivalents (FTEs) are used to standardize labor costs since workers may be part time or full ime. For example, two part-time workers equal 1 FTE. The estimates are given in terms of FTEs so the conversion is already done.

Question

1. Based on your results, how much does the captive offshoring model allow for risk? The answer is the difference between the TCOs of the two models.

	Third-Party Offshoring Model	Captive Offshoring Model
Office space: annual rental cost per square foot (assume 10,000 square feet of office space)	$11 to $13	$14 to $16
Base salary costs of workers (assume 1,000 FTEs)	$7,770 to $8,200	$9,500 to $10,300
General management staff for every 1,000 FTEs	12 to 14	16 to 18
General management salary	$55,000 to $65,000	$70,000 to $90,000
Travel and housing costs per FTE	$280 to $320	$900 to $1,060

References

Barton, P. "Exit Management: IBM v AstraZeneca." *FieldFisher.com,* December 14, 2011.

Bloomberg Businessweek. "Outsourcing Advice from the Pros." September 2, 2013. images.businessweek.com/ss/09/02/0213_outsourcing/10.htm

Boyle, C. "AstraZeneca to Axe 8,000 Jobs in Global Cull." *Times Online,* January 28, 2010.

Clark, L. "AstraZeneca Opts for Co-operation After IBM Falls Out." *ComputerWeekly.com,* March 11, 2013.

Curran, C., T. DeGarmo, & J. Sviokla. "PwC's 5th Annual Digital IQ Survey Digital Conversations and the C-suite." *PricewaterhouseCoopers LLP,* 2013.

Duckett, C. "Mobile Banking Is Kaching for CBA as App Handled over AU$9 Billion." *ZDNet.com,* August 14, 2013.

Genpact. "Sourcing—Procurement." 2014. genpact.com/home/solutions/procurement-supply-chain/sourcing-procurement

Haydamack, C. D. "Strategic Planning Processes for Information Technology." *BPTrends.com,* September 2008.

Haydamack, C. & S. Johnson. "Aligning IT with Business Goals through Strategic Planning." *Intel White Paper,* December 2008.

Insights. "Balanced Scorecard." *Bain & Company Guide.* May 8, 2013.

International Association of Outsourcing Professionas (IAOP). "The Outsourcing Life-Cycle—9 Stages." *outsourcingprofessional.org,* 2009.

Kaplan, R. S. & D. P. Norton, "Mastering the Management System." *Harvard Business Review* 86, no. 1, January 2008.

Krishnapura, S., S Achuthan, B. Barnard, L. Vipul, R. Nallapa, S. Rungta, and T. Tang. "Intel's Data Center Strategy for Business Transformation." *Intel White Paper.* January 2014.

LeMay, R. "CommBank's Kaching App: A Perfect IT/Business Alignment Case Study." *Delimiter.com,* August 16, 2013.

Lomas, N. "AstraZeneca Signs IBM Outsourcing Deal." *ZDNet UK,* July 18, 2007.

Main, A. & J. Peto. "Cloud Orchestration." *Tech Trends 2014.* Deloitte University Press (http://dupress.com/). 2013.

Martin, R. L. "The Big Lie of Strategic Planning." *Harvard Business Review,* January–February 2014.

Pagnamenta, R. "AstraZeneca to Outsource Manufacturing." *Times Online,* September 17, 2007.

Spears, J. "Six Keys to a Successful BPO Transition." Genpact White Paper. 2010.

Project Management and SDLC

Chapter Snapshot

Case 13.1 Opening Case: Keeping Your Project on Track, Knowing When It Is Doomed, and DIA Baggage System Failure

13.1 Project Management Concepts

13.2 Project Planning, Execution, and Budget

13.3 Project Monitoring, Control, and Closing

13.4 System Development Life Cycle

Key Terms
Assuring Your Learning

- **Discuss:** Critical Thinking Questions
- **Explore:** Online and Interactive Exercises
- **Analyze & Decide:** Apply IT Concepts to Business Decisions

Case 13.2 Business Case: Steve Jobs' Shared Vision Project Management Style

Case 13.3 Demo Case: Mavenlink Project Management and Planning Software

References

Learning Outcomes

1. Explain the importance of the project management life cycle, project portfolio management (PPM), and the use of the triple constraint to minimize scope creep and other project management fatal mistakes.

2. Identify the components of a project business case, statement of work (SOW), work breakdown structure (WBS), milestone schedule, Gantt chart, and project baseline.

3. Apply project monitoring and control processes to manage the triple constraint and critical path and to identify the conditions when an ongoing project should be terminated. Explain the legal need to document project changes and the business value of a project postmortem.

4. Describe the system development lifecycle (SDLC) processes, feasibility analyses, and their impact on the acceptance and success of IT implementations.

Chapter Snapshot

When most companies develop or build new products, services, markets, enterprise systems, or apps, they use a **project management** approach. Project management is a structured methodology to plan, manage, and control the completion of a project throughout its life cycle. The Project Management Body of Knowledge (PMBOK)

Guide outlines five project management process groups, shown in Figure 13.1. Each process moves the project from idea to implementation in such a way as to help ensure its successful completion. The life cycle starts with an idea or concept and project plan. If the project is approved, then the project team proceeds to perform

Figure 13.1 Overview of the project process architecture and project management life cycle. All projects, IT or otherwise, move through five phases in the project management life cycle.

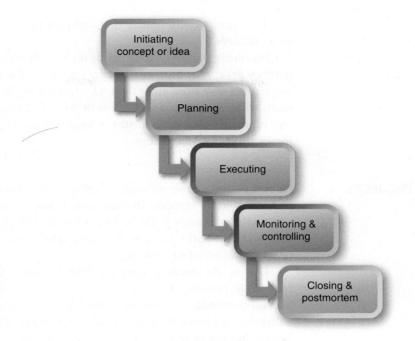

- Initiating concept or idea
- Planning
- Executing
- Monitoring & controlling
- Closing & postmortem

A **project** is a well-planned sequential series of tasks to achieve a result. Projects have a defined beginning and end, a scope, resources, and a budget. Projects are approved before they are funded and allocated resources.

Postmortem is a method for evaluating project performance, identifying lessons learned, and making recommendations for future projects.

the tasks and deliver the **project**. As part of closing the project, participants do a **postmortem** to document lessons learned in order to improve their next projects.

Projects are risky. Project management and an appropriate system development process help to get the IT project delivered on time, within budget, and according to specifications. To minimize risk of failure, the project is rigorously planned, evaluated, and monitored. Weekly status meetings, communication, and reporting are critical to find out about potential problems as far in advance as possible and fix them to avert a crisis. Project management is gaining in importance for all types of projects because of technology complexity, tighter budgets, tougher competition, and shorter time-to-delivery requirements. In short, companies cannot afford project failures or delays.

CASE 13.1 OPENING CASE

Keeping Your Project on Track, Knowing When It Is Doomed, and DIA Baggage System Failure

A majority of IT projects fail on at least one measure of success, wasting billions of dollars each year. Projects can suffer one or more of the following outcomes:

- Over budget
- Delivered late
- Rolled out with fewer features or functions than planned
- Terminated before completion
- Completed, but a failure

Except in extreme cases, the evaluation of success or failure is subjective because time and cost to complete the project are estimates. For example, exceeding the planned budget or schedule can be judged to be within an acceptable range—or not. Everyone should realize that complex projects experience some successes and some failures.

Reducing failure rates depends on what is arguably the most important IT competency area: *project management*. Too often the final stage—the postmortem—is skipped to save time and effort. However, it is during the postmortem that people learn what contributed to success or what did not. Not learning from past projects and repeating avoidable mistakes have consistently been major hurdles to improving IT project management.

KEEPING PROJECTS ON TRACK

Over a period of two months, a Fortune 500 company learned that six of its major projects were in trouble. In each case, it *seemed* as though the project failed overnight without warning. The CIO felt blindsided and executive management wanted to know who and what was to blame. The company's project management office (PMO) was asked to explain.

During the investigation, the PMO learned that the project staff felt strong but subtle pressure to keep problems to themselves. The six failing projects had executive sponsors who were politically powerful and known to attack people who delivered bad news. So, rather than report their project was in trouble, staff worked harder, hoping to recover from missed deadlines, but deadlines were still missed.

Here are three lessons learned to keep projects on track.

Set Realistic and Detailed Project Plans With Adequate Time and Resources

Projects are subject to unanticipated and uncontrollable events, so they need to have slack time built into the schedule and budget. However, project teams can be pressured to cut project costs. In response, they might reduce the time and budget allocated to training, testing, and change management. These cuts result in poor quality and low user acceptance.

Encourage Timely Feedback and Be Willing to Listen

All projects encounter difficulties. Make sure employees know they will not be punished for raising concerns, even if other project members deny problems exist. Fear blocks the flow of useful information.

Manage Risk with Regular Project Status Reviews

For the most part, no one likes formal project reviews, but they are necessary to identify and address current and potential problems.

RED FLAGS OF DOOM

Here is a list of red flags that indicate IT project problems. These red flags relate to bad planning—and do not depend on feedback from team members.

Project Has Launched Without Senior Buy-In

Failure is guaranteed without the support and buy-in of senior management. This situation can happen if a strong personality in the company has a terrific idea and begins to plan meetings and allocate resources without waiting for senior management buy-in. No one else on the team knows the project has not been approved or budgeted. Many of these projects proceed until the point where real money must be spent; then they collapse completely.

No Detailed Project Plan Exists

Any project with an estimated duration longer than two or three weeks needs a detailed rational project plan.

Meetings Are Scheduled Ignoring Team Members' Availability

Meetings that conflict with important standing meetings means that vital team members will be absent, undercutting their effectiveness. People are generally more productive and more likely to show up earlier in the day. It is better to schedule meetings before lunch, if possible.

Users Have Had Little or No Early Involvement

Large and complex projects benefit from the advice and insight of users who are familiar with how processes are done and why they are done that way. The more involvement you have from users, the greater your chance of success. If your project covers multiple departments, make sure to have a user representative from each department.

No Detailed Testing Plan Exists

Testing is essential to project success. *Unit testing* tests one facet of the system; *integrated testing* tests all components and the user interface.

No Training Budget

When faced with a budget overrun, the training budget is often sacrificed. Relying on users and help desk staff to figure out the new system for themselves means the project is in for failure. Be ready to delay the project if appropriate training is not given.

BAGGAGE HANDLING SYSTEM PROJECT AT DENVER INTERNATIONAL AIRPORT

A classic case used to illustrate a project disaster is the baggage-handling system project (Figure 13.2) for the new Denver International Airport (DIA). The project was to create the most advanced automated handling of baggage, integrating all three concourses into a single system. The terms "most advanced, automated, and integrated" clearly indicate that the system was going to be extremely complex, risky, and subject to delays. An unrealistic schedule was planned and approved even though any delay would also force the delay of the opening of the DIA. In fact, the newly completed DIA remained idle for 16 months while engineers dealt with the complexities of the baggage system. The delay added $560 million to the cost of DIA. Cost to maintain the empty airport and interest charges on construction loans cost the city of Denver $1.1 million per day throughout the delay.

Project Scaled Down; Scrapped a Decade Later

The project was scaled down from the original plan. Only baggage handling on outbound flights for one concourse was automated. Baggage to/from other concourses

Figure 13.2 The city of Denver wanted its Denver International Airport to have a competitive advantage with the world's most high-tech baggage-handling system. The system was a failure.

© Visions of America/ Shutterstock

were handled using a manual tug-and-trolley system that was quickly built when key players finally acknowledged that the automated system would never meet its goals. Ten years later, in August 2005, the automated system was scrapped because it still did not work correctly and its maintenance costs were $1 million per month.

Project Management Mistakes

DIA's baggage-handling system was a critical component in the city of Denver's plan to construct a new state-of-the-art airport that would position Denver as an air transportation hub. By automating baggage handling, aircraft turnaround time was to be cut to as little as 30 minutes. Faster turnaround meant airlines could minimize on-ground time, which would be DIA's competitive advantage.

Below is the timeline of the major events and project management mistakes:

- November 1989: DIA construction work starts.

- **Ignored experts.** In 1990, the City of Denver hired Breier Neidle Patrone Associates to do a feasibility analysis of building an integrated baggage system. Reports advised that complexity made the project unfeasible. Experts from Munich airport advised that the much simpler Munich system had taken two full years to build and that it had run 24/7 for six months prior to opening to allow bugs to be ironed out.

- Summer 1991: DIA project management team asked for bids for the automated baggage-handling system.

- **Underestimated complexity.** Fall 1991: Of the 16 companies included in the bidding process, only 3 responded. None could complete the project in time for the October 1993 opening. All three bids were rejected and the urgent search for a company that would meet the deadline continued.

- **Poor planning and impossible expectations.** In April 1992, DIA went to contract with BAE Systems to complete the project in time for the October 1993 opening—ignoring expert evidence that the timeline was impossible to achieve.

- **Lack of due diligence.** Contract terms between DIA and BAE and project specifications were hammered out in only three meetings. The rush to contract ignored the feasibility analysis. The pressure to move quickly drove them to skip critical due-diligence steps.

- **Excluded key stakeholders.** BAE and the airport project management team excluded key stakeholders—the airlines that had contracted with DIA—during the negotiations. Excluding stakeholders from discussions in which key project decisions are made is always a losing strategy.

- **Scope creep.** 1992–1993: Numerous changes in the scope of the project are made. For instance, Continental Airlines requested ski equipment handling facilities be added to its concourse.

- **Ignored interface design.** The baggage-handling system had to interface with the airport. That is, because the design of the building was started before the baggage system design was known, the designers of the physical building only made general allowances for where they thought the baggage system would go. The allowance of spaces in which the baggage system would operate represented the interface between the design of DIA and the baggage system. To make effective decisions about how to design DIA, the DIA designers should have worked with experts in designing the baggage system. DIA had sharp corners that required turns that baggage carts cannot navigate. To keep carts from falling off the rails, the speed of the system was cut from 60 cars per minute to 30 cars. This change eliminated DIA's competitive advantage of fast turnaround time for jets.

These and many other mistakes too numerous to mention doomed the DIA baggage-handling project. This case represents practically every possible project management mistake. From the outset, the decision to proceed with a single integrated system at DIA knowing that the deadline could not be met and the irrational decisions that followed made by people who lacked the necessary project management and engineering expertise contributed to project failure.

Sources: Calleam Consulting (2008), Grimes (2013), Nelson (2005), and Perkins (2014).

Questions

1. In what ways can a project fail?
2. Why is the evaluation of a project's success or failure somewhat subjective?
3. What are the benefits of a project postmortem? Why would a project not have a postmortem?
4. Assume you are a member of a project team working on a project with a six-month timeline. The materials your team needs to complete their first set of tasks will arrive three days later than their promised delivery date. The delay has a 10 percent chance of delaying completion of the project. You know that no one will tell the project manager of the delayed delivery because it is the first month of the project so it does not seem important enough to report. Would you inform the project manager of the delay? Explain your decision. Now assume you did not report the delay and such delays happened in each month afterward. What would you do and when? In your opinion, should the entire team present these problems? Explain your decisions.
5. What are three best practices to keep projects on track?
6. What are red flags indicating the project is likely to be a failure?
7. Referring to your answers in Questions 5 and 6, which of those best practices and red flags were ignored in the DIA automated luggage-handling project?
8. Referring to your answer in Question 7, why do you think each best practice and red flag were ignored?
9. In your opinion, who are the ones responsible for the failure?

13.1 Project Management Concepts

Business case is a presentation or document that outlines the justification for the start-up and funding of a project.

Enterprises face the challenge of deciding which investments to make and how to allocate scarce resources to competing projects. Typically a senior manager composes a **business case** that identifies an opportunity, problem, or need and the desired business outcomes of the project. Since not all projects are viable and not all viable projects can be funded, the business cases are reviewed. In the review process, projects compete for approval and funding.

PROJECT PORTFOLIO MANAGEMENT

Project analysis methods are used to prioritize proposed projects and allocate the budget for maximum return. Budgeting decisions apply to all business investments, such as construction to increase manufacturing capacity, entering new markets, modernizing retail stores, R&D, and acquiring IT, apps, and enterprise systems.

Investments in IT for marketing or manufacturing innovations compete head-on with investments needed to comply with new laws and regulations in finance, accounting, HR, and cybersecurity.

During project analysis, IT projects should be examined holistically—that is, in combination to identify investment synergies. This approach is known as **project portfolio management (PPM)**. PPM is a set of business practices to manage projects as a strategic portfolio. PPM ensures the alignment of programs and projects with organizational objectives. Executive management needs to review portfolios and programs, determine why projects are or are not necessary, see where money is spent, prioritize projects, stage the start of new projects, spread resources appropriately, and then keep tabs on progress.

PPM establishes a path from the concept through successful project completion. Without the necessary data, management is incapable of making informed decisions to approve the "right" new projects and to shut down projects with no hope for success:

- Map proposed projects to organizational strategies
- Assess the value that a proposed project brings to the company
- Assess the complexity of proposed projects
- Prioritize project proposals for project selection

COMPETING IT INVESTMENT PROJECTS MAY HAVE SYNERGY

The financial services sector has been compelled by strict international anti-money-laundering (AML) guidelines that require firms to *know your customer* (KYC). Master data management (MDM, Chapter 3) is needed to create a single view of the customer and AML/KYC analytics are needed for banks to manage rising compliance cost and the risk of noncompliance. To effectively motivate firms to invest in necessary defenses, regulators impose harsh sanctions when they identify failings in a firm's AML/KYC compliance systems. Several high-profile sanctions are a $1.9 billion fine for HSBC in 2012, Wachovia's $160 million settlement in 2010, and a $327 million settlement from Standard Chartered in 2012 (Gupta & Jain, 2014). It is not a surprise that AML and KYC compliance budgets have increased significantly over the past few years and get priority rankings. However, compliance projects may align well with other data-intense projects.

For example, AML laws require banks to demonstrate knowledge of where their customers live, what forms of identification they used to validate their identities, reconciliation of their demographics across products, validation that they are not on any government watch list, and understanding of their normal transaction behaviors in order to detect suspicious activity. Since much of these data are also used for marketing and credit risk analysis, maintaining the data in a common repository makes sense from business and IT perspectives of cost, consistency, and accuracy.

BASIC CHARACTER-ISTICS OF PROJECTS

A project is a series of tasks to produce one or more **deliverables**. Deliverables are items that you hand off to the client or management for their review and approval and that must be produced to complete a project or part of a project. Projects have a defined start date and finish date that determine the project duration, scope, resources, and budget. Projects differ from operations or *business as usual* based on characteristics listed in Table 13.1.

The Triple Constraint

The **triple constraint** (Figure 13.3) refers to the three attributes that must be managed effectively for successful completion and closure of any project:

1. **Scope**. The project scope is the definition of what the project is supposed to accomplish—its outcomes or deliverables. Scope is measured in terms of the project size, goals, and requirements.

TABLE 13.1	Distinguishing Characteristics of Projects

A project has these characteristics.

- Clearly defined scope, deliverables, and results
- An estimated time frame or schedule that is subject to a high degree of uncertainty
- An estimated budget that is subject to a high degree of uncertainty
- The requirement of extensive interaction among participants
- Tasks that may compete or conflict with other business activities, which makes planning and scheduling difficult
- Risky but with a high profit potential or benefits

2. **Time.** A project is made up of *tasks*. Each task has a start date and an end date. The duration of a project extends from the start date of the first task to the finish date of the last task. Time needed to produce the deliverables is naturally related to the scope and availability of resources allocated to the project.

3. **Cost.** This is the estimation of the amount of money that will be required to complete the project. Cost itself encompasses various things, such as resources, labor rates for contractors, risk estimates, and bills of materials, et cetera. All aspects of the project that have a monetary component are made part of the overall cost structure. Projects are approved subject to their costs.

These constraints are interrelated so they must be managed together for the project to be completed on time, within budget, and to specification. The major take-away from the triple constraint represented as a triangle is that you cannot change one side without changing the other sides. Ignoring the potential repercussions of adjustments to the scope, time, or cost of a project will lead to issues and may cause the project to fail.

Figure 13.3 Triple constraint.

Scope Creep

During the project, it is almost guaranteed that requests will be made that change the scope. **Scope creep** refers to the growth of the project, which might seem inconsequential—at least to the person who is requesting that change. Scope creep is the piling up of small changes that by themselves are manageable but in aggregate are significant. It is absolutely imperative that any change to the scope of the project explicitly include compensating changes in the budget, the deadline, and/or resources. Consider this scenario. The project scope is to build a new online accounting application capable of processing at least one thousand expense reports (in multiple currencies) per day, that has a budget of $200,000, and is expected to last three months. After the project is started, the scope expands to include processing of thousands of sales commissions per day. The project manager needs to renegotiate the project's duration and budget for the added functionality, testing, and user training, making sure that any requested change, no matter how small, is documented and accompanied by approval.

A standard approach for managing projects provides the following benefits:

- It establishes ground rules and expectations for the project team.
- It provides project managers, functional managers, and the operational staff with a common language that eases communication and helps ensure that everyone is on the same page.
- Managers can quickly determine which ones are proceeding smoothly and which are not when all projects follow the same processes and approaches and use the same metrics for measuring project performance.

Not using a best practices project management approach is the biggest IT project mistake a business can make. Tech Note 13.1 provides good advice on this topic. Project management helps keep projects on schedule and on budget. A good project management plan identifies anticipated costs early on to develop a realistic budget. Using resource conflict solutions, project managers can minimize the effect of funding a new project on operating capital by optimizing the allocation of workers. Coordinating tasks and clearly identifying goals or deliverables within phases reduce inefficiencies in time management that can result in being over budget.

TECH NOTE 13.1 Seven Deadly Sins of Project Management and IT Project Management—Two Views

Project Management Mistakes

Michelle Symonds (Symonds, 2014) suggested a set of *seven deadly sins of project management*, that is, the common mistakes that companies commit that contribute to project failure. As an IT project manager, these mistakes refer to project management in general rather than to IT project management, and will doom your project to failure:

1. **No project plan.** You need a list of deliverables, the tasks and resources needed to produce each deliverable, time scales, and an estimated budget.
2. **No collaboration.** If you are not collaborating with your team, you are missing opportunities to solve problems and build support.
3. **No budget tracking.** You need to track actual expenses and compare them to estimated costs throughout the project.
4. **No risk management process.** You need to monitor and keep risks under control. Maintain a risk log to record all the potential risks as well as what you are doing about them.
5. **No stakeholder management.** You need to identify each group of stakeholders relating to your project and put a plan in place for communicating and managing each group.
6. **No file organization system.** IT project managers have to handle a lot of information. From project documents to copies of e-mails, from contracts to invoices, a well-defined and workable file organization system is critical if you want to be able to find these things again.
7. **No change management process.** IT projects change. When the scope, budget, or requirements of the project change, you need to have a framework to ensure you can cope with these changes. Even minor changes can affect multiple areas of the project.

IT Project Management Mistakes

The Center for Project Management helps IT organizations implement effective project management. Over 20 years ago, the firm came up with seven most common IT project management mistakes that cause the project to fail and that are still being made:

1. Failing to stick to a project process architecture (see Figure 13.1)
2. Treating half-baked ideas as projects
3. Missing or ineffective leadership

4. Employing underskilled project managers
5. Inadequately tracking the project's tasks, milestones, and resource usage
6. Failing to fix problems as soon as they are detected
7. Failing to engage in PPM

Questions

1. What is a deliverable?
2. What is the purpose of PPM?
3. What distinguishes a project from operations?
4. What are the triple constraints?
5. How can scope creep contribute to project failure?

13.2 Project Planning, Execution, and Budget

The progression of key documents and decisions through the project management life cycle is outlined in Figure 13.4. Projects start with an idea that is explained in a business case. If the business case is accepted, a **statement of work (SOW)** is prepared. The SOW is written as a definitive statement, which means that it defines the project plan but does not offer any options or alternatives in the scope. The project plan in the SOW is reviewed; a go or no-go decision is made; if a go decision is made, the project is initiated.

PROJECT BUSINESS CASE

The project manager, senior executive, or sponsor prepares a convincing business case for consideration. Here is an example of the components of a business case.

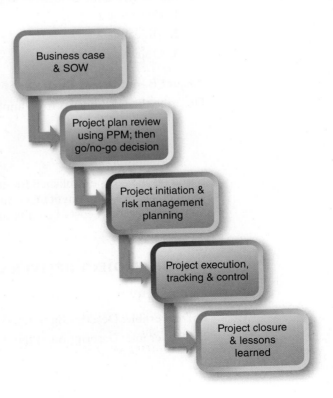

Figure 13.4 Project management key stages and activities.

Business Case Template

Project Overview Statement
Executive Summary

Project Name:

Department:

Date:

Author(s):

Project Manager(s):

Executive Sponsor(s):

Describe the pertinent facts of the project in a clear and concise way.

PROJECT BUSINESS CASE

Project Overview

Describe what is involved in executing the project.

Business Issue/Opportunity

Clearly identify the opportunity, need, or problem facing the company and why the project is necessary. Discuss the drivers that have triggered the project proposal and link them to the business need.

Project Business Goal

Describe expected benefits and how the project fits within the company's business strategy and contributes toward its goals and objectives.

Primary Project Objectives

List and describe the objectives of the project.

1. Objective 1
2. Objective 2 . . .
3. Objective n . . .

Project Benefits and Cost–Benefit Analysis

Describe the key benefits from implementing this project.

1. Benefit 1
2. Benefit 2 . . .
3. Benefit n . . .

Based on the costs established for each option, describe how those costs are weighed against the benefits. Conduct the cost–benefit analysis for each option taking into account costs, benefits, and risks.

PRIMARY PROJECT DELIVERABLES

Milestone 1

1. Deliverable: Description of the deliverable
2. Deliverable: Description of the deliverable
3. . . .

Milestone 2

1. Deliverable: Description of the deliverable
2. Deliverable: Description of the deliverable
3. ...

Milestone *n*

1. Deliverable: Description of the deliverable
2. Deliverable: Description of the deliverable
3. ...

Project Interdependencies and Inputs

Explain other projects in process or planned that have a relationship to this proposed project. List inputs that other projects may have to this project development.

- [input]
- [input]
- [input]

Project Assumptions and Constraints

List and describe all underlying technical, environmental, and resource availability assumptions upon which the project and benefits are based. List and describe constraints that can come from external or internal factors.

Project Risks

Describe known risks that apply to this project.

PROJECT KEY PERFORMANCE INDICATORS

Project Critical Success Factors or KPIs

List and describe KPIs or critical success factors that apply to this project.

PROJECT DURATION ESTIMATES AND DELIVERABLES

Project Milestone	Date Estimate	Confidence Level
Project Start Date		[High/Medium/Low]
Milestone 1		[High/Medium/Low]
Milestone 2		[High/Medium/Low]
Milestone *n*		[High/Medium/Low]
Project Completion Date		[High/Medium/Low]

APPROVALS

Prepared by _____

Project Manager

Approved by   _____

                   Project Sponsor

                   _____

                   Executive Sponsor

                   _____

                   Client Sponsor

STATEMENT OF WORK

An outline of a SOW is shown in Table 13.2. The SOW is a legal contract used to document the agreement between parties after the business terms have been

TABLE 13.2	Template for a Statement of Work
Date	[Insert date]
Client	[Insert client's name]
Job Name	[Insert project name]
Requested by	[Insert client sponsor's name]
From	[Insert project manager's name]
Summary and Objectives	A high-level description of the project and objectives
Project Scope	Description of the project scope, deliverables, and the process for how it will be performed
Schedule and Work Breakdown Structure (WBS)	List of tasks in sequential order, resources allocated to each task, and schedule
Cost or Pricing	Description of the cost (pricing) for all types of resources—labor costs, materials, equipment, overhead expenses; discussion of payment terms, including a payment schedule and if payments are based on a milestone/deliverable or a schedule, if appropriate
Key Assumptions	A crucial part of an SOW—any assumptions made when scoping and estimating the project need to be documented

Acceptance

The client named below verifies that the terms of this statement of work are acceptable. The parties hereto are each acting with proper authority of their respective companies.

Company name _____	Company name _____
Full name _____	Full name _____
Title _____	Title _____
Signature _____	Signature _____
Date _____	Date _____

accepted and a go decision is made. The **go/no-go decision** is a formal decision made by the project manager, sponsor, and appropriate executives and stakeholders.

WORK BREAKDOWN STRUCTURE

After the project objectives and scope have been defined, the next step is to identify all work or activities that need to be performed, the schedule of work, and who will perform the work. This is done by creating a **work breakdown structure (WBS)** as shown in Figure 13.5. Figure 13.6 shows a screen shot of a WBS (left side) developed using Microsoft Project. Project resources are managed according to the WBS.

Milestones

Milestones are used to manage the project work effort, monitor results, and report meaningful status to project stakeholders.

The WBS breaks a project down into the tasks or activities that must be performed, and in what order, to produce the deliverables at each milestone. Project **milestones** are very important scheduling and status devices because they enable the project manager to measure progress as the project proceeds through its planned life cycle. Lack of milestones has been a contributing factor in many project failures. Each milestone typically represents a deliverable (100 percent complete), but it may also signify the percent complete, such as 50 percent complete.

Milestone Example

Crowdfunding is raising funds for a project from the public, or *crowd*, via the Web.

Assume you are the project manager of a project for a client who wants to post a creative project on Kickstarter.com to raise funds using **crowdfunding**. You visit Kickstarter.com and do requirements analysis. You determine that you need to produce five deliverables: (1) a video, (2) a set of photos and illustrations, (3) a script that explains why the creative project deserves funding, (4) a set of pledge categories and rewards to backers, and (5) the final site with all deliverables uploaded to Kickstarter.com and tested. Each deliverable represents a milestone

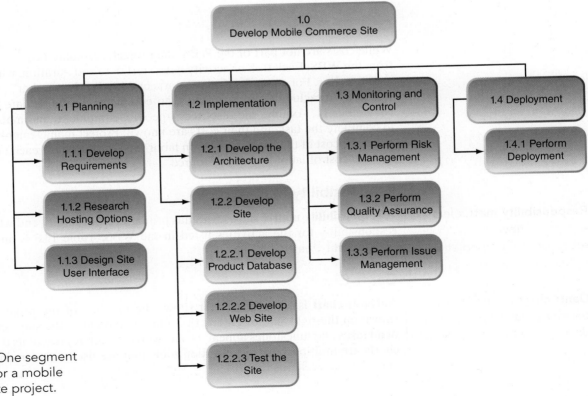

Figure 13.5 One segment of the WBS for a mobile commerce site project.

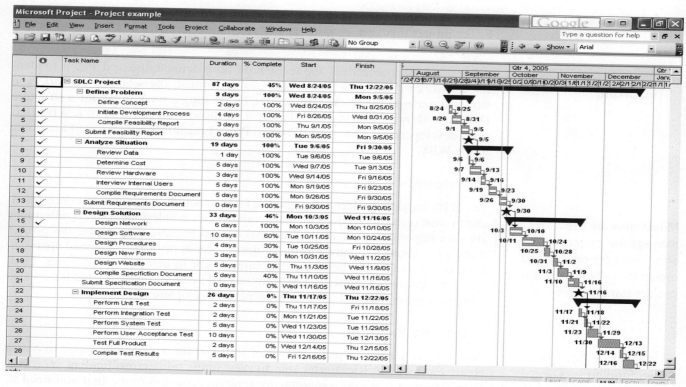

Figure 13.6 Microsoft Project screen shot of WBS (left side) and Gantt chart (right side).

in your project plan. You then rely on your milestone schedule to verify that the project is on track or to warn of the need for corrective action. Milestones should be natural, important control points in the project and easy for everyone to recognize.

Cost Estimations

While costs are not part of the WBS, the projects' estimated cost can be calculated from the WBS. Each task or activity has a start date and duration, which determines its finish date. For example, if a task starts on Monday, November 2, and takes eight work days (excluding weekend days) to complete, the finish date is Wednesday, November 11. Assume the resources—people, equipment, and materials—needed to complete the task and their costs are known. Project management software computes the cost of the project based on labor time (duration) of each task in the WBS and the cost of labor or other resource.

Responsibility Matrix

Responsibility matrix lets everyone know who is responsible for completion of tasks.

A **responsibility matrix** shows who has primary responsibility and who has support responsibility for the activities listed in the WBS. Table 13.3 is an example of a responsibility matrix.

Gantt Chart

Gantt chart is a horizontal bar chart that graphically displays the project schedule.

A **Gantt chart** is a bar chart that shows the timeline of the project schedule, as shown on the right side of Figure 13.6. On a Gantt chart, the start and finish dates of all tasks and milestones appear as bars whose length represent its duration. Gantt charts are multipurpose visualization tools that are used for planning, scheduling, and at-a-glance status reports.

TABLE 13.3 Sample Format for a Responsibility Matrix Showing Who Has Primary and Support Responsibility for WBS Tasks

WBS ID	Activity	Anna	Bart	Beth	Chas	Don
1.1	Storyboard video		S		P	
1.2	Recruit volunteers to act in video		S	P		
1.3	Record video segments				P	S
2.1	Select five photographs and images	P				S
2.2	Crop and edit photos	S				P

P = primary responsibility, S = support responsibility

Project Baseline

Baseline is a specification of the project plan that has been formally reviewed and agreed upon. It should be changed only through a formal change control process.

When the project plan is finalized and accepted, the accepted plan becomes the **baseline**, or master plan. The baseline is used for monitoring and controlling. Any change to the baseline is a deviation, or **variance**, to the plan—and it needs to be documented. Using project management software, you can save the WBS as the baseline. From then on, deviations will automatically be documented as variances from the baseline, as shown in Figure 13.7.

Work			
Scheduled:	680 hrs	Remaining:	581.2 hrs
Baseline:	528 hrs	Actual:	98.8 hrs
Variance:	152 hrs	Percent complete:	15%

Costs			
Scheduled:	$14,104.00	Remaining:	$11,751.60
Baseline:	$10,624.00	Actual:	$2,352.40
Variance:	$3,480.00		

Task Status		Resource status	
Tasks not yet started:	7	Work resources:	4
Tasks in progress:	9	Overallocated work resources:	4
Tasks completed:	0	Material resources:	0
Total tasks:	16	Total resources:	8

Figure 13.7 Work and cost variances from the agreed-upon project baseline are documented by project management software.

Questions

1. What identifies an opportunity, problem, or need and the desired business outcomes of the project?
2. What is the approach that examines projects holistically and manages them as a strategic portfolio?
3. What are the items that you hand off to the client or management for their review and approval?
4. What are the three attributes that must be managed effectively for successful completion and closure of any project?
5. What is the term for the piling up of small changes that by themselves are manageable but in aggregate are significant?
6. If the business case is accepted, what document is prepared?
7. What events are used to manage the project work effort, monitor results, and report a meaningful status to project stakeholders?
8. What is the longest path of tasks through a project?
9. What shows who has primary responsibility and who has support responsibility for the tasks listed in the WBS?
10. What is the type of bar chart that shows the timeline of the project schedule?
11. When the project plan is finalized and agreed to, what is any change to the baseline?

13.3 Project Monitoring, Control, and Closing

Monitoring and control processes are intended to occur continuously while the project work is being executed. These processes, described in Figure 13.8, depend on the baseline, milestones, responsibility matrix, and other elements from the planning stage. They keep the project team informed of project status and help them cope with challenges they encounter. Except for short, simple projects, there are going to be risks and changes that need to be kept under control and documented.

Monitoring depends on prompt and candid feedback from the project team, as you read in the opening case. In-person visits, reports, and records are also monitoring methods. Project control depends on systems and decision rules for managing variances between the project's scope, cost, schedule, and quality and the realities of project implementation.

INTEGRATED CHANGE CONTROL

Changes tend to have a trickle-down effect because of task dependencies and shared resources. For example, consider the following three activities from Table 13.3:

1.1 Storyboard a video.

1.2 Recruit volunteers to act in the video.

1.3 Record video segments.

Activity 1.3 is dependent on the completion of activities 1.1 and 1.2. Video recording cannot start until after the video has been storyboarded and actors are available.

Integrated change control processes help to manage the disruption resulting from requested changes and corrective actions across the project life cycle. Integrated change control processes are always documented and saved in the event of project failure or lawsuits related to the failure. These documents are needed to defend decisions—what did and did not happen, such as:

- Approved change requests
- Rejected change requests
- Updates to the project plan
- Updates to the scope
- Approved corrective and preventive actions
- Approved defect repair
- Validated defect repair

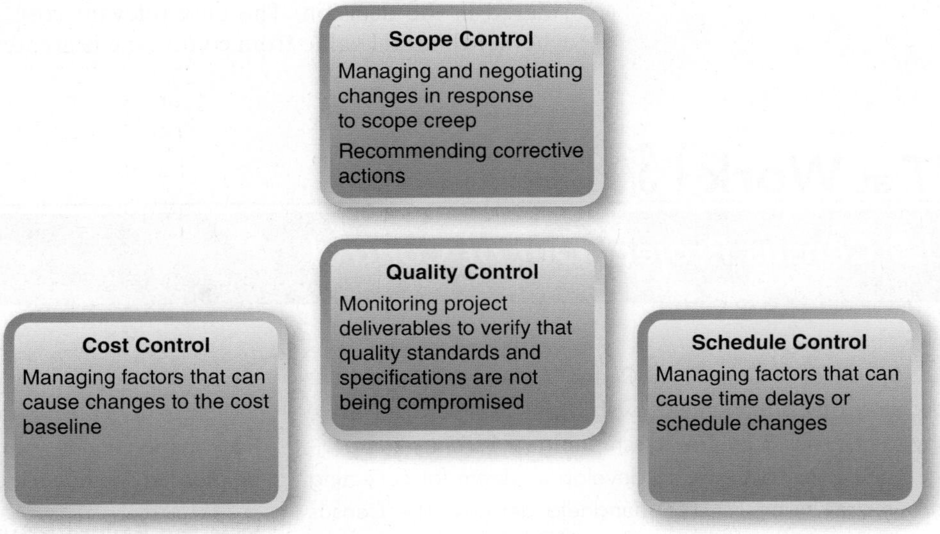

Scope Control
Managing and negotiating changes in response to scope creep
Recommending corrective actions

Quality Control
Monitoring project deliverables to verify that quality standards and specifications are not being compromised

Cost Control
Managing factors that can cause changes to the cost baseline

Schedule Control
Managing factors that can cause time delays or schedule changes

Figure 13.8 Project controls.

CRITICAL PATH

All projects have a **critical path** that extends the length of the project. Project management software shows the critical path on the Gantt chart, as in Figure 13.9. Each task or activity on the critical path is called a **critical task** or activity. Critical tasks must finish on schedule because delays will delay the project unless something is done to compensate. While it may seem that adding new people to a project is an obvious solution, in fact, it may initially slow it down. If any noncritical tasks get delayed enough, they could go critical, so both critical and noncritical paths need to be monitored.

WHEN TO KILL A PROJECT THAT IS OUT OF CONTROL

Project control is also used to identify when to declare the ongoing project a failure and kill it. Here is a common scenario:

The project is behind schedule. The scope changes almost daily. There were too few milestones identified during the planning stage to be able to monitor progress. Resources were overallocated. Because of the lack of regularly scheduled meetings, the project manager has no information on what the team members

Critical path is the longest path of tasks through a project, as shown on a Gantt chart. A delay of any task on the critical path will delay the project.

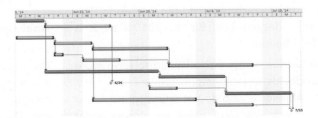

Figure 13.9 The critical path is shown as red bars. The critical path consists of the tasks from project start to finish that must be completed on time in order for the project to finish on time.

are working on at any given time. The team members are not communicating because they know that the project is on its deathbed and are afraid to say so. Many people in the company also know that the project is in trouble, except for senior management.

Sometimes, the only right way to fix a project is to cancel it. If a project suffers from one or more of conditions listed in the scenario, it has reached a point where its feasibility must be critically reexamined. It is very difficult to kill any project when millions of dollars have been spent to date—even when it is clearly the right decision. IT at Work 13.1 describes a real-world case.

The money already spent on the project, or **sunk costs**, should not be considered in the decision. The only relevant cost, from a financial point of view, is whether the total value from continuing is greater than the total cost of doing so.

IT at Work 13.1

U.S Census Project Out of Control

U.S. Secretary of Commerce Carlos M. Gutierrez issued the following official statement explaining (in an obscure way) why the Census Bureau was scrapping its $600 million project. The project plan was to develop a system for collecting census data using 500,000 handheld devices. The Census Bureau had contracted to use handheld devices from Harris Corp., but mismanagement, cost overruns, and poor planning caused the project to fail.

According to a U.S. Census Press Release:

Multiple internal and external reviews have identified continuing Census challenges across a number of areas, including adequate planning over key systems requirements, key technology requirements, specification of operational control system characteristics and functions and regional center technology infrastructure. . . . Gutierrez said that the Census Bureau will need an additional $2.2 to $3.0 billion in funding over the next five years to meet the replan needs. . . . The lifecycle cost for the Reengineered 2010 Census was estimated at $11.8 billion in the FY 2009 Budget Request, including $1.8 billion for the American Community Survey which replaced the long-form. The new estimated lifecycle cost for the 2010 Census is $13.7 to $14.5 billion.

In summary, the Census Bureau had planned to issue more than 500,000 handhelds to temporary employees to collect personal data on Americans who do not return census forms in the mail. The handhelds were being developed under a $600 million contract awarded to Harris Corp. in 2006. Stumbling over this multibillion-dollar plan for a high-tech census, the government reverted to counting the nation's 300 million people the old-fashioned way: with paper and pencil. Poor management—not poor technology—caused the government to spend an additional $3 billion for the next census.

Was the Failure a Surprise?

Senator Susan Collins, ranking member of the Committee on Homeland Security and Governmental Affairs, was not surprised by the failure. "This committee is unfortunately no stranger to tales of federal projects and contracts that have gone awry, often at a heavy cost in taxpayer funds," she said. Collins listed the usual failure reasons:

- poorly defined initial requirements and
- inability or unwillingness of management to control "requirements creep" and cost overruns.

Something larger than poor project management was at work. It was the failure of top management in the Bureau to assess and mitigate the risks inherent in such a major project. "It should be noted that the problems with this contract seemed apparent to everyone except the Census Bureau," said Senator Tom Coburn (D-Oklahoma).

Analysis of the Handheld Project Failure

The 2010 census was to have been the first true high-tech count in the nation's history. The Census Bureau had awarded a contract to purchase 500,000 of the computers, plus the computer operating system, at a cost of more than $600 million. The contract ballooned to $1.3 billion, even though the Bureau scaled back its purchase to only 151,000 handheld computers. The higher expenditure was due to cost overruns and new features ordered by the Census Bureau on the computers and the operating system. Gutierrez blamed many of the problems on "a lack of effective communication with one of our key contractors."

Census officials were being blamed for doing a poor job of spelling out technical requirements to the contractor, Harris. In addition, the handhelds proved too complex for some temporary workers who tried to use them in a test in North Carolina, and the devices were not initially programmed to transmit the large amounts of data necessary.

Harris spokesman Marc Raimondi said the cost of the contract increased as the project requirements increased: "The increased funding is required to cover additional sites, equipment, software and functions added by the bureau to the program."

Representative Alan Mollohan, chairman of the appropriations subcommittee, said the Census Bureau and Harris "contributed to today's crisis." The Census Bureau's failure to address problems with the computers early on has "turned the crisis into the emergency that we now face."

Sources: Compiled from Holmes (2008) and U.S. Census (census. gov, 2008).

Questions

1. What went wrong?
2. What should have been done that was not done?
3. Where any problems unforeseeable?
4. Consider the statement: "hope is not a plan." Does the statement apply to this project failure? Explain why or why not.
5. What are the similarities between the U.S .Census project failure and the DIA automated baggage-handling project failure?

PROJECT CLOSING AND POSTMORTEM

Closing out a project does not benefit the completed project (which is the first to be cut when costs overrun); rather, it benefits the enterprise and people who worked on the project. They gain a better understanding of what did and did not work. These lessons learned guide future projects.

Postproject reviews, or postmortems, identify the reasons the project was successful or not, strengths and weaknesses of the project plan, how problems were detected and resolved, and how the project was successful in spite of them.

CAREER INSIGHT 13.1

IT Project Management Jobs

Project management is a high-level skill and a demanding career choice. The most successful upper-level project managers typically have an MBA or other business degree and financial background to plan and manage the project budget.

A sample job description for an IT project manager is as follows:

Responsible for the coordination and completion of projects within the information technology department. Oversees all aspects of projects and project budgets. Sets deadlines, assigns responsibilities, and monitors and summarizes progress of project. Builds and maintains working relationships with team members, vendors, and other departments involved in the projects. Prepares reports for upper management regarding status of project. Requires a bachelor's degree, two to four years of experience, and knowledge of project management software. MBA is preferred. Leads and directs the work of others. A wide degree of creativity and latitude is expected. Typically reports to a senior manager or head of a unit/department.

Questions

1. What processes help to ensure that the impacts resulting from requested changes and corrective actions are managed across the project life cycle?
2. What is the length of a project?
3. Assuming no changes are made, what happens when a task on the critical path is delayed?
4. What costs should not be considered when deciding whether to kill a project?
5. When are lessons learned from a completed project identified?

13.4 System Development Life Cycle

The **system development life cycle (SDLC)** is the traditional system development method for large IT projects, such as IT infrastructure or an enterprise system. The SDLC is a structured framework that consists of a sequential set of processes, as shown in Figure 13.10. Starting with an initial idea, the SDLC processes are requirements analysis, systems analysis and design, development and testing, implementation, and maintenance. Each process consists of well-defined tasks that depend on the scope of the project. The processes are iterative, which means that they are revised when new information or conditions make a revision the smart thing to do. Iteration does not mean that system development should be subject to infinite revisions or scope creep.

IS design is highly susceptible to scope creep for many reasons. Intended users ask for additional features. People who were not intended users ask to be included. Technology changed from the time the business case was written and system development began. The actions of a competitor, supplier, or regulatory agency triggered additional requests for functionality. Because scope creep is expensive, project managers impose controls on changes requested by users. These controls help to prevent *runaway projects*—system development projects that are so far over budget and past deadline that they must be abandoned, typically with large monetary loss.

| SDLC STEPS

In general, an SDLC methodology follows the following steps.

Requirements Analysis

Deficiencies in the existing system are identified and used to specify functional and data requirements of the new system. Requirements analysis is critical to the success of the project. System development practitioners agree that the more time invested in analyzing the current system, business problem, or opportunity and

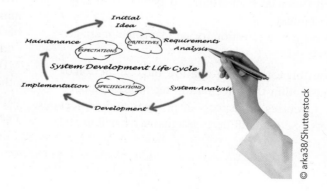

Figure 13.10 System development life cycle.

understanding problems that are likely to occur during development, the greater the probability that the IS will be a success.

System Analysis and Feasibility Studies

The proposed system is designed. Plans are laid out concerning the physical construction, hardware, software, media, dashboards, operating systems, programming, connectivity, and security issues. The feasibility of the design is tested. The feasibility study determines the probability of success of the proposed project and provides a rough assessment of the project's technical, economic, organizational, and behavioral feasibility. The feasibility study is critically important to the system development process because, done properly, the study can prevent companies from making expensive mistakes, such as creating systems that will not work, that will not work efficiently, or that people cannot or will not use. The Census Bureau case in IT at Work 13.1 is an example. The various feasibility analyses also give the stakeholders an opportunity to decide what metrics to use to measure how a proposed system meets their objectives.

- **Technical feasibility.** Technical feasibility determines if the required technology, IT infrastructure, data structures, analytics, and resources can be developed and/or acquired to solve the business problem. Technical feasibility also determines if the organization's existing technology can be used to achieve the project's performance objectives.

- **Economic feasibility.** Economic feasibility determines if the project is an acceptable financial risk and if the company can afford the expense and time needed to complete the project. Economic feasibility addresses two primary questions: Do the benefits outweigh the costs of the project? Can the project be completed as scheduled?

  Management can assess economic feasibility by using cost–benefit analysis and financial techniques such as time value of money, return on investment (ROI), net present value (NPV), and breakeven analysis. Return on investment is the ratio of the net income attributable to a project divided by the average cost of resources invested in the project. NPV is the net amount by which project benefits exceed project costs, after allowing for the cost of capital and the time value of money. Breakeven analysis calculates the point at which the cumulative cash flow from a project equals the investment made in the project.

  Calculating economic feasibility in IT projects is rarely straightforward. Part of the difficulty is that some benefits are intangible. For a proposed system that involves big data, real time analytics, or 3D printing, there may be no previous evidence of what sort of financial payback can be expected.

- **Legal and organizational feasibility.** Are there legal, regulatory, or environmental reasons why the project cannot or should not be implemented? This analysis looks at the company's policies and politics, including impacts on power distribution and business relationships.

- **Behavioral feasibility.** Behavioral feasibility considers human issues. All system development projects introduce change, and people generally resist change. Overt resistance from employees may take the form of sabotaging the new system (e.g., entering data incorrectly) or deriding the new system to anyone who will listen. Covert resistance typically occurs when employees simply do their jobs using their old methods.

  Behavioral feasibility is concerned with assessing the skills and the training needed to use the new IS. In some organizations, a proposed system may require mathematical or linguistic skills beyond what the workforce currently possesses. In others, a workforce may simply need to improve their skills. Behavioral feasibility is as much about "can they use it" as it is about "will they use it."

After the feasibility analysis, a go/no-go decision is reached. The project sponsor and project manager sign off on the decision. If it is a no-go decision, the project is put on the shelf until conditions are more favorable, or the project is discarded. If the decision is "go," then the system development project proceeds.

SYSTEM DEVELOPMENT AND TESTING

System developers utilize the design specifications to acquire the software needed for the system to meet its functional objectives and solve the business problem. Sourcing, as discussed in Chapter 12, and in-house coding are options.

Testing verifies that apps, interfaces, data transfers, and so on, work correctly under all possible conditions. Testing requires a lot of time, effort, and expense to do properly. However, the costs and consequences of improper testing, which could possibly lead to a system that does not meet its objectives, are enormous. The risk of costly lawsuits needs to be considered.

IMPLEMENTATION

Implementation, or deployment, is the process of converting from the old system to the new system. Four conversion strategies are parallel, direct cut over, pilot, and phased.

In a *parallel conversion,* the old system and the new system operate simultaneously for a period of time. That is, both systems process the same data at the same time, and the outputs are compared. This type of conversion is the most expensive but least risky.

In a *direct conversion,* the old system is cut off and the new system is turned on at a certain point in time. This type of conversion is the least expensive, but it is the most risky if the new system does not work as planned.

A *pilot conversion* introduces the new system in one location to test it out. After the new system works properly, it is rolled out.

A *phased conversion* introduces components of the new system, such as individual modules, in stages. Each module is assessed, and, when it works properly, other modules are introduced until the entire new system is operational.

MAINTENANCE

Once the new system's operations are stabilized, *audits* are performed during operation to assess the system's capabilities and determine if it is being used correctly. Maintenance must be kept up rigorously at all times. Users of the system should be kept up to date concerning the latest modifications and procedures.

Questions

1. What are the stages of the SDLC?
2. Why is information system design highly susceptible to scope creep?
3. What can be done to prevent runaway projects?
4. Explain the feasibility tests and their importance.
5. What are four conversion methods?

Key Terms

baseline
business case
critical path
critical task
crowdfunding
deliverable
Gantt chart
go/no-go decision

integrated change control
milestone
postmortem
project
project management
project portfolio
   management (PPM)

prototyping
responsibility matrix
scope creep
statement of work (SOW)
sunk cost
system development life
   cycle (SDLC)

triple constraint
variance
work breakdown structure
   (WBS)

Assuring Your Learning

DISCUSS: Critical Thinking Questions

1. Business cases take a long time to research and write. As a result, they are also time consuming to review. Explain why business cases require so much effort and detail.

2. What risks might the use of project portfolio management (PPM) minimize? Do you think PPM can guarantee honest and unbiased project approvals or not? Explain your position.

3. Do you think that projects that are needed to comply with regulations, such as the international anti-money-laundering (AML) laws that require firms to *know your customer* (KYC), should undergo the same approval requirements as discretionary projects, such as in manufacturing or marketing? Explain your reasons.

4. Why should each deliverable be made a milestone?

5. Why is the critical path an important monitoring tool?

6. How does diagramming the triple constraint as a triangle clearly demonstrate how time, scope, and cost are interrelated?

7. Refer to the Center for Project Management's list of seven IT project management mistakes. Select two of these mistakes and explain how they contribute to project failure.

8. Why should the go/no-go decision be made more than once in a project's life cycle?

9. If a project is started without a documented baseline, what risks might the project and project team face?

10. Explain how control activities are, in effect, risk management activities.

11. Why is it tough to ignore sunk costs when evaluating a failing project?

12. Why are IT projects so susceptible to scope creep?

13. What leads to a runaway project?

14. What feasibilities are needed prior to IT project approval?

15. Explain the stages of the SDLC.

EXPLORE: Online and Interactive Exercises

1. ProjectLibre is the open-source replacement of Microsoft Project. Visit the ProjectLibre website at ProjectLibre.org.
   a. Download the free software.
   b. Assume you are the project manager on a project of your choice that you are able to manage. Several project examples are delivering a tailgate party for 50 people, remodeling a kitchen, creating a YouTube video for advertising a new product, or implementing a new cloud accounting information system.
   c. Use the software to plan a project of your choice. Create a WBS and Gantt chart.

2. Research and compare the current top three open-source project management tools. What are their limitations?

3. Research the three project management vendors' software packages and find a review of each one. Write a report that compares the features of the packages, including prices, and that summarizes the reviews.

ANALYZE & DECIDE: Apply IT Concepts to Business Decisions

1. You are the project manager and need to compose a SOW for clients who want you to develop a Kickstarter.com site for their project, as discussed in the chapter.
   a. Start off by composing a SOW using a standard SOW template that you found and downloaded from the Internet.
   b. Use www.tomsplanner.com or other free Gantt chart software to create a Gantt chart for your project.
   c. Assume that after your clients review your SOW and Gantt chart, they request that you discount the price 20 percent. Based on the triple constraints, how would you respond?

2. Explore project management software on vendors' websites. Select a single project management package, download the demo, and try it. Make a list of the important features of the package. Be sure to investigate its cloud and collaboration features. Report your findings.

3. Managing a project with Microsoft Project is often the approach to IT project management, but many users prefer to use Microsoft Excel instead. The main reasons are that MS Project is too expensive, wastes too much time to set up and keep updated, and is tough to use. The debate between Excel and Project has valid arguments for either approach. Research the reviews of Excel and MS Project as project management tools. When is each software appropriate for use?

CASE 13.2

Business Case: Steve Jobs' Shared Vision Project Management Style

Steve Jobs (1955–2011) co-founded Apple Inc. and reinvented the PC, music players, phones, tablets, and digital publishing (Figure 13.11). He is regarded as technology industry's most notable luminary. He continuously managed remarkably innovative projects—extremely successful ones as well as many failures. Although widely recognized as a marketing and technology guru, Jobs was largely successful because of his project-based approach for managing his business and producing new products. His approach to executing projects ultimately changed the business world. Jobs' *shared vision* project management style offers lessons to help managers focus and motivate their team to get projects completed on schedule.

Shared Vision and Accountability
A significant part of what made Jobs successful was his persistent push to keep projects moving while communicating with his team to ensure they were working toward the shared vision. He stressed accountability and did not let anyone slide on that principle. He got to know everyone on the team and actively inspired them.

Guy Kawasaki, Apple's chief evangelist and liaison to the Mac developer community, said Jobs appreciated great work. He was well known for giving employees feedback—publicly telling them if they were great or lousy. His bluntness infuriated some people but also motivated them to either do their best or leave.

Communication
Structure, understanding, and inspiration depend on the one irreplaceable management skill: communication. Part of what made Jobs so successful was his constant push to keep projects moving while communicating with his team to ensure they were working toward a shared vision. He held regular meetings to avoid wasting time with long e-mail chains and having to address the same concerns multiple times.

Do Not Just Listen—Understand
There is a big difference between listening and understanding. Jobs made sure he understood everyone on his team and that they understood him. This is done by making people demonstrate that they understand and not simply asking them if they understand. When everyone confirms they are on the same page, they will keep moving forward.

Sources: Darton Group (2012), Isaacson (2012), and Kimbrell (2014).

Figure 13.11 Steve Jobs, CEO and founder of Apple Computers and Pixar boss, was one of the greatest project managers.

Questions
1. Steve Jobs shows the importance of people skills. Explain Jobs' way of motivating people. For example, did he try to get everyone to like him? Did he try to get everyone to get along with each other?
2. Why did Jobs' approach to project management work so well for him?
3. What lessons can project managers learn from Jobs?
4. Research Steve Jobs' management style from reputable sources. What did you learn about how people reacted to Jobs' style?
5. Create a checklist of effective project management practices.

CASE 13.3
Demo Case: Mavenlink Project Management and Planning Software

Project management software and apps continue to be improved with advanced features and integration with other technology. The decision on which project management software to use depends on the company's needs, size of business, and industry. Cloud-based or online project management applications are popular choices. Mavenlink is a vendor that provides easy-to-follow video tutorials through their online resources. With Mavenlink, you can track project timelines, collaborate on tasks, manage team activities, and integrate with Google Apps, QuickBooks, and Salesforce from a single workplace environment.

Visit Mavenlink's website at Mavenlink.com. Scroll to the bottom of the landing page and click TUTORIALS. A YouTube video will launch. Watch the video. Also search for the Mavenlink: Online Project Management on YouTube, which was posted by a client, CloudBase3.com.

Questions
1. What features support project planning?
2. What features support project monitoring and control?
3. How is change management supported?
4. What did CloudBase3 identify as shortcomings or cons of Mavenlink?

References

Calleam Consulting Ltd. "Case Study—Denver International Airport Baggage Handling System—An Illustration of Ineffectual Decision Making." www.Calleam.com. 2008.

Darton Group. "Steve Jobs and Lessons for Project Managers." *DartonGroup.com*, January 2, 2012.

Grimes, R. A. "11 Signs Your IT Project Is Doomed." *Computerworld.com*, May 6, 2013.

Gupta, S. & A. Jain. "AML and KYC Analytics—The Risk of Non-Compliance and the Cost of Compliance." Everest Group Research, 2014. genpact.com/docs/resource-/-aml-and-kyc-analytics—the-risk-of-non-compliance-and-the-cost-of-compliance

Holmes, A. "Census Program to Use Handheld Computers Said to Be in 'Serious Trouble.'" *GovernmentExecutive.com*, January 2, 2008.

Isaacson, W. *Steve Jobs*. New York: Simon & Schuster, September 2012.

Kimbrell, G. "Four Project Management Lessons You Can Learn from Software Engineers." *Forbes*, January 31, 2014.

Krigsman, M. "Who's Accountable for IT failure?" *ZDNet*, April 16, 2012.

Nelson, R. R. "Project Retrospectives: Evaluating Project Success, Failure, and Everything in Between." *MIS Quarterly Executive* 4, no. 3, September 2005.

Perkins, B. "Bart Perkins: How to Keep Projects on Track." *Computerworld.com*, April 21, 2014.

Stackpole, B. "Why Project Management in IT Is More Important Than Ever." *State Tech Magazine*, September 25, 2013.

Symonds, M. "The Seven Deadly Sins of Project Management." *The Project Management Hut*, January 17, 2014.

U.S. Census, 2008. *census.gov*

Ethical Risks and Responsibilities of IT Innovations

Chapter Snapshot

Case 14.1 Opening Case: Google Glass and Risk, Privacy, and Piracy Challenges

14.1 Privacy Paradox, Privacy, and Civil Rights

14.2 Responsible Conduct

14.3 Technology Addictions and the Emerging Trend of Focus Management

14.4 Six Technology Trends Transforming Business

Key Terms
Assuring Your Learning

- **Discuss:** Critical Thinking Questions
- **Explore:** Online and Interactive Exercises
- **Analyze & Decide:** Apply IT Concepts to Business Decisions

Case 14.2 Business Case: Apple's CarPlay Gets Intelligent

Case 14.3 Video Case: Vehicle-to-Vehicle Technology to Prevent Collisions

References

Learning Outcomes

1. Analyze the privacy paradox and the effects of IT innovations on civil rights, privacy, piracy, copyright infringement, and other social risks.

2. Distinguish and debate the complex issues of responsible conduct and irresponsible conduct, such as social media discrimination.

3. Describe the impacts of *constant connectivity* and distractions on quality of life, business, safety, and interpersonal relationships.

4. Describe the disruptive technology trends for the next three years.

Chapter Snapshot

Several of today's toughest ethical and social challenges did not even exist at the start of this decade. The latest social, mobile, cloud, and information management technologies are powerful forces. While businesses, governments, and users greatly benefit from their use, they may have harmful effects—not all of which are obvious yet. For example, what is the effect of people spending their personal and professional lives in a state of continuous disruption or partial (distracted) attention?

Are you prepared to deal effectively with ethical challenges and corporate responsibilities that social, mobile, big data, and analytics technology create in business? Anecdotal research suggests that individuals often do not even recognize when ethical issues are present. If people cannot recognize them, then it is hard to imagine how they could act responsibly.

This chapter intends to make you aware of ethical risks, legal responsibilities, what we trade off, and unresolvable controversies. These issues are examined within the context of civil rights, employment laws, regulations, research findings, and case examples. Of course, even those guidelines cannot provide easy answers to social discrimination, the demise of privacy, distractions, piracy and theft of intellectual property, and what the latest digital devices are doing to quality of life. There are no easy fixes, clear-cut judgments, answers, or solutions. As managers, you need to be able to recognize ethical issues and tip the balance toward better responsible conduct.

CASE 14.1 OPENING CASE

Google Glass and Risk, Privacy, and Piracy Challenges

In October 2013, California Highway Patrol (CHP) officer Keith Odle pulled over Cecilia Abadie for speeding along Interstate 15 in San Diego. Odle noticed that Abadie, a software developer, was wearing Google Glass (see Figure 14.1). He ticketed her for speeding and for being in violation of the distracted-driving law. California Vehicle Code Section 27602 bans people from driving while video screens are operating in the front of the vehicle, except for mapping displays such as GPS and other built-in screens. Abadie was one of the explorers who were pilot testing Google Glass, which was then not yet on the market.

While the case against Abadie was the first known instance of a Glass-related ticket, it will not be the last. At least seven states—Delaware, Illinois, Missouri, New Jersey, New York, West Virginia, and Wyoming—are considering laws prohibiting driving while using Google Glass. As stated on the CNET website (www.cnet.com), Abadie's alleged violation "does pose a thorny legal question that police, judges and drivers will have to face as these wearable devices become more prevalent" (Whitney, 2013).

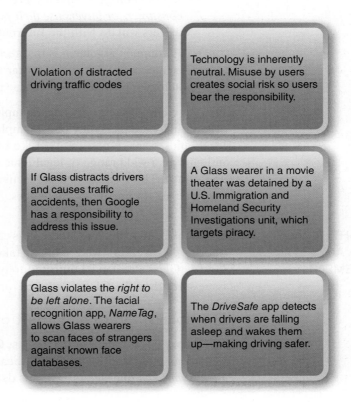

Figure 14.1 Diverse views and arguments about the consequences of wearing Google Glass.

Violation of distracted driving traffic codes

Technology is inherently neutral. Misuse by users creates social risk so users bear the responsibility.

If Glass distracts drivers and causes traffic accidents, then Google has a responsibility to address this issue.

A Glass wearer in a movie theater was detained by a U.S. Immigration and Homeland Security Investigations unit, which targets piracy.

Glass violates the *right to be left alone*. The facial recognition app, *NameTag*, allows Glass wearers to scan faces of strangers against known face databases.

The *DriveSafe* app detects when drivers are falling asleep and wakes them up—making driving safer.

DISTRACTED DRIVERS VERSUS INFORMED DRIVERS

Wearing computer-in-eyewear could be a distracted-driving violation according to the traffic code, but police must prove that the eyewear was on. The CHP officer had seen the light from Abadie's Glass screen. However, her defense attorney claimed that the Glass activated when she looked up at the officer during the stop but was not on when she was driving. The California judge dismissed her ticket saying that the CHP officer failed to prove the Glass was in operation when the driver was stopped.

One side argues that driving with a wearable computer is as risky as texting or watching TV while driving. The opposing side claims that the advantages of Glass outweigh any risks. They cite the DriveSafe app that detects when drivers are falling asleep and wakes them up—making driving safer. At present, traffic laws aim to eliminate distracted driving.

PRODUCT LIABILITY, RISK, AND RESPONSIBILITY CONTROVERSY

This case triggered many debates over the responsibility and business risk of digital technology products hitting the market. Here are several debated issues:

- *Google Glass may redefine the boundaries of companies' product liability.* Certainly, individuals have the responsibility to drive safely at all times. Does Google also bear responsibility for potential harm caused by Glass users?

- The *United Nations (U.N.) Guiding Principles on Business and Human Rights* was unanimously endorsed by the Human Rights Council in 2011. It states that companies must "avoid causing or contributing to adverse human rights impacts through their own activities, and address such impacts when they occur." Glass constitutes Google's "own activities;" therefore, according to the U.N., if Glass distracts drivers and causes traffic accidents, then Google has a responsibility to address this issue. The possible legal and ethical question is whether or not technology companies are obligated to inform users that there may be social risks (risks to others) from using their products in plain language—similar to warnings of side effects of medications.

- *Do technology companies bear any responsibility for the social risks of how consumers or buyers use their products?* Lawmakers are worried about what drivers will do with the Internet at their eyeballs.

- A common argument is that technology is inherently neutral. Misuse by users creates social risk so users bear the responsibility. Opponents argue that technology companies must manage the social risks that they contribute to or cause.

Driving violations are only one example of the effects of Glass on the legal system. Additionally, Glass is only one example of intersection of new devices and ethical, legal, and social responsibility. Like other new digital technologies, the device is influencing a wide range of legal issues, including copyright infringement, privacy, and piracy. The legal system is reactive and slower moving that IT—and may not be prepared for upcoming challenges.

COPYRIGHT, PIRACY, AND PRIVACY INFRINGEMENT

Since it is worn instead of held, Glass can record events less obtrusively than smartphones do. Wearers who want to take photos simply wink with their right eye. Google Glass also can be outfitted to prescription lenses, which introduces another issue since then the Glass is needed for correct vision.

Example 1: Piracy and Theft of Intellectual Property

In January 2014, a man in Columbus, Ohio, who was wearing prescription Google Glass was pulled out of an AMC theater about an hour into watching the movie *Jack Ryan: Shadow Recruit*. He was detained by agents from the U.S. Immigration and Customs Enforcement's Homeland Security Investigations unit, which targets piracy. After the interrogation, the agents hooked the Glass up to a computer and saw that all it was storing were personal family photos. Why and how did agents show up so quickly? AMC issued the following statement to address why it called the agency (Taylor, 2014):

> [M]ovie theft is something we take very seriously, and our theater managers contact the Motion Picture Association of America anytime it's suspected. . . . At AMC Easton 30 last weekend, a guest was questioned for possible movie theft after he was identified wearing a recording device during a film. The presence of this recording device prompted an investigation by the MPAA, which was on site. The MPAA then contacted Homeland Security, which oversees movie theft. The investigation determined the guest was not recording content.

An AMC representative explained that wearing a device that was capable of recording video, which could then be used to pirate movies, was not allowed at movies. Certainly the motion picture industry has the right to protect its products against piracy via wearable devices that can record movies in stealth. Do owners of wearables have comparable rights? Which of these conflicting rights should override the other? Now consider a similar example.

Example 2: Privacy Invasions

Privacy invasions by people wearing Google Glass who take photos or shoot video instantaneously are another violation. Some entertainment and dining places, including a restaurant in Seattle, have banned people who wear the devices. In some states, wearers who give Glass the command to record could potentially violate wiretapping laws. Should people who are out relaxing and enjoying themselves be subject to being recorded without their consent or knowledge? Whose rights should override in these cases?

PURPOSE OF GOOGLE GLASS CONFLICTS WITH PRIVACY OF OTHERS

In Google's view, the whole purpose of Glass is to have it on all the time. That is the Glass business model. The more the devices are worn, the more profitable they are. Google's response to privacy and piracy violations is that Glass is designed with explicit signals, such as the screen lighting up, to alert others when someone is taking a picture or recording video. In your opinion, is a lit screen sufficient protection?

The devices make it harder for nonwearers to remain anonymous. A facial recognition app, NameTag, allows Glass wearers to scan faces of strangers against known databases of faces. Google officially bans facial recognition apps on Google Glass. Does that ban have any meaning? Will people figure out how to get around it?

This opening case introduces current ethical challenges and competing rights decisions. Your answers to questions within the case may change once you start to wear technology—or suffer because of others who do.

Sources: Compiled from Bader (2014), Perry (2014), Davis (2014), Dobuzinskis (2013), and Taylor (2014).

Questions

1. Answer the questions within the case. Explain the basis for your answers and opinions.
2. An estimated 500 million people are expected to be wearing a Web-connected watch, camera, eyepiece, or other device by 2018. Consider how your answers to the questions within the case are different when answered from the perspective of half a billion wearers instead of just a few thousand. How have your answers and opinions changed?

3. Imagine you had a Google Glass app that monitors your surroundings and tells you when you are about to crash into something. In your opinion, should use of Glass and that app while driving be legal or illegal? Explain your reasoning.

4. Glass wearers who become accustomed to capturing their lives with wearable devices could end up violating privacy, copyright, or piracy laws without realizing it. Research each of these laws and give a description of each.

5. Use what you learned in Question #4 to give three examples of how such a violation could occur. Why might these violations be practically impossible to prevent or prove?

6. Do you think that Glass and similar wearables should be illegal? Explain your answer.

7. Do you agree with the U.N.'s position on corporate responsibility? Explain your answer.

8. Visit the SearchEngineWatch.com site. Search for "6 Funny Google Project Glass Parody Videos." Watch the original video named "Project Glass: One day…" Imagine how human interaction might change if a majority of people spent the day wearing Glass. Describe how you see interaction changing.

14.1 Privacy Paradox, Privacy, and Civil Rights

We do not live in a world without consequences and boundaries. Yet many people act as though they do, as the privacy paradox points out.

PRIVACY AND THE NEW PRIVACY PARADOX

Privacy is the right to self-determine what information about you is made accessible, to whom, when, and for what use or purpose. Privacy means we have freedom of choice and control over our personal information, including what we do not want shared with or used by others. Unauthorized disclosure of personal information is normally considered a **breach of privacy**, although what is *unauthorized* and what is *personal information* are matters of dispute, particularly when it is online.

While privacy is still the social norm, a person's privacy is based to a large extent on what choices that person has made. The amount of shared personal information is a decision that individuals make over their lifetime. This is a critical concept because online content can persist for an entire lifetime. Private content that uninhibited teenagers with bad judgment posted or sent cannot be made to disappear when they apply for jobs requiring security clearance or intense background checks—or run for public office.

Users of social sites often claim that they are concerned about their privacy. At the same time, they disclose their highly personal lives, even content that is incriminating or illegal, in their profiles or posts. The **privacy paradox** refers to this phenomenon where social users are concerned about privacy but their behaviors contradict these concerns to an extreme degree. Facebook membership has increased despite Facebook founder Mark Zuckerberg's frequent changes to default privacy settings to allow everyone to see and search for names, gender, city, and other information. Zuckerberg's position is that people "have really gotten comfortable not only sharing more information and different kinds, but more openly and with more people. That social norm is just something that has evolved over time" (Cavoukian, 2012). It is well known that Zuckerberg has a multibillion-dollar commercial interest in the elimination of online privacy, so trusting Facebook's privacy policies exemplifies the privacy paradox.

A 2013 Pew study found that 50 percent of Internet users were worried about the information available about them online, compared to 30 percent in 2009 (Rainie, Kiesler, Kang, & Madden, 2013). The results mean that 50 percent of Internet users are not worried about their online privacy. Following the news that the U.S. National Security Agency was collecting the telephone and Internet metadata of its citizens, a Washington Post–ABC poll found that only 40 percent of U.S. respondents said that it was more important to protect citizens' privacy even if it limited the ability of the government to investigate terrorist threats (Cohen & Balz, 2013).

The Global Cyber Security Capacity Centre and Oxford Internet Institute have together released a draft working paper examining the attitudes of younger people toward privacy online. The 2014 report, *A New Privacy Paradox: Young People and Privacy on Social Network Sites*, shows that, contrary to conventional wisdom, people under age 35 are actually more likely to have taken action to protect their privacy than older people (Blank, Bolsover, and Dubois, 2014). However, according to the report, the new privacy paradox is that social sites have become so embedded in the social lives of users that they must disclose information about themselves even though these sites do not provide adequate privacy controls. The consequences of the privacy paradox are far reaching.

| SOCIAL RECRUITMENT

The use of social media is so pervasive in today's workplace that it is even having an impact on the enforcement of federal laws that protect civil rights. Jonathan Segal, speaking on behalf of the Society for Human Resource Management (SHRM), explained that employers use social media for multiple reasons: to engage employees, to share knowledge among employees, and for recruitment and hiring of new employees (EEOC, 2014). The SHRM surveyed its members for several years and found that 77 percent of the surveyed companies had used social sites to recruit candidates in 2013, more than double the 34 percent rate in 2008.

Social Tools for Recruiting and Background Checks

Social recruitment refers to use of social media to find, screen, and select job candidates. Often it involves searching information the job candidate did not want considered or that is illegal to use in the hiring process.

In order to cast a wide net for potential candidates, social media are used in **social recruitment**. However, improper use of information scraped from these sites may be discriminatory and illegal. The problem starts with members who post age, race, gender, and ethnicity information—or enable it to be learned from content on their sites. To the extent that employers conduct a social media background check on job candidates, these are three best practices:

1. Have either a third party or a designated person within the company who does not make hiring decisions do the background check.

2. Use only publicly available information. Do not friend someone to get access to private information.

3. Do not request username or passwords for social media accounts.

By mid-2014, four states had enacted laws prohibiting employers from requesting passwords and usernames from applicants/employees. Other states have such laws pending, and there are several proposals before Congress to do the same on a federal level.

Social Recruiting and Discrimination

Recruiters see LinkedIn as the world's largest resume database. Depending on how job candidates control their privacy and how much they reveal through check-ins

Figure 14.2 Members expose too much information about themselves through social posts and check-ins. Employers and recruiters use social content. Laws forbid use of some types of that information in hiring practices, but what can prevent their use?

and posts (Figure 14.2), recruiters learn a great deal of information that should not be used in their decision to interview, recommend, or hire someone. In a 2009 study conducted for CareerBuilder, more than half of employers reported that the biggest factor influencing their decision not to hire an applicant was the presence of provocative photos on the candidate's social media profile, an issue more likely to affect women than men (CareerBuilder.com, 2009).

Protected Classes and Information

EEOC (Equal Employment Opportunity Commission) enforces federal laws prohibiting discrimination in employment.

Protected classes are characteristics identified by law that cannot be used in the hiring process.

Discrimination is biased or prejudicial treatment in recruitment, hiring, or employment based on certain characteristics, such as age, gender, and genetic information, and is illegal in the United States.

According to the **Equal Employment Opportunity Commission (EEOC)**, discriminatory practices are prohibited. Title VII of the Civil Rights Act of 1964, the Age Discrimination in Employment Act of 1967 (ADEA), the Americans with Disabilities Act of 1990 (ADA), and Genetic Information Nondiscrimination Act of 2008 (GINA) make it illegal to discriminate in any aspect of employment, including recruitment, hiring, and firing. GINA, the latest of these laws, was passed when results from the Human Genome Project started raising ethical dilemmas. **Protected classes** is a term used in these laws to describe characteristics that cannot be targeted for **discrimination** and harassment. Protected classes include age, disability, gender, religion, genetic information, race, national origin, and pregnancy.

If information about protected classes is used to weed out candidates, it can lead to **corporate social media discrimination**. Discrimination is not always black and white because it is prejudicial treatment (Figure 14.3) that may be tough to prove. Although job applicants might not know whether or not their social media profiles had been screened, they have several ways of finding out. For instance, an applicant might be tipped off after receiving a suspicious friend request or by talking with current employees and hiring managers who disclose the information—either purposely or accidentally—during the interview.

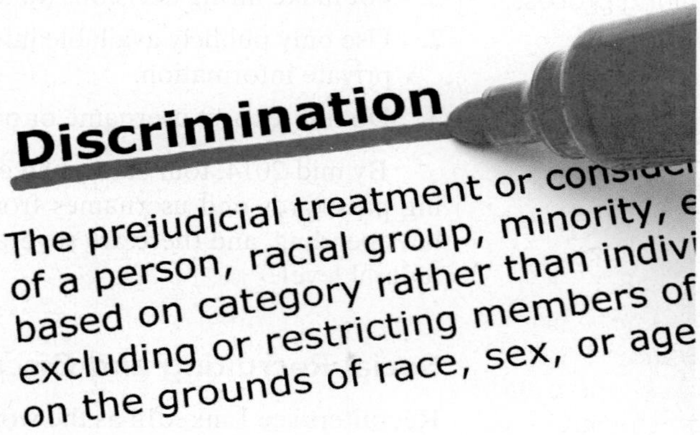

Figure 14.3 Discrimination is the result of prejudicial treatment based on protected information rather than a person's qualifications.

Discrimination
The prejudicial treatment or consider of a person, racial group, minority, e based on category rather than indivi excluding or restricting members of on the grounds of race, sex, or age

Enterprises that have not implemented formal processes for the use of social media in recruiting and selection may put themselves at risk of legal complaints because of inconsistent practices.

Civil rights are protected by federal law. If a person's civil rights are interfered with by another, the person can seek legal action for the injury. Examples of civil rights are freedom of speech, press, and assembly; the right to vote; and the right to equality in public places. Discrimination occurs when the civil rights of an individual are denied or interfered with because of their membership in a particular group or class. Various jurisdictions have enacted statutes to prevent discrimination based on a person's race, sex, religion, age, previous condition of servitude, physical limitation, national origin, and in some instances sexual orientation.

Two competing legal concerns are discrimination and negligent hiring.

- **Discrimination.** Most employers have stringent employment policies that prevent their recruiters and hiring managers from learning potentially discriminatory information about candidates. Visiting a person's social media sites, however, clearly creates the opportunity to view large amounts of information going against these nondiscriminatory practices.

- **Negligent hiring.** Employers must consider the potential risk of a negligent hiring or negligent retention lawsuit related to social networking profile information. It is possible that if a workplace violence incident occurred and the attacker's public social networking profile contained information that could have predicted that behavior, the employer may be held liable for negligence in not using readily available information during the hiring decision.

Examples and a discussion of these issues follow.

Discrimination via Social Media Scenario

Imagine that an employer reviews a candidate's activity on social media platforms and discovers the following information about her:

1. The candidate checks in via Foursquare at Woodsman Gym once or twice a day usually around 7 a.m., noon, or 6 p.m.

2. Her Facebook album is filled with party photos, like the one in Figure 14.4, showing what might be excessive drinking.

3. Her resume suggests that she is in her early 30s, but her social profile about high school indicates that her real age is late 40s.

Figure 14.4 In 2011, the Federal Trade Commission (FTC) ruled that companies that research how you spend your personal time, hobbies, and so on, do not violate your privacy. Party photos might not show illegal behavior but when posted on a social network could influence a potential employer's evaluation of a job applicant as well as disclose information about race, gender, age, and other protected characteristics.

© Bubbles Photolibrary/Alamy

4. Her posts describe her religious beliefs and customs, family's serious medical conditions, financial stress, and desire to spend as much time as possible snowboarding.

5. She makes fun of and posts insulting cartoons of people who follow a dress code at work.

Like many other job seekers, this candidate is posting, tweeting, and blogging information she would not want a recruiter or prospective employer to know about. If she is rejected because of her age, religion, or genetic condition, the company has committed social media discrimination and is very likely in violation of other laws.

Reducing the Risk of Negligent Hiring

In the past, employment law attorneys dealt with this risk by advising companies to avoid using social media in their hiring and recruitment process to avoid legal risk. However, that proposal is not realistic. By opting out of social media, recruiting firms lose a productive way to find candidates, which could cost them millions of dollars. Additionally, background checks must be conducted. Almost all employers do some form of background screening in order to avoid the risk of negligent hiring. Negligent hiring is a claim made by an injured party against an employer who knew or should have known about an employee's background that indicates a dangerous or untrustworthy character. Employers have a legal obligation to make the best effort to protect their employees and customers when they hire. Steps companies can take to balance the competing risks of negligent hiring and social discrimination are:

1. **Ask candidates to sign a disclosure statement.** Let candidates themselves disclose information found on social media. Explain to them the reason for the disclosure statement.

2. **Create a standard process and document it.** A consistent and well-documented process is needed to ensure and show compliance if there is an EEOC employment investigation.

3. **Avoid coercive practices.** Make sure recruiters do not pressure applicants to disclose protected information via social media by requiring them to disclose passwords or relax privacy settings for purposes of review by the employer.

4. **Training.** This may sound like a no-brainer, but training and repeated reminders are important to emphasize that management intends to be in compliance with laws and regulations related to social recruiting.

FINANCIAL ORGANIZATIONS MUST COMPLY WITH SOCIAL MEDIA GUIDELINES

In 2013, the Federal Financial Institutions Examination Council (FFIEC) released new guidelines titled *Social Media: Consumer Compliance Risk Management Guidance* to help financial institutions effectively manage the current risks caused by the use of social media (Ciccatelli, 2014). The activities of financial institutions are regulated by consumer protection and compliance laws. These institutions must take steps to protect their reputations and their clients—very similar to the steps that HR departments must take to comply with EEOC guidelines. Key social media guidelines for financial institutions are listed in Table 14.1.

Companies expose themselves to harsh sanctions by federal agencies when they violate the privacy policies that their customers rely upon. Unlike social discrimination, these cases are rather easy to detect and prosecute. For example, the Federal Trade Commission (FTC) charged SnapChat for, in effect, deceiving its customers with its bogus disappearing messages services. The FTC scrutinizes business practices to regulate "unfair and deceptive trade practices." The FTC has been focused on curtailing deceptive practices, even if unintentional, by businesses engaged in online commerce. While businesses should always ensure that their online advertisements are truthfully conveyed, a business with a social media presence should take particular note of the FTC's recent efforts concerning online privacy, security, and advertising. IT at Work 14.1 describes such a case.

TABLE 14.1	Key Social Media Guidelines for Financial Institutions
Guidelines	**Descriptions**
Institute policies to comply with advertising, communications, and other consumer protection laws	Perform a social media risk assessment and then implement social policies to prevent issues like spam. For example, staff should know how to react when a customer posts confidential information like a bank number on their social profiles.
Use monitoring tools	Financial institutions have added social channels that can expose their brand to additional feedback. Using social monitoring tools, they can identify issues that may cause a negative reaction and respond quickly. The use of social monitoring tools also helps banks refute inaccurate statements, protecting their brand reputation.
Train employees	Whether or not employees represent your brand on social media, their public social comments may be seen to reflect the financial institution. The best way to reduce risk is to train employees on how to use social networks professionally.

IT at Work 14.1

SnapChat Lied About Disappearing Messages and Privacy

FTC Chairwoman Edith Ramirez stated, "If a company markets privacy and security as key selling points in pitching its service to consumers, it is critical that it keep those promises" (Fitzpatrick & Kibel, 2014).

SnapChat Fined for Violating Its Own Privacy Policies and Misleading Users

The FTC charged SnapChat with violating its promises of "disappearing messages." According to the FTC's complaint:

1. SnapChat's mobile app allows consumers to send and receive photo and video messages known as snaps. SnapChat falsely marketed its app as a service for sending disappearing photo and video messages. Before sending a snap, the sender has to designate a period of time that the recipient will be allowed to view the snap.

2. Despite SnapChat's claims, the FTC contended that several methods exist by which a recipient can use tools outside of the app to save both photo and video messages,

allowing the recipient to access and view the photos or videos indefinitely. For example, when a person receives a video message, the app stores the video file in a location outside of the app's sandbox. Sandbox is the app's private storage area on the device that other apps cannot access.

3. Until October 2013, a recipient could connect his or her mobile device to a computer and use simple file browsing tools to locate and save the video file. Although this method for saving video files was widely publicized as early as December 2012, the FTC contended that SnapChat did not mitigate this flaw until October 2013.

4. SnapChat misrepresented its data collection practices by transmitting geolocation data from users of its Android app despite its privacy policy saying that it did not track or access these data.

5. SnapChat collected contact data from users' address books without notice or consent and continued to do so

without notifying users or obtaining their consent until Apple modified its operating system to provide notice with the introduction of iOS 6.

6. SnapChat's failure to secure its "Find Friends" feature resulted in a security breach that enabled attackers to compile a database of 4.6 million SnapChat usernames and phone numbers.

Settlement

SnapChat settled FTC charges alleging false promises of disappearing messages and failure to protect consumer data. Under the terms of its agreement with the FTC, SnapChat is prohibited from misrepresenting the extent to which it maintains the privacy, security, or confidentiality of users' data. SnapChat must implement a comprehensive privacy

program that will be monitored by an independent privacy professional for the next 20 years.

Questions

1. Which SnapChat claims of privacy protection were false?
2. Assume users relied on SnapChat's state privacy policies and claims about how the app worked. What potential risks did SnapChat users face?
3. If you had used the SnapChat app to send disappearing messages, what would you do when you learned of SnapChat's false claims?
4. Do you think the consequences SnapChat faced as part of its settlement with the FT are harsh enough to deter false claims? Explain.

Questions

1. Describe privacy.
2. What is the phenomenon where social users are concerned about privacy but their behaviors contradict these concerns?
3. What is the use of social media to find, screen, and select job candidates?
4. Rejecting a job candidate because of concerns about the person's health from information on his or her Facebook page is an example of what?
5. Age, disability, gender, religion, and race are examples of what?
6. Why are the legal concepts of discrimination and negligent hiring competing demands on a business?

14.2 Responsible Conduct

Any discussion about responsible conduct related to data and digital devices raises more questions than answers. Does the availability of data justify their use? Can shoppers keep their buying habits private? Can people keep their entertainment, online gaming, and other legal activities confidential? Do media have the right to publish or post highly private text messages of politicians and celebrities? Questions about data access, collection, mining, tracking, monitoring, privacy, and profiling are examples of IT capabilities that have ethical considerations. Here are cases of the power of information and analytics taken too far. Another widely cited case is Target's use of data analytics as discussed in IT at Work 14.2.

IT at Work 14.2

Target's Big Data Analytics Too Invasive

An angry man went into a Target store near Minneapolis insisting on talking to a manager: He handed a Target promotion that had been mailed to his daughter to the manager saying: "My daughter got this in the mail. She's still in high

school, and you're sending her coupons for baby clothes and cribs? Are you trying to encourage her to get pregnant?" The confused manager had no idea what was going on. The mailer had been sent by Target and addressed to the man's daughter, and it contained specials for maternity clothing and nursery furniture. A few days later he called the father to apologize again. Instead, the father apologized to the manager, explaining that he has since learned that his daughter was pregnant.

Big Data Analytics Too Invasive

How did Target know? By recognizing that there are some brief periods in a person's life when old routines change significantly and new buying habits suddenly appear.

Using big data, models of buying habits, predictive analytics, and her purchase history, Target had figured out (with about 87 percent probability) that she was pregnant. Target informed her family before she did. A lesson that Target discovered fairly quickly is that knowing about pregnancies in advance creeps out people and can be a public relations disaster (Duhigg, 2012). While Target assures compliance with all privacy laws, not breaking the law does not mean it is in the company's best interest to invade customers' privacy.

How Does Target Make Such Accurate Predictions?

Target assigns all customers a guest ID number that is linked to their credit card, name, e-mail address, and social media profile. The guest IDs become a bucket to store everything they have bought as well as demographic data.

The demographic data linked to the guest ID include age, marital status, number of kids, address, how long it takes to drive to the store, estimated salary, whether the person moved recently, other credit cards, and visited websites. Using its own predictive models, Target identifies customers who are pregnant.

Why Does Target Invest in Predictive Analytics?

Target's strategy is to capture a greater share of spending on baby items by being first to reach and promote to prospective parents. Waiting for public birth records is too late because by then parents are bombarded with offers and incentives from competing companies. Not everyone appreciates Target's strategy.

Questions

1. Is Target's data mining and predictive analytics a success, a failure, or both? Explain your answer.
2. How does Target create profiles of customers?
3. Is Target's "pregnancy predictor" a long-term competitive advantage? Explain.
4. How can this predictor upset families who receive the promotions?
5. How does Target make such accurate predictions?
6. Why does Target invest in predictive analytics?

CASES OF IRRESPONSIBLE CONDUCT

As new sets of data are collected about our lives, those data will contain a new set of predictions about us waiting to be mined. The question will be how much control we have over that process.

1. Predicting People's Behavior

Predicting people's behavior is big business—and increasingly feasible because of the volume of accessible information. For example, credit card companies can scrutinize your purchases to detect if your life is about to change—so they know what you are most interested in buying.

Canadian Tire, for instance, enabled its credit card business to create psychological profiles of its cardholders that were built using alarmingly precise correlations. Through data analytics, Canadian Tire found that cardholders who purchased carbon monoxide detectors, premium birdseed, and felt pads for the bottoms of their chair legs rarely missed a payment. On the other hand, those who bought cheap motor oil and visited a Montreal pool bar called "Sharx" were a higher risk (Ciarelli, 2010).

Depending on how intrusive, companies may face backlash from customers or be subject to investigations and fines. An example is Google's Street View Wi-Fi scandal—dubbed *Wi-Spy*.

2. Mobile Apps and Risky Behaviors

According to app security analytics firm Appthority's *App Reputation Report* (2014), 93 percent of the top 200 free apps for iOS and Androids exhibited at least one risky behavior. However, so did 89 percent of the top 200 paid apps. Just about every app requires that you click "yes" on the user agreement, which gives your consent to use your data. Types of risky behaviors are:

1. Location tracking
2. Accessing the device's address book or contact list
3. Identifying user or phone unique identifier (UDID)
4. Recording in-app purchases
5. Sharing data with ad networks and analytics companies

Mobile apps, such as Twitter, Foursquare, and Instagram, routinely gather information from personal address books and other places on your phone. Apple admits that any app that gathers a user's information without its permission is in violation. However, Apple and Android can only monitor apps available through the Apple Store and Google Play. There are countless third-party apps that are unregulated. If a user has an app that allows a company to access data on his or her phone and that phone is linked to the company's network, then privacy violations will happen.

3. Google: Google's Street View Wi-Spy Snooping Scandal

Google's Street View cars (Figure 14.5) drove along U.S. streets—and later in Europe, Canada, Mexico, and everywhere else—collecting a stream of images to feed into Google Maps. Google's engineers realized the cars could be used for **wardriving**—driving around sniffing out and mapping the physical location of the world's Wi-Fi routers. Wardriving is also a hacking technique, an invasion of privacy, and an information security risk.

Creating a database of Wi-Fi hotspot locations would make Google Maps more useful on mobile devices. Mobiles without GPS chips could use the database to approximate their physical location, and GPS-enabled devices could use the system to speed up their location-monitoring systems. When Google was building its system, a few start-ups already had created their own Wi-Fi mapping databases. However, Google was not only recording the location of people's Wi-Fi routers. When a Street View car encountered an **open Wi-Fi network**—a non-password-protected router—it recorded *all the digital traffic traveling across that router.* That is, when the car was within range of someone's open router, Google captured personal data, including login names and passwords, the full text of e-mails, Internet histories, people's medical conditions, online dating searches, streaming movies, and all other traffic.

According to the FCC (Federal Communications Commission) report, French investigators reviewed the data Google collected and found "an exchange of emails between a married woman and man, both seeking an extra-marital relationship" and "Web addresses that revealed the sexual preferences of consumers at specific residences." In the United States, Street View cars collected 200 gigabytes of private data between 2008 and 2010. The sniffing stopped only when regulators discovered the practice. Google denied any wrongdoing.

The FCC posted the following on its website: "Google's behavior also raises important concerns. Whether intentional or not, collecting information sent over Wi-Fi networks clearly infringes on consumer privacy."

The FCC determined that Google's actions were not technically illegal because snooping on unencrypted wireless data is not prohibited by the Wiretap Act. Given that Google manages so much of our personal data, this privacy invasion is an example of irresponsible conduct.

The story did not end with the FCC's decision. In May 2012, the FCC's investigation into Google's mapping project was itself being investigated. The renewed attention followed release of a mostly unredacted version of the FCC's findings in the case. The unredacted findings appear to contradict Google's claim that it inadvertently intercepted "payload data," or the content of individuals' Internet communications, in the process of gathering information from Wi-Fi networks across the globe for the Street View project. The document shows that, during preparations for the Street

Figure 14.5 Google vehicle with camera attached to photograph images used in Street View maps.

View effort, a Google engineer shared e-mails with colleagues at the firm revealing that he designed software for the project that was capable of collecting payload data. The new revelations have prompted *Consumer Watchdog,* a Washington-based advocacy group, to call for a hearing by the Senate Judiciary Subcommittee on Privacy, Technology and the Law.

4. Are FTC Fines for Privacy Violation Facebook's Business Model?

Facebook agreed to a settlement with the FTC in 2011 over charges that it deceived users about privacy. The eight-count complaint accused Facebook of changing privacy practices without notifying users, sharing users' information without their consent, and claiming to check the security of third-party applications when in fact it did not, among other charges. As part of the settlement, Facebook promises to stop making "deceptive privacy claims" and get users' permission before changing the way it shares their information. The social media company must also submit to privacy audits for 20 years. Zuckerberg wrote a blog post repeating his dedication to privacy while admitting that "we've made a bunch of mistakes." Privacy advocates do not believe that Facebook's privacy violations were anything but well-calculated decisions to test how far they could go before being charged by the FTC. In the *Daily Beast,* Dan Ryan composed what Mark Zuckerberg might have said if he dared to be brutally honest (Ryan, 2011):

> The truth is, we have no interest in protecting your privacy, and if you still believe that we do, then you are stupider than we thought, and believe me, we already thought you were pretty stupid. Think about it. The only way our business works is if we can track what you do and sell that information to advertisers.

Knowing that privacy is unprotected on Facebook, does that shift any or all responsibility to users?

These cases highlight contentious ethical issues and possibly irresponsible data-driven business practices. There rarely are easy answers to these dilemmas.

Competing Responsibilities

Most major retailers, from supermarket and drug store chains to major investment banks, rely on predictive analytics to understand consumers' shopping habits and their personal habits to market more efficiently. There are competing interests and trade-offs at work when the issue is privacy. There is also no clear-cut framework for deciding what is ethical and what is not. The personal privacy–public security debate is a prime example. Typically, privacy invasion is considered unethical. An ethically conscious corporate attitude sounds politically correct, but managers also have a responsibility to stakeholders. Monitoring may be (or seem to be) the responsible thing to do, and with intense competition marketers naturally want to use every tool or technique to gain an edge or nullify a risk.

Globalization, the Internet, and connectivity have the power to undermine moral responsibility because it becomes relatively easy to ignore harm. Despite the challenges and lack of clear answers, ethics is important because relying on the law alone to safeguard civil rights and society is insufficient. The law has its limits in large part because it changes so slowly.

THREE-DIMENSIONAL (3D) PRINTING AND BIOPRINTING— ADDITIVE MANUFACTURING DILEMMAS

Another trendy technology that has sparked ethical and other debates is the 3D printer and 3D bioprinting. Actual and planned applications include pizzas and heart valves (Martin, 2014). Prototype pizzeria 3D printers use cartridges filled with foodlike powder. In 2014, surgeons used a 3D printed model of a baby's skull in an intricate surgery to correct a serious birth defect. Bioprinting of aortic valves and 3D bioprinting technology have been used by researchers at Cornell University to fabricate living heart valves that possess the same anatomical architecture as the original valve. In 2013, a two-year-old child in the United States received a windpipe built with her own stem cells. 3D technology may seem like a win–win with no dark side or ethics challenges. Unfortunately, that is not true. Tech Note 14.1 describes the technology involved in the 3D printing process.

TECH NOTE 14.1 3D Printing Process

3D printing works by depositing tiny layers of material to create any shape. Bioprinting produces 3D biological objects or parts that are highly precise in shape and mechanical complexity. Using computer-assisted design (CAD) and/or computer-assisted manufacturing (CAM) blueprints, the bioprinter deposits ultrathin layers of living cells upon each other, following a precise geometric pattern that matches the heart valve dimensions, building the part vertically as the layers accumulate. Over hours the final tissue construct is completed.

3D Printing Dilemmas and Debated Issues

1. Despite benefits, the medical application of 3D printing to produce living tissue and organs, or 3D bioprinting, is expected to spark major ethical debates, according to Gartner (2014). 3D-bioprinted human organs may be subject to conflicting religious, political, moral, and financial interests. The 3D printing of nonliving medical devices, such as prosthetic limbs, is expected to be in high demand because of longer life spans and insufficient levels of health care in various countries. A major hurdle is determining who is legally responsible for ensuring the quality of the resulting organs and devices? Without medical malpractice insurance covering these new applications, they cannot proceed.

2. According to a study by sustainable design strategist and Berkeley mechanical engineering expert Jeremy Faludi, 3D printers can exert impacts on the environment worse than those of standard manufacturing (Martin, 2014). The carbon footprint depends on what is being made and type of printer used to make it. 3D printers use a lot more energy than conventional milling machines. 3D printers can use 100 times more electricity to produce a part than would have been used to produce the same part by nonadditive manufacturing.

3. Gartner (2014) predicts that, by 2018, at least seven of the world's top multichannel retailers will be using 3D printing technology to manufacture custom stock orders. The technology will create new business models and major challenges to intellectual property (IP)—causing an estimated loss of at least $100 billion per year in IP globally. The risks resulting from the ability to 3D print weapons are obvious.

Questions

1. By avoiding illegal conduct, do companies also act responsibly? Explain your answer.
2. What types of companies can benefit from predicting people's behavior?
3. When is predicting people's behavior a violation of privacy? Give an example.

4. When is predicting people's behavior *not* a violation of privacy? Give an example.
5. What are the ethical challenges attached to 3D printing and 3D bioprinting?
6. Research the current debate about 3D printing and bioprinting.

14.3 Technology Addictions and the Emerging Trend of Focus Management

Many people live and work in a state of continuous partial attention as they move through their day—loosely connected to friends and family through various apps on mobile and wearable devices.

Consider what you use to stay informed and how often you glance at them. You might not have noticed the gradual increase in the amount of data and information that you receive or check routinely until one day they seem to overwhelm your time. How many more things do you check today compared to a year ago? How long can you go without checking your devices without experiencing anxiety? When do you put down your mobiles and concentrate on one thing at a time? Your answers may indicate digital or connectivity overload and your tolerance for distractions.

The time between a new device or app going from *must have* to *cannot function without* is rather short. This situation is not limited to only digital natives. Studies show that adults are just as distracted as teenagers, which can also be confirmed with a casual glance at offices, airports, cafes, and so on.

DIGITAL DISTRACTIONS AND LOSS OF FOCUS

People do not need to be reminded how their lives are being taken over by tweets, texts, e-mail, social media, and annoying electronic static. Business users are more likely to suffer from too much data, rather than from data scarcity. This condition, known as **cognitive overload**, interferes with our ability to focus and be productive. Maggie Jackson (2008) suggested: "We're really facing the limit of human ability to cope with stimuli in our environment."

How big is this problem and how much does it cost? Some researchers estimate that distraction costs hundreds of billions of dollars a year in lost productivity. Gloria Mark, a professor of informatics at the University of California, Irvine, says a worker distracted by a Web search that goes rogue or a new text or tweet can take about 25 minutes to return to the task at hand and get focused again (Dumaine, 2014). Digital distraction and lack of focus in the workplace is getting the attention of senior management. When Inc. called the CEOs of technology companies Instagram, Box, and Zumba, they confirmed that the lack of focus on the job is a big concern for them.

FOCUS MANAGEMENT—THE ANTIDISTRACTION MOVEMENT

Senior management at Google, SAP, Instagram, Box, and Zumba are experimenting with new ways to diminish cognitive overload in order to help their employees stay focused. For example, at Google, employees take courses that help to sharpen their attention skills. The founders of Zumba and Box have developed their own methods to carve out focus time, such as putting aside large blocks of time to think undisturbed.

The Importance of Being Able to Focus

Nobel Prize–winning neuroscientist Eric Kandel wrote in his book *In Search of Memory* that only by intensely concentrating can a person link new ideas and facts "...meaningfully and systematically with knowledge already well-established in memory" (Kandel, 2006). He explained the importance of mental discipline to successful performance. If your mind is free of distraction, your mind is better able to absorb data, interactions, and trends and synthesize the new information with what you already know. As a result, you are more likely to come up with innovative ideas. If you are multitasking or are trying to function with only partial attention, your ability to synthesize information may be compromised.

Researchers at the Communication Between Humans and Interactive Media Lab at Stanford University studied digital distraction and focus. In 2009, researchers gave the same three cognitive tests to two different groups of test subjects:

1. **Media (high) multitaskers.** Forty-nine subjects who spent a lot of time searching the Internet, gaming online, watching TV, and hanging out on social media sites.

2. **Low multitaskers.** Fifty-two subjects who spent less time online and multitasked significantly less often.

In 2009, many believed that the Internet sharpened cognitive skills. Gaming required fast thinking and good motor skills. In contrast to widely held assumptions, the subjects who were heavy online users scored poorly on the cognitive test. One explanation for their poor performance was that they had attention deficits—less control over their attention. Because of their inability to concentrate for long, they were not able to distinguish important information from trivia. One of the researchers, Clifford Nass, whose findings are published in the *Proceedings of the National Academy of Sciences,* said "They're suckers for irrelevancy. Everything distracts them" (Ophir, Nass, & Wagner, 2009). The researchers continue to study whether chronic media multitaskers are born with an inability to concentrate or are damaging their cognitive control by willingly taking in so much at once. Science also shows that the best strategy to improve focus is to practice doing it.

Michael Merzenich, a neuroscientist, gave a biological explanation of the impacts of multitasking on focus ability. He explained that the more you focus, the more your brain releases a chemical called noradrenaline, which helps you concentrate on the task at hand. While these researchers believe that the minds of multitaskers are not working as well as they could, there are those who disagree (Ophir, Nass, & Wagner, 2009).

Questions

1. What are several potential causes of cognitive overload?
2. What are the consequences of constant distractions?
3. When a person is distracted, how long does it take to return to the task at hand and get focused again?
4. Why are senior managers interested in focus management?
5. What is the difference between the performance of high and low multitaskers on cognitive tests?
6. How can multitaskers improve their ability to focus?

14.4 Six Technology Trends Transforming Business

Accenture's *Technology Vision 2014* is an analysis of key IT trends that are expected to disrupt businesses. It is updated yearly to help organizations set their IT strategy and investment priorities. According to Vision 2014, becoming a truly digital business is crucial to how enterprises innovate and differentiate from competitors. A comparison of the disruptive technologies in 2013 and 2014 are listed in Table 14.2.

TABLE 14.2 Comparison of Technology Trends, 2013 and 2014	
2013	**2014**
Beyond the cloud	Digital-physical blur
Seamless collaboration	From workforce to crowdsource
Design for analytics	Data supply chain
Data velocity	Harnessing hyperscale
Software-defined networking	Business of applications
Active defense	Architecting resilience

Technology Vision 2014 explores the six IT trends that hold the most potential to transform businesses over the next three years. The days of innovative, technology-focused start-ups being the only market disruptors may be coming to an end. Large enterprises are starting to take advantage of their size, skills, and scale to transform into truly digital businesses.

TREND 1 DIGITAL-PHYSICAL BLUR: EXTENDING INTELLIGENCE TO THE EDGE

The convergence of several technologies is blurring the digital and physical worlds. These converging technologies are:

- The explosion of connected M2M (machine-to-machine) devices and IoT (Internet of Things)
- Greater bandwidth
- Advanced robotics, including expanding human–robot collaboration in industries beyond manufacturing
- Increased use of real time analytics

The physical–digital blur signifies a new layer of connected intelligence that augments employees, automates processes, and integrates machines into our lives. Controlling the physical world with sensors and digital devices depends on bandwidth and the ability to analyze data in real time.

Smartphones transform users' digitally augmented versions of themselves—able to create and share information in real time. Wearable devices and autonomous drones are changing the ways in which we experience the world. Intelligent interfaces are emerging that allow decisions to be made on the edge—where digital and physical worlds meet, which could be on your wrist, in your hand, or in your field of vision.

As the line between digital technology and the real world continues to blur, traditional companies are leveraging and enhancing their physical assets to create better user experiences.

TREND 2 FROM WORKFORCE TO CROWDSOURCE: THE RISE OF THE BORDERLESS ENTERPRISE

With cloud, social, and collaboration technologies, organizations can access and leverage talent and resource pools located anywhere and everywhere; in effect, an enterprise where ideas are solicited from a crowd of experts, that is, **crowdsourced**, similar to Kickstarter's crowdfunding concept.

In addition to crowdfunding, companies are using Kickstarter to provide market insight and assess product viability for a lot less than what traditional methods cost. By determining what people will actually pay for, the process influences and validates products and pricing strategies and sometimes leads to initial consumption and to product advocates. Accenture has developed initial models that show that crowdsourcing can lead to higher profits for producers.

Wikipedia relies on crowdsourcing for its content. Harnessing talent and resources to support strategic business goals will always be a challenge. Crowdsourcing can give every business access to an agile workforce that is not only better suited to solving some of the problems that organizations struggle with today but in many cases will do it for free. For example, GE currently uses crowdsourcing services to solve its most complex problems.

TREND 3 DATA SUPPLY CHAIN: PUTTING INFORMATION INTO CIRCULATION

Because of legacy systems and data silos that limit the value that organizations get out of their data, enterprise data are often underutilized. Accenture recommends that companies start treating data like a supply chain. Data need to flow easily through the entire organization—and eventually throughout the data systems of their business partners.

Achieving seamless data flows and treating data like an asset require data storage, IT infrastructure, big data platforms, and APIs. Walgreens, for example, opened its prescription API to third-party developers in order to make it easier for customers to refill their prescriptions.

Only one in five companies integrates its data across the enterprise. To truly unlock the potential of big data, companies have to treat it more like a supply chain, enabling its flow through the organization and supplier ecosystem. One way to do this, as Google has shown with Google maps data, is opening up the applications programming interface. The result—800,000 websites use Google Maps data.

TREND 4 HARNESSING HYPERSCALE: HARDWARE IS CRITICAL AGAIN

For many years, software has been the focus of managers' attention, with hardware being largely ignored. With enormous demands for processing power, hardware matters more than ever in transforming enterprises into digital businesses.

Every industry is being impacted by **hyperscale** computing systems—the super-sized, scalable, and resilient data centers pioneered by data-dependent and social media companies.

Traditional consumer goods company Unilever, tire manufacturer Pirelli, and the NBA have data processing requirements similar to technology giants Amazon and Google. All of them are faced with data challenges that hyperscale computing can help to solve, specifically huge amounts of data that need to be processed at speed—in real time. Unilever, Pirelli, and the NBA are using the sap.com platform SAP HANA to perform real time analytics on huge datasets for competitive advantage.

Ford, GM, and Toyota build vehicles that are embedded with hundreds of sensors, telematics, and real time connectivity. Data collection every day, hour, or second depends on hyperscale systems that can store and analyze these data at speed. High-performance companies are increasingly recognizing that hyperscale systems are a vital part of becoming a digital business.

Hardware is a hotbed of innovation as companies optimize their power consumption, processors, solid-state memory, and infrastructure architectures to increase data center efficiency, scale upward, and drive down costs.

TREND 5 BUSINESS OF APPLICATIONS: THERE'S AN APP FOR THAT!

Enterprises are following consumers by rapidly adopting apps to create better operational agility. Accenture says that 54 percent of the highest performing IT teams have already deployed enterprise app stores. This makes life simpler for employees and accelerates business growth.

TREND 6 ARCHITECTING RESILIENCE: BUILT TO BE FAILURE PROOF

Business runs on networks and digital technology. Technology failures are business failures. That is why companies such as Netflix use automated testing tools to attack their systems to make sure they are resilient. For example, Netflix built resiliency into its IT architecture by following two design principles: isolation and redundancy. **Isolation** means that a failure in one component cannot bring down the entire edifice, while **redundancy** means that every component is backed up by an alternative in case it fails.

IT must adopt a new mindset to ensure that systems are dynamic, accessible, and continuous—designed not just to specification but also for resilience under failure and attack.

NEXT WAVE OF	High-performing business leaders now accept that their organizations' future suc-

NEXT WAVE OF DISRUPTION WILL BE MORE DISRUPTIVE

High-performing business leaders now accept that their organizations' future success is tied to their ability to keep pace with technology. Accenture reports that its clients tell them that technology is more important than ever to their business success. Some sense that we are on the verge of a new technology revolution that will be more disruptive than previous ones. The flexibility of new technologies and architectures will naturally change how IT makes it easier for organizations to innovate.

Questions

1. What technologies are blurring the boundary between the physical and digital worlds?
2. What are the benefits of crowdsourcing?
3. Referring to trend 3, how should companies treat their data?
4. What is hyperscale?
5. What do business apps improve?
6. Why is resilience necessary?

Key Terms

breach of privacy	discrimination	open Wi-Fi network	redundancy
civil right	hyperscale	privacy	social recruitment
cognitive overload	isolation	privacy paradox	wardriving
corporate social media discrimination	negligent hiring	protected class	

Assuring Your Learning

DISCUSS: Critical Thinking Questions

1. Why will companies and recruiters continue to engage in social recruiting?

2. Visit two or more social media sites and review information that people have posted about themselves—or their friends have posted about them. What types of protected class information did you find? Give examples.

3. When organizations source their hiring to recruiting firms, how might that increase or decrease the risk of social media discrimination?

4. Consider Max Drucker's statement about employers being in a "tough spot." Explain the two risks that employers face.

5. How has IT changed the way you communicate in the last two years?

6. What changes do you predict in the way we communicate with each other in future?

7. Many questions were asked in the first two sections of this chapter—about the privacy paradox, privacy, and civil rights and responsible conduct. Answer those questions.

8. In your opinion, how does multitasking impact your performance?

EXPLORE: Online and Interactive Exercises

1. Social media discrimination is now a serious consideration for employers. Managers can evaluate vendor options such as LinkedIn Recruiter to limit liability and to remove protected information from profiles. Venture-funded startup BranchOut offers a similar tool for Facebook recruiting called RecruiterConnect.

   a. Research recruiting service providers and vendors. Select two of them.

   b. Review the website of each service or vendor.

   c. Describe the features they provide to defend against negligent hiring.

   d. Do each of them protect against social discrimination? Explain your answer and give examples.

ANALYZE & DECIDE: Apply IT Concepts to Business Decisions

1. Refer to the discrimination scenarios in this chapter. For each scenario, explain whether or not it should be used in the hiring decision.

2. In your opinion, what is the meaning of *responsible conduct* with respect to the use of social media for screening purposes?

3. Do you agree with the FTC's 2011 rule that states that searches by hiring companies into how you spend your personal time, hobbies, and the like do not violate your privacy?

4. Clerks at 7-Eleven stores enter data regarding customers' gender, approximate age, and so on, into a computer system. However, names are not keyed in. These data are then aggregated and analyzed to improve corporate decision making. Customers are not informed about this, nor are they asked for permission. What problems do you see with this practice?

5. Discuss whether cognitive overload is a problem in your work or education. Based on your experience, what personal and organizational solutions can you recommend for this problem?

6. Assume that you read about a new nonalcoholic drink discovery called "Don't-forget-a-thing." This remarkable drink, being marketed to students for $9.99 plus shipping and handling, would give the perfect recall of what he or she had read in the textbook in preparation for the exam. How would you verify the truth and accuracy of this drink—or any new drink or drug treatment—before ordering it or ingesting it? Identify five sources of trusted health, medical, or drug information.

7. The State of California maintains a database of people who allegedly abuse children. (The database also includes names of the alleged victims.) The list is made available to dozens of public agencies, and it is considered in cases of child adoption and employment decisions. Because so many people have access to the list, its content is easily disclosed to outsiders. An alleged abuser and her child, whose case was dropped but whose names had remained on the list, sued the State of California for invasion of privacy. Debate the issues involved. Specifically:

   a. Who should make the decision or what criteria should guide the decision about what names should be included and what the criteria should be?

   b. What is the potential damage to the abusers (if any)?

   c. Should the State of California abolish the list? Why or why not?

CASE 14.2

Business Case: Apple's CarPlay Gets Intelligent

At the 2014 Geneva International Motor Show, Apple unveiled CarPlay, an integration that ties Apple's mobile operating system (iOS) into automobiles.

CarPlay is Apple's iPhone in-car integration system. It lets drivers perform voice-enabled and touch-screen control of things, like making and answering calls, text messaging, and playing music, and also anticipates their needs by plotting driving routes based on their schedule and normal routine. Originally named "iOS in the Car," the service supports third-party music apps like Spotify and iHeartRadio and will be available in cars made by, for example, Ferrari, Mercedes, and Volvo.

An interesting part of the announcement were details about CarPlay's artificial intelligence (AI) capabilities. The software can scan through a user's data, such as calendar or e-mails, to try to pull up relevant destinations and driving directions. With that, Apple has made its biggest push into predictive services.

Apple already has the personal assistant Siri since the iPhone 4S release, but so far, the service has not had an emphasis on technology based on the user's context. CarPlay supports the iPhone 5, iPhone 5S, and iPhone 5C running iOS 7, which may also help drive new customers to the Apple ecosystem and push users with older iPhone models to upgrade.

Questions

1. Using privacy concepts from this chapter, identify the ways in which CarPlay can violate a user's privacy.

2. Consider the privacy paradox. How does that principle predict users' reactions to CarPlay? That is, do you expect users to be willing adopters of this AI technology?

3. Getting a customer hooked on the CarPlay technology means that the company is positioned to expand on it out of the vehicle, especially in the areas of wearables and home appliances. How might the integration of data from your car, smartphone, wearables, and home appliances impact your privacy?

4. What are your concerns about CarPlay's predictive analytics capabilities?

5. Do people who decide to use CarPlay also have a reasonable expectation of privacy? Explain.

CASE 14.3

Video Case: Vehicle-to-Vehicle Technology to Prevent Collisions

In Ann Arbor, Michigan, the U.S. Department of Transportation (DOT), the University of Michigan Transportation Research Institute, and the Michigan Department of Transportation did a pilot test of 3,000 cars, trucks, and buses equipped with vehicle-to-vehicle (V2V) communications. Based on the success of the pilot project, in 2014 the DOT announced that it would take steps to enable V2V communications to prevent collisions. V2V technology is the next generation of auto safety improvements—after seatbelts and airbags. By helping drivers avoid crashes, V2V communication will play a key role in the U.S. remaining the leader in the global automotive industry.

The technology informs drivers of changing road conditions and potential dangers in order to prevent accidents. These wireless systems are networked with traffic management systems. For example, if an agency learns that brakes have been applied several times in the same spot, a road crew could be dispatched to treat the pavement. Additionally, if a crash is detected, drivers can be diverted to alternate routes.

Visit YouTube and search *Michigan Department of Transportation* for the video, dated September 17, 2012. The video is also posted on StateTechMagazine.com where you can search the same title.

Questions

1. How much do crashes cost society?
2. What can help decrease crashes?
3. What types and percent of crashes can connected vehicle technology prevent?
4. What are other benefits of connected vehicle technology?
5. What are some of the benefits of a traffic management system?

References

Accenture. *Technology Vision 2014: Every Business is a Digital Business.* January 27, 2014. accenture.com/us-en/technology/technology-labs/Pages/insight-technology-vision-2014.aspx

Appthority. *App Reputation Report.* Summer 2014. appthority.com/resources/app-reputation-report

Bader, C. "The Risks and Responsibilities of Tech Innovation." *MIT Sloan Management Review,* June 10, 2014.

Blank, G., G. Bolsover, and E. Dubois, "A New Privacy Paradox: Young People and Privacy on Social Network Sites." *Oxford Internet Institute.* May 9, 2014. oxfordmartin.ox.ac.uk/downloads/A%20New%20Privacy%20Paradox%20April%202014.pdf

CareerBuilder.com. "Forty-Five Percent of Employers Use Social Networking Sites to Research Job Candidates, CareerBuilder Survey Finds." August 19, 2009.

Cavoukian, A. "Privacy is a Social Norm." *The Globe and Mail,* August 23, 2012.

Ciarelli, N. "How Visa Predicts Divorce." *The Daily Beast,* April 6, 2010.

Ciccatelli, A. "SEC Issues New Social Media Guidance for Financial Advisors." *Inside Counsel,* April 3, 2014.

Cohen, J. & Balz, D. "Poll: Privacy Concerns Rise after NSA Leaks." *The Washington Post,* July 23, 2013.

Davis, W. N. "Google Glass is already causing legal experts to see problems." *ABA Journal Law News.* April 1, 2014.

Dobuzinskis, A. "California Woman Ticketed for Driving with Google Glass." *Reuters,* October 31, 2013.

Duhigg, C. "How Companies Learn Your Secrets." *The New York Times.* February 16, 2012. nytimes.com/2012/02/19/magazine/shopping-habits.html?pagewanted=1&_r=2&hp&

Dumaine, B. "The Kings of Concentration." *Inc. Magazine*, May 2014.

Equal Employment Opportunity Commission. "Social Media Is Part of Today's Workplace But Its Use May Raise Employment Discrimination Concerns." Press release, *EEOC.gov*, March 12, 2014.

Fitzpatrick, A. & G. Kibel "Technology, Digital Media and Privacy Alert." *Inside Counsel*, June 17, 2014. insidecounsel.com/2014/06/17/technology-digital-media-and-privacy-alert

Gartner. "Gartner Says Uses of 3D Printing Will Ignite Major Debate on Ethics and Regulation." Press release, January 29, 2014. http://www.gartner.com/newsroom/id/2658315

Jackson, M. *The Erosion of Attention and the Coming Dark Age.* Amherst, NY: Prometheus Books 2008,

Kandel, E.R. *In Search of Memory*. New York, NY: W. W. Norton & Company, 2006.

Martin, G. "So 3-D Printers May Be Nifty and Trendy, But Environmentally Friendly? Not Necessarily." *California Magazine of UC Berkeley*, March 11, 2014.

Ophir, E., Nass, C. and Wagner, A. "Cognitive control in media multitaskers." *Proceedings of the National Academy of Sciences*. Vol. 106, No. 37. September 15, 2009.

Perry, T. "Woman wearing Google Glass found not guilty of distracted driving." *LA Times*. January 16, 2014.

Rainie, L., S. Kiesler, R. Kang, & H. Madden. "Anonymity, Privacy, and Security Online." *PEWInternet.org*, 2013.

Ryan, D. "The Truth About Facebook Privacy—If Zuckerberg Got Real." *The Daily Beast*, November 30, 2011.

Taylor, J. "Feds Interrogate Man Wearing Google Glass in Movie Theater." *BetaBeat.com*, January 21, 2014.

Whitney, L. "Google Glass Wearer Challenges Distracted Driving Charge." *CNET.com*, December 4, 2013.

Glossary

2D tag   A barcode-like image used to identify a merchant or payee.

3D bioprinting   Medical application of 3D printing to produce living tissue and organs.

3D printing   Also known as additive manufacturing, builds objects layer-by-layer to create real-world objects.

5G   Fifth generation mobile communications network.

Acceptable use policy (AUP)   Explains what management has decided are acceptable and unacceptable activities, and the consequences of noncompliance.

Access control   Limiting access to certain documents or data.

Active data warehouse   Real-time data warehousing and analytics.

Ad hoc report   An unplanned report that is generated to a mobile device or computer on demand as needed.

Additive manufacturing   See 3D printing.

Advanced persistent threat (APT)   Stealth network attack in which an unauthorized person gains access to a network and remains undetected for a long time.

Aggregation   A calculation, such as Sum, Average, or Count.

Agility   The ability to respond quickly and appropriately.

Analytical tools   Software or apps for data analysis.

Anonymous   A loose association of hacktivists.

Application controls   Safeguards that are intended to protect specific applications.

Application programming interface (API)   A gateway to facilitate the transfer of data from one website app to another.

Applications portfolio   List of major, approved IS projects that are also consistent with the long-range plan.

Assets   Things of value that need to be protected.

Asynchronous Javascript and XML   A group of technologies and programming languages that make it possible for webpages to respond to users' actions without requiring the entire page to reload.

Attack vectors   Vulnerabilities that exist in networks, operating systems, apps, databases, mobile devices, and cloud environments.

Audit   Procedure of generating, recording, and reviewing a chronological record of system events to determine their accuracy.

Augmented reality   A technology that superimposes a computer-generated image onto an image of the real world to provide information or entertainment.

Avatar   An icon, figure, or visual representation of a person in computer games, simulations, virtual worlds, or online discussion forums.

Backdoors   Type of malware that enables access to a network without logging in.

Backlinks   External links that point back to a site.

Back-office operations   Activities that support the fulfillment of orders.

Bandwidth   A network's capacity or throughput.

Barcode   A machine-readable code consisting of numbers and a pattern of thick and thin lines that can be scanned to identify the object on which the code appears.

Baseline   Specification of the project plan that has been formally reviewed and agreed upon. It should be changed only through a formal change control process.

Big data   Datasets whose size and speed are beyond the ability of typical database software tools to capture, store, manage, and analyze.

Biometric control   Automated method of verifying the identity of a person, based on physical or behavioral characteristics.

Black hat SEO   Search engine optimization tactics that try to trick a search engine into thinking a website has high-quality content, when in fact it does not.

BlackPOS   Malware designed to be installed on POS devices in order to record data from credit and debit cards swiped through the infected device.

Blog   Online journals where people regularly post personal or professional content in a variety of digital formats including text, photographs, video, and music.

Blogging platform   A software application used to create, edit and add features to a blog. Wordpress and Blogger are two of the most popular blogging platforms.

Blogosphere   A network enabling bloggers to comment on, and link to other blogs in their posts, in effect maintaining a dialogue or conversation with other bloggers.

Botnet   A network of hijacked computers that are controlled remotely, typically to launch spam or spyware.

Breach of privacy   Unauthorized disclosure of personal information.

Bring your own apps (BYOA)   Employees use their own apps instead of using apps provided by the company.

Broadband   Refers to wide bandwidth technologies that create fast, high-volume connections to the Internet and World Wide Web.

Business case   Presentation or document that outlines the justification for the start-up and funding of a project.

Business intelligence (BI)   Category of applications for gathering, storing, analyzing, and providing access to data to help enterprise users make better decisions.

Business process management (BPM)   Methods, tools, and technology to support and continuously improve business processes.

Business process reengineering (BPR)   Eliminating the unnecessary non-value-added processes, then simplifying and automating the remaining processes to significantly reduce cycle time, labor, and costs.

Business processes   Series of steps by which organizations coordinate and organize tasks to get work done.

Business record   Documentation of a business event, action, decision, or transaction.

Business-driven development approach   A development approach that starts with business strategy and work backwards to identify data sources and data that needs to be acquired and analyzed.

Business-to-business (B2B)   Markets in which the buyers, sellers, and transactions involve only organizations, not individual consumers.

Business-to-business (B2B) commerce   Selling products and services to other businesses.

BYOD   Bring your own device is a growing trend in which employees use their own devices for business purposes.

Capital budgeting   The process of analyzing and selecting investments with the highest ROI.

Cascading style sheets (CSS)   A language used to enhance the appearance of webpages written in a markup language.

Change data capture (CDC)   CDC processes capture the changes made at data sources and then apply those changes throughout enterprise data stores to keep data synchronized.

Channel conflict Competition between a manufacturer's distribution partners that sell through different channels. Channel conflict can occur at the wholesale, retail, or internal sales department level.

Circuit switching A telecom network that transmits voice or data via a dedicated channel (connection).

Click-through rates (CTR) The percentage of people who click on a hyperlinked area of a SERP or webpage.

Climate change mitigation Any action to limit the magnitude of long-term climate change.

Cloud computing A general term that refers to a style of computing in which IT services are delivered on-demand and accessible via the Internet. Common examples are Dropbox, Gmail, and Google Drive.

Cloud computing stack Cloud Computing is often described as a stack consisting of a broad range of services built on top of one another, for example SaaS, PaaS, and IaaS.

Cloud storage service Remote network storage that makes it easy to access your documents from any of the devices you work on.

Cloud strategy Short for cloud computing IT strategy.

COBIT (Control Objectives for Information and Related Technology) IT governance framework which many companies use as their IT governance guide.

Cognitive overload Condition when business users suffer from too much data that interferes with their ability to focus and be productive.

Collaborative filtering Makes recommendations based on a user's similarities to other people.

Collection analysis module Creates utility indexes that aid in providing search results.

Command and control (C&C) channel The way in which botnets are controlled remotely or used to carry out malicious activities.

Commodities Basic things that companies need to function.

Competitive advantage A difference between a company and its competitors *that matters to customers.*

Competitive forces model Model developed by Michael Porter, also called the five-forces model, to identify competitive strategies.

Computer-integrated manufacturing (CIM) Computer-integrated systems that control day-to-day shop floor activities.

Consumerization of information technology (COIT) Trend where more and more users bring their personal mobile devices and their own mobile apps to work and connect them to the corporate network.

Content-based filtering Recommends products based on the product features of items the customer has interacted with in the past.

Contract hackers Hackers available for hire or complete hack attacks that can be bought.

Core business processes Accounting, finance, sales, marketing, human resources, inventory, production, and manufacturing.

Corporate procurement or purchasing The buying of products and services by an organization for its operational and functional needs.

Corporate social media discrimination Illegal use of information about protected classes to select or weed out candidates.

Crawler control module A software program that controls a number of "spiders" responsible for scanning or crawling information on the web.

Crawler search engines Rely on sophisticated computer programs called "spiders," "crawlers," or "bots" that surf the Internet, locating webpages, links, and other content that are then stored in the SE's page repository.

Creative destruction A term coined by the economist Joseph Schumpeter in 1942 to warn that innovation can disrupt industries in capitalist societies and force established companies and business models to either adapt or fail.

Credentials Log-in information, such as username, password, or PIN.

Critical infrastructure Systems and assets, whether physical or virtual, so vital to the United States that the incapacity or destruction of such systems and assets would have a debilitating impact on security, national economic security, national public health or safety, or any combination of those matters.

Critical path Longest path of tasks through a project, as shown on a Gantt chart. A delay of any task on the critical path will delay the project.

Critical success factors (CSFS) Those things that must go right for a company to achieve its mission.

Critical task Task or activity on the critical path.

Cross-functional business process Involves two or more functions, for example, order fulfillment and product development.

Cross-sell To sell additional complimentary products or services.

Crowdfunding Raising funds for a project from the public, or crowd, via the web.

Crowdsourcing A model of problem solving and idea generation that marshals the collective talents of a large group of people.

Customer experience (CX) Building the digital infrastructure that allows customers to do whatever they want to do, through whatever channel they choose to do it.

Customer lifetime value (CLV) Formula for estimating the dollar value, or worth, of a long-term relationship with a customer.

Customer-centric Business models strive to create the best solution or experience for the customer. In contrast, product-centric models are internally focused on creating the best product.

Cycle time Time required to complete a given process.

Dashboards Data visualizations that display the current status of key performance indicators (KPIs) in easy-to-understand formats.

Data Data are the raw material from which information is produced; and the quality, reliability, and integrity of the data must be maintained for the information to be useful.

Data analytics Refers to the use of software and statistics to find meaningful insight in the data, or better understand the data.

Data center A location storing a large number of network servers used for the storage, processing, management, distribution, and archiving of data, systems, web traffic, services, and enterprise applications. Data center also refers to the building or facility that houses the servers and equipment.

Data disclosure Reporting system where data items are tagged to make them easily searchable.

Data discovery Data exploration and discovery of hidden relationships.

Data entity Anything real or abstract about which a company wants to collect and store data.

Data governance Control of enterprise data through formal policies and procedures to help insure that data can be trusted and is accessible.

Data mart Is a lower-cost, scaled-down version of a data warehouse that can be implemented in a much shorter time. Data marts serve a specific department or function, such as finance, marketing, or operations.

Data mining Is a specific analytic technique that enables users to analyze data from various dimensions or angles, categorize it, and find correlations or patterns among fields in the data warehouse.

Data science Managing and analyzing massive sets of data for purposes such as target marketing, trend analysis, and the creation of individually tailored products and services.

Data silo Stand-alone data stores available for a specific function or department, but not accessible by other ISs.

Data tampering A common means of attack that is overshadowed by other types of attacks. It refers to an attack during which someone enters false or fraudulent data into a computer, or changes or deletes existing data.

Data visualization (data viz) Tools that make it easier to understand data at a glance by displaying data in summarized formats, such as dashboards and maps, and by enabling drilldown to the detailed data.

Data warehouse Systems that integrate data from databases across an entire enterprise are called enterprise data warehouses (EDW).

Database A repository or data store that is organized for efficient access, search, retrieval, and update.

Database management system (DBMS) Software used to manage the additions, updates, and deletions of data as transactions occur; and support data queries and reporting. They are OLTP systems.

Decision model A model that quantifies the relationship between variables, which reduces uncertainty.

Decision support system (DSS) Interactive applications that support decision making.

Declarative languages A programming language that simplifies data access by requiring that users only specify what data they want to access without defining how that is to be achieved.

Deliverables The outputs or tangible things that are produced by a business process. Common deliverables are products, services, actions, plans, or decisions, such as approval or denial of a credit application. Deliverables are milestones, produced in order to achieve specific objectives.

Demand management Knowing or predicting what to buy, when, and how much.

Digital business models How a business generates revenue or profit from digital products or services.

Digital dependents The emerging generation of young people who are growing up in a world of broadband connections, constant connectivity, and related technology and who become uncomfortable if they do not have access to it.

Digital immigrants Typically a member of an older age cohort that may be increasingly comfortable with technology but much less likely to incorporate mobile technology into their shopping behavior.

Digital natives The first generation to have grown up surrounded by digital devices (i.e., computers, smartphones, digital cameras, and video recorders, etc.) and Internet connectivity.

Direct conversion Type of conversion in which the old system is cut off and the new system is turned on at a certain point in time.

Direct procurement Purchasing materials to produce finished goods.

Dirty data Data of such poor quality that they cannot be trusted or relied upon for decisions.

Discussion groups A forum to ask questions and solicit input from other members of the group.

Disruptive innovation New technologies offering the capability of transforming traditional business practices, creating new value networks, and spawning new markets.

Distributed database system A database system that allows apps on computers and mobiles to access data from both local and remote databases.

Distributed Denial of Service (DDoS) attack Attack that bombards a network or website with so much traffic that it crashes and becomes vulnerable to other threats.

Document object model (DOM) A programming API for documents. Programmers use it to manipulate (e.g., build, add, modify, delete, etc.) HTML documents.

Do-not-carry rules Security rules based on the assumption that devices will inevitably be compromised.

Dwell time The amount of time a user stays on a webpage before returning to the search engine results page.

E-commerce Process of buying, selling, transferring, or exchanging products or services or information via the public Internet or private corporate networks.

Economic order quantity (EOQ) An inventory model that is used to answer both questions of when to order and how much to order, the EOQ model takes all costs into consideration.

EEOC (Equal Employment Opportunity Commission) Enforces federal laws prohibiting discrimination in employment.

Electronic fund transfer (EFT) A transfer of funds from one bank account to another over a computerized network.

Electronic records management (ERM) A system that consists of hardware and software that manage and archive electronic documents and image paper documents; then index and store them according to company policy.

Electronic wallet (e-wallet) A software application that can store encrypted information about a user's credit cards, bank accounts, and other information necessary to complete electronic transactions, eliminating the need to re-enter the information during the transaction.

Enterprise 2.0 The use of social media tools for collaboration on company intranets to increase productivity.

Enterprise application integration (EAI) Middleware that connects and acts as a go-between for applications and their business processes.

Enterprise architecture (EA) The way IT systems and processes are structured. EA is an ongoing process of creating, maintaining, and leveraging IT. It helps to solve two critical challenges: where an organization is going and how it will get there.

Enterprise data mashup Combination of data from various business systems and external sources, often in real-time, without necessarily relying on a middle step of ETL (extract, transform, and load) from a data warehouse.

Enterprise data warehouse (EDW) A data warehouse that pulls together data from disparate sources and databases across an entire enterprise.

Enterprise graph Platform that shows how users are related to one another. It enables developers and customers to seamlessly connect people, conversations, and data across all their business services.

Enterprise IT architecture Guides the evolution and expansion of information systems, digital technology, and business processes.

Enterprise mashups Combining data from internal business sources (e.g., sales records, customer information, etc.) and/or information from external sources for enhanced usefulness and productivity.

Enterprise risk management (ERM) Risk-based approach to managing an enterprise that integrates internal control, the Sarbanes–Oxley Act mandates, and strategic planning. ERM is intended to be part of routine planning processes rather than a separate initiative.

Enterprise search tools Used by employees to search for and retrieve information related to their work in a manner that complies with the organization's information-sharing and access control policies.

Enterprise social Private (company-owned) social media, software, platforms, or apps specially designed for use by business leaders and employees to fulfill the strategic mission.

Enterprise systems Cross-functional and inter-organizational systems that support the business strategy.

E-procurement The re-engineered procurement process using e-business technologies and strategies to control costs and simplify purchasing processes.

E-sourcing Procurement methods such as auctions, RFQ processing, private exchanges, and secondary activities such as trading partner collaboration, contract negotiation, and supplier selection.

Executive information system (EIS) An information system specifically designed to support senior management.

Exploit Tool or technique that takes advantage of a vulnerability.

Extendable markup language (XML) A set of rules and guidelines for describing data that can be used by other programming languages. It makes it possible for data to be shared across the web.

Extensibility Ability to get data into and out of the cloud service.

Extensible Business Reporting Language (XBRL) A language for electronic communication of business data. Each item, such as cash or depreciation expense, is tagged with information about various attributes, such as calendar year, audited/unaudited status, currency, and so on.

Extract, transform, load (ETL) Technology involved in preparing raw data for analytics that includes three procedures: data extracted from designated databases; data transformed by standardizing formats, cleaning the data, integrating them; and data loaded into a data warehouse.

FASB Develops U.S. accounting standards and principles.

Fault tolerance Means that no single failure results in any loss of service.

Financial misrepresentation Situation in which a company has intentionally deceived one or more other parties.

Five-forces model Model developed by Michael Porter, also called the competitive forces model, to identify competitive strategies.

Flexible manufacturing systems (FMS) Systems that can accommodate the manufacture of different parts at different volumes. FMS systems schedule the manufacture of a part in the most expedient way by examining the current workload across each of eight machine tools.

Folksonomy A system of classifying and organizing online content into categories by the use of user-generated metadata such as keywords.

Formal processes Processes that are documented and have well-established steps.

Fraud risk management A system of policies and procedures to prevent and detect illegal acts committed by managers, employees, customers, or business partners against the company's interests.

Front-office operations Activities, such as sales and advertising that are visible to customers.

Gantt chart Horizontal bar chart that graphically displays the project schedule.

General controls Controls established to protect the system regardless of the specific application.

Geocoding Process that can convert postal addresses to geospatial data that can then be measured and analyzed.

Geographic information system (GIS) Captures, manages, analyzes, and displays multi-dimensional geographic data.

Geospatial data Identifies the geographic location and characteristics of natural or constructed features and boundaries on the earth, typically represented by points, lines, or polygons.

Ghost pages Webpages that are optimized to attract many people but contain a redirect command so that users are sent instead to another page to increase traffic on that page.

Giant global graph Illustration of the connections between people and/or documents and pages online.

Go/No-Go decision Formal decision made by the project manager, sponsor, and appropriate executives and stakeholders.

Goal seeking Model that starts with the desired outcome (goal) and a set of variables that impact that outcome, which are used to calculate how that outcome could be achieved and whether it's feasible to achieve that desired outcome.

Groundswell The spontaneous effort of people using online tools to obtain information, support, ideas, products, and bargaining power from each other.

Group dynamics Group processes that emerge as the members work together.

Hacktivist Short for hacker-activist or someone who does hacking for a cause. Hacking, regardless of motive, is a crime.

Hadoop Hadoop is a data processing platform that distributes computing problems across a number of servers so it is capable of processing big data.

Hashtags Descriptive keywords designated by the # sign attached to Twitter messages to make it easier for other users to find them.

Horizontal exchanges Sites where many buyers and sellers that use the same products or services conduct business transactions.

Hybrid recommendation engines Develop recommendations based on some combination of content-based filtering, collaboration filtering, knowledge-based and demographic systems.

Hybrid search engines Combine the results of a directory created by humans with results from a crawler search engine, with the goal of providing both accuracy and broad coverage of the Internet.

Hyperscale Computing systems that are the supersized, scalable, and resilient data centers pioneered by data-dependent and social media companies.

Hypertext markup language (HTML) The predominant language for webpages, used along with CSS, to describe how things will appear on a webpage.

Implementation Process of converting from the old system to the new system.

Inbound logistics Receiving of inventory, parts or products from suppliers or other sources.

Inbound marketing An approach to marketing that emphasizes SEO, content marketing, and social media strategies to attract customers. Often viewed as an alternative to traditional marketing strategies based on advertising and personal selling.

Income statement Summarizes a company's revenue and expenses for one quarter of a fiscal year or the entire fiscal year. Also known as P&L (profit and loss) or earnings statement.

Indexer module Creates look-up tables by extracting words from webpages and recording the URL where they were found.

Indirect procurement Organizations purchasing products for daily operational needs.

Industry structure Determines the range of profitability of the average competitor and can be very difficult to change.

Informal processes Processes that are typically undocumented, have inputs that may not yet been identified, and are knowledge-intensive.

Information Data that have been processed, organized, or put into context so that it has meaning and value to the person receiving it.

Information and communications technology (ICT) IT industry sector.

Information governance The control of enterprise data through formal policies and procedures. A goal of data governance is to provide employees and business partners with high quality data they trust and can access easily on demand.

Information overload Inability of a manager or decision maker to process or analyze data because of an overwhelming volume of data.

Informational search Using search engines to conduct research on a topic or product.

Insider fraud A variety of criminal behaviors perpetrated by an organization's employees or contractors.

In-store tracking Use of mobile technology to track a customer's movement through a retail store for a better understanding of individual consumer preferences as well as creating optimal store layout.

Integrated change control Processes that help to manage the disruption resulting from requested changes and corrective actions across the project lifecycle.

Interface To connect to and exchange data with apps and systems.

Internal control environment Work atmosphere that a company sets for its employees.

Internal threats Threats from employees. They are a major challenge largely due to the many ways an employee can carry out malicious activity.

Internet of Things (IoT) Refers to a set of capabilities enabled when physical things are connected to the Internet via sensors.

Internet protocol (IP) The basic technology that makes global communication over the web possible.

Intrusion detection system (IDS) Defense tool used to monitor network traffic (packets) and provide alerts when there is suspicious traffic, or to quarantine suspicious traffic.

Intrusion prevention systems (IPS) Defense system designed to take immediate action—such as blocking specific IP addresses—whenever a traffic-flow anomaly is detected.

Inventory control systems Stock control or inventory management systems.

IP address Every device that communicates with a network must have a unique identifying IP address. An IP address is comparable to a telephone number or home address.

Ipv4 The Internet protocol for over three decades, now reaching the limits of its design and running out of IP addresses.

Isolation Means that a failure in one component can't bring down the entire system.

IT consumerization The migration of consumer technology into enterprise IT environments.

IT governance Supervision, monitoring, and control of the organization's IT assets.

IT strategy Shapes the direction of IT investments over the next one to five years to maximize business value and shareholder wealth.

IT–business alignment Complex management activity of aligning IT strategy with business strategy.

Javascript An object-oriented language used to create apps and functionality on websites. Examples of Javascript apps include pop-up windows, validation of webform inputs, and images that change when a cursor passes over them.

Just-in-time (JIT) One of the two widely used models to minimize waste and deal with the complexity of inventory management. JIT inventory management attempts to minimize holding costs by not taking possession of inventory until it is needed in the production process.

Key performance indicators (KPIs) Business metrics used to evaluate performance in terms of critical success factors, or strategic and operational goals.

Keyword In the context of web search or SEO, a word or phrase that describes the content on a webpage. Search engines use keywords to match webpages with user search queries.

Keyword conversion rates The likelihood that using a particular keyword to optimize a page will result in converting a website visitor into a buyer.

Knowledge Information that has been processed, organized, and put into context to be meaningful, and to convey understanding, experience, accumulated learning, and expertise as they apply to a current problem or activity.

Lagging indicators Confirm what has already happened. They evaluate outcomes and achievements.

Latency Elapsed time (or delay) between when data is created and when it is available for a query or report.

Latency-sensitive apps Apps that depend on quick no-delay transmission, such as voice and video.

Leading indicators Indicators that help predict future events to identify opportunities.

Lean manufacturing system A system used to minimize waste and deal with the complexity of inventory management, where suppliers deliver small lots on a daily or frequent basis, and production machines are not necessarily run at full capacity.

Legacy systems Older information systems that have been maintained over several decades because they fulfill critical needs.

Link farms Websites built solely for the purpose of linking back to a promotional page.

Link spamming Generating backlinks for the primary purpose of search engine optimization, not to add value for the user.

Logistics Entails all the processes and information needed to move products from origin to destination efficiently.

Lulzsec Hacktivist group that is a spin-off of Anonymous.

Machine-to-machine (M2M) technology Enables sensor-embedded products to share reliable real-time data via radio signals.

Manufacturing execution systems (MES) Manage operations on the shop floors of factories.

Manufacturing quality control (QC) systems Systems that provide data about the quality of incoming materials and parts, as well as the quality of in-process, semifinished, and finished products.

Market share Percentage of total sales in a market captured by a brand, product, or company.

Mashup A web app that pulls data from various sources and displays that on another page to create new functionality.

Master data Data about the entities of importance to an enterprise, such as customers, products, accounts, and other business-critical data information that are needed for operations and business transactions.

Master data management (MDM) Synchronizes all business critical data from disparate systems into a master file, which provides a trusted data source.

Master file MDM links and synchronizes all critical data from those disparate systems into one file, called a master file, that provides a common point of reference.

Maverick buying Corporate purchasing outside the established approved procurement system.

Metadata Data that describe and provide information about other data.

Meta-search engines Compile search response listings by combining results from several other search engines.

MHI An international trade association that has represented the material handling, logistics and supply chain industry.

Microblog A blog that consists of frequent but very brief posts containing text, pictures or videos. Twitter is perhaps the most well-known example of a microblog.

Micropayments Transactions involving relatively small sums of money.

Microsoft cloud Provides a hybrid infrastructure and capabilities to manage enterprise apps and data.

Milestone Used to manage the project work effort, monitor results, and report meaningful status to project stakeholders.

Millennials Generation born between early 1980s to the early 2000s.

Mission Set of outcomes an enterprise wants to achieve.

Mobile biometrics Security defenses, such as voice and fingerprint biometrics, for mobile devices.

Mobile browser A web browser that is optimized to display web content effectively on a small mobile device such as a smart phone.

Mobile check-in strategy The use of mobile apps to enhance shopping behavior at retail outlets with discounts, coupons, descriptive videos, etc.

Mobile commerce or m-commerce The buying or selling of goods and services using a wireless, handheld device such as a cell phone or tablet (slate) computer.

Mobile display strategy Use by retailers of QR codes and Short Message Service (SMS) technology to encourage store customers to view short videos featuring selected merchandise.

Mobile e-commerce The use of wireless handheld devices to order and/or pay for goods and services from online vendors.

Mobile location-based marketing A marketing strategy that uses information from a mobile device's GPS or customer's mobile check-in on a social network to determine the content of marketing communications they receive on the device (e.g., advertisements, coupons, special offers).

Mobile marketing A variety of activities used by organizations to engage, communicate, and interact over Wi-Fi and telecommunications networks with consumers using wireless, handheld devices.

Mobile payment The use of systems that make transactions from smartphones and other mobile devices convenient, safe, and secure.

Mobile retailing The use of mobile technology to promote, enhance, and add to value to the in-store shopping experience.

Mobile visual search engine A search engine that uses an image instead of a text-based query to search for information on the web.

Moral hazard A situation that takes the risk (and the deterrent) out of committing fraud.

MRO supplies Items purchased for maintenance, repair, and operations, such as office supplies, and not resold to generate revenue.

Navigational search Using a search engine to locate particular websites or webpages.

Near field communication (NFC) Enables two devices within close proximity to establish a communication channel and transfer data through radio waves. NFC are location-aware technologies that are more secure than other wireless technologies like Bluetooth and Wi-Fi.

Near-field communication (NFC) technology General description covering technologies that communicate within a limited distance.

Negligent hiring Claim made by an injured party against an employer who knew or should have known about an employee's background that indicates a dangerous or untrustworthy character.

Net neutrality A principle holding that Internet Service Providers (ISPs) and their regulators should treat all Internet traffic the same way.

Network effect From the field of economics, the network effect explains how the perceived value of a product or service is affected by the number of people using the product or service.

Newsgroups Online communities similar in many ways to online bulletin boards, where members exchange messages on various topics.

NOSQL A heterogeneous group of database systems that is capable of processing large web applications.

Objectives Building blocks of strategy, these are action-oriented statements that define the continuous improvement activities that must be done to be successful. Objectives set out what the business is trying to achieve.

Occupational fraud Deliberate misuse of the assets of one's employer for personal gain.

Office graph Uses signals from email, social conversations, documents, sites, instant messages, meetings, and more to map the relationships between the people and concepts.

Offshoring Sourcing that is done off-shore.

Omni-channel retailing The effort by retailers to fully integrate both traditional and emerging methods to influence consumers.

Online analytical processing (OLAP) systems Systems for analysis of complex data, typically stored in a data warehouse or data mart.

Online transaction processing (OLTP) Events or transactions are processed as soon as they occur.

Online transaction processing (OLTP) systems Volatile systems that are designed to process and store transaction data.

Onshore sourcing Work or development that can be sourced to consulting companies or vendors that are within the same country.

Open Graph Facebook's new initiative to connect all the different relationships that exist on the Internet by linking websites to Facebook.

Open source An application programming interface (API) that anyone can use, usually for free.

Open Wi-Fi network Non-password-protected router.

Operating margin A measure of the percent of a company's revenue left over after paying for its variable costs, such as wages and raw materials. An increasing margin means the company is earning more per dollar of sales.

Operating plan Plan that defines how to execute the IT strategic plan.

Operational level Level on which managers and supervisors work most closely with the workforce and customers and play a more interpersonal role than any of the other levels of management.

Order fulfillment Set of complex processes involved in providing customers with what they have ordered on time and all related customer services.

Order fulfillment process The process of moving products from orders to the customers that includes credit check and payment collection, picking and shipping departments to pack the product, print the mailing label, and prepare for shipping, and notifying customers that their orders are on the way.

Organic search listings Search results that are heavily influenced by website content and design features.

Outbound logistics Shipping activities.

Outsource relationship management (ORM) company Company that provides automated tools to monitor and manage the outsourcing relationships.

Packet A block of data or file that is transmitted over a network to their destination.

Packet switching Transfers data or voice in packets.

Page repository A data structure that stores and manages information from a large number of webpages, providing a fast and efficient means for accessing and analyzing the information at a later time.

PageRank A Google website evaluation algorithm that counts backlinks, based on the assumption that people are more likely to link to high-quality websites than poor-quality sites.

Paid search listings A form of advertising purchased from search engine companies in which advertisers pay search engines based on how many people click on their ads.

Parallel conversion Conversion strategy in which the old system and the new system operate simultaneously for a period of time. That is, both systems process the same data at the same time, and the outputs are compared.

Patches Software programs to fix a vulnerability in a system or app.

Payload Refers to the actions that occur after a system has been infected. The payload carries out the purpose of the malware.

Payment card industry data security standard (PCI DSS) A data transmission security standard based on encryption that was created by Visa, Mastercard, American Express, and Discover to improve customers' trust in e-commerce

Pay-per-click (PPC) A form of payment based on how many viewers clink on a link to a marketer's page.

Petabyte A unit of measurement for digital data storage. A petabyte is equal to one million gigabytes.

Phishing Deceptive method of stealing confidential information by pretending to be a legitimate organization, such as PayPal, a bank, a credit card company, or other trusted source.

Planners Lab Software designed to build DSSs.

Plug-ins Buttons or features on non-Facebook sites that interact with Facebook in some way.

Postmortem Method for evaluating project performance, identifying lessons learned, and making recommendations for future projects.

Primary activities Business activities directly involved in the production of goods and services.

Privacy Right to self-determine what information about you is made accessible, to whom, when, and for what use or purpose.

Privacy paradox Refers to a phenomenon where social users claim to be concerned about privacy, but their behaviors contradict these concerns to an extreme degree.

Private cloud A single-tenant environment with stronger security and control for regulated industries and critical data. A private cloud resides within an enterprise's own network and firewall.

Private social networking service The use of social technology to create a community restricted to members selected by the SNS' owner. Private SNSs allow a greater degree of control over the network.

Process Series of steps by which organizations coordinate and organize tasks to get work done.

Production and operations management (POM) Function that is responsible for processes that transform inputs into value-added outputs.

Project Well-planned sequential series of tasks to achieve a result. Projects have a defined beginning and end; a scope, resources, and a budget. Projects are approved before they are funded and allocated resources.

Project management Structured methodology to plan, manage, and control the completion of a project throughout its lifecycle.

Project portfolio Portfolio that lists major resource projects, including infrastructure, application services, data services, and security services that are consistent with the long-range plan.

Project portfolio management (PPM) Set of business practices to manage projects as a strategic portfolio.

Propagate How a virus spreads to other networks or devices.

Protected class Characteristics identified by law that cannot be used in the hiring process.

Public cloud A shared cloud architecture run over a public network, such as the Internet. It allows multiple clients to access the same virtualized services and utilize the same pool of servers across a public network.

Quality score An ad rating determined by factors related to the user's experience.

Quick response (QR) codes A machine-readable code typically used to store a link to a URL or web address that can be read by a mobile device.

Radio frequency identification (RFID) Method of identifying unique items using radio waves. Typically, a hand-held reader communicates with a tag, which holds digital information in a chip.

Real time search tool Help to pinpoint current trends by monitoring web searches, news stories, videos views, and blog posts about a particular topic.

Really simple syndication (RSS) Allows users to subscribe to multiple sources (e.g., blogs) and have the content displayed in a single application, called an RSS Reader or RSS Aggregator, enabling readers to personalize how they want their news organized and displayed.

Real-time processing Processessing of data or transactions as they occur.

Recommendation engines Proactively identify products that have a high probability of being something the consumer might want to buy.

Red flag Fraud indicators—lavish vacations, jewelry, and cars that somebody could not afford.

Redundancy Every component is backed up by an alternative in case it fails.

Relational database A standard database model that had been used by most enterprises. Relational databases store data in tables consisting of columns and rows, similar to the format of a spreadsheet.

Relational database management system (RDBMS) System that provides access to data using a declarative language—SQL or structured query language.

Remote administration trojan (RAT) Create an unprotected backdoor into a system through which a hacker can remotely control that system.

Remote wipe capability A feature of a smart device wherein it can be instructed remotely to delete the contents.

Replicate How a virus or other malware makes copies of itself.

Resource description framework (RDF) A language used to represent information about resources on the Internet.

Responsibility matrix A document that lets everyone know who is responsible for completion of tasks.

Responsiveness Means that IT capacity can be easily scaled up or down as needed, which essentially requires cloud computing.

Retrieval/ranking module Determines the order in which pages are listed in a search engine results page.

Retweet Forwarding a Twitter message to everyone in a user's network.

Reverse supply chain Type of supply chain where products that are returned make up the supply chain; goods are moving in the reverse direction.

Rich snippets Rich, attractive listings produced on search engine result pages by websites optimized with metadata for semantic technology.

Risk Probability of a threat exploiting a vulnerability.

Rogue app monitoring Type of defense to detect and destroy malicious apps in the wild.

Rootkit A type of malware that installs itself on a network.

Router A device that transmit data packets from their source to their destination based on IP addresses, and links computers to the Internet, so users can share the connection.

RSS aggregator Enables users to pull content from a number of sources into a single location making it easier to follow news stories and blog posts from multiple sites.

RSS reader Allows users to aggregate regularly changing data, such as blog entries, news stories, audio, and video.

Safety stock Extra inventory that are used as a buffer to reduce the risk of stockout.

Scalability A system that can increase (or decrease) in size to handle data growth or the load of an increasing number of concurrent users.

Scalable Adjustable to meet changes in business needs.

Scope creep Refers to the growth of the project, which might seem inconsequential—at least to the person who is requesting that change. Scope creep is the piling up of small changes that by themselves are manageable, but in aggregate are significant.

Search engine An application for locating webpages or other content (e.g., documents, media files) on a computer network. Popular web-based search engines include Google, Bing, and Yahoo.

Search engine marketing (SEM) A collection of online marketing strategies and tactics that promote brands by increasing their visibility in SERPs through optimization and advertising.

Search engine optimization (SEO) A collection of strategies and techniques designed to increase the number of visitors to a website as a result of the website's rank on search engine results pages.

Search engine results page (SERP) The list of links and other descriptive information about webpages returned by a search engine in response to a search query.

Sell-side marketplace Organizations selling their products or services to other organizations from their own private e-marketplace or from a third-party site.

Semantic search engines Use natural language processing, contextual cues, synonyms, word variations, concept matching, specialized queries, and other strategies to create search results that are superior to those created by simple keyword-matching algorithms.

Semantic web An extension of the World Wide Web that utilizes a variety of conventions and technologies and languages developed by the W3C that allow machines to understand the meaning of web content.

Sentiment analysis Analysis of comments and social media posts to understand consumers' attitudes or feelings.

Service pack Patches released by Microsoft to update and fix vulnerabilities in its operating systems.

Shadow pages Webpages that are optimized to attract lots of people but contain a redirect command so that users are sent instead to another page to increase traffic on that page.

Sharepoint Collaborative and social platform from Microsoft.

Sharing sites Websites that make it easy for users to upload and share digital content like photos, videos or music.

Short code A short five- or six-character number used for product promotions or other interactions with customers.

Short message service (SMS) A technology used to send and receive text messages on mobile devices via a telecommunications network.

Showrooming Using mobile search engine for locating product reviews and price comparisons while shopping in brick-and-mortar stores.

SMS database strategy Compiling and tracking short message service (SMS) codes to encourage customers to opt-in to receiving coupons and other offers via text message.

Social bookmarking An app for tagging or labeling online content for later retrieval.

Social commerce Taking advantage of social media to promote sales through both online and retail channels.

Social engineering Also known as human hacking—tricking users into revealing their credentials and then using them to gain access to networks or accounts. From an IT security perspective, social engineering is a hacker's clever use of deception or manipulation of people's tendencies to trust, to try to be helpful, or to be curious.

Social graph A visual representation of the relationships and connections between individuals and groups.

Social media A collection of web applications, based on Web 2.0 technology and culture, that allows people to connect and collaborate with others by creating and sharing digital content.

Social media optimization Effective use of strategies designed to enhance a company's standing on various social media sites such as Facebook and Twitter.

Social monitoring services Allow users to track conversations taking place on the web, particularly on other social media sites.

Social network analysis (SNA) Mapping and measuring of relationships and flows between people, groups, organizations, computers, or other information or knowledge processing entities.

Social network sprawl Refers to a problem when businesses end up interacting with multiple social networks inside their own company.

Social networking service (SNS) An online platform or website that allows subscribers to interact and form communities or networks based on real-life relationships, shared interests, activities, and so on.

Social recruitment Refers to use of social media to find, screen, and select job candidates. Often it involves searching information the job candidate did not want considered or that is illegal to use in the hiring process.

Social web The new technologies, often called Web 2.0, that dramatically increase the ability of people to interact with businesses and each other, sharing and finding information, and forming relationships.

Social, mobile, and cloud (SOMOCLO) Leading digital technologies.

Software-as-a service (SaaS) A widely used model in which software is leased and available on demand instead of being owned or licensed from the vendor.

Sourcing Refers to an IT deployment strategy in which systems are developed or IT work is done by a third-party or vendor.

SPARQL Protocol and RDF Query Language Query languages used to write programs that can retrieve and manipulate data stored in RDF format.

Spiders Also known as web bots or simply "bots," spiders are small computer programs designed to perform automated, repetitive tasks over the Internet. They are used by search engines for scanning webpages and returning information to be stored in a page repository.

Spot sourcing The purchase of indirect materials in one industry as-needed, using an exchange.

Standard operating procedures (SOP) Set of well-defined, written instructions for how to perform a function or activity. SOPs provide the framework for complex processes to be managed more effectively.

Statement of work (SOW) Defines the project plan, but does not offer any options or alternatives in the scope.

Stock keeping unit (SKU) A code number, typically a machine-readable bar code, assigned to a single item of inventory.

Stockout Inventory shortage.

Strategic plan Document used to communicate the company's goals and the actions needed to achieve their goals.

Strategic planning A top management activity that sets priorities, focuses energy and human and technology resources, strengthens operations, and ensures that employees and business partners work toward common goals.

Strategy Defines the plan for how a business will achieve its mission, goals, and objectives.

Structured data Highly organized data easily included in a relational database that can be readily searched.

Structured decisions Decisions that have a well-defined method for solving and the data needed to reach a decision.

Structured query language (SQL) Standardized language for accessing databases.

Sunk cost Refers to the money already spent on the project.

Supply chain All businesses involved in the production and distribution of a product or service.

Supply chain management (SCM) The efficient management of the flows of material, data, and payments along the companies in the supply chain, from suppliers to consumers.

Supply chain visibility Awareness and sharing of POS data and data about product orders, inventory levels, demand forecasts, transportation, and logistics by trading partners from raw material to delivery to the end customer.

Support activities Activities that support primary activities.

Switch A device that transmit data packets and acts as a controller, enabling networked devices to talk to each other efficiently.

SWOT analysis Analysis of an enterprise's strengths, weaknesses, opportunities, and threats.

Synchronous communication Dialogue or conversation that takes place in real-time, without the long delays between exchanges that occur, for instance, in email or discussion board conversations.

Systematic sourcing The trading of materials that are direct inputs to manufacturing, usually in large quantities, in an environment of a long-term B2B relationship.

Tactical adoption approach Deploying cloud services incrementally results in apps and services that are patched together to create end-to-end business processes. This is a short-sighted approach.

Tactical level Level on which middle-level managers design business processes, procedures, and policies to implement strategic plans.

Tags Identifiers that describe various aspects of a webpage.

Terms of service (TOS) agreement A formal listing of the policies, liability limits, fees, and user rights and responsibilities associated with using a particular service. Users are typically required to acknowledge they have read, understand and agree to the terms of the TOS before they are allowed to use the service.

Text mining A specific analytic technique that involves interpreting words and concepts in context.

Threat Something or someone that can damage, disrupt, or destroy an asset.

Time-to-exploitation Elapsed time between when a vulnerability is discovered and when it is exploited.

Total quality management (TQM) A quality control system.

Touchpoint Any action or interaction with a customer, such as email, text, direct mail, phone call, social media message, and so on.

Traffic shaping Ability to prioritize and throttle network traffic.

Transaction processing system (TPS) A system designed to process specific types of data input from ongoing transactions.

Transactional search Using a search engine to determine where to purchase a product or service.

Transparency Being able to access current data to learn what is needed in order to make informed decisions without delay.

Triple constraint Three attributes–time, scope, and cost–that must be managed effectively for successful completion and closure of any project.

Tweet A brief 140-character message or post broadcast on Twitter, a microblogging service.

Twittersphere The universe of people who use Twitter, a microblogging service.

Uniform resource identifiers (URI) One of the features that allow data to be used by multiple applications.

Unstructured data Information that is not organized in a systematic or predefined way and more likely to contain inaccuracies or errors.

Unstructured decisions Decisions that depend on human intelligence, knowledge, and/or experience — as well as data and models to solve them.

Up-sell To sell more expensive models or features

Usenet The initial platform for online communities making it possible for users to exchange messages on various topics in public newsgroups.

Value added reseller (VAR) Customizes or adds features to a vendor's software or equipment and resells the enhanced product.

Value driver Any activity that enhances the value of a product or service to consumers, thereby creating value for the company. Advanced IT, reliability, and brand reputation are examples.

Variants Modified versions of an existing malware.

Vector Specific method that malware uses to propagate, or spread, to other machines or devices.

Vertical exchanges Sites where many buyers and sellers conduct business transactions that serve only one industry along the entire supply chain.

Vertical search engines Focus on webpages related to a particular topic and help to drill down by crawling pages that other search engines are likely to ignore.

Virtual communities Offer several ways for members to interact, collaborate, and trade with no regard for geographical or political boundaries.

Virtual machine (VM) A software-created computer or operating system.

Virtualization A technique that creates multiple operating systems that run on a single physical machine.

Voice biometrics Authentication method based on a user's voiceprint.

Voice over IP (VOIP) Network that carries voice calls by converting voice (analog signals) to digital signals that are sent as packets.

Volatility A characteristic of databases that refers to the process by which databases are constantly in use or being updated.

Vulnerability A weakness that threatens the confidentiality, integrity, or availability (CIA) of an asset.

Wardriving Refers to driving around sniffing out and mapping the physical location of the world's Wi-Fi routers. Wardriving is also a hacking technique, an invasion of privacy, and an information security risk.

Wearable technology Digital technology embedded in clothing or other things that are worn.

Web 2.0 A term used to describe a phase of World Wide Web evolution characterized by dynamic webpages, social media, mashup applications, broadband connectivity, and user-generated content.

Web directories Created by human editors and typically organized by categories, these were once the dominant method for finding web content.

Web ontology language (OWL) The W3C language used to categorize and accurately identify the nature of things found on the Internet.

What-if analysis Refers to changing assumptions or data in the model to see the impacts of those changes on the outcome.

Wide area network (WAN) Type of mobile network distributed over a large area, such as an office park

Widget A web app that pulls data from various sources and displays it on another page to create new functionality.

Wiki A collaborative app that allows multiple people to create and edit online content.

Work breakdown structure (WBS) List of tasks in a project shown in sequential order, resources allocated to each task, and schedule.

World Wide Web A network of documents on the Internet, called webpages, constructed with HTML markup language that supports links to other documents and media (e.g., graphics, video, audio, etc.).

Xmlhttprequest A Javascript object that serves as an API used by programs to retrieve data or resources from an URL without requiring a page load. It plays an important role in providing programmers with the ability to create dynamic and interactive webpages and applications.

Yammer Social network geared towards enterprises. Employees collaborate across departments, locations and business apps.

Zero-day attacks Malware so new their signatures are not yet known.

Zombie An infected computer that can be commanded to monitor and steal personal or financial data and act as spyware.